D1270274

A Guide to

THE CONSTITUTION
That Delicate Balance

A Thirteen-Week Telecourse

A Guide to

THE CONSTITUTION
That Delicate Balance

A Thirteen-Week Telecourse

George McKenna
City College of New York

 AN ANNENBERG/CPB PROJECT

 RANDOM HOUSE NEW YORK

To Sylvia

The Constitution: That Delicate Balance is produced by Media and Society Seminars, a program of the Columbia University Graduate School of Journalism, in association with WTTW/Chicago and WNET/New York. The telecourse is made possible by a grant from the Annenberg/CPB Project.

First Edition
987654321
Copyright © 1984 by Media and Society Seminars

All rights reserved under International and Pan-American Copyright Conventions. No part of this book may be reproduced in any form or by any means, electronic or mechanical, including photocopying, without permission in writing from the publisher. All inquiries should be addressed to Random House, Inc., 201 East 50th Street, New York, N.Y. 10022. Published in the United States by Random House, Inc., and simultaneously in Canada by Random House of Canada Limited, Toronto.

ISBN: 0-394-34125-2

Manufactured in the United States of America

"The one who pleads his case first seems to be in the right; then his opponent comes and puts him to the test."

PROVERBS 18:17.

Preface

In writing this guide to the telecourse based on *The Constitution: That Delicate Balance*, I have tried to keep in mind the best qualities of short textbooks. I have also kept in mind that this book must be more than a short text. Because of the uniqueness of *The Constitution: That Delicate Balance,* the guide must take on some aspects of a college classroom experience.

The common thread of most telecourses is the role of their television component. Television provides unity for the course by supplying its authoritative voice. Typically, the TV component features either a noted authority lecturing or some kind of narrative with a similarly authoritative voice-over. The program may include debates and exchanges of opinion, but it always returns to the single voice.

The Constitution: That Delicate Balance is different. It is a unique and daring experiment in television education, for it has no single voice. It is, instead, a series of programs whose participants spend their entire time arguing! No firm conclusions are supplied by anyone: certainly not by the programs' moderators, whose function is to stimulate, not resolve, argument; and not by Fred Friendly and retired Supreme Court Justice Potter Stewart, who explain key terms and provide perspective during breaks in the programs but make no final pronouncements on the issues.

The absence of this authoritative voice is not an oversight or shortcoming in the design of the programs. It is deliberate and, given the nature of the issues, it is inevitable. Over topics such as abortion, public school prayer, and affirmative action, reasonable men and women in a pluralistic society can—and *must*—disagree. These are issues not easily resolved. They may be insoluble, though even that conclusion is premature. For on all of these issues the jury is still out—and will be until these matters have received more systematic, comprehensive, and informed examination. The purpose of this series is to help provide such an examination. If it has any underlying premise, it is the premise of Oliver Wendell Holmes, Jr., that truth is best reached by the "free trade in ideas." There is no monopolist on any of these thirteen programs, no single voice that presumes to resolve everything for us. This would be a presumption contrary to the spirit of the programs and the spirit of a democratic society.

Yet the very virtues of these programs present tough challenges to the educator. Any good course in public policy and public ethics must include debate and disagreement, but it must also have unity and coherence. In the television series at hand, there are two types of unity: of theme and of purpose. The theme is the Constitution, or at least some of its more Delphic clauses and amendments. (The programs, of course, go beyond the legal issues of the Constitution to raise basic problems of policy and ethics. But the Constitution serves as a kind of gridiron, marking out the key issues.) The second unity, the unity of purpose, is best summed up by the man who developed the technique used in these programs. Their aim, according to Fred Friendly, is to put both participants and viewers "into situations so agonizing that they can escape only by thinking."

A third unity is required to turn the TV series into a course, and that is unity of organization and substance. There must be more than argument; there must be grist for the arguments. Fred Friendly and Martha Elliott's book *The Constitution: That Delicate Balance* helps to provide this grist by offering students a background in leading constitutional cases. But more is needed. Key issues should be identified and placed in their historical and political context. There should be an account of how these issues have fared in the Supreme Court and in the wider court of public opinion. Finally, the student should be helped through the exciting, bewildering maze of arguments in the TV series. How do the arguments develop? Which are most prominent? What techniques do the participants use to refute their opponents? What assumptions are made? What questions are left begging?

All these remaining areas, from the historical context to the current arguments on the TV series, need to be gathered together in a book that provides organization and coherence. This is such a book. It is intended to have some of the properties of a useful short textbook—basic substance, good organization and development, clearly marked section headings, summaries, and other guides for students and teachers. It is also meant to respect its readers, never to talk down or condescend to them. It intends to convey the sense that is it talking *with* readers; not hurling down pronouncements from Mount Olympus but entering into a series of conversations.

Given the nature of this course, the last considerations assume special importance. From the inception of this project, I have kept in mind that one way this material might be offered was as a telecourse for off-campus learners. In such a form, the course would provide students with stimulating learning materials but with limited classroom contacts. Here is a gap that needs filling; this book will try to fill it. Groping for a metaphor to characterize this book, I can only suggest "a freeze-dried professor." The metaphor is inexact, since the book is not intended to be dry, much less frozen. All it means is that the book aims at simulating the atmosphere of a college classroom: of a professor lecturing, inviting discussion, responding to questions—and complaints— from the students. In the course of a semester, this process is not always smooth; it can, at times, get somewhat shaggy and discontinuous. That is the way higher education is; it is not machine-tooled. It is a humanistic endeavor, so it has to be conducted by human beings.

The manuscript of this book was typed on a word processor. It was not, however, written by a word processor. It was written by one who has spent over twenty years teaching college and has found the experience fulfilling. In the existential give-and-take of classroom discussion, the professor and students are brought together in a joint endeavor that, at its best, begins to erase the barriers between them. If that spirit has found its way into the following pages, it may overcome whatever human imperfections they contain.

ACKNOWLEDGMENTS

Fred W. Friendly, journalist, teacher, and scholar, was the organizing genius behind the programs that inspired this book. He and his wonderful wife, Ruth, have been indefatigable in their campaign to get ordinary citizens involved in the great constitutional debates of our time. In his words, "the Constitution is too important to be left entirely to jurists." The Friendlys communicated that spirit to everyone involved in this project.

Stuart Sucherman, Executive Producer of the series, offered constant support and encouragement; a modest man, he will never realize how much he helped me. Producers Jude Dratt and David Kuhn were extremely cooperative and cordial. Martha Elliott, Fred Friendly's coauthor, supplied fascinating insights into the factual background of many of the cases studied in this book.

Indispensable advice, information, and criticism were provided by Valerie Crane and her associates, who field-tested chapters of this book; by attorney and constitutional authority Howard W. Gutman; and by Professors Wayne Brady, Philip Dolce, Robert Gilbert, Rosalie Siegel, and Martha Zebrowski, who read and commented on various chapters.

Tim Gunn, Director of Public Programs in the Education Division of public television station WNET in New York, recruited me and gave me the freedom to undertake the task as I saw fit. Good friend Marie Squerciati of WNET coordinated work on the video and written portions of the telecourse, eloquently promoted the course, and encouraged and reassured one given to occasional fainting spells. Cathy Cevoli of WNET went over the manuscript with a professional writer's eye, purging it of academese and breaking up its three-page paragraphs. The manuscript was expertly word-processed by WNET's Nancy Hayes-Davis and Alan Ellington.

At Random House, judicious editing by Jeannine Ciliotta kept the "freeze-dried professor" from digressing and bantering too much. Jeff Longcope and Bert Lummus helped develop the manuscript, and David Rothberg played an indispensable role in turning it into a book.

At the Media and Society office of Columbia University's Graduate School of Journalism, Barbara Eddings and Natalie Paine were always a great help. Michael Epstein assisted in putting together some of the appendixes to the chapters, and Cynthia McFadden provided useful information.

I am grateful to Professor Joyce Gelb, Chair of Political Science at City College of New York, for helping me secure the sabbatical leave that gave me time to work on this book.

The final acknowledgment can be stated most simply: I could do nothing without my dear Sylvia.

George McKenna
New York City
March 1984

Contents

Introduction:
Ground Rules

*"It is emphatically the province and duty of
the judicial department to say what the law is."*
CHIEF JUSTICE JOHN MARSHALL, 1803

*"In considering this question, then, we must
never forget, that it is a* constitution *we are
expounding."*
CHIEF JUSTICE JOHN MARSHALL, 1819

Some of the issues in this book touch the highest levels of statecraft. These include questions of presidential prerogative and congressional power, the right to make war and conclude treaties, the doctrine of checks and balances. Other issues may invade the lives of quite ordinary Americans: whether or not to disconnect the respirator of a dying relative, whether or not a retarded and disabled infant should undergo an operation, whether or not someone should get an abortion. The issues in this book also include the role of money in American elections, the use of racial quotas, freedom of the press and national security, euthanasia, gun control, prayer in public schools, immigration law, the right to assemble, the workings of our electoral college and our federal system. The range and mix of issues is somewhat bewildering. What holds them all together? What is the cornerstone of this book?

It is the United States Constitution.

Some of the Founding Fathers would probably be startled to find that the Constitution now encompasses all these issues. When the Constitution was written back in 1787, the laws were not much involved in people's lives; and when they were, they were usually local laws. Disputes began at the local level and ended there—unless they involved some obviously national question, like the defense of the country or a treaty with a foreign nation. But as this country has grown in size and complexity, as technology has created new problems in the course of resolving old ones, people have turned to our Constitution for answers. We did not have respirators back in 1787, nor did we have television, high-speed transportation, or thermonuclear weapons. Today we do, and to pretend that such things have no relevance to the Constitution is to attempt to keep this nation's supreme charter locked up in a glass case. That, surely, none of the Framers would have wanted.

They need not have worried. The Constitution is alive today, as vital as it ever was. We continue to turn to it for answers to our public disputes; we study it for clues about what is legitimate and illegitimate, what is arguable and what is settled, what the boundaries to our political process are. The Constitution defines the ground rules.

But it defines them with a very broad brush. It does not paint in the details. That may be one reason it endures. If the Framers had tried to spell out everything in the manner of a legal code, the Constitution would have become too rigid, too bound to the circumstances of the late eighteenth century. "We must never forget," said Chief Justice John Marshall of the Supreme Court in 1819, "that it is a *constitution* we are expounding." Its nature, he added, "requires that only its great outline should be marked, its important objects designated." It leaves the particulars to the generations of Americans who live under it, and its broad outlines are not static or inflexible. The Constitution, Marshall said, "was intended to endure for ages to come, and conse quently to be adapted to the various crises of human affairs."

Today these crises abound. Not all of them can or should be resolved by courts. But we are not as yet speaking of courts. The Constitution, indeed, is greater than the courts. It belongs to all of us. Americans revere it as a great moral charter, one of those remaining sets of standards honored by citizens of almost every persuasion. If it can be said that America has any overall "civic religion," then the two sacred documents of that religion are the Constitution and the Declaration of Independence. Of the two, the Constitution may be the more powerful, for it carries the force of law as well as of morality.

How did we get it? How did it come to be?

THE CONSTITUTIONAL CONVENTION, 1787

In the steaming Philadelphia summer of 1787, fifty-five men met to propose "revisions" of the existing charter of government, the Articles of Confederation. When they were done, it was clear that they had written a whole new charter, in some respects radically different from the Articles. At the outset, no one was sure how the Philadelphia Convention would end. At one point it almost broke up because of quarreling between representatives of the large states and the small states. But one fact was obvious: the Convention included men who had been chafing under the kind of government provided by the Articles of Confederation. These men felt that the existing government was too weak and decentralized, lacking the strong leadership they thought it needed. They wanted a central government with vigor and energy, equal to all the crises afflicting the new nation.

LEADING FIGURES AT THE CONVENTION

Who were these men? Here are a few of the more famous leaders and initiators of the Philadelphia Convention.

Alexander Hamilton of New York was one of the most impassioned proponents of a strong central government. Born in the West Indies, he came to America as a teenager and never developed any strong local attachments. Thus, he looked at America as a whole, seeing it as a nation of continental proportions instead of a patchwork of states and localities. His service as colonel in the Revolutionary War confirmed his distaste for a Congress so weak that it failed to supply its troops with sufficient food and arms. Though Hamilton was influential in organizing the Convention and even more so in getting its product ratified, his influence at the Convention itself was more limited. This may have been because of his utter candor. Behind the closed doors of the Convention, he confessed his fears about the power of "the mass of people" and proposed that presidents be elected just once, for life. Hamilton was consistently outvoted by Robert Lansing and John Yates, his fellow New York delegates.

Among the leading lights of the Virginia delegation were *George Washington* and *James Madison.* Washington, the great hero of the Revolution, presided over the Convention. He said little; his presence was enough. He had been reluctant to come and was persuaded to do so only because the organizers insisted that his presence was necessary if the work of the Convention was to be taken seriously. Tall, grave, dignified, Washington was almost as much of a legend then as he is today.

James Madison, Washington's fellow Virginian, was a contrasting figure physically —he was short, slight, and could barely be heard when he spoke—but he, too, was highly respected. He was regarded as the most learned man at the Convention, though he was only thirty-six years old. He had spent months preparing for the Convention by studying the history of ancient Greek confederacies and Italian republics. Madison also took meticulous notes of the Convention proceedings—there was no official stenographer, for the members worried about what are called "leaks" today—and his *Notes* remain one of the most important records of what transpired.

The Pennsylvania delegation included *Benjamin Franklin, James Wilson,* and *Gouverneur Morris.* Franklin, then eighty-one, was the Convention's oldest member. He had already earned his place in history as a revolutionary publicist, a statesman, an inventor, and, in the slightly exaggerated words of one of his fellow delegates, "the greatest philosopher of the present age." He was slowing down now, and his remarks had little effect on the proceedings, though they were received with respect and, on some occasions, relief: his humor helped break the tension that often developed.

James Wilson, tall, Scottish-born, with thick, wire-rimmed glasses worn halfway down his nose, became a formidable champion of a strong presidency. His keen, well-trained mind was put to the service of those who wanted to see America unified under a powerful central government headed by a single executive.

Gouverneur Morris, in the words of one contemporary account, was "a very handsome, bold, and—the ladies say—a very impudent man." Among his other distinctions were a wooden leg, an aristocratic attitude (he couldn't stand vulgar moneymakers), a keen desire for a strong central government, an elegant prose style. It was Morris who put the final polish on the language of the Constitution.

Many other members deserve honorable mention, but space permits the inclusion of only a few. *Luther Martin* of Maryland, *John Dickinson* of Delaware, and *William Paterson* of New Jersey remained out of step with majority sentiments at the Convention, but they fought a good fight for equal representation of small states in the new government. *Roger Sherman* and *Oliver Ellsworth* deserve credit for their role in preventing the Convention from breaking up over the issue of representation. Sherman offered what came to be called "the Connecticut compromise," which gave the states equal representation in the Senate and representation according to population in the House of Representatives.

The work of the Convention completed, the struggle now turned to a new front: ratification. The new charter had provided that it would become the supreme law of the land only when approved, or "ratified," by conventions in nine of the existing thirteen states.

THE FEDERALIST PAPERS

The ratification debate quickly led to the formation of two opposing factions, one of which became our first political party under the Constitution. The two factions were called the "Federalists" and the "Anti-Federalists." The Federalists, so called because they urged the adoption of the new "federal" Constitution, argued that the Constitution was necessary and would usher in an era of prosperity, stability, and concord. The Anti-Federalists argued that the Constitution was really an attempt by rich "aristocrats" to usurp the liberties of the people and crush states' rights.

A powerful propaganda vehicle for the Federalist side was a series of articles that appeared in various New York newspapers. The author of the articles was named "Publius." It turned out that "Publius" was three authors: Alexander Hamilton, James Madison, and John Jay. Jay wrote just a few of the articles; most of them were the work of Hamilton and Madison. They were later published in a volume entitled *The Federalist*.

The Federalist Papers, as they are commonly known today, were more than a sales pitch for the new Constitution. They were, and are, remarkable essays, full of insight into human nature, society, and government. Historians Charles and Mary Beard, who were not uncritical admirers of the Founding Fathers, wrote that *The Federalist* "has been widely regarded as the most profound single treatise on the Constitution ever written and as among the few masterly works on political science produced in all the centuries of history."

Thanks in part to the work of Hamilton, Madison, and Jay, the Constitution was ratified within two years. Even so, approval did not come easily. In Pennsylvania, for example, the legislature was preparing to call for a ratifying convention when three Anti-Federalists in the chamber walked out, depriving the legislature of the necessary quorum to do business. The next morning the truants were roused from their lodgings, carried triumphantly into the legislative chambers, sat upon, and counted as "present." The majority then voted to call the ratifying convention, which subsequently ratified for Pennsylvania.

THE BILL OF RIGHTS

One of the strongest arguments against the new Constitution was that it contained no explicit guarantees that the people's basic freedoms would not be abridged by the new government. It contained no "bill of rights." The Federalists replied that a bill of rights was not necessary. The new national government would have only the powers delegated to it and thus could not abridge such time-honored liberties as the right to speak and the right to a fair trial. Moreover, the Federalists argued, to guarantee *some* rights might actually be dangerous, because people might start thinking that those not mentioned could be abridged.

But demands for a bill of rights persisted. Thomas Jefferson, who had not attended the Convention, approved its work—but said it needed a bill of rights. So did another famous revolutionary, Samual Adams of Massachusetts, who conditioned his vote for ratification on a promise that a bill of rights would be added by the First Congress.

And so it was. In 1789, the First Congress added the first ten amendments to the Constitution, amendments that were ratified in 1791. The Bill of Rights guarantees freedom of speech, press, assembly, and religion. It prohibits the "establishment" of religion. It mentions "the right to keep and bear arms." It guarantees criminal suspects "due process of law," fair trials, and freedom from compulsory self-incrimination. It says that people must not be held in jeopardy twice for the same offense or be subjected to "cruel and unusual punishment." There are other guarantees as well, including one which ought to dispose of the Federalists' argument that to list some rights is to imperil those not listed. The Ninth Amendment says: "The enumeration in the Constitution, of certain rights, shall not be construed to deny or disparage others retained by the people."

Note the passive voice: the enumeration "shall not be construed. . . ." Who is it who shouldn't construe? The answer is government officials. But officials at what level of government—federal, state, or both? The Bill of Rights was originally intended to apply only to the federal government. The First Amendment begins: "*Congress* shall make no law . . ." (emphasis added). While that limiting reference to the national legislature is not found in any of the other amendments, there seems little doubt that the Framers of the Bill of Rights ended up agreeing with Representative Thomas Tucker of South Carolina, who said: "It will be much better, I apprehend, to leave the State Governments to themselves, and not interfere with them more than we do, and that is thought by many to be too much." Tucker made that remark during House debate of a Madison-inspired amendment that would have guaranteed free speech, a free press, and jury trials against infringement "by any State." Though the House passed the amendment, the Senate defeated it, and the House later concurred in the Senate's judgment.

Forty-four years later Chief Justice John Marshall placed the stamp of the judiciary upon the limited, federal-level-only interpretation of the Bill of Rights. The case was *Barron* v. *Baltimore* (1833). Of course, the *Barron* precedent has been overturned, as it were, in a piecemeal manner since 1897. Before examining this process, we need to speak about the role of courts, particularly the Supreme Court, in interpreting the Constitution.

John Marshall has already been mentioned twice in this chapter. Who was he? Why is he so important?

The fourth chief justice of the Supreme Court, John Marshall changed the institution from a weak, obscure entity—it met in the basement of the Capitol—to a center of national power that easily rivals the other two branches. Born in a log cabin near the Virginia frontier, Marshall was a distant cousin of Thomas Jefferson, with whom he often crossed swords. His portraits show a handsome man with jet-black eyes and a determined jaw. Marshall was a patriot and a fighter, serving in the Continental Army and enduring the terrible Valley Forge winter of 1777–1778. He later became a firm supporter of the new Constitution and secretary of state under John Adams. Therein, as they say, hangs a tale.

MARBURY V. *MADISON* (1803): JUDICIAL REVIEW

During the last days of the Adams administration, a series of events occurred which would culminate in a landmark Supreme Court case. That case was *Marbury* v. *Madison* (1803), and it established the principle of judicial review.

Judicial review means the authority of courts, and ultimately the Supreme Court, to declare unconstitutional acts of Congress or actions of the president. The term is never used in the Constitution, nor is such authority explicitly granted to the Supreme Court. However, the idea was not uncommon in eighteenth-century America, nor was it particularly controversial. In No. 78 of *The Federalist*, Alexander Hamilton argued that it was an essential means of enforcing the Constitution's limitations on government.

> Limitations of this kind can be preserved in practice no other way than through the medium of courts of justice, whose duty it must be to declare all acts contrary to the manifest tenor of the Constitution void.

This power to declare laws unconstitutional does not, Hamilton insisted, mean that the judicial branch is superior to the legislative branch. "It only supposes that the power of the people is superior to both. . . ." The Constitution represents the settled and carefully considered will of the people. It is the basic charter under which the people have decided to govern themselves. Legislators are merely the agents of the people, acting with a temporary grant of power but acting under the Constitution. As agents of the people, legislators are bound to respect the people's charter, including the limitations on legislative power that are written into it. And if they refuse to? That is where the judiciary plays its vital role. By declaring unconstitutional acts to be null and void, the judiciary protects the people against their agents.

In *Marbury* v. *Madison*, Marshall used reasoning similar to Hamilton's. The case arose out of the following circumstances. In the waning days of his administration, President Adams, already defeated in the election by Jefferson, began appointing his fellow Federalists en masse to judicial posts. "The Federalists," Jefferson complained, "have retired into the Judiciary as a stronghold . . . and from that battery all the works of republicanism are to be beaten down and erased." In the last hours of the Adams administration, the flood of appointments signed by the lame-duck president and sealed by his acting secretary of state—who was none other than John Marshall—became so great that Marshall mistakenly left some of the papers in his office before departing.

The next day the new secretary of state, James Madison, came upon them. One of the appointments, to the position of justice of the peace, belonged to one William Marbury. Madison withheld Marbury's appointment, thus setting the stage for a legal action of profound significance. Marbury went directly to the Supreme Court and asked for a writ of mandamus, a court order commanding Madison to deliver the appointment to him. Acting Secretary of State John Marshall had now become chief justice and, unmindful of any possible conflict of interest, was now in the position of deciding on Marbury's application for the writ. Here, surely, was a perfect example of what Jefferson feared: a Federalist chief justice beating down and erasing the works of republicanism by deciding a case involving a fellow Federalist.

Yet Marshall faced a dilemma. If he followed what would seem to be his political inclinations and granted Marbury his writ, there remained a distinct possibility that Jefferson would simply ignore it. What would happen then? Jefferson's administration had been carried into office by a large and triumphant majority. A similar pro-Jefferson majority now dominated Congress. Marshall's party was already in its dotage, while his Court was in its infancy. Both would be helpless against a defiant president, especially one as popular as Thomas Jefferson, and nothing could be more demoralizing for the Court than to issue an order and have it disobeyed with impunity. Yet the other horn of the dilemma was no more pleasant to contemplate. For if Marshall bowed to superior force and turned down Marbury's request for a writ, would this not be a concession of defeat?

Marshall sidestepped the dilemma by, in a sense, having it both ways. Much of the opinion in *Marbury* v. *Madison* was devoted to scolding Thomas Jefferson. Yes, Marbury had a right to the commission, which had been duly signed and sealed; Jefferson had no right to withhold it from him. Yes, since Marbury had a right, and the right had been violated, the laws of this country should indeed afford him a remedy. But when it came to the question of the particular relief requested by Marbury—a writ of mandamus—Marshall concluded that the Court had no power to issue it. In denying himself this power, however, Marshall claimed for the Court a far greater power: the power to declare federal laws unconstitutional.

The Court's power to issue writs of mandamus "in cases warranted by the principles and usages of law" was granted in Section 13 of the Judiciary Act of 1789. Marshall found this section unconstitutional because it sought to add to the Court's original jurisdiction. It is unnecessary for our purposes to examine Marshall's reasoning on this point. The enduring issue of the case is one which Marshall treated almost parenthetically: Where does the Court derive its authority to declare federal statutes unconstitutional? Let us see what sort of answers we can wring out of Marshall.

The question "whether an Act, repugnant to the Constitution, can become the law of the land" was, Marshall observed, "deeply interesting," but "happily, not of an intricacy proportioned to its interest." The answer was simple: if any ordinary statute could supersede the Constitution, there would be no point in having a written constitution, since legislators would not be bound by it. The trouble with Marshall's argument, however, is that it avoided a direct confrontation with the truly "interesting" question of the case. It is not hard to find adherents to the position that the Constitution should be supreme over statutes; of course the Constitution should be supreme. The real question is: Which branch of government has the sovereign power to interpret the often puzzling language of the Constitution? What does the Constitution mean by an "establishment of religion"? "Due process of law"? "Commerce among the several states"? The meaning of these and other key clauses in the Constitution is still being debated and probably will be as long as the Constitution endures. What gives the Court special insight into the meaning of this loose and elusive language? What entitles it to have the last word?

Marshall does not directly answer this question, for the simple reason that he does not raise it; but he does at least imply an answer. In doing so, he borrows heavily from Hamilton's argument in No. 78 of *The Federalist*: the argument based upon expertise or specialization. Hamilton had said that "interpretation of the laws is the peculiar province of the courts." Marshall said: "It is emphatically the province and duty of the judicial department to say what the law is." This was the major premise of his argument. The unspoken minor premise was that the Constitution is a law. Thus follows the conclusion that the courts have the peculiar duty, the sovereign authority, to interpret the Constitution.

The weakest link in the syllogism is its minor premise, that the Constitution is a law. Marshall himself did not believe the Constitution was a law in the usual meaning of that term. Earlier in this chapter we quoted from an 1819 opinion of Marshall, in which he reminded us "that it is a *constitution* we are expounding." A constitution, he said, is different than a "legal code." The distinguishing characteristic of a legal code is its "prolixity," its extensiveness, resulting from the need to spell out everything in detail. A constitution, or at least our federal Constitution, avoids that kind of precision. If it tried to spell out everything as a legal code does, it could scarcely be embraced by the human mind and "would probably never be understood by the public." The Constitution, then, is not just a lawyer's document. It is a people's document (it should be "understood by the public") and one made to be flexible, if not deliberately vague. This raises the question whether the Constitution can be considered a law, or at any rate a law of the kind which the judiciary has the peculiar "province and duty" to interpret. The legal training of judges may make them experts on prolix legal codes, but does it make them experts on a broadly worded document like the Constitution? Should not prudence and plain common sense play a great role in interpreting such a document? And do judges have a monopoly on prudence and common sense?

These questions, surprisingly enough, were not raised at the time by critics of *Marbury* v. *Madison*. Jefferson was furious at Marshall—not, however, for invalidating a section of the Judiciary Act or claiming the power of judicial review but for presuming to lecture him in the opinion. Marshall had turned a dilemma into a victory. Nothing could be done to him, nor could he even be defied, since he had commanded no one to do anything. His opinion was, as Professor Robert G. McCloskey has written, "a masterwork of indirection, a brilliant example of Marshall's capacity to sidestep danger while seeming to court it, to advance in one direction while his opponents were looking in another." The Court was "in the delightful position . . . of rejecting and assuming power in a single breath."

BARRON V. *BALTIMORE* (1833): THE BILL OF RIGHTS DOES NOT BIND THE STATES

If Marshall's opinion in *Marbury* amounted to a bold assertion of judicial power, his opinion thirty years later in *Barron* v. *Baltimore* (1833) seems almost the opposite in spirit and tone. It denies that federal courts have the authority to decide certain cases —those involving an alleged state interference with the liberties guaranteed in the Bill of Rights. One scholar, William Crosskey, went so far as to characterize Marshall's opinion in *Barron* as a "sham." Marshall, said Crosskey, expressed views he did not really believe, just to go along with the majority of the Court. Crosskey's interpretation seems strained. It is more likely that Marshall honestly did not believe that the Bill of Rights applied to the states.

John Barron was the owner of a deep-water wharf in the harbor of Baltimore, Maryland. Ditches dug by the city to promote drainage carried silt into the harbor around his wharf, filling in the water and making the wharf unsuitable for large ships. Barron sued the city for damages, claiming that the effect of its ditch digging resulted in a violation of the clause in the Fifth Amendment which prohibits the taking of property "for public use, without just compensation." In effect, his property was being "taken"—ruined—by the city of Baltimore, and he was not being compensated.

Sorry about that, John Marshall said in effect, but federal courts have no jurisdiction to hear your complaint under the Fifth Amendment. The Fifth Amendment, like the rest of the Bill of Rights, limits only the federal government. If "the framers of these amendments intended them to be limitations on the powers of the state governments, they could have . . . expressed their intention." The real intention of the Bill of Rights was to provide "security against the apprehended encroachments of the general government—not against those of the local governments." Case dismissed.

THE EROSION OF *BARRON* V. *BALTIMORE*

For thirty-five years—indeed, for almost sixty-five years—that was the end of the argument that the Bill of Rights applied to the states. But in 1868 the Fourteenth Amendment to the Constitution was ratified, and the Fourteenth Amendment very explicitly *does* apply to the states. The second sentence of the amendment begins, "No state shall. . . ." Among the things no state shall do is to "deprive any person of life, liberty, or property without the due process of the law." That "due process" clause of the Fourteenth Amendment, in the hands of Supreme Court justices, is what led to the erosion of *Barron* v. *Baltimore*. Even so, it took a long while before the erosion even began. For years lawyers tried to argue that the word "liberty" in the clause encompassed all the "liberties" contained in the Bill of Rights, thus making the first ten amendments applicable to the states. For years the Court resisted that argument.

Then, in 1897, came the case of *Allgeyer* v. *Louisiana*. In it the Court said that "the liberty mentioned in that Amendment means, not only the right of the citizen to be free from the mere physical restraint of his person, as by incarceration, but . . . the right of the citizen to be free in the enjoyment of all his faculties, to be free to use them in all lawful ways. . . ." In *Twining* v. *New Jersey* (1908), the Court, while reaffirming that the Bill of Rights did not apply to the states, nevertheless stated that "it is possible" that some of the rights safeguarded in the first eight amendments "may also be guarded against state action." In *Coppage* v. *Kansas* (1915), the Court said that the right of private property is a liberty "in the long-established constitutional sense." And in another 1915 case, *Truax* v. *Raich*, the Court said that "it requires no argument" to show that the right to work for a living was a liberty the Fourteenth Amendment was meant to secure. As constitutional scholar Charles Warren remarked sarcastically, "by the year 1915, a definition of 'liberty' which was first promulgated by the Court in the year 1897, had become its 'long-established constitutional sense' which 'requires no argument.'"

The word "liberty" in the due process clause of the Fourteenth Amendment was thus interpreted to encompass "economic liberty" and "freedom of contract," a decision which had the effect of preventing states from doing much to regulate businesses. At the same time the Court began expanding the definition of "personal freedoms." In 1923, in *Meyer* v. *Nebraska*, the Court decided that the Nebraska statute forbidding the teaching in school of any language other than English was unconstitutional. In its opinion, the Court said that the "liberty" protected in the Fourteenth Amendment meant not merely freedom from bodily restraint "but also the right of the individual to contract, to engage in any of the common occupations of life, to acquire useful knowledge, to marry, establish a home and bring up children, to worship God according to the dictates of his own conscience. . . ." This came close to saying that the "liberty" protected by the Fourteenth Amendment takes in all the liberties of the First Amendment. The Court came even closer in 1925, when it said in the case of *Gitlow* v. *New York*:

> For present purposes we *may and do assume* that freedom of speech and of the press—which are protected by the First Amendment from abridgement by Congress—are among the fundamental personal rights and "liberties" protected by the due process clause of the Fourteenth Amendment from impairments by the States. (Emphasis added.)

Since then the Court has been looking at various other parts of the Bill of Rights and deciding that they, too, are "liberties" encompassed by the Fourteenth Amendment and thus applicable to the states.

Gradually, then, *Barron* v. *Baltimore* has become obsolete. Piece by piece, in case after case, the Bill of Rights has been made applicable to the states. True, parts of it are still held not to be applicable. But its most vital parts have been "incorporated" into the Fourteenth Amendment. Elsewhere in this book, particularly in Chapter 4, the story of "selective incorporation" is told in greater length. To some people it is an inspiring story, a story of the growth of liberty. Others are troubled by it. They see it as a process that has resulted in unwarranted judicial intrusion into the affairs of states.

CONCLUSION

This introduction has tried to give a brief overview of some of the themes that run throughout this book. It has also provided some background information for the video programs and introduced key terms and concepts. It might be well for the reader to review it before watching the first TV program.

The chapters that follow contain review sections, called "Points to Remember," that summarize preceding parts. For this chapter it may be sufficient to remind the reader of what has been discussed: the "living Constitution" and how it came to be drafted in Philadelphia, the leading figures at the Convention, the struggle to ratify the Constitution and the role of *The Federalist Papers*, the later insertion of the Bill of Rights, the two cases of *Marbury* v. *Madison* and *Barron* v. *Baltimore*, and the gradual erosion of *Barron*. If you know something of the background and significance of all the above, you should be nearly ready for the following chapters and the TV programs. One last assignment: *read* the Constitution, which is at the back of the book.

Part One

The Process
of Government

Chapter 1
Ambition Against Ambition

"Ambition must be made to counteract ambition."

JAMES MADISON

"You know, we're not dealing in powdered wigs and pewter mugs here. This is street fighting. . . ."
CONGRESSWOMAN BARBARA MIKULSKI

It looks simple at first. The body of the Constitution consists of seven sections or "articles." The first three set up the three branches of our national government: Congress, the presidency, and the Supreme Court. Unlike most constitutional systems in the world today, ours is based on the principle of separation of powers. The three branches of government are elected or appointed in different ways, from different constituencies, and at different times. They also do different things. Congress makes laws, the president administers them, and the Supreme Court decides cases based on them. The Framers wanted to be sure that all three powers—legislative, executive, and judicial—did not end up in the same hands. That, James Madison said, would be "the very definition of tyranny."

There it is. Very simple. It starts to get complicated only when we look over the list of powers and duties assigned to each branch. Then we see that the president has the power to veto bills and—with the advice and consent of the Senate—make treaties with foreign countries. He is also supposed to give Congress periodic reports on "the state of the Union" and to "recommend to their Consideration such Measures as he shall judge necessary and expedient." These don't sound like executive duties. They sound legislative. Now we read over Article I, the legislative section, and find that the Senate has to approve all the president's major appointments. Doesn't that mean interfering in the executive branch's business? The Supreme Court can, we know, strike down laws passed by Congress and signed by the president. No matter how we rationalize it, we know this savors of legislative power.

What is going on here? We do not have complete separation of powers. What we have are separate branches of government *sharing* power.

Precisely, Madison would say. That is how it's supposed to be. In the same number of *The Federalist* in which he warned against the accumulation of all power in one branch, Madison also insisted that the powers must not be totally separate from one another. The great "oracle" on the subject, he said, "is the celebrated Montesquieu." Madison was referring to a French philosopher with the formidable name of Charles de Secondat, baron de la Brede et de Montesquieu (1689-1755). Montesquieu was the author of *The Spirit of the Laws*, a book much respected and quoted by Americans in the eighteenth century, which celebrated and expounded on the concept of separated powers.

Madison then went to work explaining what Montesquieu really meant. He meant "that where the *whole* power of one department is exercised by the same hands which possess the *whole* power of another department, the fundamental principles of a free constitution are subverted." But he "did not mean that these departments ought to have no *partial agency* in, or no *control* over, the acts of each other." In another paper in *The Federalist*, the famous No. 51, Madison went on to explain why the overlap of powers is essential to liberty. If each branch of government could go its own way without any outside interference, there would be no check on its powers. The American people could end up being ruled by three tyrannies.

That the three branches are designed to meddle and interfere with one another, then, is one of the beauties of our system. The president can prevent the legislators from running away with their power: he can veto their bills. His veto, in turn, can be counterchecked. Congress can override it by a two-thirds vote in both houses. The Congress can prevent the president from acting irresponsibly within his sphere of power: the Senate must approve his appointments and his treaties, and together the House and Senate can drive him from office. The Supreme Court, for its part, can strike down legislation, but it can also be interfered with in a variety of ways by the other branches if it gets too arrogant. And so it goes. "Ambition must be made to counteract ambition," said Madison. By "ambition," Madison meant the politicians' lust for power. Our system is deliberately set up to encourage those lusts to counteract themselves.

Does all this sound a little cynical? Are our liberties secure only if we pit the politicians against each other, so that they don't get together and oppress us? Madison admitted that "it may be a reflection on human nature that such devices should be necessary to control the abuses of government." But, he added, "what is government itself, but the greatest of all reflections on human nature?" If people were angels, they wouldn't need government. Most of the Founding Fathers and American revolutionaries shared this view of human nature and human organizations. Even Tom Paine, the revolutionary idealist, put forth a version of it. "Government, like clothes," he said, "is the badge of lost innocence." Madison would add something that Paine sometimes forgot: government must be firm in dealing with fallen man. Therefore, Madison said, "you must first enable the government to control the governed; and in the next place oblige it to control itself."

THE ISSUES

This brings us to the issues discussed in the video program. How well does the federal government control itself? Are the branches in balance right now, or are they tilting? The debate centers largely on the relationship between the two elected branches, the presidency and Congress, and encompasses two specific groups of issues. First, how far can Congress go in demanding information from the president? Congress, of course, is entitled to oversee the work of the executive branch. But can it demand to see confidential memos handed to the president by his aides? Can it subpoena those aides and make them recount their conversations with the president? Can it go so far as to subpoena the president? Suppose the executive officials refuse to talk—what sanctions and what means of enforcement does Congress have then? The second group of issues concerns the delegation of legislative power to the president. How far should that go? And is there any way of building into such delegations a means for pulling power back quickly if the president seems to be misusing it? What devices have been used for such purposes, and why has the Supreme Court struck down one of them?

The Video Discussion

The participants in the video debate come from a wide range of professions: a former president of the United States, former executive officials, federal judges, congressmen, professors, and prominent attorneys. The moderator is Benno C. Schmidt, Jr., dean of Columbia Law School.

List of Participants

HON. ARLIN M. ADAMS
Judge
U.S. Court of Appeals
Third Circuit

STANLEY M. BRAND
General Counsel
Office of the Clerk
U.S. House of Representatives

PHILIP W. BUCHEN
Attorney
Dewey, Ballantine, Bushby, Palmer & Wood
Former Counsel to President Ford

ARCHIBALD COX
Carl M. Loeb
University Professor
Harvard Law School
Solicitor General of the U.S., 1961–1965

LLOYD N. CUTLER
Attorney
Wilmer, Cutler & Pickering
Former Counsel to President Carter

HON. CHRISTOPHER J. DODD
U.S. Senator
Connecticut

HON. GERALD R. FORD
President of the United States,
1974–1977

HON. ORRIN G. HATCH
U.S. Senator
Utah

HON. BARBARA A. MIKULSKI
U.S. Representative
Maryland

HON. EDMUND S. MUSKIE
Attorney
Chadbourne, Parke, Whiteside & Wolff
Former Secretary of State
Former U.S. Senator
Maine

JACK NELSON
Washington Bureau Chief
Los Angeles Times

DONALD L. ROBINSON
Professor of Government
Smith College

JAMES D. ST. CLAIR
Attorney
Hale & Dorr
Former Special Counsel to
President Nixon

LT. GEN. BRENT SCOWCROFT
USAF (retired)
Chairman
President's Commission on Strategic
Forces

HON. POTTER STEWART
Justice (retired)
U.S. Supreme Court

HON. PATRICIA M. WALD
Judge
U.S. Court of Appeals
D.C. Circuit
Former Assistant Attorney General
for Legislative Affairs

HON. J. CLIFFORD WALLACE
Judge
U.S. Court of Appeals
Ninth Circuit

BEN J. WATTENBERG
Senior Fellow
American Enterprise Institute

TOM WICKER
Columnist and Associate Editor
New York Times

Program Summary

The program is divided into two parts. The first part concerns the issue of "executive privilege"—the claim of many presidents that they have a right to keep confidential executive-branch communications that relate to carrying out presidential duties. The moderator posits a hypothetical case in which records of a president's conversations with his secretary of energy and others are demanded by a congressional committee. What happens if the president instructs his secretary not to produce the records and not to testify? If Congress holds the aide and/or the president in contempt for refusing, can executive officials be jailed? If so, can they be jailed by Congress? Or would a court decision be necessary? Should courts get involved in such controversies?

In debating these questions, the issue of "reporter's privilege" comes up. If presidents have a duty to divulge sources and confidential information, don't members of the press have a similar duty? Or are the two cases fundamentally different? If so, how do they differ?

The second part of the program is concerned with delegations of power. Can Congress delegate some of its legislative power to the executive branch? If so, can it protect that power from abuse by executive officials? Why did the Supreme Court strike down the "legislative veto" in the 1983 *Chadha* case? Was it right to do so? What remaining devices does Congress have for ensuring that it can delegate power without losing it?

I: EXECUTIVE PRIVILEGE

"Executive privilege"—the right of the president to withhold information or witnesses from the other branches of government—is found nowhere in the Constitution, although it may be implied by separation of powers. The term "executive privilege" was coined in 1958, but its practice goes back to the Washington administration. In 1796 the House of Representatives, investigating the background of a controversial treaty, asked the president for papers relating to it. Washington refused, claiming that the House had no right to request such papers, since he had already supplied them to the Senate (which, unlike the House, is the president's partner in treaty making). From that time until comparatively recently, presidential refusals to supply confidential materials were rare—but so were requests for them. Presidential-congressional conflict on this issue did not escalate into open warfare until the late 1940s and early '50s, when congressional committees began a series of investigations into the issue of Communist influence in government.

We should pause here to consider the legitimate purpose of "executive privilege." Much of Congress's work is done quietly and conscientiously. On occasion, however, some congressmen cannot resist grandstanding. They conduct gaudy hearings, filled with sensational charges. In the case of *Watkins* v. *United States* (1957), the Supreme Court ruled that no congressional committee has the power to "expose for the sake of exposure," and that "no inquiry is an end in itself; it must be related to, and in furtherance of, a legitimate task of Congress." Yet the ruling is really not much help if congressmen are determined to go on a witch-hunt: they can always tie their hearings, however tenuously, to some law or proposed law. Suppose a congressional committee has no serious intent but merely wants to fish through executive files and see what it can find? Must the president yield everything requested? It would be hard not to sympathize with a president who refused to do so. On the other hand, a blanket refusal by a president to disclose *any* information under *any* circumstances would rightly be regarded with suspicion.

The issue of executive privilege, then, should be treated with caution. Unfortunately, it has not been. It has gotten tied to absolute pronouncements, which have then been reversed when circumstances changed. Examples of this syndrome can be found in reactions to the investigations of Communist influence that began in the 1940s and in the Watergate investigation of the '70s.

Investigations: Communism and Watergate

In 1947, when the House Un-American Activities Committee was investigating charges of Communist influence in the Truman administration, the president responded by reserving the right to determine whether disclosures would serve "the public interest." Among the more ardent critics of Truman's claim was a young Republican congressman named Richard M. Nixon. Later, when the Eisenhower administration came along, it found itself being investigated by a fellow Republican, Senator Joseph R. McCarthy of Wisconsin. Charging that there was evidence of Communist influence in the U.S.

Army, McCarthy asked to see some pertinent files. Eisenhower's refusal to comply contained an assertion of executive privilege even more sweeping than Truman's. He claimed that "it is not in the public interest that *any* . . . conversations or *any* documents or reproductions [relating to the investigation] be disclosed" (emphasis added).

The *New York Times*, the *Washington Post*, and other prominent media voices rejoiced at Eisenhower's refusal to produce the documents. The *Times*'s only regret was that the refusal took so long in coming. All along, the *Times* said in an editorial,

> this newspaper has maintained that the fundamental issue is an attempt on the part of the Legislative branch in the person of Mr. McCarthy to encroach upon the Executive branch, in complete disregard of the historic and constitutional division of powers that is basic to the American system of government.

The notion that a congressional committee can demand information concerning conversations between the president and his close aides struck the *Times* as wholly irresponsible.

> The committee has no more right to know the details of what went on in these inner administration councils than the Administration would have the right to know what went on in an executive session of a committee of Congress.

It would have been one thing had the *Times* said that this particular congressman was conducting not a serious investigation but a media event, and therefore deserved no cooperation from the administration. But no, the *Times* said in an earlier editorial, "it is not a personality that is at stake. . . . It is the spirit of the Constitution. It is a principle in equity." The "principle" was stated in absolute language: "No legislator, no group of legislators, has the legal, let alone the moral, right to require Government employees to violate their superiors' orders. . . ."

Twenty years later, when the Watergate scandal was being investigated by Congress, the *Times*'s editors and other leading commentators reversed themselves. Now Congress's "right to know" was paramount; the executive branch had no right to "cover up" and "hide behind" the claim of executive privilege. Today it must embarrass many people to be reminded that, back in 1954, the person who stood almost alone in warning us about the possible abuse of executive privilege was Senator Joseph McCarthy. McCarthy said:

> . . . I'm not talking about the present occupant of the White House, but we got a tremendously important question here, Mr. Chairman. That is, how far can the President go? Who all can he order not to testify? . . . We don't know who will be President, 1956, 1960, 1964. . . . Any President can, by an executive order, keep the facts from the American people. . . .

By 1973, McCarthy's warning seemed almost eerily prophetic. We will discuss what "Watergate" entailed in a later chapter. For now, let's note simply that it involved criminal activity for which administration officials eventually went to prison. In attempting to limit probes of this activity, President Nixon broadened the claim of executive privilege to cover not only documents but testimony from any "member *or former member* of the President's personal staff" (emphasis added). His attorney general went even further, announcing to a Senate committee that "executive privilege" covered not only the president's aides but any one of the 2.5 million employees of the federal government!

But little by little, Nixon began retreating. Soon his closest aides were testifying before the special Senate committee investigating the scandal. Then it was discovered that Nixon had a secret taping system in the Oval Office and at other sites, which recorded every conversation between Nixon and his visitors. The tapes' existence must have seemed a godsend to the congressional investigators. On two separate occasions, the Senate Watergate Committee tried to subpoena tapes. Yet both requests for subpoenas were rejected in district court, and the committee never appealed.

In the meantime, however, a special prosecutor had been appointed—an officer technically answerable to the president, though his name had been put forward by Congress. This prosecutor was Archibald Cox, who had served as solicitor general in the Johnson administration. (He is a participant in the video debate.) Cox, too, kept requesting tapes from Nixon—whereupon Nixon fired him. This provoked such an outcry in Congress and the press that Nixon was forced to name a new special prosecutor. If Nixon cherished any hopes that the new officer would be any easier on him, he was soon disappointed. Leon Jaworski, the new special prosecutor, wanted tapes. This time the requests brought about a historic Supreme Court case.

United States v. *Nixon* (1974): Executive Privilege Is Not Absolute

Because Jaworski's requests were resisted by Nixon, the Supreme Court soon found itself confronted for the first time with the issue of executive privilege. The case before the Court raised many unresolved questions. Is executive privilege a valid claim? Does it have a constitutional basis? What is its legitimate scope? What are its limits? All these questions hovered behind the arguments by the attorneys for the president and the special prosecutor. And while the Court confined its opinion to the immediate question before it, its opinion suggested some answers to the larger issues.

Even though he had appointed four members of the Court, Nixon lost the case by an eight-to-zero margin. He was ordered to give up the tapes to the special prosecutor. (He did, and one of the tapes was so damning that Nixon would have been impeached and convicted had he not stepped down.) Yet the opinion, written by Chief Justice Burger, was narrow in scope. In this particular case, it said, the president had to give up the tapes. Serious criminal charges had been made against members of the Nixon administration. There were going to be trials, and the tapes would be used as evidence. The requests were limited and carefully specified. They were made by a special prosecutor with authority to bring criminal charges. They would first be listened to *in camera* (privately) by a district court judge to determine their relevance. No claim had been made by the president that they contained diplomatic or military secrets. All these facts were carefully noted by Burger in denying Nixon's generalized claim of immunity.

Thus the *Nixon* decision is not very helpful to any congressional committee seeking access to a president's White House conversations. On the contrary. To begin with, Burger declared that such conversations enjoy "presumptive privilege." This means that courts must start with the assumption that their contents belong to the president and nobody else. Anyone who wants records of such talks has to show why an exception should be made. The importance of confidentiality, Burger said, "is too plain to require further discussion." The president is entitled to his aides' frank opinions; his aides "may well temper candor with a concern for appearances" if they think their words will soon be bandied about on Capitol Hill. Executive privilege, then, "can be said to derive from the supremacy of each branch within its own assigned area of constitutional duties."

Second, it is important to remember that this case involved a request not by a congressional committee but by a special prosecutor. (As already noted, the congressional requests proved fruitless. Both were rejected at the district court level and neither was appealed.) Throughout his opinion, Burger stressed the fact that the tapes were essential to prove or disprove serious criminal charges. "The ends of criminal justice would be defeated if judgments were to be founded on a partial or speculative presentation of the facts."

The case, then, did not represent a victory by Congress over the president; it represented a victory by a special prosecutor. It may be cold comfort to Nixon, but his chief appointee actually upheld and defended the concept of executive privilege even as he ruled it inapplicable in the case before him.

Video Discussion of Executive Privilege

The legal experts in the video discussion, including the judges and attorneys, know how secure executive privilege is against congressional challenge; they are cautious about bringing the issue into court. The congressmen on the panel tend to be bolder, and the media people bolder still. Boldest of all is Stanley Brand, the counsel to the clerk of the House, who is ready to subpoena the president himself if necessary.

How did the discussion reach the topic of such legal confrontations? In the hypothetical case posed by the moderator, it seems that the president, worried about America's dependence on foreign oil, talks with his close aides about using his authority under a 1955 law to impose a license fee on imported oil. The moderator turns to former President Gerald Ford. Does Congress, he asks, have a right to know the content of those conversations? No, says Ford. "It would be almost impossible for a president to carry on the operation of his office" in difficult circumstances if he could not elicit frank advice from his aides, and frankness is not compatible with publicity. What about written memos that aides give the president on the topic? They "would be just as controlled, under the executive privilege decisions as a . . . verbal or oral communication and recommendation," says Ford.

Barbara Mikulski, the cheerful, combative congresswoman from Maryland, thinks otherwise. "Oh, we're very much interested in the decision-making process. We're going to want to know what [the president's] going to do, when he's going to try to do it, and . . . why he is going to do it." Mikulski would like to hold "oversight" hearings. "Oversight," which Congress has been engaged in since the days of the Washington administration, means monitoring or checking up on the executive branch to see whether it is properly carrying out the laws passed by Congress. It is undertaken with varying degrees of thoroughness and intrusiveness, depending on the times, the parties controlling the legislature and executive, and the people doing the overseeing. In the past, especially during the heyday of the Kennedy and Johnson administrations in the 1960s, many complained that Congress was exercising too little supervision over the executive branch. More recently the complaint from Republican presidents is that congressional committees have become too intrusive and confrontational. Possibly Gerald Ford could make that complaint about Barbara Mikulski. "You know," she says at one point, "we're not dealing in powdered wigs and pewter mugs here. This is street fighting. . . ." Mikulski wants testimony and records concerning the president's conversations with his aides, and she anticipates "a major confrontation with the president."

Philip Buchen, who served as Ford's legal counsel when he was president, would advise him to provide Mikulski's committee with some but not all of the records. ("Don't send up anything you think is sensitive, that may cause us problems as a government.") The way to approach the matter, says Buchen, is to "sit down and negotiate with the committee." But Mikulski says, "it's too early to negotiate." She can do better without negotiating, because the more pressure she puts on the executive branch, "the more that a lot of information will come to me in a variety of forms."

"Ahhh!" says the moderator, and smiles knowingly. He knows that can mean only one thing. Mikulski is going to be the beneficiary of leaks from lower-level bureaucrats ("GS-13s") in the Department of Energy. Are these disloyal employees? Mikulski prefers to call them "dedicated public servants (*laughter*) with little whistles around their necks." These celebrated "whistle-blowers" occupy a corner of what turns out to be a very interesting Washington triangle.

Symbiotic Relationships: Whistle-Blowers, Congress, Press

Zoology books tell us about small birds that perch on the snouts of alligators. The birds and the alligators get along fine because the birds keep the alligators free of bugs. The two species enjoy a "symbiotic" ("living together") relationship. The video discussion discloses a similar relationship between reporters, congressmen interested in embarrassing an administration, and lower-level bureaucrats opposed to their bosses' policies. The bureaucrats leak documents that reveal the baser motives of their bosses. This information is valuable to congressmen and reporters alike.

The hypothetical case provides an example. Mikulski is not interested in the president's stated motives for imposing a license fee on imported oil—to lessen our dependence on foreign oil, to make America stronger, and all that. She wants the inside story. "I want to know why the president did what he did, apart from this pap that I've been

hearing." Her assumption that there is a "real" motive lurking behind the stated motive, and that the real motive is not very worthy, seems to be shared by the journalists.
"There have been too many examples in my own career," says Tom Wicker of the *New
York Times*, "in which presidential decisions have not been made in the spirit of pure
national interest."

But what about the motives of the whistle-blower? The moderator puts this question to Jack Nelson of the *Los Angeles Times*. Nelson replies that he will mention in
his story that the information was leaked by someone opposed to the president's policy. But then, anticipating the moderator's next question, he adds that he will *not*
include the name of the leaker. Why not? "Well, I can't afford to do that. I'd be out of
business." (There is unconscious irony here; the moderator calls attention to it by re-
minding Nelson that "that's what *he's* saying," indicating President Ford. If your business requires confidentiality, he says in effect, doesn't the president's also require it?)
The professional symbiosis between leakers, congressmen, and reporters is further
illustrated by the remarks of Stanley Brand, counsel to the clerk of the House. "I call
up my friends in the *New York Times* and the *Baltimore Sun*," he says,

> and I tell them, you know, they're trying to protect a memo from a GS-5 to a
> GS-18. . . . Do you think that's the kind of stuff that . . . ought to be subject to
> executive privilege? You know, there are 2 million GS-5s in the government, and
> the Congress would never get a shred of paper if we accepted that.

He does not need to add that the press might also have trouble getting that shred of
paper.

Ben Wattenberg has been assigned the role of President Ford's secretary of energy.
A former speechwriter for Lyndon Johnson, Wattenberg has his own media connections. He will use them to counter the bad image Mikulski and Brand are giving the administration. "I've started to make a few phone calls to some columnists I know," he
says. Mikulski is ready for the challenge: "Well, but my columnists say (*laughter*) and
my young reporters. . . ." Her distinction is subtle but significant. Wattenberg may
have some columnists on his side, but Mikulski has all the young reporters! This is no
small power to have in the 1980s.

In *The Powers That Be* (Knopf, 1979), David Halberstam describes a revolution
that occurred in the mass media during the 1960s. Effective power began slipping
away from the old owners and publishers and into the hands of working reporters and
correspondents. These men and women began setting the tone of news coverage, and
their immediate bosses either went along or eventually got replaced. It is an interesting
thesis, and in the video debate, Utah Senator Orrin Hatch adds to it by suggesting that
this new class of power wielders has an abiding professional interest in exposing administration wrongdoing. That is why, even though his heart is with Wattenberg, Hatch
thinks Mikulski and Brand will have the power of the media on their side.

> You see, there are two competing interests here. One is the interest of the president
> in being able to run the country . . . and the other is the interest of Congress to be
> able to oversee, to stop fraud, ferret out corruption. . . . I think the president loses

on executive privilege . . . in almost every case in the public media today. And I can hardly blame the press for that, because they want the information, and frankly, they generally presume that the president has something to hide. . . .

The media may be powerful, but their power is different than the power of law. What legal sanctions are there against a stonewalling president? Can he be forced to produce notes of his confidential meetings with aides? Can his secretary of energy be forced to testify even if the president forbids him to do so? These questions elicit a variety of responses during a learned discussion of scenarios that President Ford calls "ridiculous."

Brand is now going to court for "dragnet subpoenas." He wants "everything—drafts, memoranda, notes." He wants subpoenas served on the secretary of energy, the secretary of state, and the secretary of the treasury. "How about the president himself?" the moderator asks. "Sure," Brand replies. The idea of forcing the president to testify before a House committee is too much even for Barbara Mikulski. "I'm going to fetter in this guy," she says of Brand. "You don't call for the president like you're whistling for a cab." But she has no hesitation about getting a subpoena to serve on the president's secretary of energy.

The moderator now turns to Lloyd Cutler, former legal counsel to Jimmy Carter. What would he tell the secretary of energy? The secretary, Cutler says, should go and testify but "respectfully decline to answer a very limited category of questions—those relating to advice to the president." But that is just the information Mikulski wants!

What happens next? Mikulski can try to persuade the full House to cite the secretary for contempt of Congress. But she has little appetite for this option. Her preference is to encourage her young reporters to make the secretary look "contemptible in the eyes of the American people (laughter)." Mikulski does not want to pursue a full House vote on contempt for two reasons. First, it might create a "backlash against [her] own cause." Second, she would have to squander so many of her "bargaining chips" in persuading her colleagues to vote for the contempt citation that she could not ask any more favors of them for a long time.

But the moderator wants to push the hypothetical case to its conclusion: Suppose the House does vote to cite Wattenberg for contempt? What then? In that case, Mikulski says, we arrest him. Who arrests him? The sergeant-at-arms of the House of Representatives, says Mikulski. The vision of Jack Russ, former chief page of the House, marching over to the White House to arrest the secretary of energy does not seem quite credible to the panelists. And the image approaches the psychedelic when Stanley Brand informs the panelists that "there's a jail in the basement of the Capitol (laughter)." No one objects when President Ford calls the whole scenario "ridiculous."

It's judges who bring the discussion back to reality. Appeals Court Judge Patricia Wald makes no secret of her desire to avoid the issue of executive privilege versus congressional subpoenas. "We've been able to avoid it for 200 years more or less." She would "figure out some way to avoid it without leaving Mr. Wattenberg in the basement." Arlin Adams, another appeals court judge, agrees. "We ought to do everything within our power to get the parties directly to solve their differences. . . . I think the most important thing is to make sure that Mr. Wattenberg is released from his confinement."

Archibald Cox thinks the jailing of Wattenberg is "quite intolerable," and suggests a way to get him out: the president's lawyers should go to court and contend that Congress has no reason for holding him, since the whole matter is beyond the courts' jurisdictions—it is a "political question." The concept of "political questions" will be discussed in Chapter 2. For now, it is enough to note that even the former Watergate special prosecutor seems to doubt that Congress can coerce a president's assistant to testify if the president orders him not to. With the apparent exception of Stanley M. Brand, no one on the panel has very much enthusiasm for court tests of executive privilege.

Points to Remember

1. The Framers of the Constitution believed in separation of powers, but they also believed that there should be some overlap of powers in order to encourage "checks and balances."
2. Executive privilege—the practice, not the term—goes back to the Washington administration. However, presidents' reasons for withholding documents and information have varied with administrations.
3. Not until the late 1940s was executive privilege asserted as a general principle. That was when Congress began investigating charges that the administration harbored Communist agents.
4. During the period of Communist investigations, the *New York Times* and other major media asserted that Congress had no right to demand records of conversations within the executive branch. Twenty years later, during the Watergate investigations, they reversed their position.
5. Executive privilege in relation to Congress (that is, the president's assertion of the right to withhold material from congressional investigators) has never successfully been challenged in court. However, in *United States* v. *Nixon* (1974), the Supreme Court held that executive privilege is not an absolute right and ordered the president to turn over materials to a special prosecutor.
6. *United States* v. *Nixon* qualified executive privilege but also gave it judicial recognition. The Court said that records of the president's conversations enjoy "presumptive privilege," meaning that anyone seeking access to them must convince the Court that an exception should be made. In the *Nixon* case the Court considered it important that the tapes were relevant to pending criminal trials.
7. The video discussion of executive privilege reveals that "whistle-blowers," some congressmen, and the press sometimes work together when they have a common interest in exposing the misdeeds of an administration.
8. Most of the panelists would like to avoid legal showdowns on the issue of executive privilege. The politicians would rather rely on the press and public opinion; the judges and attorneys prefer negotiation.

II: DELEGATING LEGISLATIVE POWER

This chapter began by mentioning the three branches of the federal government: Congress, the presidency, and the Supreme Court. The Congress passes laws, the president administers them, and the Supreme Court decides cases involving them. All very simple —yet not so simple. The three compartments are not hermetically sealed from one another; on the contrary, they leak. The president can veto legislation passed by Congress, which gives him a legislative role. The Senate must approve presidential appointments, which gives it an executive role. The Supreme Court can strike down legislation and presidential decisions, which gives it both a legislative and an executive role. The leakage, James Madison assured us in *The Federalist*, is quite intentional; its purpose is to give each branch a means of defense against the other branches, so that no single branch can take over the whole government; for that, he said, "is the very definition of tyranny." This intentional overlap of powers for the purpose of preventing their accumulation in one branch is called "checks and balances."

The system makes sense. But it has its own difficulties. In theory, separation of powers and checks and balances complement each other. In reality, there is tension between them. Separation of powers means that each branch minds its own business; checks and balances means that each branch minds the other branches' business, at least a little bit—the legislature may disapprove executive appointments, the executive may veto the work of the legislature, and so on. This leads to some interesting jurisdictional fights.

We saw one of those fights played out in the first part of the program. In effect, Gerald Ford was telling Congress: "My White House conversations with my aides are entirely my own business." Some of the members of Congress were answering: "No, Mr. President, not entirely your business. We have the task of overseeing your branch to make sure it is faithfully enforcing the laws." Meanwhile, the judges and the Washington attorneys were wondering whether it was any of *their* business. On the one hand, they seemed to think that the problems should be worked out by the president and Congress; on the other hand, they didn't want to see Ben Wattenberg imprisoned in the Capitol basement.

In the second part of the program, the jurisdictional battle gets more complicated. At issue is the topic of legislative vetoes, in which Congress delegates power to the president but reserves the right to take back that power if even one house of Congress so decides. The Supreme Court struck down the practice just four months before the panelists debated it.

Before we can talk about legislative vetoes, though, we have to say something about delegations of power. The dictionary defines the verb "to delegate" as "to appoint someone to perform a task." We may delegate a lawyer to represent us in court, or delegate a friend to write a letter for us. The clear meaning is that the act be done in accordance with our intentions and on the basis of rather specific instructions. Delegating power is not the same as abdicating it.

The Supreme Court has repeatedly upheld the right of Congress to delegate legislative power to the executive branch. But the Court has changed its views on how specific the guidelines must be for the use of this legislative power. In a 1931 case, the Supreme Court said that "Congress cannot delegate any part of its legislative power except under a limitation of a prescribed standard." But what kind of standard was meant? How specific should it be? At one point in the program, retired Supreme Court Justice Potter Stewart is asked whether courts should "be worried about overly broad delegations of power to the president." He replies that "this harks back to a long time, many years ago, when I was in law school." Justice Stewart was in law school in the 1930s. In those days every American law student cut his teeth on the case of *Schechter Poultry Corp.* v. *United States* (1935), also known as the "sick chicken case."*

Schechter: The Sick Chicken Case

In 1933 Congress passed the National Industrial Recovery Act (NIRA). It authorized the president to promulgate "codes of fair competition" for trades and industry throughout the United States. (In fact, the codes were largely developed by leaders of the various industries, but they carried the sanction of the executive branch.) Soon there were several hundred codes that contained provisions concerning unfair trade practices, minimum wages and prices, and maximum hours. Schechter, who operated a slaughterhouse in Brooklyn, was convicted of violating a number of codes promulgated by the executive commission. He appealed on two grounds: first, the national government had no business trying to regulate him, since his business was not involved in interstate commerce; second, the executive branch commission that set up the "codes of fair competition" had been given too broad a delegation of legislative power. The Supreme Court agreed with him on both counts.

In Chapter 13 we shall examine the Supreme Court's view of interstate commerce. It is the second point, concerning the delegation of legislative power, that interests us here. The Court said that the NIRA "supplies no standards for any trade, industry or activity." Instead of prescribing rules of conduct for industries, the act left everything up to the president. His discretion "is virtually unfettered." In a concurring opinion, Justice Benjamin Cardozo said, "This is delegation running riot."

The reason Justice Stewart may have connected the *Schechter* decision with his youth is that in some respects it seems tied to the 1930s. The Court never formally overturned the decision, but in subsequent cases it approved delegations of legislative power at least as sweeping as those it had struck down in *Schechter.* More recently, however, some approving references to *Schechter* have cropped up in both Supreme Court decisions and political science literature. In *National Cable Television Association* v. *United States* (1974), for example, the majority opinion of Justice William O. Douglas put a narrow construction on the fee-setting authority of administrative agencies in order to avoid the charge that the agencies had been given unrestricted legislative power. He cited the *Schechter* case as a standard. In a 1969 work, political scientist

*It is not altogether clear *why* it is called "the sick chicken case." Schechter was convicted not of selling diseased poultry but of violating labor and trade regulations. Maybe it was these practices, rather than the chickens, that were considered unwholesome.

Theodore Lowi also suggested that *Schechter* embodied a sound principle of law, namely that the legislature ought to do the legislating. Acknowledging that a great deal of discretion had been handed over to the executive branch since 1935, Lowi contended that it was time to rein in some of that discretion. The Supreme Court, he said, should go back to the spirit of *Schechter*:

> The Court's rule must once again become one of declaring invalid and unconstitutional any delegation of power to an administrative agency that is not accompanied by clear standards of implementation.

Yet whatever Lowi or anyone else might think, the fact is that the executive branch of government has been given more and more authority to promulgate rules that govern our lives. The increase in administrative rule making is reflected in the phenomenal growth of the *Federal Register*, in which most of these rules must be published. In 1960, the *Register* contained 14,479 pages. By 1970, the figure had risen to 20,032; by 1975 it was 60,221; and by 1980 the *Register* contained more than 87,000 pages! In theory, of course, these are not really laws—just rules for "implementing" laws passed by Congress. Yet in practice the bureaucrats have enormous discretion; they promulgate everything from automobile safety standards to the ratio of girls to boys in public school gym classes.

All these delegations may be essential for the governing of modern America. With all our social and economic problems, our burgeoning, complex technology, our international involvements, our domestic needs, it would be pure nostalgia to think we could go back to the government we had a century ago. Yet it is just here that the dilemma arises. If we do need regulations, who should make them? If the executive branch makes them, then bureaucrats are exercising what amounts to legislative power. Yet if Congress decides it wants to make all the rules, how can it possibly do so? Congress has a hard enough time passing the most general statute. It lacks the speed and flexibility to deal with the particulars of regulation. Thus the dilemma: Congress can either risk abdicating its lawmaking function or else risk insanity by trying to write over 87,000 pages of rules to implement its statutes. There has got to be a way out.

Congress thought it found one in the legislative veto.

The Legislative Veto

Here is how it worked. Congress would pass a law delegating broad decision-making authority to the executive branch. But it would retain the right to strike down any executive decision it didn't like. Congress inserted such provisions into at least 126 statutes. Some statutes said both houses of Congress had to agree to reverse the executive decision; other statutes said that if even one house disapproved, the president's decision would be reversed. The principle was the same: Congress gave authority to the president but retained the right to veto his decisions. Many legislative experts considered this a great way to retain both legislative authority and flexibility. The Supreme Court said it was unconstitutional.

Chadha: Legislative Veto Is Unconstitutional

The pivotal case was *Immigration and Naturalization Service* v. *Chadha et al.*, decided in June 1983. Just a few months earlier, two political scientists had confidently predicted that the Court would uphold the veto. It is "highly probable," they said, that some form of the veto would survive judicial challenge. After all, it has "been used for half a century in a wide variety of important policy areas, ranging from executive reorganization to trade agreements, arms sales, and executive impoundments." Right. Yet it did not survive. Why?

To see the Court's reasoning, we should first understand the background of the case. Until 1940 Congress had always regulated immigration through precisely written statutes that the Justice Department had to enforce to the letter. No allowance was made for an immigrant's individual hardship. If such cases did arise, the only remedy was a "private bill" naming the individual and providing a remedy in his or her case only. This was obviously a very cumbersome solution. James Sundquist, an authority on Congress, picks up the story:

> Eventually, someone said: Let's simplify all this. Whenever the two branches agree, let the Attorney General do on his own what has heretofore been done through private bills; when they disagree, reserve for the Congress the power that it has always had to say no. So a two-house legislative veto was written into law in 1940, and converted into a one-house veto in 1952.

Enter Jagdish Rai Chadha, an East Indian born in Kenya. Chadha came to the United States in 1966 on a nonimmigrant student visa. His visa expired in 1972, but he didn't leave the country. In 1973, the Immigration and Naturalization Service (INS) ordered him to show cause why he should not be deported. A hearing was held, during which Chadha managed to convince an immigration judge that being deported would cause him "extreme hardship." His deportation was suspended, and the suspension was reported to Congress.

If Congress had taken no action, the story would have ended there. But Congress, or rather one house of Congress, did act. A congressional subcommittee reviewed Chadha's case and concluded that he should have been deported. The full House agreed and voted to deport him. When the House vote was carried back to the immigration judge, he told Chadha he had no alternative but to deport him. Chadha sued, and the case wound up in Supreme Court.

The majority opinion, written by Chief Justice Burger, must have infuriated some members of Congress. It sounded like a lecture on the topic "How to Pass a Law." Here is the way laws are passed, said Burger. A bill passes through both houses of Congress and is then presented to the president for his signature. If he signs it, it becomes law. If he does not, it fails to become a law unless both houses of Congress pass it again by two-thirds majorities. A bill must go through all these steps; otherwise it is not law. Now, Burger continued, here is what Congress has done in this case. It has delegated some of its legislative power to the executive branch. That is all right. But it also wants to overrule the executive without bothering to pass a new law! When the legislature acts (except in certain cases carefully specified in the Constitution), it must act through *both* houses and then *present* the bill to the president. It has not done that here. It has tried to legislate through one house only. That attempt violates Article I of the Constitution.

Though the political scientists mentioned earlier were wrong in predicting that the Court would sustain the legislative veto, they were right about one thing: over the past half-century the veto has been put into an astounding number and variety of statutes— trade agreements, energy laws, budget control measures, campaign regulations, pension plan regulations, veterans' education laws, the War Powers Resolution (see the next chapter), and many others. When the Court struck down the legislative veto in *Chadha*, it knocked out 207 legislative veto provisions in 126 laws. It may have gone even further and killed off some whole statutes. At this writing the lawyers are still trying to figure out how many of the legislative veto provisions are *severable* from the rest of the laws. Some statutes say or imply that if the veto provisions are declared invalid by courts, the rest of the statute survives. Others make it clear that the veto is an integral part of the statute, so that if it is invalidated the whole law is demolished.

The effects of *Chadha*, then, are still incalculable. No one can be certain whether it is going to cause a horrible mess or have some good effect on our system, forcing Congress to tend more closely to its legislative responsibilities. For Chief Justice Burger, these effects—good or bad—are beside the point. Conceding that it might be more efficient to allow laws to be changed by the action of only one house, Burger said that the Framers of the Constitution "ranked other values higher than efficiency." Their common desire was to define and limit the power of the newly created federal government. That is why they insisted that all legislation be passed by both houses and presented to the president for his signature. The Framers knew that this procedure would "often seem clumsy, inefficient, even unworkable." But this was one of the "hard choices" consciously made "by men who had lived under a form of government that permitted arbitrary government acts to go unchecked."

Video Discussion of Legislative Veto

In the video discussion the moderator asks Gerald Ford to assume he believes "it's essential to the national interest to impose a license fee on imported oil."

> Now you have the power under the Trade Expansion Act, as I understand it, to . . . do whatever you think is necessary to stop [the imported oil]. You can tax it. You can bar it. You can do whatever you want. Now, Mr. President, is that a presidential kind of a problem for Congress to put in your lap?

Ford thinks it *is* necessary for Congress to hand him the problem, because it calls for quick action. Ask Congress for a tax increase of $2 or $5 a barrel on imported oil and you will have a long wait. "With all respect to my friends in Congress, they don't act promptly or expeditiously on tax matters because of their apprehension about political ramifications."

Oddly enough, Senator Christopher Dodd of Connecticut seems just as ready to circumvent the legislative process. He doesn't mind that the license fee comes from the White House. But he thinks that the president's advisers should include members of Congress.

> I noticed when you set up your first meetings, you included everybody—the secretary of state, the president's chief legal adviser, the attorney general. But you didn't include any members of Congress at all in those discussions, and I'm quite confident that the Framers, the fathers, of that legislation never intended for this to be so exclusively a unilateral executive decision that they would be excluded from the process. . . .

This is a startling suggestion. Carried to its conclusion it would abolish separation of powers, for it would make members of Congress part of the president's cabinet.

Political science professor Donald Robinson is appalled. He thinks the Framers of the Constitution would no longer recognize their document:

> They intended for the branch that is elected by the people to make the policy, and the job of the president is to carry that policy out, to take care that the laws are faithfully executed. . . . I think for the president to make policy for this country turns the Constitution upside down.

But, counters the moderator, "he's just doing what Congress has invited him to do." Robinson has his answer ready: "That's a good point. Congress is a co-conspirator in turning the constitutional process upside down."

Professor Robinson's argument is so forceful and clear that it brings back into focus the theme of this chapter: separation of powers. In stating his point, however, he may have gone too far. He has harkened back to the *Schechter* decision of 1935, which struck down a delegation of power to the president. Since then, as already noted, the Court has approved some extremely broad grants of legislative power to the executive branch.

Is *Schechter* still a live precedent? Many constitutional authorities think not. If Christopher Dodd is ready to blur separation of powers by bringing members of Congress into the president's cabinet, Donald Robinson may tend toward the other extreme by emphasizing the separateness of the two branches. Actually, the Framers of the Constitution did not believe these branches should be completely separate. They believed in an overlap of powers which they considered necessary for checks and balances to work.

Perhaps, then, the legislative veto would fit right into the spirit of checks and balances. It allowed Congress to give power to the president without losing complete control of it. Isn't that what James Madison had in mind? Another James, James Sundquist, puts it this way:

> The legislative veto is an additional check and balance that the Founding Fathers did not think of. If it violated the Constitution's language, it actually served to reinforce the very constitutional principle that the Chief Justice chose to cite in striking it down.

The argument is worth considering. But the fact remains that the legislative veto no longer exists. "Not after June 21, 1983," Brand acknowledges.

Points to Remember

1. In the *Schechter* case of 1935, the Supreme Court struck down as overly broad a delegation of legislative power to the president. Since then, however, the Court on many occasions has approved broad delegations of such power to the president. Many constitutional authorities now consider *Schechter* to be moribund, although others think it is ripe for revival.
2. In order to combine speed and flexibility with legislative control, Congress in the 1940s invented the legislative veto. By this method Congress delegated broad powers to the president but reserved the right to veto any of his decisions by passing a resolution in one or both houses.
3. In the *Chadha* case of 1983, the Supreme Court declared the legislative veto unconstitutional. Since the veto has been written into 207 places in 126 laws, the effect of *Chadha* may be far-reaching. In deciding the case, Chief Justice Burger said that no matter how useful the veto might have been, it violated Article I of the Constitution because it attempted to pass legislation without passing it in both houses and presenting it to the president for his signature.
4. In the video discussion, President Ford supports broad grants of power to the president when speed and flexibility are essential. Senator Dodd suggests that members of Congress be brought into executive decision making in such cases. Professor Robinson claims that broad grants of legislative power to the president turn the Constitution "upside down."

SUMMARY

Early in the video discussion, emphasizing Congress's need to be aggressive, Barbara Mikulski said, "You know, we're not dealing in powdered wigs and pewter mugs here. This is street fighting. . . ." Mikulski's statement gives the impression that the Founding Fathers spent their time bowing to each other and doing the minuet. Actually, they could probably hold their own in any street fight. In his youth Ben Franklin was as formidable a wrestler as he was a debater. Hamilton was an almost insanely courageous fighter during the Revolution. Jefferson was nearly captured by the British, who would have hanged him as a rebel. Washington's exploits hardly need to be recounted. These men could also talk tough—about the British, the French, and each other. Jefferson considered Hamilton an arrogant upstart. Hamilton regarded Jefferson as a sneak and a hypocrite. John Adams was famous for his tart comments on people and institutions. If these men could return to Philadelphia, they would warm the heart of Barbara Mikulski. They knew how to fight.

But just as they could act aggressively, they also knew that others could do the same. They suspected that aggressiveness is part of human nature, and that if it is not restrained it can become very nasty indeed. That is one purpose of government—to place limits on our aggressiveness. The trouble is that governments are themselves composed of human beings. Thus, government must not only control the governed; it must control itself. The best way of effecting that end, the Founding Fathers seemed to agree, was to separate the three branches of government, yet to give each branch just enough power over the others to prevent them from exercising unrestrained power. Let the politicians meddle just a bit with each other's powers. Let them fight it out.

The two issues considered in this chapter—executive privilege and the legislative veto—have been among the chief areas of combat between the legislative and executive branches. In the late '40s and early '50s, legislative committees grilled executive officials and demanded to see the records of executive deliberations. The executive fought back with claims of executive privilege. This happened again in the '70s, during the Watergate period. The tension continues today, roused by issues as varied as energy, environment, taxes, and war.

Yet even as the branches fight, they cooperate. The legislature delegates some of its power to the president, for it knows that it cannot deal with the particulars of lawmaking. Yet although it leaves much in the hands of the executive, it also tries to construct retrieval mechanisms. One of them, the legislative veto, was struck down by the Supreme Court in 1983. But Congress will continue to seek other ways of protecting delegated powers—or else it may stop or cut back on its delegations. Because it needs to, Congress will often cooperate with the executive; but there is no evidence that it is about to surrender its power to him.

The two elected branches, then, need each other, distrust each other, and jealously guard their territories against each other. Each has its own weapons of offense and defense. Each uses them, with varying degrees of success, in the contests that break out periodically in our history and that, thus far at least, have ended in no final victory for either side. "A harmonious system of mutual frustration," one critic called it. But for those of us who are neither presidents nor legislators and do not wish to be pushed around too much by either, the stalemate has certain advantages.

Documents

UNITED STATES V. NIXON, 418 U.S. 683 (1974)

This case grew out of a suit by a special prosecutor to obtain secret White House tape recordings and other materials which the prosecutor believed might be pertinent to upcoming trials of individuals accused of "Watergate" crimes. President Nixon, claiming "executive privilege," had denied the prosecutor access to the materials.

In a unanimous ruling the Court upheld the subpoena request of the special pro-secutor. (Justice William Rehnquist took no part in the decision because he had served in the Nixon Justice Department.)

Below are excerpts from the Court's opinion, as delivered by Chief Justice Warren Burger.

Opinion of the Court, Chief Justice Berger.

[W]e turn to the claim that the subpoena should be quashed because it demands "con-fidential conversations between a President and his close advisors that it would be inconsistent with the public interest to produce." The first contention is a broad claim that the separation of powers doctrine precludes judicial review of a President's claim of privilege. The second contention is that if he does not prevail on the claim of abso-lute privilege, the court should hold as a matter of constitutional law that the privilege prevails over the subpoena *duces tecum.**

In the performance of assigned constitutional duties each branch of the Govern-ment must initially interpret the Constitution, and the interpretation of its powers by any branch is due great respect from the others. The President's counsel, as we have noted, reads the Constitution as providing an absolute privilege of confidentiality for all Presidential communications. Many decisions of this Court, however, have unequiv-ocally reaffirmed the holding of Marbury v. Madison, 1 Cranch. 137 (1803), that "[i]t is emphatically the province and duty of the judicial department to say what the law is." *Id.*, at 177. . . .

Our system of government "requires that federal courts on occasion interpret the Constitution in a manner at variance with the construction given the document by another branch." Powell v. McCormack, 395 U.S., at 549. And in Baker v. Carr, 369 U.S., at 211, the Court stated:

"[D]eciding whether a matter has in any measure been committed by the Con-stitution to another branch of government, or whether the action of that branch exceeds whatever authority has been committed, is itself a delicate exercise in constitutional interpretation, and is a responsibility of this Court as ultimate in-terpreter of the Constitution."

Notwithstanding the deference each branch must accord the others, the "judicial Power of the United States" vested in the federal courts by Art. III, § 1, of the Con-stitution can no more be shared with the Executive Branch than the Chief Executive, for example, can share with the Judiciary the veto power, or the Congress share with the Judiciary the power to override a Presidential veto. Any other conclusion would be contrary to the basic concept of separation of powers and the checks and balances that flow from the scheme of a tripartite government. The Federalist, No. 47, p. 313

---

*A writ ordering a person to appear in court and to bring along books, writings, or other relevant materials in his or her possession.

(S. Mittell ed. 1938). We therefore reaffirm that it is the province and duty of this Court "to say what the law is" with respect to the claim of privilege presented in this case. Marbury v. Madison, *supra,* 1 Cranch. at 177.

In support of his claim of absolute privilege, the President's counsel urges two grounds, one of which is common to all governments and one of which is peculiar to our system of separation of powers. The first ground is the valid need for protection of communications between high Government officials and those who advise and assist them in the performance of their manifold duties; the importance of this confidentiality is too plain to require further discussion. Human experience teaches that those who expect public dissemination of their remarks may well temper candor with a concern for appearances and for their own interests to the detriment of the decisionmaking process. Whatever the nature of the privilege of confidentiality of Presidential communications in the exercise of Art. II powers, the privilege can be said to derive from the supremacy of each branch within its own assigned area of constitutional duties. Certain powers and privileges flow from the nature of enumerated powers; the protection of the confidentiality of Presidential communications has similar constitutional underpinnings.

The second ground asserted by the President's counsel in support of the claim of absolute privilege rests on the doctrine of separation of powers. Here it is argued that the independence of the Executive Branch within its own sphere . . . insulates a President from a judicial subpoena in an ongoing criminal prosecution, and thereby protects confidential Presidential communications.

However, neither the doctrine of separation of powers, nor the need for confidentiality of high-level communications, without more, can sustain an absolute, unqualified Presidential privilege of immunity from judicial process under all circumstances. The President's need for complete candor and objectivity from advisers calls for great deference from the courts. However, when the privilege depends solely on the broad, undifferentiated claim of public interest in the confidentiality of such conversations, a confrontation with other values arises. Absent a claim of need to protect military, diplomatic, or sensitive national security secrets, we find it difficult to accept the argument that even the very important interest in confidentiality of Presidential communications is significantly diminished by production of such material for *in camera* inspection with all the protection that a district court will be obliged to provide.

The impediment that an absolute, unqualified privilege would place in the way of the primary constitutional duty of the Judicial Branch to do justice in criminal prosecutions would plainly conflict with the function of the courts under Art. III. In designing the structure of our Government and dividing and allocating the sovereign power among three co-equal branches, the Framers of the Constitution sought to provide a comprehensive system, but the separate powers were not intended to operate with absolute independence.

"While the Constitution diffuses power the better to secure liberty, it also contemplates that practice will integrate the dispersed powers into a workable government. It enjoins upon its branches separateness but interdependence, autonomy but reciprocity." Youngstown Sheet & Tube Co. v. Sawyer, 343 U.S., at 635 (Jackson, J., concurring).

To read the Art. II powers of the President as providing an absolute privilege as against a subpoena essential to enforcement of criminal statutes on no more than a generalized claim of the public interest in confidentiality of nonmilitary and nondiplomatic discussions would upset the constitutional balance of "a workable government" and gravely impair the role of the courts under Art. III.

Since we conclude that the legitimate needs of the judicial process may outweigh Presidential privilege, it is necessary to resolve those competing interests in a manner that preserves the essential functions of each branch. The right and indeed the duty to resolve that question does not free the Judiciary from according high respect to the representations made on behalf of the President.

The expectation of a President to the confidentiality of his conversations and correspondence, like the claim of confidentiality of judicial deliberations, for example, has all the values to which we accord deference for the privacy of all citizens and, added to those values, is the necessity for protection of the public interest in candid, objective, and even blunt or harsh opinions in Presidential decisionmaking. A President and those who assist him must be free to explore alternatives in the process of shaping policies and making decisions and to do so in a way many would be unwilling to express except privately. These are the considerations justifying a presumptive privilege for Presidential communications. The privilege is fundamental to the operation of Government and inextricably rooted in the separation of powers under the Constitution. In Nixon v. Sirica, 159 U.S.App.D.C. 58, 487 F.2d 700 (1973), the Court of Appeals held that such Presidential communications are "presumptively privileged," *id.*, at 75, 487 F.2d, at 717, and this position is accepted by both parties in the present litigation. We agree with Mr. Chief Justice Marshall's observation, therefore, that "[i]n no case of this kind would a court be required to proceed against the president as against an ordinary individual." United States v. Burr, 25 F.Cas., at 192.

But this presumptive privilege must be considered in light of our historic commitment to the rule of law. This is nowhere more profoundly manifest than in our view that "the twofold aim [of criminal justice] is that guilt shall not escape or innocence suffer." Berger v. United States, 295 U.S., at 88. We have elected to employ an adversary system of criminal justice in which the parties contest all issues before a court of law. The need to develop all relevant facts in the adversary system is both fundamental and comprehensive. The ends of criminal justice would be defeated if judgments were to be founded on a partial or speculative presentation of the facts. The very integrity of the judicial system and public confidence in the system depend on full disclosure of all the facts, within the framework of the rules of evidence. To ensure that justice is done, it is imperative to the function of courts that compulsory process be available for the production of evidence needed either by the prosecution or by the defense.

Only recently the Court restated the ancient proposition of law, albeit in the context of a grand jury inquiry rather than a trial,

"that 'the public . . . has a right to every man's evidence,' except for those persons protected by a constitutional, common-law, or statutory privilege, United States v. Bryan, 339 U.S. 724, 730 (1949); Blackmer v. United States, 284 U.S. 421, 438 (1932). . . ." Branzburg v. Hayes, United States, 408 U.S. 665, 688 (1972).

The privileges referred to by the Court are designed to protect weighty and legitimate competing interests. Thus, the Fifth Amendment to the Constitution provides that no man "shall be compelled in any criminal case to be a witness against himself." And, generally, an attorney or a priest may not be required to disclose what has been revealed in professional confidence. These and other interests are recognized in law by privileges against forced disclosure, established in the Constitution, by statute, or at common law. Whatever their origins, these exceptions to the demand for every man's evidence are not lightly created nor expansively construed, for they are in derogation of the search for truth.

In this case the President challenges a subpoena served on him as a third party requiring the production of materials for use in a criminal prosecution; he does so on the claim that he has a privilege against disclosure of confidential communications. He does not place his claim of privilege on the ground they are military or diplomatic secrets. As to these areas of Art. II duties the courts have traditionally shown the utmost deference to Presidential responsibilities. . . . No case of the Court, however, has extended this high degree of deference to a President's generalized interest in confidentiality. Nowhere in the Constitution, as we have noted earlier, is there any explicit reference to a privilege of confidentiality, yet to the extent this interest relates to the effective discharge of a President's powers, it is constitutionally based.

The right to the production of all evidence at a criminal trial similarly has constitutional dimensions. The Sixth Amendment explicitly confers upon every defendant in a criminal trial the right "to be confronted with the witnesses against him" and "to have compulsory process for obtaining witnesses in his favor. Moreover, the Fifth Amendment also guarantees that no person shall be deprived of liberty without due process of law. It is the manifest duty of the courts to vindicate those guarantees, and to accomplish that it is essential that all relevant and admissible evidence be produced.

In this case we must weigh the importance of the general privilege of confidentiality of Presidential communications in performance of the President's responsibilities against the inroads of such a privilege on the fair administration of criminal justice. The interest in preserving confidentiality is weighty indeed and entitled to great respect. However, we cannot conclude that advisers will be moved to temper the candor of their remarks by the infrequent occasions of disclosure because of the possibility that such conversations will be called for in the context of a criminal prosecution.

On the other hand, the allowance of the privilege to withhold evidence that is demonstrably relevant in a criminal trial would cut deeply into the guarantee of due process of law and gravely impair the basic function of the courts. A President's acknowledged need for confidentiality in the communications of his office is general in nature, whereas the constitutional need for production of relevant evidence in a criminal proceeding is specific and central to the fair adjudication of a particular criminal case in the administration of justice. Without access to specific facts a criminal prosecution may be totally frustrated. The President's broad interest in confidentiality of communications will not be vitiated by disclosure of a limited number of conversations preliminarily shown to have some bearing on the pending criminal cases.

We conclude that when the ground for asserting privilege as to subpoenaed materials sought for use in a criminal trial is based only on the generalized interest in confidentiality, it cannot prevail over the fundamental demands of due process of law in the fair administration of criminal justice. The generalized assertion of privilege must yield to the demonstrated, specific need for evidence in a pending criminal trial.

IMMIGRATION AND NATURALIZATION SERVICE V. CHADHA (1983)

In this case the Court ruled unconstitutional the "legislative veto," the provision, which had been inserted into a number of statutes, permitting one or both houses of Congress to negate by resolution powers delegated to the president.

Chief Justice Warren Burger delivered the opinion of a six-member majority. (Justice Lewis Powell filed a separate concurring opinion. Dissenting were Justices Byron White and William Rehnquist.)

Excerpts from the opinion follow.

Opinion of the Court, Chief Justice Burger.

Chadha is an East Indian who was born in Kenya and holds a British passport. He was lawfully admitted to the United States in 1966 on a nonimmigrant student visa. His visa expired on June 30, 1972. On October 11, 1973, the District Director of the Immigration and Naturalization Service ordered Chadha to show cause why he should not be deported for having "remained in the United States for a longer time than permitted." App. 6. Pursuant to § 242(b) of the Immigration and Nationality Act (Act), 8 U. S. C. § 1254(b), a deportation hearing was held before an immigration judge on January 11, 1974. Chadha conceded that he was deportable for overstaying his visa and the hearing was adjourned to enable him to file an application for suspension of deportation under § 244(a)(1) of the Act, 8 U. S. C. § 1254(a)(1). . . .

After Chadha submitted his application for suspension of deportation, the deportation hearing was resumed on February 7, 1974. On the basis of evidence adduced at the hearing, affidavits submitted with the application, and the results of a character investigation conducted by the INS, the immigration judge, on June 25, 1974, ordered that Chadha's deportation be suspended. The immigration judge found that Chadha met the requirements of § 244(a)(1): he had resided continuously in the United States for over seven years, was of good moral character, and would suffer "extreme hardship" if deported. . . .

Once the Attorney General's recommendation for suspension of Chadha's deportation was conveyed to Congress, Congress had the power under § 244(c)(2) of the Act, 8 U. S. C. § 1254(c)(2), to veto the Attorney General's determination that Chadha should not be deported. Section 244(c)(2) provides:

"(2) In the case of an alien specified in paragraph (1) of subsection (a) of this subsection—
if during the session of the Congress at which a case is reported, or prior to the close of the session of the Congress next following the session at which a case is reported, either the Senate or the House of Representatives passes a resolution stating in substance that it does not favor the suspension of such deportation, the Attorney General shall thereupon deport such alien or authorize the alien's voluntary departure at his own expense under the order of deportation in the manner provided by law. If, within the time above specified, neither the Senate nor the House of Representatives shall pass such a resolution, the Attorney General shall cancel deportation proceedings."

The June 25, 1974 order of the immigration judge suspending Chadha's deportation remained outstanding as a valid order for a year and a half. [Then the House of Representatives passed a resolution vetoing the suspension.]

After the House veto of the Attorney General's decision to allow Chadha to remain in the United States, the immigration judge reopened the deportation proceedings to implement the House order deporting Chadha. Chadha moved to terminate the proceedings on the ground that § 244(c)(2) is unconstitutional. The immigration judge held that he had no authority to rule on the constitutional validity of § 244(c)(2). On November 8, 1976, Chadha was ordered deported pursuant to the House action.

Chadha appealed the deportation order to the Board of Immigration Appeals again contending that § 244(c)(2) is unconstitutional. The board held that it had "no power to declare unconstitutional an act of Congress" and Chadha's appeal was dismissed. App. 55–56.

Pursuant to § 106(a) of the Act, 8 U. S. C. § 1105a(a), Chadha filed a petition for review of the deportation order in the United States Court of Appeals for the Ninth Circuit. The Immigration and Naturalization Service agreed with Chadha's position before the Court of Appeals and joined him in arguing that § 244(c)(2) is unconstitutional. In light of the importance of the question, the Court of Appeals invited both the Senate and the House of Representatives to file briefs *amici curiae*.

After full briefing and oral argument, the Court of Appeals held that the House was without constitutional authority to order Chadha's deportation; accordingly it directed the Attorney General "to cease and desist from taking any steps to deport this alien based upon the resolution enacted by the House of Representatives." *Chadha v. INS*, 634 F. 2d 408, 436 (CA9 1980). The essence of its holding was that § 244(c)(2) violates the constitutional doctrine of separation of powers.

We granted certiorari . . . and we now affirm. . . .

Explicit and unambiguous provisions of the Constitution prescribe and define the respective functions of the Congress and of the Executive in the legislative process.

Since the precise terms of those familiar provisions are critical to the resolution of this case, we set them out verbatim. Art. I provides:

> "All legislative Powers herein granted shall be vested in a Congress of the United States, which shall consist of a Senate *and* a House of Representatives." Art. I, § 1. (Emphasis added).

> "Every Bill which shall have passed the House of Representatives *and* the Senate, *shall*, before it become a Law, be presented to the President of the United States; ..." Art. I, § 7, cl. 2. (Emphasis added).

> "*Every* Order, Resolution, or Vote to which the Concurrence of the Senate and House of Representatives may be necessary (except on a question of Adjournment) *shall be* presented to the President of the United States; and before the Same shall take Effect, *shall be* approved by him, or being disapproved by him, *shall be* repassed by two thirds of the Senate and House of Representatives, according to the Rules and Limitations prescribed in the Case of a Bill." Art. I, § 7, cl. 3. (Emphasis added).

These provisions of Art. I are integral parts of the constitutional design for the separation of powers. We have recently noted that "[t]he principle of separation of powers was not simply an abstract generalization in the minds of the Framers: it was woven into the documents that they drafted in Philadelphia in the summer of 1787." *Buckley* v. *Valeo*, 424 U. S., at 124. ...

The Presentment Clauses

The records of the Constitutional Convention reveal that the requirement that all legislation be presented to the President before becoming law was uniformly accepted by the Framers. Presentment to the President and the Presidential veto were considered so imperative that the draftsmen took special pains to assure that these requirements could not be circumvented. During the final debate on Art. I, § 7, cl. 2, James Madison expressed concern that it might easily be evaded by the simple expedient of calling a proposed law a "resolution" or "vote" rather than a "bill." 2 M. Farrand, The Records of the Federal Convention of 1787 301–302. As a consequence, Art. I, § 7, cl. 3, *ante*, at 25, was added. *Id.*, at 304–305.

The decision to provide the President with a limited and qualified power to nullify proposed legislation by veto was based on the profound conviction of the Framers that the powers conferred on Congress were the powers to be most carefully circumscribed. It is beyond doubt that lawmaking was a power to be shared by both Houses and the President. In the Federalist No. 73 (H. Lodge ed. 1888), Hamilton focused on the President's role in making laws:

> "If even no propensity had ever discovered itself in the legislative body to invade the rights of the Executive, the rules of just reasoning and theoretic propriety

would of themselves teach us that the one ought not to be left to the mercy of the other, but ought to possess a constitutional and effectual power of self-defense." *Id.*, at 457–458. . . .

The Constitution sought to divide the delegated powers of the new federal government into three defined categories, legislative, executive and judicial, to assure, as nearly as possible, that each Branch of government would confine itself to its assigned responsibility. The hydraulic pressure inherent within each of the separate Branches to exceed the outer limits of its power, even to accomplish desirable objectives, must be resisted.

Although not "hermetically" sealed from one another, *Buckley* v. *Valeo, supra,* 424 U. S., at 121, the powers delegated to the three Branches are functionally identifiable. When any Branch acts, it is presumptively exercising the power the Constitution has delegated to it. . . .

Examination of the action taken here by one House pursuant to § 244(c)(2) reveals that it was essentially legislative in purpose and effect. In purporting to exercise power defined in Art. I, § 8, cl. 4 to "establish an uniform Rule of Naturalization," the House took action that had the purpose and effect of altering the legal rights, duties and relations of persons, including the Attorney General, Executive Branch officials and Chadha, all outside the legislative branch. Section 244(c)(2) purports to authorize one House of Congress to require the Attorney General to deport an individual alien whose deportation otherwise would be cancelled under § 244. The one-House veto operated in this case to overrule the Attorney General and mandate Chadha's deportation; absent the House action, Chadha would remain in the United States. Congress has *acted* and its action has altered Chadha's status.

The legislative character of the one-House veto in this case is confirmed by the character of the Congressional action it supplants. Neither the House of Representatives nor the Senate contends that, absent the veto provision in § 244(c)(2), either of them, or both of them acting together, could effectively require the Attorney General to deport an alien once the Attorney General, in the exercise of legislatively delegated authority, had determined the alien should remain in the United States. . . .

Finally, we see that when the Framers intended to authorize either House of Congress to act alone and outside of its prescribed bicameral legislative role, they narrowly and precisely defined the procedure for such action. There are but four provisions in the Constitution, explicit and unambiguous, by which one House may act alone with the unreviewable force of law, not subject to the President's veto:

(a) The House of Representatives alone was given the power to initiate impeachments. Art. I, § 2, cl. 6;

(b) The Senate alone was given the power to conduct trials following impeachment on charges initiated by the House and to convict following trial. Art. I, § 3, cl. 5;

(c) The Senate alone was given final unreviewable power to approve or to disapprove presidential appointments. Art. II, § 2, cl. 2;

(d) The Senate alone was given unreviewable power to ratify treaties negotiated by the President. Art. II, § 2, cl. 2.

Clearly, when the Draftsmen sought to confer special powers on one House, independent of the other House, or of the President, they did so in explicit, unambiguous terms. These carefully defined exceptions from presentment and bicameralism underscore the difference between the legislative functions of Congress and other unilateral but important and binding one-House acts provided for in the Constitution. These exceptions are narrow, explicit, and separately justified; none of them authorize the action challenged here. On the contrary, they provide further support for the conclusion that Congressional authority is not to be implied and for the conclusion that the veto provided for in § 244(c)(2) is not authorized by the constitutional design of the powers of the Legislative Branch.

Since it is clear that the action by the House under § 244(c)(2) was not within any of the express constitutional exceptions authorizing one House to act alone, and equally clear that it was an exercise of legislative power, that action was subject to the standards prescribed in Article I. The bicameral requirement, the Presentment Clauses, the President's veto, and Congress' power to override a veto were intended to erect enduring checks on each Branch and to protect the people from the improvident exercise of power by mandating certain prescribed steps. To preserve those checks, and maintain the separation of powers, the carefully defined limits on the power of each Branch must not be eroded. To accomplish what has been attempted by one House of Congress in this case requires action in conformity with the express procedures of the Constitution's prescription for legislative action: passage by a majority of both Houses and presentment to the President.

The veto authorized by § 244(c)(2) doubtless has been in many respects a convenient shortcut; the "sharing" with the Executive by Congress of its authority over aliens in this manner is, on its face, an appealing compromise. In purely practical terms, it is obviously easier for action to be taken by one House without submission to the President; but it is crystal clear from the records of the Convention, contemporaneous writings and debates, that the Framers ranked other values higher than efficiency. The records of the Convention and debates in the States preceding ratification underscore the common desire to define and limit the exercise of the newly created federal powers affecting the states and the people. There is unmistakable expression of a determination that legislation by the national Congress be a step-by-step, deliberate and deliberative process.

The choices we discern as having been made in the Constitutional Convention impose burdens on governmental processes that often seem clumsy, inefficient, even unworkable, but those hard choices were consciously made by men who had lived under a form of government that permitted arbitrary governmental acts to go unchecked. There is no support in the Constitution or decisions of this Court for the proposition that the cumbersomeness and delays often encountered in complying with explicit Constitutional standards may be avoided, either by the Congress or by the President. See *Youngstown Sheet & Tube Co.* v. *Sawyer*, 343 U. S. 579 (1952). With all the obvious flaws of delay, untidiness, and potential for abuse, we have not yet found a better way to preserve freedom than by making the exercise of power subject to the carefully crafted restraints spelled out in the Constitution.

SELECTED READINGS

Baruch, Jeremiah. "Vetoing the Veto." *Commonweal*, August 12, 1983, pp. 421–424.
Jeremiah Baruch is the "pseudonym of a Washington writer with a position in
government." He characterizes *INS* v. *Chadha* as "an arthritically conceived and
articulated decision" and predicts that, by "foreclosing the efficient allocation of
congressional decision-making," it will increase the chances of hasty, ill-considered
action by Congress.

Berger, Raoul. *Executive Privilege: A Constitutional Myth.* Cambridge, Mass.: Harvard
University Press, 1974.
A leading authority on the separation of powers examines the historical basis for
contemporary claims of executive privilege. He concludes not only that the Founders did not intend such a privilege but that executive privilege amounts to a "shield
for executive unaccountability." This thorough analysis addresses privilege in relation to both domestic and foreign policy and both Congress and the courts.

Breslin, Jimmy. *How the Good Guys Finally Won.* New York: Viking, 1975.
A moving and amusing account of "impeachment summer," or the last months of
the Nixon administration. Breslin brings the characters involved to life, while discussing the Nixon tapes, executive privilege, and the grand confrontation between
the president and Congress.

Congressional Digest, December 1983, pp. 296–314.
The issue contains pro and contra arguments on whether Congress "should act
now to preserve the legislative veto." Those favoring such action include Senator
Dennis Deconcini and Representatives James Broyhill and Elliot Levitas. Those
opposed include Senator Wendell Ford and Representatives Neal Smith and John
Moakley.

Cronin, Thomas E. "A Resurgent Congress and the Imperial Presidency." *Political Science Quarterly* 95 (Summer 1980): 209–237.
Political scientist and former White House staff member Cronin examines presidential-congressional interaction since the so-called resurgence of congressional
power. He argues that, while congressional control of the presidency has not been
as great as some had hoped, in many ways it has been quite effective. Yet he also
argues that it is difficult to prevent misuse of presidential power without "ham-
stringing the President who would use those same powers for purposive and
democratically acceptable ends."

Destler, I. M. "Dateline Washington: Life After the Veto." *Foreign Policy*, Fall 1983,
pp. 181–186.
A former Carnegie Endowment director criticizes Chief Justice Burger's "simplistic and sweeping" opinion in *Chadha.* "Future Presidents may well rue the day
that their predecessors encouraged the Court to strike down an innovative, flexible mechanism for power sharing between the branches."

Dixon, Robert G., Jr. "Congress, Shared Administration, and Executive Privilege." In
Harvey C. Mansfield, Sr., *Congress Against the President. Proceedings of The
Academy of Political Science* 32, no. 1 (1975).
Dixon, a former assistant U.S. attorney general, examines the history of the doc-

trine of executive privilege, the complexities and subtleties seen in the doctrine since *United States* v. *Nixon*, and the strains that a president's potential assertion of executive privilege puts on his relations with Congress.

Fisher, Louis. *Presidential Spending Power.* Princeton, N.J.: Princeton University Press, 1975.

Professor Fisher examines the history of the budgeting and appropriations process from the presidency of George Washington through that of Richard Nixon. He is concerned with the powers that have come to the presidency through several legal or questionably legal practices: reprogramming and transferring appropriated funds, covert financing of CIA operations, and presidential impoundment of funds. He examines in particular the legacy of Richard Nixon and Congress's 1974 decision to control presidential impoundments.

Friedman, Leon, ed. *United States v. Nixon: The President Before the Supreme Court.* New York: Chelsea House, 1974.

A collection of documents tracing the controversy that culminated in the Supreme Court's "Nixon tapes" case. Starting with District Court Judge Sirica's order, the book includes the U.S. Court of Appeals decision, both sides' petitions to the Supreme Court, briefs, and oral arguments before the Court, as well as the Court's decision. A valuable reference work for anyone seeking a fuller understanding of the case.

Sorensen, Theodore C. *Watchmen in the Night: Presidential Accountability after Watergate.* Cambridge, Mass.: MIT Press, 1975.

Former Kennedy aide and confidant Sorensen asks: "Was Nixon an aberrant?" and "Was Watergate a deterrent?" He then looks at how the Congress, the courts, and the public might bring some measure of accountability to the presidency. This is a short and readable introduction to the general problem of presidential accountability in the age of the imperial presidency.

Sundquist, James L. *The Decline and Resurgence of Congress.* Washington, D.C.: The Brookings Institution, 1981.

The "resurgence" that congressional scholar James Sundquist examines is that of congressional power in the years after the Nixon administration and the Watergate crisis. He considers the general structural and political factors that make congressional leadership difficult and provides detailed analysis of Congress's assertion of authority over the budget, the administration, and wartime policy.

Wayne, Stephen J. *The Legislative Presidency.* New York: Harper & Row, 1978.

This excellent, slim volume by a political science professor at George Washington University provides a thorough introduction to the institutionalized management techniques designed to bring as much cooperation as possible to presidential-congressional relations.

West, William, and Cooper, Joseph. "The Congressional Veto and Administrative Rule-making." *Political Science Quarterly* 98 (Summer 1983): 285-304.

West and Cooper explain the complex aspects of the administrative process that led to Congress's decision to exercise a constitutional check on executive power through the legislative veto. The authors consider the veto's practical more than its constitutional advantages and disadvantages.

GLOSSARY

Ambition. In Madison's usage, the lust for power. Such lust tempts people to "vex and oppress" each other.

Checks and balances. A system of governmental organization that, by slightly over-lapping the functions of the branches, stimulates rivalry among the branches.

Delegation of power. The transfer of legislative power to the executive branch for the purpose of applying it to specific cases.

Executive privilege. The president's claim of confidentiality regarding the conversations of top-level administrators.

Federal Register. A government publication that records the president's executive orders.

In camera. In the judge's chamber. An *in camera* examination of subpoenaed materials takes place behind closed doors, in the judge's chamber.

Legislative veto. A device permitting one or both houses of Congress, by a resolution, to negate powers delegated to the president. Declared unconstitutional in the Supreme Court's 1983 *Chadha* decision.

Separation of powers. The assignment of different functions to different branches of government—that is, lawmaking to the legislature, administration to the executive, application of legal sanctions to the judiciary.

Special prosecutor. During the "Watergate" period of 1973-74, executive-branch investigation and prosecution was taken out of the hands of the attorney general (who was himself a suspect) and turned over to someone specially appointed to deal with the charges made against Nixon administration officials. The first special prosecutor, Archibald Cox, was dismissed by President Nixon, who replaced him with Leon Jaworski.

Symbiotic relationship. A mutually beneficial relationship between two or more separate animal species. Used metaphorically in this chapter to describe the relationship between congressmen hostile to an administration, disgruntled bureaucrats ("whistle-blowers"), and the press.

Whistle-blower. A disgruntled bureaucrat, usually in the middle levels of power, who leaks stories to the press about waste, corruption, incompetence, or general misconduct among his superiors.

Chapter 2
The President's War Powers

*"Mr. [Roger] Sherman [of Connecticut] said he
considered the Executive magistracy as nothing
more than an institution for carrying the will of the
legislature into effect. . . ."*

JAMES MADISON's *Notes*
Constitutional Convention, 1787

*"We elect a king for four years and give him
absolute power within certain limits, which after all
he can interpret for himself."*

WILLIAM H. SEWARD
Secretary of State under Abraham Lincoln

In the early 1980s, in lands as far away as Lebanon and as close as Central America, America found itself involved in a variety of military activities. In Lebanon, U.S. Marines, originally sent there as part of an international force to facilitate the peaceful evacuation of the Palestine Liberation Organization, were being used to demonstrate American support for a shaky government besieged by Syrian- and Soviet-backed forces. In El Salvador, American advisers were trying to help the government survive an insurgency by Communist-supported guerrillas. And in neighboring Nicaragua, the country accused of being the most direct supporter of those guerrillas, rebels aided by the American CIA were trying to overthrow the Marxist "Sandinista" government.

These U.S. military operations went by a variety of names: "covert assistance," "peacekeeping missions," "advice and support." To observers on the scene, they looked like wars. Weapons were fired, projectiles whistled through the air, explosions went off, blood was shed, people died. But if they were wars, they were wars of a special kind: they were undeclared.

MEMORIES OF VIETNAM

As America moves through the 1980s, "undeclared war" still evokes memories of Vietnam. Even historians find it hard to recall precisely how we got into that war. The involvement just crept up on us. It started under Eisenhower with economic aid and a few advisers, rose to 16,000 advisers under Kennedy, suddenly sprang into the full-fledged commitment of half a million troops under Johnson, and spread into Cambodia under Nixon. It ended, under Ford, in humiliating defeat.

Nobody wants another Vietnam. But that statement has a double meaning. To some it means we must never give the president the kind of power we gave Kennedy, Johnson, and Nixon. To others it means we must never let another country be devoured by the Soviet empire.

The advocates of the first point of view argue that the president should be more closely checked by Congress and, if necessary, by the Supreme Court. The advocates of the second approach say that the president must not be hamstrung by Congress or the courts as he attempts to counter Soviet advances. These contradictory political viewpoints have undoubtedly influenced the current debate over the president's constitutional war powers.* Nevertheless, the constitutional issues deserve to be studied in their own right.

THE ISSUES

The United States Constitution says that the president "shall be Commander-in-Chief of the military forces . . . when called into the actual service of the United States," but it vests the authority "to declare war" with Congress. Does it follow, then, that any presidentially initiated military engagement violates the Constitution? If so, does that mean that all the conflicts America entered without congressional declarations, including the Korean War of 1950–53, violate the Constitution? But perhaps formal declaration is not necessary as long as there is congressional *authorization*. Is *that* always necessary?

Behind these questions are larger questions. Is the president supposed to be merely the servant of Congress, or does he possess powers independent of Congress? Are there circumstances in which his powers might be even greater than those of Congress? What happens if the president and Congress have conflicting views? Can Congress take the president to court? If it does and wins, must the president abide by the Court's decision?

The Video Discussion

These are the central issues debated by the panelists in the video discussion of the president's war powers. The moderator is Benno C. Schmidt, Jr., dean of Columbia University School of Law.

---

*The two different versions of "the lessons of Vietnam" were described by Democratic Representative Jim Wright of Texas during a debate in Congress. Vietnam, he said, "means different things to different people. When some say Vietnam, they mean we'd be damn fools ever to get involved in another war like that. To others, Vietnam conjures up a vision of the ultimate in cowardice. They feel we abandoned the effort before we won, and should have stayed the course." Quoted in Steven V. Roberts, "War Powers Debate Reflects Its Origin," *New York Times*, 2 October 1983, Sec. IV, p. 4.

List of Participants

HON. ARLIN M. ADAMS
Judge
U.S. Court of Appeals
Third Circuit

LAURENCE I. BARRETT
Senior White House
Correspondent
Time Magazine

JOHN BRADEMAS
President
New York University
U.S. Representative
Indiana, 1959–1981

PHILIP W. BUCHEN
Attorney
Dewey, Ballantine, Bushby, Palmer
& Wood
Former Counsel to President Ford

ARCHIBALD COX
Carl M. Loeb
University Professor
Harvard Law School
Solicitor General of the U.S.,
1961–1965

HON. CHRISTOPHER J. DODD
U.S. Senator
Connecticut

HON. GERALD R. FORD
President of the United States,
1974–1977

HON. ORRIN G. HATCH
U.S. Senator
Utah

ADM. BOBBY R. INMAN
USN (retired)
Chairman, President, and Chief Executive Officer, Microelectronics and
Computor Technology Corporation
Director
National Security Agency, 1977–1981

HON. BARBARA A. MIKULSKI
U.S. Representative
Maryland

HON. EDMUND S. MUSKIE
Attorney
Chadbourne, Parke, Whiteside & Wolff
Secretary of State, 1980–1981
U.S. Senator
Maine, 1959–1980

LT. GEN. BRENT SCOWCROFT
USAF (retired)
Chairman
President's Commission on Strategic
Forces

HON. POTTER STEWART
Justice (retired)
U.S. Supreme Court
1958–1981

HON. J. CLIFFORD WALLACE
Judge
U.S. Court of Appeals
Ninth Circuit

BEN J. WATTENBERG
Senior Fellow
American Enterprise Institute

TOM WICKER
Columnist and Associate Editor
New York Times

Program Summary

The program is divided into three parts, the first of which turns on the issue of American covert aid. In a hypothetical country called "Sierra Madre," a Marxist-Leninist regime has seized power. It is now supporting a guerrilla insurgency against the government of "El Dorado," a neighboring country that is friendly to the United States. The president decides to give the regime a taste of its own medicine. He plans secretly to assist exiles from Sierra Madre who are trying to overthrow the regime. The participants debate the wisdom and morality of covert assistance.

The second part of the program concerns more direct military involvement by the president. To help the friendly country threatened by guerrilla insurgency, he sends them a substantial group of advisers. Five or six of these advisers get killed by the guerrillas. Is that war? If so, does it need Congress's approval? Here much of the discussion centers upon the War Powers Act of 1973. How does it work? Is it a good law? There is also discussion of the precedents for war making: to what extent have past presidents deferred to Congress in matters of war and peace?

The third part of the program is based on the assumption that the president and Congress disagree over whether the president is violating the War Powers Act, and they cannot work out their disagreement. Can Congress take the president to court and get a hearing? The argument here concerns the doctrine of "political questions," which the Court invokes in certain types of cases when it thinks that courts have no business deciding them.

The Scholars' Change of Heart

Before considering the particulars covered in the program, we should keep in mind some background facts. One fact that may surprise the reader is that those who once championed the widest-ranging presidential "activism" in foreign affairs and war making have now changed their minds.

In the 1950s and early '60s, scholars and writers on the presidency were saying that the president should have a great deal of leeway in foreign affairs, particularly regarding the use of military force. They usually added that this was what the Framers of the Constitution wanted and the way things have worked since the early days of the Republic. In 1951 Arthur Schlesinger, Jr., a famous historian who later served in the Kennedy administration, wrote an indignant letter to the *New York Times* complaining about a position taken by Republican Senator Robert Taft. Senator Taft had questioned the right of President Truman to enter the Korean War without a congressional declaration of war. "Senator Taft's statements are demonstrably irresponsible," Schlesinger wrote. He went on to argue that ever since President Jefferson ordered military force used against Mediterranean pirates, "American Presidents have repeatedly committed American forces abroad without Congressional approval."

Another Harvard historian, Henry Steele Commager, wrote an article in the *New York Times Magazine* on the same theme, citing many historic precedents and arguments that seemed to support presidential war making. The issue, he said, "arose—and was settled—in one administration after another." George Kennan, a statesman-scholar and former ambassador to the Soviet Union, declined to criticize President Eisenhower's policy in Indochina because, he said, "having elected a government, we will be best advised to let it govern and to let it speak for us in the councils of the nations."

James Reston, a *New York Times* columnist and member of the paper's editorial board, worried about what happens when the legislative branch gets too involved in foreign affairs. "When the Senate of the United States tries to direct the nation's foreign policy, it almost always gets into trouble." Senator William Fulbright, who then headed the Senate Foreign Relations Committee, seemed to agree. In a 1961 lecture he suggested that the long deliberations of legislatures are not well suited to resolving crises in foreign affairs. "The question I put [is] whether in the face of the harsh necessities of the 1960s we can afford the luxury of eighteenth century procedures for measured deliberation."

But between 1966 and 1970, something strange happened. All these journalists, scholars, and statesmen reversed their views. In the space of four years, presidential experts were arguing—often in the same forums—that the president did not possess unilateral war-making powers, never had possessed them, never was intended to possess them, and never should possess them.

What caused this astonishing reversal? One reason may be the kind of men who occupied the White House between the close of 1963 and the autumn of 1974. Lyndon Johnson and Richard Nixon had what the author of a widely acclaimed book on presidential "character" called "active-negative" personalities. The scholars did not like these men; they especially disliked Richard Nixon.

But the larger reason for the scholars' change of heart was Vietnam. Many of these writers supported the war in its early stages; as late as the summer of 1965, Schlesinger was publicly defending it in a nationally televised "teach-in." But as the war escalated without noticeable results except an increase in violence, the scholars turned against it. They also began to wonder if the "activist presidency" they had been promoting might have helped bring it on. And so they went back to the old texts and read them differently.

Now, it turned out, some of the precedents for presidential wars have been misunderstood: they could really be interpreted as instances of presidents deferring to Congress. Now, too, it seemed that the Founding Fathers had left no doubt that Congress must authorize wars. As for the Supreme Court, its decisions were really meant to limit presidential claims to unilateral power. And so it went—all the evidence that had been cited in support of presidential war powers underwent a sea change: it now proved the opposite.

This reversal raises an important question. In Schlesinger's 1951 letter to the *New York Times*, Senator Taft and his supporters were accused of "rewriting American history according to their own specifications" and foisting off "their current political prejudices as eternal American verities." Could similar charges be made against all those, including Schlesinger, who changed their views so drastically between 1966 and 1970? Without presuming to answer that question, what all of us—teachers and students, writers and readers—need to remember is that scholars are human beings. Their reading, for example, of "what the Founding Fathers thought" may be influenced to some degree by what they *wish* the Founding Fathers had thought.

This does not mean that the past is inaccessible. It means that it must be approached cautiously. We must be careful not to imagine that what we think is right was also on the minds of America's early leaders. With that as a warning, let us briefly examine the Founding Fathers' views on presidential war making.

Presidential War Making: The Founders' Views

We can be certain of one thing about the Founders' intentions: they did not intend the presidency to be a weak institution. The president's role was not to be simply that of carrying out the will of Congress. True, there were some men at the convention who wished to have it so. According to the *Notes* of James Madison:

> Mr. [Roger] Sherman [of Connecticut] said he considered the Executive magistracy as nothing more than an institution for carrying the will of the legislature into effect, and that the person or persons ought to be appointed by and accountable to the legislature only, which was the depository of the supreme will of the Society.

Had Sherman's views prevailed, the president would have ended up as a clerk or servant of Congress. But they did not. By the end of the convention it was decided that the president would not be "appointed by and accountable to the legislature" but would be independently elected for four-year terms and removable only by impeachment. It was decided, moreover, that he would be a "person," not "persons." Remembering the feebleness of the plural executive under the Articles of Confederation, the Framers decided that a single independent executive was needed.

Later, in *The Federalist*, Alexander Hamilton explained the connection between what he called "energy in the executive" and the single executive. "Decision, activity, secrecy, and despatch," which Hamilton considered the basic ingredients of an energetic executive, "will generally characterize the proceedings of one man in a much more eminent degree than the proceedings of any greater number. . . ."

The Framers also gave the chief executive important powers and responsibilities. Among other things he can veto legislation, appoint public ministers, consuls, and judges (with the approval of the Senate), make treaties (with two-thirds Senate approval), and pardon offenses against the United States. He is also to "Take care that the laws be faithfully executed." Finally, he serves as "Commander in Chief of the Army and Navy of the United States, when called into the actual Service of the United States."

Critics of presidential war powers fasten upon the last phrase. The president is commander in chief only when troops are called into actual service. The president commands the armies, in other words, but Congress declares war. In *The Federalist*, No. 69, Hamilton underscored that point. One of the differences, he said, between the president and the king of England is that the president's power as commander in chief "would amount to nothing more than the supreme command and direction of the military and naval forces," while the power of the British king "extends to the declaring of war and to the raising and regulating of fleets and armies—all of which, by the Constitution under consideration, would appertain to the legislature."

Yet Hamilton's remark must be taken in context. In No. 69 of *The Federalist*, Hamilton was trying to reassure his readers that a single executive would not be a king. Therefore he stressed the differences between the two positions. In No. 75 of *The Federalist*, however, Hamilton made it clear that he considered the war- and treaty-making power as the "joint possession" of the legislative and executive branches, a view he continued to hold while serving in Washington's cabinet.

Although Hamilton's overall views may not have been typical of the Founders, this particular opinion was widely shared by them. Note, for example, that Congress is given the exclusive power not to "make" war but to "declare" it. The word "make" was originally proposed at the convention but was rejected. The Framers did not wish to deny the president the power "to repel sudden attacks." Thus war making was not to be an exclusively congressional power.

Indeed, it would have been out of character for the men who sat at the Philadelphia convention to make the president a mere servant of the legislature. Most of them were in Philadelphia because they worried about the weakness of the existing government. They worried about the power of the French, Spanish, and English forces surrounding the new nation. They worried about internal troubles, from the occasional rampages of the Indians to more serious upheavals, such as the one led by Daniel Shays, a former captain in the Revolutionary army. The Framers wanted a strong government to deal with such crises, and they knew that strong government was impossible without a strong executive.

The philosophers they read reinforced that view. Among their favorites were the Baron de Montesquieu (1689–1755) and John Locke (1634–1704), both advocates of "balanced government." Each branch of government, said Montesquieu, should have powers over the other branches; the resulting tension would keep the system balanced. (See the previous chapter.) In the words of constitutional scholar Edward S. Corwin— one scholar whose views on the presidency never changed—the Constitution is an "invitation to struggle" among the branches of government.

Prerogative

John Locke was a strong believer in government by settled laws. He also thought the legislature should be the lawmaking branch (which is what the term "legislature" literally means). However, his theory left considerable power in the hands of the executive, particularly in the field of foreign affairs. And there was another important element in Locke's thinking: his theory of executive "prerogative." The dictionary defines "prerogative" as "an exclusive right or privilege." According to Locke, the executive should, as a general rule, carry out the settled laws of the kingdom. But occasions would arise when the executive has an exclusive right "to act according to discretion for the public good without the prescription of law *and sometimes even against it*" (emphasis added). Locke, in other words, gave the executive certain undefined emergency powers, including the power to act against the will of the legislature.

How seriously was this theory taken by the Founders? It is hard to say. Locke was, on the whole, extremely influential, but "prerogative" occupies only one chapter of his *Second Treatise on Government.* Other parts of the *Treatise*, particularly the parts on revolution, were quoted so often by the Founders that some of Locke's language appeared in the Declaration of Independence. The principal author of the Declaration, Thomas Jefferson, was a strong believer in legislative power who disagreed with Hamilton about the scope of presidential powers. But Jefferson might have remembered Locke's comments on "prerogative" when, a year after leaving office as president, he wrote to a friend:

> A strict observance of the written laws is doubtless *one* of the high duties of a good citizen, but it is not *the highest*. The laws of necessity, of self-preservation, of saving our country when in danger, are of a higher obligation. . . . To lose our country by a scrupulous adherence to written law, would be to lose the law itself, with life, liberty, property and all those who are enjoying them with us; thus absurdly sacrificing the end to the means.

This idea would be reasserted a half-century later by Abraham Lincoln, who assumed enormous extralegal powers during the Civil War. Lincoln's "war powers" will be described later in this chapter. For now, it is enough to say that even in 1787 the presidency was seen as a strong institution sharing powers of war and peace with the Congress.

With this as preface, we can now turn to the video discussion. The discussion, as we said, falls into three parts: Covert Action, Presidential War Powers, and Suing the President.

I: COVERT ACTION

"Decision, activity, secrecy, and despatch." For Alexander Hamilton those were the ingredients of an "energetic" executive, the kind he wanted the country to have. Notice that he included "secrecy" among his list of virtues. Today, many critics of presidential power think that secrecy, at least when combined with hostile actions in the absence of a formal declaration of war, is not a virtue but a vice. That is clearly the view of some participants in the discussion of the not-very-hypothetical case of "Sierra Madre" and "El Dorado."

The moderator turns to Admiral Bobby Inman, former national security director, and posits this situation: some exiles from Sierra Madre come to him and ask for help from the United States in their own guerrilla operation in Sierra Madre, which has for its aim the overthrow of the Sierra Madre government. The moderator then asks Inman how he decides whether the United States should help.

Inman is cautious. First, he says, the secretary of state tries all diplomatic means of persuading Sierra Madre not to help the guerrillas in El Dorado. Only if that attempt fails does the talk in Washington turn to covert action. And even then the discussion has to be disciplined; it can't be a casual "gee, they're good people who would like to overthrow a government."

But for former Secretary of State Edmund Muskie, any discussion of covert action is too casual. Central America "is so unstable and volatile an area by definition" that

American interests cannot be advanced "by the kind of off-the-cuff, casual . . . involvement in . . . the purposes of a dissident guerrilla group."

Former Air Force General Brent Scowcroft, who headed a commission that advised President Reagan on the MX missile, sides with Inman. For him, the emphasis has to be on secrecy. Plans to help the exiles can work—but they have to be concealed. The moderator presses him: "Concealed from whom?" Scowcroft probably knows how dangerous it would be to answer "concealed from the American people." So he says, "concealed from . . . the world at large"—a good answer, except that he spoils it by adding that cynical bureaucratic expression, "plausibly deniable."

Gerald Ford remembers Vietnam. He says that no president ever wants to thrust the United States "into a quagmire." Presidents "just don't get on their horse and go charging with covert aid, or anything else, to make a point or two." For Ford, the decision whether or not to provide covert aid depends on circumstances. How well thought out is the plan? Does it really serve our long-term interests? Is our nation's security involved? Then there is the paramount question: can the operation be kept secret? "If you start out with the assumption that for one reason or another it's going to be out on the table, and in every newspaper, forget it." Ford is critical of all the congressional committees and subcommittees that, in the wake of Vietnam, "began to pick and look and expose and publish information about intelligence activities." The press didn't even have to work hard to get the stuff. "It was just out there on the marketplace."

Senator Orrin Hatch of Utah has some of the same concerns, although he notes that many leaks to the press come from the bureaucracy itself. In any case, "there is a propensity on the part of members of Congress to . . . substitute themselves for the executive branch." The president, says Hatch, should make decisions about covert aid; he is the one with "access to all . . . the important and pertinent information." This wins a smile from former Congressman John Brademas, now president of New York University. He remembers, he says sarcastically, "the great triumph of the CIA and the Bay of Pigs."

Brademas is referring to the Kennedy administration's disastrously unsuccessful attempt in 1961 to sponsor an invasion of Communist Cuba by Cuban exiles. The invasion force, trained by the CIA, was to storm ashore at Cuba's Bay of Pigs and retake the island from Fidel Castro. But there weren't enough troops, they were poorly armed, they picked the wrong invasion site, they underestimated Castro's strength, and the United States failed to give them air cover because it did not want its involvement to be too obvious. Castro's forces quickly routed the invaders. Brademas raises this horrible example of covert action to show how wrong Senator Hatch is to assume that the president has access to all "the important and pertinent information."

Yet Brademas's position is puzzling. Does he mean that there should be no covert assistance programs because some have failed miserably? (Later, Ford will say that there have been many more successes than failures, but the successes don't get publicized.) Or does Brademas mean that there should be covert assistance but that Congress should be in on planning it? But Congress, General Scowcroft says, is not very good at keeping secrets. A covert operation planned by congressmen would quickly become an overt operation. It would then lose its effectiveness as a unique tool of foreign policy.

Tom Wicker has been waiting to reply to General Scowcroft. He is still thinking about Scowcroft's "plausibly deniable" remark. Unlike Brademas, Wicker is not going to get trapped in pragmatic arguments about covert action. His argument is based on the principle that covert action is morally wrong. Turning to the general, he says that "plausibly deniable" is just a nice way of saying that "you need to be able to lie your way out of this." Covert action must be wrong, because to protect its secrecy American officials have "to lie and lie and lie again" to the American public.

Senator Christopher Dodd of Connecticut agrees with Wicker. Back in the 1960s a folksinger named Phil Ochs wrote a satiric song with this line in it: "I believe in God and Senator Dodd and keepin' ol' Castro down." But *that* Senator Dodd was not the one on our panel; it was his father, Tom Dodd, known in the Senate for his staunch anti-Communism. The present Senator Dodd is different. To his supporters he is a refreshing new voice in American politics, a man who has broken with the stale Cold War thinking of the past. To his critics he is a wholly innocent appeaser of Communists, a man prepared to let the Soviet empire expand deeply into our hemisphere.

This Senator Dodd, like Wicker, is opposed to covert action on principle. It is immoral. He looks around the room and gestures. "We forget that in this very hall, a group of people sat down and decided that the system wasn't necessarily to be efficient." Does he mean the Founders would have objected to covert action? His point seems more general, that the Founders were men of principle. They decided, he says, that "our means were our ends." Does he mean that ends can never justify means? That would rule out war under any circumstances. More likely he means that covert action is never justified. "If it makes sense to overthrow the Nicaragu—." He corrects himself: " . . . the government of Sierra Madre, then we ought to have the courage to come before the Congress of the United States, and say, we want your help to do this." But why? All the world would then know of our plans.

Suppose it were 1943 and American intelligence had figured out a way to smuggle exiles back into the Third Reich to overthrow Hitler. Should the president have to come before Congress and say, "We want your help to do this?" But then World War II was a declared war. Suppose, then, it were 1951 and the CIA wanted to smuggle anti-Communist Koreans into North Korea to help overthrow the government. But, some would say, America's involvement in Korea was a response to an attack by North Korea. But aren't the actions planned in Sierra Madre also a response to that country's support of guerrillas in El Dorado?

The reader can see the drift of the argument. The debate about covert action is really a debate about the president's legitimate war powers. If there is a broad consensus that the president is acting legitimately—as there was during World War II—then secrecy is also broadly accepted. "Loose lips sink ships," we used to say. Even lying may be forgiven. The Roosevelt administration lied about the enormous damage done to American shipping by Japanese kamikaze planes without causing a public uproar. But if there is substantial disagreement about the president's power to conduct the war in the first place—as seems to be the case regarding the wars in Central America—then we can expect congressmen and others, in the words of Gerald Ford, to "pick and look and expose and publish."

The question, then, is the power of the president to involve the nation in military action without a congressional declaration of war.

Points to Remember

1. Between 1966 and 1970 many leading presidential scholars reversed their views on presidential war powers. They had formerly maintained that the Founders gave the president power to enter wars without congressional authorization. Now they said that constitutional history and precedent offer no support to such claims.
2. The Framers of the Constitution intended the president to be more than a servant of Congress. They believed in balanced power, with the president and Congress sharing responsibility for the nation's defense. The Congress has the power to "declare" war, but the president may "make" war when necessary to repel attacks. The Founders were students of John Locke, who left room for executive "prerogative" in certain situations.
3. The arguments pro and con in the first part of the video debate about covert action serve to introduce the larger question of whether the president has the right to take us into any sort of military action without explicit congressional authorization.

II: PRESIDENTIAL WAR POWERS

"Mr. President," the moderator says, "suppose you have concluded . . . that a substantial group of American military personnel ought to be dispatched to El Dorado, the ally of the United States that's engaged in this guerrilla insurgency." The case at hand involves sending El Dorado 400 or 500 military advisers. "Now, is that a decision that the Constitution gives you the responsibility for making? Or does Congress have the last word on it?" These are really two different questions, and former President Ford answers yes to both. Yes, the Constitution gives the responsibility to the president and yes, Congress has the last word on it. If Congress does not like the dispatch of advisers, it can always shut off funds; that is surely the last word. Yet the decision to send advisers in the first place belongs to the president. He is the commander in chief.

Senator Dodd disagrees.

We're sending down 400 military people into a hostile environment. That's for sure. Now, it seems to me at that particular juncture . . . that you'd be hard pressed to argue that the Constitution doesn't demand that the shared power, and the shared responsibility of the . . . legislative and executive branch be invoked, and that Congress should be brought into that decision-making process—clearly has to be brought in.

General Scowcroft defends the former president's version of shared power—Congress can cut off funds but the president makes the initial decision by himself. Dodd's version is "clearly wrong," he thinks, because the president is commander in chief of our armed forces. "If that does not include the right to deploy those forces, then it has no meaning."

Former Secretary of State Muskie is asked for his views. Muskie does not think the issue of the president's power in this case is a constitutional one. Rather, it turns upon the meaning of a statute, the War Powers Act of 1973. Under that act, says Muskie, "it might be wise" if the president told Congress what he was doing in El Dorado. But statutes never talk about actions "it might be wise" to take. They either require actions or do not require them. Does the War Powers Act require the president to report his action to Congress? Well, "there would be a debate as to whether or not the War Powers Act requires it, and whether, if it requires it, it is constitutional." Muskie's remarks lead the discussion to the wisdom and constitutionality of the War Powers Act of 1973.

The War Powers Act of 1973: Sixty- to Ninety-Day Wars

The War Powers Act (or Resolution, which is its official citation) was passed in 1973 over President Nixon's veto. It was intended to prevent "another Vietnam," another war the nation gets enmeshed in by a series of presidential initiatives. In theory, Congress could have ended the Vietnam War anytime it wanted simply by refusing to vote any more funds for it. (That *is* the way Congress finally put an end to American involvement in Cambodia in the 1970s.) But this is easier said than done. Once a war has begun, it is not so easy for Congress to risk being called "unpatriotic" by cutting off funds for it. So Congress devised a means to end a presidentially-initiated war simply by doing nothing. Here is how it works:

1. *Notification.* If the president introduces American troops into any situation where hostility is imminent or into a foreign nation equipped for combat, he must notify the Speaker of the House of Representatives and the president pro tempore of the Senate within 48 hours. The notification must be in writing; it must set forth the reasons and justification for the introduction, and give some estimate of how long the troops will be there.

2. *Sixty- to Ninety-Day Limit.* Unless the Congress declares war, authorizes war, or extends the time period, the president must bring the troops home within sixty days. However, if he certifies that he needs more time in order to protect the troops while they are being withdrawn, he can have another thirty days to bring them home.

3. *Consultation.* The president must answer any questions about the war that Congress raises and submit periodic progress reports on the war.

In the video discussion, former President Ford says the act lacks "intestinal fortitude." It is "gutless." To understand what he means, we should begin with the remarks of Barbara Mikulski, congresswoman from Maryland. Mikulski is asked whether she agrees with former President Ford or Senator Dodd. "I'm with Senator Dodd," she answers unhesitatingly.

It's the whole issue of imminent hostilities. There are 500 advisers. What are they doing there? Where are they doing it? Are they in airplanes? Are they in helicopters? Are they on the ground? And if someone is shooting at El Dorado military, and we're standing right side by side with walkie-talkies advising them how to fight, it's pretty darn sure that somebody's going to be shot.

All right then, says the moderator. If we're in a war, then the president must bring those advisers home in sixty days, right? Wrong, says Mikulski. "The War Powers Act . . . is not automatically triggered by the opinions of Senator Dodd and myself. The president has to trigger the War Powers Act."

This is what sparks Ford's complaint about the act's lack of "intestinal fortitude." Let us assume, says Ford, that Mikulski is right, that this is a war. In that case Congress has always had two options. It can approve the president's action or it can disapprove it and, by majority vote, bring the troops home. But Ford complains that the act says, in effect: "If *nothing* is done by the Congress, then Congress can be assumed to have ordered the president to bring the troops home." This is the quality that strikes Ford as "gutless." Congressmen "ought to face up to it one way or the other—either approve it or disapprove it. And for them to say, well, we'll sit back in our cozy way and do nothing, and get the same result, I think is inexcusable, indefensible."

Whatever the merits of Ford's complaint, he is right that the act gives Congress a passive role. The passivity shows up in two ways. First, as Mikulski notes, the act has to be "triggered" by the president. It is he who starts the clock ticking on the sixty- to ninety-day limit by conceding that the act is applicable. As yet, no president has done that.* Second, as soon as the sixty (or, if necessary, ninety) days are up, the president has to bring the troops home. Congress has had to do nothing.

Oddly enough, the charge that the War Powers Act lacks guts is shared not only by self-proclaimed "hawks" like Gerald Ford but by some "doves" as well. *New York Times* editor and columnist Tom Wicker has opposed presidential war making since the late '60s; he is sympathetic to the intentions of those who wrote the War Powers Act. Nevertheless, he says, he opposed the act when it was first passed because he suspected it would lead to exactly what had recently happened in Lebanon. In 1983 Congress ended up authorizing the president to keep troops in Lebanon for another eighteen months, something it probably would not have done were it not for the pressure generated by the War Powers Act. Now, Wicker says, suppose those troops come under

---

*President Ford introduced American forces into a combat situation when he used the navy to rescue American seamen from the ship *Mayaguez*, which had been seized by Cambodian Communists. Ford notified Congress but never conceded that the War Powers Act applied. Jimmy Carter introduced American forces into a hostile environment when he sent American airmen into Iran in a futile attempt to rescue American hostages in Iran. Ronald Reagan sent an invasion force into Grenada without conceding that he had triggered the timer on the War Powers Act. The same applies to his continuing use of American advisers in El Salvador. As for the "peacekeeping" force of marines sent to Lebanon, in October 1983 President Reagan won an eighteen-month extension of the marines' presence there without conceding that he had triggered the War Powers Act. He even suggested that the act's "arbitrary and inflexible deadlines" might be unconstitutional.

fire. "When troops are under fire abroad, what's Congress going to do? Tell the president to take them out? I don't think so."

Unknown to Wicker or anyone else in the room, at the very time he made these remarks the first news was arriving of a truck-bomb attack on marine headquarters in Lebanon, an attack that ultimately claimed the lives of 240 marines. The tragedy underscores Wicker's point. Congress had just authorized an eighteen-month stay for the marines. Now it would have to renege on that agreement if it were to try to force the president to remove the marines from Lebanon. And the agreement itself would never have been hammered out were it not for the War Powers Act. Arguably—this seems to be Wicker's point—an act intended to limit presidential wars ended up licensing one. "May I say," Gerald Ford says, "that I am pleased that Tom Wicker and I share the same view vis-à-vis the War Powers Act." Actually, they have opposite views. Ford thinks the act hamstrings the president; Wicker thinks it greatly expands his power.

Both could be wrong. At the end of the War Powers Act is a section purporting to "interpret" it. Among other things, this section says that nothing in the act is intended to "alter" the existing constitutional authority of the president or Congress or give the president any additional powers that "he would not have had in the absence of this joint resolution." In reply to Ford, the section seems to say: "This act will *not* hamstring the president because it is not taking away any power he would have otherwise had under the Constitution." In reply to Wicker, it seems to say: "This will *not* give the president any new powers to conduct wars; it leaves his existing powers just as they were."

Presidents and Precedents

Presidents have been known to take bold initiatives in foreign and military affairs without bothering about Congress. Unchallenged, those initiatives become precedents for further initiatives. The history of the presidency, according to constitutional scholar Edward S. Corwin, "is a history of aggrandizement."

Yet, Corwin added, "the story is a highly discontinuous one." It is the discontinuities that most interest Senator Dodd. He takes on a difficult task in the discussion, for he tries to prove a negative: that the historical record of the presidency does *not* provide many examples of unilateral presidential war making. In Dodd's words, until the presidency of Theodore Roosevelt, "most presidents were very, very respectful of the shared responsibility of Congress in this area." The word "most" saves his assertion, since few nineteenth-century presidents went to war without congressional authorization. But there were some outstanding exceptions:

- President Jefferson ordered his navy to fight off attacks by Barbary pirates in the Mediterranean Sea.*

---

*Dodd says that Jefferson "sought the approval of Congress before he would engage the Barbary pirates," but this is somewhat misleading. Jefferson and his cabinet authorized the American naval commander, who was on his way to Malta to get water, to disable but not sink or seize any ship that fired upon him *on the way to Malta.* But on the way back he should seize the disabled ship and tow it back with him. Without telling Congress of these standing orders, Jefferson went before it and asked for the constitutional authority to do what he had every intention of doing anyway. See Abraham Sofear, "The Presidency and Foreign Affairs: Practice Under the Framers," *Law and Contemporary Problems*, Spring 1976, pp. 25–27.

- President Monroe ordered then-General Andrew Jackson to chase the Seminole Indians into Florida territory. Jackson did, and was soon fighting Spaniards and Englishmen as well.
- President Tyler unilaterally disposed American land and naval forces in such a way as to threaten Mexico.
- President Polk sent American troops into territory claimed by Mexico, thus provoking the Mexican-American war.
- President Fillmore sent Commodore Perry to deliver a polite ultimatum to the Japanese: treat American seamen more gently or be "severely chastised."
- President Pierce sent a naval expedition to Greytown, Nicaragua, to extract an apology and monetary damages from Greytown officials for an insult to Pierce's minister to Central America. (The official's nose was bloodied when someone in an angry crowd threw a bottle in his face.) Because Greytown officials refused to apologize, the town was shelled and burned to the ground.
- Then there was President Lincoln. Abraham Lincoln deserves a special place in the history of presidential aggrandizement because of the enormous lengths to which he carried the war powers.

Lincoln and War Powers

Earlier in this chapter, Locke's theory of "prerogative" was discussed. To repeat, by "prerogative" Locke meant the executive's power to act "without the prescription of law *and sometimes even against it*" (emphasis added). Lincoln frequently acted without congressional authorization. Sometimes he even violated the Constitution.

When the Civil War broke out in April 1861, Lincoln delayed convening Congress because he wanted no congressional interference. He then appropriated $2 million from the Treasury, even though the Constitution forbids such appropriations except by Congress. He amalgamated state militias and added 41,000 soldiers and sailors to the national force, even though the Constitution says that *Congress* should "raise and support armies." He suspended the writ of habeas corpus in various places, even though that power is granted only to *Congress* during emergencies. He proclaimed a blockade of Southern ports, even though that amounted to an act of war. He arrested and detained without trial persons he suspected of treason, though his actions violated several provisions of the Bill of Rights.

Lincoln later justified these constitutional violations by comparing himself to a surgeon who must amputate a patient's arm or leg in order to save his life. Lincoln was "amputating" some constitutional provisions in order to save the Union. Years later, Lincoln's former secretary of state, William H. Seward, still could not get over the enormous reach of power in Lincoln's presidency. "We elect a king for four years," he said, "and give him absolute power within certain limits, which after all he can interpret for himself."

But Seward's remark seems to generalize from a particular set of circumstances. Lincoln's presidency was an exception: the Civil War was no distant clash, but the domestic rebellion of a whole section of the country. America has never been so close to dissolution. Until a crisis of that magnitude occurs again, presidents will have a hard time using Lincoln's actions as precedents.

Yet the presidents of the 1980s and 1990s need not use Lincoln. There are, as Senator Dodd concedes, plenty of examples from this century:

- Without congressional authorization, President Theodore Roosevelt "took" the Panama Canal Zone. "I took the Canal Zone, and let Congress debate, and while the debate goes on the canal does also," he said.
- The same Roosevelt intervened several times in Latin America and the Caribbean, sending American marines into Santo Domingo, Haiti, Nicaragua, and Honduras.
- President Woodrow Wilson sent expeditionary forces into Mexico; the force bombarded and occupied the city of Veracruz.
- Before America entered World War I, Wilson ordered the arming of American merchant ships.
- More than a year before Congress declared war on the Axis powers in World War II, President Franklin Roosevelt entered into an agreement with the British to give them overage American destroyers in return for the use of British military bases in the Caribbean. The agreement violated several statutes.
- In the summer of 1941, several months before war was declared, Roosevelt sent American warships to convoy British ships, even though Britain was at war with Germany. During that same period Roosevelt instituted a "shoot on sight" policy against German submarines.

Wisely, then, Senator Dodd exempts twentieth-century presidents from his observation that past presidents "were very, very respectful of the shared responsibility of Congress" in war making.

Points to Remember

1. The War Powers Act of 1973 was intended to prevent "another Vietnam," a protracted war entered into by a president without explicit congressional authorization.
2. The main provisions of the War Powers Act require that the president (a) notify Congress within forty-eight hours of any military engagement he enters into; (b) automatically withdraw troops within sixty days unless Congress acts, though he may have an additional 30 days if necessary to insure the safety of the retreat; and (c) consult with Congress about the engagement and answer any questions Congress asks.
3. The sixty- to ninety-day limit must be triggered by the president, who notifies Congress that hostilities have begun. After its expiration, the president is supposed to withdraw the troops unless Congress says otherwise. To date, no president has conceded that the War Powers Act is applicable to any hostile situation.
4. The act has been criticized by self-declared hawks as well as by some doves. The hawks think the act constrains the president too much; the doves fear it may license presidential wars. The act itself states that it neither adds to nor detracts from existing presidential powers.

5. There are numerous precedents for presidents sending American forces into hostile situations. They stretch back to the Jefferson administration, though most of them occurred in the twentieth century. Abraham Lincoln, who faced the unique challenge of the Civil War, repeatedly violated the Constitution in order to save the Union.

III: SUING THE PRESIDENT

The third part of the program concerns legal challenges to the president's war powers. The moderator asks U.S. Appeals Court Judge J. Clifford Wallace to assume that a soldier who has been ordered by the president to fight in El Dorado decides to challenge that order. He takes the president to court, contending that the president has no authority to fight this undeclared war. "Now," the moderator says, "how should a federal district judge respond to that kind of a judicial challenge to the president's power?" Judge Wallace answers: "Very carefully (*laughter*)."

Judges are usually wary of legal challenges to the president's war powers for two reasons. First, they tend to feel that the president has more independence in foreign affairs in general—and military affairs in particular—than he does in domestic affairs. Second, since judges themselves usually have limited experience in military and foreign affairs, they feel that they should try to keep out of conflicts between president and Congress over such matters. Military and foreign affairs, they feel, are "political questions," and should be decided by the political branches. Let us examine each of these points in turn, and look at some leading Supreme Court cases which apply to them.

Foreign and Military Powers of Presidents

The first clear-cut challenge to a president's power to conduct war without a congressional declaration occurred in the midst of the Civil War. In the *Prize Cases* (1863), the plaintiffs, ship owners whose vessels were seized by the Union Navy for trying to run Lincoln's blockade of Southern ports, sued for damages on the ground that Lincoln's blockade was unconstitutional. They argued that a blockade is an act of war and that Lincoln ordered the blockade without a congressional declaration of war. By a margin of five to four, the Court rejected their contention. In upholding the constitutionality of Lincoln's blockade, the Court took note of the fact that the Civil War had been thrust upon the president by uncontrollable circumstances. He had no alternative but to respond "without waiting for Congress to baptize it with a name."

The *Prize Cases* can be cited to support the president's power to put down domestic rebellion or resist foreign invaders. But the decision will not work very well for anyone trying to justify presidential wars in other lands. "By the Constitution," the Court said, "Congress alone has the power to declare a national or foreign war." The president "has no power to initiate or declare a war either against a foreign nation or a domestic state." But what if the president responds to attacks on American personnel stationed in a foreign land? Is that the same as countering an invasion? The Court did not answer that question.

One question the Court *has* ruled on is that of presidential discretion in foreign policy. In domestic affairs, said the Court in 1936, the president is on a short leash: Congress may not give him much discretion. But in foreign affairs, everything is different, for the president is "the sole organ of the federal government in the field of international relations."

The 1936 case *United States* v. *Curtiss-Wright Corporation* arose out of the following circumstances. In 1934 Congress passed a joint resolution authorizing the president to stop the sale of arms to Bolivia and Paraguay, countries that were then engaged in a war in the jungles of South America. President Roosevelt imposed an arms embargo, and the Curtiss-Wright Corporation was found guilty of violating it. The corporation appealed its conviction on the ground that Congress had no right to delegate to the president its power to make laws.

Today, when Congress almost routinely delegates power to the president, such an argument would seem slightly bizarre. But in those days the Court was extremely suspicious of any delegation of power to the executive. The Curtiss-Wright Corporation might have thought it had a good chance of winning. But it lost badly, in an eight-to-one decision. For the Court, the fact that the case involved foreign affairs made all the difference. In domestic affairs, said the Court, the president's power has to be deduced from specific grants of power listed in the Constitution. But in foreign affairs his power is not so tied down; instead, it actually predates the Constitution and grows out of the fact that we are a sovereign nation and need someone to represent us in the world. This makes the president the "sole organ" of foreign relations. It gives him "plenary and exclusive power" in foreign affairs.

Curtiss-Wright seemed to legitimize extremely broad use of presidential discretion in foreign affairs and, by inference, in military affairs. It may help explain why President Truman's entrance into the Korean War without a congressional declaration was so widely supported. And, once we were in the war, it may have been one of the factors that tempted Truman to act even more boldly at home.

Here is what happened. At the end of 1951 the nation's steel mills and steel unions could not resolve their differences over wages. So the unions struck, paralyzing the steel industry while we were at war. President Truman seized the steel mills and put in effect a wage settlement more or less acceptable to the unions but opposed by the companies. The steel companies went to court, charging that the president had no authority to seize domestic industries. The Truman administration argued that the president possessed certain "inherent" powers, flowing from the office itself, as well as the more specific powers of chief executive and commander in chief, and that these powers justified seizure of the steel mills.

The Supreme Court issued its decision in the case of *Youngstown Sheet and Tube Co.* v. *Sawyer* (1952), more commonly called the steel seizure case. The Court denied Truman's claims by a margin of six to three, although the decision contained seven separate opinions. The formal "opinion of the Court," delivered by Justice Hugo Black, was based on the premise that "the Founders of this Nation entrusted the lawmaking power to the Congress alone in both good and bad times." But the opinion in the steel seizure case that is most frequently cited today is the concurring opinion of Justice Robert Jackson.

Jackson was not prepared to stamp "unconstitutional" on every presidential act undertaken without congressional authorization. Instead, he proposed a sliding scale. When the president acts according to a statute, his power is at the highest. When he acts in the absence of a statute but also in the absence of a congressional prohibition, his acts belong in a gray area, a "zone of twilight." His actions might or might not be unconstitutional, depending on circumstances. But when the president acts in the teeth of a congressional prohibition, his power is "at its lowest ebb." Jackson would not say that such actions are always unconstitutional. But he required that the president prove the congressional prohibition to be outside the jurisdiction of Congress. Truman's steel seizure, said Jackson, belonged in the third category; his power was at its "lowest ebb."

If we look back on presidential war powers since the Korean War, most of the actions taken by presidents seem to belong in the "twilight zone." Eisenhower's use of the CIA to overthrow leftist governments and to fly spy planes over the Soviet Union, Kennedy's attempt to invade Cuba in 1961 and his 1962 blockade of Cuba during the "Cuban missile crisis," Johnson's invasion of the Dominican Republic in 1965—in all these cases Congress played a passive role. It never said, "do it" or "don't do it." It said nothing.

Vietnam itself was largely a "twilight" war. Congress neither authorized it nor forbade it. The Senate did pass a resolution in 1964 authorizing the president "to take all necessary measures to repel any armed attack against the forces of the United States and to prevent further aggression," but no president ever claimed that American participation in the war depended on that resolution. When the Senate repealed it in 1971, President Nixon said he could carry on the war without it. And he did.

How does all this affect the topic of court challenges to the president's war powers? In general, how do courts handle such challenges? "Very carefully," says Judge Wallace. His answer has more implications than have so far been explained. To understand them, we must turn to a second category of cases. We have examined the cases the Court has decided. Now we must examine the kind of case the Court refuses to decide—cases involving "political questions."

Political Questions

The Supreme Court's doctrine of "political questions" dates back to 1849, when the Court decided—or nondecided—the case of *Luther* v. *Borden.* During 1841-42 in the state of Rhode Island, two factions were warring against each other. Each claimed to be the legitimate government of Rhode Island. Luther, a representative of one faction, had his home broken into by Borden, an agent of the rival faction, and brought suit for trespass. Borden countered that he was representing the legitimate government of Rhode Island, which was suppressing an insurrection from Luther's group. The issue then became: Which is the real government of Rhode Island?

The Court simply refused to decide the issue. It said that the subject was "political in its nature" and belonged in the hands of the political branches—president and Congress. The procedures used by courts "would be utterly unfit," it said, to resolve the crisis.

Since *Luther* v. *Borden*, the Court has often cited its doctrine of "political questions" as the reason for its refusal to rule on certain issues. Yet the particular types of issues the Court considers "political" are sometimes difficult to pin down. For years the Court held that disputes over how legislative districts are apportioned belong in the category of "political questions." But it reversed itself in *Baker* v. *Carr* (1962), when it held for the first time that such disputes are indeed "justiciable" (capable of being decided by courts).

What about disputes concerning the president's military acts in foreign lands? Are they "justiciable"? Or are they inherently "political questions?" The undeclared war in Vietnam provided an occasion for testing these questions in the late '60s and early '70s.

Political Questions: The Vietnam War

On at least seven occasions during the Vietnam War, the Supreme Court refused to hear challenges to the legality and constitutionality of the war. Among the reasons the Court stated for its refusal was that such issues were inherently political and must be resolved by the political branches or through the political process. From most of those decisions Justice William O. Douglas dissented, and in one of them, *Mora* v. *McNamara* (1967), Justice Potter Stewart also wrote a dissent.

Mora v. *McNamara* resembles the hypothetical situation posed by the moderator. Mora was a draftee about to be sent to Vietnam; he and two other draftees brought suit to challenge their orders on the ground that they were instruments for carrying out an illegal and unconstitutional war. In his dissent from the Court's refusal to hear the case, Justice Stewart said, "These are large and deeply troubling questions." The Court, he added, cannot make them go away "simply by refusing to hear the case of three obscure Army privates."

Recent Court Challenges

During the Vietnam War a slogan emanating from Communist Cuba said that the United States would soon be faced with "two, three, many Vietnams." In the early 1980s the prophecy seemed to be coming to pass in Central America. By a variety of military and economic means, the United States was trying to support the government of El Salvador against Communist insurgents and harass, if not overthrow, the Marxist-Leninist rulers of Nicaragua, who were aiding the insurgents in El Salvador. To many it sounded like Vietnam again. There were also court challenges to the policies. In one of them, "Ronald Wilson Reagan" was named among the defendants and accused of, among other things, violating the War Powers Act. On August 1, 1983, the suit was dismissed by a federal district court judge in Washington, D.C. Among the grounds for dismissal was that the case presented "political questions" beyond the jurisdiction of courts.

But three months later, in November 1983, another legal challenge to the Reagan administration's support of covert action in Nicaragua was sustained. A federal district court judge in California ordered the Reagan administration to study charges, brought by California Congressman Ronald Dellums and others, that its aid to anti-Sandinista rebels in Nicaragua violated the Neutrality Act of 1794. The Neutrality Act makes it a criminal offense to furnish money for a military enterprise against a country with which the United States is at peace. After the judge ordered the Reagan administration to answer these charges, attorneys for the administration urged him to reconsider. They said that the Neutrality Act has nothing whatever to do with the president's actions but is aimed solely at private citizens. Early in 1984 the judge reaffirmed his ruling. At this writing the administration is appealing.

It is unlikely that the Supreme Court today would consider the merits of any challenges of the kind just described. Judge Wallace knows that, and so do all the other legal experts on the panel. Their only disagreement is over whether the Court *should* listen to such challenges. Archibald Cox thinks it should. If the president is violating the War Powers Act by keeping forces in El Dorado, says Cox, then there has to be a judicial remedy. Judge Wallace is not so sure. "The solution is not always the courts," he says. His tendency would be "to let the political process go its own way." U.S. Appeals Court Judge Arlin Adams is more emphatic: "I think it is a conventional political question. . . . I don't think some judge, like myself, appointed for life, without any military qualifications, should make this awesome decision."

We come now to the climax of the program—the part that stunned some members of the audience and panel. The moderator asks Philip Buchen, who served as President Ford's legal counsel, what he would do if the Supreme Court did sustain a challenge to the president and ordered the president to bring American forces home from El Dorado. "I'd say forget it," Buchen answers. "Keep your troops there."

There is a pause. Then Judge Adams signals the moderator.

MODERATOR: Judge Adams?

JUDGE ADAMS: I would go and see my very good friend Phil Buchen and try to persuade him not to take that position. As strongly as I feel that he's right, I don't think he . . . we can ever defy. . . .

Nor is President Ford ready to take the advice of his former counsel. "If the court of highest jurisdiction makes a decision, as wrong as I think it was, I would . . . abide by that decision." Even before President Ford's remark, Buchen has already begun qualifying himself. What he meant is that as a matter of legal right the president does not *have to* obey the order. But as a matter of political wisdom the president *should* obey it.

It would have been more interesting if Buchen had stuck to his guns. Earlier in the program, Archibald Cox posited a situation in which a president simply decided he wanted to declare war on the Soviet Union. If we can imagine that improbable situation, why can't we imagine a situation in which judges issue orders jeopardizing the security of the United States? If we can, why rule out the possibility of disobeying them?

A precedent exists. When the Civil War broke out, the military arrested a Southern sympathizer named John Merryman and held him without trial. Merryman applied to Supreme Court Justice Roger Taney, who was presiding over a circuit court at the time, for a writ of habeas corpus (a writ that would force the administration to bring formal charges against him and release him if it could not prove them in a court of law). Taney issued the writ, claiming that Lincoln had no right to suspend it. It didn't matter. Merryman remained confined to the military fort. Though he was eventually released, Lincoln had in the meantime defied an order from the chief justice of the Supreme Court.

Did Lincoln have a right to do so? Perhaps the circumstances need to be taken into account. Our nation had just plunged into civil war. The momentum seemed to be on the side of the secessionists. If there was ever a time when "decision, activity, secrecy, and despatch" were needed, now was the time. Yet Lincoln broke the law and, however briefly, defied the chief justice of the Supreme Court.

In a comparable situation today, would the president be justified in disobeying an order from the nation's highest court? We may ponder the question without worrying too much about what the constitutional "experts" might say. At bottom the question is a moral one, and nobody is an expert on morality.

Points to Remember

1. The Court has considered the president's power in military and foreign affairs in three major cases. In the *Prize Cases* (1863), the Court said that President Lincoln could blockade Southern ports without congressional authorization. In *United States v. Curtiss-Wright* (1936), the Court characterized the president as the "sole organ" of foreign relations, whose power in that area is derived not from specific clauses in the Constitution but from the fact of national sovereignty. In the steel seizure case, *Youngstown Sheet and Tube v. Sawyer* (1952), the Court said that President Truman's seizure of the mills—which the Truman administration defended as necessary to settle a strike during wartime—violated the Constitution.
2. Justice Jackson's concurring opinion in the steel seizure case is often cited today. In it he referred to a "twilight zone" of presidential power, an area in which Congress has neither authorized nor forbidden presidential action. Within that zone, Jackson said, a president's unilateral actions may be justified under certain circumstances. Many presidential actions since that time, including the use of the CIA for covert activities, belong in that "twilight zone." Vietnam seemed to be a "twilight war."
3. The moderator posited a situation in which a serviceman about to be sent into a hostile situation sues the president, arguing that the war is undeclared and therefore illegal and unconstitutional. During the Vietnam War, the Court refused to hear such cases on the ground that they involve "political questions." The Court's "political questions" doctrine goes back to the case of *Luther v. Borden* (1849), when the Court refused to decide which government of Rhode Island was the legitimate one, saying that such questions should be left to the political branches of government.

SUMMARY

This chapter began with two quotations. The first, from James Madison's *Notes* of the Constitutional Convention of 1787, summarizes the view of Connecticut's Roger Sherman. Sherman believed that the executive branch should be nothing more than "an institution for carrying the will of the legislature into effect." The second is from William H. Seward, President Lincoln's secretary of state, who claimed that the president is an elected king with absolute power.

Both views are extreme. We know that the Framers of the Constitution did not follow Sherman's suggestion and make the president, as James Wilson put it disgustedly, a mere "minion" of the legislative branch. The Founders created a single, independently elected executive with a variety of impressive powers and duties. The presidency, then, is a powerful and highly respected institution. The president leads the armies and serves as the sole organ of American foreign relations. He is given the power to repel attacks on the United States, which means his actions can affect the fate of the earth. At the same time it is silly and reckless to call him an elected "king" who can set his own limits. More than once, Congress and the courts have set limits and humiliated presidents who have seen fit to ignore them.

Perhaps the question comes down to the kind of people elected to the office of president and the kind of situations confronting the nation. A president with democratic instincts and common sense, acting in situations perceived as genuine emergencies, will be trusted by the American people, and that trust is almost certain to be translated into the leeway to act decisively. The American people know that the Hamiltonian virtues of "decision, activity, secrecy, and despatch" are not the hallmarks of Congress. If they are to be found anyplace in the government, it is in the executive branch. Americans want their president to act with sobriety and restraint, but they have made it clear that they will not tolerate presidential weakness and indecision.

Yet they have made it equally clear that they do not want "another Vietnam"—however we interpret that expression. They do not want any more twilight wars that begin without thought and end without honor. They want public deliberation before America assumes long-term military commitments. And they know, though they may not always acknowledge it, that Congress is an institution that provides the best forum for national deliberation. In a sense, then, the two elected branches of government complement one another: the president acts; the Congress deliberates, makes laws, and oversees the actions of the executive. In practice, of course, the two keep bumping into one another, each accusing the other of meddling and usurping. But that, too, is as it should be. President and Congress keep each other in line by the application of force and counterforce. It is a struggle the Constitution continues to invite.

Documents

U.S. V. CURTISS-WRIGHT CORPORATION, 299 U.S. 304 (1936)

In 1934 Congress passed a joint resolution authorizing the president to stop the sale of arms to Bolivia and Paraguay, which were engaged in a war in the Chaco jungles of South America. Pursuant to that resolution, President Roosevelt imposed an arms embargo. The Curtiss-Wright Corporation was later found guilty of violating that embargo. It appealed on the ground that Congress had no right to delegate its power to make laws.

Writing for an eight-to-one majority, Justice George Sutherland contended that the president's power in foreign affairs does not depend upon specific grants in the Constitution but predates the Constitution; it grows out of the very fact of national sovereignty. Thus, the president possesses "plenary and exclusive power" in the field of foreign affairs.

Excerpts from the opinion follow.

Opinion of the Court, Mr. Justice Sutherland.

First. It is contended that by the Joint Resolution the going into effect and continued operation of the resolution was conditioned (a) upon the President's judgment as to its beneficial effect upon the re-establishment of peace between the countries engaged in armed conflict in the Chaco; (b) upon the making of a proclamation, which was left to his unfettered discretion, thus constituting an attempted substitution of the President's will for that of Congress; (c) upon the making of a proclamation putting an end to the operation of the resolution, which again was left to the President's unfettered discretion; and (d) further, that the extent of its operation in particular cases was subject to limitation and exception by the President, controlled by no standard. In each of these particulars, appellees urge that Congress abdicated its essential functions and delegated them to the Executive.

Whether, if the Joint Resolution had related solely to internal affairs, it would be open to the challenge that it constituted an unlawful delegation of legislative power to the Executive, we find it unnecessary to determine. The whole aim of the resolution is to affect a situation entirely external to the United States, and falling within the category of foreign affairs. The determination which we are called to make, therefore, is whether the Joint Resolution, as applied to that situation, is vulnerable to attack under the rule that forbids a delegation of the lawmaking power. In other words, assuming (but not deciding) that the challenged delegation, if it were confined to internal affairs, would be invalid, may it nevertheless be sustained on the ground that its exclusive aim is to afford a remedy for a hurtful condition within foreign territory?

It will contribute to the elucidation of the question if we first consider the differences between the powers of the federal government in respect of foreign or external affairs and those in respect of domestic or internal affairs. That there are differences between them, and that these differences are fundamental, may not be doubted.

The two classes of powers are different, both in respect of their origin and their nature. The broad statement that the federal government can exercise no powers except those specifically enumerated in the Constitution, and such implied powers as are necessary and proper to carry into effect the enumerated powers, is categorically true only in respect of our internal affairs. In that field, the primary purpose of the Constitution was to carve from the general mass of legislative powers *then possessed by the states* such portions as it was thought desirable to vest in the federal government, leaving those not included in the enumeration still in the states. . . . That this doctrine applies only to powers which the states had is self-evident. And since the states severally never possessed international powers, such powers could not have been carved from the mass of state powers but obviously were transmitted to the United States from some other source. During the Colonial period, those powers were possessed exclusively by and were entirely under the control of the Crown. By the Declaration of Independence, "the Representatives of the United States of America" declared the United (not the several) Colonies to be free and independent states, and as such to have "full Power to levy War, conclude Peace, contract Alliances, establish Commerce and to do all other Acts and Things which Independent States may of right do."

As a result of the separation from Great Britain by the colonies, acting as a unit, the powers of external sovereignty passed from the Crown not to the colonies severally, but to the colonies in their collective and corporate capacity as the United States of America. Even before the Declaration, the colonies were a unit in foreign affairs, acting through a common agency—namely, the Continental Congress, composed of delegates from the thirteen colonies. That agency exercised the powers of war and peace, raised an army, created a navy, and finally adopted the Declaration of Independence. Rulers come and go; governments end and forms of government change; but sovereignty survives. A political society cannot endure without a supreme will somewhere. Sovereignty is never held in suspense. When, therefore, the external sovereignty of Great Britain in respect of the colonies ceased, it immediately passed to the Union. See *Penhallow* v. *Doane,* 3 Dall. 54, 80, 81. That fact was given practical application almost at once. The treaty of peace, made on September 3, 1783, was concluded between his Britannic Majesty and the "United States of America." . . .

The Union existed before the Constitution, which was ordained and established among other things to form "a more perfect Union." Prior to that event, it is clear that the Union, declared by the Articles of Confederation to be "perpetual," was the sole possessor of external sovereignty, and in the Union it remained without change save in so far as the Constitution in express terms qualified its exercise. The Framers' Convention was called and exerted its powers upon the irrefutable postulate that though the states were several their people in respect of foreign affairs were one. . . .

It results that the investment of the federal government with the powers of external sovereignty did not depend upon the affirmative grants of the Constitution. The powers to declare and wage war, to conclude peace, to make treaties, to maintain diplomatic relations with other sovereignties, if they had never been mentioned in the Constitution, would have vested in the federal government as necessary concomitants of nationality. Neither the Constitution nor the laws passed in pursuance of it have any force in foreign territory unless in respect of our own citizens (see *American Banana*

Co. v. *United Fruit Co.,* 213 U.S. 347, 356); and operations of the nation in such territory must be governed by treaties, international understandings and compacts, and the principles of international law. As a member of the family of nations, the right and power of the United States in that field are equal to the right and power of the other members of the international family. Otherwise, the United States is not completely sovereign. . . .

Not only, as we have shown, is the federal power over external affairs in origin and essential character different from that over internal affairs, but participation in the exercise of the power is significantly limited. In this vast external realm, with its important, complicated, delicate and manifold problems, the President alone has the power to speak or listen as a representative of the nation. He *makes* treaties with the advice and consent of the Senate; but he alone negotiates. Into the field of negotiation the Senate cannot intrude; and Congress itself is powerless to invade it. . . .

It is important to bear in mind that we are here dealing not alone with an authority vested in the President by an exertion of legislative power, but with such an authority plus the very delicate, plenary and exclusive power of the President as the sole organ of the federal government in the field of international relations—a power which does not require as a basis for its exercise an act of Congress, but which, of course, like every other governmental power, must be exercised in subordination to the applicable provisions of the Constitution. It is quite apparent that if, in the maintenance of our international relations, embarrassment—perhaps serious embarrassment—is to be avoided and success for our aims achieved, congressional legislation which is to be made effective through negotiation and inquiry within the international field must often accord to the President a degree of discretion and freedom from statutory restriction which would not be admissible were domestic affairs alone involved. Moreover, he, not Congress, has the better opportunity of knowing the conditions which prevail in foreign countries, and especially is this true in time of war. He has his confidential sources of information. He has his agents in the form of diplomatic, consular and other officials. Secrecy in respect of information gathered by them may be highly necessary, and the premature disclosure of it productive of harmful results. Indeed, so clearly is this true that the first President refused to accede to a request to lay before the House of Representatives the instructions, correspondence and documents relating to the negotiation of the Jay Treaty—a refusal the wisdom of which was recognized by the House itself and has never been doubted.

The marked difference between foreign affairs and domestic affairs in this respect is recognized by both houses of Congress in the very form of their requisitions for information from the executive departments. In the case of every department except the Department of State, the resolution *directs* the official to furnish the information. In the case of the State Department, dealing with foreign affairs, the President is *requested* to furnish the information "if not incompatible with the public interest." A statement that to furnish the information is not compatible with the public interest rarely, if ever, is questioned.

When the President is to be authorized by legislation to act in respect to a matter intended to affect a situation in foreign territory, the legislator properly bears in mind the important consideration that the form of the President's action—or, indeed, whether he shall act at all—may well depend, among other things, upon the nature of the confidential information which he has or may thereafter receive, or upon the effect which his action may have upon our foreign relations. This consideration, in connection with what we have already said on the subject, discloses the unwisdom of requiring Congress in this field of governmental power to lay down narrowly definite standards by which the President is to be governed. As this court said in *Mackenzie* v. *Hare,* 239 U.S. 299, 311, "As a government, the United States is invested with all the attributes of sovereignty. As it has the character of nationality it has the powers of nationality, especially those which concern its relations and intercourse with other countries. *We should hesitate long before limiting or embarrassing such powers."* (Italics supplied.)

In the light of the foregoing observations, it is evident that this court should not be in haste to apply a general rule which will have the effect of condemning legislation like that under review as constituting an unlawful delegation of legislative power. The principles which justify such legislation find overwhelming support in the unbroken legislative practice which has prevailed almost from the inception of the national government to the present day. . . .

Practically every volume of the United States Statutes contains one or more acts or joint resolutions of Congress authorizing action by the President in respect of subjects affecting foreign relations, which either leave the exercise of the power to his unrestricted judgment, or provide a standard far more general than that which has always been considered requisite with regard to domestic affairs. . . .

The result of holding that the joint resolution here under attack is void and unenforceable as constituting an unlawful delegation of legislative power would be to stamp this multitude of comparable acts and resolutions as likewise invalid. And while this court may not, and should not, hesitate to declare acts of Congress, however many times repeated, to be unconstitutional if beyond all rational doubt it finds them to be so, an impressive array of legislation such as we have just set forth, enacted by nearly every Congress from the beginning of our national existence to the present day, must be given unusual weight in the process of reaching a correct determination of the problem. A legislative practice such as we have here, evidenced not by only occasional instances, but marked by the movement of a steady stream for a century and a half of time, goes a long way in the direction of proving the presence of unassailable ground for the constitutionality of the practice, to be found in the origin and history of the power involved, or in its nature, or in both combined. . . .

Both upon principle and in accordance with precedent, we conclude there is sufficient warrant for the broad discretion vested in the President to determine whether the enforcement of the statute will have a beneficial effect upon the re-establishment of peace in the affected countries; whether he shall make proclamation to bring the resolution into operation; whether and when the resolution shall cease to operate and to make proclamation accordingly; and to prescribe limitations and exceptions to which the enforcement of the resolution shall be subject. . . .

The judgment of the court below must be reversed and the cause remanded for further proceedings in accordance with the foregoing opinion.

Reversed.

THE WAR POWERS RESOLUTION OF 1973

Congress's determination to ensure that there would be "no more Vietnams" was embodied in the War Powers Resolution, which was passed over President Nixon's veto in 1973.

In a "national emergency," the resolution states, the President may conduct a war for sixty days and no more unless Congress has declared or authorized war in the meantime. But the resolution provides for an additional thirty days' extension if the president declares that "unavoidable military necessity" requires continuing military action in the course of withdrawing the troops.

The resolution also contains notification procedures. Within forty-eight hours of hostilities, the president must submit a written report to Congress setting forth his justification for troop commitment, his statutory and constitutional authority for doing so, and his estimate of how long the war will last. He must also answer any questions about the war raised by Congress and must submit periodic reports on the war's progress.

Excerpts from the resolution follow.

Short Title

Section 1.   This joint resolution may be cited as the "War Powers Resolution."

Purpose and Policy

Sec. 2.   (a) It is the purpose of this joint resolution to fulfill the intent of the framers of the Constitution of the United States and insure that the collective judgment of both the Congress and the President will apply to the introduction of United States Armed Forces into hostilities, or into situations where imminent involvement in hostilities is clearly indicated by the circumstances, and to the continued use of such forces in hostilities or in such situations.

(b) Under article I, section 8, of the Constitution, it is specifically provided that the Congress shall have the power to make all laws necessary and proper for carrying into execution, not only its own powers but also all other powers vested by the Constitution in the Government of the United States, or in any department or officer thereof.

(c) The constitutional powers of the President as Commander-in-Chief to introduce United States Armed Forces into hostilities, or into situations where imminent involvement in hostilities is clearly indicated by the circumstances, are exercised only pursuant to (1) a declaration of war, (2) specific statutory authorization, or (3) a national emergency created by attack upon the United States, its territories or possessions, or its armed forces.

Consultation

Sec. 3.   The President in every possible instance shall consult with Congress before introducing United States Armed Forces into hostilities or into situations where imminent involvement in hostilities is clearly indicated by the circumstances, and after every such introduction shall consult regularly with the Congress until United States Armed Forces are no longer engaged in hostilities or have been removed from such situations.

Reporting

Sec. 4. (a) In the absence of a declaration of war, in any case in which United States Armed Forces are introduced—

(1) into hostilities or into situations where imminent involvement in hostilities is clearly indicated by the circumstances;

(2) into the territory, airspace or waters of a foreign nation, while equipped for combat, except for deployments which relate solely to supply, replacement, repair, or training of such forces; or

(3) in numbers which substantially enlarge United States Armed Forces equipped for combat already located in a foreign nation;

the President shall submit within 48 hours to the Speaker of the House of Representatives and to the President pro tempore of the Senate a report, in writing, setting forth—

(A) the circumstances necessitating the introduction of United States Armed Forces;

(B) the constitutional and legislative authority under which such introduction took place; and

(C) the estimated scope and duration of the hostilities or [involvement].

Congressional Action

Sec. 5. . . . (b) Within sixty calendar days after a report is submitted or is required to be submitted pursuant to section 4(a)(1), whichever is earlier, the President shall terminate any use of United States Armed Forces with respect to which such report was submitted (or required to be submitted), unless the Congress (1) has declared war or has enacted a specific authorization for such use of United States Armed Forces, (2) has extended by law such sixty-day period, or (3) is physically unable to meet as a result of an armed attack upon the United States. Such sixty-day period shall be extended for not more than an additional thirty days if the President determines and certifies to the Congress in writing that unavoidable military necessity respecting the safety of United States Armed Forces requires the continued use of such armed forces in the course of bringing about a prompt removal of such forces.

(c) Notwithstanding subsection (b), at any time that United States Armed Forces are engaged in hostilities outside the territory of the United States, its possessions and territories without a declaration of war or specific statutory authorization, such forces shall be removed by the President if the Congress so directs by concurrent resolution. . . .

Interpretation of Joint Resolution

Sec. 8. (a) Authority to introduce United States Armed Forces into hostilities or into situations wherein involvement in hostilities is clearly indicated by the circumstances shall not be inferred—

(1) from any provision of law (whether or not in effect before the date of the enactment of this joint resolution), including any provision contained in any appropriation Act, unless such provision specifically authorizes the introduction of United States Armed Forces into hostilities or into such situations and states that it is intended to constitute specific statutory authorization within the meaning of this joint resolution; or

(2) from any treaty heretofore or hereafter ratified unless such treaty is implemented by legislation specifically authorizing the introduction of United States Armed Forces into hostilities or into such situations and stating that it is intended to constitute specific statutory authorization within the meaning of this joint resolution. . . .

(d) Nothing in this joint resolution—

(1) is intended to alter the constitutional authority of the Congress or of the President, or the provisions of existing treaties; or

(2) shall be construed as granting any authority to the President with respect to the introduction of United States Armed Forces into hostilities or into situations wherein involvement in hostilities is clearly indicated by the circumstances which authority he would not have had in the absence of this joint resolution. . . .

WAR POWERS VETO

Following is the White House text of President Nixon's message to Congress concerning his veto of the War Powers Resolution. (Congress later overrode the veto.)

TO THE HOUSE OF REPRESENTATIVES:

I hereby return without my approval House Joint Resolution 542—the War Powers Resolution. While I am in accord with the desire of the Congress to assert its proper role in the conduct of our foreign affairs, the restrictions which this resolution would impose upon the authority of the President are both unconstitutional and dangerous to the best interests of our Nation.

The proper roles of the Congress and the Executive in the conduct of foreign affairs have been debated since the founding of our country. Only recently, however, has there been a serious challenge to the wisdom of the Founding Fathers in choosing not to draw a precise and detailed line of demarcation between the foreign policy powers of the two branches.

The Founding Fathers understood the impossibility of foreseeing every contingency that might arise in this complex area. They acknowledged the need for flexibility in responding to changing circumstances. They recognized that foreign policy decisions must be made through close cooperation between the two branches and not through rigidly codified procedures.

These principles remain as valid today as they were when our Constitution was written. Yet House Joint Resolution 542 would violate those principles by defining the President's powers in ways which would strictly limit his constitutional authority.

Clearly Unconstitutional. House Joint Resolution 542 would purport to take away, by a mere legislative act, authorities which the President has properly exercised under the Constitution for almost 200 years. One of its provisions would automatically cut off certain authorities after sixty days unless the Congress extended them. Another would allow the Congress to eliminate certain authorities merely by the passage of a concurrent resolution—an action which does not normally have the force of law, since it denies the President his constitutional role in approving legislation.

I believe that both these provisions are unconstitutional. The only way in which the constitutional powers of a branch of the Government can be altered is by amending the Constitution—and any attempt to make such alterations by legislation alone is clearly without force.

Undermining Foreign Policy

While I firmly believe that a veto of House Joint Resolution 542 is warranted solely on constitutional grounds, I am also deeply disturbed by the practical consequences of this resolution. For it would seriously undermine this Nation's ability to act decisively and convincingly in times of international crisis. As a result, the confidence of our allies in our ability to assist them could be diminished and the respect of our adversaries for our deterrent posture could decline. A permanent and substantial element of unpredictability would be injected into the world's assessment of American behavior, further increasing the likelihood of miscalculation and war.

If this resolution had been in operation, America's effective response to a variety of challenges in recent years would have been vastly complicated or even made impossible. We may well have been unable to respond in the way we did during the Berlin crisis of 1961, the Cuban missile crisis of 1962, the Congo rescue operation in 1964, and the Jordanian crisis of 1970—to mention just a few examples. In addition, our recent actions to bring about a peaceful settlement of the hostilities in the Middle East would have been seriously impaired if this resolution had been in force.

While all the specific consequences of House Joint Resolution 542 cannot yet be predicted, it is clear that it would undercut the ability of the United States to act as an effective influence for peace. For example, the provision automatically cutting off certain authorities after 60 days unless they are extended by the Congress could work to prolong or intensify a crisis. Until the Congress suspended the deadline, there would be at least a chance of United States withdrawal and an adversary would be tempted therefore to postpone serious negotiations until the 60 days were up. Only after the Congress acted would there be a strong incentive for an adversary to negotiate. In addition, the very existence of a deadline could lead to an escalation of hostilities in order to achieve certain objectives before the 60 days expired.

The measure would jeopardize our role as a force for peace in other ways as well. It would, for example, strike from the President's hand a wide range of important peacekeeping tools by eliminating his ability to exercise quiet diplomacy backed by subtle shifts in our military deployments. It would also cast into doubt authorities which Presidents have used to undertake certain humanitarian relief missions in conflict areas, to protect fishing boats from seizure, to deal with ship or aircraft hijackings, and to respond to threats of attack. Not the least of the adverse consequences of this resolution would be the prohibition contained in section 8 against fulfilling our obligations under the NATO treaty as ratified by the Senate. Finally, since the bill is somewhat vague as to when the 60 day rule would apply, it could lead to extreme confusion and dangerous disagreements concerning the prerogatives of the two branches, seriously damaging our ability to respond to international crises.

Failure to Require Positive Congressional Action. I am particularly disturbed by the fact that certain of the President's constitutional powers as Commander in Chief of the Armed Forces would terminate automatically under this resolution 60 days after they were invoked. No overt Congressional action would be required to cut off these powers—they would disappear automatically unless the Congress extended them. In effect, the Congress is here attempting to increase its policymaking role through a provision which requires it to take absolutely no action at all.

In my view, the proper way for the Congress to make known its will on such foreign policy questions is through a positive action, with full debate on the merits of the issue and with each member taking the responsibility of casting a yes or no vote after considering those merits. The authorization and appropriations process represents one of the ways in which such influence can be exercised. I do not, however, believe that the Congress can responsibly contribute its considered, collective judgment on such grave questions without full debate and without a yes or no vote. Yet this is precisely what the joint resolution would allow. It would give every future Congress the ability to handcuff every future President merely by doing nothing and sitting still. In my view, one cannot become a responsible partner unless one is prepared to take responsible action.

Strengthening Cooperation Between the Congress and the Executive Branches. The responsible and effective exercise of the war powers requires the fullest cooperation between the Congress and the Executive and the prudent fulfillment by each branch of its constitutional responsibilities. House Joint Resolution 542 includes certain constructive measures which would foster this process by enhancing the flow of information from the executive branch to the Congress. Section 3, for example, calls for consultations with the Congress before and during the involvement of United States forces in hostilities abroad. This provision is consistent with the desire of this Administration for regularized consultations with the Congress in an even wider range of circumstances.

I believe that full and cooperative participation in foreign policy matters by both the executive and the legislative branches could be enhanced by a careful and dispassionate study of their constitutional roles. Helpful proposals for such a study have already been made in the Congress. I would welcome the establishment of a non-partisan commission on the constitutional roles of the Congress and the President in the conduct of foreign affairs. This commission could make a thorough review of the principal constitutional issues in Executive-Congressional relations, including the war powers, the international agreement powers, and the question of Executive privilege, and then submit its recommendations to the President and the Congress. The members of such a commission could be drawn from both parties—and could represent many perspectives including those of the Congress, the executive branch, the legal profession, and the academic community.

This Administration is dedicated to strengthening cooperation between the Congress and the President in the conduct of foreign affairs and to preserving the constitutional prerogatives of both branches of our Government. I know that the Congress shares that goal. A commission on the constitutional roles of the Congress and the President would provide a useful opportunity for both branches to work together toward that common objective.

RICHARD NIXON

THE WHITE HOUSE,
October 24, 1973

SELECTED READINGS

Bickel, Alexander, "Congress, the President and the Power to Wage War." *Chicago-Kent Law Review* 48 (1971): 131-147.

> Bickel, late professor of constitutional law at Yale University, provides an excellent and highly readable overview of the constitutional, political, and pragmatic questions surrounding the president, Congress, and war powers. Although the article predates the War Powers Act, it is still timely—particularly in its discussion of constitutional questions raised by the Gulf of Tonkin Resolution.

Corwin, Edward S. *The President: Office and Powers.* 4th ed. New York: New York University Press, 1957.

> The greatest constitutional authority in our history here argues that the language of the Constitution invites struggle between the executive and legislative branches for the privilege of directing American foreign policy. Corwin further argues that additional presidential power and authority derive from the president's capacity as executive of the law of nations.

Dolce, Philip, and Skau, George, eds. *Power and the Presidency.* New York: Scribner's, 1976.

> An excellent compendium of essays on presidential power, including pieces by James MacGregor Burns, Louis Koenig, and Arthur Schlesinger, Jr. The essays are intelligently arranged by categories: historical studies, analyses of contemporary issues, and "views from the top."

Ehrlich, Thomas. "The Legal Process in Foreign Affairs: Military Intervention—A Testing Case." *Stanford Law Review* 27 (1975): 637-652.

> Ehrlich, professor of law at Stanford University, examines the executive decision-making process in the area of military intervention short of full-scale war—with an eye to suggesting possible legal controls on the power of the president. He considers legal controls possible within the executive branch, others developed and imposed by Congress (including the War Powers Act), and still others imposed by the legal profession.

Henkin, Louis. *Foreign Affairs and the Constitution.* Mineola, N.Y.: Foundation Press, 1972.

A detailed analysis of the foreign affairs powers and authority of the president, the Congress, and the Supreme Court, particularly in relation to international law. The analysis includes careful consideration of constitutional commentary and case law from the time of the nation's founding.

Henkin, Louis. "Is There a 'Political Question' Doctrine?" *Yale Law Review* 85 (1976): 597–625.

While admitting that there *is* a political questions doctrine, Henkin argues that the federal courts' reliance upon and application of that doctrine have been significantly less frequent than political scientists and lawyers have claimed.

Pious, Richard M. *The American Presidency.* New York: Basic Books, 1979.

Pious is one of the leading presidential scholars writing today. In this major book on the presidency, he focuses on both the president's constitutional authority and on presidential responses in crisis situations.

Schlesinger, Arthur M., Jr. *The Imperial Presidency.* Boston: Houghton Mifflin, 1973.

"The constitutional Presidency—as events so apparently disparate as the Indochina War and the Watergate affair showed—has become the imperial Presidency and threatens to be the revolutionary Presidency." Schlesinger's analysis of past and recent exercises of presidential power explores the shift in the constitutional balance of powers away from the Congress and toward the president in both the foreign and domestic spheres. In particular, he addresses questions raised by national emergencies and war making.

Scigliano, Robert. "The War Powers Resolution and the War Powers." In *The Presidency in the Constitutional Order*, edited by Joseph M. Bessette and Jeffrey Tulis. Baton Rouge, La.: Louisiana State University Press, 1981.

This excellent essay examines the genesis, purpose, language, and application of the War Powers Resolution. It considers the resolution in relation to the Constitution and to the political thought of Locke and Montesquieu and addresses the problem of prerogative powers.

Sofaer, Abraham D. "The Presidency, War, and Foreign Affairs: Practice under the Framers." *Law and Contemporary Problems* 40 (Spring 1976): 12–38.

A survey of the relations between presidents and Congresses from Washington through Monroe and of the gradual development of executive power. Sofaer argues that, while past presidents were powerful, they did not claim the inherent powers recent presidents have claimed and were far more deferential to congressional opinion and authority.

GLOSSARY

Bay of Pigs. The site of an unsuccessful attempt, by CIA-sponsored Cuban exiles, to invade Communist Cuba in 1961.

Covert action. Secret government involvement in an attempt to destabilize or overthrow another government.

Cuban missile crisis. Despite assurances to the contrary, the Soviet Union in 1962 began shipping nuclear missiles to Cuba for deployment against targets in the Western
Hemisphere. In response, the Kennedy administration established a naval blockade
of Cuba until the Soviets removed the missiles.

Habeas corpus. If someone is held by the authorities without being formally charged
with any crime, he or she can apply to a court for a "writ of habeas corpus"—an
order forcing the authorities to acknowledge that they are holding the person (the
term literally means "we have the body") and to hold a trial.

"Plausibly deniable." A bureaucratic term of art meaning that an executive official
can deny American involvement in some controversial activity without sounding
like an out-and-out liar.

Political question. Also called a "nonjusticiable question." An issue that courts refuse
to decide because they think it can only be resolved by the political process or by
the elected branches of government.

Prerogative. A term used by the British philosopher John Locke (1634–1704) to
describe what he considered to be the right, even the duty, of a nation's chief executive: to act without the prescription of law, and, on certain occasions, even
against the law.

"Zone of twilight." A term used by Supreme Court Justice Robert Jackson, concurring in the steel seizure case, to describe presidential acts that are neither authorized nor forbidden by Congress.

Chapter 3
Somehow It Works . . .
or Does It?

*"Is our presidential nomination and election
system a disaster waiting to happen? Can we replace
a disabled President who won't let go?"*
          FRED FRIENDLY

"Practical politics consists in ignoring the facts."
          HENRY ADAMS

When it comes to putting political candidates in the White House and taking them out of it, the American system seems at first to work pretty well. What in many countries is settled by bullets is settled here by ballot and ritual.

True, our presidential election system is hard to explain to foreigners. Parts of it are hard to explain to ourselves. We have what we call an "electoral college" that works just the opposite of the way it was supposed to work. The Framers of the Constitution wanted it to be an elite body of wise and sober gentlemen who would use their discretion in picking a president. It is now a group of political robots who, with an occasional exception, vote as they are expected to vote.

Then there is the role of political parties in the election process. Parties are never mentioned in the Constitution; the Founders distrusted them. Yet today there is no way anybody is going to get elected president without first getting the backing of a party.

Finally, there is the contingency that every system must in some way anticipate: what if the chief executive becomes physically or mentally incapacitated? Who takes over, when, how, and for how long? The Twenty-Fifth Amendment tries to spell out the answers to all these questions. But the evidence we have so far indicates that the president's staff—a small, dedicated group of personal aides—takes over the functions of government during periods of presidential disability. *They* aren't even mentioned in the Twenty-Fifth Amendment.

Well, Americans might say, so what? The actual operation of our system is not entirely consistent with the way the Constitution says it works, but it works all right. Perhaps, for a practical people, that is enough. "If it ain't broke, don't fix it," Americans say.

If the issue were just a theoretical one, there wouldn't be much to argue about. But our history has also revealed some practical weaknesses in the system: sometimes it does *not* seem to work very well. On three occasions, in 1824, 1876, and 1888, the electoral college system gave us presidents who received fewer popular votes than one of their opponents. It could happen again. What would we do then? How would we feel about our new president? How much authority would that new chief executive have to run the country? Would the majority of people who voted for the loser take the outcome in good grace? It is not pleasant to contemplate the answers.

Then there is our nominating system, involving political parties. For years politicians got nominated by currying favor with party leaders, the "bosses." That system caused such hard feelings that in 1968 it led to riots at the site of the Democratic Convention in Chicago. Now the process is handled differently. Politicians get nominated by currying favor with those who vote in the party elections and caucuses held in various states. The trouble is that only 25 to 30 percent of eligible party voters bother to show up for these events. So the party nominee is usually very popular with small, intense minorities but not so popular with the party rank and file. In fact, some of these nominees in recent years seem to be regarded by voters in the general elections as inept, extreme, or both. The "bosses" may have given us better nominees—yet we can't go back to them. What to do?

The practical problems of presidential disability are the most frightening of all. Suppose the president of the United States, the one who can, in Lyndon Johnson's chilling words, "mash that button," becomes incapable of making rational decisions. Despite the elaborate procedures spelled out in the Twenty-Fifth Amendment, everything then seems to rest with the president's personal staff. Is that what we really want? Decisions that could be apocalyptic left in the hands of a group of people neither elected nor officially appointed—a group of cronies who may hardly be known outside their own inner circle? Clearly, the whole procedure needs to be rethought.

The Video Discussion

Rethinking the topic of presidential disability and the other issues is a distinguished panel of journalists, professors, jurists, and political activists. The panel is moderated by Professor Arthur R. Miller of Harvard Law School.

List of Participants

LAURENCE I. BARRETT
Senior White House Correspondent
Time Magazine

ARCHIBALD COX
Carl M. Loeb University Professor
Harvard Law School
Former Solicitor General of the U.S.

LLOYD N. CUTLER
Former Counsel to President Carter

TERRY DOLAN
Chairman
National Conservative Political
Action Committee

FRED GRAHAM
Law Correspondent
CBS News

HON. ORRIN G. HATCH
U.S. Senator
Utah

ALEXANDER HEARD
Chancellor Emeritus
Professor of Political Science
Vanderbilt University

ANN F. LEWIS
Political Director
Democratic National Committee

LAWRENCE D. LONGLEY
Professor of Government
Lawrence University

HON. BARBARA A. MIKULSKI
U.S. Representative
Maryland

HON. EDMUND S. MUSKIE
Former U.S. Secretary of State
Former U.S. Senator
Maine

JACK NELSON
Washington Bureau Chief
Los Angeles Times

JODY POWELL
National Political Columnist
Dallas Times Herald
Former Press Secretary to President Carter

DONALD L. ROBINSON
Professor of Government
Smith College

HON. POTTER STEWART
Justice (retired)
U.S. Supreme Court
1958-1981

JACK VALENTI
President
Motion Picture Association of
America, Inc.
Former Special Assistant to
President Johnson

HON. J. CLIFFORD WALLACE
Judge
U.S. Court of Appeals
Ninth Circuit

BEN J. WATTENBERG
Senior Fellow
American Enterprise Institute

TOM WICKER
Columnist and Associate Editor
New York Times

Program Summary

The program is divided into three parts. The first part is concerned with the issue of party nominations. The moderator sets up a situation in which the candidate who has been the front-runner in the primaries is reported to have had a homosexual affair. The moderator then assigns the participants a variety of roles and asks how they would act. What should a party leader do? How should delegates vote if they got elected as supporters of the candidate? What could a lawyer do for an irate voter who voted for a delegate pledged to the candidate and now discovers that the delegate is going to vote for someone else? Behind these questions are the real issues: What is the purpose of political parties? Are they strictly private organizations? Are their nominating procedures really democratic?

The second part of the program moves beyond the nominating stage to the general election. At issue is the electoral college system. The central question: What happens if a candidate who loses the popular vote wins in the electoral college? How would journalists carry the story? How would political leaders react to it? Would they try to persuade some of the electors to change their votes? How should the losing candidate react? Should he fight the result or persuade his supporters to accept it? Finally, suppose the election gets thrown into the House of Representatives for decision. How should members vote? Should they vote by party lines? Should they vote as their district has voted? Or should they be guided by the popular votes in their states or in the nation as a whole? In the video debate, the consensus seems to be that House members should be guided by the popular-vote majorities in their districts.

The third part of the program centers on the theme of presidential disability. The moderator presents various situations. Suppose the president is slightly injured in an assassination attempt. Suppose he is going into the hospital for a tonsillectomy. Suppose he is going mad. The panelists try to anticipate how the people around the president would react in these situations. At issue is the workability of the Twenty-Fifth Amendment. Some panelists doubt whether the procedures set forth in the amendment would ever be followed in the case of prolonged presidential disability.

I: NOMINATION PROCEDURES

To understand the background of the first round of discussion, we need to know something about political parties.

Not only is there no mention of political parties in the Constitution, there was a widely shared feeling among America's first generation of leaders that parties were subversive institutions, conspiracies against the general good. The word "party" derives from "part," meaning that it seeks only a "partial" good, the good of its members, at the expense of the good of the whole. In his Farewell Address, George Washington condemned "all combinations and associations . . . with the real design to direct, control, counteract or awe the regular deliberations of the constituted authorities." Thomas Jefferson said, "If I could not go to heaven but with a party, I would not go there at all."

Such strong sentiments did not prevent Washington and Jefferson from belonging to parties. Washington was the living symbol of the Federalists, the nation's first party under the new Constitution, and Jefferson soon became leader of the Republicans, who took him not to heaven but to the presidency in 1800.

If people who spoke so forcefully against "combinations and associations" became members of them, it suggests that political parties are well-nigh unavoidable in the American political system. In the video discussion of the nomination process, the importance of parties is established at the very outset. The moderator says he wants to run for president and asks what the qualifications for the office are. He is told that he has to be a natural-born citizen, must have resided in this country for fourteen years, and must be at least thirty-five years old. Since he meets all these requirements, he wonders whether all he has to do is "look in the *Yellow Pages*, call up the Board of Electors in each state, and say, 'Put my name on the ballot.'" No, the panelists tell him, it's a little more complicated than that. You have to get nominated by a party. The moderator persists: But why? The Constitution requires only that I be a natural-born citizen, a resident of America for fourteen years, and thirty-five years old.

Terry Dolan, head of the National Conservative Political Action Committee, gives the most succinct answer: "There's a difference between running and winning. If you want a chance of winning, you should have a party." Whatever disagreements there may be between Dolan and some other members of the panel, there is no argument here. Even in local races it is hard for anyone to win as an independent. In a presidential race, an independent candidacy is a quixotic venture.

Take John Anderson. In 1980 he failed to get the Republican nomination. Instead of supporting the Republican nominee, Ronald Reagan, Anderson ran as an independent, calling himself the "national unity" candidate. He is a distinguished-looking man and an impressive public speaker. He had interesting, arguable positions on the issues and some very dedicated campaign workers. He was endorsed by movie stars and other celebrities and was on the news practically every night. Some people feared and others hoped that he might just pull it off. The result? Less than 7 percent of the popular vote.

Ballot Access to Independents

Independents have such a hard time partly because of discrimination by state election laws and officials. They make it hard for independents to get on the ballot when they require, for example, special petitions with thousands of signatures (which the officials squint very hard at, looking to invalidate signatures wherever they can), early filing deadlines, and high filing fees. The Supreme Court has examined some of these practices and found them to be unconstitutional. In *Williams* v. *Rhodes* (1968), George Wallace's American Independent party and another minor party challenged the procedures for getting on the ballot in Ohio. The state kept the major parties on the ballot if they had obtained 10 percent of the vote or more at the last election. But new parties and independents had to go through an elaborate rigmarole, including a very early submission of petitions (with signatures totaling 15 percent of the vote in the last gubernatorial election), the creation of a party structure, and the holding of primary elections. The Court said those requirements amounted to discrimination, and it struck them down.

In some later cases in other states, the Court upheld certain petition requirements as reasonable safeguards that did not "freeze the political status quo." But in 1983 Ohio's ballot requirements were successfully challenged again. The case was *Anderson* v. *Celebrezze*. At issue was an Ohio statute requiring independent candidates to file their petitions and related materials by March 20 in order to get on the November ballot. John Anderson sued, claiming the statute amounted to an unconstitutional restriction on ballot access, and that it discriminated against his candidacy. The Supreme Court agreed.

The Usefulness of Political Parties

Still, Anderson's poor showing even where his name was on the ballot suggests that American voters generally prefer candidates with party endorsements. There may be good reasons for this preference. Parties help to define candidacies, placing them in contexts ordinary people can understand. Party labels simplify the choices for voters, making it possible to vote with some degree of rationality without having to look up all the candidates' positions on issues. For these reasons and others, many political scientists look favorably upon political parties, seeing them as instruments of democracy. Besides simplifying choices, parties can help get out the vote, inject energy and enthusiasm into campaigns, and, perhaps most importantly, help link the people to the government. If the American people want programs A, B, and C, they should vote Democrat; if they want programs D, E, and F, they should vote Republican.

In reality, of course, American party platforms straddle many fences and fuzz over many issues, and party candidates aren't always loyal to the platforms anyway. But on the whole there *are* significant differences between Democrats and Republicans in Congress and between Democratic and Republican presidents. Cynics used to say that the major American parties are Tweedledum and Tweedledee. Could anyone who watched the 1984 presidential election say that?

Are Parties Strictly Private?

Legally, our political parties occupy an indistinct area between official and private organizations. In the video discussion, former Supreme Court Justice Potter Stewart says that parties "are . . . voluntary associations, and . . . as such, protected by the First Amendment to the Constitution. And any rules that they want to make . . . as voluntary associations . . . take precedent over any state laws." This needs a little qualification. A series of Supreme Court decisions from 1927 to 1953 has made it clear that political parties are not "voluntary associations" in the same sense as, say, church choirs or amateur softball teams. Parties are tied to the machinery of election; they put people into office. Thus, they have certain responsibilities that go along with the public purposes they serve.

The cases that elicited these conclusions concerned the exclusion of black voters from primary elections. A primary is an election a party holds to see who will be nominated, or endorsed, by the party as its candidate at the general election. *Nixon v. Herndon* (1927) involved a Texas law which mandated the exclusion of blacks from Democratic primaries. The Supreme Court struck down the law, saying that it violated the Fourteenth Amendment. Texas obediently repealed the law—and passed a new one. This law said that the authority to decide who could participate in primaries should rest with the executive committees of the parties. The Democratic executive committee then ruled that no blacks could participate in its primaries. This law, too, in the case of *Nixon* v. *Condon* (1932), was struck down by the Court. It reasoned that the law had really made the party's executive committee an agency of the state by officially mentioning it and giving it the power to decide who should vote. Texas then repealed *all* laws touching on the qualifications for voting in primary elections and just let the Democrats exclude blacks on their own. At first this passed muster. In a 1935 case the practice was upheld by the Court. But in a later case, *Smith* v. *Allright* (1944), the 1935 decision was overturned. From that time on, racial exclusion from primary elections, even in the absence of official state endorsement, was no longer allowed by the Court.

The white Democrats of Texas tried one last "legal" way of excluding blacks from primaries. They started holding "preprimary" elections under the auspices of the Jaybird Democratic Association, a "voluntary club" of Democrats that excluded blacks. Typically, the winners of these contests would then run unopposed in the Democratic primaries. But in *Terry* v. *Adams* (1953), the Court struck down the practice. Though there were different opinions in the case, the majority seemed to agree that it amounted to another way of trying to deny blacks their right to vote.

Political parties, then, are more than "private" organizations, at least in terms of their duty to avoid racial exclusivity. But in other respects they *are* private. When Justice Stewart says their rules take precedent "over any state laws," he probably has in mind the case of *Democratic Party* v. *LaFollette* (1981), which involved a conflict between Wisconsin state law and the internal rules of the Democratic party. Wisconsin law mandates "open" primaries—primaries in which you don't have to be a registered party member in order to vote. This allows Republicans to vote in Democratic primaries and vice versa. Yet at the Democratic presidential convention of 1980, the party refused to seat some delegates picked in this manner. The delegates sued, but the Supreme Court backed the party's right to seat delegates in the manner its rules prescribe. Wisconsin can mandate "open" primaries if it likes, but neither party has to be bound by the rule in deciding which delegates to seat.

Caucuses

Not all states use primary elections as a means of selecting delegates to presidential nominating conventions. Some, such as Iowa, Hawaii, Nevada, and Oklahoma, use caucuses. Caucuses are meetings of registered party members. They usually begin at the neighborhood or "precinct" level, where delegates are picked to represent them at a higher level in the state, most often at the county level. The county caucuses, in turn, pick delegates to the state convention, which then selects delegates for the national convention.

In the past, most delegates to party conventions were either appointed outright by party officials or picked by the caucus method. And, not to put too fine a point on it, the caucuses were controlled by the local party organizations. Party workers from the local clubhouse showed up at them and voted as it was suggested that they vote. These old ways were sharply challenged in 1968, when insurgents within the

Democratic party sought to win the presidential nomination for Senator Eugene McCarthy of Minnesota. McCarthy had positioned himself as the anti-Vietnam War candidate, and he was challenging Vice-President Hubert Humphrey, the candidate favored by most party leaders and by President Johnson.

The Democrats After 1968: The New Rules

McCarthy's followers tried to play by the old rules, but the rules—or sometimes the lack of rules—worked against them. For example, McCarthy's people would show up at the place where the local caucus was supposed to be held, only to discover that the meeting place had suddenly been changed. By the time they found the new place, all the delegates would have been picked, and of course they would all be pro-Humphrey.

The end result was that Humphrey got the nomination. But it proved to be a hollow victory, for the party was so bitterly divided—the bitterness helped set the stage for the riots between police and demonstrators around the Chicago hotel where the convention was held—that it probably helped Richard Nixon win the 1968 election.

The Democrats were determined not to repeat the debacle of '68. So they "reformed" themselves. The word is in quotation marks because not everybody agrees that the changes were improvements. A special Commission on Party Structure and Delegate Selection was established, cochaired by George McGovern, then a South Dakota senator, and Representative Donald Fraser. By 1970 the McGovern-Fraser Commission issued a report whose major recommendations included these:

1. *"Fair-play rules."* Party caucuses must be open to all members, announced in advance, held in public places, and governed by written rules.

2. *Affirmative action.* Women, minorities, and young people eighteen or more years old must be represented at the convention "in reasonable relationship to their presence in the state's population." Those supporting this change called it "broadened representation." Those opposing it called it a "quota system."

3. *Altered delegate selection procedures.* Delegates must be selected within a year of the presidential election, and three-quarters of them must be selected by caucuses (which must follow "fair-play rules") or by primaries.

In 1972 the Democrats implemented these suggestions, with the result that their presidential convention looked much different—and acted differently—than it did in previous years. There were many more blacks, women, and young people in attendance, and they were better educated and more affluent than in previous years. They tended to be people with the time, interest, and income required to spend much of their time in unpaid political activity. They nominated George McGovern, who inherited much of Eugene McCarthy's anti-Vietnam War constituency. The "outs" of 1968 had become the "ins" of 1972 in the leadership of the Democratic party. In the process, the party began to change its texture: from a blue-collar, white ethnic and white Southerner, Catholic, Southern Protestant, city "machine" coalition into a younger organization of college professors, graduate students, lawyers, doctors, feminist leaders, antiwar clergy, middle-class blacks, consumer activists, environmentalists, and social workers. Supporters of the new rules changes say that they broadened the party and lent new legitimacy to it. Opponents tend to argue that the changes turned the party from a grass-roots organization to an elitist body that no longer has much in common with the mass of nominal Democrats.

The Proliferation of Primaries

One certain result of the changes adopted between 1968 and 1972 is that there has been an explosion of primary elections. In 1968, only seventeen states picked delegates to presidential conventions by means of primaries. By 1980, the number had increased to thirty-seven. Each state has its own rules for primaries. In some states primaries are just "beauty contests," ranking the popularity of candidates but leaving actual delegate selection to caucuses. In most states primaries actually yield delegates "pledged" to vote for particular candidates at the convention. In other words, when you vote for candidate X, you are actually voting for convention delegates who support candidate X. Each state also sets its own dates for primaries, so that they are strung out between January and June of the election year, with the convention following a month or two later.

The timing and rules of primaries raise some troubling issues. What if something happens to a candidate who has piled up a huge number of delegates during the early primaries? Are "his" delegates still obliged to vote for him? Or can they switch their vote to one of his opponents? These issues are the central focus of the first part of the video discussion. Before turning to them, let us summarize what has been said.

Points to Remember

1. Though the Founding Fathers never mentioned parties in the Constitution and distrusted them profoundly, parties have become essential to anyone planning a serious race for the presidency. Many students of politics consider them as useful instruments of democracy, since they simplify choice, help get out the vote, stimulate enthusiasm, and help to make officials more responsible to the electorate.
2. Our parties are voluntary associations, but since they serve the public function of electing people to office, there are certain things they may not do, such as exclude people from membership because of race. In general, however, the autonomy of their internal rules is protected by the courts.
3. In the past, delegates to conventions were picked mainly by caucuses controlled by local party organizations or else were appointed by party leaders. Today, primary elections play a critical role in the selection of delegates. Primaries are now important to both parties, but the changes were initiated by the Democrats between 1968 and 1972 as a result of protests over the way Hubert Humphrey got the nomination in 1968. Other rules changes initiated by the Democrats included "fair-play rules" for caucuses and "affirmative action" in selecting women, blacks, and young people as delegates.

The Video Discussion: "The Cameron Scandal"

"Ms. Lewis," says the moderator, turning toward Ann Lewis, political director of the National Democratic Committee, "you're sitting at breakfast one morning and you open up your newspaper and, lo and behold, page one: There's a story that Chris Cameron, this dynamic governor from the Midwest who's got a lock, now, on your party's convention, had a homosexual affair twelve years ago. How do you react?"

Lewis starts off by informing the moderator that Cameron does not, in fact, have a "lock" on the nomination. He might have if this were 1980, when "pledged" delegates were strongly bound to the candidates they were associated with. But the present rules are more relaxed; the delegates are only "expected, in good conscience, to reflect the wishes of the people who elected them." In short, a Cameron delegate can switch at the convention and vote for another candidate. And Lewis makes it clear that delegates have a right to switch in certain circumstances. After all, the goals of the party are "to win elections and to govern." It can't do either if it nominates Cameron.

Jody Powell, former press secretary to President Carter, agrees with Lewis. If he were Cameron's campaign manager, he would advise him to get out of the race. But what if Cameron denies the charge, and, indeed, it turns out that the evidence for it isn't solid? Then, Powell says, he would tell him to stay in the race and would help him fight the charge. But suppose that in the meantime the charges are all over the media and Cameron delegates are starting to get cold feet; some of them are switching because they know that, true or not, the charges will greatly hurt the party during the general election. The moderator reminds the panelists of what Ann Lewis said: that her party was interested in winning elections. Tom Wicker of the *New York Times* replies that "the practical answer to that might be that if you throw Cameron over the side and go to the guy who's been consistently losing all the primaries, you're probably going to lose even more badly than you would have anyway." In one stroke Wicker has joined decency and compassion together with the prime maxim of machine politics: "Don't back no losers."

Suppose, however, that the convention delegates ignore Wicker's advice. They switch their votes from Cameron to the number-two candidate. Is that fair? Is it legal? The moderator pretends to be a voter who has cast his ballot for a Cameron delegate and then discovers the delegate has decided to switch. The outraged voter demands to know what kind of "shell game" is going on. "They con me into thinking I'm voting for a candidate, when, in fact, I'm voting for one of their functionaries who, under their rules, can do whatever he or she wants." Lloyd Cutler, who served as President Carter's legal counsel, says, "That's exactly right." That's the way the system is supposed to work. It's a *representative* system. You're voting for the delegates, not the candidates. Congresswoman Barbara Mikulski agrees, and reminds the moderator that delegate selection is a year-long process; during that time anything could happen to a front-runner. He "could have been killed in an automobile accident." She thinks about it for a moment. This one, she adds, "was hit by the front page."

The indignant Cameron voter is not appeased by Mikulski's explanation. He wants "his" delegate to vote as pledged. Can he get any relief from the courts? It doesn't seem so. He gets no encouragement from former Solicitor General Archibald Cox, nor from the judges he approaches, U.S. Appeals Court Judge J. Clifford Wallace or former

Supreme Court Justice Potter Stewart. It's here that Stewart refers to the parties as "voluntary associations" enjoying the freedom to make their own rules concerning delegates. With the exceptions mentioned earlier in the chapter (the "white primary" cases), Justice Stewart's statement can serve as a conclusion. The outraged voter can write angry letters, switch parties, or picket the convention, but there is no way he can legally compel Cameron delegates to vote Cameron.

It is time to move on to the general election. Once again, the voter goes to the polls. Once again he or she votes for somebody for president. And—once again—it turns out that the voter is not voting for a candidate but for delegates, or, more precisely, electors.

II: THE ELECTORAL COLLEGE

Here is how the system was supposed to work. Each state gets an allotment of "electoral votes" equal to its total number of representatives plus its two senators. If a state has five congressmen, it gets seven electoral votes; if it has eight, it gets ten electoral votes; and so on. The electoral votes are cast by "electors," who, it was assumed, would be wise and upright citizens respected for their good judgment. Each elector would then exercise this good judgment by casting two votes, at least one of which must be for someone outside of his or her state. (The Founders wanted to avoid the parochialism of all the state "favorite sons" being picked.) Then the ballots of all the electors in all the states would be counted; the candidate with the majority would become president and the runner-up vice-president.

It was an aristocratic idea: a group of wise men interposed between the people and the presidency. It was to be government *for* the people, but not directly *by* them. But by 1800 the idea had become a fiction. By then, parties had taken over the whole electoral system. The parties offered voters competing "slates" of electors who were "pledged" to the parties' candidates for president and vice-president. Thomas Jefferson and Aaron Burr, the Republican party's candidates, were running for president and vice-president respectively. The two won a majority of electoral votes. The trouble was that the Jefferson-Burr electors turned out to be such perfect party dummies that the two were tied. That triggered another constitutional provision: if nobody gets a majority of electoral votes, the election is thrown into the House of Representatives for decision. For this special House vote, each state, regardless of its population, is assigned one vote. In the House, the Federalists had a clear majority, and some of them were thinking of voting for Burr. But Alexander Hamilton, who disliked Jefferson but deeply distrusted Burr (he was eventually killed by Burr in a duel), prevailed upon his fellow Federalists to vote for Jefferson. Eventually, after several inconclusive ballots, Jefferson was elected president and Burr vice-president.

To prevent a repetition of this sort of tie, the Twelfth Amendment was adopted in 1804. It says that the electors must cast separate ballots for president and vice-president. That means that the president and vice-president on the same ticket are not running against each other but against competing candidates for president and vice-president.

"Faithless Electors" and "Winner Take All"

Today, as in 1800, when voters go to the polls to cast their ballots for president, they are not really voting for president. They are voting for slates of electors pledged to a particular presidential candidate. In all save a few states, the electors are not bound by law to vote for the candidate to whom they are pledged, and there have been some cases of "faithless electors" who turned against their party's candidate. But the number of such cases have been so few that they have never posed any threat to the outcome of an election. Electors are, almost without exception, friends of the party leaders; their most distinguishing trait is loyalty to the ticket—which, presumably, is the way voters would want it to be.

A more serious issue arises from what is called the "unit rule" or "winner take all" feature of the electoral college. If a candidate wins the majority of popular votes in a state, *all* that state's electoral votes go to him or her. Even if the loser lost by a razor-thin margin, he or she gets zero electoral votes from the state. For example, in the state of Massachusetts in 1980, Reagan beat Carter by a very small margin of popular votes; the percentage was 50.1 to 49.9. Yet Reagan got all of Massachusetts's fourteen electoral votes. The effect of this is to (choose your word) "distort" or "amplify" the extent of a winner's victory in the nation as a whole. In popular votes, the 1980 national percentages were Reagan, 51.6; Carter, 41.7; Anderson, 6.7. But in electoral votes it was Reagan, 489; Carter, 49; Anderson, 0. In itself there may be nothing wrong with this practice. A win, after all, is a win. It might even be good for national unity and for the authority of the presidency to "amplify" the extent of the victor's victory. But suppose that, in every state a candidate loses, he loses by the tiniest margin of popular votes. Suppose further that in every state he wins, he wins by huge and therefore "wasted" margins. In both cases popular votes have accumulated that really do the candidate no good in the electoral college. They are either far in excess of what he needs or not enough to tip the state's electoral votes into his column. What happens then? The mathematics of the situation will result in a popular-vote victory but a loss in the electoral college. The candidate will therefore lose the election even though he beat his opponent in popular votes. This happened to Grover Cleveland in 1888, and there were two earlier elections, in 1824 and 1876, in which an apparent popular-vote winner lost the presidency.

What if it were to happen again? In the video discussion it does—to President Baker.

The Video Discussion of Electoral College

President Baker and his challenger, Mr. Abel, "have waged this very tough, honorable campaign," says the moderator. The morning after election night we wake to find that the president has a 2-million-vote majority but that Abel has won the electoral vote by 271 to 267.

President Baker is indignant. He calls up Lloyd Cutler and asks him what he can do to reverse the verdict of the electoral college. Cutler advises him that "you might have a good shot at disqualifying one of those electors, or persuading three of them to change their vote."

MODERATOR: Hmmm. In other words, to submarine the electoral college.

CUTLER: Not to submarine it, to carry out the original constitutional provision that it was to be a deliberative body.

Cutler will try to turn the electors back into a body of wise and sober individuals who make up their own minds—the original dream of the Founding Fathers. And the moderator is going to help him, by assembling a team consisting of Cutler, Jody Powell, Ann Lewis, and Terry Dolan. Their mission: to change the minds of Abel-pledged electors and get them to switch their votes.

What does the team think of their assignment? Powell will have nothing to do with it. It sounds to him like "an effort to . . . in effect subvert the processes" of presidential elections. Dolan sees nothing wrong with it. Since the electoral college "is supposed to be deliberative," he says, "I don't see anything wrong with trying to convince electors to change their minds." Ann Lewis not only agrees with Cutler and Dolan but is ready to start planning strategy. "I would be looking for electors to whom I could appeal, I think, on two grounds: on patriotism, and on process, on fair play." All she needs is to get four Abel electors to abstain. She will say to them: "Do you want to participate in the first time in our history in so many years in which the popular vote is undermined?" If she can get them to abstain, the election will be thrown into the House of Representatives, for the vote would then be tied, 267 to 267.

Tom Wicker is appalled at the thought of a presidential election being thrown into the House, and many political analysts would agree. In the first place, it would delay the outcome of the election for an indefinite period. During that interim the American people would have no president except the person in office—who might or might not be the loser—and no prospect of a successor. It would be a strange and possibly strained period in our history. Second, the House vote would be far more undemocratic than anything the electoral college vote could have given us. For in that special election each state would be allotted one vote *regardless of its population.* Sparsely populated states like Alaska and Wyoming would have the same vote as New York and California. Third, a House election would invite all manner of wheeling and dealing as supporters of the candidates sought to get votes. Some of the deals might become unsavory, not to say crooked.

Needless to say, there is no crookedness or impropriety in any of the deals Ann Lewis is proposing in order to get the election thrown into the House. The moderator introduces her to "Jack Judas." Mr. Judas, an Abel elector, might consider switching to Baker or abstaining. But he "wants something" for his vote. The moderator is not quite sure what Mr. Judas wants. "It could be small, it could be big." But Lewis knows that it must be big. "See, there's no small in that bargain." The presidency of the United States is at stake, "so any bargain is a very large one." And she will have no part in it.

Still, the very fact that any kind of deal making is possible bothers Professor Lawrence Longley, who teaches government at Lawrence University. He thinks the electoral college is "ill equipped to serve as a deliberative body . . . or to barter or bargain for who should be president." Longley himself was chosen as a Democratic elector in the 1980 race, perhaps in part because he had written a scholarly book on the topic but more likely because the state party chairman trusted him to vote as he was pledged to vote. Longley characterizes the electors as "a state-by-state collection of political hacks and fat cats." Moderator: "Or academics who have written books." Longley: "Occasionally."

Longley's view is challenged by another government professor, Donald Robinson of Smith College. Robinson thinks that the electoral college "has served a useful purpose." He acknowledges that "the room for mischief is enormous," and for that reason would like to make electoral votes "automatic": when a candidate carries a state, he or she gets all the state's electoral votes, "and no monkey business." But he thinks the electoral college serves as a good "safety valve." If "something is discovered" between election day and the time the electors vote in December, "it gives us a chance, if the occasion is serious enough, for a second thought." Evidently, then, Robinson does not want the electoral votes to be "automatic" in every case. If "something is discovered" about the winner, then evidently the electors *can* engage in a bit of "monkey business" by changing their votes.

Congresswoman Barbara Mikulski agrees with Longley and disagrees with Robinson. It is not clear, though, that Longley would agree with her reasoning. She would abolish the electoral college because "I don't see the electoral college taking care of women and minorities and as a vehicle for ensuring affirmative action." This is a puzzling statement. It seems to be based on a misunderstanding of the peculiar bias or "tilt" in the electoral college. It may be interesting to probe it.

Mikulski has long been a supporter of the feminist movement, so by "women" she probably means causes championed by that movement, such as the Equal Rights Amendment. By "minorities" she probably means black leaders and civil rights activists. By "affirmative action" she means what is sometimes referred to as "quota systems." (See Chapter 12.) These causes are most popular in the big industrial states of the Northeast and Middle West and least popular in the South and West (except for California). The big industrial states are also the "big jackpot" states in the electoral college system. New York, for example, has 36 electoral votes to offer, in contrast, say, to Wyoming with 3 electoral votes, or Idaho, with 4. The upshot is that smart presidential candidates spend their time wooing voters in the big states. Big states are states with big cities. And who lives in big cities? Blacks, intellectuals, and feminists—the people whose causes Mikulski champions. Therefore, her stated reason for opposing the electoral college—that it fails to serve "women and minorities"—is difficult to understand.

Lately, of course, big states are also states with big suburbs, and not all suburban constituencies are friendly to the causes Mikulski supports. What is more, the electoral college does give a two-vote bonus to each state regardless of size, which helps the least populous states gain influence. Nevertheless, many members of Congress from urban constituencies are fearful of abolishing the electoral college, lest its abolition dilute their strength during presidential elections. This is one reason why it has not been abolished.

A House Election

In any event, for the Abel-Baker election it is too late to abolish the electoral college. It has now, the moderator assumes, been thrown into the House. (Those four Abel electors must have decided to abstain.) Mikulski is part of the Maryland congressional delegation. Which candidate will she vote for—Baker, the incumbent, who won the popular vote but lost the electoral vote, or Abel, the challenger, who did the opposite? "I vote Baker," she says. Why? The moderator suggests three alternatives: because Baker won the popular vote in her congressional district, because he won the popular vote in the state of Maryland, or because he won the popular vote in the nation as a whole. Mikulski answers "yes." The moderator tries again. Which people do you represent, "the people in your district, the people in your state, or the people in the nation as reflected in the total vote count?" Mikulski is still ambiguous. "We [she?] would cast them along . . . along the lines our districts and states went."

But what if the state went one way and the district another? Mikulski doesn't comment. But Jack Valenti, president of the Motion Picture Association and a former aide to President Lyndon Johnson, has a ready answer. He would vote his district. But, the moderator presses him, what if your district's popular vote went for the Republican candidate and you are a Democratic congressman? Valenti says he would still vote for the Republican, because it would be smart politics to do so. His district must contain quite a few Republicans if it preferred the Republican presidential candidate. If he went against their wishes, he might be ousted in the next election.

Tom Wicker then turns the discussion from politics to statesmanship. If President Baker lost in the electoral college, it would be the president's duty "on that cold November morning to get up and tell the people that he lost, and lost constitutionally." Nobody was cheated. The system worked as the Constitution prescribes. In the interests of the nation, therefore, the president should urge all the electors not to follow "any of these blandishments."

Would any political candidate be so high-minded? Would you if you won the popular vote but lost the electoral college?

Points to Remember

1. The electoral college was supposed to interpose electors between the people and the presidency. The electors would use their good judgment in deciding for whom to vote. But by 1800 the electors had become rubber stamps of the majority vote in each state. This resulted in a tie vote between Jefferson and Burr, which was finally resolved by the House of Representatives.
2. In our history there have been a few cases of "faithless electors" pledged to one candidate who switched their votes to another. These cases have been so few that they have never even come close to affecting the outcome of an election.

3. A more serious issue grows out of our "winner take all" system, which awards all the state's electoral votes to the candidate who wins a majority of popular votes in the state. This system "distorts" or "amplifies" the extent of a winner's victory nationwide. It could result in the defeat of a candidate who had gotten more popular votes than his or her opponent. On three occasions, most notably in 1888, a popular-vote victor has been defeated in the electoral college.

III: PRESIDENTIAL DISABILITY

Maybe President Baker made the generous concession speech that Tom Wicker urged upon him. In any event, Mr. Abel is now president. He is, in fact, on tour in a Third World country "when, in the middle of a public ceremony, a grenade is thrown; it explodes; the president is injured but not seriously; he . . . is quite groggy." What happens then? Who takes over for the president? For how long? By what procedure?

The discussion has turned to a topic often ignored or forgotten—until circumstances force it back to our attention. Most recently, on March 30, 1981, the circumstances were brought about by the criminally sick mind of John W. Hinckley, Jr. Hinckley's deed, and the deeds of others like him, are discussed in Chapter 5. Here we are concerned only with the other end of the scenario: What happens in cases of presidential disability?

In Reagan's case, the period of disability was almost miraculously short. Thanks to his robust physical health and the wonders of modern surgery, the president—who had a bullet fired into his chest—was back in his office twelve days later, announcing "I feel fine" and joking with reporters.

A century earlier, President James Garfield was not so fortunate. On July 2, 1881, while waiting for a train, he was shot in the back by a disappointed office-seeker named Charles Guiteau. With today's medicine, he would probably have survived. But it turned out that Garfield's doctors finished the work that Guiteau had begun. They probed the wound to find the bullet, turning the probe around and around in Garfield's back. Then the probe got stuck inside and was removed with great difficulty. The unsterilized instrument opened up channels for a septic infection, and in those days there were no antibiotics.

So the long deathwatch began. At times the president seemed to rally, and for a time it was even hoped that he would recover. Then his condition worsened again, and toward the end he was hallucinating. It took eighty days for him to die, and during that period there was scarcely any activity in the White House. Work piled up. Appointed posts went unfilled, correspondence unanswered, and the promised civil service reforms—of the type that deprived Guiteau of the patronage job he so badly wanted—were never brought to their conclusion.

Still, America at that time was not a world power, nor was the world itself caught up in the kind of furors that have set it on fire in this century. Life was simpler, slower, and less complicated than it would be a generation later; the American presidency was hardly a pivotal office in the affairs of the globe.

It had become one by the twentieth century, especially when America became involved in what was then called The Great War. Our president then was Woodrow Wilson. Wilson's wife died during his first term of office, and he remarried in December 1915. The second Mrs. Wilson was an attractive widow sixteen years his junior. She had had two years of formal schooling. Wilson, the former college professor, was blissful.

The First Woman President

Two years after Wilson's remarriage, America entered World War I. The war aged Wilson as nothing else had done, furrowing his face with deep lines and turning his hair white. He was appalled at the mass slaughter and determined that it must never happen again. When peace finally came in 1918, Wilson sailed to Europe to participate in the Paris Peace Conference. When he returned he was already exhausted, but he was a man with a mission. That mission was to secure Senate ratification for American participation in the newly formed League of Nations. This international body, Wilson was convinced, would be an instrument for settling disputes by diplomacy instead of war. But leading senators were less enthusiastic about American participation in the League; they feared it would entangle the United States in the petty quarrels and intrigues of Europe and perhaps even draw us into new wars.

Wilson was furious at the senators, but he was not deterred. He redoubled his efforts to pressure the Senate into ratification and set out on a national speaking tour to build public sentiment in favor of the League. He got as far as Pueblo, Colorado, before he collapsed, apparently of a stroke, and was brought back to the White House. There he suffered a second stroke, which partially paralyzed his right side. The former Chief Usher of the White House later described Wilson's condition:

> He just lay helpless. True, he had been taking nourishment, but the work the doctors had been doing on him just about sapped his remaining vitality. All his natural functions had to be artificially assisted and he appeared as helpless as one could possibly be and live.

Over the next ten months, Wilson's condition improved somewhat and then stabilized, but he still could not sit up without assistance, and we know today that both his speech and his mind were adversely affected by the illness. Hardly any of this was known then, however, for the Wilsons lived behind closed doors in the White House. All official business was transacted through the door of the president's room by Mrs. Wilson. In *When the Cheering Stopped*, a book on those last pathetic months of the Wilson administration, Gene Smith quotes the journalist Ray Stannard Baker, who wrote in his diary at the time that it seemed "as though our Government has gone out of business." And yet, Smith adds, "business of a kind was being transacted."

> By far the majority of all letters to the President were ignored, and dozens of bills were becoming law without his signature, but certain matters were acted upon.

Over the wide left margins of an elegantly typed letter, down to the bottom space under the typing, up the right margin and then across the top, weaving in and out of the title of the writer and his seal of office, there were each day penciled notes by a woman who had a total of just two years of formal schooling and whose round and enormous script resembled that of a twelve-year-old. The reader of these notes—Secretary of War, of Labor, or whatever—would have to rotate his returned letter in his hands and sometimes continue on to the envelope to find out what the message in the childish handwriting was. For each scrawl began, "The President says" or "The President wants" and there was no one in the world to say that the President from his sickroom in the southwest portion of the second floor did *not* say or did *not* want.

At that time, of course, there was no Twenty-Fifth Amendment. Yet even in Article II of the Constitution there is mention of disability. It says that in the event of the president's "Inability to discharge the Powers and Duties of the said Office, the Same shall devolve on the Vice President." What was Wilson's vice-president doing during his illness? The answer is that he was staying as far away from the White House as possible. Thomas Riley Marshall, Wilson's running mate in 1912 and 1916, was a nonentity, brought on to balance the ticket. He enjoyed being vice-president, since the job entailed few responsibilities, and he had neither the desire nor the least ability to serve as president of the United States. Today he is remembered by trivia enthusiasts for his one great utterance: "What this country needs is a good five-cent cigar."

Since Wilson's time there have been other periods of presidential disability. Warren G. Harding lay a semi-invalid for four days before his death. Franklin Roosevelt was comatose for over two hours before his death. Dwight D. Eisenhower suffered an intestinal blockage, a stroke, and a heart attack while in the White House. His heart attack alone kept him away from work for a total of 143 days. John F. Kennedy, of course, was assassinated. Lyndon Johnson was hospitalized for a gallbladder operation. During the strange "Watergate" period of the Nixon presidency, both the physical and mental health of the president were severely strained. (If Woodward and Bernstein's account in *The Final Days* is to be believed, Nixon at one point began talking to paintings hanging in corridors of the White House.) Then there was the twelve-day period of Reagan's hospitalization. His joking question to the aides who visited him in the hospital sums up the whole issue: "Who's minding the store?"

The Twenty-Fifth Amendment

There is, of course, the Twenty-Fifth Amendment, adopted in 1967. But that is a very complicated piece of machinery, perhaps too complicated. It also raises as many questions as it answers. Section 3 of the amendment says that whenever the president transmits to the president pro tempore of the Senate and the Speaker of the House his written declaration that he is unable to discharge his duties, power shall then pass to the vice-president, who will serve as acting president. Does that mean that the president *should* notify Congress any time he becomes ill or temporarily disabled? Section 3 never makes the answer clear, but in the video discussion of presidential disability, the participants with experience in such matters suggest the great unlikelihood of a president sending such a notice to Congress unless he were at his last extremity. Such reluctance could, in certain circumstances, set section 4 of the amendment in motion. This is the most complicated section. It was intended to deal with a variety of possibilities, including the possibility that a president could be physically or mentally impaired and refuse to admit it. It is loaded down with checks and balances, and it goes roughly like this:

1. If the vice-president and either a majority of the cabinet or a majority of a special body appointed by Congress notify the Speaker of the House and the president pro tempore of the Senate (from here on simply referred to as "Congress") that the president is disabled, then the vice-president becomes acting president.
2. But if the president then writes Congress his own note, saying, "No, I'm not disabled," he takes his power back.
3. *However*, if, within four days, the same body mentioned in item 1 above, writes back and says, "Yes, he is indeed disabled," then:
4. If two-thirds of both houses of Congress agree that the president is disabled, the vice-president resumes his role as acting president. If that vote cannot be mustered, the president is presumed not to be disabled.

It sounds like legalism run riot. Yet it may, on some future occasion, save the nation from a president unable to perform his functions but unwilling to step down.

The Video Discussion of Presidential Disability

In the video discussion Lloyd Cutler and former Secretary of State Edmund Muskie make it clear that the formal procedures set forth in section 3 of the Twenty-Fifth Amendment (the president "transmits . . . his written declaration that he is unable to discharge the powers and duties of his office") are not likely to be followed except in the most extreme cases. The moderator has talked about a president temporarily disabled by grenade fragments. Should he notify Congress that he is disabled and ask that the vice-president take over his functions? Cutler does not think it necessary. What about other instances of temporary disability? What if the president goes into the hospital for a tonsillectomy? Should the president notify Congress of his disability? Cutler: "I think presidents would be most reluctant to do that." The moderator says, "You make it sound like . . . some macho problem (*laughter*)." Muskie, the former secretary of state, has been listening to all this—and getting impatient. He reminds the moderator that "the power of the presidency is not something you can . . . lightly . . . pass around the table as though you were passing fruit." Then he says something that would interest James Madison because it speaks to the great issue of human nature:

> Whoever has these powers for however long and . . . his or her supporters, his or her believers, you know, when they have those powers they're going to be conscious . . . of the power that is theirs.

In other words, once the vice-president and his retine have tasted presidential power, they may not find it easy to give up after the president announces that he is well and fit to resume his functions.

Jack Valenti adds his own contribution to this discussion of power and human nature by citing the real case of President Johnson's gallbladder operation. "There were a few of his aides around him," he says, "and nobody else got into that hospital room." It sounds almost like a repetition, on a smaller scale, of President Wilson's isolation with *his* "aide." What about the vice-president? In the event of a serious and long-term disability, Valenti says, the vice-president "would be giving the orders," but the president's staff would be right there beside him "to give whatever legitimacy a White House staff can confer on anybody."

This is quite a reversal. How can a staff, an ad hoc group of personal aides, confer "legitimacy" on the vice-president, who gets his authority from the Constitution? One would think rather that the vice-president would lend legitimacy to them. Well, "make no mistake about it," Valenti says, the "apparatus of the White House" is "in the hands of the staff and the president. Now that's not in the Constitution, but that's the way it is."

Later in the program the power of the staff comes up again. The moderator asks Laurence Barrett, senior White House correspondent for *Time*, what went on while Reagan was hospitalized with his wounds. Why wasn't the Twenty-Fifth Amendment invoked? Barrett answers: "The White House staff made a pretty much unilateral decision not to . . . invoke it, or not to begin the process that would invoke it." The question of whether to invoke the amendment came up twice. "And in the second of the two instances [Vice-President] Bush was not even consulted. Nor were any of the principal [cabinet] officers." The moderator notes that this is the second time the discussion has gotten around to the role of the staff: "not the president, not the cabinet, not the vice-president." Barrett replies: "Well, in certain circumstances, and this is one of them, the White House staff is a far more powerful body, even though it's extralegal, than any of the aforementioned."

Then he reveals an interesting piece of information. Just after Reagan was shot, the White House counsel drafted or obtained papers that would formally notify Congress of the president's disability, as provided in section 3 of the Twenty-Fifth Amendment. Staff members were present in the White House Situation Room, a military planning room, during the emergency meeting chaired by then-Secretary of State Al Haig, who was the senior cabinet member. (Vice-President Bush was flying back from Texas.) Somehow the papers were left out, and one of the staff members saw Haig perusing them. The staff member promptly locked the papers up in his safe. The moderator: "Imprisoned the Twenty-Fifth Amendment." Barrett: "Metaphorically, yes."

Cutler thinks that Reagan's staff was right not to invoke the Twenty-Fifth Amendment. Barrett's own opinion is not clear, but he is convinced that the amendment will never be invoked as long as "there's any borderline situation where a case could plausibly be made" that the president is not disabled. Nobody on the panel disagrees with either Cutler's opinion or Barrett's predictions.

Points to Remember

1. President Reagan's disability lasted only twelve days, but in previous presidencies there have been prolonged periods of disability. James Garfield was bedridden for 80 days before he died; Woodrow Wilson was disabled for at least 280 days; and Dwight D. Eisenhower spent 143 days recovering from his heart attack.
2. The Twenty-Fifth Amendment was intended to provide specific mechanisms for ensuring continuity in cases of temporary or permanent disability. Section 3 of the amendment prescribes procedures by which the president can notify the Congress of his disability and pass along his power to the vice-president. Section 4 is intended to deal with situations in which the president and the vice-president and cabinet officials differ on whether in fact the president is disabled.
3. Some participants in the video discussion are convinced that in real situations of presidential disability, the president's power is transferred more to his staff than to any of the officers mentioned in the Constitution.

SUMMARY

Two sides of the American political system confront each other in this chapter. On one side is the formal, the official, the words inscribed upon parchment. On the other is the informal, the improvised, the nitty-gritty activities of men and women forced to make decisions.

The chapter started off with a discussion of political parties. These were informal from their very inception in early America. They were also widely distrusted and never mentioned in the Constitution. All the Constitution says about qualifications for office is that the person must be at least thirty-five, be a natural-born citizen, and have been a resident of the United States for fourteen years. But in point of fact, as the participants in the video discussion remind the moderator, any serious candidate for president must have the endorsement of a party.

Parties themselves have become more formal in recent years. The rules changes initiated by the Democrats between 1968 and 1972 standardized and regularized procedures that were once conducted informally. Caucuses are now governed by written rules intended to ensure fairness. Primary elections have proliferated. But just how meaningful and useful have these formal procedures been in the life of parties? The video discussion has focused on an issue resulting from a scandal that impairs the ability of a candidate to win an election. To what extent are "his" delegates bound to vote for his nomination? Would a strict adherence to a rule of "pledged" voting result in irrationality—a party that must run a candidate who is sure to lose?

The same tension between the official and the informal is found in the electoral college. It was supposed to be an aristocratic institution of wise and sober electors who would use their discretion in picking a president for us; it has become a motley assortment of party robots. Which do we want it to be? Do we want a collection of yes-people who register the will of the voters in each of the states? Or are there occasions when we might want them to revert to being real decision makers—people who use their discretion? If, by a mathematical fluke, which has already occurred in American history, the "automatic" operation of the electoral college results in a minority president—then what? We have seen that some of the panelists are ready for the Founders' wise and sober electors to return.

In the case of presidential disability, we see again the two hemispheres of politics, each challenging the other. We have an ingenious machine in the Twenty-Fifth Amendment, full of cams and gears, which is meant to solve the problems occasioned by a sick or injured president. On the other hand, we have a president and his staff determined, during actual periods of disability, not only to ignore that machinery but to keep it locked up and far away from anyone who might plan to set it in operation.

Which aspect of our political system, the informal part or the legal, is the practical, real, and vital part? We can anticipate the answer of the political pro. Politicians tend to regard official procedures as stage properties, public facades behind which the "real" business of politics is conducted. Sometimes, however, what seems "practical" is really quite irrational. In 1968 the good old informal procedures of the Democratic party backfired, resulting in a disastrous party split and the election of a Republican to the White House. The informal operation of our electoral college may also turn out to be a ticking time bomb, giving us some day a president who has lost the popular vote to his opponent. On a far more serious scale, the informal "staff" solutions to the problems occasioned by presidential disability could lead, at some point, to a presidency lacking in authority, a crippled presidency unable either to exercise power or to let go of it.

Documents

AN ARGUMENT FOR ABOLISHING THE ELECTORAL COLLEGE

by William T. Gossett*

In 1969, William T. Gossett, then president of the American Bar Association, testified before a Senate committee that was considering alternatives to the electoral college. Below are excerpts from his testimony.

There is no more vital issue facing the Nation today than that of electoral reform. Our most recent presidential election surely demonstrated that the electoral college is potentially hazardous to our nation. It also confirms the conclusion of the American Bar Association Commission on Electoral College Reform that "the electoral college

*From Statement of William T. Gossett, President of the American Bar Association, U.S. Congress, House of Representatives, Committee on the Judiciary, *Hearings, Electoral College Reform*, 91st Congress, 1st Session, 1969, pp. 198–209. Footnotes have been omitted.

method of electing a President of the United States is archaic, undemocratic, complex, ambiguous, indirect, and dangerous."

If [in 1968] there had been a shift of a relatively few popular votes in Ohio and Missouri, or if President Nixon had lost California, or if Mr. Wallace had carried three border states, no presidential candidate would have had a majority of the electoral votes. The choice of President would then have shifted to the electoral college, in which the electors pledged to George C. Wallace would have held the balance of power. Mr. Wallace certainly would have been tempted to play the role of a President-maker during the forty-one day period between election day and the meeting of the electors. If Mr. Wallace should have decided against any such role and his electors had voted for him, then the choice of President would have shifted to the House of Representatives under an inequitable one state–one vote formula susceptible to political wheeling and dealing and frustration of the popular will. One can only speculate as to the outcome of an election by the House. The twenty-six populated states, representing sixteen percent of the nation's total population, would have had the power to elect the President. It is conceivable that no candidate might have been able to obtain the votes of twenty-six states by Inauguration Day and that in consequence a Vice President selected by the Senate would have had to assume the powers and duties of the President that day. It is also conceivable that the House and Senate might have selected a split ticket by Inauguration Day. It is also conceivable that neither House might have been able to make a choice, in which event the Speaker of the House of Representatives would have become the Acting President.

Had a deadlock occurred in the 1968 election, it could have had the most perilous of consequences for our country and the office of President. Yet, unless our system is changed, we will suffer the risk of such consequences in every future presidential election. . . . No sooner was the Constitution adopted than proposals were introduced in Congress to reform the electoral college. The first proposal was introduced in 1797, and since then more than 500 proposals have been offered. The major plans of reform— the district, proportional, automatic and direct vote plans—have their roots in proposals introduced in Congress during the nineteenth century. . . .

The workings of the electoral college over the past 190 years show that it is something completely different from that envisioned by the Framers. Thanks to the extraordinary notes of James Madison, we know that the Framers of the Constitution encountered much difficulty in deciding on a method of electing the President. More than fifteen different methods were proposed at the Constitutional Convention, including election by the Congress, the state legislatures, and the people. Some of these proposals were first adopted and then reconsidered and rejected. Among the supporters of popular vote were James Madison, "the master-builder of the Constitution," James Wilson, one of the great lawyers of his age, Gouverneur Morris of Pennsylvania, John Dickinson of Delaware and Daniel Carroll of Maryland.

Not until the final weeks of the Convention was the electoral college adopted. Election by Congress was rejected because it was felt that the President would be subservient to the Legislative Branch and it opened the door for "intrigue, cabal or faction." A direct vote by the people was criticized on the grounds that the people were too "uninformed" and would be "misled by a few designing men." One delegate said that an election by the people would be like referring a "trial of colours to a blind man." What seemed to move the delegates to accept the electoral system were certain practical considerations, dictated not by political ideals but the social realities of the time—realities that no longer exist. These were centered largely in the limited communications and relatively low literacy of the period, which made it virtually impossible for the people to know the candidates, rendered them subject to deception and would have inclined them to vote only for someone from their own state. This made it likely that the largest state, having the largest vote, usually would elect its candidate. On the other hand, the delegates assumed that the electors, to whom the people would delegate their franchise, would be the wise men of the community, with their disinterested role protected by the requirement that they not be officeholders or candidates.

The Electoral College was thus envisioned by the Framers as a kind of elite gathering in which the most distinguished and talented persons in the various states would participate. These electors would deliberate and cast an informed and independent vote for President.

Since it was felt that the large states would have considerable influence in the electoral voting, the Framers, in an effort to allay the fears of the small states, provided for the House of Representatives to choose the President, with each state having the same influence, where no candidate received a majority of the electoral votes. The Convention debates indicate that many of the Framers were of the view that most elections would be thrown into Congress.

We know that the design of the Framers in creating the electoral college was not fulfilled. Political parties appeared and the electors' role became a purely mechanical one of voting for their party's candidate. As they became partisan functionaries, their names and reputations became far less known to the citizens than those of the candidates. As a Committee of the Congress noted in 1826, electors "have degenerated into mere agents, in a case which requires no agency, and where the agent must be useless, if he is faithful, and dangerous if he is not."

Participation by the American people in presidential elections has come slowly. Since the Constitution left it to the states to determine the manner of selecting the electors, in the first eleven elections a number of states gave the right of choice to the members of their legislatures rather than to the people. It was not until late in the Nineteenth Century that every state had entrusted the right of choice to the people. Today, of course, due to state law the people choose the electors, who are expected to register the will of their constituents in the electoral college.

Experience has shown, however, that the electoral college is riddled with defects which could operate to frustrate the will of the people.

First, it can happen that the popular will of the majority of the nation can be defeated by mathematical flukes. Under the winner-take-all or unit vote rule for allocating a state's electoral votes a candidate could win an electoral victory and yet receive fewer popular votes than his opponent. Success in twelve key states alone would give a candidate an electoral majority, regardless of his margin of victory in those states and regardless of whether he received any votes in the other thirty-eight states. Three times in our history—1824, 1876 and 1888—the popular vote loser was elected President. In fifteen elections a shift of less than one percent of the national vote cast would have made the popular-vote loser President. I think it would be tragic for the popular-vote winner to be rejected again, particularly since the people have come to measure a President's success by his popular vote margin. This aspect of the electoral college allowing for the election of the popular-vote loser violates our most fundamental principle of government by consent of the governed.

Second, it can happen that the choice of the President is thrown into the House of Representatives, where each state has but a single vote. While it has been 144 years since the House of Representatives has had to choose a President, we have had seven narrow escapes since then, including the elections of 1968, 1960 and 1948. A shift of less than one percent of the popular vote in a few key states would have thrown those elections into Congress with the consequent risk of political deals and possibly the election of a President who was rejected by a majority of the voters. This feature of our system is clearly a political monstrosity, fully distorting the most elementary principles of self-government.

Third, presidential electors can take matters into their own hands and reject the will of the people who chose them. The so-called constitutional independence of electors can take various forms. It can take the form of pledged electors defecting as in our most recent election, 1960, and 1956: of unpledged elector movements, as in 1960: or third party electors being instructed by their presidential candidate to vote for one of the major candidates. Under the electoral college system, the decision of the people is meaningless unless it is approved by, in effect, another body of government. Such a barrier between the people and their President is both anachronistic and abhorrent.

The electoral college system violates fundamental democratic principles in other ways:

The winner-take-all feature of the system suppresses at an intermediate stage all minority votes cast in a state. The winner of the most popular votes in a state, regardless of his percentage of the votes cast, receives all of that state's electoral votes. The votes for the losing candidates are in effect discarded while those for the winner are multiplied in value. As Senator Thomas Hart Benton stated in 1824: "To lose their votes, is the fate of all minorities, and it is their duty to submit; but this is not a case of votes lost, but of votes taken away, added to those of the majority, and given to a person to whom the minority is opposed."

The present system discriminates among voters on the basis of residence. While a small state voter might seem to enjoy an electoral vote advantage because his state receives two electoral votes regardless of size, a large state voter is able to influence more electoral votes, and it is in the large industrial states that presidential elections are usually won or lost. There is no sound reason why every citizen should not have an equal vote in the election of our one official who serves as the symbol and spokesman for all the people.

The electoral college system fails to reflect the actual strength of the vote turnout in each state. Under the system each state casts its assigned electoral votes regardless of voter turnout. Thus, voters in states where the turnout is small are given a premium. It is not uncommon to find a great disparity in the vote turnout in states having the same number of electoral votes.

To remedy these evils, the American Bar Association proposes a system of direct popular election, with the following major features:

A candidate must obtain at least forty percent of the popular vote to be elected President. The ABA Commission felt that a majority vote requirement was not desirable because it would frequently happen that no candidate had a majority and therefore a second election would be required to decide the outcome. In this regard, it should be noted that one-third of our Presidents received less than a majority of the total popular vote cast. Additionally, the Commission felt that a majority vote requirement might encourage proliferation of the parties, since a small group might have the potential to cause the election to be resolved under the machinery established for a contingent election. In arriving at a forty percent plurality, the Commission was of the view that it was high enough to furnish a sufficient mandate for the Presidency and low enough so that the first election would decide the contest.

The ABA recommends that in the event no candidate receives at least forty percent of the popular vote, a national runoff should be held between the top two candidates. The Commission felt that a runoff was preferable to an election by Congress because it would avoid the possibility of political wheeling and dealing and assure the election of the popular vote winner. The Commission also believed that a national runoff, together with a forty percent plurality requirement, would operate to discourage proliferation of the parties. The Commission reasoned that it would rarely occur that no major candidate had at least forty percent, even with minor party candidates in the field. However, if that happened, the people would choose between the top two. As the Commission stated in its report:

> A runoff between the highest two would seem to have the tendency to limit the number of candidates in the field in the original election because it is improbable that a minor candidate would be one of the top two; and the influence of such a group would be asserted more effectively as now, before the major party nominations and platforms are determined. . . .

The advantages of direct popular election over other proposals are numerous. It is the only method that would eliminate once and for all the principal defects of our system: the "winner-take-all" feature and its cancellation of votes; the inequities arising from the formula for allocating electoral votes among the states; the anachronistic and dangerous office of presidential elector; and the archaic method by which contingent elections are handled. There would no longer be "sure states" or "pivotal states" or "swing voters" because votes would not be cast in accordance with a unit rule and because campaign efforts would be directed at people regardless of residence. Factors such as fraud and accident could not decide the disposition of all a state's votes. Direct election would bring to presidential elections the principle which is used and has worked well in elections for Senators, Representatives, governors, state legislators, mayors, and thousands of other officials at all levels of government. That principle, "one person, one vote," would make the votes cast by all Americans in presidential elections of equal weight. All votes would be reflected in the national tally. None would be magnified or contracted. All citizens would have the same chance to affect the outcome of the election. Finally, under a popular vote system, presidential elections would operate the way most people think they operate and expect them to operate....

A DEFENSE OF THE ELECTORAL COLLEGE

by Martin Diamond*

In 1977 the American Enterprise Institute published a monograph by the late Martin Diamond, a political scientist, who answered Gossett's critique of the electoral college and offered his own defense of the institution. Excerpts follow.

In 1967, a distinguished commission of the American Bar Association recommended that the Electoral College be scrapped and replaced by a nationwide popular vote for the President, with provision for a runoff election between the top two candidates in the event no candidate received at least 40 percent of the popular vote. This recommendation was passed by the House in 1969, came close to passage in the Senate in 1970, and is now once again upon us. It is this proposal that has just been endorsed by President Carter and that is being pressed upon Congress under the leadership of Senator Bayh.

The theme of this attack upon the Electoral College is well summarized in a much-quoted sentence from the 1969 ABA Report: *"The electoral college method of electing a President of the United States is archaic, undemocratic, complex, ambiguous, indirect, and dangerous."* These six charges may seem a bit harsh on a system that has worked well for a very long time, but they do provide a convenient topical outline for a brief defense of the basic principles and procedures of the Electoral College.

An "Archaic" System?

The word *archaic* evokes all those Herblock and other cartoons that portray the Electoral College (or any other feature of the Constitution that is being caricatured) as a deaf, decrepit, old fogey left over from the colonial era. This is the characteristic rhetoric and imagery of contemporary criticism of our now nearly two-centuries old Constitution. But we ought not (and perhaps lawyers, especially, ought not) acquiesce too readily in the prejudice that whatever is old is archaic, in the ABA's pejorative use of that word. On the contrary, it may be argued that the proper political prejudice, if we are to have one, ought to be in favor of the long-persisting, of the tried and true— that our first inclination in constitutional matters ought to be that old is good and

*From *The Electoral College and the American Idea of Democracy.* Copyright © 1977, The American Enterprise Institute for Policy Research. Reprinted by permission.

older is better. We should remind ourselves of some Aristotelian wisdom reformulated by James Madison in *The Federalist*, Number 49, when he warned that tinkering with the Constitution would deprive the system of government of "that veneration which time bestows on everything, and without which perhaps the wisest and freest governments would not possess the requisite stability." ...

But it is not necessary, in defense of the Electoral College, to rely on such sober (but startling nowadays) reasoning as that of Madison, because the Electoral College happens not to be an archaic element of our constitutional system. Not only is it not at all archaic, but one might say that it is the very model of up-to-date constitutional flexibility. Perhaps no other feature of the Constitution has had a greater capacity for dynamic historical adaptiveness. The electors became nullities; presidential elections became dramatic national contests; the federal elements in the process became strengthened by the general-ticket practice (that is, winner-take-all); modern mass political parties developed; campaigning moved from rather rigid sectionalism to the complexities of a modern technological society—and all this occurred tranquilly and legitimately within the original constitutional framework (as modified by the Twelfth Amendment). The Electoral College thus has experienced an immense historical evolution. But the remarkable fact is that while it now operates in historically transformed ways, in ways not at all as the Framers intended, it nonetheless still operates largely to the ends that they intended. What more could one ask of a constitutional provision? ...

An "Undemocratic" System?

The gravamen of the "undemocratic" indictment of the Electoral College rests on the possibility that, because votes are aggregated within the states by the general-ticket system, in which the winner takes all, a loser in the national popular vote may nonetheless become President by winning a majority of the electoral votes of the states. This is supposedly the "loaded pistol" to our heads, our quadrennial game of Russian roulette; indeed, no terms seem lurid enough to express the contemporary horror at this possibility. This is what shocks our modern democratic sensibilities and, once the issue is permitted to be stated in this way, it takes a very brave man or woman to defend the Electoral College. But, fortunately, courage is not required; it suffices to reformulate the issue and get it on its proper footing.

In fact, presidential elections are already just about as democratic as they can be. We already have one-man, one-vote—*but in the states*. Elections are as freely and democratically contested as elections can be—*but in the states*. Victory always goes democratically to the winner of the raw popular vote—*but in the states*. The label given to the proposed reform, "direct popular election," is a misnomer; the elections have already become as directly popular as they can be—*but in the states*. Despite all their democratic rhetoric, the reformers do not propose to make our presidential elections more directly democratic, they only propose to make them more directly *national*, by entirely removing the states from the electoral process. Democracy thus is not the question regarding the Electoral College, federalism is: should our presidential election remain in part *federally* democratic, or should we make them completely *nationally* democratic?

Whatever we decide, then, democracy itself is not at stake in our decision, only the prudential question of how to channel and organize the popular will. That makes everything easier. When the question is only whether the federally democratic aspect of the Electoral College should be abandoned in order to prevent the remotely possible election of a President who had not won the national popular vote, it does not seem so hard to opt for retaining some federalism in this homogenizing, centralizing age. When federalism has already been weakened, perhaps inevitably in modern circumstances, why further weaken the federal elements in our political system by destroying the informal federal element that has historically evolved in our system of presidential elections? The crucial general-ticket system, adopted in the 1830s for reasons pertinent then, has become in our time a constitutionally unplanned but vital support for federalism. Also called the "unit rule" system, it provides that the state's entire electoral vote goes to the winner of the popular vote in the state. Resting entirely on the voluntary legislative action of each state, this informal historical development, combined with the formal constitutional provision, has generated a federal element in the Electoral College which sends a federalizing impulse throughout our whole political process. It makes the states as states dramatically and pervasively important in the whole presidential selection process, from the earliest strategies in the nominating campaign through the convention and final election. Defederalize the presidential election—which is what direct popular election boils down to—and a contrary nationalizing impulse will gradually work its way throughout the political process. The nominating process naturally takes its cues from the electing process; were the President to be elected in a single national election, the same cuing process would continue, but in reverse.

It is hard to think of a worse time than the present, when so much already tends toward excessive centralization, to strike an unnecessary blow at the federal quality of our political order. . . .

A "Complex" System?

The ABA Report does not make clear what is "complex" about the Electoral College or why complexity as such is bad. Perhaps the fear is that voters are baffled by the complexity of the Electoral College and that their bafflement violates a democratic norm. It must be admitted that an opinion survey could easily be devised that shows the average voter to be shockingly ignorant of what the Electoral College is and how it operates. But, then, opinion surveys almost always show the average voter to be shockingly ignorant of whatever a survey happens to be asking him about. It all depends upon what kind of knowledge the voter is expected to have. I would argue that most voters have a solid working knowledge of what a presidential election is all about. They know that they are voting for the candidate of their choice and that the candidate with the most votes wins in their state. And when watching the results on television or reading about them in the papers, they surely discover how the election came out. However ignorant they may be of the details of the Electoral College, their ignorance does not seem to affect at all the intention and meaning of their vote, or their acceptance of the electoral outcome. What more is necessary than that? What is the use of making the process less complex?

However, the animus against the complexity of the Electoral College surely goes deeper than a fear that voters are unable to explain it when asked. There seems to be a hostility to complexity as such. This hostility has a long history. It goes back at least to those French Enlightenment thinkers who scolded John Adams for the unnecessary complexity, for example, of American bicameralism. However such complexity had helped to mitigate monarchical severities, of what possible use could bicameralism be, they asked, now that America had established popular government? When the people rule, they insisted, one branch is quite enough; no complexity should stand in the way of straightforwardly recording and carrying out the popular will. The answer to them, and to all like minded democratic simplifiers ever since, derives from the very essence of American democracy, which is precisely to be complex. The American idea of democracy, as argued above, is to take into account both local and national considerations, and also to moderate democracy and blend it with as many other things as are necessary to the public good. That blending necessitates complexity. . . .

An "Ambiguous" System?

This charge is rather puzzling. It is so far off the mark that a rebuttal is hardly required; rather, it supplies the opportunity to point out a particular advantage of the Electoral College in comparison with its proposed substitute. Far from speaking unclearly or confusingly, the Electoral College has delivered exceptionally prompt and unequivocal electoral pronouncements. . . .

To judge fairly the charge of ambiguity, then, the Electoral College must be compared in this regard with other electoral systems and, especially, with the 40 percent plus/runoff system proposed by President Carter and Senator Bayh as its replacement. Under the proposed system, the nation forms a single electoral district; the candidate who gets the most popular votes wins, provided the winning total equals at least 40 percent of the total number of votes cast; failing that, there would be a runoff election between the two candidates who had the most votes. Let us consider the prospects for ambiguity under this proposed system, in comparison with the actual experience under the Electoral College.

The American electorate has a fundamental tendency to divide closely, with "photo finish" elections being almost the rule rather than the exception. The Electoral College almost always announces these close election outcomes with useful amplification. In purely numerical popular votes, an election outcome might be uncertain and vulnerable to challenge; but the Electoral College replaces the numerical uncertainty with an unambiguously visible constitutional majority that sustains the legitimacy of the electoral result. If this magnifying lens is removed, the "squeaker" aspect of our presidential elections will become more visible and, probably, much more troubling. For example, the problem of error and fraud, no doubt endemic in some degree to all electoral systems, could very well be aggravated under the proposed national system, because every single precinct polling place could come under bitter scrutiny as relevant to a close and disputed national outcome. In contrast, under the Electoral College, ambiguity of outcome sufficient even to warrant challenge is infrequent and is always limited to but a few states. Indeed, the massive and undeniable fact is that, for a whole century, the Electoral College has produced unambiguous outcomes in every single presidential election, accepted by the losing candidate and party and by the whole American people with unfaltering legitimacy. . . .

A "Dangerous" System?

It is not possible here to discuss all the dangers that alarm critics of the Electoral College, for example, the faithless electors, or a cabal of them, or the problem of the contingency election in the House of Representatives. Some pose real enough problems and would have to be dealt with in a fuller discussion. But the present remarks are limited to the main danger that the reformers fear, namely, the popular-vote/electoral-vote discrepancy. This is the loaded pistol pointed to our heads, the threat that necessitates radical constitutional revision. Now the funny thing about this loaded pistol is that the last time it went off, in 1888, no one got hurt; no one even hollered. As far as I can tell, there was hardly a ripple of constitutional discontent, not a trace of dangerous delegitimation, and nothing remotely resembling the crisis predicted by present-day critics of the Electoral College. But it must be sadly acknowledged that, the next time it happens, there might well be far greater public distress. It would be due, in large part, to the decades of populistic denunciation of the Electoral College; a kind of self-confirming prophecy would be at work. . . .

Experience has demonstrated that the dangers incident to the present system are neither grave nor likely to occur. But what of the dangers incident to the proposed reform? It is as important to speculate about them as to frighten ourselves with imaginary possibilities under the Electoral College. Three dangers seem seriously to threaten under the proposed reform: weakening the two-party system, weakening party politics generally, and further imperializing the presidency.

Many have warned that the 40 percent plus/runoff system would encourage minor parties and in time undermine the two party system. The encouragement consists in the runoff provision of the proposed reform, that is, in the possibility that minor parties will get enough votes in the first election to force a runoff. Supporters of the proposed change deny this likelihood. For example, the ABA Report argues that a third party is unlikely to get the 20 percent of the popular vote necessary to force a runoff. Perhaps so, and this has been very reassuring to supporters of the reform. But why does it have to be just "a" third party? Why cannot the runoff be forced by the combined votes of a half dozen or more minor parties that enter the first election? Indeed, they are all there waiting in the wings. The most powerful single constraint on minor-party presidential candidacies has always been the "don't throw your vote away" fear that caused their support to melt as election day approached. . . .

Minor party votes now shrink away as the election nears and practically disappear on election day. As is well known, this is because minor-party supporters desert their preferred candidates to vote for the "lesser evil" of the major candidates. But the proposed reform would remove the reason to do so. On the contrary, as in multiparty parliamentary systems, the voter could vote with his heart because that would in fact also be the calculating thing to do. There would be plenty of time to vote for the lesser evil in the eventual runoff election. The trial heat would be the time to help the preferred minor party show its strength. Even a modest showing would enable the minor party to participate in the frenetic bargaining inevitably incident to runoff elections. And even a modest showing would establish a claim to the newly available public financing that would simultaneously be an inducement to run and a means to strengthen one's candidacy. . . .

Not only might the change weaken the two-party system, but it might well also have an enfeebling effect on party politics generally. The regular party politicians, which is to say, the state and local politicians, would become less important to presidential candidates. This tendency is already evident in the effect the presidential primaries are having; regular party machinery is becoming less important in the nominating process, and the individual apparatus of the candidates more important. The defederalizing of the presidential election seems likely to strengthen this tendency. No longer needing to carry states, the presidential candidates would find the regular politicians, who are most valuable for tipping the balance in a state, of diminishing importance for their free-wheeling search for popular votes. They probably would rely more and more on direct-mail and media experts, and on purely personal coteries, in conducting campaigns that would rely primarily on the mass media. The consequence would seem to be to disengage the presidential campaign from the party machinery and from the states and to isolate the presidency from their moderating effect. If "merchandising" the President has become an increasingly dangerous tendency, nationalizing and plebiscitizing the presidency would seem calculated only to intensify the danger.

This raises, finally, the question of the effect of the proposed reform on the presidency as an institution, that is, on the "imperial presidency." The populistic rhetoric that denounces the Electoral College as undemocratic has had, since the time of the New Deal, a corollary inclination to inflate the importance of the presidency. In recent years, however, we have all learned to be cautious about the extent of presidential power. Yet the proposed change could only have an inflating effect on it. The presidency has always derived great moral authority and political power from the claim that the President is the only representative of all the people. Why increase the force of that claim by magnifying the national and plebiscitary foundations of the presidency? This would be to enhance the presidential claims at just the moment when so much fear had been expressed about the "imperial presidency."

Many who deal with the Electoral College are concerned chiefly with its consequences for partisan purposes. They support or oppose it because of its alleged tendency to push the presidency in a liberal direction. As for myself, I am not at all sure what those partisan effects used to be, are now, or will become in the future. Accordingly, it seems a good time to rise above party considerations to the level of constitutional principle. On that level, it seems quite clear to me that the effects of the proposed change are likely to be quite bad. And it likewise seems quite clear to me that the Electoral College is easy to defend, once one gets the hang of it. It is a paradigm of the American idea of democracy. Thus to defend it is not only to help retain a valuable part of our political system, but also to help rediscover what the American idea of democracy is.

SELECTED READINGS

Anderson, Patrick. *The President's Men.* Garden City, N.Y.: Doubleday, 1968.
Anecdotal accounts of presidential staff members—their deeds and occasional mis-
deeds—during the administrations of F.D.R., Truman, Eisenhower, Kennedy, and
Johnson.

Bayh, Birch. *One Heartbeat Away.* Indianapolis, Ind.: Bobbs-Merrill, 1968.
Senator Bayh's account of his leadership in the campaign to draft, pass, and secure
ratification of the Twenty-Fifth Amendment.

Best, Judith. *The Case Against Direct Election of the President.* Ithaca, N.Y.: Cornell
University Press, 1975.
The author reviews all the arguments for abolishing the electoral college and finds
them wanting. While conceding that the present system "has defects," she concludes that it supplies a necessary balance in our governmental system by favoring
urban areas (against the bias of Congress toward small-town areas). Her basic philosophy: why swap a system whose consequences are well known for one whose
virtues are based on sheer speculation?

Crotty, William J. *Decision for the Democrats: Reforming the Party Structure.* Baltimore: Johns Hopkins University Press, 1978.
A defense of the changes made in the rules of the Democratic party between 1968
and 1972 by someone who participated in making them. "The party," Crotty
argues, "was opened and, in the process, made more responsive to and representative of its rank and file."

Feerick, John D. *The Twenty-Fifth Amendment: Its Complete History and Earliest
Applications.* New York: Fordham University Press, 1976.
A comprehensive history and analysis of the Twenty-Fifth Amendment. Starting
with an account of some of the important instances of presidential disability,
which suggested the need for such an amendment, it then examines the struggle to
get the amendment passed, the application of the amendment during the resigna-
tions of Nixon and Agnew, and some of the amendment's strengths and weaknesses.

Ladd, Everett Carll, Jr. *Where Have All the Voters Gone?* New York: Norton, 1978.
A critique of the "reforms" made in the Democratic party since 1968. Far from
benefiting rank-and-file voters, the author charges, the rules changes have largely
served "upper-middle-class groups," who have had the time, money, and interest
to become political activists.

Longley, Lawrence D., and Braun, Alan G. *The Politics of Electoral College Reform.*
2d ed. New Haven, Conn.: Yale University Press, 1975.
The authors recommend a new constitutional amendment to institute direct election of the president and contend that a direct popular vote would not favor any
special interests. Longley is a participant in the video discussion covered in this
chapter.

Michener, James A. *Presidential Lottery: The Reckless Gamble in Our Electoral System.* New York: Random House, 1969.
This best-selling novelist, who once served as president of Pennsylvania's electoral

college, makes a case for the abolition of the electoral college system. "The peculiar weakness of this system, and one which totally disqualifies it, is that the vital decisions are made by members of the Electoral College bound by no law, no tradition, no restraint, and little common sense."

Sindler, Allan P. *Unchosen Presidents.* Berkeley, Calif.: University of California Press, 1976.

The author comes to grips with a contingency that became reality with the accession of Gerald Ford to the presidency in 1974: What should we do if an *appointed* vice-president becomes president upon the resignation of a president? Should our system be changed to permit a special new election in such cases? Sindler considers this option and others.

Sobel, Lester A. *Presidential Succession: Ford, Rockefeller and the Twenty-Fifth Amendment.* New York: Facts on File, 1975.

The book contains a brief section on the history of presidential succession, but its main focus is on the events leading to the retirement of Nixon and Agnew. Though less a book than a news index, it is rich in information.

GLOSSARY

"Beauty contest."   A primary election that does not yield convention delegates but merely indicates how popular the candidates are with the voters.

Caucuses.   In presidential elections, a series of meetings at the local, or "precinct," level that produces delegates pledged to candidates at a higher (usually county) level, that in turn leads to the selection of delegates to a state convention. The state convention then picks delegates to the national convention.

Delegate.   A person with authority to vote for a presidential party candidate at the party's convention. Most delegates are "pledged" to a particular candidate, and in the past they were bound to vote for him or her. Now, however, they can switch their votes if they think someone else will make a better candidate.

"Faithless elector."   A member of the electoral college who was "pledged" to the party's candidate but who voted for someone else.

Federalists.   The party whose most famous leaders included George Washington, John Adams, and Alexander Hamilton and that championed the new Constitution. The party favored a strong central government, a strong presidency, and the promotion of Eastern commercial interests. Beaten in the 1800 election by the Jeffersonian Republicans, it ceased to exist after 1816.

Jeffersonian Republicans.   Also called the Democratic Republicans, this party championed popular government, equality of opportunity, and states' rights. It romanticized the yeoman farmer and generally appealed to rural interests, though it later grew to include the interests of the urban working class. A distant ancestor of today's Democratic party.

Presidential staff.   A small group of close aides to the president. Unlike cabinet officials, these aides do not have to have their appointments confirmed by the Senate.
   Also called the president's "kitchen cabinet."
Primary election.   An election to determine who should be the nominee of a political
   party.
Unit rule.   See "Winner take all."
"Winner take all."   The understanding that *all* of a state's electoral votes will go to the
   candidate who won a majority of popular votes in that state.

Part Two

Criminal Justice in America

Chapter 4
"A Creeping, Crawling Crud"

"The criminal is to go free because the constable has blundered."
CHIEF JUDGE BENJAMIN CARDOZO
New York State Court of Appeals, 1926

"The criminal goes free, if he must, but it is the law that sets him free."
JUSTICE TOM CLARK
U.S. Supreme Court, 1961

"Go ahead. Make my day."
CLINT EASTWOOD

In Buffalo, New York, over the 1983 July Fourth holiday, Willie Williams came home and found his ten-year-old daughter missing. For hours he searched for her, increasingly anxious. The next morning she returned, dazed, shocked, and wearing only a pillowcase. She told her father she had been raped, and she gave him a description of her alleged attacker, including his address. Together with some neighbors, Willie Williams went to the apartment of the man she described; he beat and stabbed him nearly to death. It turned out that the man had had a record of fifty previous arrests, on charges ranging from robbery to rape, and that he had been let out of jail on $250 bail for allegedly committing an act almost identical to the attack on Williams's daughter.

How did other citizens react to Willie Williams's act of vigilante justice? Everyone praised him. Cops congratulated him in his cell. A deluge of checks came through the mail to help him pay for his defense. Neighbors set up a fund for him. Well-wishers from around the country phoned in their congratulations. In the end, a judge turned him loose after one night in jail, and no charges were ever filed against him.

How does one react to this true story? Perhaps in the same way people react to the act described in the hypothetical example in the video debate entitled *Criminal Justice and a Defendant's Right to a Fair Trial*. As described by the moderator, the hypothetical case involves the rape of a nun by a man who then carved crosses on her chest with a knife. (Sad to say, the case is not wholly hypothetical but is based on an actual incident in New York City.) "Raping a nun and placing these crosses on her body was an act of an animal," says New York Mayor Edward Koch. Defense lawyer A. Charles Peruto calls the perpetrator "a creeping, crawling crud." Whoever it was that raped Willie Williams's ten-year-old daughter would seem to fit the same description. But does that justify vigilantism—taking the law into one's own hands?

107

THE ISSUES

Maybe the question is wrongly put. Maybe the real question is: What drives law-abiding men like Willie Williams to take the law into their own hands and commit acts of violence? Is it a lack of faith in our system of criminal justice? Are our courts and our judges putting people who are a menace to society back on the streets? Are guilty people going free because of "technicalities" in the law—the failure of a police officer to give a suspect all the correct warnings before the suspect confesses, the failure to obtain the proper warrant before conducting a search? How important to our system of justice are these technicalities?

There is another set of issues. Don't even "creeping, crawling cruds" deserve a good defense in criminal trials? Don't they need a competent lawyer to defend them vigorously? Don't we have to assume that they are innocent until proven guilty? Aren't they entitled to the same protection against dirty tricks by prosecutors and police that the rest of us are entitled to? Finally, isn't it just possible that some of those "cruds" may turn out to be not guilty, and that fair procedures may bring out that startling revelation?

These are the central issues discussed in the televised debate. The present chapter will study them in terms of their origins as federal issues—how they came to be part of the central agenda of the United States Supreme Court and how they have been treated by the Court. With that as background, it will examine how the issues are handled by the participants in the Philadelphia panel.

THE PROBLEM

The problem is violent crime—murder, rape, armed robbery, aggravated assault—particularly what appears to be a staggering increase in such crime since the early '60s. Some of this apparent increase may simply be due to better crime reporting, but even as such reporting has improved, the number of reported incidents of violent crime has grown appreciably. By 1980 violent crime in America had increased 60 percent over its 1971 level. According to 1981 crime data, a murder was taking place every 23 minutes, a rape every 6 minutes, and a burglary every 8 seconds. While the increase in crime appears to be a worldwide phenomenon, violent crime is far more severe in the United States than in most major industrialized countries. For example, there are more criminal homicides in New York City (whose *rate* of homicide is lower than that of a number of other American cities) than in all of Great Britain or Japan, which have respectively 9 and 15 times the population of New York.

During the same period in which this dramatic increase in violent crime has occurred, American courts have imposed a number of restrictions on the procedures that law-enforcement authorities may use in obtaining valid evidence for convicting defendants. In 1961, for example, the Supreme Court ruled that evidence obtained without a proper search warrant may not be used in state trials. In 1964, the Court ruled that criminal suspects may have their lawyers present during police questioning. And in 1966, the Court ruled that arrests are not valid unless defendants have been advised of their right to remain silent, warned that anything they say may be used against them, told that they have a right to a lawyer, and, if they lack funds, are entitled to the services of a lawyer free of charge. Rightly or wrongly, many people suspect (and successful political campaigns have been built upon these suspicions) that there may be some connection between the increase in violent crime and the multiplication of procedural safeguards available to crime suspects. More importantly, it offends their sense of justice that, in the words of Benjamin Cardozo, "the criminal is to go free because the constable has blundered."

There are, of course, answers to these concerns. Aside from denying that there is any causal link between the Supreme Court rulings and the increase in violent crime, defenders of the rulings can say, as Supreme Court Justice Tom Clark said in 1961, that "nothing can destroy a government more quickly than its failure to observe its own laws, or worse, the charter of its own existence." The "charter" referred to is the United States Constitution. The Constitution may sometimes be inconvenient to law-enforcement authorities. But if we condone its violation, our nation itself is imperiled.

What *does* the Constitution say about procedural safeguards? To get some perspective on this question, we need to step back from our immediate concerns about crime and violence. We must take a longer view of American constitutional law and particularly of the changing relationship between the states and the federal government in matters of law enforcement.

NINETEENTH AND EARLY TWENTIETH CENTURY: AUTONOMY OF STATE GOVERNMENT

At the outset, the important fact to remember is that ours is a federal system, a system consisting of national and state governments, each in some respects autonomous. The national government regulates interstate and foreign commerce, coins money, conducts foreign policy, protects the nation against foreign enemies, and engages in other business considered "necessary and proper" for carrying out the powers delegated to it in Article I, section 8, of the Constitution. Everything else is reserved to state governments (or to local governments, subject to state governments). The "everything else" includes much of the day-to-day business of life: getting married, getting divorced, driving a car, cashing a check, living securely in one's home, or walking the streets unmolested. Narrowing it down to the area of crime and punishment, the overwhelming majority of such cases are handled in state and local courts. The cases begin there, and they end there. In order for a case to have a chance of reaching federal courts, a substantial "federal question" must be raised: there must be a showing that a state practice collides with a federal statute or with the United States Constitution.

For all of the nineteenth century and the first part of the twentieth century, the issue of the procedural rights of those accused of violating state laws—how such people are to be treated by police and by courts—was left in the hands of state officials. If a person complained of mistreatment by police or mishandling of his or her case in a court, it could be appealed through the state system, right up to the state's highest court. But it could go no further; the case could not be taken into federal courts on the ground that some right of the appellant's under the Bill of Rights had been violated. The reason for this should be clear from what has been said in the Introduction. In the case of *Barron* v. *Baltimore* (1833), Chief Justice John Marshall said that the Bill of Rights applied only to the federal government, not to the states. Of course, a number of developments have occurred since *Barron*, the most important being the adoption of the Fourteenth Amendment in 1868, which prevented states from denying "due process of law" to their residents.

But what did "due process" mean? Was it the same kind of due process as is mentioned in the Fifth Amendment? If so, did it incorporate any of the other guarantees of the Fifth Amendment, such as the protection against double jeopardy ("nor shall any person be subject for the same offense to be twice put in jeopardy of life or limb") and self-incrimination (being compelled in a criminal case "to be a witness against" oneself)? Did this new "due process clause," as some argued, incorporate *all* of the Bill of Rights and apply it to the states? If it did not, what *did* it do? What *does* it mean? From 1884 to 1923, the Court's answer was, "Not very much," or at least, "Not very much when it comes to the rights of the accused." (The Court thought that the due process clause meant a great deal in the protection of private property rights.)

In 1884, in the case of *Hurtado* v. *California*, the Court refused to hold that the Fourteenth Amendment's due process clause compelled the states to use the grand jury method of indicting suspects. The Fifth Amendment states that "no person shall be held in answer for a capital, or otherwise infamous crime" unless there is first an indictment through a grand jury. But states had not considered themselves bound by this federal requirement; and the California Constitution prescribed a different method of obtaining indictments, a so-called "information," or prosecutor's affidavit, which, it claimed, protected the defendant's rights just as well as a grand jury procedure. The Court agreed, thus denying that the due process clause incorporated the grand jury provision of the Fifth Amendment. Sixteen years later, in *Maxwell* v. *Dow* (1900), the Court said that the states were not held to the same standards as the federal government in jury trials, and the 1908 case of *Twining* v. *New Jersey* held that the Fourteenth Amendment did not protect a person against compulsory self-incrimination, though that is specifically forbidden in federal cases under the Fifth Amendment.

The first sign of the Supreme Court's willingness to take a closer look at state criminal procedures came in the case of *Moore* v. *Dempsey* (1923), when the Court held that a federal court must conduct a hearing on the facts after state prisoners alleged that their trials lacked due process. Over the next ten years, it became increasingly clear that these and other abuses were not uncommon in state proceedings. In the 1931 report of the Wickersham Commission, entitled *Lawlessness in Law Enforcement*, numerous examples of police improprieties were cited, including physical and psychological coercion, the use of tricks by state authorities during plea bargaining, and the holding of suspects incommunicado for long periods. Then, in 1932, came the decision in *Powell* v. *Alabama*, which brought to public attention some of the seamier aspects of state law enforcement.

POWELL V. ALABAMA (1932): "THE SCOTTSBORO BOYS"

The background for this case began on a freight train slowly moving through the Alabama countryside. In one of its gondola cars were two groups of youths, white and black. Among the whites were two girls. A fight broke out between the black and white boys, and it ended with the whites being ejected from the car. But the two white girls remained. What happened then is still not certain, but it became the basis of this case. When the train approached the village of Scottsboro, it was met by the sheriff and a posse; the black youths were ordered out of the car and charged with rape. Soon, white mobs were starting to form, and the situation became so tense that the defendants were moved to a neighboring town. The seven "Scottsboro boys," as they became known, were quickly tried in three separate proceedings, and, in the space of a single day, found guilty of rape and sentenced to death.

All seven defendants were ignorant, illiterate, and penniless. They could neither afford a lawyer nor defend themselves. They were provided with only the most cursory and casual defense by court-appointed attorneys. The whole atmosphere was charged with tension and the threat of violence. Was this a fair trial—did the defendants receive "due process of law" under the Fourteenth Amendment? No, answered the Court, in an opinion by Justice George Sutherland. It was the first time in our history that the Supreme Court reversed a state criminal conviction because of unfair trial procedures.

In reversing the Alabama court system, however, Justice Sutherland crafted his opinion carefully. He did not say that the due process clause of the Fourteenth Amendment applies the Bill of Rights to state criminal proceedings, even though the Sixth Amendment guarantees the right "to have the assistance of Counsel." Instead, he stuck very closely to the facts of this particular case: the ignorance, poverty, and illiteracy of the defendants, their confinement and surveillance, their isolation from friends and families, and above all the fact that their lives were at stake. In such circumstances "it is the duty of the court, whether requested or not, to assign counsel."

By itself, this careful narrowing of the decision would provide little guidance for future cases; after all, how many *perfect* replicas of the Scottsboro case are there? But the Court laid down principles for other cases. The due process clause of the Fourteenth Amendment does not incorporate the Bill of Rights, the Court said, but it does incorporate certain basic principles of liberty and justice. Quoting from two earlier cases, the Court spoke of "fundamental principles of liberty and justice which lie at the base of all our civil and political institutions" and "immutable principles of justice which inhere in the very idea of free government." For a state to abridge *these* is to abridge the due process clause of the Fourteenth Amendment. Decisions regarding the constitutionality of state criminal procedures, then, do not turn upon the specific clauses of the Bill of Rights but upon the question of whether these basic principles have been violated. The Court determined that they were violated in the case of the Scottsboro boys. It left to future courts what other practices of state authorities would violate these "immutable principles of justice." Before the decade was over, the Court would grapple with another landmark case of state criminal procedures. This time its decision went against the defendant.

PALKO V. *CONNECTICUT* (1937): ABSORPTION

The opinion of *Palko* v. *Connecticut* (1937) was delivered by Justice Benjamin Cardozo, the same Cardozo who, as New York state judge, had condemned the idea that because "the constable has blundered" the "criminal is to go free." In this case Cardozo gave considerable leeway to the constable. At issue was the application of a Connecticut provision that allowed the state to appeal from rulings and decisions in its criminal courts on points of law. Palko, who was convicted of murder in the second degree and given a life sentence, was retried after a successful state appeal. This time he was found guilty of first-degree murder and given a death sentence. All during these appeals, Palko objected that the state was holding him twice in jeopardy for the same offense, a practice forbidden to the federal government by the Fifth Amendment. The question in the case was whether this specific provision applied to states. The Court said that it did not.

But *Palko* was more than a decision against a defendant in jeopardy of life and limb. It was an attempt by the Court to tidy up all of its previous rulings on the applicability of the Bill of Rights to the states. Some of them had gone one way and some the other. In *Gitlow* v. *New York* (1925), the Court had ruled that the free speech provisions of the First Amendment applied to states as well as the federal government. In *Near* v. *Minnesota* (1931), discussed in Chapter 8, the Court ruled that the First Amendment's free press guarantee also bound the states. Yet in *Hurtado* v. *California* (1884), the Court ruled that the grand jury requirement in the Fifth Amendment did *not* bind state authorities. And in *Twining* v. *New Jersey* (1908), it said the same of the Fifth Amendment's ban on compulsory self-incrimination. Even the *Powell* case carefully avoided saying that the Sixth Amendment's guarantee of the right to counsel applied with the same force to states as it did to the federal government. Justice Sutherland had stressed the special hardships the defendants faced in this case, the implication being that there might be other cases where the defendant's lack of counsel would not violate fundamental principles of justice.

In short, some amendments, or fragments of amendments, would seem to apply to both the states and the federal government, while others apply only to the federal government. By the time of *Palko* in 1937, the situation looked like this:

Apply to Both States and Federal	*Apply Only to Federal*
Free speech (in First Amendment)	Ban on self-incrimination (in Fifth Amendment)
Free press (in First Amendment)	Grand jury indictments (in Fifth Amendment)
Right to court-appointed counsel in cases like *Powell* v. *Alabama* (a "fundamental principle")	Right to court-appointed counsel in noncapital cases (implicit in Sixth Amendment)
	Right to jury trial in civil cases (in Seventh Amendment)

How could the Court justify this dichotomy? Why do some Bill of Rights provisions get on the left-hand side and others on the right-hand side? Why are some incorporated into the Fourteenth Amendment's due process clause and some not? What is the rationale for sorting them out like this? The answer to these questions had already been touched upon by Justice Sutherland in the *Powell* case. It remained for Justice Cardozo to attempt a more comprehensive statement.

"Reflection and analysis," Cardozo said, should help us to arrive at the "rationalizing principle" for the dichotomy. Consider some of the items on the right-hand side, such as the requirements of grand jury indictments and the right to a jury trial in civil cases "where the value in controversy shall exceed twenty dollars," found in the Fifth and Seventh Amendments of the Bill of Rights. These rights "may have value and importance," Cardozo said, but they are not "of the very essence of a scheme of ordered liberty." The same could be said of immunity from compulsory self-incrimination. "This, too, might be lost, and justice still be done." On the other hand, if confessions were tortured out of suspects, the line would be crossed: basic human rights would be violated. Similarly, the items listed in the left-hand column—free press and the right to competent court-appointed counsel for defendants as helpless as the Scottsboro boys—are "of the very essence of a scheme of ordered liberty."

Justice Cardozo did not provide a complete catalogue of which amendments or clauses in the Bill of Rights were incorporated into the due process clause of the Fourteenth Amendment. In fact, he avoided using the word "incorporate," preferring instead the word "absorption." Absorption is a metaphor that appears to be borrowed from physiology. One thinks of the digestive process. Food enters the intestines and its nutrients are absorbed into the bloodstream. The Bill of Rights, then, is a great mix of material, some of it digestible by the Fourteenth Amendment and some—a kind of roughage?—applicable only to the federal government. The organizing principle, the principle that identifies what is absorbable, "had its source in the belief that neither liberty nor justice would exist if they were sacrificed. . . ." Applying this reasoning to the particular case of Palko, Cardozo asked whether the "kind of double jeopardy" in this case subjected Palko to a "hardship so acute and shocking that our polity will not endure it." No, Cardozo answered. Judgment affirmed.

CRITIQUE OF THE *PALKO* OPINION

Cardozo's "absorption" theory seems to rest on highly subjective considerations. Who is to say what rights are "of the very essence of a scheme of ordered liberty"? How do we determine which rights are so basic that "neither liberty nor justice would exist if they were sacrificed"? What litmus test exists for indicating the rights whose abrogation will cause a "hardship so acute and shocking that our polity will not endure it"? Behind the verbiage there seems to be nothing but Benjamin Cardozo's view of what rights *he* considers important. The suspicion is reinforced by some of his own examples. He sees nothing particularly shocking about compulsory self-incrimination. The immunity from it "might be lost, justice still be done." Many think differently. At the time Cardozo was writing his opinion, the so-called purge trials were occurring in the

Soviet Union, during which defendants were "confessing" to all sorts of crimes they had not committed. We know today that these confessions were coerced—not necessarily by torture—and that they were a shocking travesty of justice. Justice Cardozo is entitled to his opinion about coerced confessions, but it is just that: an opinion, not a self-evident proposition. The same is true of his pronouncement on the immediate issue in the case, double jeopardy. Because the state said that there were errors in the first trial of Palko, which resulted in a term of life imprisonment for him, the state decided to have another go at him; this time Palko was sentenced to death. Leave aside the double jeopardy clause of the Fifth Amendment and simply ask, with Cardozo, whether Palko's "hardship" was of a kind "so acute and shocking that our polity will not endure it." Cardozo did not think so, and therefore concluded that Palko's right to immunity from double jeopardy was not "fundamental." Others are almost certain to disagree with all of the above. One constitutional scholar summed up the difficulty in Cardozo's approach this way: "It distinguishes between rights which are fundamental and those which are not, and it silently assumes that all or most Americans will agree on which rights are and which are not fundamental." The Cardozan standard "is both majestic in its sweep and intellectually exasperating."

AN ALTERNATIVE: TOTAL INCORPORATION OF THE BILL OF RIGHTS

The Supreme Court justice who eventually became most exasperated by the Cardozan formula was Hugo Black. Black's views on the First Amendment will be studied in Chapter 8. He was a First Amendment absolutist, believing that because the amendment says "Congress shall make no law" abridging free speech, it meant just that: *no* law. But there was another, related aspect of Black's views that interests us here. Black believed that the due process clause of the Fourteenth Amendment incorporated the entire Bill of Rights, making all of it applicable to the states. There is a neatness and simplicity in this approach. Justice Black was appropriately named: he was a black-and-white man. "Congress shall make no law" meant *no* law, and the Bill of Rights should be applied, clause by clause, letter by letter, to the states exactly as it is applied to the federal government. He considered the Cardozan formula a morass of verbiage almost certain to produce subjective, capricious rulings. He disparagingly referred to it as the "natural law" approach. "Natural law" is a philosophy based on the premise that there exist certain ethical norms that stand above and apart from the laws of the state. The great problem for natural-law philosophers has always been determining the actual content of these abstract standards and showing that they are rooted in something firm and objective that we can all agree upon. What Justice Black was saying to his colleagues on the bench was this: If the philosophers can't agree on what rights are "fundamental," or essential to "a scheme of ordered liberty," how are we supposed to do it? In Black's view, it all seemed to border on hocus-pocus.

Black's complaint is understandable. But we must consider some weaknesses in his alternative approach. Black would take the first eight amendments of the Constitution and apply them wholesale to the states. In most cases this would cause no great difficulties. But consider some of the clauses in the Bill of Rights, such as the Seventh Amendment's requirement that "in suits of common law, where the value in controversy shall exceed twenty dollars" there must be trial by jury. In 1789, $20 was a fortune for the average person. Today a child could spend it treating his friends to the movies. Should federal courts force states to hold jury trials for civil suits involving $20.01? The reader only has to imagine the enormous disruption such a ruling would produce in our state court system—as if there were not enough delay and confusion there! Some of the other provisions in the Bill of Rights may also be less than essential for the preservation of justice, such as grand jury indictments (many states use other procedures that still safeguard essential rights of defendants). And what about the Second Amendment, the right "to keep and bear arms"? If the Court were to make this binding on states (reversing an 1896 ruling), would it pump new life into the whole gun-control controversy, leading to a deluge of new cases? Clearly, the Black approach has its own dangers—the intellectual danger of absurdity and the practical danger of opening the floodgates to litigation, turmoil, confusion.

ADAMSON V. *CALIFORNIA*: THE GRAND BATTLE

The two approaches, the Black and the Cardozan, came into sharpest confrontation in the 1947 case of *Adamson* v. *California.* By that time Black had gotten three other members of the Court to agree with him that all of the Bill of Rights was incorporated into the due process clause of the Fourteenth Amendment. Also by that time, Justice Cardozo had died, but his approach was accepted by the majority of the Court and defended vigorously by Justice Felix Frankfurter. Frankfurter was a former Harvard law professor appointed to the Court by President Franklin D. Roosevelt (who also appointed Black). Although the *Adamson* case was decided by Justice Reed, it is best remembered for Justice Frankfurter's concurring opinion and Justice Black's dissent. The two opinions remain as classic antithetical statements on the issue of incorporation versus "absorption."

Adamson, the defendant in the case, was convicted of murder in the California courts, but he appealed on the ground that California had violated his Fifth Amendment right not to have to testify against himself. Unlike most states, California allowed state prosecutors to comment to the jury on a defendant's failure to take the witness stand. Adamson refused to be put on the stand during his trial, because California law also allowed prosecutors to impeach the testimony of a defendant by pointing out to the jury the defendant's previous convictions. Not wanting to allow the discussion of his previous convictions, Adamson chose not to take the stand, which then allowed the prosecutor to comment adversely on his silence. Thus wedged between a rock and a hard place, Adamson appealed; it sounded to him like compulsory self-incrimination.

Perhaps it was, but was it "a hardship so acute and shocking that our polity will not endure it"? That was the *Palko* test. In *Adamson* the Court ruled that Adamson had not suffered such a hardship. Therefore, even assuming that California's procedure might not be acceptable if this were a federal case—even if it violated the Fifth Amendment's protection against self-incrimination—all that is irrelevant because *the Four-*

teenth Amendment does not incorporate the Bill of Rights. Frankfurter's concurring opinion in the case lent support to the Court's opinion by a long recitation of examples in which the Court had refused to apply the Bill of Rights to the states. To overturn these, Frankfurter said, would lead to chaos. In effect, Frankfurter's opinion brought up to date, with fresh examples, the Cardozan philosophy of a decade earlier.

Justice Black's lengthy dissent was based upon a single premise: that *Barron* v. *Baltimore*—the 1833 ruling that the Bill of Rights did not apply to the states—had been completely overturned by the passage of the Fourteenth Amendment. Much of his opinion was devoted to historical references purporting to show that the chief framers of the amendment meant to do precisely that: to wipe away *Barron* in order to make sure that each of the eight amendments applied with equal force to state and national governments.

Justice Black's philosophy of total incorporation did not prevail in *Adamson*, though it came close. (It was a five-to-four decision.) With the loss of two members who supported him, Black's support dwindled further in later cases. Nevertheless, it might be argued that over the next twenty years Black's defeat in principle was more than compensated by a practical victory, a victory in fact.

The last sentence is what TV newscasters call a "tease." It usually signals the beginning of a commercial. Here it means a different kind of time-out: a factual review.

Points to Remember

1. From the ratification of our Constitution in 1789 up through the early years of the twentieth century, federal courts adopted a "hands-off" attitude toward the procedures used in state criminal cases.
2. *Powell* v. *Alabama* (1932), the case involving the Scottsboro boys, marked the first time the Court reversed state criminal convictions on procedural grounds. However, the Court carefully avoided saying that the Fourteenth Amendment incorporated any specific provision of the Bill of Rights.
3. In *Palko* v. *Connecticut* (1937), the Court flatly denied that the due process clause of the Fourteenth Amendment incorporated the Bill of Rights. It said that the due process clause "absorbed" into itself certain basic, fundamental rights, the denial of which would subject a person to "a hardship so acute and shocking that our polity will not endure it."
4. The *Palko* formula has certain problems, the main ones being vagueness and vulnerability to subjective interpretation.
5. Justice Hugo Black became the archenemy of the "absorption" theory. His approach was to insist that the due process clause incorporated all of the Bill of Rights. This has its own problems, the main one being that it would force the states to grant rights—such as jury trials for civil suits involving paltry sums—that may not any longer be considered fundamental.

6. Justice Black's view almost prevailed in the case of *Adamson* v. *California* (1947). But, by a five-to-four decision, the Court resisted the view that the due process clause of the Fourteenth Amendment incorporates the Bill of Rights.

Now we turn again to the "tease," the possibility that Justice Black, who lost the *Adamson* battle, may have won the war after all. In a nutshell, what has been happening since the *Adamson* decision is this: the major procedural protections in the Bill of Rights have been absorbed through the due process clause of the Fourteenth Amendment and applied to the states. The Court has simply been broadening the application of the *Palko* rule about rights so basic "that neither liberty nor justice would exist if they were sacrificed." The incorporation of the Bill of Rights has been selective, not total, but it has been wide-ranging.

SELECTIVE INCORPORATION: FOUR CASES

Wolf v. *Colorado*: A Partial Victory

Four major cases can be cited as evidence that the procedural protections in the Bill of Rights have been extended to defendants in state cases. In *Wolf* v. *Colorado* the Court held that the immunity against "unreasonable searches and seizures" was one of those basic liberties—a "core" liberty, the Court called it—that *Palko* considered essential to a just system of government. From the standpoint of defendants' rights, however, it was only a partial victory, for the court ruled that the evidence seized could still be used against the defendant at the trial. To the defendant, Wolf, the Court was saying yes and no: yes, the federal prohibition against unreasonable searches and seizures also applies to states; no, you may not demand that the evidence seized be excluded from your trial.

The precedent the Court was struggling with in the *Wolf* case was a 1914 federal case, *Weeks* v. *U.S.* In that case the Court ruled that the Fourth Amendment barred the use of evidence secured through illegal search and seizure. The Court reasoned that there would not be much point in guaranteeing people protection against such searches if the fruit of them could be used in trials. But there was an ambiguity in *Weeks*. Did it mean that the "exclusionary rule"—the·rule barring the government from using illegally seized evidence at the trial—was a part of the Fourth Amendment itself or simply a rule of administration binding upon federal courts? This subtle point of law, which was never fully resolved between 1914 and 1949, played a major role in the case. The court in *Wolf* considered the exclusionary rule not as an integral part of the Fourth Amendment but simply as a judge-made rule binding *federal* courts. Did it also bind state courts? In order to do that, it would have to pass the *Palko* test: it would have to be so basic that neither liberty nor justice could survive without it. It fails that test, the Court ruled, so it does not apply to states.

The case has its ironies. Aside from the major irony that the court was letting a man be punished on the basis of evidence seized in violation of the Constitution, there was the irony that the case was decided by Justice Frankfurter, Black's chief opponent in the *Adamson* case. Though Frankfurter vehemently opposed wholesale incorporation of the Bill of Rights, he was prepared to do some selective incorporation. The final irony is that Black in this case concurred with Frankfurter on both parts of the ruling. He agreed that the Fourth Amendment was incorporated (and continued to insist that all of the Bill of Rights was incorporated), and he also agreed that the exclusionary rule is not part of the Fourth Amendment.

There was something inherently unstable about *Wolf*. How can a court say that people are entitled to protection against unreasonable searches and seizures yet allow state officials to use the evidence obtained through such searches? It offends our everyday logic. Before very long it began to offend the Court's logic. But before we see what happened to *Wolf*, let us turn to an intervening case that involved both the Fourth and Fifth Amendments. This was a case that, more clearly than *Wolf*, caused "a hardship so acute and shocking" that the Court refused to tolerate it.

Rochin v. *California*: The Stomach Pump

Rochin v. *California* (1952) grew out of the following facts. California law-enforcement officials broke into a man's bedroom in search of illegal drugs. The suspect promptly gulped down some capsules. The officials then rushed him to a hospital, pried open his mouth, put a tube down his stomach, and pumped his stomach, causing him to vomit up the capsules. They introduced them as evidence at his trial, and he was convicted. If ever a case seemed to fit the *Palko* test, this was the one. The Court held that "this is conduct that shocks the conscience." The case involved a kind of mixture of Fourth and Fifth Amendment rights—the Fourth Amendment's search-and-seizure provision and the Fifth Amendment's protection against self-incrimination. It hardly mattered. The methods used were "too close to the rack and the screw to permit of constitutional differentiation." They were simply intolerable, and the Court barred the use of the evidence.

Mapp v. *Ohio*: A Reversal of *Wolf*

Chapter 8 of Friendly and Elliot's book recounts the fascinating circumstances behind the case of *Mapp* v. *Ohio* (1961). Police broke into a woman's rooming house without a proper warrant and seized obscene materials. The question the Court considered central was whether such materials could be used against her at the trial. Answer: no. The Court thus reversed *Wolf* v. *Colorado*, or a least that part of the *Wolf* case that held the federal exclusionary rule inapplicable to state proceedings. Now the *Weeks* rule barring the use of illegally seized evidence in federal cases was extended to state cases as well. For the Court majority it was a kind of completion of *Wolf*. The "admission of the new constitutional right by *Wolf* could not consistently tolerate denial of its most important constitutional privilege, namely, the exclusion of the evidence which an accused had been forced to give by reason of the unlawful seizure." Without the

exclusionary rule, the right of the Fourth Amendment would remain an "empty promise." For the three dissenters—one of them Justice Frankfurter, the author of *Wolf*—it
was a straitjacket placed upon state law enforcement. They referred again to then-judge
Cardozo's famous decision in the New York State Court of Appeals where he repudiated the notion that "the criminal is to go free because the constable has blundered."

Although the Court in *Mapp* came close to saying that the exclusionary rule is a
constitutional command, not merely a rule of judicial administration, it did not finally
resolve the question. At this writing the Court is considering other cases involving the
question of whether the exclusion of illegally seized evidence is constitutional or
whether in certain cases it may be modified by practice and experience.

In one case before the high court, a major California drug prosecution got derailed
by a court ruling that the police had obtained a search warrant for a private home
without "probable cause" to believe that a crime had been committed there—even
though the search warrant request followed a month-long surveillance indicating that
drug transactions were being made. In another case awaiting decision by the Supreme
Court, police in Massachusetts investigating a murder had their key evidence thrown
out because they used the wrong standard form in obtaining a search warrant from a
judge.

These are the uses of the exclusionary rule that are particularly frustrating to law-
enforcement officials. They contend that many courts have applied the letter of the
law at the expense of its spirit—and at the expense of society. They argue for a "good-
faith exception" to the exclusionary rule, to apply to cases, like the above, in which
officials may not have followed all the exact forms but had good reason to suspect
criminal activity. Many in Congress agree with that view, and bills are presently pending that would allow improperly obtained evidence to be admitted in federal criminal
trials if law-enforcement officials acted in the "good-faith belief" that they were acting
properly. The Reagan White House has taken a similar view. It has written a legal brief
supporting the Massachusetts and California police in the cases before the Supreme
Court. Former Attorney General William French Smith wrote a law review article entitled "The Exclusionary Rule Be Damned," and his designated successor, Edwin
Meese, has frequently spoken out against the rule.

Supporters of the exclusionary rule fear that weakening it will correspondingly
weaken the rule's "deterrent" value, which is meant to encourage police to exercise
care in their searches. They fear that weakening it may also lead to *bad* faith by police
officers. Said one: "The good-faith exception is an open invitation to police perjury.
They could fabricate their good-faith belief in fact or law from whole cloth, and no
one could contradict them."

Gideon v. *Wainwright*: Right to Counsel

New York Times columnist Anthony Lewis has written a moving account of the case
of *Gideon* v. *Wainwright* (1963). His book *Gideon's Trumpet* is the story of a man
with little education and no money who managed to get his case before the Supreme
Court, where it was argued by some of the most brilliant—and expensive—legal talents
in America. A dry summary of the facts: Clarence Gideon, defendant in a petty lar-

ceny case in Florida, was refused a court-appointed lawyer. Since he could not afford
to hire one, he defended himself as best he could but lost the case. He appealed on
Sixth Amendment grounds. (The Sixth Amendment says that accused persons have the
right to "the Assistance of Counsel.") But does the Sixth Amendment apply to the
states? In *Powell* v. *Alabama* the Court had held that the Scottsboro boys had suffered
a violation of basic rights by the failure of the court to supply competent counsel. But
Powell was a special case. Racism was clearly involved, the atmosphere was charged
with tension and intimidation, and the youths were on trial for their lives. Here there
was no racism, since all of the parties were white; there was no particular tension; and
the crime was a minor one. Moreover, in an earlier case, *Betts* v. *Brady* (1942), the
Court had held that the Sixth Amendment's right of counsel, at least as it was interpreted in federal cases, did not apply to the states. The *Gideon* decision did not
attempt to distinguish the facts in the case from those in *Betts* or otherwise walk
around it. The Court simply reversed *Betts*, holding that any defendant in a criminal
case has a right to a competent court-appointed attorney if he or she cannot afford
one—and that such a right belongs among those "fundamental" rights basic to freedom
and justice.

The decade of the 1960s was already well under way at the time of the *Gideon*
decision. But the two most famous and controversial victories for the rights of criminal
suspects had not yet been decided. These two cases are the ones that seem to be most
associated with the charge that the Supreme Court has "handcuffed the police." In the
public's perception, they are, perhaps, emblems of '60s-style "permissiveness." The
decisions referred to are *Escobedo* and *Miranda*.

ESCOBEDO AND *MIRANDA* CASES: POLICE INTERROGATIONS

In *Escobedo* v. *Illinois* (1964), a five-to-four majority dramatically expanded the constitutional right to counsel. A suspect brought in for questioning asked for but was
denied the right to have his lawyer present during the interrogation. Under persistent
questioning, he made a damaging statement that was used against him during his trial,
and he was found guilty of murder. In overturning his conviction, the Court for the
first time extended the right to counsel back to the police station, during the preliminary investigation, at least at the point "when the process shifts from investigatory to
accusatory—when its focus is on the accused and its purpose is to elicit a confession."
The Court had come a long way from the days when it left state criminal procedure
solely in the hands of state authorities. In a sharply worded dissent, Justice Byron
White complained that the right to counsel had now become "an impenetrable barrier
to any interrogation once the accused has become a suspect."

Miranda v. *Arizona* (1966) consolidated four separate cases involving police interrogation. In each of the cases the defendant had not been advised of his right to
remain silent and consult counsel. Unlike Escobedo, none of the defendants had asked
for and been denied counsel. The defendants' central claim, then, was not the Sixth
Amendment's right to counsel but the Fifth Amendment's protection against compulsory self-incrimination. The Supreme Court supported their claim.

> Our holding . . . briefly stated . . . is this: the prosecution may not use statements, whether exculpatory or inculpatory, stemming from custodial interrogation of the defendant unless it demonstrates the use of procedural safeguards effective to secure the privilege against self-incrimination. By custodial interrogation, we mean questioning initiated by law enforcement officers after a person has been taken into custody or otherwise deprived of his freedom of action in any significant way.

Miranda Warnings

What kind of "procedural safeguards" did the Court consider essential during police questioning of suspects in custody? By now, most people have probably heard of "*Miranda* warnings." Before "custodial" questioning can begin, the police must notify the suspect that:

1. The suspect has a right to remain silent.
2. Anything the suspect says may be used as evidence against him or her.
3. The suspect has a right to have an attorney present.
4. If the suspect lacks the money to hire an attorney, a court must appoint one if he or she desires.

Any "custodial" confession obtained before the police have notified the suspect of the above rights is invalid. Once again, the Court had come a long way since the early years of the century. Does the reader remember the 1908 case of *Twining* v. *New Jersey*? That was the case in which the Court held that the Fifth Amendment's protection against compulsory self-incrimination did not apply to the states. Without being formally overturned, the force of that decision was now spent. Clearly, since 1908 there had been a gradual broadening of the Supreme Court's concept of rights. The catalogue of state procedures that, in the Court's view, entailed hardships "so acute and shocking" as to be unendurable, had grown dramatically. Now it was not only the use of physical coercion that troubled the Court majority but "the very fact of custodial interrogation," which "exacts a heavy toll on individual liberty and trades on the weaknesses of individuals."

The question on the minds of many is whether the Court went too far in protecting the rights of criminal suspects. Has justice been done when a case is lost because a suspect blurted out his confession before receiving his *Miranda* warnings? Is this, perhaps, weighting the scales of justice so much on the side of the accused that society itself is not properly protected? In the 1968 presidential election campaign, these kinds of issues were raised, and they have become perennial campaign issues since. Yet they cannot be dismissed as mere demagoguery; at least it serves no purpose to do so. Politicians are sensitive barometers of opinion. The opinions and feelings have to be "out there" to begin with in order to attract the attention of the politicians.

Nor were these concerns voiced only by lay people unfamiliar with the mandates of the Constitution. *Miranda* was a five-to-four decision, and its dissenting opinions raised many of the same concerns as those that continue to trouble the nonexpert. "The thrust of the new rules," said Justice John Harlan, "is to negate all pressures . . . and ultimately to discourage any confession at all." If the aim of the Court is to ensure that confessions are voluntary, Harlan said, this is "voluntariness with a vengeance."

Suspects' Rights Since *Miranda*

The string of cases that culminated in *Miranda* emerged in large part from the Court presided over by the late Chief Justice Earl Warren. Within a year after the election of President Nixon in 1968, Warren had died. In 1969, Nixon named a new chief justice, Warren E. Burger. In the next four years, Nixon appointed three more Supreme Court justices. The four new members of the Court were, as a group, generally more "conservative" on the issue of suspects' rights than were the justices they replaced. Probably as a result of these new appointments, the Court seemed to modify its direction. In *Harris* v. *New York* (1971), the Court allowed statements made by a defendant who did not receive proper *Miranda* warnings to be used in court to contradict his testimony. In 1974, in the case of *Michigan* v. *Tucker*, the Court ruled that evidence obtained by police after an incomplete warning of legal rights to a suspect could still be used against the suspect. There were other such cases that seemed to weaken *Miranda*, yet there were also some decisions that reinforced it. In *Jenkins* v. *Anderson* (1980), the Court ruled that a suspect's silence after being read his *Miranda* rights could not be used against him. In the 1979 case of *Dunaway* v. *New York*, the Court ruled that even after having had his *Miranda* rights read to him, a suspect could not be convicted on the basis of his subsequent confession if he had been held for questioning without valid grounds. The most spectacular and grisly of all the Burger Court cases reaffirming *Miranda* was *Brewer* v. *Williams* (1977). Pamela Powers, a ten-year-old girl, was abducted on Christmas Eve, sexually molested, murdered, and thrown into a culvert. Before the body was found, a suspect turned himself in to the police. The police promised him that he would not be interrogated until they drove him to the police station. On the way there, however, a detective suggested that if they could find the girl's body they could give it a "Christian burial." Moved, the suspect directed the police to the girl's body, and this evidence was used against him at his trial. The Supreme Court overturned his conviction and ordered a new trial because the detective's remark anounted to interrogation, during which process "he has a right to legal representation."

In cases involving search and seizure, the Court more clearly blunted the point of its *Mapp* decision of 1961. In *Terry* v. *Ohio* (1968), the Court ruled that the police may "stop and frisk" a suspect on the street without a warrant if there is reasonable suspicion that the suspect is armed and dangerous. In 1983, the Court extended *Terry* by ruling that the police can conduct a "protective" search of the passenger area of a car without a warrant—even if the suspect is out of the car and in custody. (The six-to-three decision in the case, *Michigan* v. *Long*, was written by Justice Sandra Day O'Connor.)

Conclusion: while the record is mixed, on the whole the Supreme Court in recent years has tended to trim and modify its earlier precedents concerning the rights of the accused. Even so, there have been no major reversals of the precedents. They remain today as fundamental, landmark decisions giving criminal suspects rights that would have been almost unthinkable in the early years of this century.

And they remain as controversial as ever. "Law and order" is as powerful a rallying cry as it was a decade ago, perhaps even more so now that "liberals" also pledge themselves to it. Is this concern an understandable one? Does it have an element of mean-spirited authoritarianism in it, a spirit opposed to lawful government? Or is it possible that both of these assessments are true—or partly true? The debate in Philadelphia helps to illuminate the various facets of the arguments concerning the rights of criminal suspects. But before turning to *Criminal Justice and a Defendant's Right to a Fair Trial*, it is time to summarize the main points made since our last time-out.

Points to Remember

1. Despite the defeat of Justice Black's "incorporation" theory in the *Adamson* case, the Court has selectively incorporated—or "absorbed"—most of the provisions in the first eight amendments, making them as applicable to the states as to the federal government.

2. In *Wolf* v. *Colorado*, in 1949, the Court said that the Fourth Amendment's protection against "unreasonable searches and seizures" applied to the states. However, it also ruled that the evidence seized in state cases could be used against the defendant at the trial. That last part of the ruling was overturned by a later decision, *Mapp* v. *Ohio* (1961).

3. In *Rochin* v. *California* (1952), the Court ruled that pumping a suspect's stomach against his will is a "conscience-shocking" act violative of those basic liberties referred to by Justice Cardozo in the *Palko* case.

4. In *Gideon* v. *Wainwright* (1963), the Court added another specific basic liberty which the states, as much as the federal government, must respect: the right to a court-appointed attorney even for relatively minor criminal offenses. This was a vast extension of its ruling in *Powell* v. *Alabama* (1932), which seemed to limit the right to the peculiar circumstances of the Scottsboro affair. *Gideon* reversed an earlier case, *Betts* v. *Brady* (1942), which denied the right to court-appointed counsel in noncapital cases.

5. In two cases, *Escobedo* v. *Illinois* (1964) and *Miranda* v. *Arizona* (1966), the Court carried suspects' rights still further. In *Escobedo* it ruled that a suspect was entitled to have his lawyer present during preliminary questioning by the police, at least at the point when the questioning began to center on the suspect, and that any incriminating admissions made without the attorney present could not be used in court. In *Miranda* it laid down the four statements the police must make before questioning anyone in their custody: You have a right to remain silent; anything you say may be used against you; you have a right to have an attorney present; and the state must appoint one if you cannot afford one.

6. In later cases the force of *Mapp* and *Escobedo* may have been weakened by decisions that seemed to qualify them, including decisions justifying "stop-and-frisk" and the use in court of statements by defendants who had not received proper *Miranda* warnings.

The Video Discussion

We turn now to the video discussion of defendants' rights as moderated by Professor Charles H. Nesson of Harvard Law School.

List of Participants

JEANNE BAKER
Attorney
Baker & Fine
Former General Counsel
Massachusetts Civil Liberties Union

MAX FRANKEL
Editorial Page Editor
New York Times

MICHAEL GARTNER
President and Editorial Chairman
Des Moines Register & Tribune

EDWARD I. KOCH
Mayor
New York City

MARIO MEROLA
District Attorney
Bronx County, New York City

JAMES F. NEAL
Attorney
Neal & Harwell

A. CHARLES PERUTO
Attorney
Peruto, Ryan & Vitullo

HON. R. EUGENE PINCHAM
Judge
Circuit Court
Cook County, Illinois

WILLIAM RASPBERRY
Columnist
Washington Post

DAN RATHER
Managing Editor
CBS Evening News

FRANK L. RIZZO
Former Mayor
Philadelphia

JOHN SEIGENTHALER
Publisher
The Tennessean

SAMUEL K. SKINNER
Attorney
Sidley & Austin
Former U.S. Attorney
North District of Illinois

HON. POTTER STEWART
Retired Justice
U.S. Supreme Court

HON. RENA K. UVILLER
Acting Justice
New York State Supreme Court

WILLIAM H. WEBSTER
Director
Federal Bureau of Investigation

BENJAMIN WARD
(then) Commissioner
Department of Correction
New York City
Currently Police Commissioner
New York City

Program Summary

The moderator begins with the hypothetical case of "Butch Barnes," a man accused of raping a nun and carving crosses on her chest. This heinous crime is posited in order to put the civil libertarians and defense counsels to the ultimate test: Do they really want to defend a man whom Attorney A. Charles Peruto calls "a creeping, crawling crud"?

The program consists of roughly four parts. The first begins with Butch Barnes's phone call to Peruto. He's been accused of the crime. Will Peruto take his case? This part is an extended reflection on why defense attorneys take cases, what cases they would rather not take (this is obviously one), what role money has in inducing them to take cases, and how they conduct the defense of their clients, including some rather delicate ethical problems that arise if the defendant wants to lie on the stand or possesses evidence that might be incriminating.

The second part gets us into the thorny issue: What happens if the constable blunders? What if it's a bad arrest? The cop, infuriated by the crime, throws the suspect against the wall, gives him no *Miranda* warnings, grabs evidence without a warrant, and scares the suspect into confessing. Should the confession and the evidence be suppressed in a courtroom?

The third part concerns newspaper coverage of the trial and its possible consequences for the defendant. The moderator asks reporters and editors if they feel the need to restrain their pretrial coverage of a crime of this sort. Then he asks judges if they would ever feel the need to impose a "gag rule" on the press or to hold the trial in private in order to protect the defendant's rights. Finally, he asks defense attorneys how they would attempt to protect their clients against a prejudicial atmosphere arising from hostile media coverage.

The fourth and last part is a reflection on the implications of the second part. Suppose there has been a bad arrest. Should the evidence and the confession be thrown out even if both are highly incriminating? Is the exclusionary rule a sound principle of law? Where does it come from? Should it be abandoned or modified? The participants grapple with these questions until the end of the program, when Fred Friendly and former Supreme Court Justice Potter Stewart offer some concluding thoughts on the issues.

Let us examine these four parts in greater detail.

I: SUSPECTS AND THEIR LAWYERS

The moderator's first question to the defense attorneys is: Will you take the case? All of them are highly reluctant to do it, even Jeanne Baker, former general counsel of the Massachusetts Civil Liberties Union. They all agree with Peruto that Butch Barnes is a "creeping, crawling crud." Then the trap is sprung. It is not clear whether the moderator deliberately set a trap or whether it just materialized, but after Baker, Peruto, and attorney James Neal had all indicated that they would take the case only if it were assigned to them by a judge, Judge R. Eugene Pincham of Illinois indignantly reminds them that Butch Barnes has, thus far, only been *accused* of the crime. In none of his remarks to the attorneys had Barnes actually said he did it, and none of the attorneys bothered to ask him whether he did it. Here were three famous defense attorneys assuming the guilt of the man they were supposed to defend!

After this initial embarrassment, the discussion continues—and gets more embarrassing. Butch tells his attorney that he has committed the crime. The topic is now money. Does the prospect of a fat fee make it easier to defend such a man? On this issue the discussion begins to assume a jocular tone which some viewers find offensive. (For some reason it seems to offend professors more than students.) Perhaps there are depths of cynicism here. It sounds that way when James Neal remarks that "you're getting up there pretty close to making a nice fella out of this guy when you start talking about a hundred thousand dollars." But we have to remember how the discussion evolved into this pattern. It was really Peruto, prodded by the moderator, who set it on its path. Peruto is a street-smart defense attorney who is, nevertheless, deeply repelled by the prospect of defending this "crud." Far from acting mercenary, he at first tells the moderator, "I don't care if he's Du Pont. He doesn't have that kind of money for this kind of case." But the moderator goads and scolds Peruto: "What is all this baloney I always hear about 'the right of a criminal to a good defense, and I'm a defense lawyer' and all this stuff?" The moderator is appealing to Peruto's sense of professionalism and his conviction that our system of justice requires the best defense a person can get. These kinds of idealistic appeals (and, possibly, Peruto's sense that this dialogue is an interesting game) help persuade Peruto to consider taking the case. Only then does the discussion get mercenary.

With the fee question settled, the discussion turns to the conduct of the defense. Suppose the defendant starts bringing in all sorts of incriminating evidence, such as the nun's rosary and prayer book. Peruto faces a dilemma. If he holds this stuff or even notes it, he is covering up a felony. But if he hands it over to authorities, what kind of defense attorney is he? He resolves the dilemma by—literally—averting his eyes. He fixes on a spot somewhere near the ceiling and tells his client, "Take your belongings and you get out of here with them." Again, it sounds cynical, but how else does one resolve this ethical dilemma? Much the same dilemma is presented by Butch Barnes's insistence that he, Barnes, must get on the stand and tell lies. Peruto's approach is to distance himself from his client—"it's his trial, not mine"—and at the same time protect him by trying to dissuade him from testifying. Another attempt, perhaps less than successful, to avoid the horns of a dilemma.

II: THE CONSTABLE BLUNDERS

How relieved are the defense attorneys to reach this part of the discussion! Baker is delighted that she can now "do some lawyering," and Peruto has stopped looking at the ceiling. Now they are both talking confidently about the legal protections available to Barnes. It seems that the cops charged into his room, casually waved a scrap of paper they said was a warrant, and threw him up against the wall. "Whose are these?" they said of the rosary beads, and Butch told them everything. It sounds like a combination of *Mapp* and *Miranda*. The defense attorneys would move to suppress both the evidence and the confessions because of an improper warrant and the failure to give Barnes his *Miranda* warnings. But does it bother them that the exclusion of this damning evidence could put a vicious maniac back on the street? "I'd rather think it was in the sense of the preservation of the presumption of innocence," says Peruto. "Cut through it, though," the moderator persists. How do you explain this to your daughter? What would you tell her? Peruto: "Go to medical school."

James Neal is not so ready to give up trying to justify the exclusionary rule. He says that he would tell his daughter that "if we didn't have this exclusionary rule, then we would have the police running around violating our constitutional rights." Sure, "it is unfortunate that this kind of a man will go free, but this is the price we pay for our wonderful system of justice." He pauses, sighs. "And I guess she wouldn't understand."

III: PRETRIAL PUBLICITY

In this section the discussion turns to the effect of heavy media coverage of a particularly grisly and violent case. Can a defendant get a fair trial under such circumstances? In the days when media were not as closely linked as they are today, the best solution was change of venue: move the trial to a different area where the news of it has been less intense. But in these days of national TV networks, newpaper chains, wire services, and the like, change of venue seems to have little effect. Another solution is to screen the jurors, excluding those who have followed the case too closely and acquired bias from the media's coverage. But it is just here that a new dilemma arises. The moderator skillfully puts it to Judge Pincham: the danger is that the screening process may give you either twelve hypocrites—jurors who admitted they followed the story but swore that they never formed opinions—or twelve ignoramuses—who never read the newpapers or followed the story on radio or TV. Judge Pincham is unfazed: "Oh, we'd get twelve if it took an eternity. And it might do that. But we'd get twelve." Even the statement "by the honorable Mayor" (he refers to New York Mayor Koch's statement that whoever did this was "an animal") would not be as prejudicial as one might think, says Pincham. The same is true of Dan Rather's coverage of the events. "In time you can get twelve jurors that would hear this case on the evidence, independent of the evidence that has been excluded. . . ." Peruto is having none of this. "We're kidding ourselves. Nobody can have that kind of knowledge, knowing that this physical evidence was found, knowing that there was a confession and say, 'Well, I'm going to put that out of my mind.'" It is like putting a drop of ink in a quart of milk, shaking the bottle vigorously, then trying to pull the drop out again. Baloney!"

IV: THE EXCLUSIONARY RULE

"Let's focus on the main question," says the moderator. "We have talked about the scenario that introduces it, but the main question is whether or not it makes sense. Does it, Mayor Koch?"

"No, it doesn't," Koch answers. He refers approvingly to a recent decision by a federal appeals court that it is a "rule of reason" rather than a strict constitutional requirement. Whether or not the evidence obtained by an illegal search is admitted should depend upon a number of factors, including the willfulness and malice of the arresting officers. After all, if the Supreme Court itself is divided by five-to-four votes on what police procedures are illegal, how are cops to know all the legal minutiae?

Mario Merola, District Attorney of the Bronx, is asked his opinion. He thinks that there isn't any question but that it has "helped the defense." He worries that we are forgetting about the victim of violent crime. And he suggests that judges ought to "restrict" the application of the exclusionary rule. FBI Director William Webster says that the exclusionary rule "in theory" advances professionalism in law enforcement, but he leaves open whether it does so in practice. He suggests that a "blanket, mechanical application" of the rule "does not serve the interests of justice." His position seems close to that of Mayor Koch. The last of the law-enforcement officials to comment on the rule is Benjamin Ward, who was then New York City's Correction Commissioner. (Ward has since become the city's Police Commissioner.) He is asked whether it has diminished respect for law-enforcement officers. He doesn't think so, and he doesn't find it a big problem, though he seems to agree with the others that the courts are right "to fashion some distinctions" concerning its use.

What is interesting is that none of these law-enforcement officials has utterly rejected the exclusionary rule. Nesson is looking for an argument and can't find one. "I don't hear anyone saying, 'I'm against the exclusionary rule.'" At that point a voice is heard off camera: "Didn't ask me." The camera swings to William Raspberry, *Washington Post* columnist. Raspberry explains:

> [I]t doesn't make any sense at all to exclude the solid, reliable evidence, physical and otherwise . . . that the cops find in that room. . . . I don't see whose interests are served by excluding it. Obviously if you're talking about coerced confessions that's something else again. If you're talking about a cop breaking and entering obviously there are some problems. If you're talking about . . . a blurted-out confession that—and the cop didn't—didn't put his hand over the suspect's mouth and shut him up while he read him his *Miranda* rights, I think it's—I think it's absurd.

There is a bit of hyperbole in this argument. Cops don't have to put their hands over suspects' mouths while they read them their *Miranda* warnings. It is simply that the confession made before the warnings are given cannot be used in court. If, later, under proper circumstances, the defendant repeats the confession, it is then valid evidence. We ought also to remember that a suspect does not necessarily "get off" because evidence is suppressed. Possibly Butch Barnes could have been convicted because of other evidence he left at the scene, or because he later bragged about his crime, or because of information acquired by the police from independent sources.

While we are on the subject of facts, it might be well to note some other facts about the exclusionary rule in practice. First, there is absolutely no empirical evidence that the exclusionary rule has had anything to do with the increase in violent crime since the time of the *Mapp* decision in 1961. Second, the number of cases thrown out of court or resulting in acquittals because of improper searches is minuscule. On the federal level, a 1979 study by the General Accounting Office put the figure at less than 0.5 percent, and at the state level it is not much higher (in 1980 California had the largest number, 4.8 percent, because of numerous "drug busts"). Third, and this may be a point for the other side of the controversy, there is no conclusive evidence that the adoption of the exclusionary rule has made the police any more professional or careful about avoiding Fourth and Fifth Amendment violations.

SUMMARY

William Raspberry's remarks may contain some exaggerations and misleading premises, but they strike responsive chords among Americans today. A decade or more ago it was fashionable in some circles to deride the slogan of "law and order," reducing it to one word, "lawnorder," which was then called "a code word for racism." This has fallen from fashion, and deservedly: blacks seem to be at least as concerned as whites about violent crime, for the very good reason that a disproportionate number of them are victims of it.

Even if there is no causal relationship between the increase in violent crime since the time of the 1961 *Mapp* decision and the decisions the Court was making during the '60s, the decisions still offend many people's sense of justice. Why, they say, should an obviously guilty person go free just because of technicalities? One can give all the answers—that "technical" violations often amount to violations of the Bill of Rights, that very few suspects actually do go free because of excluded evidence—yet sense that the answers are not enough. In the first place, there are answers to the answers: (1) there *are* some obviously guilty persons, such as the Christmas Eve killer in *Brewer* v. *Williams*, who actually led police to the body yet got the evidence suppressed; (2) no matter how small the percentage of cases thrown out of court on Fourth Amendment grounds, even one Butch Barnes sprung from jail is too many; and (3) technical violations may not always be violations of the United States Constitution.

Second, entirely apart from specific gripes about our court system is the more

general complaint that, as the phrase goes, "things have gotten out of hand." The suspicion of many people is that the scales have become unbalanced, that the criminals
are getting all the rights and society's safety is being slighted. Leaving aside the polem-
ical part of this statement, we can say that it contains one germ of truth: it acknowledges that there has been considerable movement toward the protection of suspects'
rights since the early years of the century. This chapter has surveyed the movement.
The catalogue of rights that, in the language of the *Palko* formula, are "of the very
essence of a scheme of ordered liberty" has grown steadily and impressively.

From one perspective, the movement amounts to progress toward a more humane
and just society. From another philosophical perspective, it is evidence of a society
whose legal structure has become increasingly flaccid, increasingly nonchalant about
protecting society from those who prey upon it. Both sides of the argument can review
the same history, consider the same cases, watch the same argument on TV—yet see
everything differently. Some day, perhaps, the consensus may be that one of these
visions was the correct one. In the meantime, those not yet entirely wed to either can
only wish the debate to continue.

Documents

MIRANDA V. ARIZONA 384 U.S. 436 (1966)

*Miranda v. Arizona held that the Fifth Amendment privilege against self-incrimination
requires that individuals taken into custody or otherwise deprived of their freedom
must be warned that they have a privilege against self-incrimination and a right to remain silent and to have counsel present during interrogation.*

Mr. Chief Justice Warren delivered the opinion of the Court.

The cases before us raise questions which go to the roots of our concepts of American criminal jurisprudence: the restraints society must observe consistent with the
Federal Constitution in prosecuting individuals for crime. More specifically, we deal
with the admissibility of statements obtained from an individual who is subjected to
custodial police interrogation and the necessity for procedures which assure that the
individual is accorded his privilege under the Fifth Amendment to the Constitution
not to be compelled to incriminate himself.

. . .

Our holding will be spelled out with some specificity in the pages which follow
but briefly stated it is this: the prosecution may not use statements, whether excul-
patory or inculpatory, stemming from custodial interrogation of the defendant unless
it demonstrates the use of procedural safeguards effective to secure the privilege against
self-incrimination. By custodial interrogation, we mean questioning initiated by law
enforcement officers after a person has been taken into custody or otherwise deprived

of his freedom of action in any significant way. As for the procedural safeguards to be employed, unless other fully effective means are devised to inform accused persons of their right of silence and to assure a continuous opportunity to exercise it, the following measures are required. Prior to any questioning, the person must be warned that he has a right to remain silent, that any statement he does make may be used as evidence against him, and that he has a right to the presence of an attorney, either retained or appointed. The defendant may waive effectuation of these rights, provided the waiver is made voluntarily, knowingly and intelligently. If, however, he indicates in any manner and at any stage of the process that he wishes to consult with an attorney before speaking there can be no questioning. Likewise, if the individual is alone and indicates in any manner that he does not wish to be interrogated, the police may not question him. The mere fact that he may have answered some questions or volunteered some statements on his own does not deprive him of the right to refrain from answering any further inquiries until he has consulted with an attorney and thereafter consents to be questioned.

. . .

Today, then, there can be no doubt that the Fifth Amendment privilege is available outside of criminal court proceedings and serves to protect persons in all settings in which their freedom of action is curtailed in any significant way from being compelled to incriminate themselves. We have concluded that without proper safeguards the process of in-custody interrogation of persons suspected or accused of crime contains inherently compelling pressures which work to undermine the individual's will to resist and to compel him to speak where he would not otherwise do so freely. In order to combat these pressures and to permit a full opportunity to exercise the privilege against self-incrimination, the accused must be adequately and effectively apprised of his rights and the exercise of those rights must be fully honored.

It is impossible for us to foresee the potential alternatives for protecting the privilege which might be devised by Congress or the States in the exercise of their creative rule-making capacities. Therefore we cannot say that the Constitution necessarily requires adherence to any particular solution for the inherent compulsions of the interrogation process as it is presently conducted. Our decision in no way creates a constitutional straitjacket which will handicap sound efforts at reform, nor is it intended to have this effect. We encourage Congress and the States to continue their laudable search for increasingly effective ways of protecting the rights of the individual while promoting efficient enforcement of our criminal laws. However, unless we are shown other procedures which are at least as effective in apprising accused persons of their right of silence and in assuring a continuous opportunity to exercise it, the following safeguards must be observed.

To summarize, we hold that when an individual is taken into custody or otherwise deprived of his freedom by the authorities in any significant way and is subjected to questioning, the privilege against self-incrimination is jeopardized. Procedural safeguards must be employed to protect the privilege, and unless other fully effective means are adopted to notify the person of his right of silence and to assure that the exercise of the right will be scrupulously honored, the following measures are required. He must be warned prior to any questioning that he has the right to remain silent, that anything he says can be used against him in a court of law, that he has the right to the presence of an attorney, and that if he cannot afford an attorney one will be appointed for him prior to any questioning if he so desires. Opportunity to exercise these rights must be afforded to him throughout the interrogation. After such warnings have been given, and such opportunity afforded him, the individual may knowingly and intelligently waive these rights and agree to answer questions or make a statement. But unless and until such warnings and waiver are demonstrated by the prosecution at trial, no evidence obtained as a result of interrogation can be used against him.

Mr. Justice Harlan dissented from the judgment of the Court on the grounds that the due process clauses of the Fifth and Fourteenth Amendments are the proper foundation of suspects' rights in the custody and interrogation context and that the Court's broad requirement might diminish the effectiveness of law enforcement.

Mr. Justice Harlan, dissenting.

I believe the decision of the Court represents poor constitutional law and entails harmful consequences for the country at large. How serious these consequences may prove to be only time can tell. But the basic flaws in the Court's justification seem to me readily apparent now once all sides of the problem are considered.

. . .

The new rules are not designed to guard against police brutality or other unmistakably banned forms of coercion. Those who use third-degree tactics and deny them in court are equally able and destined to lie as skillfully about warnings and waivers. Rather, the thrust of the new rules is to negate all pressures, to reinforce the nervous or ignorant suspect, and ultimately to discourage any confession at all. The aim in short is toward "voluntariness" in a utopian sense, or to view it from a different angle, voluntariness with a vengeance.

To incorporate this notion into the Constitution requires a strained reading of history and precedent and a disregard of the very pragmatic concerns that alone may on occasion justify such strains. I believe that reasoned examination will show that the Due Process Clauses provide an adequate tool for coping with confessions and that, even if the Fifth Amendment privilege against self-incrimination be invoked, its precedents taken as a whole do not sustain the present rules. Viewed as a choice based on pure policy, these new rules prove to be a highly debatable, if not one-sided, appraisal of the competing interests, imposed over widespread objection, at the very time when judicial restraint is most called for by the circumstances.

. . .

How much harm this decision will inflict on law enforcement cannot fairly be predicted with accuracy. Evidence on the role of confessions is notoriously incomplete, see Developments, *supra,* n. 2, at 941–944, and little is added by the Court's reference to the FBI experience and the resources believed wasted in interrogation. See *infra,* n. 19, and text. We do know that some crimes cannot be solved without confessions, that ample expert testimony attests to their importance in crime control, and that the Court is taking a real risk with society's welfare in imposing its new regime on the country. The social costs of crime are too great to call the new rules anything but a hazardous experimentation.

While passing over the costs and risks of its experiment, the Court portrays the evils of normal police questioning in terms which I think are exaggerated. Albeit stringently confined by the due process standards interrogation is no doubt often inconvenient and unpleasant for the suspect. However, it is no less so for a man to be arrested and jailed, to have his house searched, or to stand trial in court, yet all this may properly happen to the most innocent given probable cause, a warrant, or an indictment. Society has always paid a stiff price for law and order, and peaceful interrogation is not one of the dark moments of the law.

MAPP V. OHIO 367 U.S. 643 (1961)

Mapp v. Ohio *held that the search-and-seizure provisions of the Fourth Amendment prohibit a state from using evidence seized in an illegal search in a criminal prosecution.*

Mr. Justice Clark delivered the opinion of the Court.

. . .

Today we once again examine *Wolf's* constitutional documentation of the right to privacy free from unreasonable state intrusion, and, after its dozen years on our books, are led by it to close the only courtroom door remaining open to evidence secured by official lawlessness in flagrant abuse of that basic right, reserved to all persons as a specific guarantee against that very same unlawful conduct. We hold that all evidence obtained by searches and seizures in violation of the Constitution is, by that same authority, inadmissible in a state court.

Since the Fourth Amendment's right of privacy has been declared enforceable against the States through the Due Process Clause of the Fourteenth, it is enforceable against them by the same sanction of exclusion as is used against the Federal Government. Were it otherwise, then just as without the *Weeks* rule the assurance against unreasonable federal searches and seizures would be "a form of words," valueless and undeserving of mention in a perpetual charter of inestimable human liberties, so too, without that rule the freedom from state invasions of privacy would be so ephemeral and so neatly severed from its conceptual nexus with the freedom from all brutish means of coercing evidence as not to merit this Court's high regard as a freedom "implicit in the concept of ordered liberty."

. . .

The ignoble shortcut to conviction left open to the State tends to destroy the entire system of constitutional restraints on which the liberties of the people rest. Having once recognized that the right to privacy embodied in the Fourth Amendment is enforceable against the States, and that the right to be secure against rude invasions of privacy by state officers is, therefore, constitutional in origin, we can no longer permit that right to remain an empty promise. Because it is enforceable in the same manner and to like effect as other basic rights secured by the Due Process Clause, we can no longer permit it to be revocable at the whim of any police officer who, in the name of law enforcement itself, chooses to suspend its enjoyment. Our decision, founded on reason and truth, gives to the individual no more than that which the Constitution guarantees him, to the police officer no less than that to which honest law enforcement is entitled, and, to the courts, that judicial integrity so necessary in the true administration of justice.

Mr. Justice Harlan dissented from the judgment of the Court on the grounds that the Fourteenth Amendment allows states to determine the specifics of their own trial procedures. He also argued that the Court jeopardized its integrity by making a decision on an issue not really central to the case before it.

Mr. Justice Harlan, dissenting.

In overruling the *Wolf* case the Court, in my opinion, has forgotten the sense of judicial restraint which, with due regard for *stare decisis*, is one element that should enter into deciding whether a past decision of this Court should be overruled. Apart from that I also believe that the *Wolf* rule represents sounder Constitutional doctrine than the new rule which now replaces it.

From the Court's statement of the case one would gather that the central, if not controlling, issue on this appeal is whether illegally state-seized evidence is Constitutionally admissible in a state prosecution, an issue which would of course face us with the need for re-examining *Wolf.* However, such is not the situation. For, although that question was indeed raised here and below among appellant's subordinate points, the new and pivotal issue brought to the Court by this appeal is whether § 2905.34 of the Ohio Revised Code making criminal the *mere* knowing possession or control of obscene material, and under which appellant has been convicted, is consistent with the rights of free thought and expression assured against state action by the Fourteenth Amendment. That was the principal issue which was decided by the Ohio Supreme Court, which was tendered by appellant's Jurisdictional Statement, and which was briefed and argued in this Court.

In this posture of things, I think it fair to say that five members of this Court have simply "reached out" to overrule *Wolf.* With all respect for the views of the majority, and recognizing that *stare decisis* carries different weight in Constitutional adjudication than it does in nonconstitutional decision, I can perceive no justification for regarding this case as an appropriate occasion for re-examining *Wolf.*

The action of the Court finds no support in the rule that decision of Constitutional issues should be avoided wherever possible.

. . .

I am bound to say that what has been done is not likely to promote respect either for the Court's adjudicatory process or for the stability of its decisions. Having been unable, however, to persuade any of the majority to a different procedural course, I now turn to the merits of the present decision.

. . .

A state conviction comes to us as the complete product of a sovereign judicial system. Typically a case will have been tried in a trial court, tested in some final appellate court, and will go no further. In the comparatively rare instance when a conviction is reviewed by us on due process grounds we deal then with a finished product in the creation of which we are allowed no hand, and our task, far from being one of overall supervision, is, speaking generally, restricted to a determination of whether the prosecution was Constitutionally fair. The specifics of trial procedure, which in every mature legal system will vary greatly in detail, are within the sole competence of the States. I do not see how it can be said that a trial becomes unfair simply because a State determines that evidence may be considered by the trier of fact, regardless of how it was obtained, if it is relevant to the one issue with which the trial is concerned, the guilt or innocence of the accused. Of course, a court may use its procedures as an incidental means of pursuing other ends than the correct resolution of the controversies before it. Such indeed is the *Weeks* rule, but if a State does not choose to use its courts in this way, I do not believe that this Court is empowered to impose this much-debated procedure on local courts, however efficacious we may consider the *Weeks* rule to be as a means of securing Constitutional rights.

. . .

I regret that I find so unwise in principle and so inexpedient in policy a decision motivated by the high purpose of increasing respect for Constitutional rights. But in the last analysis I think this Court can increase respect for the Constitution only if it rigidly respects the limitations which the Constitution places upon it, and respects as well the principles inherent in its own processes. In the present case I think we exceed both, and that our voice becomes only a voice of power, not of reason.

SELECTED READINGS

Fellman, David. *The Defendant's Rights Today.* Madison, Wisc.: University of Wisconsin Press, 1976.
  Fellman's book covers defendants' rights in many areas, including rights at the time of arrest, the right to counsel, rights in the context of searches and seizures, and rights against self-incrimination. The volume is both a convenient handbook of rights and a scholarly commentary on the case law and principles involved in each of the rights considered.
Friendly, Henry J. "The Bill of Rights as a Code of Criminal Procedure." *California Law Review* 53 (October 1965): 929-956.
  Federal Appeals Court Judge Friendly argues that, in a federal system of govern-

ment, the due process clause of the Fourteenth Amendment should not be understood as requiring rigid uniformity of procedure among states.

Henkin, Louis. "'Selective Incorporation' in the Fourteenth Amendment." *Yale Law Journal* 73 (1963): 74–88.

Professor Henkin examines the cases concerning the doctrine of selective incorporation and argues that, while there are good reasons why all the substantive liberties found in the Bill of Rights ought also to be incorporated into the Fourteenth Amendment concept of "liberty," there are not such good reasons why all the procedural provisions in the Bill of Rights ought also to be incorporated into the Fourteenth Amendment concept of due process.

Jacob, Herbert. *Justice in America*, 4th ed. Boston: Little, Brown, 1984.

An excellent, quick introduction to the organization, procedures, and personnel of both the state and federal judiciaries. Note, in particular, the chapters on policy-making by the courts and criminal trials.

Lewis, Anthony. *Gideon's Trumpet*. New York: Random House, 1960.

This is the moving story of Clarence Gideon and of the case of *Gideon* v. *Wainwright*, which established the constitutional right of the indigent to an attorney in noncapital state criminal prosecutions. Lewis clearly and thoroughly explains the procedural, political, and legal aspects of the federal judicial process. The book is "must" reading for all new students of the judicial process and constitutional law.

Silberman, Charles E. *Criminal Violence, Criminal Justice*. New York: Random House, 1978.

Silberman introduces the reader to two related cultures: the culture of crime, in which poverty plays a part, and the institutional culture of the criminal justice system. The book is essential reading for anyone who thinks there are simple solutions to crime or simple reforms for the criminal justice system. It contains an extensive bibliography.

Stewart, Potter. "The Road to *Mapp* v. *Ohio* and Beyond: The Origins, Development and Future of the Exclusionary Rule in Search-and-Seizure Cases." *Columbia Law Review* 83 (October 1983): 1365–1409.

Retired U.S. Supreme Court Justice Potter Stewart explains the historical origin of the Fourth Amendment, the judicial development of the exclusionary rule in case law, and the practical and constitutional arguments against the exclusionary rule.

GLOSSARY

Absorption.   Justice Benjamin Cardozo's theory that only some elements of the Bill of Rights apply to the states through the due process clause of the Fourteenth Amendment—specifically, those elements that are "of the very essence of a scheme of ordered liberty."

Double jeopardy. Holding someone twice "in jeopardy of life or limb"; for example, retrying someone already acquitted of a capital crime for the same offense. The practice is prohibited by the Fifth Amendment.

Due process. A clause, found in both the Fifth and Fourteenth Amendments, prohibiting the federal and state governments respectively from depriving people of "life, liberty, or property, without due process of law."

Exclusionary rule. A rule preventing the use of illegally seized evidence against a defendant in a criminal trial.

Incorporation. Applying parts of the Bill of Rights to the states through the due process clause of the Fourteenth Amendment. Justice Hugo Black favored *total incorporation*—applying the entire Bill of Rights. Instead, Supreme Court majorities have *selectively incorporated* the Bill of Rights.

Miranda warnings. A term referring to the case of *Miranda* v. *Arizona* (1966), in which the Supreme Court ruled that before any suspects under arrest can be questioned by the police, they must first be warned of their right to remain silent, their right to have an attorney present, their right to a court-appointed attorney should they lack the means to hire one, and the fact that anything they say may be used in evidence against them.

Pretrial publicity. Intensive news coverage of a crime and of the criminal suspect(s) prior to a trial; the coverage may prejudice jurors.

Procedural safeguards. Constitutional guarantees that individuals suspected of crimes are treated fairly by law-enforcement officials.

Search warrant. Court-obtained permission, given to law-enforcement officials, to search someone's premises.

Chapter 5
Criminal and Insane

"How do you punish somebody who is insane?"
GERRY SPENCE

"Even though we had the doctors and the professors there, they did not prove anything either with all their knowledge and degrees."
MARYLAND T. COPELIN
Juror in the Hinckley trial

THE CASE OF JOHN W. HINCKLEY

On March 30, 1981, a twenty-seven-year-old drifter named John W. Hinckley, Jr., fired six bullets at President Ronald Reagan as the president emerged from a Washington hotel. One of the shots hit Reagan, inflicting a dangerous chest wound; two went wild; and the other three wounded Secret Service Agent Timothy McCarthy, a Washington policeman named Thomas Delahanty, and James Brady, President Reagan's press secretary. Brady, shot through the forehead, was the most seriously wounded. Since Hinckley used exploding bullets, the shot inflicted extensive, apparently irreversible brain damage.

Hinckley committed the act in full view of scores of witnesses—indeed, in front of news cameras. There was no question about his having done it. Yet, after an eight-week trial, thousands of pages of testimony, and a total cost to all sides of about $3 million, he was acquitted by a twelve-member jury in Washington, D.C., on grounds of insanity. He now resides in St. Elizabeth's Hospital, a mental institution in the District of Columbia. He will probably be there for a long time, though his case is subject to review every six months. If he is judged no longer sick or dangerous enough to require institutionalization, he will be released. As Hinckley quite accurately pointed out in one of his occasional phone calls to the *Washington Post*, if the doctors give the go-ahead and get a judge's approval, "I'm going to walk out the door whether the public likes it or not."

The Hinckley case brought to a boil what was already simmering in the public's consciousness: an angry suspicion that the insanity defense was—literally—letting people get away with murder and mayhem. The president of the United States was wounded in the chest and his press secretary permanently maimed, yet the admitted perpetrator was declared "not guilty" and sent to a hospital for what might turn out to be a limited

138

stay. "It's a Mad, Mad Verdict" was the title of a *New Republic* article on the trial. Lawmakers and the public were ready to go further: they wondered whether the whole concept of insanity defenses was not fundamentally crazy. Radical changes in the laws were called for by public officials. A United States Senate subcommittee conducted hearings to consider changing federal law on the subject; five of the jurors in the Hinckley case were summoned to testify. Commentators, even those with strong libertarian sympathies, wondered whether something had gone wrong in the application of what had once been considered a humane standard. As for the general public, a 1981 Associated Press–NBC News poll showed that 87 percent thought that too many murderers were not sent to jail because of insanity pleas; 70 percent favored total elimination of the insanity defense.

Hinckley's Competence

It was not as if John Hinckley were totally mad. If he were a raving lunatic, staggering about with his eyes rolling in their sockets, he most likely would be declared incompetent to stand trial. "Incompetence" is a legal term that means the defendant is so mentally impaired that he does not even understand the charges against him and is not able in any way to participate in his defense. If that were the case, the defendant would be confined to an institution until competent to stand trial; there would have to be a civil proceeding to determine whether permanent confinement were necessary. None of this applied to Hinckley. He was competent enough to make airline reservations, pay his bills, check in and out of motels as he roamed the country stalking Ronald Reagan and, before him, Jimmy Carter. There are degrees of madness, and John Hinckley's did not amount to incompetence.

Hinckley's "Illness"

What, then, was the nature of his illness? That is not easy to answer. There were several thousand pages of testimony at the trial, much of it from psychiatrists who could not agree on the nature of his illness. Was he "schizophrenic"? "Delusional"? Or merely "anomic"? Behind all the jargon were confusion and uncertainty; the experts simply could not agree. One of the jurors, a fifty-two-year-old cafeteria worker, expressed the frustration of many others on the jury: "Even though we had the doctors and the professors there, they did not prove anything either with all their knowledge and degrees." Yet the burden of proof had been placed upon the prosecution. It had to prove to the jury "beyond a reasonable doubt" that Hinckley was sane! In the case of a man who tried to kill the president because he had a crush on movie actress Jodie Foster, that was obviously a heavy burden of proof. "I sacrificed myself and committed the ultimate crime in hopes of winning the heart of a girl," he wrote. What *do* we do with such a person?

The Video Discussion

The video debate revolves around a hypothetical case that closely resembles the Hinckley case and raises many of the same issues. What do we do with the Hinckleys, the obviously disturbed people who commit violent crimes? How do we determine whether such people are competent to stand trial? What happens if a defendant is adjudged incompetent? Suppose he is adjudged competent but he insists on conducting his own very crazy defense: Should he be allowed to do so? Finally, and most importantly, is the insanity defense a just and fair one? Does it need to be abolished or modified? There are many other issues in the debate, but these are the ones the participants keep circling as they grope for answers to the moderator's challenges. The moderator is Harvard Law Professor Charles R. Nesson.

List of Participants

HON. ARTHUR L. ALARCON
Judge
U.S. Court of Appeals
Ninth Circuit

HON. BARNEY FRANK
U.S. Representative
State of Massachusetts

VINCENT J. FULLER
Attorney
Williams & Connolly

WILLARD GAYLIN, M.D.
President
The Hastings Center for Bioethics

RUDOLPH W. GIULIANI
U.S. Attorney
Southern District of New York
Former Associate Attorney General,
Department of Justice

HON. IRVING R. KAUFMAN
Judge
U.S. Court of Appeals
Second Circuit

HON. JOAN DEMPSEY KLEIN
Presiding Justice
California Court of Appeal

MARIO MEROLA
District Attorney
Bronx County, New York City

BILL MOYERS
Senior News Analyst
CBS News

LOREN H. ROTH, M.D.
Professor of Psychiatry
University of Pittsburgh;
Codirector
Law and Psychiatry Program
Western Psychiatric Institute
and Clinic

GERRY SPENCE
Attorney
Spence, Moriarity & Schuster

HON. POTTER STEWART
Retired Justice
U.S. Supreme Court

ALAN STONE, M.D.
Professor of Law and Psychiatry
Harvard Law and Medical Schools

HON. JAMES R. THOMPSON
Governor
State of Illinois

Program Summary

The moderator begins by outlining the hypothetical. "Here's the story," he says.

> Oscar King was a candidate for the Senate in Piedmont. He's been a prominent actor, a lot of movies, not great, kind of Westerns, John Wayne kind of character. Gotten out of the acting business, gone into politics. He looked like a good prospect for the Senate. Harvey Brink, young fellow, twenty-five, college dropout, always had trouble keeping a grip on reality. Somehow he had gotten fascinated with Oscar King. Had watched all of his movies and decided that he should be King's strategist in his campaign, and so had written some memos for him, sent them off to him, heard nothing.
>
> And as time went on, Brink got fixated with the idea that in fact, King was not the hero he thought he was, but in fact a very evil person. As he listened to his speeches he would imagine King speaking to him, threatening things. And one day when King was talking to a group of businessmen, Harvey Brink in the audience pulled out a thirty-eight and shot King—dead.

The program is then divided roughly into three parts. The first part concerns the question of competence. What are the standards for determining competence to stand trial? What procedures and strategies does a defense lawyer use at this initial stage of an insanity defense? What strategies are resorted to by the prosecution? What happens if someone is found incompetent to stand trial? Can he or she be kept in confinement indefinitely? Can an incompetent defendant be "restored" to competence?

The second part begins with the assumption that Harvey Brink is found competent to stand trial. But that is an extremely minimal standard. A very disturbed person can be held competent, and Harvey Brink seems to fit that description. This part centers on the issue of whether a mentally ill person should be allowed to conduct his or her own defense. Can an attorney plead an insanity defense without the defendant's permission? What techniques do defense attorneys use with disturbed people in order to persuade them to use an insanity defense? Who is in charge of the management of the case? Can such defendants fire their lawyers and argue their cases themselves?

The third and last section reaches the heart of the insanity defense issue. Are the psychiatrists who testify at such trials really supplying objective evidence—or is it all speculation and subjective impressions? Do the psychiatrists really serve as "hired guns" for the prosecution and defense? What is the central issue in an insanity trial—insanity or guilt? Are the two related? How does the question of intent relate to insanity? Can insane people really be considered to have intent? How do we assess responsibility in the case of an insane defendant? Should the insanity defense be abandoned or modified?

It is the last section which is the most controversial and confusing. The moderator works his way up to it by considering two areas for which standards are clearer.

I: COMPETENCE TO STAND TRIAL

The first question to consider is whether the accused is competent to stand trial. Again, it must be emphasized that the question of competence is different, at least in degree, from the question of whether the defendant is insane. An incompetent person is so detached from reality as to be unable to understand the charges and to participate in the defense. Someone with the mentality of a two-year-old could be classified as incompetent.

What does the state do with such a person? The first question to ask is whether the person is permanently or only temporarily incompetent. A killer could be so deranged at the time of the deed as to be incompetent to stand trial, yet he or she could become competent in a matter of weeks or months, perhaps with psychiatric help, so as to be able to stand trial. This psychological possibility is often closely bound to the strategy of the defense. The remarks of attorney Gerry Spence at the beginning of the program show the outlines of a typical defense strategy at the outset of a trial.

Gerry Spence is a "country slicker." He wears a buckskin jacket and cowboy boots everywhere and has a soft Wyoming drawl. But he has a regional and, increasingly, national reputation for his ability to win huge damage awards for clients and to get acquittals for others in seemingly hopeless cases. He knows the legal minutiae as well as any lawyer but pretends he is just an ordinary guy trying to solve problems through common sense and compassion.

Compassion is Spence's stock in trade. The first thing he wants to do with his client in this case is to "have a sense of him. He's a human being and . . . he's afraid, and he's in a strange place, and he's committed . . . a horrible crime." By this time the moderator has started portraying himself as the disturbed Harvey Brink, and Spence says to him, "I'd like to kind of walk with you hand in hand through your life." Spence sounds like a preacher. But the preacher in this case is concerned with earthly salvation. "You know," he says, "the law is a game in a way," and the "next thing the state wants to do in its game is kill him." To keep his client from being killed, Spence is going to press the state from the very beginning. The beginning is a competency hearing. Is Spence's client fit to stand trial? Spence's opening gambit is to win a "no" answer, or at least a "no—not yet." He wants to use "competency" as a means of delaying the trial. And why does he want to do that? His voice is soothing, the preacher-tone is evident: "Time heals anger, and that would be nice—if we could get a little healing to occur here so that justice could do a better job." But he had already put it more candidly. He wants the delay so that "people will soften up down the line; maybe they'll feel better a year from now, maybe they'll forget." From the outset of the legal proceedings, then, it appears that the question of the defendant's state of mind is not an issue independent of the strategies of both sides but inextricably connected with them. The defense wants its client declared temporarily incompetent so as to delay the trial and thus dull people's memories of the crime. The prosecution has a contrary interest. What strategy will the prosecutors pursue?

Spence jumps in with his own answer: "They're going to hire an incompetent psychiatrist!" Here we have the first reference to the role of psychiatrists in the courtroom.

Spence's gibe exemplifies a frequently heard suggestion made about psychiatrists—namely, that they serve as "hired guns" for whichever side of the case pays their fees. Thus, a prosecutor will get himself a psychiatrist who will certify that Harvey Brink is indeed competent to stand trial. When the moderator turns to Mario Merola, district attorney of the Bronx, to ask if that is indeed a "foregone conclusion," Merola demurs, but very mildly. "Well, it's not a foregone conclusion, but. . . ." Moderator: "But close, huh?" Merola says that "the inexactness of the science of psychiatry" means that you can get psychiatrists on all sides of insanity cases—which sounds as if he pretty well agrees with Spence.

At this stage of the trial, the psychiatrist's role is relatively modest. All that has to be determined is whether the defendant is competent. Merola is ready to go to court once he gets a testimony that (1) Harvey knew Oscar, (2) Harvey aimed the gun at him and hit him, and (3) Harvey was convinced that he was shooting at Oscar "and not at a windmill." Since all these criteria fit Oscar—just as they fit John Hinckley—he is competent to stand trial. Even Spence does not object.

But suppose Oscar were not competent. What then? Vincent Fuller, another of the attorneys on the panel, seems to suggest that Oscar could be held in a mental hospital, without any trial, indefinitely. If that is what he is saying, he may be mistaken. The Supreme Court has spoken on the issue.

Jackson v. *Indiana* (1972): No Indefinite Confinement Without Trial

Theon Jackson was a twenty-seven-year-old deaf mute with the mental level of a preschool child. He was charged with petty theft (stealing $4 from one woman and $5 from another), but psychiatrists and a deaf-school interpreter testified that he was unable to understand the charges, even in sign language. All agreed that his prognosis was dim, that his condition appeared to be irreversible. The trial judge found that Jackson "lack[ed] comprehension sufficient to make his defense" and ordered him sent to a mental hospital until the state health department certified him as "sane." That meant, in all probability, for life. Without a trial, Theon Jackson was given a life sentence for stealing $9.

The Supreme Court overturned the judge's confinement order on the grounds that it violated Jackson's constitutional rights of "equal protection of the laws" and "due process of law." Jackson had now been held in a hospital for three years. Assuming that he remained incompetent, he had to be either released or given a civil trial to decide whether the state had a right to hold him in the hospital.

Of course, Theon Jackson was no Harvey Brink. He had not killed anyone; nor was there any showing that he was dangerous. The Court hedged on the question of whether a violent incompetent could be held indefinitely without trial. Federal law seems to leave room for it, and the Court distinguished *Jackson* from a federal case on the ground that Jackson was not considered dangerous. But since no one could say that of Harvey Brink, Fuller might be able to argue that in this case indefinite confinement does not necessarily violate the Constitution.

But all of this becomes, as the lawyers say, moot—neither here nor there. For Harvey Brink is held to be competent. He may be crazy, but he is not that crazy. He knows the charges against him and can participate in his defense.

But can he run his own defense the way he wants? Can he testify at the trial even if his lawyer tells him it is against his interests and safety to do so? Can he order his lawyers about? Can he fire them if he likes, and handle his own defense? This brings us to Part II of the video discussion.

II: COMPETENCE TO DEFEND ONESELF

Yossarian, the hero of Joseph Heller's World War II novel *Catch-22*, spends much of his time trying to get out of dangerous combat duty. One way to get out of it is to convince the company doctor that he is insane. Probing the doctor a bit, Yossarian asks about one of the other pilots. Is he crazy? Yes, of course, says the doctor. "He has to be crazy to keep flying combat missions after all the close calls he's had." But before he can be grounded, he first has to request it.

> "That's all he has to do to be grounded?"
> "That's all. Let him ask me."
> "And then you can ground him?" Yossarian asked.
> "No. Then I can't ground him."
> "You mean there's a catch?"
> "Sure there's a catch," Doc Daneeka replied. "Catch-22. Anyone who wants to get out of combat duty isn't really crazy."

There is something about this convoluted reasoning that may be relevant to insanity defenses. Someone who is really crazy would not plead insanity, for really crazy people do not consider themselves insane. Therefore, the fact that someone pleads insanity is proof that he or she is not insane.

Of course, there is a resolution to this dilemma; it comes through the role of the defendant's attorney. It was not John Hinckley who stood before the jurors and argued, eloquently and cogently, that he was mad. It was his attorney who did it for him and who did all the other things necessary to his defense. Typically, the defendant in any criminal case leaves the management of the defense to his attorney, and this is especially true when the defendant is mentally disturbed.

But suppose the defendant refuses to plead insanity. The moderator tries this out on attorney Fuller by impersonating Harvey Brink: "I'm not crazy. What do you think I shot this guy for? Because I was crazy? I shot him because he was an evil person and he was about to do the world great damage."

Fuller is pleased to hear this kind of talk from his client. It shows just how crazy he is. "I may have a fantastic case of insanity." What he has forgotten is that an attorney cannot plead insanity for his client unless he gets the client's permission—and Harvey is in no mood to give such permission. He has to be persuaded. Fuller is confident he can do that. The moderator wonders whether such "persuasion" does not often amount to manipulation. As if to prove the point, Gerry Spence gives the moderator an idea of how he would "persuade" Brink to plead insanity. We're going to talk, says Spence, about the fact that "you're afraid of what's going to happen to you in the future, you feel trapped." Then he makes his pitch: "I know what that's about, I have feelings like that myself. I sometimes am afraid too, and sometimes am trapped. And we want out of this trap." The moderator terms this the "get-into-bed-with-him-and-bring-him-along theory." Spence's approach raises an ethical question. Is it right for an attorney to manipulate a client into pleading insanity?

On the one hand, the Sixth Amendment ensures that the accused shall enjoy "the Assistance of Counsel for his defense," which means he deserves the best defense he can get; in this case his counsel has determined that an insanity plea is the best strategy. As Spence says in another connection, "It sure beats the hell out of the gas chamber." On the other hand we recognize the defendant as an individual, and if individualism means anything, it means that people should have a right to decide what to do with their lives. Harvey Brink has been held competent to stand trial. Since that is the case, is he not competent to manage his own defense? Or are there degrees of competence? A defendant may understand the charges and be able to *participate* in the defense. But does *participating* mean the same as *managing*?

Not as far as Fuller is concerned—or at least, not while Fuller is representing him. Brink can always fire me, he says, and find some attorney who will go along with his irrational defense strategy. But even then Fuller is not ready to concede that Brink has any right to manage his own defense. He does not understand how, in a case like Brink's, "a court could permit a defendant to waive an insanity defense."

What does the law say about such an issue? As is often the case, the law says many things, some of which lend support to Fuller's view. One thing it seems to say, though, is that a criminal defendant competent to stand trial is competent to handle his or her own defense. The leading Supreme Court case is *Faretta* v. *California*, decided by a six-to-three majority in 1975.

Faretta v. *California*: A Defendant May Conduct His Own Defense

Anthony Faretta, charged with grand theft in California, wanted to conduct his own defense. He had no law degree, but he wanted to be his own lawyer. At first the judge agreed, albeit reluctantly, but later, after questioning Faretta about his preparation of the case, he changed his mind and refused even to allow Faretta to serve as co-counsel. Faretta, against his will, was given a public defender. He was found guilty, and he appealed to the Supreme Court, charging that his Sixth Amendment right to counsel was abrogated.

In the last chapter we discussed the right to counsel as it evolved from the case of "the Scottsboro boys," *Powell* v. *Alabama* in 1932, to *Gideon* v. *Wainwright* in 1963. Now, in a way, we have the obverse issue: not whether defendants have the right to state-appointed counsel but rather whether they have the right to *refuse* counsel. In his majority opinion, Justice Stewart's answer was: yes, or at least, yes in cases involving defendants like Faretta.

Faretta was no lawyer, but he had his wits about him and had acquired an amateur's knowledge of law. He also knew the dangers of forsaking legal representation; he was going into the trial with his eyes open. "The record affirmatively shows that Faretta was literate, competent, and understanding, and that he was voluntarily exercising his free will." To force a lawyer upon such a defendant is to violate "the logic of the [Sixth] Amendment." The amendment "speaks of the 'assistance' of counsel, and an assistant, however expert, is still an assistant." To force him upon the defendant would be to make him "master"!

Yet Fuller could also appeal to the majority opinion in *Faretta* to support his view that Harvey Brink needs counsel whether he wants it or not. Faretta was fully lucid. Harvey Brink is at best confused, if not totally out of touch. In order to represent himself, Justice Stewart said, quoting from an earlier case, the accused must "knowingly and intelligently" renounce the benefit of counsel. Citing another precedent, he said that the record must establish that the defendant "knows what he is doing and his choice is made with eyes open." Whether Brink's "eyes" are fully "open" is a serious question. Moreover, in an earlier case, *Mayberry* v. *Pennsylvania* (1971), the Court suggested that a judge may appoint standby counsel to protect a defendant from himself. Speaking for the Court, Chief Justice Warren Burger said, "A criminal trial is not a private matter. The public interest is so great that the presence and participation of counsel, even when opposed by the accused, is warranted in order to vindicate the process itself." However, standby counsel seems to mean just that—standby. In the words of a federal appeals court, he "is to be seen, but not heard. He is not to compete with the defendant or supersede his defense."

How do the judges on the panel handle the issue of whether Brink has a right to be his own lawyer? They all sympathize with Fuller's position, but they are cautious about forcing Brink to retain an attorney. Judge Joan Dempsey Klein, who presides over California's Court of Appeal, is undoubtedly familiar with *Faretta* v. *California.* She agrees that "he's got a constitutional right for self-representation. . . . Even crazy people have some sort of a constitutional right allegedly to represent themselves." Her approach is to put a lot of pressure on him not to do it. She would say, "Look, you can't do it. You cannot." She puts so much into what seems at first a bluff that she ends up convincing herself. "I have that discretionary right, as I understand the status of the law, and I would not allow him to represent himself." This contradicts her earlier assertion that "even crazy people" can represent themselves, but now she says that her ruling "would probably be affirmed on appeal."

Judge Arthur Alarcon, a federal appeals court judge, says "I'm not as sure" it would be affirmed, though his opinion is so loaded down with qualifications that he never completes a sentence. He ends up by saying that *if* the defendant "has the mental capacity to represent himself . . ." and then passes the buck to "some psychiatrist to assist me in making that decision." Judge Irving Kaufman, another appeals court judge, clearly sides with Fuller. He does not want Brink representing himself. His way of getting around the *Faretta* precedent is simply to change the hypothetical. He supposes that Brink is going to fire his lawyer on the eve of summation and thus force the trial to begin all over again, delaying a verdict indefinitely. (In terms of *Catch-22*, that would prove he was not crazy after all.) "But," the moderator says, "if he doesn't want to go to a new trial, if he just wants to proceed" and make a thoroughly bizarre defense that his lawyer thinks is crazy, why can't he? Kaufman ends up by falling back on the *Mayfair* decision that a criminal trial is not a private affair and that backup counsel is sometimes warranted.

Why do these three judges want to force counsel upon an unwilling defendant? Probably because they are themselves trained in the law. They know how intricate and esoteric it is and how little chance even a level-headed layman has of adequately representing himself in a criminal trial. And if the old proverb "One who is his own lawyer has a fool for a client" is true for a normal person, how much more true it is for someone who is a fool to begin with, someone like Harvey Brink. The three judges can perhaps be faulted for their handling of precedents and their judicial reasoning but not for their goodwill and their sense of justice.

Before discussing the insanity defense, let's review some of the important points made so far.

Points to Remember

1. The first thing to consider in a legal proceeding in which a defendant's sanity may be an issue is whether the defendant is competent to stand trial. The standards for competence are minimal. Usually, they mean that the defendant is able to understand the charges and participate in the defense.
2. If the defendant is adjudged incompetent, he or she may not be held indefinitely in a mental hospital without a civil trial to determine whether this incompetence is permanent.
3. Defendants who are held competent and thus able to participate in their defense may represent themselves without counsel, at least if they have knowingly and intelligently forgone such assistance and if they have understanding and free will. However, a judge may appoint standby counsel, though the counsel cannot supersede a defendant's own handling of the case. At this writing, the very last clause above—requiring the standby counsel not to supersede the defendant—is being considered by the Supreme Court. All the rest is well settled.

    But much has not been settled, either because the law is uncertain or because of ethical considerations that do not admit of final answers. Without pretending to resolve such issues, we can at least identify them.

Unresolved Issues

1. Is it ethically right for a defense attorney to delay a trial so that people's memories of the crime will fade? Is justice served if the defense attorney concentrates

solely on defending his or her client? Does the attorney have any duty to a larger public?

2. Is it right for a defense attorney to use manipulative techniques to get his or her client to plead insanity?

3. Is it right for a judge to "pressure" defendants, by bluffing and bullying if necessary, to get them to accept counsel? Is it right for the judge to acquiesce in an obviously disturbed defendant's decision to conduct his or her own defense? Is there a point at which a defense becomes so bizarre that the judge must intervene and appoint counsel?

III: THE INSANITY DEFENSE

The first thing to remember about the word "insanity" is that it is not a term used by the psychiatric profession today. Psychiatrists and psychologists talk at great length about specific "disorders," to which they give various complicated names, but they do not talk about people being "insane." The word "insanity" is a lay term, based on the assumption that there is a certain line separating people who are in touch with reality from those who are not. But the mind experts, at least since the time of Sigmund Freud, are reluctant to draw such a line. With over 400 varieties of mental disorders to deal with, the experts focus upon the diseases' shadings and degrees and specific effects; they do not focus upon—indeed, they have trouble seeing—some great divide between sanity and craziness. From a psychiatric standpoint, to say that someone is "insane" is about as helpful as saying that he is bonkers, nuts, or wacko.

Mens Rea: Evil Intent

This is not, however, to say that the word "insane" should be expunged from the dictionary. The word, or at least the concept it embodies, is basic to the whole notion of moral responsibility for our deeds, a legacy of Western religion which even nonreligious people hold sacred. In criminal law, it is expressed by the term *mens rea* ("culpable mind"). With most crimes, conviction requires proof not only of a particular act (*actus reus*) but also of a particular mental state accompanying the act (*mens rea*).

A moment's reflection will tell us why both are necessary. A two-year-old child playing with a gun may kill someone, but no one would call it murder. Even though the child caused someone's death, there was no "culpable mind." What if the killer were not a two-year-old child but a thirty-year-old with the mental capacity of a two-year-old? It hardly seems different. It gets to be a tougher call only when the perpetrator is not a moron but an emotionally disturbed person. Even so, the concept is the same: people should not be held morally or legally responsible if they lack mental culpability.

This notion is as old as the Judeo-Christian teaching about sin. Any traditional Christian knows that there can be no sin without "consent of the will." As early as the fifth century, St. Augustine was teaching that insane people could not be punished for any illegal act they committed while insane because they lacked the will to do the act. By the sixteenth century, the concept was being worked into Anglo-Saxon jurisprudence by commentators. In 1582, William Lambard raised the question whether an act could be considered felonious if committed by "a man or a natural fool or a lunatic in the time of his lunacy, or a child who apparently has no knowledge of good or evil." In his view, the only answer was that it could not, since such persons "cannot be said to have any understanding will."

"Understanding will" conjoins two quite different mental faculties. "Understanding" is cognitive: it tells the person about what is going on; "will" is action-oriented: it gives orders to the body to do something. Ideally, each faculty should work properly and the two should work together. The understanding supplies the will with correct information and the will then gives the appropriate orders. But if the cognitive element is malfunctioning, it supplies false information, and if the will is impaired, it acts inappropriately or compulsively.

M'Naghten Rule

The M'Naghten rule, the first serious attempt to crystallize an insanity defense, puts the emphasis on cognition. It dates back to 1843 in England and arose from the following circumstances. One Daniel M'Naghten (pronounced McNAWten) attempted to assassinate the prime minister of England, Robert Peel. He did not realize, however, that Peel was riding in a different carriage, with Queen Victoria. He ended up shooting to death the secretary of Peel, who was riding in the prime minister's carriage. M'Naghten was acquitted on the grounds that he was suffering delusions of persecution and could not be held accountable.

Many, however, were not pleased with the verdict, and the queen herself asked the House of Lords to gather together the nation's leading judges and formulate a rule to cover such cases. They did, and by an overwhelming majority they repudiated the rationale behind M'Naghten's acquittal and formulated what now, rather ironically, is called the M'Naghten rule. The rule states that a person cannot be held guilty of a crime if:

> At the time of the committing of the act, the party accused was labouring under such a defect of reason, from disease of the mind, as not to know the nature and quality of the act he was doing; or, if he did know it, that he did not know he was doing what was wrong.

The emphasis is on cognition: knowing. If you shoot someone because you think he is a clay pigeon, or because you think he is a KGB agent about to shoot you, you cannot, under the M'Naghten rule, be found guilty of murder. Suppose, however, that you shoot him, knowing he is human and not about to kill you, because you are driven by such fury that you have no control over your impulses. Then the M'Naghten rule does not apply. But should such a person be considered guilty? The question is still unresolved.

Though the M'Naghten rule prevailed as a standard in all American courts for more than a century—about twenty states still use M'Naghten or variations of it—it struck many jurists as inadequate, largely because of its failure to take account of the second element of *mens rea*: the role of will. The development of modern, "scientific" psychology helped focus attention on compulsive behavior, behavior resulting not from misperception but from impairment of the will.

Durham Rule

The first important legal formulation of a broader concept of insanity came from Judge David Bazelon, of the U.S. Court of Appeals for the District of Columbia, in the 1954 case of *Durham* v. *United States.* It states that a defendant is not criminally responsible "if his unlawful act was the product of a mental disease or defect." The trouble with this rule, in the opinion of its critics, is that it is so broad and vague that it could excuse anybody. It could excuse Adolf Hitler.

Indeed, use of the Durham rule apparently resulted in a sharp increase in acquittals. Dr. William Winslade, a psychoanalyst and lawyer who directs UCLA's Program in Medicine, Law and Human Values, cites the following figures:

In the District of Columbia thirty-four acquittals on the basis of not guilty by reason of insanity had been given during the four years previous to the application of the Durham rule. In the four years after Durham was held to be the proper standard, the number of acquittals from insanity pleas rose to one hundred and fifty.

Criticism of Durham intensified during the late '50s and the '60s, as outpatient treatment and deinstitutionalization meant that a killer acquitted by reason of insanity would not necessarily be confined to a mental institution for life. By 1972 the Durham rule was overturned even in the District of Columbia. Every state except New Hampshire had also repudiated it.

American Law Institute Rule

In the meantime, a new standard had appeared. Formulated by the American Law Institute, it was intended to be broader than M'Naghten but not as general as the Durham rule. It says that a person is not responsible for criminal conduct if at the time of committing it "he lacks substantial capacity either to appreciate the criminality of his conduct or to conform his conduct to the requirements of law." This may be, as one critic called it, a "linguistic bowl of mush," but its intention is evident. It aims to combine the cognitive standard of M'Naghten with one that leaves room for a disorder of the will (inability "to conform his conduct").

The American Law Institute rule is now the dominant standard in America. With slight variations, it is now used by a majority of states and federal appeals courts. It has been endorsed by the American Bar Association and by some of America's most distinguished lawyers, psychiatrists, and professors, many of whom also helped to draft it. How well has it worked? That is probably impossible to answer, not only because the standards for "well" vary according to one's perspective (e.g., does it mean more acquittals or more convictions?) but also because it is being used in a variety of criminal cases, each one, in a way, unique. The focus here will be on the rule's weaknesses. Our intention is not simply to find fault but to identify the areas that have helped to fuel the controversy over insanity pleas.

We can start with the Hinckley case. Among the aspects of the case that have drawn fire—we shall mention some others shortly—is its reliance upon the American Law Institute rule. According to reporter Stuart Taylor, a Harvard Law graduate who covered the trial for the *New York Times*, the standard failed to do one of the things it is supposed to do—make it clear "that mental illness does not constitute legal insanity unless it reaches a degree that seriously impairs self-control." He quotes one of the jurors, a forty-eight-year-old parking-lot attendant, as offering this explanation for his acquittal vote: "I believe that he did have a mental problem. I think he was a little mixed up."

But it was not only the Hinckley case that raised questions about the American Law Institute's standard of insanity. At least two other cases in recent years, one in San Francisco and the other in New York, have served to undermine public confidence in it.

Dan White: Diminished Capacity

The more recent of the two cases set in motion events that are still unfolding. It began on November 27, 1978, when Dan White, a former policeman and a member of the San Francisco City Council, shot the mayor to death, reloaded his pistol, and then did the same to another member of the city council. White was furious with the mayor for reneging on a promise to reappoint him to the council, and he was sure that the other council member, Harvey Milk, had plotted against him.

There are two versions of the Dan White case: the press version and the correct version. In the press, the case is often called "the Twinkie defense." It seems that White's attorney managed to convince a jury that his client had been driven mad by eating too much junk food. What really happened was that his attorney, with the help of five psychotherapist witnesses, convinced a jury that White suffered from a "diminished capacity" to control his behavior because of his mental illness, described variously as "unipolar depressive reaction," "manic-depressive illness," "episodes of depression," and "depression of a fairly severe degree." Bingeing on junk food was cited only as one of the *symptoms* of Dan White's illness (along with insomnia and loss of sexual interest).

White was not acquitted, but the two-count indictment of first-degree murder was reduced by the jury to voluntary manslaughter on both counts, the least serious charge possible. He was sentenced to seven years in prison, got two years off for good behavior, and was released on January 6, 1984—five years after shooting to death the mayor of San Francisco, reloading his pistol, then doing the same to a member of the city council.

The Torsney Case: *Catch-22* in Reverse

At least White has done some time in prison for his killing. That is more than can be said of Robert Torsney, a New York City police officer who on Thanksgiving Day,

1976, shot and killed a fifteen-year-old black teenager without provocation. Torsney, along with two other officers, was answering a radio call reporting a man with a gun lurking about a housing project. After interviewing someone in the project, they walked out and encountered a group of teenagers. One of them, fifteen-year-old Randy Evans, asked if his apartment had been searched, whereupon Torsney drew his revolver and fired at him from the distance of 2 feet. Torsney maintained that he acted in self-defense because he thought he saw the youth pull something silvery from his pocket, but his fellow officers saw no such movement, and a subsequent search found nothing silvery on the youth's person or on the ground.

Apparently, Torsney's own attorney thought the self-defense justification a weak one, for he decided to plead insanity. Psychiatrists were brought to the stand, one of whom testified that Torsney might have suffered a "psychomotor seizure," causing him to fire involuntarily (although an EEG of Torsney's brain waves recorded no abnormalities); later he said he believed Torsney suffered from something called "automatism of Penfield." At the trial Torsney himself stuck to his self-defense line while his attorney insisted that he lacked "substantial capacity," in the words of a New York State statute partly modeled on the American Law Institute rule, "to know or appreciate either the nature and consequence" of his conduct "or that such conduct was wrong."

The case turned out to be something like *Catch-22* in reverse. In Joseph Heller's novel the hero, Yossarian, was trying to stay out of combat; in a New York City court-room Robert Torsney was trying to stay out of prison. But in the novel the system kept working against Yossarian: the very fact that he was trying to get himself declared insane was taken as proof that he was sane. At the Torsney trial the system worked the opposite way: every piece of proof the prosecution produced showing that Torsney had not acted in self-defense was used by Torsney's attorney to prove that he was crazy. The prosecution showed that there was no silvery object, no gun at all, on or around the body of Randy Evans. Well, then, Torsney's attorney said to the jury, "if there was no gun, then this man is sick." The all-white jury agreed. Torsney was found not guilty by reason of insanity and sent off to a mental hospital for treatment.

Then, nine months after the conclusion of the trial, staff of the mental hospital announced that they could find nothing wrong with Torsney; no "psychomotor" impairment, no "automatism of Penfield," no psychosis of any sort. All he had was an "impulsive and explosive" personality—a short temper. They recommended his release. This set in motion a switching of positions familiar to prosecutors and defense attorneys in insanity cases. Now the defense was arguing that Torsney was sane and the prosecution was insisting that he was insane. In most cases the flip-flop can be justified, despite its seeming illogic, by the fact that the patient has received treatment. The defense attorney can say, "All right, my client was insane at the time he did the act, but after nine months of treatment, he is better." But in Torsney's case there was no treatment—because there was nothing to treat! A judge reluctantly ordered Torsney's release. His decision was overturned on appeal but finally upheld by New York State's highest court, the Court of Appeals, in a four-to-three decision. Two years and seven months after shooting an unarmed youth to death without provocation, Robert Torsney went home to stay.

Cases like Torsney's, White's, and Hinckley's have brought to a head the public's doubt about the wisdom and fairness of insanity defenses. (The plural, defen*ses*, is used because the standards vary from state to state. As already noted, the majority of states use the American Law Institute standard, while almost all the others use variations on M'Naghten. The Supreme Court has refused to impose any single standard on states, believing that diversity and experimentation are best.) It can be argued, of course, that these cases are exceptional, and that focusing on them exaggerates the problem. Insanity pleas represent only a small percentage of defenses in the criminal justice system, and only about 25 percent of them are successful. One criminal attorney has called it the "fireplug rule." Jurors, he said, think the defendant is sane unless they are convinced that he believes himself to be a fireplug. Of those defendants who do get acquitted, only a tiny percentage are released outright instead of being sent to mental hospitals. But if even 100 people a year—which may be about the number it comes down to—are set free despite having committed serious crimes, it is enough to represent a danger to others and to outrage the public's sense of justice.

Changing the Rules: Some Proposals

The last part is what's really important. Even if people like John Hinckley never return to the streets, it strains our concept of justice to think that someone can commit a heinous act, one that everyone agrees he or she has committed, yet be declared "not guilty." The Hinckley case may well have been the last straw. Everywhere, from the halls of Congress and prestigious law journals to popular magazines, came proposals for changing the rules about insanity defenses. Below are some of the major proposals.

1. *Abolish the Insanity Plea.* The most radical proposal is also the simplest: just do away with the plea. Let people be responsible for their actions, period. The advantage of this is that it would sweep away all the psychological jargon, all the probing into the recesses of people's minds, all the conflicting testimony of the mind "experts." The disadvantage is that it would knock out what has been one of the central criteria for criminal behavior: *mens rea*, "culpable mind." As previously noted, this standard goes back several centuries and is based upon the idea that we should not hold people criminally responsible for what they do without bad intent. Shall we punish a two-year-old for shooting someone? Shall we punish morons? Because of the obvious flaws in this proposal, a more moderate version of it is more popular: to allow a finding of guilty but insane.

2. *Guilty but Insane.* Many critics of the present system would feel comfortable with a verdict of this sort in cases like Hinckley's (though it does not seem to fit Dan White or Robert Torsney). Hinckley was certainly deranged, but he knew what he was doing and had a clear sense that it was wrong; he just thought the trade-off (doing wrong but getting famous) was worth it. *New York Times* reporter Stuart Taylor called him "simultaneously sick and evil." Such a person may not belong behind prison bars, but perhaps he ought not to be called innocent. Giving the jury an option of "guilty but insane" permits society to protect the principle of responsibility yet mix it with compassion; Hinckley could be "sentenced" to a mental hospital.

Despite these advantages, "guilty but insane" has drawbacks. First, it may confuse a jury—as if juries were not confused enough. Usually, "guilty but insane" is presented as another option a judge could present to a jury while instructing them. They now have three choices: guilty, not guilty, and not guilty by reason of insanity. Now they would have a fourth to consider: guilty but insane.* It might be too much for lay people to handle. Moreover, it does not really resolve the issue of principle it seeks to resolve. Its aim is to hold people, at least theoretically, responsible for their deeds. But once we say someone is guilty but insane, we have straddled the fence—not a good thing to do if we are trying to clarify principles. In what sense is the defendant guilty if he is truly insane? If we are to preserve the principle of *mens rea*, then we must take account of the defendant's mental state as an element of guilt. "Guilty but insane" seeks to ignore it but—not ignore it. It is muddy, if not muddled.

3. *Keep Psychiatrists out of Courtrooms.* One obvious result of the trials of Hinckley, White, and Torsney was an intensification of the public's distrust of "shrinks." Not that the public has ever had unquestioning respect for them: in cartoons and comedy sketches they are often depicted as wearing propeller beanies and swatting at imaginary flies. But the spectacle at the Hinckley trial of "experts" tossing around all kinds of jargon and never reaching any agreement was too much even for those who tried to listen. One of the jurors summed it up: "They couldn't prove him insane, they couldn't prove that he was sane." In the video debate, Bronx District Attorney Merola puts it delicately when he refers to "the inexactness of the science of psychiatry."

Others, more rudely, suggest that psychiatry is not a science at all but a kind of occult art, on the order of palmistry or reading the entrails of birds. Unlike true science, say these critics, psychiatry lacks objective standards. If, let us say, the ceiling of a hotel collapsed and a trial were held to determine whether there was negligence in construction, engineers might be called in as expert witnesses. If so, they would have to produce hard evidence (from stress tests, from the strength and weight of I-beams, and so on) to back up their opinions. Psychiatry seems to lack such objective evidence, so the court must fall back on "expert" hunches and speculations. No court would ever accept an engineer's testimony that the hotel ceiling was improperly constructed "because I say so and I'm an expert." Yet the courts come very close to doing just that in insanity trials.

Moreover, these critics continue, psychiatry is not only subjective but also fundamentally antithetical to law because it seems, on the whole, to reject the premise that human beings have free will. It tends to assume that people are driven by emotions resulting from early childhood experiences; at least, that is how it explains people's abnormal behavior. To explain is to understand, and to understand is to forgive. "I'm depraved on accounta I'm deprived," one of the gang members in *West Side Story* explains to the cop. But if people are depraved because they are deprived—if they are driven by compulsions caused by childhood traumas—then perhaps nobody belongs in prison, not even Mafia hit men. They all deserve treatment, not punishment. Justice gives way to therapy.

---

*The reason for using "guilty but insane" as a fourth option instead of using it to replace "not guilty by reason of insanity" is that there are people who *do* consider themselves fireplugs, and it seems absurd to consider them "guilty" in any sense of the word.

Defenders of psychiatry protest that this is a wild caricature of the discipline, and they may be right. But even its defenders—in fact, especially its defenders—agree that psychiatry must not be allowed to dominate the courtroom. The legal question involved in an insanity case cannot be answered by psychiatry. The legal question is whether the defendant is morally responsible for his actions. No psychiatrist worthy of the name would ever want to touch that question, at least not as a psychiatrist. Perhaps a moral philosopher could be called in as an expert witness on it, but not a psychiatrist.

But it is one thing to say that psychiatry should not be allowed to dominate the proceedings and quite another to say psychiatric testimony should be barred from the trial. It is the duty of both defense and prosecution to bring as much light to bear as possible on the issues of the case. If psychiatrists can help to shed factual light on what is finally a legal question, then it seems foolish to bar their testimony. The jurors may decide to take it with a grain of salt. Well and good, but at least they ought to hear it.

In fact, according to Judge Irving Kaufman, they ought to hear more of it. In an article published in the *New York Times Magazine* ten months before his participation in the video debate, Judge Kaufman suggested panels of independent psychiatrists.

4. *Panels of Independent Psychiatrists.* One of the common complaints about psychiatrists at trials is that they get folded into the adversary system. The prosecution introduces psychiatrists who testify to the defendant's freedom from compulsions and delusions, and the defense gets its own psychiatrists to testify that the defendant is an emotional wreck.* The suspicion is that some psychiatrists work as "hired guns," selling their services to the highest bidder. What is needed, says Kaufman, is some independent testimony from psychiatrists not tied to either side of the case. They would be appointed by the judge and appear at the trial to testify as "the court's experts." From what has already been said about the Hinckley trial, the reader may have guessed the major weakness of this proposal: it risks plunging the jurors into still more confusion. After sitting through hours of psychiatric testimony by each side, they would have to endure still more of it by judge-appointed psychiatrists. Jurors, many of them men and women of modest education, have enough trouble understanding psychiatrists even when the psychiatrists are guided by attorneys. Now we would have "neutral" psychiatrists, loose cannon, whose testimony would probably be so full of qualifications that nobody could draw any conclusions from it. This does not seem calculated to clarify the confusion surrounding insanity trials.

5. *Put the Burden of Proof on the Defendant.* This suggestion commands support across the ideological spectrum. Even a former American Civil Liberties Union attorney suggested it in an article in *The Nation* shortly after the Hinckley trial. Indeed, it was the Hinckley trial that made the present system an embarrassment even to libertarians. For the judge in the trial did not require the defense to prove that Hinckley was insane; he required the prosecution to prove that he was *sane* "beyond a reason-

---

*"Dr. David M. Bear, a defense psychiatrist whose glittering curriculum vitae include the top academic ranking in Harvard's College Class of 1965, told me after the verdict that he had spent 'at least twenty to twenty-five hours' rehearsing his testimony [for the Hinckley trial] with defense lawyers." Stuart Taylor, Jr., "Too much Justice," *Harper's*, September 1982, p. 63.

able doubt." This is a staggering burden of proof. How do we go about proving that *any* assassin or would-be assassin is sane "beyond a reasonable doubt"? Opinions differ about whether the judge was forced to place this burden of proof on the prosecution or whether he did it out of an excess of caution, fearing that otherwise his ruling might be overturned on appeal. What all sides seem to agree upon is that Congress ought to take the matter in hand and pass a law making it clear that the burden of proof must rest upon the defense to show that its client was insane "beyond a reasonable doubt." The only question remaining is whether such a law, which has already been adopted by a number of states, would survive a serious constitutional challenge.

In a 1970 case, *In re Winship*, the Supreme Court held that the government must prove beyond a reasonable doubt that the defendant is guilty. If, according to *mens rea*, one's mental state is an element of guilt, it seems to follow that sanity must also be established by the government. The logic of this is hard to defeat, yet the result of the logic seems to violate common sense. Perhaps the present burden of proof would not seem so intolerable if "sanity" were given a broader meaning—or, putting it the other way around, if "insanity" were given a narrower definition.

6. *Narrow the Definition of Insanity.* In the 1950s it was considered "scientific" and "progressive" to abandon, or at least revise, the old M'Naghten rule. M'Naghten limited the definition of insanity to cognitive disfunction: the defendant thinks he or she is shooting a clay pigeon instead of a human being. The Durham and American Law Institute rules expanded the definition of insanity to take into account a person's inability to control his or her behavior. That would seem to describe Hinckley, Torsney, and White.

The question is whether such a definition does not cast too wide a net. Anyone with a hot temper or a low boiling point would now seem to qualify as insane. Anyone involved in an angry argument who ends it with a pistol shot could claim to suffer from poor impulse control. The person's lawyer could produce numerous examples from the past showing how easily the defendant flew off the handle; relatives could be brought in to testify to his or her bad temper (which is what occurred in the Torsney trial). What happens, then, is that viciousness becomes a virtue. The very behavior that people should be ashamed of is used to exonerate them. The question is whether it might not be a good idea to stick with the M'Naghten rule without any of the modern additions to it.

This is worth considering, but we should also remember that the intellect and the will are both parts of the mind. If an individual's perceptions are so flawed as to make him or her innocent of the deeds he commits, why can't that person's will be similarly impaired? "That which I know is right I cannot do," said St. Paul. There may also be people of whom it can be said, "That which they know is wrong they are compelled to do." What should society do with such people when they commit horrible deeds? How should they be classified? Are they guilty, insane, or both? Should they be locked up until they are cured, or merely till they are no longer dangerous? Or should they be locked up for life? Should we treat them or punish them?

The Video Discussion of Insanity Defense

The video discussion of the insanity defense is itself divided into three parts. The first part concentrates on the role of psychiatrists as "hired guns," something Judge Kaufman called attention to in his *New York Times Magazine* article. The moderator asks the three psychiatrists on the panel if they would be willing to testify for the defense of Harvey Brink. Earlier, Gerry Spence had characterized the insanity trial as a kind of "game," and everyone seems to accept this characterization; a number of the participants pick up the word and use it themselves.

The selection of the "right" psychiatrist, it appears, is part of the game. The defense wants one who is articulate and whose testimony will jibe with the defense claim. Dr. Willard Gaylin knows the drift of this game and declines to play it. Dr. Loren Roth seems more inclined to play. He will let himself be interviewed by the defense attorney and, if it seems like an interesting case, he will testify to the defendant's insanity if he thinks he is insane. Dr. Alan Stone shares Roth's willingness to play. But it is doubtful that the defense—or the prosecution, for that matter—would be interested in his testimony, for, he warns us, it would be full of qualifications. Now Judge Joan Dempsey Klein gets a bit impatient. Psychiatrists, she says, "are behavioral scientists, they are the people who are supposedly at the cutting edge of the knowledge of human behavior. Now, if I can't rely on help from them, where am I going to get it and where is the juror going to get it?" Dr. Stone replies, "The jury should be confused; we shouldn't clear it up for them, because to clear it up for them is to distort the realities, right?" The reader might want to ask whether that *is* right. Dr. Stone is nobody's hired gun. The problem, rather, is that he is going to leave the jurors in a state of confusion—and then justify it as a form of enlightenment!

It is just this, apparently, that happened in the case of the Hinckley jurors; they resolved the confusion by voting "not guilty" and letting it go at that. In the present case, the confusion is captured in this exchange between the moderator and Dr. Stone:

MODERATOR: Dr. Stone, let's just see what they're confused about here. They're not confused that Harvey Brink shot Oscar King. . . .
STONE: Right.
MODERATOR: Oscar King is as dead as a doornail. . . .
STONE: Right.
MODERATOR: No doubt.
STONE: Right.
MODERATOR: They are not confused that Harvey Brink is as crazy as a bedbug.
STONE: Right.
MODERATOR: What they are confused about is whether he is guilty. . . .
STONE: Absolutely.
MODERATOR: . . . whatever the hell that means.
STONE: Right, right.

The confusion, then, results from the fact that law and psychiatry seem to be operating along different tracks. It was said before in this chapter, but it needs to be emphasized: "insanity," at least as the term is used in trials involving insanity pleas, is not a psychiatric term; it is a legal term. It means "not accountable for one's actions." Put another way, it means, "there is no *mens rea.*" No psychiatrist can answer these questions. A psychiatrist, who may be able to determine that the defendant is suffering from a certain illness, has no expert knowledge of whether the illness has destroyed the person's sense of moral accountability. That is itself a moral question, and it is doubtful whether anybody is an expert on morals. Anyway, psychiatrists are not.

Why not, then, simply eliminate the insanity defense? Why not try people for what they have done, and get them off the streets? That is the no-nonsense approach taken by Congressman Barney Frank, and he presents it so forcefully that, for a time, it silences potential critics. True, he softens his proposal by suggesting two trials for the defendant, one to determine guilt and the other to decide whether the defendant should be sent to prison or a mental institution, but it is still a fairly severe test. Henceforward, says Frank, guilt should depend solely on what a person does, not what is on his or her mind. Even the psychiatrists do not dispute this proposal, though Dr. Gaylin puts a strange twist on his assent. "There are certain crimes that are so heinous that a juror wants them punished, and I think that for purposes of the social order, it may be well that we pay that small price of injustice in one case, so we will send absolutely crazy people to punishment." In other words, if it makes the jurors and society feel better to assign punishment, then let them do it.

Judge Irving Kaufman is shocked that nobody has challenged Barney Frank's suggestion that juries find people guilty solely for their deeds. "Nobody paid attention to whether or not the man had any intention or whether he had a *mens rea.* . . . I haven't heard intention mentioned here at all. That's my point. We have bypassed that crucial finding that the jury has to make in this case." Judge Kaufman has brought us back to the crucial question, the question introduced at the beginning of this third section. He has also set off Gerry Spence: "I thought I could never agree with Judge Kaufman, but I find that I embrace him. . . ." Spence says a number of things, talking around his subject, but then he drives straight to the heart of it: "How do you punish somebody who is insane?" The moderator agrees that "that really is the hard question." Whatever our answer may be, it seems that Spence has ended by asking the right—the painful—question.

Points to Remember

1. Ordinarily, people cannot be found guilty of crimes unless their "culpable acts" are committed with a "culpable mind," or *mens rea.*
2. For many centuries, jurists and philosophers have tended toward the conclusion that a truly insane person cannot be held responsible for his or her actions.
3. The first serious attempt to define insanity in Anglo-Saxon law was the M'Naghten rule of 1843. It is still used as the standard in about twenty states. It emphasizes cognitive impairment: the individual did not know what he or she was doing or did not know that it was wrong.
4. Dissatisfaction with the M'Naghten rule led to broader tests for insanity. The Durham rule of 1954 defined it simply as "mental disease or defect." By the 1960s,

the Durham rule was widely considered to be too loose, so a tighter definition was attempted by the American Law Institute: the mental disease or defect must be one that results in the failure to appreciate the wrongfulness of one's conduct or the inability to control it.

5. Recent cases, notably those of John Hinckley, Dan White, and Robert Torsney, have intensified public criticism of the use of insanity pleas in criminal cases.

6. These cases have also brought forth a number of suggestions for reforming the system. The most popular of these suggestions are: (a) reversing the burden of proof by placing it on the defendant and (b) introducing an alternative verdict: guilty but insane.

SUMMARY

This chapter has taken us through the three stages of an insanity trial, confronting us with three corresponding issues. First, is the defendant competent to stand trial? Second, is the defendant competent to take charge of his or her defense? Third, what criteria are we to use in deciding whether or not the defendant is legally insane? Each of these questions raises a number of related issues. The competency issue raises the question of what to do with incompetent defendants. To that question, fortunately, we have an answer. We know that we cannot simply warehouse someone in a mental institution indefinitely without a trial. That is what they do in the Soviet Union, but the case of *Jackson* v. *Indiana* (1972) made it clear that we cannot do it here.

The questions get tough when we come to the second part. Suppose the defendant is so crazy that he or she insists on taking over the defense? Would a defense attorney be right to use a bit of trickery and manipulation to dissuade such a client from trying to run the defense? Would a judge be right to bluff and intimidate the defendant into letting his or her lawyer do the defending? All this, in the words of Gerry Spence, "beats the hell out of the gas chamber." But in America we believe that individuals have the right to conduct their own defenses. *Faretta* v. *California* (1975) made this into a constitutional principle.

Of course, Faretta was perfectly sane. Harvey Brink may be competent to stand trial, but is he competent to defend himself at the trial? Are there degrees of competence that should be taken into account before we let mentally disturbed persons defend themselves? Can we break in and stop the defendant if the defense becomes sufficiently bizarre? All this has yet to be resolved.

It is when we get to the third section that we approach the most formidable issues: Are psychiatrists reliable witnesses in insanity trials? Is their discipline really a science, in the sense that it can present objective evidence? Do psychiatrists who testify really become advocates? Would it be better if psychiatric testimony were kept out of such trials? Would it be better simply to do away with the insanity defense and let people be tried for their deeds alone?

The last question really goes to the heart of the matter. As a congressman, Barney Frank is in the business of listening to what people in his congressional district think about the insanity defense, and there is no question about it: they are increasingly impatient with the way that it is being used. But what is the solution? Should it be done away with? Should it be replaced or supplemented with a "guilty but insane" option for the jury? Should there be, as Frank argues, two trials, one to determine guilt—based on deeds alone—and one to determine whether the convicted person should be sent to prison or a mental hospital?

Such proposals need to be considered very seriously. In considering them, however, we also need to keep in mind our legal tradition, which holds that people should not be held criminally responsible unless they commit criminal deeds with *mens rea*—"culpable mind"—or evil intent. Of course, it gets much more difficult when we deal with the problem of emotional illness. Should we limit our definition of legal insanity to serious cognitive confusion (the M'Naghten rule) or use a broader definition (the Durham and American Law Institute rules)? Somehow, in some way, at some point in the proceedings, we have to get at the question of intent. *Mens rea* is a tradition at least as old as Christianity, one which grows from the conviction that people are not guilty unless their will has assented to their deeds. The human heart is a very dark place, but what goes on there is not irrelevant to law. It may be that Gerry Spence tilts too far to the side of compassion, at the expense of justice and community safety. But he has at least raised the right question: "How do you punish somebody who is insane?" Whether we want to or not, we must find an answer, or answers, to this question. Perhaps defendants like Hinckley, Torsney, and White can be simultaneously sick and evil; perhaps they deserve treatment *and* punishment.

Documents

JACKSON V. *INDIANA*, 406 U.S. 715 (1971)

In this case the Court ruled that a criminal suspect adjudged incompetent to stand trial cannot be held indefinitely in a mental institution without further legal proceedings.

Opinion of the Court, Mr. Justice Blackmun.

We are here concerned with the constitutionality of certain aspects of Indiana's system for pretrial commitment of one accused of crime.

Petitioner, Theon Jackson, is a mentally defective deaf mute with a mental level of a pre-school child. He cannot read, write, or otherwise communicate except through limited sign language. In May 1968, at age 27, he was charged in the Criminal Court of Marion County, Indiana, with separate robberies of two women. The offenses were alleged to have occurred the preceding July. The first involved property (a purse and its contents) of the value of four dollars. The second concerned five dollars in money. The record sheds no light on these charges since, upon receipt of not guilty pleas from Jackson, the trial court set in motion the Indiana procedures for determining his competency to stand trial.

As the statute requires, the court appointed two psychiatrists to examine Jackson. A competency hearing was subsequently held at which petitioner was represented by counsel. The court received the examining doctors' joint written report and oral testimony from them and from a deaf school interpreter through whom they had attempted to communicate with petitioner. The report concluded that Jackson's almost non-existent communication skill, together with his lack of hearing and his mental deficiency, left him unable to understand the nature of the charges against him or to participate in his defense. One doctor testified that it was extremely unlikely that petitioner could ever learn to read or write and questioned whether petitioner even had the ability to develop any proficiency in sign language. He believed that the interpreter had not been able to communicate with petitioner to any great extent and testified that petitioner's "prognosis appears rather dim." The other doctor testified that even if Jackson were not a deaf mute, he would be incompetent to stand trial, and doubted whether petitioner had sufficient intelligence ever to develop the necessary communication skills. The interpreter testified that Indiana had no facilities that could help someone as badly off as Jackson to learn minimal communication skills.

On this evidence, the trial court found that Jackson "lack[ed] comprehension sufficient to make his defense," § 9-1706a, and ordered him committed to the Indiana Department of Mental Health until such time as that Department should certify to the court that "the defendant is sane."

Petitioner's counsel then filed a motion for a new trial, contending that there was no evidence that Jackson was "insane," or that he would ever attain a status which the court might regard as "sane" in the sense of competency to stand trial. Counsel argued that Jackson's commitment under these circumstances amounted to a "life sentence" without his ever having been convicted of a crime, and that the commitment therefore deprived Jackson of his Fourteenth Amendment rights to due process and equal protection, and constituted cruel and unusual punishment under the Eighth Amendment made applicable to the States through the Fourteenth. The trial court denied the motion. On appeal the Supreme Court of Indiana affirmed with one judge dissenting. — Ind. —, 255 N.E. 2d 515 (1970). Rehearing was denied with two judges dissenting. We granted certiorari, 401 U.S. 973 (1971).

For the reasons set forth below, we conclude that, on the record before us, Indiana cannot constitutionally commit the petitioner for an indefinite period simply on account of his incompetency to stand trial on the charges filed against him. Accordingly, we reverse.

. . .

[We hold] that Indiana's indefinite commitment of a criminal defendant solely on account of his incompetency to stand trial does not square with the Fourteenth Amendment's guarantee of due process.

A. *The Federal System.* In the federal criminal system, the constitutional issue posed here has not been encountered precisely because the federal statutes have been construed to require that a mentally incompetent defendant must also be found "dangerous" before he can be committed indefinitely. But the decisions have uniformly articulated the constitutional problems compelling this statutory interpretation.

The federal statute, 18 U.S.C. §§ 4244 to 4246, is not dissimilar to the Indiana law. It provides that a defendant found incompetent to stand trial may be committed "until the accused shall be mentally competent to stand trial or until the pending charges against him are disposed of according to law." § 4246. Section 4247, applicable on its face only to convicted criminals whose federal sentences are about to expire, permits commitment if the prisoner is (1) "insane or mentally incompetent" and (2) "will probably endanger the safety of the officers, the property, or other interests of the United States, and . . . suitable arrangements for the custody and care of the prisoner are not otherwise available," that is, in a state facility. See *Greenwood* v. *United States,* 350 U.S., at 373–374. One committed under this section, however, is entitled to release when any of the three conditions no longer obtains, "whichever event shall first occur." § 4248. Thus a person committed under § 4247 must be released when he no longer is "dangerous."

In *Greenwood,* the Court upheld the pretrial commitment of a defendant who met all three conditions of § 4247, even though there was little likelihood that he would ever become competent to stand trial. Since Greenwood had not yet stood trial, his commitment was ostensibly under § 4244. By the related release provision, § 4246, he could not have been released until he became competent. But the District Court had in fact applied § 4247, and found specifically that Greenwood would be dangerous if not committed. This Court approved that approach, holding § 4247 applicable before trial as well as to those about to be released from sentence. 350 U.S., at 374. Accordingly, Greenwood was entitled to release when no longer dangerous, § 4248, even if he did not become competent to stand trial and thus did not meet the requirement of § 4246. Under these circumstances, the Court found the commitment constitutional.

Since *Greenwood,* federal courts without exception have found improper any straightforward application of §§ 4244 and 4246 to a defendant whose chance of attaining competency to stand trial is slim, thus effecting an indefinite commitment on the grounds of incompetency alone. [Case citations omitted.]

The holding in each of these cases was grounded in an expressed substantial doubt that §§ 4244 and 4246 could survive constitutional scrutiny if interpreted to authorize indefinite commitment.

These decisions have imposed a "rule of reasonableness" upon §§ 4244 and 4246. Without a finding of dangerousness, one committed thereunder can be held only for a "reasonable period of time" necessary to determine whether there is a substantial chance of his attaining the capacity to stand trial in the foreseeable future. If the chances are slight, or if the defendant does not in fact improve, then he must be released or granted a §§ 4247–4248 hearing.

B. *The States.* Some States appear to commit indefinitely a defendant found incompetent to stand trial until he recovers competency. Other States require a finding of dangerousness to support such a commitment or provide forms of parole. New York has recently enacted legislation mandating release of incompetent defendants charged with misdemeanors after 90 days of commitment, and release and dismissal of charges against those accused of felonies after they have been committed for two-thirds of the maximum potential prison sentence. The practice of automatic commitment with release conditioned solely upon attainment of competence has been decried on both policy and constitutional grounds. Recommendations for changes made by commentators and study committees have included incorporation into pretrial commitment procedures of the equivalent of the federal "rule of reason," a requirement of a finding of dangerousness or of full-scale civil commitment, periodic review by court or mental health administrative personnel of the defendant's condition and progress, and provisions for ultimately dropping charges if the defendant does not improve. One source of this criticism is undoubtedly the empirical data available which tends to show that many defendants committed before trial are never tried, and that those defendants committed pursuant to ordinary civil proceedings are, on the average, released sooner than defendants automatically committed solely on account of their incapacity to stand trial. Related to these statistics are substantial doubts about whether the rationale for pretrial commitment—that care or treatment will aid the accused in attaining competency—is empirically valid given the state of most of our mental institutions. However, very few courts appear to have addressed the problem directly in the state context.

In *United States ex rel. Wolfersdorf* v. *Johnson*, 317 F. Supp. 66 (SDNY 1970), an 86-year-old defendant committed for nearly 20 years as incompetent to stand trial on state murder and kidnaping charges applied for federal habeas corpus. He had been found "not dangerous," and suitable for civil commitment. The District Court granted relief. It held that petitioner's incarceration in an institution for the criminally insane constituted cruel and unusual punishment, and that the "shocking circumstances" of his commitment violated the Due Process Clause. The court quoted approvingly the language of *Cook* v. *Ciccone*, 312 F. Supp. 822, 824 (WD Mo. 1970), concerning the "substantial injustice in keeping an unconvicted person in . . . custody to await trial where it is plainly evident his mental condition will not permit trial within a reasonable period of time."

In a 1970 case virtually indistinguishable from the one before us, the Illinois Supreme Court granted relief to an illiterate deaf mute who had been indicted for murder four years previous but found incompetent to stand trial on account of his inability to communicate, and committed. *People ex rel. Myers* v. *Briggs*, 46 Ill. 2d 281, 263 N. E. 2d 109 (1970). The institution where petitioner was confined had determined, "[I]t now appears that [petitioner] will never acquire the necessary communication skills needed to participate and cooperate in his trial." Petitioner, however, was found to be functioning at a "nearly normal level of performance in areas other than communication." The State contended petitioner should not be released until his competency was restored. The Illinois Supreme Court disagreed. It held:

> "This court is of the opinion that this defendant, handicapped as he is and facing an indefinite commitment because of the pending indictment against him, should be given an opportunity to obtain a trial to determine whether or not he is guilty as charged or should be released." 263 N. E. 2d, at 113.

C. *This Case.* Respondent relies heavily on *Greenwood* to support Jackson's commitment. That decision is distinguishable. It upheld only the initial commitment without considering directly its duration or the standards for release. It justified the commitment by treating it as if accomplished under allied statutory provisions relating directly to the individual's "insanity" and society's interest in his indefinite commitment, factors not considered in Jackson's case. And it sustained commitment only upon the finding of dangerousness. As Part A, *supra*, shows, all these elements subsequently have been held not simply sufficient, but necessary to sustain a commitment like the one involved here.

The States have traditionally exercised broad power to commit persons found to be mentally ill. The substantive limitations on the exercise of this power and the procedures for invoking it vary drastically among the States. The particular fashion in which the power is exercised—for instance, through various forms of civil commitment, defective delinquency laws, sexual psychopath laws, commitment of persons acquitted by reason of insanity—reflects different combinations of distinct bases for commitment sought to be vindicated. The bases that have been articulated include dangerousness to self, dangerousness to others, and the need for care or treatment or training. Considering the number of persons affected, it is perhaps remarkable that the substantive constitutional limitations on this power have not been more frequently litigated.

We need not address these broad questions here. It is clear that Jackson's commitment rests on proceedings that did not purport to bring into play, indeed did not even consider relevant, *any* of the articulated bases for exercise of Indiana's power of indefinite commitment. The state statutes contain at least two alternative methods for invoking this power. But Jackson was not afforded any "formal commitment proceedings addressed to [his] ability to function in society," or to society's interest in his restraint, or to the State's ability to aid him in attaining competency through custodial care or compulsory treatment, the ostensible purpose of the commitment. At the least, due process requires that the nature and duration of commitment bear some reasonable relation to the purpose for which the individual is committed.

We hold, consequently, that a person charged by a State with a criminal offense who is committed solely on account of his incapacity to proceed to trial cannot be held more than the reasonable period of time necessary to determine whether there is a substantial probability that he will attain that capacity in the foreseeable future. If it is determined that this is not the case, then the State must either institute the customary civil commitment proceeding that would be required to commit indefinitely any other citizen, or release the defendant. Furthermore, even if it is determined that the defendant probably soon will be able to stand trial, his continued commitment must be justified by progress toward that goal. In light of differing state facilities and procedures and a lack of evidence in this record, we do not think it appropriate for us to attempt to prescribe arbitrary time limits. We note, however, that petitioner Jackson has now been confined for three and one-half years on a record that sufficiently establishes the lack of a substantial probability that he will ever be able to participate fully in a trial.

SELECTED READINGS

Dutile, Fernand N., and Singer, Thomas H. "What Now for the Insanity Defense?" *Notre Dame Law Review* 58, no. 5 (1983): 1104–1111.

Two professors of law examine the Hinckley verdict and consider possible new policy directions for legislatures, courts, judges, juries, and mental health professionals.

Fingarette, Herbert. *The Meaning of Criminal Insanity.* Berkeley, Calif.: University of California Press, 1972.

This excellent volume examines the medical concept of mental disease, the legal concept of insanity, and the intersection and relations between the two. The treatment is thorough but also somewhat technical. The volume contains an excellent bibliography. See also D. McDonald, "Mental Disabilities and Criminal Responsibility: An Interview with Herbert Fingarette," *The Center Magazine* 15 (November–December 1982): 8-16.

Gerard, J. B. "Insane Hinckley Verdict." *Policy Review* 23 (Winter 1983): 79-83.

Gerard, professor of law at the Washington University School of Law in St. Louis, takes the case of John Hinckley as a point of departure to explain the insanity defense and the problems it has raised for the administration of criminal justice. He carefully distinguishes insanity and the defense, which are matters of law, from the psychological and medical matters of mental health and mental illness.

Hart, H. L. A. *Law, Liberty, and Morality.* Stanford, Calif.: Stanford University Press, 1963.

The most renowned legal philosopher writing in English today examines the relation between law and morality in several areas, including punishment and retribution, public morals, prostitution, and homosexuality. See the same author's *Punishment and Responsibility,* New York: Oxford University Press, 1968; and *Punishment and the Elimination of Responsibility,* London: Athlone Press, University of London, 1962.

Szasz, Thomas. *Law, Liberty, and Psychiatry.* New York: Macmillan, 1963.

Psychiatrist and professor Szasz takes a careful look at his own profession and then examines its relation to the criminal law and to public policy. In addition to considering the insanity defense in criminal cases, Szasz considers the overall constitutional situation and rights of mental patients. The volume contains a number of short case studies. See the same author's *Psychiatric Justice,* New York: Macmillan, 1965.

Symposium on Mental Health. *Law and Contemporary Problems* 45, no. 3 (1982).

The symposium includes papers on a wide variety of problems confronting both mental health practitioners and the criminal justice system. Of particular interest are Alan Meisel, "The Rights of the Mentally Ill under State Constitutions," and Michael Perlin and Robert Sadoff, "Ethical Issues in the Representation of Individuals in the Commitment Process."

Taylor, Stuart, Jr. "Too Much Justice." *Harper's,* September 1982, pp. 56-66.

Lawyer and journalist Taylor explains how the apparently simple case arising from John Hinckley's attempt to assassinate President Ronald Reagan became complicated, expensive, and difficult to resolve. Taylor compares the Hinckley case to other celebrated cases of murder, assassination, and attempted assassination. He asks whether there is any wisdom in the insanity defense as it is now understood and argues for the adoption of an alternative standard of "guilty but mentally ill."

GLOSSARY

American Law Institute rule. The most recent and most highly regarded rule for determining whether a defendant should be found guilty by reason of insanity. It says that a person is not responsible for a criminal act if at the time of committing it "he lacks substantial capacity to appreciate the criminality of his conduct or to conform his conduct to the requirements of law."

Competence. The ability of a defendant to understand the charges against him or her and to participate in the defense.

Diminished capacity. An impairment of the will, resulting in a lessened ability to control one's behavior. A jury reduced the verdict against San Francisco Councilman Dan White from first-degree murder to voluntary manslaughter because of White's "diminished capacity."

Durham rule. Derived from the judge's opinion in *Durham* v. *United States* (1954), this rule says that a person should be found not guilty by reason of insanity "if his unlawful act was the product of a mental disease or defect."

Guilty but insane. A possible jury verdict in which the defendant could be found guilty but would be subject to a second hearing to determine whether he or she should be imprisoned or sent to a mental hospital.

"Hired gun." In the context of this chapter, a psychiatrist who regularly hires himself out to the prosecution or the defense in insanity trials to bolster the assertion that the accused is either sane or insane.

M'Naghten rule. The rule, dating back to 1843, which states that a person may not be found guilty of a criminal act if at the time of committing it he did not know what he was doing or, if he did, did not know it was wrong.

Mens rea. Evil intent (literally, "culpable mind"). In the tradition of Anglo-American law, a person is not considered "guilty" of a criminal act unless it was committed with evil intent.

Chapter 6
Jail ... Prison ...
Something Worse

*"I've seen the jails and prisons where people are
sent to receive their 'deserts.' I've seen them often,
and my heart starts bleeding every time I enter
them and aches when I leave."*
DR. KARL MENNINGER

"If you can't do the time, don't do the crime."
PRISON SLOGAN

In this chapter, the subject is again our criminal justice system: how it works, how it doesn't work, what rights accused people have under our system, what authority the state has in fighting crime. In Chapters 4 and 5, the focus has been on what happens before the conclusion of the trial. What kind of search was conducted of the suspect's home or person? Can the evidence from an illegal search be used in a trial? How was the suspect treated during interrogation? Was the suspect coerced into self-incrimina-tion? What kind of trial did the defendant receive? Was it fair?

This chapter starts to cross a line. At a certain point—after the suspect has had all the *Miranda* warnings, has been represented by counsel at a trial, and has pleaded "not guilty" or "not guilty by reason of insanity," after witnesses against the suspect have been cross-examined and illegally obtained evidence has been excluded from the court-room—after all that, the suspect may still be found guilty. What happens then? If he or she is imprisoned, what is the reason for it? How long is the imprisonment to last? Under what conditions will it continue? What does the state hope to accomplish by it? What sorts of punishments fit what sorts of crimes? Is there any crime so heinous and inhuman that it deserves capital punishment? If so, how should capital punishment be meted out? What is fair and unfair procedure? *What are the rights of the guilty?*

THE RIGHTS OF THE GUILTY

To Americans besieged by violent crime it may seem to be carrying "rights" too far when we start to speak of "the rights of the guilty." Why should guilty people have rights? A moment's reflection is enough to provide an answer. As late as the early years of the eighteenth century, it was not uncommon to execute prisoners by "break-ing them on the wheel." The prisoner was bound hand and foot to a large wheel. In front of a large, cheering audience the executioner stepped forward, holding a heavy iron bar, like a crowbar. After twirling it a few times for effect, he would swing with all his might and break the prisoner's shins. Then he would break the prisoner's wrists. Then, working both extremities toward the middle of the body, he would break in succession the prisoner's knees, elbows, thighs, upper arms, shoulders, and hips. By that time the prisoner was usually dead and did not need to be finished off by blows to the chest and face.

Even if we assume that every one of those doomed prisoners was guilty, we still recoil in horror from the punishment. They were guilty—yet they still had some rights. At least they had a right not to be put to death like that. "The rights of the guilty" expresses a basic conviction of Americans, a conviction that even the most hardened offenders are entitled to a certain level of humane treatment. Far from being a recent invention of judges and law processors, it goes back to 1791, when the Eighth Amendment was adopted. This amendment reads: "Excessive bail shall not be required, nor excessive fines imposed, nor cruel and unusual punishments inflicted."

Before we go any further, a qualification is needed. We said above that our discussion here *starts* to cross the line from the rights of the accused to the rights of the convicted. The language was chosen carefully. In some ways this discussion *straddles* the line. It talks about the rights of people in jail and not yet tried, then discusses the rights of those already convicted. There is a certain untidiness in that, but the untidiness is inherent in the Eighth Amendment. The amendment begins by talking about "excessive bail." Bail is a monetary payment to a court by a person accused of a crime but not yet tried for it. It is a bond, a kind of deposit paid to guarantee that the person will show up for his or her trial. Of course, the defendant may "jump bail" and go into hiding. If this happens, the bail money is forfeited (it would otherwise be returned at the beginning of the trial), and the defendant will be subject to punishment for running away in addition to the other charges.

The Eighth Amendment's mention of bail makes it straddle the line between the rights of the guilty and the rights of the accused. Since bail applies to those accused of crimes but not yet tried for them, the Eighth Amendment is meant to apply not only to punishments and the rights of the guilty but also to the treatment of those awaiting trial.* For such individuals, there are two alternatives to bail. One is "personal recognizance," meaning that they are released until their trial on their own personal assurance that they will show up. This is sometimes used in cases where the offense is minor or when the defendant is well known and is highly unlikely to run away before trial.

The other alternative is jail. Although the word "jail" is often used broadly to describe any place of incarceration, it is used here to describe the place where accused

---

*Actually, those in jail are protected by more than the Eighth Amendment's prohibition against excessive bail. More broadly, they are protected by the due process clauses of the Fifth Amendment (for federal jails) and the Fourteenth Amendment (for state jails). Pretrial detainees are presumptively innocent. Therefore, the authorities are barred not only from punishing them in a "cruel and unusual" manner but from punishing them at all. "Punishments" can only be meted out to those who are guilty of a crime. All a pretrial detainee has to prove in order to make a valid constitutional claim against the authorities is that he or she is being punished (not merely confined). Such a case is, properly speaking, not an Eighth Amendment case but a due process case.

felons are confined while awaiting trial. Unlike a prison, it is not a place intended for punishment or rehabilitation. Its purpose is to make sure that the accused is on hand for trial. Some people are accused of crimes carrying such severe penalties that bail would not be sufficient to ensure their showing up for trial; from their own standpoint, they would be better off "jumping bail" and losing the money than facing the prospect of a life prison term or execution. Therefore, they are held in jail without bail. Others, facing the possibility of lesser though still severe penalties, may be held in jail because they cannot afford the bail.

What needs to be kept in mind—and is very easy to forget—is that *all these jailed individuals are innocent*. Perhaps that sounds outrageous, but it is legally correct. Under our system of criminal law, people are presumed innocent until proven guilty. If, tomorrow, by some fluke, you were to be accused of rape or murder, you would not therefore become guilty of rape or murder. The same has to be said of all those now residing in American jails. All of them, no matter what their previous record of convictions, must be presumed innocent of the crime they are charged with.

The Video Discussion

All the participants in the video discussion have considerable experience in prison administration, or in the federal or state judiciary, or in the mass media. Some of them, we shall see, have been involved in disputes similar to those in the hypothetical case. The moderator is Professor Charles Nesson of Harvard Law School.

List of Participants

HON. ARTHUR L. ALARCON
Judge
U.S. Court of Appeals
Ninth Circuit

DAVID W. BURKE
Vice-President and
Assistant to the President
ABC News

NORMAN A. CARLSON
Director
Federal Bureau of Prisons

W. J. ESTELLE, JR.
Director
Texas Department of Corrections

HON. BARNEY FRANK
U.S. Representative
Massachusetts

RUDOLPH W. GIULIANI
U.S. Attorney
Southern District of New York
Former U.S. Associate Attorney General

EDWARD R. HAMMOCK
Chairman
New York State Board of Parole

HON. JOAN DEMPSEY KLEIN
Presiding Justice
California Court of Appeal

HON. POTTER STEWART
Retired Justice
U.S. Supreme Court

MARIO MEROLA
District Attorney
Bronx County, New York

THOMAS B. STODDARD
Legislative Director
New York Civil Liberties Union

BILL MOYERS
Senior News Analyst
CBS News

HON. JAMES R. THOMPSON
Governor
Illinois

HON. DALLIN H. OAKS
Justice
Utah Supreme Court

HON. EDWIN TORRES
Justice
New York State Supreme Court

HON. R. EUGENE PINCHAM
Judge
Circuit Court of Cook County (Illinois)

BENJAMIN WARD
Police Commissioner
New York City
Former Commissioner

ROGER ROSENBLATT
Senior Writer and Essayist
Time Magazine

New York City Department
of Correction

Program Summary

The moderator begins the first part of the program by discussing the relationship between the jails, the prisons, the parole board, and the governor in the fictional state of Piedmont. Participants, who in real life represent such institutions, tell him that each operates independently of the others. He then posits a situation in which Piedmont's jails are "chockablock full" of pretrial detainees and a federal judge rules that any further overcrowding will violate the Constitution. He raises two basic issues: What measures can and should be taken to ease the overcrowding problem? And where should the fault or blame lie if dangerous people are returned to the streets as a result of the federal judge's ruling? Participants debate these questions with a good deal of finger pointing. The governor blames the judge for meddling. The judge blames the governor for not solving the overcrowding problem. The legislator blames the public for not caring. Eventually the question comes down to sentencing. Perhaps if state judges used alternatives to prison sentencing, the problem of overcrowding would be eased.

The second part of the program focuses on the question of who should go to prison. The prosecutor is not prepared to ask for incarceration of prostitutes and car thieves (unless the latter are involved in a major operation). Then more serious crimes are discussed: a woman who shoots her lover in a jealous rage, a nursing-home operator who defrauds the public. What are the criteria for deciding who should go to prison and who should pay a fine or do community service? Does it turn on whether the per-petrator is violent? Malicious? A recidivist? A big-shot criminal? A rational person, capable of responding to deterrence? Behind the discussion lies the more basic ques-tion of the purpose of punishment: incapacitation, rehabilitation, deterrence, or retribution.

The third segment, on capital punishment, begins when the moderator posits a situation where one of the prisoners stomps a guard to death. The moderator asks the prison administrator if capital punishment is then appropriate. What will it accom-plish? If it is justified, should it be televised? Much of this discussion turns upon whether publicizing capital punishment is appropriate. The underlying question is whether capital punishment is itself a shameful act. If it should be hidden, is it just?

I: OVERCROWDED JAILS

To appreciate the issue in the first part of the program, it might be helpful to picture it as a complicated game of musical chairs. Jail is the first stop in confinement for those accused of felonies. After that the person is brought before a judge, informed of the charges, and asked how he or she pleads. After that the person may be released on bail or returned to jail. If the accused has pleaded "not guilty," a trial is scheduled. At the conclusion of the trial, the person may be found not guilty and released. If he or she is found guilty, a prison sentence may be imposed. The prisoner will then be removed from jail and placed in a federal or state "correctional institution." In simplified form, the possibilities look like this:

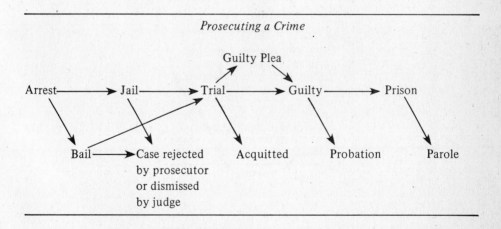

Prosecuting a Crime

As the diagram reveals, the system leaks like a sieve. All along the route are avenues—indicated by the downward arrows—that permit arrestees to escape incarceration. A defendant may "jump bail" and disappear. A prosecutor may decide that the case has no merit or that the police have blundered so much in making the arrest (see Chapter 4) that the evidence will be thrown out of court. In either case the prosecutor would probably decide not to prosecute. The judge may throw out the case. The defendant may be found (or plead) guilty but be let off on probation. Finally, the criminal may be sent to prison for a time but let out on parole. (Together, probation and parole are granted to three quarters of those sentenced.) And this is not even taking account of "plea bargaining," the process by which the prosecutor agrees to drop serious charges against a defendant in exchange for a guilty plea of a misdemeanor.

It may be gathered that only a small percentage of those arrested for serious crimes end up going to prison. In 1981, according to *The New York Times*, only 1 percent of felony arrests in New York City led to terms in state prison. Indeed, only 20 percent of felony arrests are even prosecuted as felonies. The other 80 percent are plea-bargained down to misdemeanors. A special assistant to Bronx District Attorney Mario Merola tells what happens in the Bronx: "If a guy punches a cop in the nose, the cop might arrest him and charge him with assault. When we get the case, we might say, 'Are you kidding?' and dismiss it or reduce it to resisting arrest, a misdemeanor."

Yet in spite of the leakiness of the system, both jails and prisons are full to overflowing with accused and convicted felons. More crimes and more arrests may have something to do with this increase, but the reason most frequently cited is the public's demand for "toughness" on criminals. Legislators in state after state have been enacting mandatory prison terms for a variety of crimes; even when parole is possible, parole boards are acting cautiously in the wake of public anger about paroled offenders who repeat their crimes. The result: between 1980 and 1982, the inmate population of America's prisons increased 12.1 percent; in the ten-year period between 1972 and 1982, it increased 94 percent. The graph illustrates the growth of the nation's prison population.

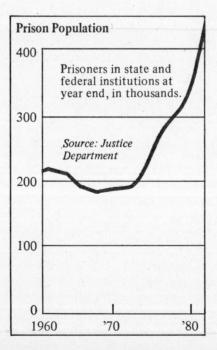

Prison Population

Prisoners in state and federal institutions at year end, in thousands.

Source: Justice Department

The same "get tough" policy has also increased our jail population. When a guilty plea will still result in a long prison term, many defendants prefer to plead not guilty. That means there must be a trial. More trials mean more congestion in the court dockets. That, in turn, slows down the processing of cases, which means that the jails get crowded with defendants awaiting trial. What happens then? We can let the panelists pick up the story.

After talking to Benjamin Ward, then jail commissioner for New York City (now head of the city's Police Department); W. J. Estelle, head of Texas prisons; Norman Carlson, director of the Federal Bureau of Prisons; Edward Hammock, head of the New York State Parole Board; and Illinois Governor James Thompson, the moderator finds that they all operate their "shops" independently of one another. None of them controls the other, even though they all feed into one another. (We are assuming that they all work for the same fictional state of Piedmont.) Nor does any overall coordinator govern the flow of defendants and convicts from one place to the other. The moderator then asks them to assume that all the jails in Piedmont are overcrowded. What is more, a federal judge has imposed a limit on the number of prisoners allowed in jail; if the limit is exceeded, Commissioner Ward is going to have to start releasing inmates without bail. When Ward approaches his limit, he releases a number of inmates on a Friday, certain that the weekend will bring in a fresh batch of arrestees. Then he goes fishing for the weekend.

The Finger Pointing

Now we reach the main issue of this segment: Whose fault is it that this event had to happen? (When it occurred in New York City, one official called it "legalized jailbreak.") Ward thinks at least part of the blame rests with the federal judge. When Ward gets back from his fishing trip, he plans to call a press conference to explain to the public that he had to let prisoners out because he was under a court order from Judge Alarcon. He is going to make sure that it is called "the Alarcon release order." "That's what you want the press to know, isn't it?" the moderator says, and he puts into words what he knows is on Ward's mind. "I didn't set this order. This isn't my order. This is Judge Alarcon's order. These people are getting out because Judge Alarcon, that's A-L-A-R-C-O-N . . . (Laughter), is letting them." But the judge is not going to take the blame. He says he is merely enforcing the Constitution, whose Eighth and Fourteenth Amendments have been violated by the overcrowding. The problem hasn't been created by him but by the governor and the authorities who are supposed to provide sufficient jail space.

Ward seems to agree, adding that the problem is also created by state judges who set high bails or hold suspects without bail just to "give this person a taste of jail." The moderator turns to New York State Judge Edwin Torres. "Judge Torres, is he talking about you?" "Doesn't sound like me," Judge Torres answers. He goes on to explain why he thinks the Alarcon order is "infernal." It is infernal because Alarcon fails to understand the reason why jails are full. Jail overcrowding has nothing to do with judges who set bail too high. It has to do with delays resulting from the logistics of moving inmates back and forth from jail to court.

One cannot sentence a prisoner without a probation report. So now starts the comic opera. The probation officer is taken ill. Or the probation officer is . . . on vacation, or the typists are not available or on strike. Or the prisoner wants to get married. (*Laughter*) Or the prisoner has been assaulted . . . and/or the prisoner has assaulted his lawyer. (*Laughter*) You see? So we go from there. So this . . . in turn necessitates delay.

If the release order cannot be blamed on the federal judge or on the slowness of state judicial proceedings, where does the fault lie? Perhaps it lies with the governor and the legislature for not building enough jails. Governor Thompson disagrees. First of all, he resents the intrusion of the federal judiciary into affairs that should concern governors and legislators. "What's Alarcon doing in this business anyway?" State elected officials, not appointed federal judges, are supposed to determine spending priorities in the states. Second, Thompson wonders aloud whether there isn't already too much money being spent on housing prisoners. Ward had said that it cost $84 a day per inmate, and that "is more than taxpayers pay when they check into a hotel on vacation"; they can hardly be blamed for thinking of jails as country clubs for criminals.

So the circle is complete. The jailer who has released accused felons says, "It's not my fault. A federal judge ordered it." The federal judge says, "It's not my fault. The jail was overcrowded." The state judge says, "It's not my fault. It takes so long to process these cases. We need more jail space." The governor says, "That's not my fault. We already spend too much on jails. The people who elected me think we're coddling criminals."

The situation in Piedmont is far from imaginary. Due to steadily growing prison population coupled with an increase in lawsuits by "prisoners' rights" organizations, overcrowding has become a major issue in federal courts. District court judges, who man the lowest level of federal courts, have often sided with prisoners and demanded that local authorities remedy the situation. The authorities have often appealed these decisions, only to find appeals court judges supporting the rulings of the district courts. The Supreme Court has been less sympathetic to the argument that overcrowding amounts to "cruel and unusual punishment," or punishment of any sort. But its rulings still leave room for lower-court judges to pressure local authorities into making hard choices: either to make more room or to start freeing inmates.

The issue of overcrowded jails has been considered in the Supreme Court case of *Bell* v. *Wolfish* (1979).

Bell v. *Wolfish*: Double Bunking Does Not Violate the Constitution

Bell v. *Wolfish* originated in a U.S. District Court in Manhattan. At issue were the conditions and practices in the Manhattan Correctional Center, a federal jail. In the words of Justice William Rehnquist, who wrote the Supreme Court's majority opinion in the case, inmates "served up a veritable potpourri of complaints" against the institution. They objected to the search procedures used in the jail, which included body-cavity searches. They objected to room searches. They objected to the institution's "publisher only" rule, barring the receipt of books in the mail unless the books came directly from a publisher or book club. And among the conditions of the jail they objected to was the practice of "double bunking," putting two inmates in rooms originally designed for one. The district court judge, Morris Lasker, agreed with the inmates that these practices violated due process of law and ordered the facility to stop them. He was upheld by a court of appeals, but when the case reached the Supreme Court, the decisions were reversed.

The inmates' case had rested largely upon the "presumption of innocence." They were not convicts but pretrial detainees. In America people are presumed innocent until they are found guilty. Pretrial detainees are therefore innocent; yet in this case they were being treated like convicted felons. In replying to this argument, the Supreme Court agreed that the presumption of innocence "plays an important role in our criminal justice system." However, "it has no application to a determination of the rights of a pretrial detainee during confinement before his trial has even begun."

The Court's point was this: once we admit that these presumptively innocent citizens can be detained, held behind bars, despite their "innocence," we have to admit that the authorities have a right "to employ devices that are calculated to effectuate this detention." Such devices may include cell searches, body searches, mail restrictions, and so on. As for the practice of "double bunking," the Supreme Court said there is not "some sort of 'one man, one cell' principle lurking in the Due Process Clause of the Fifth Amendment." Rehnquist even lectured the lower federal courts on the necessity of minding their own business. Their business is the Constitution and laws of the United States, not the details of prison administration. He quoted from the appeals court opinion: "Concern with the minutiae of prison administration can only distract the court from detached consideration of the one overriding question presented to it: does the practice or condition violate the Constitution?" The trouble, said Rehnquist, was that the appeals court "failed to heed its own admonition not to 'second-guess' prison administrators."

In spite of the Court's firm rejection of the inmates' claims in this case, it did not slam the door shut on future suits by inmates. If jail overcrowding is so great as to cause inmates "to endure genuine privations and hardship over an extended period," then it "might raise serious questions under the Due Process Clause. . . ." This dictum became the opening wedge for new decisions in the lower federal courts upholding inmates' claims.

The Lasker Release Order

One of the most controversial of these new lower-court decisions was handed down a month before the panelists met to debate this issue; in fact, one of the panelists, New York City jail commissioner Benjamin Ward, was a principal in the case. The district court judge was Morris Lasker, the same judge whose ruling was overturned in *Bell* v. *Wolfish*. Ironically, Lasker now used Rehnquist's *Wolfish* dictum about "genuine privations and hardships over an extended period" to order New York City's Department of Correction to reduce overcrowding, even if that meant opening up its jails and releasing inmates.

The case began in 1980, a year after *Wolfish*, when Lasker, responding to the petitions of inmates, began setting limits or "caps" on the number of inmates who could be housed in the city's jails. The city asked for time to correct the hardships which Lasker said had resulted from overcrowding. Three years later, in the spring of 1983, Lasker scheduled new hearings. After determining that the hardships still remained, Lasker ordered that his population caps be strictly enforced. That could mean releasing prisoners on reduced bail or no bail, although Lasker suggested other means, such as increasing pretrial services and letting defendants use credit cards for posting bail. At the beginning of November 1983, city officials began releasing inmates held on low bail ($1,500 or less). At first the city required detainees to post 10 percent of their bail, and 477 were released under that rule. But that still did not bring the inmate population down to the cap set by Judge Lasker, so the city began letting them out without any bail. Another 136 inmates were then released, bringing the jails down to the cap. The inmate release was then discontinued, at least for the time being.

In all, 613 inmates—some of them with long criminal records, others charged with crimes like rape and robbery*—were turned loose. It was the first time in New York City's history that this had happened. Within two days, one of the free inmates, Dean Craig, age thirty-six, was rearrested on a rape charge. (He was later acquitted.) Over the next month, another seventy-four were rearrested on a variety of other charges. In Manhattan, according to District Attorney Robert Morgenthau, about a third of the released detainees also failed to show up for their court appearances. Morgenthau said that the percentage was about double what would have been expected had the inmates been released under customary bail procedures.

Why had Judge Lasker set the population limits that resulted in these releases? In his 1983 decision, he contended that jail congestion had caused a variety of privations and hardships, from unsanitary kitchens to lack of sufficient recreation. While acknowledging that improvements in these conditions had been made since 1980, Lasker concluded that the facilities, "despite the vigorous efforts of their administrators, appear unable adequately to support even their current levels of population." Some of the conditions described by Judge Lasker, like the dirty kitchens and the vermin-infested cells, sound serious indeed, though the city claimed they could be remedied without population caps. Some of the other deprivations seem less than conscience-shocking. For example, Lasker noted that classes the inmates signed up for were often closed out and "the copying machine is frequently out of ink and paper." It is arguable that the entire opinion violates the spirit of *Bell* v. *Wolfish*, for it seems to be deeply concerned "with the minutiae of prison administration." Thus, the city's Correction Department

---

*Two separate studies, one by Manhattan District Attorney Robert Morgenthau and the other by *The New York Daily News*, confirmed that a sizable number of those released were either career criminals or charged with dangerous, violent crimes. "They fall into two categories," Morgenthau said, "those with serious crimes, such as murder, rape or robbery, or those with extensive arrest records, such as the pickpocket with 25 previous arrests." *The New York Times*, May 23, 1983, p. B3. *The News* survey revealed "a high proportion of career criminals who have run up as many as 24 arrests and 11 convictions." *The News* selected seventeen inmates at random and reviewed their records. "The records showed that the 17 have been responsible for a total of 124 arrests and 61 convictions for crimes, which included robbery, grand larceny and narcotics offenses." *The New York Sunday News*, November 13, 1983, p. 3.

stood a chance of getting Judge Lasker's decision reversed had it appealed its case to the U.S. Supreme Court.

The intriguing question is why it did not appeal. Perhaps the answer is that the city was really quite pleased with the decision. The video discussion lends some support to this hypothesis. The moderator says to Commissioner Ward: "So Judge Alarcon's order turns out to be a pretty good thing for you. I mean, you get to hold press conferences. You get to make the system respond. Your population drops." And Ward answers: "Never said it was a bad order except in the simplicity of the release mechanism." Significantly, in the wake of Judge Lasker's order in New York City, Mayor Edward Koch, usually outspoken on the subject of "law and order," had a surprisingly mild reaction. He blamed the prisoner release not on Judge Lasker's decision but on the slowness of the *state* judges in processing cases. Afterward, at a public meeting on the subject, Judge Lasker said the mayor was being unfair to the state judiciary. So it comes down to the reverse of finger pointing; it was *nobody's* fault that 613 former jail inmates were walking the streets.

It was not Judge Lasker's fault; he was merely enforcing the Constitution as he read it. It was not Commissioner Ward's fault; he was doing what he had to do. It was not the city's fault; it had no more funds to build jails. It was not the state judges' fault; the delays were built into the system. It was not the public's fault; they were already being taxed to death. Just as everyone was innocent, everyone—or *almost* everyone—gained from the decision. Judge Lasker got to see his orders implemented. Commissioner Ward got some relief from overcrowding. Mayor Koch got to make speeches about the slowness of justice. The state judges got vindicated by Judge Lasker. And the inmates got out of jail. There were many winners, but there may have also been losers—those who might have been victimized by released inmates.

Points to Remember

1. Jails, in contrast to prisons, are not intended as places of punishment. They are places of detainment, housing those accused of crimes until their trials. Their inmates are presumptively innocent.

2. Only a small percentage of those arrested end up doing time in prison. Even so, the prison population in America has nearly doubled since the early 1970s, in part because of public demand for a "get tough" approach to criminals. The jail population has also increased at an alarming rate, causing congestion and pressure upon existing facilities.

3. Although recent Supreme Court decisions have admonished federal judges not to get too involved in the details of prison administration, the lower federal courts have been pressing prison and jail administrators to improve inmates' living conditions and provide them with more space.

4. In *Bell* v. *Wolfish* (1979), the Supreme Court said the practice of double bunking does not, by itself, violate the Constitution. It also said jail administrators can set rules which may invade the privacy of pretrial detainees as long as the rules are reasonably related to the administration of their jails.
5. But in *Bell* the Court also acknowledged that overcrowding which results in genuine privation and hardship over an extended period might indeed constitute punishment without a trial, in violation of the due process clause of the Fifth or Fourteenth Amendment. In New York City in 1983, a district judge decided that the jails were doing just that; his decision culminated in the release of 613 inmates on low bail or no bail. There is some evidence that city officials were not altogether displeased with the judge's decision, for it relieved overcrowding. But it also raised questions about the safety of the public.

II: WHAT ARE PRISONS FOR?

The first and second parts of the video discussion are almost seamlessly connected. They really grow out of the same problem: overcrowding in jails and prisons. If these facilities are filled beyond capacity, then we have to make some hard choices. Who really deserves to be in prison? Who, on the other hand, may be better off with a stiff fine, or with a probationary sentence, or with some sort of community service? Overcrowding thus forces us to think as never before about the whole purpose of prison. What is it for? What, realistically, can we expect it to accomplish?

The program's second part begins when the moderator turns to Bronx District Attorney Mario Merola. "Mr. Merola," he says, "you have your hand on the intake part of the system." He means that if Merola decides not to prosecute someone, then one less body has to be accommodated in prison. Who, then, does he think should serve time? Prostitutes? Never, says Merola. What about car thieves? Car thieves, Merola answers, do not go to jail unless they are part of some big operation, a "chop shop" that cuts up cars and sells the pieces—a big business in many cities. Next the moderator mentions crime that is more serious but still nonviolent. "Sixty-year-old guy. He's made a lot of money ripping off people in nursing homes. In it with his son. Fraud. How about him?" Community service and a stiff fine, Merola answers. Then the moderator turns to the subject of violent crime. A thirty-five-year-old nurse, in love with a doctor, finds he's been cheating on her. She shoots him with a thirty-eight. Again, community service, although Merola is willing to allow that if there is enough prison space, she should go there. Merola doesn't like these choices. If he had his way, all felons would do some time. But overcrowding doesn't permit such "luxury."

There follows a discussion of why Merola has decided as he has. Judge Pincham is much more inclined to incarcerate the nursing-home crook than he is the nurse who shoots her lover. The former is acting maliciously. The nurse, on the other hand, has committed a crime of passion which she is unlikely to repeat. Congressman Barney Frank agrees that "the nursing-home guy is probably one of the prime candidates to be locked up," for he has committed a "calculated, rational crime" that can be deterred by imprisonment. On the other hand, Frank doesn't see why the nurse should be out free, doing community service. At the very least, she should have to give any would-be lover a "reverse *Miranda* warning" which says, "Hi, I'm so-and-so, and if we hit it off, I might shoot you."

Behind the joke is a serious question: What kind of offender belongs in prison? Is prison only for the violent? Then the nurse belongs there but not the nursing-home owner. Is it for the rational, calculating criminal? Then the nursing-home owner belongs there but not the nurse. Is it for big, rich criminals? Then the "chop shop" owner should go to prison, but not the petty car thief. Is it for recidivists, those chronic thieves who steal almost out of habit? Then the little car thief should go to prison but possibly not the nursing-home operator. The larger question behind all this remains: What is the purpose of prison?

Broadly speaking, four purposes have been identified. Each has its advocates, and each has enjoyed its seasons of prominence. The four purposes are:

1. *Rehabilitation.* A "prison," as we understand the term today, is a modern institution. We think of a prison as a place of long-term confinement. Before the nineteenth century, criminals were rarely kept long behind bars. Political or religious dissenters might be imprisoned or kept under house arrest, but ordinary criminals were disposed of quickly: they would have their cheeks branded, or their ears chopped, or their backs flogged and be let go; or else they would be put to death. Then came the nineteenth century and the rise of Protestant pietism, the belief that the principles of the Gospel ought to govern society. The most pietistic of all sects was the Quakers: they established the "penitentiary," a place where the criminal could "repent" of misdeeds while sitting in solitary confinement. Long periods of reflection would rehabilitate the criminal, preparing him to face society as a reformed person. But experience showed that strict solitude led instead to insanity. Programs of instruction, labor, and spiritual counseling were then added. These too failed. At best, they encouraged fraud and fakery by prisoners, who pretended to be "born again" in order to get out of prison.

No sooner did nineteenth-century pietism start to crumble than twentieth-century psychology took its place. Indeed, some might even say that the advocates of rehabilitation had traded one religion for another. A number of observers, such as historian Christopher Lasch and sociologist Peter Berger, have contended that psychotherapists serve as clergy for a secular culture: they hear confessions, absolve people of guilt, help them find paths to regeneration. This new "religion" claimed a new purpose for prisons of the twentieth century: crime was a kind of sickness, of which people needed to be "cured." Prisons were to be places where people got educated, learned skills, did work therapy, and received intensive psychological counseling. They were no longer "penitentiaries" but rather "correctional centers." They were not supposed to "punish" criminals but to "treat" them.

In the '30s and '40s, Dr. Karl Menninger, a psychiatrist, pioneered in the new approach to rehabilitation. In *The Crime of Punishment*, Menninger reflected on his life's work: "Do I believe there is effective treatment for offenders, and that they *can* be changed? *Most certainly and definitely I do*" (emphasis Menninger's). The majority of violent criminals, said Menninger, are "curable." "The willfulness and the viciousness of offenders are part of the thing for which they have to be treated." The corollary to this is that prisoners should have opportunities for parole. If criminals are sick, then they should be released when they are well. This, in turn, meant indeterminate sentences ("five to twenty years") so prisoners could be monitored to see if their behavior improved. If it did, what further reason was there to hold them?

In recent years, the philosophy of rehabilitation has fallen from favor, even among academics and intellectuals. Its critics point to two weaknesses in it. First, defining criminality as mental illness seems to deny human responsibility. If everyone who commits a crime is just sick, then no one is guilty of anything. What's more, as soon as criminals are "cured," they should be released. Yet something about this offends our concept of justice. Second, there is not much evidence that rehabilitation works. The best-known critic of rehabilitation, political scientist James Q. Wilson of Harvard, cites statistics showing the rates of recidivism (repeating crimes) among ex-offenders from model rehabilitative prisons compared to those from prisons where prisoners lack supportive services. The result: no appreciable difference. It may be nice, it may be humane, to give prisoners plenty of counseling and training, but it does not seem to have much effect on their behavior.

2. *Deterrence.* Professor Wilson is sometimes caricatured by his critics as an advocate of "locking 'em up and throwing away the key." Actually, if Wilson can be associated with any slogan, it is "the certainty of punishment, not the severity." Wilson is appalled by the leakiness of our criminal justice system—that, for example, 99 percent of all felony arrests in New York City do not lead to even a day in state prison. Crime pays! To make it *not* pay, would-be criminals should know that they will certainly do some time if they get caught. Even if the penalty is only a year, the would-be criminal may be deterred by *knowing* that it *will* be imposed. Following this philosophy, a number of states have done away with indeterminate sentencing, taking discretion out of the hands of judges and parole boards, in order to make punishments more predictable. Minnesota, for example, has adopted a "grid" system that quantifies a convict's criminal past and current offense and assigns the appropriate sentence. Any judge who wants to impose a greater or lesser penalty must justify the alternative in writing.

"Wicked people exist," says Wilson. They should be punished. "And many people neither wicked nor innocent, but watchful, dissembling, and calculating of their opportunities, ponder our reaction to wickedness as a cue to what they might profitably do." We should take the profit out of crimes by affixing definite punishments to them. Then we can say to someone thinking about committing wickedness: "If you can't do the time, don't do the crime."

Are there any weaknesses in this approach? One obvious shortcoming is that it probably would have no effect on the nurse, the one who shot the doctor in a jealous rage. That is a crime of passion, not of calculation, and is probably undeterrable by the threat of punishment. The police blotters of every city are full of such crimes: a man stabs his brother-in-law after a family quarrel, a man finds his wife with another man and shoots them both, a friendly card game culminates in a killing. Add to this the killings, maimings, and armed robberies committed by people under the influence of liquor or drugs. Wilson's picture of the "watchful, dissembling, and calculating" criminal may be simplistic. It fits the nursing-home operator and the "chop shop" proprietor, but it does not fit a large category of other criminals. Even the car thief may be stealing not out of rational calculation but because he needs heroin and will take any chance to get it. Furthermore, the theory of deterrence assumes that each locality has an honest and efficient police force. It hardly does any good to have a system of certain *punishments* if the criminal knows that he will probably not get *arrested*. A great deal of crime in America is carried out with impunity because overburdened, demoralized, and sometimes corrupt police have learned to look the other way.

3. *Incapacitation.* This is really a horrible term. It sounds like breaking the criminal's legs! Yet all it means is confinement—preferably for a long time—keeping the criminal locked up and off the streets. Those who favor deterrence also tend to favor incapacitation, probably because it has the same no-nonsense quality. James Q. Wilson makes a strong case for it. Citing statistics compiled by a University of Pennsylvania professor and his colleagues on 10,000 Philadelphia youths, Wilson notes that only 6 percent of them committed five or more offenses before they were eighteen. "Yet these few chronic offenders accounted for *over half* of all the recorded delinquencies and about *two-thirds* of all the violent crimes committed by the entire cohort" (emphasis Wilson's). Just locking up these hardened cases would make people's lives much safer.

Just as incapacitation is related to deterrence, it may share some of the same weaknesses. It is, perhaps, a bit simplistic. Locking criminals up is one thing, but at some point—unless we give them all life sentences—we have to let them out again. And what happens after that? Unless we assume that prison has rehabilitated them, which the advocates of incapacitation usually deny, chances are they will return to crime, perhaps with a vengeance and with new techniques learned from other convicts. Incapacitation also runs head-on into the sobering reality mentioned earlier in this chapter: the annual 12 percent increase in our prison population. Where are we going to *put* all the people we wish to incapacitate?

4. *Retribution.* Not long ago, this rationale for prison was not even discussed in enlightened circles. It was considered primitive and irrational. The idea of "paying back" the criminal, which is what "retribution" literally means, can be found in the Old Testament law of "an eye for an eye, a tooth for a tooth." Jesus seemed to preach a different doctrine: "Let him who is without sin cast the first stone," and "Forgive one another, even as the Father forgives you." Again, as with the philosophy of rehabilitation, a Christian doctrine was secularized in the early years of this century, when the philosophy of "help" and "therapy" for criminals became fashionable. What sense did it make to "pay back" criminals if they could hardly help what they were doing when they committed their crimes? What on earth could be accomplished by retribution? It seemed like senseless brutality.

In recent years, however, retribution has made a comeback. Some writers, like the philosopher Walter Berns, have used it as their chief argument for capital punishment. Others use it more broadly, as a way of justifying punishments when all other rationales fail. It speaks to something deep and basic in the human soul. Let the reader try this experiment. Suppose Martin Bormann, or one of the other Nazi murderers still at large, were apprehended. Should he be imprisoned? If the answer is yes, then the next question is why. To rehabilitate him? By now he would be about ninety-five, a little past the stage of rehabilitation. To deter others? But his crimes were so unique, it is doubtful that the deterrence "message" would mean very much to others. To incapacitate him, get him off the streets before he commits more mass murders? That hardly seems likely! The only alternative left is retribution—to *pay him back* for his role in mass murder.

The problem with retribution is that it seems to have no built-in limits. "Paying back" seems to lead, logically and inexorably, to "paying back in kind." If we owe Jack $2, we have to pay him back $2. If we owe him $200, we have to pay him back $200. Now suppose Jack has set fire to his girlfriend. It seems to follow that we have to pay him back by doing the same to him. The account book has to be balanced. Obviously, we recoil from this. We say, "It doesn't have to follow at all. We are humane people, not savages. We figure out appropriate punishments; we set limits to what we allow ourselves to do." But the psychological hazard of retribution is that it lifts the lid on some very dangerous emotions. Who among us has not felt these emotions after hearing about—or experiencing—a particularly vile crime?

Returning to the hypothetical examples mentioned in the video debate, we can see how the various participants line up. Judge Pincham and Congressman Frank seem to support the idea of retribution, though they apply it in different ways. Both would imprison the nursing-home operator, even though he is nonviolent, and the reasons they give suggest the idea of "paying back." Frank says, "I don't want that bum doing community service." On the other hand, Pincham is ready to let the nurse off with community service, while Frank would imprison her not for the sake of retribution but simply to keep her off the streets, or perhaps out of doctors' bedrooms, given her tendency toward homicidal jealousy.

Both Frank and Roger Rosenblatt, essayist for *Time* magazine, seem to agree on the value of deterrence, which is one reason they would both lock up white-collar criminals. "Punishment," says Rosenblatt, is for "the law-abider, too. It keeps the law-abider in line, so you don't just let people off that easily for crimes." On the other hand, Illinois Governor Thompson seems to think of prison primarily in terms of incapacitation. Get the muggers and the rapists off the streets. This annoys Tom Stoddard of the New York Civil Liberties Union, who is the panel's foremost defender of rehabilitation. He and Thompson get into an extended argument about whether it is cheaper to keep people in prison or let them out to do supervised community service.

Points to Remember

1. Prisons, as places of long-term confinement, are relatively new in Western history. They began under Quaker auspices as "penitentiaries," places designed for "penitence." Later, under the influence of modern psychology and social work, they were intended as "correctional centers."
2. Imprisoning criminals has been justified under one or more heads: (a) rehabilitation, (b) deterrence, (c) incapacitation, and (d) retribution. Each of these rationales has its supporters and critics. It is now up to the reader to review at least one

argument for and against each of these rationales. Which of the four seems the most defensible? Or are combinations called for? What about the cases of the prostitute, the car thief, the "chop shop" owner, the corrupt nursing-home proprietor, and the nurse who killed her lover—what *should* society do with such people?

III: THE DEATH PENALTY

Rather abruptly, the moderator introduces a new topic into the discussion. A twenty-seven-year-old prisoner serving a life term stomps a guard to death. The moderator turns to Rudolph Giuliani, a federal prosecutor. "Mr. Giuliani, you've got a death penalty statute in Piedmont. You go for it with this fellow?" "Sure," Giuliani answers, "No question about it." Others, however, and not just Giuliani's fellow panelists, have some very serious questions. They have had them for hundreds of years, though their questioning has become more intense during the last two decades. The issue deserves a closer look.

The discussion in the video portion takes a rather strange turn. Most of what remains of it seems to turn upon the desirability of showing an execution on TV. CBS News commentator Bill Moyers opposes it. Judge Joan Klein accuses him of being "sanctimonious" and finds his desire to protect viewers from scenes of violence "singularly peculiar" in light of CBS's violence-filled programming. That's not the point, says Moyers. He only wants to protect the condemned man's dignity and to avoid making a "spectacle" of his death. Earlier, Moyers had put the case in terms of privacy rights: "Certain moments should remain private." But, as several panelists remind him, an execution is not exactly a private act. It is a solemn state ceremony, with official witnesses present, including members of the press.

If an execution is a public act, what is wrong with showing it to the public? Nothing at all, says Tom Stoddard of the New York Civil Liberties Union. An opponent of capital punishment, Stoddard hopes that televising an execution will nauseate people to such an extent that they will demand its abolition. Rudolph Giuliani, the U.S. prosecutor, wants it shown for the opposite reason: it might deter anyone who may be contemplating murder. He favors capital punishment. Utah Supreme Court Judge Dallin Oaks also favors it, but he opposes showing it on TV. His reason: watching it will "brutalize" viewers. *Time*'s Roger Rosenblatt wonders if that is not inherent in capital punishment. It *is* brutal; therefore, the American people should have to see what their cherished death penalty leads to.

But the brutality of the death penalty is not a sufficient argument against it. Many things are brutal: a soldier getting blown apart by a land mine, an intruder getting shot in the face by a woman he is trying to rape, a time bomb exploding at a Nazi High Command meeting. Arguably, none of these events, or even reenactments of them, should be shown on TV. But that does not mean they are always unjustified. The death penalty cannot be opposed simply because it involves violence or because watch-

ing it on TV may brutalize viewers. It has to be opposed because it is unjust or unconstitutional. How do we test for that?

Let us start with an extreme. We return to the example with which the chapter began: breaking people on the wheel, smashing their bones with a crowbar. *That*, surely,
is immoral; *that*, surely, violates the Eighth Amendment's ban on "cruel and unusual
punishment." But why? What is it about the practice that shocks our consciences? At
least two characteristics stand out. First, it involves the wanton, deliberate infliction
of pain. The pain is not incidental to the punishment; it is the whole point of it. The
historical evidence suggests that what the Founders meant by "cruel and unusual punishment" was punishment that involved "tortures" and other "barbarous" methods.
Breaking on the wheel is certainly torturous. But what about "barbarous?"

This brings us to the second characteristic. Suppose we were to put someone to
death by dropping a 5,000-pound safe on his head. It would not be torturous; he
probably would not feel a thing. But it would be "barbarous." (It would also be "unusual," but what the Framers meant by "unusual" is less certain than what they meant
by "cruel.") Barbarity is somehow tied to the denial of human dignity. Hanging a dead
man's head on a fence is not torturous but is barbaric—it is a deliberate, horrible affront to his dignity. So is breaking someone on the wheel: it would be barbaric even if
it were not torturous. In that sense, too, it is "cruel."

What else is "cruel?" The Supreme Court has ruled, at least in federal cases, that
punishments grossly disproportionate to the crimes committed can be considered cruel.

Weems v. *United States* (1910): The Need for Proportionality

Weems, a former Coast Guard official in the Philippine Islands, which at that time
were under U.S. jurisdiction, was convicted of defrauding the government of 612 pesos.
Using a provision of the old Spanish code, a judge sentenced him to fifteen years' imprisonment, chained at the ankle and wrist, doing hard and painful labor. In an opinion by Justice McKenna, the Court majority ruled that this punishment was "cruel"
because of its disproportionality. McKenna conceded that the Framers of the Eighth
Amendment may have had a narrower view of "cruel"; they were thinking about dis-
embowelments, breaking on the wheel, and so forth. Nevertheless, he added, we need
not be limited to considering those kinds of punishments in interpreting "cruel," for
"*a principle, to be vital, must be capable of wider application than the mischief which
gave it birth*" (emphasis added). What does that mean? It means we have to keep up
with the times in interpreting the Constitution; we have to apply it to today's circumstances. Governments are not going to disembowel people anymore. But they may do
other "cruel" things that never occurred to the Framers.

The logic of the *Weems* opinion was developed further in a case decided almost
fifty years later by the Court of Chief Justice Earl Warren.

Trop v. *Dulles* (1958): "Evolving Standards"

Under an act derived from a Civil War statute, a court-martial held that Trop, a native-
born American guilty of wartime desertion, should lose his citizenship. Trop appealed

to the Supreme Court and won. Speaking for a five-member majority, Chief Justice Warren ruled that such a penalty subjected Trop to "a fate forbidden by the principles of civilized treatment guaranteed by the Eighth Amendment." True, there was no physical torture.

> There is instead the total destruction of the individual's status in organized society. It is a form of punishment more primitive than torture, for it destroys for the individual the political existence that was centuries in the development.

In a famous passage, Warren justified his reading of the Eighth Amendment—a reading some consider strained if not utterly arbitrary—by positing the following principle of interpretation. The Eighth Amendment, he said, "must draw its meaning from the evolving standards of decency that mark the progress of a maturing society." What on earth is that supposed to mean?

What it means is that the Court of Earl Warren had enormous, almost boundless, faith in human progress. It believed that human societies are "evolving," rising upward from barbarism and cruelty. We are getting better each day; we are ascending. We must not be content, therefore, with the standards of the past. We measure ourselves against the higher standards of today. Critics of this approach find in it a perfect recipe for judicial arrogance. Using it, they say, permits judges to amend the Constitution on their own, simply by deciding what *they* think is "enlightened" and "civilized." If Warren were alive, he could well reply that he did not mean the ruling to be so subjective. Indeed, in the *Trop* case he went out of his way to cite an example of a practice that some judges might oppose but which the American people still support: the practice of capital punishment. "Whatever the moral arguments may be against capital punishment" (and Warren added that "they are forceful"), the death penalty "is still widely accepted" and thus "cannot be said to violate the constitutional concept of cruelty." In other words, judges have no right to substitute their morality for the norms of society.

Why, then, did the Court overrule the death penalty in *Furman* v. *Georgia* (1972)? The answer is that it did not. The "swing" members of the Court, who swung a narrow majority against the capital punishment laws being tested in the case, did not say the Constitution forbids capital punishment. They said it forbids meting out capital punishment in an "arbitrary and capricious" way.

Furman v. *Georgia*: "Arbitrary and Capricious" Executions

Furman v. *Georgia* is difficult to summarize, not only because it contains some 50,000 words and deals with three separate cases but also because the majority never found any agreed-upon reasons for its ruling against the death penalty in the cases before it. All five justices in the majority agreed that the Eighth Amendment prohibited the states from executing the convicts then being held on death row. Two justices, William Brennan and Thurgood Marshall, voted against the death penalty under any circumstances. One, William O. Douglas, voted against the death penalty because he believed it was applied in a racially discriminatory manner. The other two—the "swing members," Byron White and Potter Stewart—considered it unconstitutional because it was imposed in such an arbitrary and capricious fashion that no one could ever predict who would be sentenced to death and who would be spared. (Stewart compared it to being hit by a bolt of lightning.)

This was, at best, a fragmented majority. And it was opposed by a solid minority of four: Chief Justice Burger and Justices Powell, Blackmun, and Rehnquist. Anyone compiling a list of bad predictions over the past fifteen years will have to include that of NAACP attorney Jack Greenberg, who, in the wake of the *Furman* decision, joyfully asserted: "There will no longer be any more capital punishment in the United States." Four years after this confident prediction, the Supreme Court approved the use of the death penalty in the case of *Gregg* v. *Georgia* (1976).

Gregg v. *Georgia*: **Constitutional Executions**

Some intervening events probably affected the Court's decison.

- Almost immediately after *Furman*, state legislatures began enacting new death penalty statutes designed to meet the objections raised in *Furman*. By 1976, thirty-five had done so.
  The people of California voted in a referendum by a two-to-one margin to bring back their own death penalty, which had been struck down by their state's highest court.
- Justice William O. Douglas, who probably would have voted against the death penalty in any form, retired and was replaced by John Paul Stevens, a nominee of President Ford.

The first two events are important because they tended to weaken one argument for abolishing the death penalty—an argument borrowed from *Trop* v. *Dulles*. In the *Trop* case of 1958, Chief Justice Warren had talked about "the evolving standards of decency that mark the progress of a maturing society." This prompted Justices Brennan and Marshall to offer the following argument in *Furman*: even though the Framers of the Bill of Rights did not mean to abolish capital punishment,* we have moved so far beyond them in our standards of decency that we now consider it barbarous and cruel. True, the statutes are still on the books, but they are old and seldom applied anymore. What about the fact that Chief Justice Warren had specifically said in *Trop* that the American people do *not* consider capital punishment "cruel and unusual"? Well, that was then. A lot of changes came over Americans between 1958 and 1972. Standards had now evolved to the point where the death penalty simply lacked the legitimacy it once had.

---

*Legislative history and the Constitution itself leave no doubt that the Framers of the Eighth Amendment did not mean to abolish capital punishment. The same Congress that wrote the Eighth Amendment also passed death penalty statutes. Furthermore, the Fifth Amendment (written by the same Congress that wrote the Eighth) states that grand jury indictments are necessary in cases involving "capital" crimes. The Fifth Amendment also prohibits holding someone twice "in jeopardy of life or limb." Finally, the Fifth Amendment prohibits government from depriving people of "*life*, liberty, or property" (emphasis added) without due process of law, which means that government *may* deprive people of their lives if due process is used.

But all that seemed to be disproved by the developments between 1972 and 1976: the consistent support of the death penalty in public opinion polls, the California referendum, and above all the new death penalty statutes. "Evolving standards"? The American people's obvious support for the death penalty during the '70s showed that their standards just hadn't evolved that much!

Justice Stewart took note of all this in his majority opinion in *Gregg*. He also noted Georgia's effort to avoid the "arbitrary and capricious" imposition of the death penalty, which Stewart and White considered to be the chief problem of the old laws. The new Georgia statute contains the following features:

1. *Bifurcation.* The statute provides for two jury trials, one to determine the defendant's guilt, the other to decide whether he or she should be imprisoned or executed. In that way, evidence concerning the defendant's character that had been excluded at the first trial can be weighed in deciding whether his or her life should be spared. It constitutes another layer of protection for the defendant.

2. *Guidelines.* In deciding whether or not to sentence someone to death, juries are not left with unlimited discretion. They must consult a series of guidelines, which spell out "aggravating circumstances." Was the murder committed by someone who had already been convicted for murder? Was it committed in the course of a major felony, like first-degree burglary? Did the murder also endanger the lives of others? There are ten guidelines in all, and unless the jury finds that at least one is met, it cannot call for the death penalty.

3. *Court review.* The Georgia statute provides for state supreme court review of each death sentence to see whether it was imposed under the influence of passion, prejudice, or some arbitrary factor. The state's highest court is also authorized to review the "proportionality" of a death sentence—that is, to determine whether the sentence is "excessive or disproportionate" when compared to other sentences meted out by juries in the state. This provision reflects the Supreme Court's decision in the *Weems* case of 1910, in which the Court struck down a sentence for being disproportionate to the crime.

Delays in Execution: Cruel and Unusual?

A number of states have adopted new capital punishment statutes resembling Georgia's. Florida's statute is almost identical to it, and under it, as of this writing, two men have already been put to death. One of them, Robert Sullivan, held the record for the longest stay on death row—he had been there for ten years. The delay resulted from the lengthy appeals process afforded to Sullivan. After appealing his case through the state system, Sullivan was able to appeal it through the federal system and then again through both systems. All others convicted and sentenced under the new laws are entitled to take the same time-consuming steps. In consequence, the death rows of America have been filling up with condemned prisoners trying to win appeals or at least to buy more time. There are more than 1,200 of them, and their number is growing rapidly.

There is evidence that some members of the Supreme Court may be growing impatient with this lengthy appeals process. In Sullivan's case, the Supreme Court voted seven to two to reject his last appeal. In a written comment accompanying the Court's verdict, Chief Justice Burger noted that the appeals had lasted ten years and had brought the case before the Supreme Court four times. He then added:

> The argument so often advanced by the dissenters that capital punishment is cruel and unusual is dwarfed by the cruelty of 10 years on death row inflicted upon this guilty defendant by lawyers seeking to turn the administration of justice into a "sporting contest."

Four months earlier, in August 1983, the Supreme Court handed down a decision that would permit federal courts to expedite the review process. In a case originating in Texas, *Barefoot* v. *Estelle* (1983), the Court permitted a federal appeals court to telescope two hearings into one. If adopted widely, this "expedited procedure" could cut down on the time between death sentences and executions. "This is the dynamite that will blow open the dam," said the prosecutor of Thomas Barefoot.

Proportionality: The New Issue

In a situation that was certainly unusual if not cruel, one Texas prisoner was already being prepared for execution in 1983 when he won a new delay. James Autry was half an hour away from death by lethal injection—in fact, he was already strapped down in a hospital gurney with intravenous tubes in each arm—when Justice Byron White of the Supreme Court granted him a new stay. The reason: Autry had not been granted a "proportionality review" by the Texas courts. The reader may recall the third provision of the Georgia law that the Court upheld in *Gregg* v. *Georgia*. This was the provision for state court review of death sentences to see if, among other things, they were proportional. If others with the same background were getting off much more lightly for the same crime, then the state court might strike the death sentence in a particular case. Stewart had praised this provision in the Georgia law. But did that mean that a proportionality review was necessary? At this writing, a Supreme Court ruling on this issue is imminent. The Court's ruling will be too late for Autry—he was executed in March 1984. However, it may affect the fate of others who have not received proportionality reviews.

Points to Remember

1. The Framers of the Eighth Amendment were not opposed to capital punishment. By "cruel and unusual punishment," they meant punishment that involves "tortures" and other "barbarous" methods. The Supreme Court has interpreted this to mean the deliberate, wanton infliction of pain and/or the use of degrading punishment.
2. The Supreme Court has also, in the case of *Weems* v. *U.S.* (1910), outlawed punishments that are grossly disproportionate to crimes (e.g., fifteen years in chains and hard labor for petty embezzling).

3. In *Trop* v. *Dulles* (1958), the Court said that today's courts should not be bound
    to the standards of "cruel and unusual" that prevailed in 1791. The Eighth
    Amendment should draw its meaning from our "evolving standards." The assump-
    tion was that our country is progressing morally—that its standards are improving.
4. In *Furman* v. *Georgia* (1972), the Court outlawed the death penalty in the three
    cases brought before it. However, only two of the justices thought the death pen-
    alty per se was unconstitutional. The "swing justices" thought it was unconstitu-
    tional only because it was applied arbitrarily and capriciously.
5. In *Gregg* v. *Georgia* (1976), the Supreme Court upheld the death penalty under
    certain circumstances and with what the Court deemed proper safeguards against
    arbitrariness, passion, and prejudice. It rejected the argument that the death penal-
    ty per se violates the Eighth Amendment.
6. Delays in carrying out the death sentence have resulted from an extensive and
    complicated appeals process. In 1983 the Court allowed a lower federal court to
    expedite this process.
7. The new issue to be tested by the Supreme Court is that of proportionality. Is it
    necessary for state courts to hold proportionality reviews before an execution can
    take place? To what extent should federal courts become involved in the question
    of proportionality? At this writing these questions are still unresolved.

SUMMARY

This chapter began by considering the problems inherent in pretrial detention, in
which the presumption of innocence is always required. The main problems result
from overcrowding. The public's new "get tough" attitude has caused the nation's jail
population (like its prison population) to soar. The resulting congestion often results
in a deterioration of conditions. Coincident with this population increase has been the
increased willingness of lower federal courts to order officials to improve conditions.
Although the Supreme Court has cautioned against excessive judicial involvement in
the minutiae of jail administration, some federal judges have gone to the length of is-
suing "release orders." In one Manhattan case, detainees were released with no bail or
a fraction of their bail and some were rearrested on new felony charges. Overcrowding
in jails and prisons has forced public officials to think hard about who should be incar-
cerated. That raises the question of what a prison is for. To rehabilitate? To deter? To
incapacitate? To "pay back"? Each of these purposes has its own rationale; each has
also been criticized.

How does capital punishment fit these four justifications for punishment? Obviously, it does not rehabilitate the prisoner, though a doomed person's anticipation of
death may effect wholesome changes in personality and outlook. Does it deter others
from committing similar crimes? The answer is much in dispute. Death penalty abolitionists cite a 1959 study that could find no evidence of deterrence; supporters like to
cite a 1975 study by Isaac Ehrlich entitled *The Deterrent Effect of Capital Punishment.* As for incapacitation, execution may be the surest means of accomplishing that

—since the criminal is irrevocably off the streets—but there are other ways of achieving it. "I can weld the door shut on him," says W. J. Estelle, head of Texas prisons. Finally, there is retribution, "paying back" the murderer by taking his or her life in return. To some, this rationale is barbarous. For others, it is evidence of a civilized society, a society determined not to tolerate those who would destroy civilization. The Supreme Court at first gave the abolitionists of capital punishment reason for hope. However, its 1972 decision prohibited capital punishment only when meted out in "arbitrary and capricious" fashion. In 1976 a solid Court majority held that capital punishment is not in itself a violation of the Eighth Amendment.

There remains that very strange, almost mystical notion, spelled out in the 1958 case of *Trop* v. *Dulles*, that American morality is traveling onward and upward. America is blessed with "evolving standards of decency," an evolution that marks our "progress" as a "maturing society."

Is our society "maturing"? Or is it regressing? Americans in the 1980s may not be as hopeful as they were in the 1950s. The fact that thirty-eight states rushed to pass new death penalty laws after the Supreme Court's 1972 decisions makes some people wonder about the direction of our "evolution." Others question the guiding assumption of *Trop* v. *Dulles* for quite different reasons. They do not want the Constitution to "evolve" at all except by the process of amendment. They worry about judges who may read their own moral views into the Constitution and then announce that these are the new, "evolved" standards of American justice. If the Court majority was ever tempted to do so in the case of the death penalty, it resisted the temptation in *Gregg* v. *Georgia*. Instead, it bowed to the fact that Americans today, like those who framed the Eighth Amendment in 1789, are prepared to "pay back" murderers by killing them.

Documents

FURMAN V. GEORGIA 408 U. S. 238 (1972)

In Furman, *which struck down Georgia's and Texas's capital punishment statutes, each member of the Court majority wrote a separate opinion expressing his reason for agreeing in the judgment. The judgment itself was very brief. It is reprinted below.*

Judgment of the Court.

. . .

Certiorari was granted limited to the following question: "Does the imposition and carrying out of the death penalty in [these cases] constitute cruel and unusual punishment in violation of the Eighth and Fourteenth Amendments?" 403 U. S. 952 (1971). The Court holds that the imposition and carrying out of the death penalty in these cases constitute cruel and unusual punishment in violation of the Eighth and Fourteenth Amendments. The judgment in each case is therefore reversed insofar as it leaves undisturbed the death sentence imposed, and the cases are remanded for further proceedings.

So ordered.

In the light of the Court's subsequent decision in Gregg v. Georgia *(1976), which upheld the principle of capital punishment, it appears that the controlling opinions in* Furman *were those of Justices Potter Stewart and Byron White. Both suggested that capital punishment may not be unconstitutional per se but was in this case because of the manner in which it was applied. Their concurrent opinions are reprinted below.*

Mr. Justice Stewart, concurring.

The penalty of death differs from all other forms of criminal punishment, not in degree but in kind. It is unique in its total irrevocability. It is unique in its rejection of rehabilitation of the convict as a basic purpose of criminal justice. And it is unique, finally, in its absolute renunciation of all that is embodied in our concept of humanity.

For these and other reasons, at least two of my Brothers have concluded that the infliction of the death penalty is constitutionally impermissible in all circumstances under the Eighth and Fourteenth Amendments. Their case is a strong one. But I find it unnecessary to reach the ultimate question they would decide. See *Ashwander* v. *Tennessee Valley Authority,* 397 U.S. 288, 347 (Brandeis, J., concurring).

. . .

. . . I cannot agree that retribution is a constitutionally impermissible ingredient in the imposition of punishment. The instinct for retribution is part of the nature of man, and channeling that instinct in the administration of criminal justice serves an important purpose in promoting the stability of a society governed by law. When people begin to believe that organized society is unwilling or unable to impose upon criminal offenders the punishment they "deserve," then there are sown the seeds of anarchy— of self-help, vigilante justice, and lynch law.

The constitutionality of capital punishment in the abstract is not, however, before us in these cases. For the Georgia and Texas legislatures have not provided that the death penalty shall be imposed upon all those who are found guilty of forcible rape. And the Georgia Legislature has not ordained that death shall be the automatic punishment for murder. In a word, neither State has made a legislative determination that forcible rape and murder can be deterred only by imposing the penalty of death upon all who perpetrate those offenses. . . .

Instead, the death sentences now before us are the product of a legal system that brings them, I believe, within the very core of the Eighth Amendment's guarantee against cruel and unusual punishments, a guarantee applicable against the States through the Fourteenth Amendment. . . . In the first place, it is clear that these sentences are "cruel" in the sense that they excessively go beyond, not in degree but in kind, the punishments that the state legislatures have determined to be necessary. . . . In the second place, it is equally clear that these sentences are "unusual" in the sense that the penalty of death is infrequently imposed for murder, and that its imposition for rape is extraordinarily rare. But I do not rest my conclusion upon these two propositions alone.

These death sentences are cruel and unusual in the same way that being struck by lightning is cruel and unusual. For, of all the people convicted of rapes and murders in 1967 and 1968, many just as reprehensible as these, the petitioners are among a capriciously selected random handful upon whom the sentence of death has in fact been imposed. My concurring Brothers have demonstrated that, if any basis can be discerned for the selection of these few to be sentenced to die, it is the constitutionally impermissible basis of race. . . . But racial discrimination has not been proved, and I put it to one side. I simply conclude that the Eighth and Fourteenth Amendments cannot tolerate the infliction of a sentence of death under legal systems that permit this unique penalty to be so wantonly and so freakishly imposed.

For these reasons I concur in the judgments of the Court.

Mr. Justice White, concurring.

The facial constitutionality of statutes requiring the imposition of the death penalty for first degree murder, for more narrowly defined categories of murder or for rape would present quite different issues under the Eighth Amendment than are posed by the cases before us. In joining the Court's judgment, therefore, I do not at all intimate that the death penalty is unconstitutional *per se* or that there is no system of capital punishment that would comport with the Eighth Amendment. That question, ably argued by several of my Brethren, is not presented by these cases and need not be decided.

The narrower question to which I address myself concerns the constitutionality of capital punishment statutes under which (1) the legislature authorizes the imposition of the death penalty for murder or rape; (2) the legislature does not itself mandate the penalty in any particular class or kind of case (that is, legislative will is not frustrated if the penalty is never imposed) but delegates to judges or juries the decisions as to those cases, if any, in which the penalty will be utilized; and (3) judges and juries have ordered the death penalty with such infrequency that the odds are now very much against imposition and execution of the penalty with respect to any convicted murderer or rapist. It is in this context that we must consider whether the execution of these petitioners violates the Eighth Amendment.

I begin with what I consider a near truism: that the death penalty could so seldom be imposed that it would cease to be a credible deterrent or measurable to contribute to any other end of punishment in the criminal justice system. It is perhaps true that no matter how infrequently those convicted of rape or murder are executed, the penalty so imposed is not disproportionate to the crime and those executed may deserve exactly what they received. It would also be clear that executed defendants are finally and completely incapacitated from again committing rape or murder or any other crime. But when imposition of the penalty reaches a certain degree of infrequency, it would be very doubtful that any existing general need for retribution would be measurably satisfied. Nor could it be said with confidence that society's need for specific deterrence justifies death for so few when for so many in like circumstances life imprisonment or shorter prison terms are indeed sufficient, or that community values are measurably reenforced by authorizing a penalty so rarely invoked.

Most important, a major goal of the criminal law—to deter others by punishing the convicted criminal—would not be substantially served where the penalty is so seldom invoked that it ceases to be the credible threat essential to influence the conduct of others. For present purposes I accept the morality and utility of punishing one person to influence another. I accept also the effectiveness of punishment generally and need not reject the death penalty as a more effective deterrent than a lesser punishment. But common sense and experience tell us that seldom-enforced laws become ineffective measures for controlling human conduct and that the death penalty, unless imposed with sufficient frequency, will make little contribution to deterring those crimes for which it may be exacted.

. . .

. . . The short of it is that the policy of vesting sentencing authority primarily in juries—a decision largely motivated by the desire to mitigate the harshness of the law and to bring community judgment to bear on the sentence as well as guilt or innocence —has so effectively achieved its aims that capital punishment within the confines of the statutes now before us has for all practical purposes run its course.

Judicial review, by definition, often involves a conflict between judicial and legislative judgment as to what the Constitution means or requires. In this respect, Eighth Amendment cases come to us in no different posture. It seems conceded by all that the Amendment imposes some obligations on the judiciary to judge the constitutionality of punishment and that there are punishments that the Amendment would bar whether legislatively approved or not. Inevitably, then, there will be occasions when we will differ with Congress or state legislatures with respect to the validity of punishment. There will also be cases in which we shall strongly disagree among ourselves. Unfortunately, this is one of them. But as I see it, this case is no different in kind from many others, although it may have wider impact and provoke sharper disagreement.

In this respect, I add only that past and present legislative judgment with respect to the death penalty loses much of its force when viewed in light of the recurring practice of delegating sentencing authority to the jury and the fact that a jury, in its own discretion and without violating its trust or any statutory policy, may refuse to impose the death penalty no matter what the circumstances of the crime. Legislative "policy" is thus necessarily defined not by what is legislatively authorized but by what juries and judges do in exercising the discretion so regularly conferred upon them. In my judgment what was done in these cases violated the Eighth Amendment.

I concur in the judgments of the Court.

GREGG V. GEORGIA, 428 U.S. 153 (1976)

In this case, which upheld capital punishment, Justice Potter Stewart announced the judgment of the Court, then went on to give his reasons for upholding the use of capital punishment in this case. He was joined in his opinion by Justices Lewis Powell and John Paul Stevens.

Judgment of the Court and opinions of Justices Stewart, Powell, and Stevens.

We address initially the basic contention that the punishment of death for the crime of murder is, under all circumstances, "cruel and unusual" in violation of the Eighth and Fourteenth Amendments of the Constitution. In Part IV of this opinion, we will consider the sentence of death imposed under the Georgia statutes at issue in this case.

The Court on a number of occasions has both assumed and asserted the constitutionality of capital punishment. In several cases that assumption provided a necessary foundation for the decision, as the Court was asked to decide whether a particular method of carrying out a capital sentence would be allowed to stand under the Eighth Amendment. But until *Furman* v. *Georgia*, 408 U. S. 238 (1972), the Court never confronted squarely the fundamental claim that the punishment of death always, regardless of the enormity of the offense or the procedure followed in imposing the sentence, is cruel and unusual punishment in violation of the Constitution. Although this issue was presented and addressed in *Furman*, it was not resolved by the Court. Four Justices would have held that capital punishment is not unconstitutional *per se;* two Justices would have reached the opposite conclusion; and three Justices, while agreeing that the statutes then before the Court were invalid as applied, left open the question whether such punishment may ever be imposed. We now hold that the punishment of death does not invariably violate the Constitution.

Of course, the requirements of the Eighth Amendment must be applied with an awareness of the limited role to be played by the courts. This does not mean that judges have no role to play, for the Eighth Amendment is a restraint upon the exercise of legislative power.

. . .

. . . in assessing a punishment selected by a democratically elected legislature against the constitutional measure, we presume its validity. We may not require the legislature to select the least severe penalty possible so long as the penalty selected is not cruelly inhumane or disproportionate to the crime involved. And a heavy burden rests on those who would attack the judgment of the representatives of the people.

. . .

In sum, we cannot say that the judgment of the Georgia Legislature that capital punishment may be necessary in some cases is clearly wrong. Considerations of federalism, as well as respect for the ability of a legislature to evaluate, in terms of its particular State, the moral consensus concerning the death penalty and its social utility as a sanction, require us to conclude, in the absence of more convincing evidence, that the infliction of death as a punishment for murder is not without justification and thus is not unconstitutionally severe.

Finally, we must consider whether the punishment of death is disproportionate in relation to the crime for which it is imposed. There is no question that death as a punishment is unique in its severity and irrevocability. *Furman* v. *Georgia*, 408 U. S., at 286-291 (BRENNAN, J., concurring); *id.*, at 306 (STEWART, J., concurring). When a defendant's life is at stake, the Court has been particularly sensitive to insure that every safeguard is observed. *Powell* v. *Alabama*, 287 U. S. 45, 71 (1932); *Reid* v. *Covert,*

354 U. S. 1, 77 (1957) (Harlan, J., concurring in result). But we are concerned here only with the imposition of capital punishment for the crime of murder, and when a life has been taken deliberately by the offender, we cannot say that the punishment is invariably disproportionate to the crime. It is an extreme sanction, suitable to the most extreme of crimes.

We hold that the death penalty is not a form of punishment that may never be imposed, regardless of the circumstances of the offense, regardless of the character of the offender, and regardless of the procedure followed in reaching the decision to impose it.

. . .

The basic concern of *Furman* centered on those defendants who were being condemned to death capriciously and arbitrarily. Under the procedures before the Court in that case, sentencing authorities were not directed to give attention to the nature or circumstances of the crime committed or to the character or record of the defendant. Left unguided, juries imposed the death sentence in a way that could only be called freakish. The new Georgia sentencing procedures, by contrast, focus the jury's attention on the particularized nature of the crime and the particularized characteristics of the individual defendant. While the jury is permitted to consider any aggravating or mitigating circumstances, it must find and identify at least one statutory aggravating factor before it may impose a penalty of death. In this way the jury's discretion is channeled. No longer can a jury wantonly and freakishly impose the death sentence; it is always circumscribed by the legislative guidelines. In addition, the review function of the Supreme Court of Georgia affords additional assurance that the concerns that prompted our decision in *Furman* are not present to any significant degree in the Georgia procedure applied here.

For the reasons expressed in this opinion, we hold that the statutory system under which Gregg was sentenced to death does not violate the Constitution. Accordingly, the judgment of the Georgia Supreme Court is affirmed.

It is so ordered.

BELL V. WOLFISH, 441 U.S. 520 (1979)

In this case the Supreme Court majority reversed lower-court rulings that conditions at the Manhattan Correctional Center (MCC), a federal institution whose inmates included pretrial detainees, amounted to "punishment" before trial, in violation of the Fifth Amendment's due process clause.

In evaluating the constitutionality of conditions or restrictions of pretrial detention that implicate only the protection against deprivation of liberty without due process of law, we think that the proper inquiry is whether those conditions amount to punishment of the detainee. For under the Due Process Clause, a detainee may not be punished prior to an adjudication of guilt in accordance with due process of law. A person lawfully committed to pretrial detention has not been adjudged guilty of any crime. He has had only a "judicial determination of probable cause as a prerequisite to [the] extended restraint of [his] liberty following arrest." *Gerstein* v. *Pugh, supra,* 420 U.S., at 114. And, if he is detained for a suspected violation of a federal law, he also has had a bail hearing. [See 18 U.S.C. §§ 3146, 3148.] Under such circumstances, the Government concededly may detain him to ensure his presence at trial and may subject him to the restrictions and conditions of the detention facility so long as those conditions and restrictions do not amount to punishment, or otherwise violate the Constitution.

Not every disability imposed during pretrial detention amounts to "punishment" in the constitutional sense, however. Once the Government has exercised its conceded authority to detain a person pending trial, it obviously is entitled to employ devices that are calculated to effectuate this detention. Traditionally, this has meant confinement in a facility which, no matter how modern or how antiquated, results in restricting the movement of a detainee in a manner in which he would not be restricted if he simply were free to walk the streets pending trial. Whether it be called a jail, a prison, or a custodial center, the purpose of the facility is to detain. Loss of freedom of choice and privacy are inherent incidents of confinement in such a facility. And the fact that such detention interferes with the detainee's understandable desire to live as comfortably as possible and with as little restraint as possible during confinement does not convert the conditions or restrictions of detention into "punishment."

. . .

Based on affidavits and a personal visit to the facility, the District Court concluded that the practice of "double-bunking" was unconstitutional. The court relied on two factors for its conclusion: (1) the fact that the rooms were designed to house only one inmate, 428 F.Supp., at 336–337; and (2) its judgment that confining two persons in one room or cell of this size constituted a "fundamental denia[l] of decency, privacy, personal security, and, simply, civilized humanity . . . ." *Id.,* at 339. The Court of Appeals agreed with the District Court. In response to petitioners' arguments that the rooms at the MCC were larger and more pleasant than the cells involved in the cases relied on by the District Court, the Court of Appeals stated:

> "[W]e find the lack of privacy inherent in double-celling in rooms intended for one individual a far more compelling consideration than a comparison of square footage or the substitution of doors for bars, carpet for concrete, or windows for walls. The government has simply failed to show any substantial justification for double-celling." 573 F.2d, at 127.

We disagree with both the District Court and the Court of Appeals that there is some sort of "one man, one cell" principle lurking in the Due Process Clause of the Fifth Amendment. While confining a given number of people in a given amount of space in such a manner as to cause them to endure genuine privations and hardship over an extended period of time might raise serious questions under the Due Process Clause as to whether those conditions amounted to punishment, nothing even approaching such hardship is shown by this record.

. . .

Respondents also challenged certain MCC restrictions and practices that were designed to promote security and order at the facility on the ground that these restrictions violated the Due Process Clause of the Fifth Amendment, and certain other constitutional guarantees, such as the First and Fourth Amendments. The Court of Appeals seemed to approach the challenges to security restrictions in a fashion different from the other contested conditions and restrictions. It stated that "once it has been determined that the mere fact of confinement of the detainee justifies the restrictions, the institution must be permitted to use reasonable means to insure that its legitimate interests in security are safeguarded." 573 F.2d, at 124. The court might disagree with the choice of means to effectuate those interests, but it should not "second-guess the expert administrators on matters on which they are better informed. . . . Concern with minutiae of prison administration can only distract the court from detached consideration of the one overriding question presented to it: does the practice or condition violate the Constitution?" *Id.*, at 124–125. Nonetheless, the court affirmed the District Court's injunction against several security restrictions. The court rejected the arguments of petitioners that these practices served the MCC's interest in security and order and held that the practices were unjustified interferences with the retained constitutional rights of *both* detainees and convicted inmates. *Id.*, at 129–132. In our view, the Court of Appeals failed to heed its own admonition not to "second-guess" prison administrators.

SELECTED READINGS

Alpert, Geoffrey P., ed. *Legal Rights of Prisoners.* Beverly Hills and London: Sage, 1980.
> This wide-ranging series of articles on the legal rights of prisoners includes a comparison of prisoner access to courts in the United States and Europe, several studies of women prisoners, and articles placing prisoners' rights in historical perspective.

American Bar Association Project on Minimum Standards for Criminal Justice. *Standards Relating to Sentencing Alternatives and Procedures.* New York: Institute of Judicial Administration, 1968.
> This report by the ABA's Advisory Committee on sentencing and review examines various model penal codes and makes policy recommendations to judges and lawyers involved in sentencing.

American Friends Service Committee. *Struggle for Justice.* New York: Hill and Wang, 1971.
> This study—already a classic—is a simple yet thorough introduction to the problems of crime and punishment in the United States.

Berns, Walter. *For Capital Punishment.* New York: Basic Books, 1979.
> A professor of political philosophy places arguments for and against capital punishment in historical perspective, examines the history of the use of capital punishment in the United States, looks at the directions of relevant Supreme Court

opinions over the last few decades, and considers the morality of capital punishment in the United States today.

Casper, Jonathan D. "Having Their Day in Court: Defendant Evaluations of the Fairness of Their Treatment." *Law and Society Review* 12 (Winter 1978): 237-251. Convicted felons express their sense of the fairness of their own sentences and the system of sentencing in American courts.

Frankel, Marvin. *Criminal Sentences: Law Without Order.* New York: Hill and Wang, 1973. Federal District Judge Frankel (now retired) examines the problems associated with indeterminate sentences and asks whether vagueness in the laws regarding sentencing really serves justice.

Gaylin, Willard. *Partial Justice; A Study of Bias.* New York: Knopf, 1974. Gaylin, director of the Hastings Center, which sponsors studies on medical ethics, interviewed sitting judges in order to identify possible bias in their sentencing.

Gross, Hyman, and von Hirsch, Andrew, eds. *Sentencing.* New York: Oxford University Press, 1981. This excellent volume, which contains articles by legal philosophers, political scientists, historians, judges, and attorneys, considers a multiplicity of issues associated with criminal sentencing. Topics addressed include philosophies and varieties of punishment and the problem of discretion for prosecutor, jury, and judge. The volume contains substantial additional bibliography.

Rothman, David J. "Decarcerating Prisoners and Patients." *Civil Liberties Review* 1 (Fall 1973): 8-30. Rothman, an historian, examines the goals, successes, and unintended consequences of the policies of deinstitutionalization in both prisons and mental hospitals. He considers the roles of attorneys, judges, and prisoners and patients themselves in the deinstitutionalization process.

Woll, Robert. "The Death Penalty and Federalism: Eighth Amendment Constraints on the Allocation of State Decision-making Power." *Stanford Law Review* 35 (1983): 787-829. This is a technical and complex but thorough and informative examination of the special problems the principle of federalism brings to state adoption and implementation of the death penalty. Woll discusses many of the post-*Furman* death penalty cases in detail.

GLOSSARY

Bail. Money that an accused person lets the court hold to ensure that the accused will show up for the trial. If the accused cannot afford bail, he or she must remain in jail while awaiting trial. (See **Pretrial detention.**)

Community service. A penalty in lieu of incarceration. The service assigned could consist of working in a hospital or nursing home or performing any other function that in some measure "pays back" the community for the offender's misdeeds.

Determinate sentence. A sentence in which the term, or length of punishment, is spelled out by the state, leaving little or no discretion to the judge. The opposite is an indeterminate sentence, which leaves considerable discretion in the hands of the judge.

Plea bargain. An agreement between a prosecutor and a defense attorney that the defendant will plead guilty provided the charge is reduced.

Presumptively innocent. In American law, the accused is assumed to be innocent until proven guilty. Therefore, all individuals held in pretrial detention are presumptively innocent.

Pretrial detention. Holding an accused person in jail while he or she awaits trial.

Probation. Releasing a prison inmate before the maximum term has expired. The determination to do so is usually made by a probation board on the basis of evidence that the prisoner no longer poses a danger to society.

Work release. Any prison program that allows prisoners to spend part of their prison time working in the community. Unlike **community service**, the participating individuals must spend at least part of their term within the prison.

Part Three

Liberties and Responsibilities

Chapter 7
Money, Politics, and the First Amendment

*"We have allowed the basic idea of our demo-
cratic process—representative government—to slip
away. The only question is whether we are serious
about trying to retrieve it."*

ELIZABETH DREW

*"The latent causes of faction are thus sown in
the nature of man. . . ."*

JAMES MADISON

In 1973 and 1974 the Watergate investigations uncovered a series of shocking abuses of power by the White House. The investigations also revealed that enormous amounts of money had been funneled into President Nixon's reelection committee in 1972. Much of the money came from a small number of very wealthy contributors. President Nixon's top ten contributors gave him more than $4 million. One of them, W. Clement Stone of Chicago, gave him $2 million in 1972 alone and had given him $4.7 million between 1968 and 1972. According to Stone, Nixon told him on at least two occasions, "Clem, you and I know that I wouldn't be here if it weren't for you."

The scandal of money in the 1972 elections became the impetus for reform. In 1974 Congress seemed determined to do something about what Walter Mondale, then a senator, called "the profound, smelly, stinking corruption of money in politics." So Congress passed a series of measures that limited the amount of money that could be spent and contributed in federal elections, provided for public disclosure of who contributes to these campaigns and in what amounts, gave candidates the option of receiving public funds to finance their campaigns in order to lessen their dependence on private contributors, and set up the Federal Elections Commission to oversee the whole process and make sure the laws were obeyed. These new provisions passed both houses of Congress by comfortable margins and were signed by the first post-Watergate president, Gerald Ford.

The years went by. Now it was the 1980s. In 1972 the total amount spent in the American election process, national and state, had totaled $425 million. In the 1980 election, it was up to $1.203 billion! Campaign money was still coming from wealthy people. It was also coming from a relatively new source: political action committees, or PACs. There were PACs representing businesses, labor unions, and trade associations. There were also many "independent" PACs representing a variety of points of view and positions on issues like the Equal Rights Amendment, abortion, and aid to parochial schools. At the end of 1974, there were only 600 PACs. By the end of 1982, there were about 3,400—an increase of nearly 500 percent. The PACs, plus the parties, plus corporations, plus labor unions, plus government itself were all funneling money into our campaigns. "In other words," concludes reporter Elizabeth Drew in her book *Politics and Money*, "contributions of the size that were given to the Nixon campaign of 1972 and that so shocked the nation—and paved the way for public financing of Presidential elections—can still be made." Drew quotes Senator Daniel Inouye of Hawaii: "I think we're back about where we were before the laws were passed."

THE PROBLEM

What bothers many Americans about the role of money in our campaigns is that it seems to give rich people and rich interests an enormous amount of power. America is supposed to be a democracy. In a democracy, the rich are not supposed to have more political clout than the nonrich. One person, one vote. When you and W. Clement Stone go into the voting booth you are completely equal. His vote has the same weight as yours and no more. The difference is that, for many months before the election, he has also been "voting" with his dollars by helping to fund the candidates of his choice. Maybe you have, too, but he has a lot more wealth to do it with. His candidates have gotten an extra boost—a very important boost. "When a politician's success depends on a combination of dollars and votes, the nation is clearly less democratic than it would be if a victory depended on votes alone," said the late Senator Philip A. Hart, during congressional hearings on the measures that were enacted in 1974.

Nor is this all. It seems fair to assume that most people who contribute to political campaigns do not have the spirit of St. Francis of Assisi, who gave away everything and expected no earthly reward. When people give money they usually want something back. They may want an influential post in an administration; they may want to obtain favorable consideration for some proposal that will benefit them; they may want a regulation enacted, abolished, or modified. They may not get any of these things. But if they have put up a substantial amount of money, they are certain to get a respectful hearing. Politicians are not ingrates. They are grateful, of course, to all their constituents, but they are especially grateful to those who have given them not just votes but large chunks of money to run their campaigns. That, again, seems to violate the spirit of one person, one vote.

At least that is how many critics of the present system see things. But the critics have also been criticized. They have been called utopians, bent upon changing human nature by legislation. They have been called timid reformers, tinkering with the effects of our capitalist system instead of working to abolish it. Thus we come to the issues examined in this chapter.

THE ISSUES

Have the critics of our present system been exaggerating the problem of money in politics? What caused the problem? Is the problem still with us? Was the 1974 law a rational approach to reform? Did it violate the First Amendment? Was the Supreme Court right to strike down parts of it? How is money connected to the role of "media consultants" and political commercials? Should political ads on TV be abolished? Do "political action committees" (PACs) violate the spirit of democracy? Do we need new laws to control them? Do we need new laws to control the effects of money in campaigns?

The Video Discussion

These are the main issues that underlie the controversy explored in the video debate. The moderator is former Federal Communications Commissioner Tyrone Brown.

List of Participants

FLOYD ABRAMS
Attorney
Cahill, Gordon & Reindel

JOHN B. ANDERSON
Chairman
National Unity Committee
Former U.S. Representative
Illinois

DAVID S. BRODER
National Political Correspondent
and Columnist
Washington Post

DAVID W. BURKE
Vice-President and
Assistant to the President
ABC News

JOHN TERRENCE DOLAN
Chairman
National Conservative Political
Action Committee

REV. ROBERT F. DRINAN, S.J.
Professor of Law
Georgetown University Law Center
President
Americans for Democratic Action
Former U.S. Representative
Massachusetts

CHARLES FERRIS
Attorney
Mintz, Levin, Cohn, Ferris, Glovsky
and Popeo
Former Chairman
Federal Communications Commission

HON. BARNEY FRANK
U.S. Representative
Massachusetts

DAVID L. GARTH
Political Consultant
The Garth Group, Inc.

WILLIAM J. GREEN
Former Mayor of Philadelphia
Former U.S. Representative
Pennsylvania

MEG GREENFIELD
Editorial Page Editor
Washington Post

HON. HENRY J. HYDE
U.S. Representative
Illinois

HON. NANCY LANDON KASSEBAUM
U.S. Senator
Kansas

JOHN V. LINDSAY
Former Mayor of New York
Former U.S. Representative
New York

HON. RICHARD G. LUGAR
U.S. Senator
Indiana

HON. ABNER J. MIKVA
Judge
U.S. Court of Appeals
D.C. Circuit
Former U.S. Representative
Illinois

BILL MOYERS
Senior News Analyst
CBS News

HON. POTTER STEWART
Retired Justice
U.S. Supreme Court

GLENN E. WATTS
President
Communications Workers of America
AFL-CIO

EDDIE N. WILLIAMS
President
The Joint Center for Political Studies

Program Summary

The program is divided into four parts. The first is a discussion of some of the major provisions in the Federal Election Campaign Amendments of 1974, including the provisions struck down by the Supreme Court in *Buckley* v. *Valeo* (1976). Discussion centers particularly on whether the Supreme Court made a rational distinction between limitations on spending (which the Court considered to be an abridgment of free speech) and limitations on contributions (which the Court considered to be within the legitimate domain of legislatures). The second part concerns the role of political consultants in campaigns. The issue is whether they facilitate the democratic process by helping to stimulate debate and education on the issues or whether they distort it by oversimplification, manipulation, and personal attack. The third part of the program centers on the topic of political action committees. Some of the participants think PACs are divisive, negative forces in our political campaigns that weight the scales unfairly against the candidates the PACs oppose. Others praise PACs as units of political activism that restore some balance to a political process distorted by biased media coverage. Still others neither condemn nor praise them but suggest that their multiplicity and diversity cause them to check and balance each other. The fourth part serves as a kind of wrap-up. It goes back to the efforts to control spending through legislation, with particular attention to the public financing provisions of the Federal

Election Campaign Amendments of 1974. It again raises the question discussed in the first part, about the wisdom of the Supreme Court's decision in *Buckley* v. *Valeo*.

Watergate: Symbol of Corruption

To understand the background of the debate over the Supreme Court's decision in *Buckley* v. *Valeo* (1976), we have to begin with Watergate. Watergate was the real impetus for the 1974 reforms passed by Congress, the reforms the Court reviewed in the *Buckley* case.

Watergate. A whole generation has grown up with dim memories of it. We need to begin with some simple questions and answers.

Q: What *is* Watergate?

A: Watergate is a hotel complex in Washington, D.C. In 1972 the Democrats had their national headquarters there.

Q: And?

A: And a group of burglars were caught trying to install a "bug," a secret listening device, in one of the phones there. It was soon found that some of the burglars were connected with the Committee to Re-Elect the President (CREEP). Then Congress, the press, a special prosecutor, and even a federal judge started investigating, and they found that the conspiracy kept going higher and higher.

Q: Was Nixon in on it?

A: Not directly. But some of his closest aides were.

Q: What was Nixon guilty of?

A: Covering it up. According to his own secret tapes—which the Supreme Court made him surrender—Nixon conspired to derail an FBI investigation of Watergate by instructing his aides to tell the FBI to keep out of it. When all this was revealed, Nixon was forced to resign. The votes were there in both houses of Congress to impeach and convict him. So he quit.

This is an inadequate summary; there is not enough space to tell the whole story. But perhaps all we need remember is that by 1974 Watergate was more than a story. It was a symbol. "Watergate" now stood for everything sneaky and dirty in American politics. In the area of campaign finance, it stood for all the big contributions that came into Nixon headquarters. It stood for "laundering" money—sending it down to a Mexican bank account and then back up to Miami in order to wash off the name of the original contributor. It stood for shakedowns of corporations—implied promises to help them if they contributed and hurt them if they didn't. It stood for suitcases full of money flying into Washington on corporate jets.

Congress was determined to do something about this. In 1974 it did.

Federal Election Campaign Amendments, 1974

The same Congress that forced the resignation of Richard Nixon also passed a series of amendments to the Federal Election Campaign Act of 1971. Together, the original law and the new amendments contained the following provisions:

1. *Spending Limits.* All candidates for federal elections (Senate, House, and presidency) were limited in the amount they could spend. Different formulas were used for each office, for primaries, and for general elections.

2. *Contribution Limits.* Individuals were allowed to contribute no more than $1,000 to each candidate in each federal election or primary. There were also limits on the amounts people could give to political parties and PACs.

3. *Disclosure.* Candidates were required to file periodic reports disclosing the names and addresses of everyone who donated more than $100 and listing all expenditures of more than $1,000.

4. *Public Financing.* Presidential—but not Senate or House—candidates had the option of accepting money to help pay for both primaries and general elections. The money was provided by a special fund which was fed by "tax checkoffs."* The idea was to lessen politicians' dependence on private donations.

5. *Federal Elections Commission.* A special Federal Elections Commission was set up—the majority of its members to be appointed by Congress—to oversee the whole process, disburse the funds, and release the lists of contributors to the public.

Previous attempts had been made to regulate campaign financing. Back in 1907, Congress had prohibited corporations from contributing to federal campaigns. The ban had little effect. Corporations contributed to state parties and the money leaked back into federal elections; anyway, disclosure requirements were sketchy at best. In 1925 Congress tried to strengthen disclosure requirements by passing the Federal Corrupt Practices Act. Even with its later amendments, the act was so porous that Lyndon Johnson was amused; he called it "more loophole than law." The Taft-Hartley Act forbade direct campaign contributions from labor unions, but unions found their own way around the law by setting up their own "political action committee," COPE (Committee on Political Education), to funnel money into campaigns. But 1974 seemed to be a watershed. Congress had tackled the issue of campaign financing more earnestly than it had ever done in the past and produced the most sweeping, comprehensive campaign reforms in the nation's history.

But within ten years this law, too, had become ineffective.

Why? What happened?

What happened first was that the law was challenged in court, and in 1976 the Supreme Court declared parts of it unconstitutional.

Buckley v. *Valeo*: Spending Limits Violate the First Amendment

Everyone has heard the saying "Politics makes strange bedfellows." In 1976 the old saw acquired new life, when a very odd assortment of plaintiffs sat in the Supreme Court chambers and heard the Court support at least part of their case against the 1974 amendments. The plaintiffs included James Buckley, the Conservative-Republican senator from New York, who was up for reelection; Eugene McCarthy, the peace Democrat of '68, who was now running for president as an Independent; the American Conservative Union; the New York Civil Liberties Union; and the Conservative Victory

*The system is explained more fully later in this chapter. See pp. 222-223.

Fund. They ran the gamut from New Right conservatives to antiwar liberals, yet they all thought that the limitations on spending and contributions curbed free speech. If you can't spend money or collect it beyond a certain point, then you can't buy the time and space to be heard.

The Supreme Court agreed—in part. It ruled that the spending limitations in the 1974 amendments violated the First Amendment's protection of free speech.* Restricting the amount of money one person or group can spend on political communication during a campaign "reduces the quantity of expression by restricting the number of issues discussed, the depth of their exploration, and the size of the audience reached." Why is that? The Court noted that we live today in a society dominated by mass media. Unless candidates can buy media spots, they are as good as silenced. To limit the amount they may spend is, therefore, to limit their right to speak. The Court used the analogy of gasoline in a car. "Being free to engage in unlimited political expression subject to a ceiling on expenditures is like being free to drive an automobile as far and as often as one desires on a single tank of gasoline." Yet the Court upheld the amendments' limitations on contributions. This may seem inconsistent. (It did to Justices Burger and White, both of whom concurred in part and dissented in part.) If spending limits cut off free speech, don't contribution limits do the same? Using the Court's analogy of driving on a single tank of gasoline, haven't we limited gas supply if we limit contributions? Not at all, said the Court. We have simply forced the candidate to buy gas from a variety of small stations rather than from one or two big outlets.

The contribution limits specify that each contributor may give no more than $1,000 per candidate for each election. The candidates, then, must solicit funds from a large number of contributors. Nothing wrong with that. But isn't it unfair to the contributors? If candidates can spend as much as they want, why can't contributors contribute as much as they want? But the issue here is not the free circulation of money; it is free speech. Contribution limits entail "only a marginal restriction upon the contributor's ability to engage in free communication." He or she can still buy ads, or contribute to the candidate's party, or contribute to any of a number of independent "political action committees." In short, contribution limits do not "in any way infringe the contributor's freedom to discuss candidates and issues."

I: *BUCKLEY* V. *VALEO* DEBATED

Was it fair for the Supreme Court to strike down the limits on spending but leave the contribution limits intact? In the video debate, the participants explore this issue by means of a hypothetical case. "Congressman Ernest," a role assigned to former Illinois

---

*The Court also held unconstitutional the method of appointing members of the Federal Election Commission. The amendments provided that most of the members be appointed by Congress. The Court held this to be a usurpation of presidential power. The president, said the Court, not the Congress, has the power to appoint members of an administrative agency. Soon after the *Buckley* decision, Congress remedied this constitutional flaw by reconstituting the Federal Elections Commission with all members appointed by the president.

Congressman John Anderson, wishes to run for president. All the participants seem to agree that his first concern is money. Where is he going to get the million or so he needs for publicity? The answer, says Massachusetts Congressman Barney Frank, is that he's going to ask contributors for it. Can they contribute as much as they want? No, says attorney Floyd Abrams, who notes the $1,000-a-person limitation on contributions.

Now the moderator starts to thicken the plot. Congressman Ernest is a person of modest means. But in the state of "Centralia," a self-made millionaire, an industrialist named Harry Alger, has also decided to run for president. He also needs publicity. But he doesn't need to solicit contributions. All he has to do is open his checkbook and buy his own ads. Thanks to the Supreme Court, there can be no legal limits placed upon his spending. Is that fair? Like *Buckley* v. *Valeo*, the question creates some interesting alliances. Illinois Congressman Henry Hyde and Floyd Abrams, who would not agree on much else, agree on this: yes, it is fair, or at least it is what the Constitution requires. "I feel that spending one's own money in political advocacy is a form of free speech," says Hyde; this is also Abrams's position.

Almost everyone else on the panel disagrees. Anderson thinks that the rich man's candidacy will have a "chilling effect" on contributions to his own campaign. He undoubtedly speaks from the heart, since Anderson himself ran for president as an Independent in 1980 and saw his contributors start to freeze as the major parties got their campaigns going. Former New York Mayor John Lindsay, who once tried for the Democratic nomination, agrees with Anderson and adds: "I think that the Supreme Court in the *Buckley* case has wreaked havoc in the political system." Even former Supreme Court Justice Potter Stewart seems less than wholehearted in his defense of the *Buckley* decision. The Court, he says, "upheld all it could" of the 1974 amendments. What about the difference the Court found between spending limits and contribution limits? Stewart: "It's not big and it may be arbitrary." He corrects himself: "It may seem arbitrary or capricious." But, well, "it is the Court's duty to strike down anything . . . that it finds violates the Constitution of the United States."

Strangely enough, Terry Dolan is more persuasive in defending *Buckley*. Dolan heads a group called the National Conservative Political Action Committee (NCPAC). His group opposes most of the Supreme Court's decisions on abortion, school prayer, and busing, and Dolan thinks that its *Buckley* decision was also fairly "ridiculous." But he sympathizes with the Court, because the law it had to work with was worse than ridiculous. The 1974 amendments, Dolan believes, could accurately be called "the incumbency protection law." The overwhelming majority of congressmen keep getting reelected. "The only time they aren't reelected is when their opponent outspends them. The spending limitations, therefore, were meant to keep themselves in power. And there is no question that the incumbents knew it when they passed this bill."

Dolan's charge is provocative. And there are facts which lend some weight to it. The most important fact is that the majority of congressmen have resisted all attempts to extend public financing to congressional elections. As already mentioned, the 1974 amendments provided the option of public financing for presidential candidates. One reason behind this was to let fresh faces come into presidential contests. During the primaries, anyone who can raise $100,000 in small contributions from twenty states or more will get a matching check for $100,000. Why not have something on that order for congressional races? That way new people might be encouraged to run for Congress. The idea was first raised in 1974 and the Senate passed it, but it was defeated in the House. Every so often it gets brought up again and gets defeated again. Why? Probably because congressmen would rather not subsidize people to run against them! Yet they had no hesitation in limiting the amount of money any would-be opponent could spend in running against them.

The only trouble with Terry Dolan's position is that it may have its own consistency problems. If we skip ahead for a moment to Part IV of this debate, we see the moderator asking Dolan if he has any problems with public financing of congressional elections. "Oh, certainly," Dolan answers, "I think it's a ridiculous position." But if Dolan really thinks incumbents have an unfair advantage, why not give some money to challengers? His answer is that only 30 percent of the public has ever used the tax-checkoff system, so that we have 30 percent "appropriating money from the U.S. Treasury, which I think is a novel idea." Aside from the fact that the 30 percent are appropriating their *own* dollars, thus diverting them from the Treasury, there is nothing at all "novel" about a fraction of the American people benefiting from tax options. Businessmen do it all the time. Anyway, if, as Dolan maintains, our campaigns are underfunded ("We spend more advertising dog food in America"), then one would think he should welcome more funds injected into them by public financing. His opposition to it seems puzzling at first. We shall return to it later in the chapter.

Why is so much money needed in campaigns? Why is it that money is the very first topic brought up when someone considers a race? Why do elections have to cost over $1 billion? Even adjusting for inflation, this increase has been staggering. Why?

One reason is decline of the "boss."

In the vocabulary of politics, there are "yea" words and "boo" words. "Boss" is a boo word. It conjures up the image of a cigar-chomping scoundrel who runs a corrupt political organization. There is some truth in the caricature, but all the word "boss" really has to mean is "local political party leader." There used to be many such leaders in the party. Some of them were mayors, some were governors, some were senators, some were county and district leaders. They were the individuals who determined who would get their parties' nomination. If the panelists in the video discussion were meeting not in 1983 but in '43 or '53 and the moderator asked them what they needed first if they were planning to run for president, the answer would probably not be money. It would be support of the party leaders. These men got together and decided who would get the party nomination. (They gave us some excellent candidates: Franklin Roosevelt, Thomas Dewey, Adlai Stevenson, John F. Kennedy.) They also funded the elections. True, the candidates helped raise money for their parties, but money was not a preoccupation.

Then came the political reformers. The reformers disliked and distrusted the bosses. They wanted to democratize the nomination process, take power away from the bosses. The bosses and their followers had great contempt for reformers. It was the contempt of professionals for amateurs. They called them "morning glories" because their political fervor bloomed quickly but died out just as fast. The bosses sneered at these "good government" types—"goo goos," they called them, insinuating that they were babies trying to play a man's game.

But by the end of the '60s, the bosses had lost their grip. The morning glories had learned to stick it out. The goo goos had grown up. To get nominated now you do not have to curry favor with party leaders. You have to curry favor with the voters by entering a long string of primary elections held in various states. If you are to win these primary elections, your name must become well known to millions of voters, and you must be liked. How do you get to be well known and liked during this long primary season? You must spend enormous sums of money. And you will not get it from any bosses. You must somehow contrive to get it for yourself or have top staff people get it for you. That is one reason campaign expenses have gone up so high.

What do you get for your money? You get newspaper ads, radio and TV spots, printed materials, ballpoint pens, bumper stickers, pins. But you need someone to coordinate all this, put it all together, package it. So you spend more money and hire David Garth.

Who is David Garth? David Garth is a political consultant. He sells candidates to the voting public. He is an image maker. Back in '43, image makers were unnecessary for getting the nomination; even during the general elections, they played a marginal role. Most people voted by party. But party loyalty started declining during the '50s and declined rapidly during the '60s and '70s. People started splitting their tickets and switching from one party to another as they moved from one election to another. And they started registering as "Independents." The party leadership—the bosses—lost power. So the equation, somewhat oversimplified, came to this: Decline of party loyalty, decline of bosses = rise of money, rise of media consultants.

II: POLITICAL CONSULTANTS AND ADVERTISING

The second part of the video discussion begins when the moderator says to "Congressman Ernest" (John Anderson): "Your recognition outside your district is very low. How are you going to get it up?" Television is Anderson's first answer. But he needs someone to show him how to use it. So his next thought is: "I guess in most cases now, we go to someone like David Garth and . . . ask him what do I do." David Garth is best known for helping to introduce Hugh Carey to the voters of New York State. Carey, then a Brooklyn congressman with little recognition outside his district, was running for governor. A stiff figure with a less than captivating personality, Carey needed a new image. So Garth ran a campaign emphasizing Carey's warmth and humanity. In TV commercials, Carey was pictured walking down the mean streets of a New York slum with his jacket slung over his shoulder. The voice-over mentioned his Catholicism, his compassion, his determination to help everyone. A modest man, but determined. Carey won.

In the discussion, Garth is a little sensitive about his craft. The moderator asks him if part of his service is to "develop the appropriate image." Yes, Garth answers, but "that's a very bad word." Moderator: "Well, what would you use?" Garth: "Project."

(*Laughter.*) Project what? Garth: "What he cares about, what he stands for." Then the moderator asks a wonderfully naive question: "Why does he need your help to do that? He knows what he stands for." Well, but he's got to communicate it, says Garth, he's got to get his campaign organized. Moderator: "You're going to package it?" Garth doesn't like that word, either. "I think fifty years ago it was called campaign manager." But fifty years ago they didn't have TV. The way to "project" the candidate is, first, to buy commercials and, second, to get free coverage by "staging" news events. About that term Garth is not at all embarrassed. When the moderator says, "You're staging a situation," Garth answers, "Absolutely . . . absolutely." Earlier, Garth had cited some typical ways of staging events for the news cameras. A "classic situation" is "a closed factory; you put the man . . . the person running for Congress in that kind of a situation."

The moderator starts to wonder if something is wrong with American campaigns if candidates must spend so much of their time rounding up money and staging fake news events. What about discussing issues? What about genuine debates? Well, Garth just wishes that the TV networks would provide more free time for an intelligent discussion so that he would not need to puff his candidates. Now the heat has been deflected off Garth and onto the network news departments. David Burke, vice-president of ABC News, thinks Garth's criticism is unjust. The networks provide plenty of time for debates. It's just that the candidates try to manipulate the agenda and the coverage. Who, then, controls the election process? "The candidate," Burke answers. What is more, he adds, the candidate tries to control the news as well. "He wants a half an hour to sit there in a controlled-style environment to make a pitch."

David Broder, columnist for the *Washington Post*, reacts to this as print journalists often react to their colleagues in the electronic media when the latter claim that they are being ill used by campaigners. "I think my colleagues from the electronic side are being disingenuous." *They* are controlling TV, Broder says, and TV is the heart of the campaign. Therefore, they are controlling the campaign. Congressman Barney Frank joins the attack. "I think Mr. Burke burlesques us." Nobody wants a half an hour alone to present his or her views. "No one would watch except your very close relatives, and you can only lose them." What politicians want is issue coverage. But communicating views on the issues "is to the people in journalism the most boring thing about the campaign." That is why politicians have to stage events.

Who is right in this debate? Is Burke right to complain that politicians try to use TV news to promote themselves? By Garth's own admission, he is in the business of "staging" events in order to get his clients on the air. Are Garth, Broder, and Frank right to complain that TV news seems uninterested in issues? *The Unseeing Eye*, a 1976 book by political scientists Thomas Patterson and Robert McClure, lends support to that complaint. After systematically studying TV news coverage, Patterson and McClure concluded that TV news provides "plenty of good pictures but very little hard information." The TV news staffs have a penchant for "action" coverage: pictures of the candidate wading into crowds, getting cheered or booed, pressing the flesh, mounting a truck or platform—*doing* something. Thus, we learn next to nothing about the candidates' personal fitness for office or their views on issues. "Instead, television news emphasizes superficial pictures of the candidates in action."

Political Ads: Better than News?

The most surprising conclusion of Patterson and McClure's book was that viewers learn more about the issues from some of the 30-second commercials for candidates than they do from news coverage of them. That is because the most effective commercials for a candidate (at least for a candidate who is already well known) are commercials emphasizing issues rather than images. These ads may discuss the issues in a selective and biased way. But at least they contain information, and viewers tend to remember it. TV news coverage, on the other hand, leaves little on the viewers' minds except pictures of candidates coming and going, hustling and bustling. To test and perhaps update this conclusion,* the reader might try to recall the last political campaign. What sticks in your mind from the TV news coverage of it? Did it all seem like noise and hoopla? Or do you remember serious discussion of issues? And what about the political commercials? Were they all just "image making," or did they communicate—in however biased a fashion—some sense of the issues in the campaign?

If Patterson and McClure are right, then perhaps the suggestion of Elizabeth Drew needs rethinking. In her book *Politics and Money*, Drew suggests that political ads on TV be banned. Aside from the First Amendment problems with that suggestion, it sounds like a way of reducing still further the amount of information voters receive during a campaign season. True, she suggests replacing the ads with "free air time" for the candidates, but that raises more problems than it solves.

First, there is no such thing as "free" air time. Somebody will pay for it. Either the networks will, in lost revenues, or the Treasury will. If the networks lose the money, they will make up for it by charging advertisers more. The advertisers will then pass it along by charging more for their products. Thus, consumers will pay. If the money comes from the Treasury, then of course taxpayers will pay. The second problem is deciding who gets to share this air time besides the Democratic and Republican candidates. What about the Conservative candidate? The Socialist-Labor candidate? The Libertarian candidate? The Right-to-Life candidate? The Liberal candidate? And so on. The prospect of free air time might even create more parties. Drew does not tell us whether free air time would also be doled out during primary season. If so, then not only all the parties but all the candidates seeking the nomination of all the parties would get some air time. It sounds like madness.

It is no answer to these problems to say, as Drew does, that in Europe they do not permit candidates to purchase air time. The European party system is very different from the American; so is the European concept of civil liberties. Since 1776 one of America's boasts is to have fashioned a political system somewhat different from Europe's!

---

*In a more recent book by Thomas Patterson, *The Mass Media Election* (Praeger, 1980), it is acknowledged that some of the election "specials" during the 1976 elections (including the Carter-Ford debates) helped inform viewers. But the news coverage itself "apparently has not added much to the voters' issue awareness" (p. 169).

Points to Remember

1. The Watergate scandal was the impetus behind the attempt to reform our system of campaign finance in 1974. In that year Congress passed a series of amendments to the Federal Election Campaign Act of 1971.
2. The 1974 amendments contained five provisions: spending limits, contribution limits, disclosure, public financing, and the establishment of the Federal Elections Commission to make sure all the provisions were properly carried out.
3. In the 1976 case of *Buckley* v. *Valeo*, the Supreme Court struck down the spending limitations, holding that they violated the free speech clause of the First Amendment. It left standing the limits on contributions because such limitations entail "only a marginal restriction upon the contributor's ability to engage in free communication."
4. The preoccupation with fund raising that characterizes American political campaigns is in part attributable to the disintegration of party leadership ("bosses") and party loyalty. Independent-minded voters must now be wooed during both primary and general elections. This requires large expenditures for advertising.
5. Modern campaigns rely upon TV. They use media consultants like David Garth. Many critics are concerned about the increase in "image making" at the expense of the discussion of issues. Others suggest that the "staging" of events by candidates is a response to the priorities of TV news programs, which do not provide adequate coverage of issues. One study concluded that voters learn more from political advertisements on TV than they do from TV coverage of political campaigns.

III: POLITICAL ACTION COMMITTEES (PACs)

The third part of the program begins when the moderator turns to Terry Dolan and asks: "Mr. Dolan, what is a political action committee?" Terry Dolan is the right man to ask. He heads the National Conservative Political Action Committee (NCPAC), a group that helped Ronald Reagan get elected in 1980. Although Dolan has since become rather disenchanted with President Reagan—he thinks the president has shifted away from "conservatism"—the rest of NCPAC's leadership continues to support the president.

But it is not so much NCPAC's support of candidacies as its opposition to them that has made the group controversial. In 1980 NCPAC set its sights on a number of candidates it considered too "liberal" on a variety of issues, ranging from abortion to the Panama Canal. It then produced a series of "negative" ads calling voters' attention to those candidates who supported the "wrong" side of the issues. In this way NCPAC may have helped defeat a number of "liberals." To its opponents, NCPAC seems to use tactics reminiscent of the late Senator Joe McCarthy. To its supporters, it is trying to restore some balance and fairness to a political process distorted by "liberal" media coverage.

Without getting involved in that dispute, we can simply observe that NCPAC is doing what other groups in America have been doing since the nation's founding: exercising its First Amendment right to cuss out its enemies. Civil rights and antiwar groups did it during the '60s. In the early '70s, environmental groups compiled a list of congressmen they called "the dirty dozen"—ones who had opposed environmental legislation. More recently, nuclear freeze groups have compiled a list they call "the doomsday dozen," who have opposed the freeze. Feminist groups have their own targets—congressmen who voted against the Equal Rights Amendment. It may not be nice to do that, but American politics has never been a particularly genteel sport.

Aside from its ideology and tactics, though, there is something else about NCPAC that bothers its critics—a quality it shares with all other PACs. NCPAC serves as a giant funnel, letting contributors pour money into campaigns in amounts that seem to violate the spirit of the 1974 amendments. Again, all PACs do this, including those supporting "liberal" causes. Because PACs are, in theory, not tied to a political party or a candidate's election committee, they are not limited either in the amount they can spend or collect from contributors. Yet, by their ads and other activities, they can help a party candidate get elected. NCPAC probably helped Ronald Reagan get elected, and helped other Republicans get into office during the 1980 election, by its scathing attacks on their opponents. It acted as a kind of bulldog for "conservative" Republicans, one that could not be regulated or limited by law. NCPAC's activities thus raise some serious issues about all PACs. To what extent are they really "independent"? Is their phenomenal growth since 1974—from 600 to 3,400—something to be concerned about? Have they made a shambles of the attempt to control campaign spending?

These, no doubt, are questions on the moderator's mind as he addresses the head of NCPAC. Dolan, a slight, soft-spoken man, has an air of self-assurance that his critics find unpleasant but which may serve as cover for an underlying wariness; he is determined not to be trapped in any framework of discussion that assumes there is something wrong with PACs. The wariness starts to surface after he has explained to the moderator that there are two types of PACs, those affiliated with businesses, labor unions, and trade associations, and those, like his, that are wholly "independent." As if he has not heard him, the moderator asks Dolan: "But what organization is your political action committee connected with?"

DOLAN: No one . . . it's totally independent.
MODERATOR: It exists for itself?
DOLAN: Just for itself.
MODERATOR: Unconnected?
DOLAN: Unconnected.
MODERATOR: A loose cannon.
DOLAN: If you want to call it that—as loose as the Republican party is, I guess.
(*Laughter*)

Some of the laughter may be at Dolan's expense. What he apparently means is that his group is just as independent as the major parties. But the fact that he singled out the Republican party is probably taken by some as an admission that NCPAC is a satellite of Ronald Reagan's party.

Yet there is support on the panel for Dolan's assertion of "independence." It comes from an unexpected quarter: from David Garth, the professional media consultant. Garth's support is backhanded. His complaint about PACs is that, while they think their political ads are helping a candidate, they may have a destructive effect. The party candidate has "totally no control" over the ads, the style of which is sometimes "outrageous." The ads, then, can "backfire." Garth's annoyance is that of a professional who has watched too many muddled performances by amateurs. But if he is right, the conspiracy theory of PACs does not stand up very well. If PACs are nothing but hired guns of the major parties, then why are the parties unable to control them?

John Anderson is more critical than Garth. His complaint centers not just on PAC commercials but on the very existence of PACs. "They're destroying the parties." In Anderson's view, political parties are good institutions. They serve the function of "mediating the various conflicts in our society." But they are gradually being displaced by these well-funded PACs, which divide the American people instead of uniting them. The complaint, with its corresponding defense of political parties, is certainly arguable, but there is some irony in the fact that it is coming from John Anderson. In 1980 Anderson, along with several others, contended for the Republican nomination. He lost, of course, to Ronald Reagan, but unlike the other losers he refused to support the winner; instead, he bolted the party and ran as an independent.

The irony is not lost on Congressman Henry Hyde, Anderson's former Illinois colleague in the House of Representatives. "I think it's a delight," Hyde says, "to welcome John back into the fold of supporting the two-party system!" Hyde goes on to defend the proliferation of pressure groups as an insurance that no single one will have undue influence. "The more that PACs proliferate, the less influence any individual PAC has. . . . Their influence is diminished by their proliferation."

There is some interesting political philosophy in Hyde's statement. The philosophy is challenged by Father Robert Drinan, a former congressman who used to disagree with Hyde on other issues as well. For Drinan, organizations and interests have no business getting involved in the campaign process by backing candidates. It never used to be that way. "We've never had . . . bankers and realtors and funeral directors" contributing to candidates. As history this is a very dubious statement, as David Broder points out:

> American political history is replete with examples of every industry, every large conglomeration of people, putting money into politics; what's changed under the new system is that much more of it is reported than used to be the case.

But Drinan is not really making a historical statement. He is stating a theory. The theory is that individuals, not interest groups, should contribute to campaigns. "Whose theory is that?" asks the moderator. Drinan replies: "That's the traditional American theory, and Mr. Broder would admit that it is."

So we have two distinct, clashing views. Hyde says, in a sense, the more PACs the better, since that way no one or few will have too much influence. Drinan insists that individual voters, not PACs or other special interests, should be the ones involved in

American election campaigns. He adds that he is stating the "traditional American theory." Is he?

The trouble is that there is no one "traditional American theory." There are at least two. The first, championed most vigorously by Thomas Jefferson, is very close to Drinan's. Jefferson believed in individualism and was convinced that if the individual could just be left alone by selfish interests, he would vote intelligently and without bias. Human beings are by nature innocent. They can be corrupted by excessive wealth and other bad influences, but if these are removed—and Jefferson believed that in our new land they could be removed—we can trust the individual voter. But there is a second "traditional American theory," and its most articulate spokesman was a friend of Jefferson, James Madison. Since Madison specifically addressed the topic of interest groups, his theory deserves a closer look. The eighteenth-century version of PACs were what Madison called "factions," and he singled them out for examination in No. 10 of *The Federalist*.

James Madison on "Factions"

Madison defined a faction as any group bound together by an interest that runs counter to the rights of others or to the "permanent and aggregate interests of society." Madison did not like factions. But the question was what to do about them—eliminate them or learn to live with them? There are two ways to eliminate them: either extinguish liberty or find some way of talking everyone into sharing the same opinions. If we extinguish liberty, we can put an end to factions, for "liberty is to faction as air is to fire." Just arrest them, or at least limit their right to speak. The trouble is that extinguishing oxygen will smother us all in the course of putting out the fire. In less metaphorical language, once we abridge the liberties of some, we risk abridging the liberty of all. What about talking everyone into adopting the same opinions? That, Madison said, is impossible, for factions "are sown in the nature of man."

"The nature of man." What has that got to do with PACs? Simply this. People, Madison held, are by nature full of willfulness and selfishness. There is no sense trying to use the voice of sweet reason to win everyone over to the "good" side. Our reason is always subservient to our "self-love." We are full of pride. We will fight each other over "the most frivolous and fanciful distinctions." But the most common and durable source of factions is "the various and unequal distribution of property." Unless we give everyone the same amount and even the same kind of property, we can expect factions to thrive. Since Madison assumed his readers were not prepared to plunge into socialism (and even if they were, he still thought people would fight each other), he saw no acceptable way of eliminating the *cause* of faction. All we can do is try to control its *effects*.

Here Madison began to build his case for federalism, a system of government that divides authority between a national government and a number of state governments. We need not follow that argument in detail (federalism is discussed in Chapter 13). All we need to see is that Madison's argument rests on the beauty of diversity. The more states, the more territory, the more diversity. And the more diversity—the "greater variety of parties and interests"—the less likelihood there is of any group taking over the whole country. The interests check and balance each other. The cure for the mischiefs of faction is therefore more faction. The more factions the better. Let a thousand factions bloom. Madison would undoubtedly endorse Henry Hyde's view that the influence of PACs "is diminished by their proliferation."

Do PACs Check and Balance Each Other?

There is recent, albeit unintentional, support for the Madison-Hyde thesis in Elizabeth Drew's book *Politics and Money*. Drew's intention is to refute it. "An argument is sometimes made that since everyone is in the game—since all interests are raising and distributing money—it all evens out in the end." That premise, she says, is fallacious, and she quotes Kansas Senator Robert Dole to prove its fallacy. "As Robert Dole says, 'there aren't any Poor PACs or Food Stamp PACs or Nutrition PACs or Medicare PACs.'" Yet there are Food Stamps, and there is Medicare, and there are nutrition programs, and there is antipoverty spending! The absence of PACs for these programs has not prevented their institution and growth. Numerous interest groups support them on Capitol Hill. (They are also supported in the national media, which regularly feature stories on "hunger in America.")* Drew's book is replete with examples of interest groups checking interest groups: the banking industry checking the securities industry, the candy manufacturers checking the sugar interests, NCPAC threatening the political future of Wall Street Democrats, Arab interests competing with Jewish interests, movie and television interests fighting the Sony Corporation and other manufacturers of videotape machines. It goes on and on. One congressman even complained to Drew that one of the reasons Congress has not passed a number of bills is that "you get PACs fighting PACs, so it is just easier to do nothing."

Yet there is also evidence on the other side, evidence that the PACs are not so evenly divided. Business PACs spend more than labor PACs and in recent years have gotten almost flawlessly coordinated. There is, for example, NABPAC, the National Association of Business Political Action Committees, a giant coalition of business PACs, which gives its 225 member PACs advice on everything from lobbying techniques to briefings on upcoming legislation. Political scientist Michael Parenti may have an arguable point when he asserts that "those who control the wealth of society enjoy a persistent and pervasive political advantage."

Whether PACs are evenly or unevenly divided, the din of their battles resounds in the Capitol every day that Congress sits. This points up what may be the real problem with PACs. The noise of their incessant fighting may be drowning out the quieter voice of reason. The proliferation of PACs and the cross-pressures they put on congressmen may be leaving legislators exhausted from battle fatigue, unable to think about the good of their country or their constituencies. They want to avoid getting caught in the cross fire of PACs. So they hunker down and do nothing or follow only what seems to be the safest route, not the wisest. If this is happening today because of PACs—and

*As Barbara Walters puts it, "If you want to be a reporter, you are going to have to see poverty and misery, and you have to be involved in the human condition." Quoted in *Time*, December 12, 1983, p. 82.

there is evidence, in Drew's book and elsewhere, that it is—then the proliferation of PACs is indeed a cause for concern. Why did it happen? Why have PACs grown 500 percent since 1974?

Why PACs Have Grown: Three Reasons

1. Former Congressman John Anderson has already called attention to one reason, though he may have mistaken cause for effect. He talks about the disintegration of political parties and worries that PACs may be a contributing factor. It probably works the other way: the breakdown of party loyalty and party leadership (bosses) has contributed to the growth of PACs. In the old days congressmen used to respond to cues from party leaders and committee chairmen in Congress. The slogan, carefully impressed on the minds of freshman congressmen, was: "If you want to get along, go along." This may not have been very democratic, but it made individual congressmen less vulnerable to pressure from special interests. Elections, too, were less influenced by special-interest money, for the reason discussed earlier: voters were more loyal to one or another of the two major parties, and the nomination process was handled almost exclusively by party leaders. There was not as much need to woo voters by expensive advertising.

2. The scope of government has grown enormously since the 1960s. It regulates more and more interests. Naturally, those interests want to make sure they are not harmed by Washington; if possible, they will see if they can be helped by it. That is one reason the "bankers and realtors and funeral directors" Father Drinan refers to are forming PACs and sending them off to the nation's capital to lobby. The stakes are very high. As Edward Magnuson, senior writer for *Time* magazine, put it: "A single clause tucked away in the Federal Register of regulations . . . can put a small-town manufacturer out of business or rejuvenate an industry that was on the brink of bankruptcy. The lobbyist who gets the clause removed, or puts it in, can be worth his salary for 100 lifetimes."

3. Finally, the proliferation of PACs was caused in part by the Federal Election Campaign Amendments of 1974—the ones that were intended to lessen the effect of money in campaigns—and in part by *Buckley* v. *Valeo*. Congress in 1974 limited the amount of money that could be contributed to parties and candidates. It also legitimized PACs. Labor unions had had PACs since the 1940s, in order to counter the spending of big business. Now labor wanted to make sure its PACs were not outlawed. So it prevailed upon the Democrats to allow a special place for them in the law. (By now business had its own PAC, so it sided with labor.)

Now the reader must consider these two provisions together: Congress sought to limit individual contributions to parties and candidates. But it allowed PACs to contribute to them and also to make "independent expenditures" supporting them. True, it also sought to limit the amounts PACs could contribute and spend. But the Supreme Court struck down all spending limits, including the amounts PACs could spend. So here is what Congress did: by placing limits on the amount people could contribute to candidates and parties, it merely diverted the money to other spending units. PACs then became the logical alternative.

America is an extraordinarily wealthy country. It has many individuals and interests with lots of money. Some of that money is going to find its way into the electoral process. Limit the openings for it at one place and it will diligently search for other places to enter. Even Elizabeth Drew, who keeps hoping that "the mind of man" can devise workable limits, admits that contributors are persistent and indefatigable. In apparent agreement, she quotes Ronald Reagan's former campaign manager: "If there are people with money, they're going to surface."

The Socialist and the "Boss"

It is just here that the socialist and the old-style "boss" may share a common reaction to the efforts of reformers. The socialist tends to regard efforts to control the flow of money into campaigns as at best superficial, at worst something like rearranging the deck chairs on the *Titanic*. The real problem, says the socialist, is the distribution of wealth in our society. As long as there are fabulously rich classes who wish to maintain their position, there is no way we can keep them from spending to do it. The solution must be the redistribution of wealth, the leveling of class distinctions. The old-style boss is unenthusiastic about socialism, but he would agree that legal reforms are futile. The problem, he would say, is not class inequality but human nature. Human beings are by nature selfish. They get into politics for what they can get out of it. We bosses, they would say, used to manage things reasonably well. We helped ourselves *and* the community. We were brokers, mediating among groups. But the reformers took us out, and now the whole game is played with raw cash.

Both the socialist and the boss may be wrong. The boss may be too pessimistic about human nature. Are we really selfish by nature? Are we really uninterested in politics except for what we can get out of it? The socialist may be pointing the way to a "remedy" that could turn out to be worse than the disease.

In any case, the 1974 reforms may not have been as futile as the socialist and the boss think they are. Thanks to the amendments, we now have better accounting of who contributes what to our campaigns. We also have a Federal Elections Commission which, while appointed by the president, is not as much under the president's thumb as is the attorney general, who used to be in charge of enforcement. Finally, the 1974 amendments set up a new system of financing elections: having the federal government help fund campaigns. This last innovation deserves more discussion. First, though, a summary of some points made above.

Points to Remember

1. Political action committees (PACs) were allowed by the 1974 amendments, although they were limited in the amount they could spend. Those spending limits were struck down by the Supreme Court in the *Buckley* case.

2. Some PACs are affiliated with labor unions, others with business and trade associations. Still others are called "independent." The independent PACs include those

supporting "liberal" and "conservative" views on a variety of issues, from abortion to the Panama Canal.

3. One criticism of the independent PACs is that they are not truly independent, but serve as the "bulldogs" of candidates by criticizing their opponents. Another criticism of PACs is that they use divisive, "negative" advertisements. However, this is a long tradition in American politics. For years, interests have exercised their right to attack their opponents verbally.

4. Another criticism of PACs is that they distort the electoral process. However, there is evidence that Henry Hyde may be right: the proliferation of PACs means that they check and balance each other. That was also James Madison's point in *Federalist* No. 10.

5. Since 1974, PACs have grown from 600 to 3,400, an increase of 500 percent. This phenomenon had at least three causes: (a) the breakdown of party loyalty and party leadership (bosses) who once served to control and mediate the struggles of pressure groups; (b) the increase in the number of interests regulated by Washington; and (c) the legitimization of PACs in the 1974 amendments and the effort to limit direct contributions to parties and candidates (these limitations had the effect of diverting money into PACs).

IV: PUBLIC FINANCING

Earlier in the chapter, NCPAC's Terry Dolan was quoted as saying that American campaigns are actually underfinanced. "We spend more advertising dog food in America." Dolan's view is shared by America's foremost expert on campaign finance, Herbert Alexander. Alexander, who has been studying the subject since 1962, warned Congress in 1973 that spending and contribution limits would not work. His approach to reducing candidates' dependence on big contributors would be to provide public subsidies for campaigns. If candidates could be weaned away from large private contributors by the prospect of receiving public money, they would not be in the debt of anyone except the American people. Congress partially implemented this philosophy in the 1974 amendments, which provided for partial public financing of presidential elections. As mentioned earlier, it rejected public financing of congressional elections, perhaps because congressmen were not interested in funding the campaigns of their opponents.

Here is how the system works. Your yearly income tax form has a box to check if you want $1 of your tax money ($2 on joint returns) diverted into a special fund to subsidize presidential elections. This fund is then used in two ways: first, to help candidates running in primary elections fund their races, all the while encouraging them to seek contributions from numerous small contributors rather than from a few big contributors; second, to help fund the general election.

In the primary races, the system works by matching grants. If you can raise $100,000 in small contributions ($5,000 or less) in at least twenty states, the federal government will present you with a matching $100,000. Now suppose you have won the Democratic or Republican nomination. You can now elect to have the federal government contribute to your general-election campaign. But if you do, you must accept spending limits. (The Supreme Court did not strike down these spending limits, because nobody is forced to take the government's money. Just turn it down and you can spend as much of your own as you like.) Of course, the whole system is extraordinarily leaky. Between PAC expenditures and "soft" money (money spent by *state* parties, which is not regulated by the federal government), enormous amounts of money still make their way into presidential elections. But perhaps some of these loopholes can be closed. In any case, the concept is interesting: induce candidates to take the money of many so that they will not be dependent on the few.

Almost everyone on the video panel who comments on the topic of public financing seems to like the idea. Floyd Abrams, who agrees with the Supreme Court that spending limitations violate the First Amendment, sees no problem when the spending limits are tied to the acceptance of public money. John Lindsay likes public financing as an antidote to what he considers the corruption of wealth—"in the sense that the only people who are running for office any longer are those who either have huge amounts of money or access to it." Father Drinan thinks the concept of public financing should be extended to congressional races. "I think that's one way of equalizing the . . . advantage of the incumbent."

The one participant who doesn't approve is Terry Dolan, who finds the idea "ridiculous." As already mentioned, Dolan's opposition is at first puzzling. If he really thinks our campaigns are underfinanced and the present system is stacked against challengers, it would seem logical to support public financing of both presidential and congressional elections. In fairness to Dolan, however, part of his "conservative" philosophy is his opposition to large-scale government welfare programs. He would not be very consistent in *that* philosophy if he ended up supporting welfare to politicians!

The remainder of the program is a kind of wrap-up. It returns to the questions laid down in the first segment, particularly to the issue of the Supreme Court's distinction between spending limitations (which the Court said violated the First Amendment) and contribution limitations (which the Court upheld). John Anderson, Barney Frank, and others on the panel believe that the distinction between the two is arbitrary and capricious. *Washington Post* columnist David Broder disagrees. "A contribution, it seems to me, is an effort to give voice to the candidate or cause that person is supporting. Expenditures are voice." An effort to "give voice" as opposed to the "voice" itself. Does the reader accept that distinction? Does it make sense?

It might be a fitting ending to Part IV if the reader were to return to *Buckley* v. *Valeo* and ask whether the Supreme Court was right to consider spending limits as a violation of the First Amendment. Broder thinks they are, and he is "disturbed that there are so many liberals in this room who cannot see . . . that you are treading on very dangerous grounds when you say to an individual in this country, 'You may not spend your own money legitimately in the cause of seeking public office in this country.'" Abrams, Dolan, and Justice Stewart agree with him. Virtually everyone else on the panel disagrees.

SUMMARY

At the turn of the century, Tammany Hall, then a powerful Democratic organization in New York City, was run by a man named George Washington Plunkitt. Plunkitt was not only a wily politician but also a philosopher. He had about two years of formal education but many years of experience. Sitting high on the shoe-shine stand in front of City Hall, Plunkitt would dispense advice to anyone who cared to listen. And his prime piece of advice was this: If you want to be successful in politics, you must "study human nature and act accordin'." His complaint about reformers ("ray-formers," he called them) was that they had not done that. They did not study human nature but tried to change it by legislation. Reformers thought they could take self-seeking out of politics.

If Plunkitt were alive today, he would probably say that much of the problem with money in politics results from the well-meaning efforts of reformers. They weakened political parties and insisted on primary elections. That meant candidates had to rely on media campaigns, which made them even more dependent on money. Then the reformers tried to dam up the flow of money with the 1974 amendments. But the money just flowed around the dam. Now some of them would like to ban political advertisements. But, Plunkitt would say, the money will still find its outlet.

Plunkitt was not much of a reader, but if he read Elizabeth Drew's *Politics and Money*, he might catch some points that other reviewers have missed. For example, Drew reveals that one of the changes insisted upon by congressional reformers—opening up congressional committee meetings to the public—"has strengthened the lobbyists' hand and reduced the legislators' ability to legislate." The reason special-interest groups got called "lobbyists" is that they used to have to hang around the lobbies of Congress waiting for legislators to emerge. Now they can go right into the committee hearings and keep score. "Sometimes," Drew says, "they even signal to a member how to vote on a certain amendment." Thus the work of "ray-formers." They demanded "open meetings," and they opened them to PAC-men.

There are answers to Plunkitt. One answer is that times have changed since the turn of the century. Higher education is now the rule rather than the exception. Public welfare has replaced many of the "charitable" functions of political parties (jobs for unemployed relatives, free coal deliveries to widows). The mass media, especially TV, are powerful whether we want them to be or not. The kind of kinship and ethnic ties that sustained parties have declined or at least been redirected. By the 1960s the old party organizations were already going the way of the dinosaurs. The reformers may be naive and clumsy, but by struggling with the new they have made it clear that the ordinary, comfortable ways of managing politics have to be reconsidered. American politics has a Humpty-Dumpty quality. Old patterns are constantly being shattered; they can never be put back the way they were. Maybe, though, they can be improved.

Documents

BUCKLEY V. VALEO, 424 U.S. 1 (1976)

The majority opinion in this case was an unsigned per curiam *("by the court") opinion. Only Justices William Brennan, Potter Stewart, and Lewis Powell joined all portions of it.*

These appeals present constitutional challenges to the key provisions of the Federal Election Campaign Act of 1971 [and] related provisions, [as] amended in 1974. [The challenged laws] in broad terms [provide:] (a) individual political contributions are limited to $1,000 to any single candidate per election, with an overall annual limitation of $25,000 by any contributor; independent expenditures by individuals and groups "relative to a clearly identified candidate" are limited to $1,000 a year; campaign spending by candidates for various federal offices and spending for national conventions by political parties are subject to prescribed limits; (b) contributions and expenditures above certain threshold levels must be reported and publicly disclosed; (c) a system for public funding of Presidential campaign activities is established; [and] (d) a Federal Election Commission is established to administer and enforce the Act....

[The majority summarized its conclusion as follows: "[W]e sustain the individual contribution limits, the disclosure and reporting provisions, and the public financing scheme. We conclude, however, that the limitations on campaign expenditures, on independent expenditures by individuals and groups, and on expenditures by a candidate from his personal funds are constitutionally infirm." Moreover, the composition of the Federal Election Commission was held unconstitutional. The excerpts that follow focus on the contribution and expenditure provisions. Other parts of the decision are noted elsewhere in this book.]

I. Contribution and Expenditure Limitations

. . .

The Act's contribution and expenditure limitations operate in an area of the most fundamental First Amendment activities. Discussion of public issues and debate on the qualifications of candidates are integral to the operation of the system of government established by our Constitution....

A restriction on the amount of money a person or group can spend on political communication during a campaign necessarily reduces the quantity of expression by restricting the number of issues discussed, the depth of their exploration, and the size of the audience reached. This is because virtually every means of communicating ideas in today's mass society requires the expenditure of money. [The] expenditure limitations contained in the Act represent substantial rather than merely theoretical restraints on the quantity and diversity of political speech. [E.g., the] $1,000 ceiling on spending "relative to a clearly identified candidate" would appear to exclude all citizens and groups except candidates, political parties and the institutional press from any significant use of the most effective means of communication. . . .

By contrast with a limitation upon expenditures for political expression, a limitation upon the amount that any one person or group may contribute to a candidate or political committee entails only a marginal restriction upon the contributor's ability to engage in free communication. A contribution serves as a general expression of support for the candidate and his views, but does not communicate the underlying basis for the support. The quantity of communication by the contributor does not increase perceptively with the size of his contribution, since the expression rests solely on the undifferentiated, symbolic act of contributing. At most, the size of the contribution provides a very rough index of the intensity of the contributor's support for the candidate. A limitation on the amount of money a person may give to a candidate or campaign organization thus involves little direct restraint on his political communication, for it permits the symbolic expression of support evidenced by a contribution but does not in any way infringe the contributor's freedom to discuss candidates and issues. While contributions may result in political expression if spent by a candidate or an association to present views to the voters, the transformation of contributions into political debate involves speech by someone other than the contributor.

Given the important role of contributions in financing political campaigns, contribution restrictions could have a severe impact on political dialogue if the limitations prevented candidates and political committees from amassing the resources necessary for effective advocacy. There is no indication, however, that the contribution limitations imposed by the Act would have any dramatic adverse effect on the funding of campaigns and political associations. The overall effect of the Act's contribution ceilings is merely to require candidates and political committees to raise funds from a greater number of persons and to compel people who would otherwise contribute amounts greater than the statutory limits to expend such funds on direct political expression, rather than to reduce the total amount of money potentially available to promote political expression.

The Act's contribution and expenditure limitations also impinge on protected associational freedoms. Making a contribution, like joining a political party, serves to affiliate a person with a candidate. In addition, it enables like-minded persons to pool their resources in furtherance of common political goals. The Act's contribution ceilings thus limit one important means of associating with a candidate or committee, but leave the contributor free to become a member of any political association and to assist personally in the association's efforts on behalf of candidates. And the Act's contribution limitations permit associations and candidates to aggregate large sums of money to promote effective advocacy. By contrast, the Act's $1,000 limitation on independent expenditures "relative to a clearly identified candidate" precludes most associations from effectively amplifying the voice of their adherents. [In] sum, although the Act's contribution and expenditure limitations both implicate fundamental First Amendment interests, its expenditure ceilings impose significantly more severe restrictions on protected freedoms of political expression and association than do its limitations on financial contributions. . . .

Expenditure Limitations. The Act's expenditure ceilings impose direct and substantial restraints on the quantity of political speech. [It] is clear that a primary effect of these expenditure limitations is to restrict the quantity of campaign speech by individuals, groups, and candidates. The restrictions, while neutral as to the ideas expressed, limit political expression "at the core of our electoral process and of First Amendment freedoms."

1. *The $1,000 limitation on expenditures "relative to a clearly identified candidate."* Section 608 (e) (1) provides that "[n]o person may make any expenditure . . . relative to a clearly identified candidate during a calendar year which, when added to all other expenditures made by such person during the year advocating the election or defeat of such candidate, exceeds $1,000." The plain effect of § 608 (e) (1) is to prohibit all individuals, who are neither candidates nor owners of institutional press facilities, and all groups, except political parties and campaign organizations, from voicing their views "relative to a clearly identified candidate" through means that entail aggregate expenditures of more than $1,000 during a calendar year. The provision, for example, would make it a federal criminal offense for a person or association to place a single one-quarter page advertisement "relative to a clearly identified candidate" in a major metropolitan newspaper. . . .

[Unconstitutional vagueness] can be avoided only by reading § 608 (e) (1) as limited to communications that include explicit words of advocacy of election or defeat of a candidate. [We] turn then to the basic First Amendment question—whether § 608 (e) (1), even as thus narrowly and explicitly construed, impermissibly burdens the constitutional right of free expression. The Court of Appeals summarily held the provision constitutionally valid on the ground that "section 608 (e) is a loophole-closing provision only" that is necessary to prevent circumvention of the contribution limitations. We cannot agree. [T]he constitutionality of § 608 (e) (1) turns on whether the governmental interests advanced in its support satisfy the exacting scrutiny applicable to limitations on core First Amendment rights of political expression.

We find that the governmental interest in preventing corruption and the appearance of corruption is inadequate to justify § 608 (e) (1)'s ceiling on independent expenditures. First, assuming arguendo that large independent expenditures pose the same dangers of actual or apparent quid pro quo arrangements as do large contributions, § 608 (e) (1) does not provide an answer that sufficiently relates to the elimination of those dangers. Unlike the contribution limitations' total ban on the giving of large amounts of money to candidates, § 608 (e) (1) prevents only some large expenditures. So long as persons and groups eschew expenditures that in express terms advocate the election or defeat of a clearly identified candidate, they are free to spend as much as they want to promote the candidate and his views. [It] would naively underestimate the ingenuity and resourcefulness of persons and groups desiring to buy influence to believe that they would have much difficulty devising expenditures that skirted the restriction on express advocacy of election or defeat but nevertheless benefited the candidate's campaign. [Second], the independent advocacy restricted by the provision does not presently appear to pose dangers of real or apparent corruption comparable to those identified with large campaign contributions. The parties defending § 608 (e) (1) contend that it is necessary to prevent would-be contributors from avoiding the contribution limitations by the simple expedient of paying directly for media advertisements or for other portions of the candidate's campaign activities. [But] controlled or coordinated expenditures are treated as contributions rather than expenditures under the Act . . . . By contrast, § 608 (e) (1) limits expenditures for express advocacy of candidates made totally independently of the candidate and his campaign. Unlike contributions, such independent expenditures may well provide little assistance to the candidate's campaign and indeed may prove counterproductive. The absence of pre-arrangement and coordination of an expenditure with the candidate or his agent not only undermines the value of the expenditure to the candidate, but also alleviates the danger that expenditures will be given as a quid pro quo for improper commitments from the candidate. Rather than preventing circumvention of the contribution limitations, § 608 (e) (1) severely restricts all independent advocacy despite its substantially diminished potential for abuse. While the independent expenditure ceiling thus fails to serve any substantial governmental interest in stemming the reality or appearance of corruption in the electoral process, it heavily burdens core First Amendment expression. [Advocacy] of the election or defeat of candidates for federal office is no less entitled to protection under the First Amendment than the discussion of political policy generally or advocacy of the passage or defeat of legislation.

It is argued, however, that the ancillary governmental interest in equalizing the relative ability of individuals and groups to influence the outcome of elections serves to justify [this limitation]. But the concept that government may restrict the speech of some elements of our society in order to enhance the relative voice of others is wholly foreign to the First Amendment, which was designed "to secure 'the widest possible dissemination of information from diverse and antagonistic sources,'" and "'to assure unfettered interchange of ideas for the bringing about of political and social changes desired by the people.'" New York Times v. Sullivan. The First Amendment's protection against governmental abridgment of free expression cannot properly be made to depend on a person's financial ability to engage in public discussion. . . .

2. *Limitation on expenditures by candidates from personal or family resources.* The Act also sets limits on expenditures by a candidate "from his personal funds, or the personal funds of his immediate family, in connection with his campaigns during any calendar year." § 608 (a) (1). These ceilings vary from $50,000 for Presidential or Vice Presidential candidates to $35,000 for Senate candidates, and $25,000 for most candidates for the House of Representatives. [The] candidate, no less than any other person, has a First Amendment right to engage in the discussion of public issues and vigorously and tirelessly to advocate his own election and the election of other candidates. [The] ceiling on personal expenditures by a candidate in furtherance of his own candidacy thus clearly and directly interferes with constitutionally protected freedoms. The primary governmental interest served by the Act—the prevention of actual and apparent corruption of the political process—does not support the limitation on the candidate's expenditure of his own personal funds. [T]he use of personal funds reduces the candidate's dependence on outside contributions and thereby counteracts the coercive pressures and attendant risks of abuse to which the Act's contribution limitations are directed. . . .

3. *Limitations on campaign expenditures.* Section 608 (c) of the Act places limitations on overall campaign expenditures by candidates seeking nomination for election

and election to federal office. Presidential candidates may spend $10,000,000 in seeking nomination for office and an additional $20,000,000 in the general election campaign. [There are also ceilings for campaigns for the House and Senate.] [No] governmental interest that has been suggested is sufficient to justify [these restrictions] on the quantity of political expression. [The] campaign expenditure ceilings appear to be designed primarily to serve the governmental interests in reducing the allegedly skyrocketing costs of political campaigns. [T]he mere growth in the cost of federal election campaigns in and of itself provides no basis for governmental restrictions on the quantity of campaign spending and the resulting limitation on the scope of federal campaigns. The First Amendment denies government the power to determine that spending to promote one's political views is wasteful, excessive, or unwise. In the free society ordained by our Constitution it is not the government but the people—individually as citizens and candidates and collectively as associations and political committees—who must retain control over the quantity and range of debate on public issues in a political campaign. [W]e hold that § 608 (c) is constitutionally invalid.

Chief Justice Warren Burger dissented in part from the judgment of the Court. He agreed with the Court that the expenditure limitations were unconstitutional, but, unlike the Court, thought that the limitations on contributions were also unconstitutional.

Chief Justice Burger, concurring in part and dissenting in part.

Contribution and expenditure limits. I agree fully with that part of the Court's opinion that holds unconstitutional the limitations the Act puts on campaign expenditures. [Yet] when it approves similarly stringent limitations on contributions, the Court ignores the reasons it finds so persuasive in the context of expenditures. For me contributions and expenditures are two sides of the same First Amendment coin. . . .

The Court attempts to separate the two communicative aspects of political contributions—the "moral" support that the gift itself conveys, which the Court suggests is the same whether the gift is of $10 or $10,000, and the fact that money translates into communication. The Court dismisses the effect of the limitations on the second aspect of contributions. [On the premise] that contribution limitations restrict only the speech of "someone other than the contributor" [rests] the Court's justification for treating contributions differently from expenditures. The premise is demonstrably flawed; the contribution limitations will, in specific instances, limit exactly the same political activity that the expenditure ceilings limit, and at least one of the "expenditure" limitations the Court finds objectionable operates precisely like the "contribution" limitations. The Court's attempt to distinguish the communication inherent in political *contributions* from the speech aspects of political *expenditures* simply will not wash. We do little but engage in word games unless we recognize that people—candidates and contributors—spend money on political activity because they wish to communicate ideas, and their constitutional interest in doing so is precisely the same whether they or someone else utter the words. The Court attempts to make the Act seem less restrictive by casting the problem as one that goes to freedom of association rather than freedom of speech. I have long thought freedom of association and freedom of expression were two peas from the same pod. [It] is not simply speculation to think that the limitations on contributions will foreclose some candidacies. The limitations will also alter the nature of some electoral contests drastically.

Justice Byron White also concurred in part and dissented in part. In an opinion that was the mirror-image of Chief Justice Burger's, White agreed with the Court that the contribution limits did not violate the Constitution but disagreed that the expenditure limits did.

Justice White, concurring in part and dissenting in part.

. . .

I dissent [from] the Court's view that the expenditure limitations [violate] the First Amendment. Concededly, neither the limitations on contributions nor those on expenditures directly or indirectly purport to control the content of political speech by candidates or by their supporters or detractors. What the Act regulates is giving and spending money, acts that have First Amendment significance not because they are themselves communicative with respect to the qualifications of the candidate, but because money may be used to defray the expenses of speaking or otherwise communicating about the merits or demerits of federal candidates for election. The act of giving money to political candidates, however, may have illegal or other undesirable consequences: it may be used to secure the express or tacit understanding that the giver will enjoy political favor if the candidate is elected. Both Congress and this Court's cases have recognized this as a moral danger against which effective preventive and curative steps must be taken.

Since the contribution and expenditure limitations are neutral as to the content of speech and are not motivated by fear of the consequences of the political speech of particular candidates or of political speech in general, this case depends on whether the nonspeech interests of the Federal Government in regulating the use of money in political campaigns are sufficiently urgent to justify the incidental effects that the limitations visit upon the First Amendment interests of candidates and their supporters. Despite its seeming struggle with the standard by which to judge this case, this is essentially the question the Court asks and answers in the affirmative with respect to the limitations on contributions. [The] Court thus accepts the congressional judgment that the evils of unlimited contributions are sufficiently threatening to warrant restriction regardless of the impact of the limits on the contributor's opportunity for effective speech and in turn on the total volume of the candidate's political communications by reason of his inability to accept large sums from those willing to give.

The congressional judgment, which I would also accept, was that other steps must be taken to counter the corrosive effects of money in federal election campaigns. One of these steps is § 608 (e) [the expenditure limits]. Congress was plainly of the view that these expenditures also have corruptive potential; but the Court strikes down the provision, strangely enough claiming more insight as to what may improperly influence candidates than is possessed by the majority of Congress that passed this Bill and the President who signed it. [It] would make little sense to me, and apparently made none to Congress, to limit the amounts an individual may give to a candidate or spend with his approval but fail to limit the amounts that could be spent on his behalf. Yet the Court permits the former while striking down the latter limitation. . . .

Let us suppose that each of two brothers spends one million dollars on TV spot announcements that he has individually prepared and in which he appears, urging the election of the same named candidate in identical words. One brother has sought and obtained the approval of the candidate; the other has not. The former may validly be prosecuted under § 608 (e); under the Court's view, the latter may not, even though the candidate could scarcely help knowing about and appreciating the expensive favor. For constitutional purposes it is difficult to see the difference between the two situations. I would take the word of those who know—that limiting independent expenditures is essential to prevent transparent and widespread evasion of the contribution limits.

SELECTED READINGS

Alexander, Herbert E. *Financing Politics*. 2d ed. Washington, D.C.: Congressional Quarterly Press, 1980.
  Alexander, the leading authority on election financing and finance reform, examines the patterns of election financing that have emerged since the passage of campaign finance legislation in the early 1970s. After explaining the Federal Election Campaign Act of 1971 and its 1974 amendments, he considers the relative strengths of individual and group contributors in the political process and the special roles of corporate, labor, and other political action committees. His chief concern is the relationship between the principle of "one man, one vote" and the unequal distribution of financial resources.
Barber, James D. *The Pulse of Politics: Electing Presidents in the Media Age*. New York: Norton, 1980.
  A leading student of the presidency looks at "the interplay of Presidential campaigners and the journalists who tell their running stories," covering presidents and journalists since the days of Theodore Roosevelt. Barber worries about the presentation of campaigns and politics as great "games," unrelated to the difficult problems of governance.
Crouse, Timothy. *The Boys on the Bus: Riding with the Campaign Press Corps*. New York: Ballantine, 1976.
  Crouse delivers an amusing inside view of the media's coverage of the Nixon-McGovern campaign—with an especially wry look at the ways campaigners strive to produce media events. The relationship between campaigners and journalists is revealed to be cooperative and friendly as often as it is antagonistic.

Drew, Elizabeth. *Politics and Money: The New Road to Corruption.* New York: Macmillan, 1983.

Washington journalist Drew examines the practices and problems of campaign financing and fund raising under the federal election reforms of the 1970s. In many respects, she concludes, the letter of the law regarding limitations on contributions is observed while the spirit of the law is overlooked. Drew is especially concerned with how the very necessity of fund raising is altering the nature of representation in Congress.

Jacobson, Gary. *Money in Congressional Elections.* New Haven, Conn.: Yale University Press, 1980.

Professor Jacobson examines the politics of campaign finance reform since the Nixon administration and the patterns of contributions from individual and institutional donors. Legal restrictions on campaign spending, he concludes, usually benefit incumbents rather than challengers.

Kraus, Sidney, and Davis, Dennis. *The Effects of Mass Communications on Political Behavior.* New York: Praeger, 1980.

This valuable volume explores our current ability to "measure, assess and evaluate" the media's effect on politics.

Patterson, Thomas E. *The Mass Media Election.* New York: Praeger, 1980.

A study of the decline of the American political party and of the media's efforts to perform the agenda-setting and information-providing functions parties once performed. Patterson concludes that the media can present electoral competition and controversy but are poorly equipped to cover candidates' philosophies and preferred policies.

Rubin, Bernard. *Media, Politics, and Democracy.* New York: Oxford University Press, 1977.

A professor of communications examines the role of the media in several significant areas: national agenda setting, influencing the values of children, manipulation and censorship, and the electoral process. This readable volume offers a number of brief case studies of media influence.

Sabato, Larry J. *The Rise of Political Consultants.* New York: Basic Books, 1981.

An excellent overview of the variety of services political consultants offer their clients and of the impact of political consultants on the electoral process and representative government. Two of the political consultant's special tools—the media and direct mail—are examined in detail. Appendixes list individual and institutional political consultants by specialty.

Thayer, George. *Who Shakes the Money Tree?* New York: Simon and Schuster, 1973.

A history of campaign finance since George Washington's time. The book reveals, for example, that when Washington was running for the Virginia House of Burgessess, it cost him a quart and a half of liquor per voter to run his campaign.

GLOSSARY

Boss. A derogatory name for a political party leader.

Faction. A term used by James Madison for a special interest group, or what today is sometimes called a pressure group. Madison defined "faction" as any group motivated by a common interest contrary to the rights of others or to the long-term interests of society.

Image making. The attempt to make a political candidate look good in the mass media while avoiding any discussion of issues; for example, showing the candidate jogging or playing with his children instead of saying what he stands for.

Lobbyist. Someone who attempts to influence government decisions. So called because such individuals usually could be found in the lobbies of the Capitol Building, waiting for congressmen to enter and leave the House and Senate chambers.

Media consultant. A person who makes a living by managing or "packaging" the campaigns of political candidates—work which includes creating appropriate political advertisements.

Negative ads. Radio and TV ads that do not promote any particular candidate but confine themselves to attacking a candidate.

Party loyalty. The disposition to support a particular political party year after year, through good and bad. Party loyalty has declined in America over the past two decades.

Political action committee (PAC). A group which solicits contributions in order to support or oppose particular candidates and causes during campaign periods and to lobby the government.

Socialist. One who believes that the private ownership of business should be abolished and replaced by some system of public or state ownership.

Tax checkoff. A provision on income tax forms permitting each taxpayer to earmark $1 ($2 on joint returns) of tax payment to be diverted into a special fund to finance presidential primaries and general elections.

Chapter 8
Shouting Fire:
Rights and Duties of the Press

"The Founding Fathers wanted a free press, not a 'responsible' one."

ALAN BARTH
Washington Post

"We do not have absolute power, just power without accountability."

JEREMIAH O'LEARY
Washington Times

When the United States invaded Grenada in 1983, reporters were excluded from the battle scene until the operation was virtually over. Journalists were indignant. "The American government," said NBC commentator John Chancellor, "is doing whatever it wants to, without any representative of the American public watching what it is doing."

The assumption behind Chancellor's statement was that the American press is a "representative of the American public." Almost immediately, that assumption was challenged—by the American public. Some 500 letters and phone calls flooded into NBC's offices, informing the network by a margin of five to one that they supported the exclusion of the press from the Grenada operation. ABC News anchor Peter Jennings said that his mail was running "99 percent" in favor of the press ban. The trade publication *Editor and Publisher* surveyed several newspapers and found that letters to the editor were running three to one for excluding the press. Richard Salant, a former network executive who headed the National News Council, told the annual meeting of the Society of Professional Journalists that he had proposed to network officials that they include in one of their polls a question on the issue of press bans. "Hell no!" they answered. "It would run five to one against us!" Even that might have understated the reaction. *Time* magazine reported that its letters were running eight to one in favor of excluding the press.

Alarmed at these public reactions, journalists began invoking hallowed traditions. This was the first time, they complained, that American military forces had barred the press from a war zone. During World War II the press had even gone ashore with our troops. To that point Secretary of State George Schultz had a ready answer. In past wars, he said, American reporters were on "our" side. "These days, in the adversary journalism that's developed, it seems as though reporters are always against us. And when you are trying to conduct a military operation, you don't need that." By "adversary journalism," Schultz meant the kind of reporting that focuses on wrongdoing by one's own government. Since the Vietnam War and "Watergate," this type of reporting has become popular among members of the press.

But the American public may be turning against it. In a special cover story, *Time* magazine said that many of the letters to editors about the Grenada press ban "seemed to reach beyond the battlefield issue to reflect deep, far-reaching resentment of the press." One letter cited in the article, from a woman in California, said: "Journalists are so much out of touch with majority values, such as honor, duty, and service to country, that they are alienated from the society they purport to serve." Another, from a man in Colorado, said: "The media have frequently misused sensitive and explosive events as opportunities for personal glory and financial gain." These kinds of feelings are probably behind the widespread loss of confidence in the press since the mid-'70s. In 1976 almost 30 percent of Americans told pollsters that they had "a great deal of confidence" in the press. By 1978 the percentage had fallen to slightly more than 20. In 1983 only 13.7 percent expressed great confidence in the press.

The immediate issue in this chapter is press freedom, particularly as it relates to the topic of national security. The issue is easy to formulate. What actions can the press get away with? What are its legal rights, and what are the limitations on those rights? But this chapter also has a larger concern, one that has nothing directly to do with legal coercion. It is the question of the press's moral responsibilities. Does the press have any? If so, what are they? Is it enough that the press gets its facts straight and prints newsworthy stories? Or do reporters have the moral obligation to keep in mind what the woman in California wrote about: "honor, duty, and service to country"? Does it matter whether a reporter is motivated by nothing except (in the words of the man from Colorado) "personal glory and financial gain"? Or should a reporter pursue larger, more selfless goals?

Moral issues are hard to resolve. All of us have moral viewpoints, and the viewpoints differ. Even "honor, duty, and service to country" are not as easy to define as they once may have been. Yet we cannot avoid moral issues as we talk about press freedom and responsibility. Moral issues are different from legal rights, but they are at least as important. During the video discussion of press freedom, retired Supreme Court Justice Potter Stewart says, "Just because you have a right to do something doesn't mean it's right to do it." That sums it up. Americans may not rush to impose legal limits on the press, but they think the press itself must recognize moral limits. And that may be what lies behind the current mood of resentment at the press.

That resentment, and the corresponding loss of confidence in the press, may go no further than feelings. Yet the danger exists that people or groups may seize on this public mood to argue that legal actions should follow. In December 1983, even as the press ban in Grenada was being debated, an ABC News poll revealed that 67 percent of those polled would support censorship of the news media if they felt "national security" were at stake. It is in everyone's interest, but not least the press's interest, that thoughtful people inside and outside of the press should probe the legal and moral dimensions of press freedom today.

The Video Discussion

In the video program, a distinguished panel of journalists, judges, attorneys, political leaders, and former administration officials takes up the thorny issues raised by freedom of the press versus national security. The moderator is Professor Benno C. Schmidt, Jr., dean of Columbia University Law School.

List of Participants

FLOYD ABRAMS
Attorney
Cahill, Gordon & Reindel

HON. GRIFFIN B. BELL
Attorney
King & Spalding
Former U.S. Attorney General

HON. ROBERT H. BORK
Judge
U.S. Court of Appeals
District of Columbia

PHILIP BUCHEN
Attorney
Dewey, Ballantine, Bushby,
Palmer & Wood
Former Counsel to President Ford

HODDING CARTER III
Host
Inside Story
Former Assistant Secretary of State
Bureau of Public Affairs

LYLE DENNISTON
Supreme Court Reporter
Baltimore Sun

HON. HARRY T. EDWARDS
Judge
U.S. Court of Appeals
District of Columbia

MAX FRANKEL
Editorial Page Editor
New York Times

HON. ORRIN G. HATCH
U.S. Senator
Utah

BRIT HUME
Correspondent
ABC News

HON. FRANK J. MCGARR
Chief Judge
U.S. District Court
Northern District of Illinois

JACK NELSON
Washington Bureau Chief
Los Angeles Times

DAN RATHER
Managing Editor
CBS Evening News

VAN GORDON SAUTER
President
CBS News

HON. JAMES SCHLESINGER
Consultant in Residence
Georgetown University Center for
Strategic and International Studies
Former Director
Central Intelligence Agency
Former U.S. Secretary of Defense

HOWARD SIMONS
Managing Editor
Washington Post

HON. POTTER STEWART
Justice (retired)
U.S. Supreme Court

SAMUEL K. SKINNER
Attorney
Sidley & Austin
Former U.S. Attorney
Northern District of Illinois

WILLIAM H. WEBSTER
Director
Federal Bureau of Investigation

Program Summary

The program is divided into four parts, corresponding to four "stages" of news gathering and publishing. Stage 1, "the covert action plan," concerns the CIA's formulation of a top-secret plan to destabilize the hostile government of "Sierra Madre" by training a force of exiles for military action against it and helping opposition forces within the country. Stage 2, "the leak," involves the question of how far reporters will go in soliciting a story from a "source." Will they receive stolen documents? Will they steal documents themselves? Do they care about the motives of the leaker? Do journalists have any responsibilities besides getting and printing stories?

Stage 3, "publication," concerns the kinds of considerations journalists must take into account before deciding whether or not to run a story. Should they check first with government officials? Should they kill a story if government officials ask them to? Should they worry about the story's possible impact on national security? Stage 4, "keeping the story under wraps," concerns the issue of temporary restraining orders (TROs). Are there circumstances in which a judge should restrain in advance the broadcast or publication of a news story?

I: THE COVERT ACTION PLAN

The first part of the discussion is a kind of preface. The moderator sets the stage for the argument by talking about the CIA's plan to train exiles for covert action against the anti-American government of "Sierra Madre." We have met Sierra Madre before, in Chapter 2. It appears to be a thinly disguised Nicaragua. (In that program, Senator Christopher Dodd even slipped at one point and started to call it Nicaragua.) Chapter 2 examined whether the president, and thus the CIA, had a right to conduct such operations without consulting Congress. Here the question is somewhat different. It is whether the American people have a "right to know" whether such plans are being made in the executive branch.

Former CIA Director James Schlesinger says the public has no such right. There are certain issues, he says, "that should not be discussed in public"—because to provide certain information in public "means one provides it to other countries." Former Attorney General Griffin Bell seems to disagree. At least he would start off with the assumption that the public has a "right to know."

Justice Stewart disagrees. In fact, he is angry that the term "right to know" is "loosely bandied about by a lot of intelligent people, including some of my former colleagues" on the Supreme Court. According to Stewart, a "right to know" is found nowhere in the Constitution, and the phrase's constant use can only lead to "fuzzy and sloppy thinking." This does not mean Stewart would support bans on reporting or other forms of censorship. On the contrary, he says, once a reporter gets hold of a story, "he's entitled under the First Amendment to print it." But he does not think the CIA director or any other government official has an obligation to hand the story to reporters or to any other member of the public. Legally speaking, the game seems to be one of "finder's keepers." Once the story is in the reporter's hands, it is his to do with as he wishes.

But in Stewart's view there is more than a game involved in the business of exposing government security secrets. Even at this early stage, Stewart begins to raise the ethical issues as opposed to the purely constitutional ones. Exposing the government's covert plan for Sierra Madre, he says, "involves great questions of ethics and morality and responsibility and so on. Not constitutional questions."

II: THE LEAK

In Chapter 1, we discussed the "symbiotic" relationship that often exists between reporters and "leakers." The two help each other. The leaker, usually a middle-level bureaucrat who has an ax to grind with his superiors, goes to the press to embarrass his or her bosses or derail their policies. The reporters, of course, are delighted to get information that might make a good news story. Scarcely a day goes by without evidence of leaks appearing in the press. Stories that begin "According to reliable sources within the _____ Department" are typical products of a leak.

Understandably, then, a warm relationship often exists between leakers and reporters. Reporters sometimes refer to leakers as "whistle-blowers," conjuring up the image of public-spirited citizens who summon the police—in this case the American public—against wrongdoers. The real motives of leakers are rarely questioned by reporters. This is evident in the remarks of the reporters on the panel. "I have never been, and I'm not now, particularly interested in the motives of leakers," says Brit Hume, ABC news correspondent. CBS anchor Dan Rather says, "It's not the number-one question on my mind." All Rather claims to care about is whether the story is true and newsworthy.

But that raises a new question. Suppose the leaker's story is not true. Suppose, out of sheer malice, the leaker is lying. Generally speaking, the reporters on the panel are reluctant to accept this hypothesis. Later in the program, *Baltimore Sun* reporter Lyle Denniston will talk about "an ongoing relationship between a reporter and a source." If the source "comes to you with new information and there is no easily or immediately verifiable means available to you, you go with it." You print it, that is, without even checking with the head of the CIA? Denniston: "I would expect that Mr. Schlesinger would probably ultimately lie to me about it anyway." Wait a minute, says the moderator. You're ready to believe the source without question, but you assume his boss is lying? Denniston: "Well, it's been my experience after a lot of years in Washington that lying increases the closer you get to the top." The logical implication is that the biggest liar of all is the president of the United States!

No reporter on the panel challenges the substance of what Denniston has said. (Hume thinks his position is "absurd," but only because *his* audience likes to hear both sides of the story.) Dan Rather, in fact, has his own version of it. There are certain kinds of leaks Rather might not broadcast even if they were true. Those are "offensive leaks." An offensive leak is one made by a very high government official to a reporter with the intention of "sending a message" to a hostile country. For example, the head of the CIA might tell Rather, on a not-for-attribution basis, that our country was *thinking* of invading Sierra Madre—his purpose being to frighten the rulers of that country. Rather might not carry that story because he doesn't like to be "used." Yet as the moderator reminds Rather, he doesn't mind being used by middle-level bureaucrats who leak antigovernment secrets.

If the journalists on the panel have any bias, it seems to be an antigovernment bias. This comes out most dramatically right after Dan Rather's comments. The moderator turns to Lyle Denniston and asks if *he* minds being used by a leaker. Not at all, says Denniston.

MODERATOR: Used by someone who's committed a crime?
DENNISTON: Exactly. Exactly.
MODERATOR: Or used by someone who is breaching his oath of office . . . breaching his trust?
DENNISTON: Professor Schmidt, as a journalist I have only one responsibility and that is to get a story and print it.
MODERATOR: Would you steal it yourself?
DENNISTON: I would.
MODERATOR: Right off Mr. Schlesinger's desk?
DENNISTON: Exactly. And hopefully without his knowing it.
MODERATOR: Would you hold a gun to his head? . . .
DENNISTON: Mayhem might well be ruled out, but I'm not even sure of that.
MODERATOR: But breaking and entering?
DENNISTON: Breaking and entering is benign.

There is nervous laughter in the room. The moderator asks Denniston how he can justify such an attitude toward the government. Denniston answers:

It isn't a question of justification in terms of the law. It's a question of justifying it in terms of the commercial sale of information to interested customers. That's my only business. That's the only thing I do in life is to sell information, hopefully for a profit.

In terms of style, Lyle Denniston is an embarrassment to his journalistic colleagues. Some of them even suggest that he may be playing "devil's advocate." But the substance of his remarks does not seem to arouse much disagreement. Would Brit Hume accept stolen documents? "I'd take a Xerox, frankly." Even this may not be necessary, advises Floyd Abrams, an attorney who often represents the *New York Times* in court cases. If Abrams were Hume's attorney, he "would advise him the chances of prosecution [were] so slight, the chances of conviction slighter still," that he could go ahead and accept the stolen documents. For a moment it sounds as though Hume is going to raise the moral issue of whether it is right to accept documents stolen from the government. He says: "Mind you, Professor Schmidt, that it is *not* the question of prosecution that concerns me." What concerns him is all the bad publicity he might get for accepting stolen documents. "That would perhaps change the focus of the story," he says, meaning that *he* would become the story. Hume is not worried about morality but about his "credibility."

How does Jack Nelson, bureau chief of the *Los Angeles Times*, feel about accepting stolen government documents? "Oh, I might be a little concerned," Nelson says. He would "rather" they not be stolen. "But in the end it wouldn't make any difference." That is also Dan Rather's view. "As a professional, my job is to publish and be damned," he says. If the story is true and newsworthy, he'll probably run it. Does it bother him that the documents came to him "with this taint of criminality"? Rather replies: "Some, but frankly not a great deal."

All of this is too much for Frank McGarr, a blunt-speaking U.S. appeals court judge from Illinois. He says:

> I'm amazed and appalled at most of the comments I heard this morning from the newsmen. I'm actually shocked to hear somebody say "I wouldn't touch the stolen document, I'll just let him read it to me." Or to hear somebody else argue, you know, "the national security is no great problem, it's news and I have the right and duty to publish it." Or, "I'd break the law in furtherance of my commercial duty to publish them." That's what a fence does. He breaks the law in furtherance of his pursuit of his commercial goal. There has been no respect for the law, for the legal problem implied here, by anyone who has spoken for the media here today, and I'm amazed by it.

Denniston's remarks about the commercial motives of reporters are probably misleading—at least when it comes to those in the position of Dan Rather or of Washington reporters for papers like the *New York Times* and the *Washington Post*. Such individuals are not wholly shielded from bottom-line concerns, but they need not be obsessed with ratings or circulation as they decide what stories to report. What evidence we have suggests that mercenary considerations are not uppermost in the minds of journalists for the "prestige press." What may be more important in shaping their "product" is their view of America and its institutions.

Political Views of Reporters

We have already seen evidence of this view in the video discussion. It seems to include these propositions:

1. The CIA has no business interfering in other countries, even if those countries' actions threaten the security of the United States, without a formal declaration of war

by Congress. (Jack Nelson calls the CIA a "rogue elephant" for "going to war without declaring war.")

2. If the CIA does intervene, the press has the duty to expose such covert actions. The public has a right to know, and the press represents the public.

3. The motives of leakers are not important *unless* a leaker is a high government official. A reporter should not be "used" by the government, but it is all right to let himself be used by someone opposed to the government.

4. High government officials are more likely to be liars than those lower down in the bureaucracy.

5. There is nothing wrong with receiving "top secret" documents stolen from the government, though it might be wise to copy them and give back the originals. (Max Frankel of the *New York Times* says that isn't really stealing anyhow, because all government information belongs to the American people.)

That such views are broadly shared among journalists from the major media was revealed in a major study by political scientists S. Robert Lichter and Stanley Rothman which was published in the October/November 1981 issue of the journal *Public Opinion*. Lichter and Rothman conducted lengthy interviews with journalists from the *Washington Post*, the *Wall Street Journal, Time, Newsweek, U.S. News and World Report*, the three commercial networks, PBS, and major broadcasting stations. The results showed that journalists from these media were not only much more affluent and better educated than the average American but that their views on political issues were markedly different from those of most Americans. For example, 81 percent of the journalists voted for Senator George McGovern in the presidential election of 1972, though McGovern's support from the public at large was only 38 percent, and 91 percent of them preferred the pro-choice position on abortion, a position favored by 47 percent of the general public.

As to the issues relating to this chapter, what stands out in the Lichter and Rothman study is the suspicion with which journalists regard the government. Some 56 percent of them thought that the United States causes poverty in the world by exploiting Third World countries; 51 percent were convinced that American foreign policy was interested mainly in protecting American business; 57 percent considered the use of U.S. resources to be immoral; 55 percent either disagreed or strongly disagreed with the statement that the CIA should sometimes undermine hostile governments.

These views lie at the roots of the "adversary journalism" that Secretary of State Schultz complained about in 1983. They may explain why the journalists on the panel will accept documents stolen from the government, publicize the secret plans of the CIA, and accept the word of a whistle-blower as against that of a high government official. They may also explain why the Reagan administration did not allow journalists to come along when it invaded Grenada.

III: PUBLICATION

By hook or by crook, the reporter in our hypothetical case has gotten the documents. Does he publish them? If he does, what risks does he take? Will the courts protect him? How strong is the First Amendment's guarantee of free speech and a free press?

The First Amendment says, "Congress shall make no law . . . abridging the liberty of speech, or of the press. . . ." That *sounds* absolute: "no law." In practice, though, America has always put a number of restraints upon free speech and press, including laws against libel and slander, against pornography, and against advertising products considered dangerous or unhealthy. When it comes to the advocacy of political doctrines, America has had very few restrictions, at least when compared with other countries. But even here the rights of speech and press are not absolute. At times, government has restricted them, and has done so with the approval of the Supreme Court.

The *Schenck* Case: "Clear and Present Danger"

The benchmark Supreme Court decision on freedom of speech is *Schenck* v. *United States* (1919). During World War I, Charles Schenck, general secretary of the Socialist party, mailed to potential draftees 15,000 leaflets that compared conscription to slavery and urged readers to "assert your rights." Schenck did nothing physical to obstruct the draft; his actions were wholly verbal. Yet he was arrested under the Espionage Act of 1917 and sentenced to prison for draft obstruction. Schenck claimed that his activities were protected by the First Amendment. The Supreme Court disagreed.

The Court's opinion in *Schenck* v. *United States* was written by Justice Oliver Wendell Holmes, Jr., a famous jurist. Holmes agreed that during normal times Schenck's leaflets would be protected by the First Amendment. But during a wartime emergency, they constituted a "clear and present danger" of an evil—draft obstruction—that government had a right to prevent.

What is meant by "clear and present danger"? Holmes gave an example that has become as famous as Holmes himself. "The most stringent protection of free speech would not protect a man in falsely shouting fire in a theatre and causing a panic." Certain forms of speech are not mere advocacy; what they really amount to is incitement. And anyone who incites people to commit acts the government has a right to prevent is not protected by the First Amendment.

But why not? In other cases, Holmes showed himself to be a fearless champion of free speech. He insisted that Americans should be allowed to hear every type of doctrine, even "dangerous" doctrines like communism. He favored "free trade in ideas." Why, then, did he allow the government to imprison Schenck, a comparatively tame socialist? In Holmes's mind the critical factor was incitement. If someone merely advocates a doctrine, no matter how radical, listeners have time to think it over. But if someone shouts "Fire!" in a dark theater, the response is, quite literally, a knee-jerk reaction. People's freedom to think has been taken away from them. Such expressions "have all the effect of force."

In spite of Holmes's reverence for the First Amendment, then, he believed that the absolute-sounding language of the amendment must be qualified. In certain circumstances—a wartime emergency being one of them—government may punish certain types of speech activity. First Amendment freedoms must be balanced against other values that government has a right to protect. One of those values is the security of the nation.

Holmes's approach has always had its critics. Some deny that any kind of "balancing" is appropriate when First Amendment freedoms are at stake. After all, the First Amendment says that Congress shall make "no law" abridging freedom of speech and press. The late Supreme Court Justice Hugo Black often cited the absolute language of the First Amendment, and he could get impatient, even sarcastic, with those who resisted his literal reading of it. "I understand," he said, "that it is rather old-fashioned and shows a slight naivete to say that 'no law' means 'no law.'" Alexander Meiklejohn, a famous political and social commentator, agreed with Black. He once suggested that if Holmes's doctrine of "clear and present danger" were pushed to its conclusion, it might justify the arrest of a dissenting Supreme Court justice during an "emergency" period.

But free-speech absolutism has its own difficulties. Does it mean that government may never regulate advertising? Should the Mafia be allowed to solicit hit men in the want-ad section? Should people be allowed to advertise heroin? Meiklejohn got around these difficulties by adding a number of qualifications (distinguishing, for example, between political and nonpolitical speech and allowing only qualified protection to the latter), but these qualifications diluted the original force of his argument. Black was more consistent (he did not even believe in laws against libel and slander), but even he qualified his position. He refused to regard picketing as a form of speech, and he would not allow the right of assembly—also guaranteed in the First Amendment—to outweigh the claim of private property rights.

There are federal statutes that could be used to punish the press for publishing certain kinds of secret information. Most of these statutes are aimed at protecting secret codes and prescribe stiff punishments for publishing any information that could be used by a hostile country to decipher our codes. A more recent statute would go further; it makes it a felony to publish the names of American secret intelligence agents. The statute was enacted after an American CIA agent, whose name and activities were publicized in a left-wing publication, was assassinated.

In the past, laws were rarely necessary to discourage the press from publicizing covert "national security" activities of our government. During World War II, journalists were often privy to extremely sensitive military information and voluntarily censored themselves. Even in the absence of declared war, journalists kept secrets. In 1961, the *New York Times* learned of the Kennedy administration's plan to use a force of anti-Castro Cubans to invade Cuba. But the *Times* deliberately muted its reporting of the plan to avoid jeopardizing the operation. (The invasion attempt was a humiliating failure, and Kennedy later said that it might have been better if the *Times* had publicized the plan, thus forcing the administration to abort it.)

But times have changed since 1961. Early in 1984, on ABC's *Nightline*, host Ted Koppel said he would have broadcast the Reagan administration's plan to invade Grenada if he could have found independent confirmation of the tip he received from a Caribbean official that an invasion was imminent. Although Jack Nelson, on the same *Nightline* program, said he would not report such information, other journalists on the video panel seem to agree with Koppel's apparent position: if a highly sensitive leak can be confirmed, the journalist should not be deterred from publicizing it. No one disagrees with Dan Rather when he says, "If we'd established it was true, we'd probably run it."

Howard Simons, managing editor of the *Washington Post*, has even worked out a philosophy on the subject. "I think it's his job, Jim Schlesinger's job, to keep secrets," he says. "That's his job. My job is to find 'em." Simons views American society as an aggregation of people with jobs to perform. As often as not, the jobs are adversarial; they work in opposition to each other. This view of American society is so widely shared by the other panelists that it becomes the basis for a game played later in the program. Each of the players assumes a role—prosecutor, judge, journalist, defense attorney. The prosecutor is out to "get" the journalist, and he shops around for a tough judge. The journalist goads *his* attorney to find a lenient judge. The assumption behind the game is that American society can be seen as an arena filled with competing interests.

There is much to be said for this view. It bears some resemblance to James Madison's philosophy of "checks and balances," which was discussed in Chapter 1. The relentless competition between interests may be what preserves freedom in America. Yet as a vision of society, this image lacks any concept of the *common* good. All it envisages is continuous struggles between self-serving interests. Simons's view may even be more Madisonian than Madison's. The author of *The Federalist* No. 10 wrote about "the permanent and aggregate interests of the community." It is not clear that Simons believes in overall community interests, or, if he does, whether he thinks it is his "job" to take them into account.

Points to Remember

1. The "symbiotic" relationship between "leakers" and reporters is evident in the way the journalists on the panel regard those in government who supply them with news embarrassing to the administration. The journalists are not much interested in the motives of leakers. They tend to assume that the leakers are more likely to tell the truth than are those who head departments.
2. A 1981 study of journalists from major media revealed that their views on key issues are markedly different from those of most Americans. Most major journalists distrust the government's motives in foreign affairs, think the United States exploits the people of the Third World, and regard U.S. foreign policy as a means of protecting American business interests. They also oppose the use of "covert action" even against governments hostile to the United States.
3. The First Amendment guarantees free speech and press, but key Supreme Court decisions have said that First Amendment rights are not absolute. In *Schenck* v. *United States* (1919), the Court held that government may limit free speech in circumstances that present a "clear and present danger" of an evil which government

has a right to prevent. To illustrate the meaning of "clear and present danger," the Court used the example of someone shouting "Fire!" in a crowded theater.

4. None of the journalists on the video panel raises any objection to the idea of receiving "top secret" information stolen from the government. Some specifically affirm that they would accept it. Lyle Denniston of the *Baltimore Sun* says that he might break into a government office and steal it himself.

5. The journalists on the panel would not be deterred from publishing a story simply because a government official told them it would damage the nation's security. The managing editor of the *Washington Post* sees the relationship between journalists and government officials as being adversarial: it is the job of the officials to keep secrets and the job of journalists to find them.

IV: KEEPING THE STORY "UNDER WRAPS"

The discussion now turns to the role of government and the courts in restraining publication. Suppose that a newspaper or a television news department has received the stolen "top secret" documents. Suppose it plans to go ahead and publish (or broadcast) them. Is there any way it can be stopped?

Here we must make a crucial distinction. There are plenty of enforceable laws on the books that prescribe punishment for speech and press activities: libel and slander laws as well as laws against obscenity, misleading advertising, and so on. There are laws against the theft of government documents, and there are probably laws that could be used to punish journalists for receiving and publishing the information they contain, at least in certain circumstances. *None of those are at issue here.* The central issue is whether the government may restrain *in advance* the publication of certain information—something quite different from punishing someone after the information has been published.

In the last part of the program, there is much talk about TROs, or temporary restraining orders. A TRO, issued by a judge, tells people that they must not do something until a formal judicial hearing has determined whether they have a right to do it. Otherwise, if the action goes forward before the hearing can be held, "irreparable" or "irreversible" harm will be done to one of the parties; no matter what fines or punishments are meted out later, they won't undo the harm done.

For example, a judge may issue a TRO to a construction company that is going to tear down a historic building. Since no monetary award can compensate for such damages, the demolition must be stopped until it is determined that the company has a right to do it. But what if the "action" in question is a proposed speech or the publication of a document? In such a case—as the reader can see in the video program—it is very difficult for the government to obtain a TRO. The government's only hope is to demonstrate to a judge that "irreparable harm" will almost surely result if the publication goes forward. Even then, the government has a hard case. For over 300 years our legal tradition has been opposed to the prior restraint of speech activities.

Prior restraint, also called "previous restraint," sets off alarm bells in the heads of American jurists. Historically the expression is most commonly associated with seventeenth-century England, where the royal authorities tried to silence dissenters before they could even get started. A license had to be obtained before anyone could issue a pamphlet, newspaper, or any other printed matter, and licenses were issued at the pleasure of the Crown. The poet John Milton and others cried out against the practice. Even if, Milton wrote, "all the winds of doctrine were let loose to play upon the earth," as long as truth is in the field we do an injury "by licensing and prohibiting to misdoubt her strength." Let truth and falsehood grapple with each other; "whoever knew truth put to the worse, in a free and open encounter." Before the end of the seventeenth century, Milton's eloquent appeal had borne fruit: licensing was abolished. In the next century Sir William Blackstone, the great English jurist, summed up what had now become common practice in England and America. "Every freeman has an undoubted right to lay what sentiments he pleases before the public; to forbid this is to destroy the freedom of the press." Before the First Amendment, indeed before the American Revolution, prior restraint was already outlawed in Anglo-American courts. Whatever else the First Amendment means, it certainly means that under ordinary circumstances the government has no business trying to stop anyone from expressing in public "what sentiments he pleases."

This does not mean, of course, that such a person cannot be punished afterward. It would be hard to find any eighteenth-century thinker, even the most libertarian, advocating the abolition of all laws punishing slander, libel, sedition, and so on. Again, Blackstone summed up the common understanding. Liberty of the press "consists in laying no *previous* restraints upon publications, and not in freedom from censure for criminal matter when published." If someone punishes "what is improper, mischievous or illegal, he must take the consequences of his temerity."

Near v. *Minnesota* (1931): Prior Restraint Is Unconstitutional

The first Supreme Court case to deal with the issue of prior restraint was *Near* v. *Minnesota* (1931). Jay M. Near published a brash, anti-Semitic newspaper, *The Saturday Press*, that accused officials in Minneapolis, Minnesota, of being in the pay of "Jew gangsters." Acting under a 1925 Minnesota statute that provided for shutting down as a public nuisance any "malicious, scandalous and defamatory newspaper," the authorities did just that to Near's scandal sheet. Near appealed to the Supreme Court, claiming that the shutdown amounted to a form of prior restraint and thus violated the First Amendment.

By a vote of five to four, the Court agreed with Near. "The fact," said Chief Justice Charles Evans Hughes, "that the liberty of the press may be abused by miscreant purveyors of scandal does not make any the less necessary the immunity of the press from previous restraint in dealing with official misconduct." Hughes added that if the publisher has committed libel or some other punishable offense, he can always be punished later. But he can never be restrained in advance of publication.

Well, hardly ever. There is, perhaps, an exception. Lawyers call it "the *Near* dictum," or sometimes "the *Near* troopship dictum." What is referred to is the "one, single, rather narrow exception," as former Supreme Court Justice Potter Stewart calls it in the video discussion. Stewart notes that the exception was mentioned "in dictum," parenthetically, and he wonders whether its specifics have much relevance today. In prefacing its dictum, the Court made reference to the *Schenck* case:

> [T]he protection even as to previous restraint is not absolutely unlimited. But the limitation has been recognized only in exceptional cases: "When a nation is at war many things that might be said in time of peace are such a hindrance to its effort that their utterance will not be endured so long as men fight and that no Court could regard them as protected by any constitutional right." *Schenck* v. *United States*, 249 U.S. 47, 52 (1919).

So even in *Near*, the Court majority could not put *Schenck* out of its mind. It remembered Holmes's allegory of the darkened theater, the lunatic yelling "Fire!," the stampede to the exits, and the inevitable trampling and crushing. All this suggests the idea of irreparable harm. Such harm did not occur in the *Near* case, so prior restraint was not justified. But there might be cases where it would occur if the government allowed something to be said or printed, and in such cases prior restraint would certainly be justified.

> No one would question but that a government might prevent actual obstruction to its recruiting service or the publication of the sailing dates of transports or the number and location of troops.

> Forty years after *Near*, the Court was asked to consider whether this narrow category of exceptions might at last be applicable. Would irreparable harm befall the nation if a newspaper published excerpts from forty-seven volumes of highly classified material spirited out of the Defense Department? That was the question the Court had to answer in the so-called Pentagon Papers case, *New York Times* v. *United States* (1971).

The Case of the Pentagon Papers

The story of the Pentagon Papers goes back to 1967, when Robert McNamara, President Johnson's secretary of defense, began having second thoughts about American involvement in Vietnam. He assembled a special "task force" and asked its members to write a review of U.S. involvement, which stretched back to the late 1940s. He advised them to "let the chips fall where they may." The result was a mammoth study that documented the role of American policymakers in deceiving the American public, casually disregarding both national and international law, cynically sending young men off to fight a war which the decision makers conceded was unwinnable, manipulating both the press and the Congress, and knowingly inflicting terrible losses on the civilian population of Vietnam.

The report was stamped "top secret," but one member of the task force was determined to make it public. His name was Daniel Ellsberg.

Ellsberg, an employee of the RAND Corporation (a Defense Department "think tank") had once been a passionate hawk, but shortly after visiting Vietnam he underwent a change of heart. As one of the compilers of the Pentagon Papers, Ellsberg had easy access to the document; he smuggled it out and photocopied all 7,000 pages. After some unsuccessful attempts to persuade members of Congress to make it public, he passed a copy to the *New York Times*. Three months later the *Times* began publishing parts of it.

Why the three-month delay? During that time the newspaper had a special team sifting through the Papers, deciding which were the best parts to print. It may be that nobody will ever know the bases on which those decisions were made, for the whole operation was kept top secret. A special room was set aside for it, and those who worked on it were sworn to secrecy. In other words, the *Times* behaved very much like the government, and demanded the same loyalty from its staff.

Once the *Times* started publishing the Pentagon Papers, the Nixon administration asked a district court judge to restrain any further publication pending a hearing on the merits. The judge granted the injunction—the first time in American history that a newspaper was restrained in advance by a court from publishing a specific article.

What were the merits of the case? The government argued that the Pentagon Papers were stamped "top secret" for good reason: they contained information that, if made public, could do irreparable harm to the security of the United States. The *Times* countered that none of the material which it published or planned to publish was of such a nature, although a lot of it could be embarrassing to those who got us into Vietnam. The case was decided by the Supreme Court, with unusual haste, two weeks after the original restraining order was served on the newspaper. (By this time Ellsberg had also leaked a copy of the Pentagon Papers to the *Washington Post*. The government, after being turned down by a lower court, secured a restraining order from a court of appeals after the *Post* began printing excerpts from the Papers. The *Post*, then, appeared with the *Times* in this case.) For the majority of the Court the real issue was whether the First Amendment protected newpapers against prior restraint by the government. By a margin of six to three, the Court ruled that it did.

Though the justices divided into a majority and a minority, they all had such different views that each wrote a separate opinion. On the majority side, Justices Hugo Black and William O. Douglas took the absolutist view: under no circumstances would they approve of prior restraint. Black even proclaimed that the *Times* and *Post* deserved commendation for trying to stop the government "from deceiving the people and sending them off to distant lands to die of foreign fevers and foreign shot and shell." Justice Brennan opened the door to prior restraint by the narrowest crack: only if publication "must inevitably, directly, and immediately cause the occurrence of an event kindred to imperilling the safety of a transport already at sea." Justices Stewart and White, the centrists in the case, were not so specific. They would allow prior restraint when disclosure would "surely result in direct, immediate, and irreparable damage to our Nation or its people." Neither, however, was ready to join Justice Black in pinning any medals on the *Times* and the *Post*. They thought criminal prosecutions against the newspapers might be in order, and Justice White even suggested some statutes the government might use in prosecuting them.

Justice Thurgood Marshall took an entirely different approach. Not aligning himself with anyone else in the majority, Marshall said that the real issue was "whether this Court or the Congress has the power to make law." His answer was that of course only Congress can pass laws, and since Congress had passed no law providing for prior restraints on newspapers, the Court had no business imposing prior restraint. Though Marshall's argument was unshared on the Court in 1971, it is used by a number of participants in the video debate. "We're not to make policy," says U.S. Appeals Court Judge Harry Edwards. "We enforce and apply laws for the Constitution, and you're asking us to make policy. We won't do it."

The two dissenters in the case were Chief Justice Warren Burger and Justice John Marshall Harlan. Harlan's dissent focused on the "frenzied train of events" that forced the Court to decide on a case of such magnitude, involving a document of 7,000 pages and 2.5 million words, in less than a week. The Court majority, said Harlan, "has been almost irresponsibly feverish in dealing with these cases." As to the merits of the case, Harlan suggested that the president, as "sole organ" of foreign relations, ought to be given proper deference by the courts; if it is the president's view that certain material will harm the national interest if published, that opinion should not lightly be overruled by a court—as he believed it was in this case.

Substantively, Burger's dissent was not much different from Harlan's. He seemed especially irked by the argument that even a short delay in publishing constituted a violation of the First Amendment. Since the *Times* itself withheld the Papers from publication for three months, couldn't it spare a little more time? That way the government could go over the Papers in an orderly way and decide what could be declassified and what should remain confidential.

Burger and Harlan considered the issue one that could be resolved by negotiation. Let the government and the *Times* sit down together and work things out, or at least narrow their areas of disagreement, on the question of what could be published without jeopardizing the nation's security. But for the press this case was, and is, a matter of principle. A newspaper's story was being held up by an injunction; meanwhile, its editors were being asked to negotiate with the government over what they could and could not print. In the video discussion, Dan Rather sums up the press's viewpoint: "I'm not going to give it a week's delay and get bogged down with a bunch of government lawyers. We're going to run it tonight."

In spite of the substantive similarities between the dissenting views of Harlan and Burger, there was an emotional tone to Burger's that set it apart. Burger was, very simply, horrified by the behavior of the *New York Times*.

To me it is hardly believable that a newspaper long regarded as a great institution in American life would fail to perform one of the basic and simple duties of every citizen with respect to the discovery or possession of stolen property or secret government documents. That duty, I had thought—perhaps naively—was to report forthwith, to responsible public officers. This duty rests on taxi drivers, Justices, and the *New York Times*.

Burger's argument is forcefully put. But consider its logical implications. The Pentagon

Papers were massive in bulk, but qualitatively they were no different than any other "leak" to a newspaper. What if Daniel Ellsberg had not delivered 7,000 pages to the *Times* but only one page? Or what if he had "leaked" information orally? Would the *Times* have been morally obliged to "report forthwith" to government officials, and ask permission before publishing? Putting the issue more broadly, should the press be "responsible"? If "responsibility" means having to negotiate with the government before publishing information which the government considers dangerous, then how is a "responsible" press any different from a government-controlled press?

Points to Remember

1. Prior restraint of speech, as opposed to punishment after a speech, is almost never permitted by American courts.

2. In *Near* v. *Minnesota* (1931), the Supreme Court held that the state's shutdown of a Minnesota newspaper amounted to a form of prior restraint and thus violated the First Amendment.

3. In the *Near* case the Court recognized, parenthetically, a narrow category of exceptions to its prohibition of prior restraint. Included in that category were speech activities such as "the publication of the sailing dates of transports or the number and location of troops" during wartime. This exception has been called "the *Near* dictum."

4. The government invoked the *Near* dictum when it tried to prevent the *New York Times* and other newspapers from publishing articles based on top secret papers removed from the Pentagon by Daniel Ellsberg. However, it lost its case before the Supreme Court in *New York Times* v. *United States* (1971). The Court majority felt that the government failed to prove that publication of the Papers would result in immediate, grave, and irreparable harm to the security of the United States. The dissenters contended that the Court was acting precipitously and irresponsibly, that more time was needed to study the Papers in order to decide what could be published, and that the executive branch was not being given the deference it deserved.

5. Part IV of the video discussion centers around whether the government can obtain a TRO against publication of a "leak." Most of the legal authorities on the panel would deny the TRO, since there is no statute passed by Congress permitting the issuance of one in such cases.

SUMMARY

The discussion you have watched between leading journalists, public officials, and legal authorities would have been unthinkable a generation ago. No one with the stature of the journalists on the panel would ever have sat down and matter-of-factly confessed a willingness to break laws, break into offices, receive stolen documents with "top secret" stamps on them, and assume that high administration officials are liars and manipulators. The bland response of most of the public officials on the panel would also have been unthinkable. With the exception of Justice Potter Stewart and Judge Frank McGarr, none of these panelists registers shock or indignation. For good or for ill, "national security" no longer has the urgent sound it once had.

Vietnam changed everything. Go back to the period just before the Vietnam War started escalating. Read John F. Kennedy's Inaugural Address of 1961. "Let the word go forth," Kennedy said, "that the torch has been passed to a new generation of Americans," a generation "unwilling to witness or permit the slow undoing of those human rights to which this nation has always been committed, and to which we are committed today at home and around the world." In speaking of the erosion of "human rights," Kennedy was not thinking particularly about South Africa or the Somoza regime in Nicaragua. He was worrying about the steady advance of the Soviet empire in the world. He saw this as a threat to our nation's security, and he was prepared to fight it.

So was the *New York Times.* The *Times,* in fact, chided Kennedy for not being firm enough in standing up to the Communist forces in Vietnam. Shortly before his death, Kennedy said that the war in Vietnam must be "their war," a war for the Vietnamese to fight. No, said the *Times* in an editorial, it was "our war—a war from which we cannot retreat and which we dare not lose." But as the war escalated in the late '60s, journalists began to turn against it. They reported on its violence and on the excesses on the American and South Vietnamese side, on the bar girls and the narcotics in South Vietnam, on the corruption of South Vietnamese officials. They wondered about the purpose of the war and complained of being lied to by American officials. (One Defense Department official even asserted a "right to lie.") As the journalists' reports on Vietnam became increasingly critical, American officials reacted angrily. Some of them impugned the patriotism of journalists and tried to intimidate them. Journalists reacted with their own kind of anger—and something more than anger. A deep cynicism about public officials crept into their thinking, a cynicism about the deeds of public officials, about their motives, and about the ideal which public officials so often invoked: patriotism.

Patriotism. Love of country. Today, in prominent newspapers like the *New York Times* and the *Washington Post*, the word is often put in quotation marks. It is "patriotism." This is the post-Vietnam treatment of the term—holding it with a forceps. Yet for nearly two centuries of American history it had been treated differently. It was warmly embraced by the American Revolutionists and the Founding Fathers. Both the Federalists and the Anti-Federalists claimed to be the "true" patriots. Still later, the Jeffersonians and the followers of John Adams fought each other under its banner. Even Henry David Thoreau, the American anarchist, wanted to be called a citizen and a patriot. For Henry Clay, patriotism was "the sublimest of public virtues." It was still regarded that way in the twentieth century and became the supreme standard under which America fought in two world wars and Korea. In the more protracted struggle with the Soviet Union, it remained the standard. But sometime—it is hard to say what year—between the inauguration of John F. Kennedy in 1961 and the ouster of Richard M. Nixon in 1974, patriotism became "patriotism."

Perhaps this is evidence that the American press is maturing, that it can no longer be intimidated by flag waving. But if patriotism is obsolete, or at any rate irrelevant to the practice of journalism, what ethical standards should journalists use in deciding what stories to print? In the last part of the video discussion, Howard Simons says, "We're not in the business of drawing moral values . . . if we report something." But surely journalists are not the kind of people who subordinate their consciences to their jobs. They must have standards, at least implicit ones. What would cause them to pull back, to refrain from doing something or printing something even at the cost of a great story? Brit Hume hints at one answer when he says he would not carry a story if it endangered the life of hostages. The problem is that in today's world whole societies are hostages to decisions made in Moscow and Washington, to terrorism, subversion, revolution, and imperialism. If Justice Oliver Wendell Holmes was correct to say that no one has a right to falsely shout "Fire!" in a crowded theater, then what of the world today? Is it not itself a great crowded theater? What moral implications does that have for journalists?

If this chapter and the video discussion have demonstrated anything, it is that the American press today can get away with a great deal without being held legally accountable. The remaining question is whether the press considers itself accountable in any moral sense, whether it agrees with Justice Stewart that "just because you have a right to do something doesn't mean it's right to do it." At the end of the program Justice Stewart has a final word to say about journalists. Perhaps it can serve as a provisional conclusion, or at least as a provocation:

> Well, I hope they act responsibly and with self-restraint and with good judgment. Because it seems to me that if in violation of the canons of judgment and self-restraint . . . a journalist someday published some information that's going to end up in a tremendous catastrophe, that, that alone will trigger a modification of the First Amendment. And that, it seems to me, would be a tragic event in American society.

Documents

SCHENCK V. UNITED STATES, 249 U.S. 47 (1919)

Charles Schenck and others sent out leaflets during World War I protesting against the draft and urging young men to "assert your rights." Schenck was charged with conspiracy to obstruct the draft and other violations of the Espionage Act of 1917. He appealed to the Supreme Court, charging that his First Amendment rights were being violated.

In his opinion for the Court, Justice Oliver Wendell Holmes, Jr., said that Schenck's activities constituted a "clear and present danger." Below are excerpts from Holmes's famous opinion.

Opinion of the Court, Mr. Justice Holmes.

This is an indictment in three counts. . . . The defendants were found guilty on all the counts. They set up the First Amendment to the Constitution forbidding Congress to make any law abridging the freedom of speech, or of the press, and bringing the case here on that ground have argued some other points also of which we must dispose. . . .

The document in question upon its first printed side recited the first section of the Thirteenth Amendment, said that the idea embodied in it was violated by the Conscription Act and that a conscript is little better than a convict. In impassioned language it intimated that conscription was despotism in its worst form and a monstrous wrong against humanity in the interest of Wall Street's chosen few. It said "Do not submit to intimidation," but in form at least confined itself to peaceful measures such as a petition for the repeal of the act. The other and later printed side of the sheet was headed "Assert Your Rights." It stated reasons for alleging that any one violated the Constitution when he refused to recognize "your right to assert your opposition to the draft," and went on "If you do not assert and support your rights, you are helping to deny or disparage rights which it is the solemn duty of all citizens and residents of the United States to retain." It described the arguments on the other side as coming from cunning politicians and a mercenary capitalist press, and even silent consent to the conscription law as helping to support an infamous conspiracy. It denied the power to send our citizens away to foreign shores to shoot up the people of other lands, and added that words could not express the condemnation such cold-blooded ruthlessness deserves, &c., winding up "You must do your share to maintain, support and uphold the rights of the people of this country." Of course the document would not have been sent unless it had been intended to have some effect, and we do not see what effect it could be expected to have upon persons subject to the draft except to influence them to obstruct the carrying of it out. The defendants do not deny that the jury might find against them on this point.

But it is said, suppose that that was the tendency of this circular, it is protected by the First Amendment to the Constitution. Two of the strongest expressions are said to be quoted respectively from well-known public men. It well may be that the prohibition of laws abridging the freedom of speech is not confined to previous restraints, although to prevent them may have been the main purpose, as intimated in *Patterson* v. *Colorado*, 205 U.S. 454, 462. We admit that in many places and in ordinary times the defendants in saying all that was said in the circular would have been within their constitutional rights. But the character of every act depends upon the circumstances in which it is done. *Aikens* v. *Wisconsin*, 195 U.S. 194, 205, 206. The most stringent protection of free speech would not protect a man in falsely shouting fire in a theatre and causing a panic. It does not even protect a man from an injunction against uttering words that may have all the effect of force. *Gompers* v. *Bucks Stove & Range Co.*, 221 U.S. 418, 439. The question in every case is whether the words used are used in such circumstances and are of such a nature as to create a clear and present danger that they will bring about the substantive evils that Congress has a right to prevent. It is a question of proximity and degree. When a nation is at war many things that might be said in time of peace are such a hindrance to its effort that their utterance will not be endured so long as men fight and that no Court could regard them as protected by any constitutional right. It seems to be admitted that if an actual obstruction of the recruiting service were proved, liability for words that produced that effect might be enforced. The statute of 1917 in § 4 punishes conspiracies to obstruct as well as actual obstruction. If the act (speaking, or circulating a paper), its tendency and the intent with which it is done are the same, we perceive no ground for saying that success alone warrants making the act a crime. *Goldman* v. *United States*, 245 U.S. 474, 477. . . .

Judgments affirmed.

NEAR V. *MINNESOTA*, 283 U.S. 697 (1931)

Jay Near published a sleazy anti-Semitic newspaper, The Saturday Press, *which accused officials in Minneapolis, Minnesota, of being in the pay of "Jew gangsters." Acting under a Minnesota law, local officials closed his newspaper as a "public nuisance." Near appealed to the Supreme Court, charging that the closing amounted to a form of "prior restraint" forbidden by the First Amendment.*

By a margin of five to four, the Court agreed with Near. Excerpts from the majority opinion, by Chief Justice Charles Evans Hughes, follow.

Opinion of the Court, Chief Justice Hughes.

The district court made findings of fact, which followed the allegations of the complaint and found in general terms that the editions in question were "chiefly devoted to malicious, scandalous and defamatory articles" concerning the individuals named. The court further found that the defendants through these publications "did engage in the business of regularly and customarily producing, publishing and circulating a malicious, scandalous and defamatory newspaper," and that "the said publication" "under said name of The Saturday Press, or any other name, constitutes a public nuisance under the laws of the State." Judgment was thereupon entered adjudging that "the newspaper, magazine and periodical known as The Saturday Press," as a public nuisance, "be and is hereby abated." The judgment perpetually enjoined the defendants "from producing, editing, publishing, circulating, having in their possession, selling or giving away any publication whatsoever which is a malicious, scandalous or defamatory newspaper, as defined by law," and also "from further conducting said nuisance under the name and title of said The Saturday Press or any other name or title." . . .

The statute, for the suppression as a public nuisance of a newspaper or periodical, is unusual, if not unique, and raises questions of grave importance transcending the local interests involved in the particular action. It is no longer open to doubt that the liberty of the press and of speech is within the liberty safeguarded by the due process clause of the Fourteenth Amendment from invasion by state action. It was found impossible to conclude that this essential personal liberty of thei citizen was left unprotected by the general guarantee of fundamental rights of person and property. . . . Liberty, in each of its phases, has its history and connotation and, in the present instance, the inquiry is as to the historic conception of the liberty of the press and whether the statute under review violates the essential attributes of that liberty. . . .

First. The statute is not aimed at the redress of individual or private wrongs. Remedies for libel remain available and unaffected. The statute, said the state court, "is not directed at threatened libel but at an existing business which, generally speaking, involves more than libel." It is aimed at the distribution of scandalous matter as "detrimental to public morals and to the general welfare," tending "to disturb the peace of the community" and "to provoke assaults and the commission of crime." In order to obtain an injunction to suppress the future publication of the newspaper or periodical, it is not necessary to prove the falsity of the charges that have been made in the publication condemned. In the present action there was no allegation that the matter published was not true. It is alleged, and the statute requires the allegation that the publication was "malicious." But, as in prosecutions for libel, there is no requirement of proof by the state of malice in fact as distinguished from malice inferred from the mere publication of the defamatory matter. The judgment in this case proceeded upon the mere proof of publication. The statute permits the defense, not of the truth alone, but only that the truth was published with good motives and for justifiable ends. It is apparent that under the statute the publication is to be regarded as defamatory if it injures reputation, and that it is scandalous if it circulates charges of reprehensible conduct, whether criminal or otherwise, and the publication is thus deemed to invite public reprobation and to constitute a public scandal. The court sharply defined the purpose of the statute, bringing out the precise point, in these words: "There is no constitutional right to publish a fact merely because it is true. It is a matter of common knowledge that prosecutions under the criminal libel statutes do not result in efficient repression or suppression of the evils of scandal. Men who are the victims of such assaults seldom resort to the courts. This is especially true if their sins are exposed and the only question relates to whether it was done with good motive and for justifiable ends. This law is not for the protection of the person attacked nor to punish the wrongdoer. It is for the protection of the public welfare."

Second. The statute is directed not simply at the circulation of scandalous and defamatory statements with regard to private citizens, but at the continued publication by newspapers and periodicals of charges against public officers of corruption, malfeasance in office, or serious neglect of duty. Such charges by their very nature create a public scandal. They are scandalous and defamatory within the meaning of the statute, which has its normal operation in relation to publications dealing prominently and chiefly with the alleged derelictions of public officers.

Third. The object of the statute is not punishment, in the ordinary sense, but suppression of the offending newspaper or periodical. The reason for the enactment, as the state court has said, is that prosecutions to enforce penal statutes for libel do not result in "efficient repression or suppression of the evils of scandal." Describing the

business of publication as a public nuisance does not obscure the substance of the proceeding which the statute authorizes. It is the continued publication of scandalous and
defamatory matter that constitutes the business and the declared nuisance. In the case
of public officers, it is the reiteration of charges of official misconduct, and the fact
that the newspaper or periodical is principally devoted to that purpose, that exposes it
to suppression. In the present instance, the proof was that nine editions of the newspaper or periodical in question were published on successive dates, and that they were
chiefly devoted to charges against public officers and in relation to the prevalence and
protection of crime. In such a case, these officers are not left to their ordinary remedy
in a suit for libel, or the authorities to a prosecution for criminal libel. Under this
statute, a publisher of a newspaper or periodical, undertaking to conduct a campaign
to expose and to censure official derelictions, and devoting his publication principally
to that purpose, must face not simply the possibility of a verdict against him in a suit
or prosecution for libel, but a determination that his newspaper or periodical is a public nuisance to be abated, and that this abatement and suppression will follow unless
he is prepared with legal evidence to prove the truth of the charges and also to satisfy
the court that, in addition to being true, the matter was published with good motives
and for justifiable ends.

This suppression is accomplished by enjoining publication, and that restraint is the
object and effect of the statute. . . .

The objection has been made that the principle as to immunity from previous restraint is stated too broadly, if every such restraint is deemed to be prohibited. That is
undoubtedly true; the protection even as to previous restraint is not absolutely unlimited. But the limitation has been recognized only in exceptional cases: "When a
nation is at war many things that might be said in time of peace are such a hindrance
to its effort that their utterance will not be endured so long as men fight and that no
Court could regard them as protected by any constitutional right." *Schenck* v. *United
States*, 249 U. S. 47, 52. No one would question but that a government might prevent
actual obstruction to its recruiting service or the publication of the sailing dates of
transports or the number and location of troops. On similar grounds, the primary requirements of decency may be enforced against obscene publications. The security of
the community life may be protected against incitements to acts of violence and the
overthrow by force of orderly government. The constitutional guaranty of free speech
does not "protect a man from an injunction against uttering words that may have all
the effect of force. *Gompers* v. *Buck Stove & Range Co.*, 221 U. S. 418, 439." *Schenck*
v. *United States, supra.* These limitations are not applicable here.

Fourth. The statute not only operates to suppress the offending newspaper or periodical, but to put the publisher under an effective censorship. . . .

If we cut through mere details of procedure, the operation and effect of the statute in substance is that public authorities may bring the owner or publisher of a newspaper or periodical before a judge upon a charge of conducting a business of publishing
scandalous and defamatory matter—in particular that the matter consists of charges
against public officers of official dereliction—and, unless the owner or publisher is able
and disposed to bring competent evidence to satisfy the judge that the charges are true
and are published with good motives and for justifiable ends, his newspaper or periodi-

cal is suppressed and further publication is made punishable as a contempt. This is of the essence of censorship.

The question is whether a statute authorizing such proceedings in restraint of publication is consistent with the conception of the liberty of the press as historically conceived and guaranteed. In determining the extent of the constitutional protection, it has been generally, if not universally, considered that it is the chief purpose of the guaranty to prevent previous restraints upon publication. The struggle in England, directed against the legislative power of the licenser, resulted in renunciation of the censorship of the press. The liberty deemed to be established was thus described by Blackstone: "The liberty of the press is indeed essential to the nature of a free state; but this consists in laying no *previous* restraints upon publications, and not in freedom from censure for criminal matter when published. . . ."

The statute in question cannot be justified by reason of the fact that the publisher is permitted to show, before injunction issues, that the matter published is true and is published with good motives and for justifiable ends. If such a statute, authorizing suppression and injunction on such a basis, is constitutionally valid, it would be equally permissible for the legislature to provide that at any time the publisher of any newspaper could be brought before a court, or even an administrative officer (as the constitutional protection may not be regarded as resting on mere procedural details) and required to produce proof of the truth of his publication, or of what he intended to publish, and of his motives, or stand enjoined. If this can be done, the legislature may provide machinery for determining in the complete exercise of its discretion what are justifiable ends and restrain publication accordingly. And it would be but a step to a complete system of censorship. The recognition of authority to impose previous restraint upon publication in order to protect the community against the circulation of charges of misconduct, and especially of official misconduct, necessarily would carry with it the admission of the authority of the censor against which the constitutional barrier was erected. . . .

Equally unavailing is the insistence that the statute is designed to prevent the circulation of scandal which tends to disturb the public peace and to provoke assaults and the commission of crime. Charges of reprehensible conduct, and in particular of official malfeasance, unquestionably create a public scandal, but the theory of the constitutional guaranty is that even a more serious public evil would be caused by authority to prevent publication. "To prohibit the intent to excite those unfavorable sentiments against those who administer the Government, is equivalent to a prohibition of the actual excitement of them; and to prohibit the actual excitement of them is equivalent to a prohibition of discussions having that tendency and effect; which, again, is equivalent to a protection of those who administer the Government, if they should at any time deserve the contempt or hatred of the people, against being exposed to it by free animadversions on their characters and conduct." There is nothing new in the fact that charges of reprehensible conduct may create resentment and the disposition to resort to violent means of redress, but this well-understood tendency did not alter the determination to protect the press against censorship and restraint upon publication. . . .

Judgment reversed.

Justice Pierce Butler and three other justices dissented from the Near *decision. Below are excerpts from the dissent, which was written by Justice Butler.*

Mr. Justice Butler, dissenting.

The decision of the court in this case declares Minnesota and every other state powerless to restrain by injunction the business of publishing and circulating among the people malicious, scandalous and defamatory periodicals that in due course of judicial procedure has been adjudged to be a public nuisance. It gives to freedom of the press a meaning and a scope not heretofore recognized and construes "liberty" in the due process clause of the Fourteenth Amendment to put upon the states a Federal restriction that is without precedent. . . .

The record shows, and it is conceded, that defendants' regular business was the publication of malicious, scandalous, and defamatory articles concerning the principal public officers, leading newspapers of the city, many private persons and the Jewish race. It also shows that it was their purpose at all hazards to continue to carry on the business. In every edition slanderous and defamatory matter predominates to the practical exclusion of all else. Many of the statements are so highly improbable as to compel a finding that they are false. The articles themselves show malice. . . .

The Minnesota statute does not operate as a *previous* restraint on publication within the proper meaning of that phrase. It does not authorize administrative control in advance such as was formerly exercised by the licensers and censors, but prescribes a remedy to be enforced by a suit in equity. In this case there was previous publication made in the course of the business of regularly producing malicious, scandalous, and defamatory periodicals. The business and publications unquestionably constitute an abuse of the right of free press. The statute denounces the things done as a nuisance of the ground, as stated by the state supreme court, that they threaten morals, peace, and good order. There is no question of the power of the State to denounce such transgressions. The restraint authorized is only in respect of continuing to do what has been duly adjudged to constitute a nuisance. . . .

It is well known, as found by the state supreme court, that existing libel laws are inadequate effectively to suppress evils resulting from the kind of business and publications that are shown in this case. The doctrine that measures such as the one before us are invalid because they operate as previous restraints to infringe freedom of press exposes the peace and good order of every community and the business and private affairs of every individual to the constant and protracted false and malicious assaults of any insolvent publisher who may have purpose and sufficient capacity to contrive and put into effect a scheme or program for oppression, blackmail or extortion.

The judgment should be affirmed.

Mr. Justice Van Devanter, Mr. Justice McReynolds, and Mr. Justice Sutherland concur in this opinion.

NEW YORK TIMES CO. V. *UNITED STATES*, 403 U.S. 713 (1971)

The "Pentagon Papers Case" arose out of the following circumstances. A New York Times reporter was handed several volumes of classified documents that had been removed from Pentagon files without authorization. When the Nixon administration learned of the Times's plan to publish the documents, it went to court and obtained a temporary stay on publication. The case then went to the Supreme Court, which had to decide whether the temporary stay should be continued.

By a margin of six to three, the Court decided that continuing the stay would violate the First Amendment.

Each member of the majority wrote a separate opinion. Below are excerpts from the opinion of Justice Hugo Black.

Mr. Justice Black's opinion.

. . . In my view it is unfortunate that some of my Brethren are apparently willing to hold that the publication of news may sometimes be enjoined. Such a holding would make a shambles of the First Amendment.

Our Government was launched in 1789 with the adoption of the Constitution. The Bill of Rights, including the First Amendment, followed in 1791. Now, for the first time in the 182 years since the founding of the Republic, the federal courts are asked to hold that the First Amendment does not mean what it says, but rather means that the Government can halt the publication of current news of vital importance to the people of this country.

In seeking injunctions against these newspapers and in its presentation to the Court, the Executive Branch seems to have forgotten the essential purpose and history of the First Amendment. When the Constitution was adopted, many people strongly opposed it because the document contained no Bill of Rights to safeguard certain basic freedoms. They especially feared that the new powers granted to a central government might be interpreted to permit the government to curtail freedom of religion, press, assembly, and speech. In response to an overwhelming public clamor, James Madison offered a series of amendments to satisfy citizens that these great liberties would remain safe and beyond the power of government to abridge. Madison proposed what later became the First Amendment in three parts, two of which are set out below, and one of which proclaimed: "The people shall not be deprived or abridged of their right to speak, to write, or to publish their sentiments; *and the freedom of the press, as one of the great bulwarks of liberty, shall be inviolable."* The amendments were offered to *curtail* and *restrict* the general powers granted to the Executive, Legislative, and Judicial Branches two years before in the original Constitution. The Bill of Rights changed the original Constitution into a new charter under which no branch of government could abridge the people's freedoms of press, speech, religion, and assembly. Yet the Solicitor General argues and some members of the Court appear to agree that the general powers of the Government adopted in the original Constitution should be interpreted to limit and restrict the specific and emphatic guarantees of the Bill of

Rights adopted later. I can imagine no greater perversion of history. Madison and the other Framers of the First Amendment, able men that they were, wrote in language they earnestly believed could never be misunderstood: "Congress shall make no law . . . abridging the freedom . . . of the press . . ." Both the history and language of the First Amendment support the view that the press must be left free to publish news, whatever the source, without censorship, injunctions, or prior restraints.

In the First Amendment the Founding Fathers gave the free press the protection it must have to fulfill its essential role in our democracy. The press was to serve the governed, not the governors. The Government's power to censor the press was abolished so that the press would remain forever free to censure the Government. The press was protected so that it could bare the secrets of government and inform the people. Only a free and unrestrained press can effectively expose deception in government. And paramount among the responsibilities of a free press is the duty to prevent any part of the government from deceiving the people and sending them off to distant lands to die of foreign fevers and foreign shot and shell. In my view, far from deserving condemnation for their courageous reporting, the New York Times, the Washington Post, and other newspapers should be commended for serving the purpose that the Founding Fathers saw so clearly. In revealing the workings of government that led to the Vietnam war, the newspapers nobly did precisely that which the Founders hoped and trusted they would do.

Among the three dissenters in the case was Chief Justice Warren Burger. Below are excerpts from his dissenting opinion.

Chief Justice Burger, dissenting.

. . . The newspapers make a derivative claim under the First Amendment; they denominate this right as the public "right to know"; by implication, the Times asserts a sole trusteeship of that right by virtue of its journalistic "scoop." The right is asserted as an absolute. Of course, the First Amendment right itself is not an absolute, as Justice Holmes so long ago pointed out in his aphorism concerning the right to shout "fire" in a crowded theater if there was no fire. There are other exceptions, some of which Chief Justice Hughes mentioned by way of example in Near v. Minnesota ex rel. Olson. There are no doubt other exceptions no one has had occasion to describe or discuss. Conceivably such exceptions may be lurking in these cases and would have been flushed had they been properly considered in the trial courts, free from unwarranted deadlines and frenetic pressures. An issue of this importance should be tried and heard in a judicial atmosphere conducive to thoughtful, reflective deliberation, especially when haste, in terms of hours, is unwarranted in light of the long period the Times, by its own choice, deferred publication.

It is not disputed that the Times has had unauthorized possession of the documents for three to four months, during which it has had its expert analysts studying them, presumably digesting them and preparing the material for publication. During all of this time, the Times, presumably in its capacity as trustee of the public's "right to know," has held up publication for purposes it considered proper and thus public knowledge was delayed. No doubt this was for a good reason; the analysis of 7,000 pages of complex material drawn from a vastly greater volume of material would inevitably take time and the writing of good news stories takes time. But why should the United States Government, from whom this information was illegally acquired by someone, along with all the counsel, trial judges and appellate judges be placed under needless pressure? After these months of deferral, the alleged "right to know" has somehow and suddenly become a right that must be vindicated instanter.

Would it have been unreasonable, since the newspaper could anticipate the Government's objections to release of secret material, to give the Government an opportunity to review the entire collection and determine whether agreement could be reached on publication? Stolen or not, if security was not in fact jeopardized, much of the material could no doubt have been declassified, since it spans a period ending in 1968. With such an approach—one that great newspapers have in the past practiced and stated editorially to be the duty of an honorable press—the newspapers and Government might well have narrowed the area of disagreement as to what was and was not publishable, leaving the remainder to be resolved in orderly litigation, if necessary. To me it is hardly believable that a newspaper long regarded as a great institution in American life would fail to perform one of the basic and simple duties of every citizen with respect to the discovery or possession of stolen property or secret government documents. That duty, I had thought—perhaps naively—was to report forthwith, to responsible public officers. This duty rests on taxi drivers, Justices, and the New York Times. . . .

SELECTED READINGS

Abrams, Floyd. "The Pentagon Papers a Decade Later." *New York Times Magazine*, June 1981, pp. 4ff.

A retrospective study of the Pentagon Papers case by one of the attorneys who represented the *Times* and who is also a participant in the video discussion. Abrams contends that events since 1971 have vindicated the position taken by the *Times.*

Black, Hugo. "The Bill of Rights." *New York University Law Review*, April 1960, pp. 865-881.

The late Supreme Court justice presents his understanding of the Bill of Rights. He explains why he feels that the authors of these American rights intended them to be absolute and unqualified.

Christian, Shirley. "Covering the Sandinistas." *Washington Journalism Review*, March 1982, pp. 33-38.

A Pulitzer Prize-winning reporter for the *Miami Herald* contends, on the basis of content analysis, that the *Washington Post*, the *New York Times*, and CBS provided biased reports of the Nicaragua revolution in 1978 and 1979. "Probably not since Spain has there been a more open love affair between the foreign press and one of the belligerents in a civil war."

Friendly, Fred W. *Due to Circumstances Beyond Our Control.* New York: Random House, 1967.

An account of the author's association with Edward R. Murrow, of some of the most important programs he and Murrow produced (including the controversial program on Senator Joseph McCarthy), and of the reasons why Friendly resigned from CBS.

Friendly, Fred. W. *The Good Guys, the Bad Guys, and the First Amendment.* New York: Random House, 1976.

A study of the political use of FCC rules. Particularly revealing are the first five chapters, where Friendly shows how Kennedy administration officials made systematic use of the FCC's "fairness doctrine" to harass "right-wing" broadcasters.

Friendly, Fred W. *Minnesota Rag.* New York: Random House, 1981.

A vivid account of the events and personalities that brought the case of *Near* v. *Minnesota* before the Supreme Court and of the arguments that convinced the Court majority in 1931 to oppose the restraint of Near's newspaper.

Lichter, S. Robert, and Rothman, Stanley. "Media and Business Elites." *Public Opinion*, October/November 1981, pp. 42-60.

The authors conducted extensive interviews with journalists from leading media, including the three commercial networks, the *New York Times*, and the *Washington Post.* The results show that journalists are considerably more "liberal" than most Americans. The journalists also distrust the motives and policies of governing officials.

Mill, John Stuart. *On Liberty* (many editions).

Mill's slim volume, written in England in 1859, has become a classic defense of individual liberty.

Strong, Frank R. "Fifty Years of 'Clear and Present Danger': From Schenck to Brandenburg—and Beyond." *Supreme Court Review*, 1969, pp. 41-80.

The author examines the history of the "clear and present danger" doctrine and the cases in which it has played an important role. He explains why the doctrine has always been difficult to define.

Ungar, Sanford J. *The Papers and the Papers.* New York: Dutton, 1972.

The most comprehensive account of the political battle that culminated in the Supreme Court decision in the Pentagon Papers case, *New York Times* v. *United States* (1971). Written with gusto if not with total objectivity by a *Washington Post* reporter.

GLOSSARY

Derivative right. A right not expressly stated in a statute or constitution but derived from or implied by an express right. Retired Supreme Court Justice Potter Stewart says that the public's "right to know" is "at the most" a derivative right.

Gag order. A judge's order to journalists not to publish accounts of court proceedings until their conclusion.

Offensive leak. A leak to the press of confidential information by high government officials for the purpose of warning or threatening officials of an adversary regime.

Pentagon Papers. A forty-seven-volume study of America's involvement in Vietnam from the end of the 1940s to the mid-1960s. Written by Pentagon staffers, it was intended to be an internal document and was classified "top secret." In 1971, Daniel Ellsberg, a former policy analyst from the RAND Corporation (a Pentagon-affiliated "think tank"), secretly removed the entire study and gave photocopies of it to reporters. The *New York Times* and other newspapers published portions of it.

Precedent. A prior decision by a court establishing a rule for certain cases. American courts sometimes reverse precedents but in principle honor the rule of *stare decisis*, "let the decision stand."

Prior restraint. Government-imposed restraint of the press in advance of publication. In *Near* v. *Minnesota* (1931) and *New York Times* v. *United States* (1971), the Supreme Court ruled that prior restraint violates the First Amendment.

Rogue elephant. An instrument which no longer serves its original purpose but has gotten out of hand and become destructive. In the video discussion, Jack Nelson of the *Los Angeles Times* calls the CIA a "rogue elephant."

TRO (temporary restraining order). A court-ordered restraint on an activity pending formal review of it in court. The halt is ordered so as to prevent irreparable harm to one of the parties during the time it takes for the case to be brought to court and resolved.

Chapter 9
"Praise the Lord and . . . ."

*"We are a religious people whose institutions
presuppose a Supreme Being."*
WILLIAM O. DOUGLAS
Majority opinion, *Zorach* v. *Clausen* (1952)

*"If a religious leaven is to be worked into the
affairs of our people, it is to be done by individuals
and groups, not by the Government."*
WILLIAM O. DOUGLAS
Dissenting opinion, *McGowan* v. *Maryland* (1961)

Let us begin with a prayer:

> Almighty God, we acknowledge our dependence upon Thee, and we beg thy bless-
> ings upon us, our parents, our teacher, and our country.

That was the prayer whose daily recitation in New York public classrooms provoked a legal challenge that culminated in a Supreme Court decision outlawing the
recitation of prayers in public schools.

Note that the prayer refers to God but not to Jesus, the Blessed Virgin, or any figure associated with a particular religion. It was intended to be a "nondenominational"
prayer. It was composed by the New York State Board of Regents specifically for that
purpose.

It was also "voluntary," in the sense that any child who did not want to say it
could either stand silent or leave the room while it was being said. For some people
such a practice is not really voluntary, but many other "voluntary" activities, from
saluting the flag to sex education, are handled the same way.

Why, then, was saying this prayer at the start of the school day outlawed by the
Supreme Court? The Court concluded that such exercises violate the "establishment"
clause of the First Amendment. This point will be explained later in the chapter.
Legally, constitutionally, the "school prayer issue" turns upon it.

But school prayer is more than a legal issue. It is also a political one. In March
1984 the Senate voted 56 to 44 in favor of a constitutional amendment allowing vocal
prayer in public schools—11 votes short of the necessary two-thirds but enough to
show that the issue is a potent one. About 80 percent of Americans want prayers restored to public schools, and President Reagan made it one of his major themes in the
1984 presidential election.

Public school prayer is a deeply emotional issue. After all, it touches on what for many Americans are the ultimate questions of human life and purpose. Sometimes the emotions it brings to the surface make reasoned discussion difficult. School prayer is the kind of issue that can make people yell at each other, call each other names like "Godless," "bigot," and "bitter, reactive people." It is an issue that makes compromise very difficult. The contending sides cannot split the difference, allowing, say, half a prayer or three-quarters of a prayer. (Silent prayers, which have already been invalidated by some courts, have never satisfied either side.) It seems to be all or nothing.

SCHOOL PRAYER, GUN CONTROL, AND THE RIGHT TO ASSEMBLE

There are other such issues. Abortion, which is studied in the next chapter, is one. Two other issues in the same category—in the press they are often called "social issues"—are gun control and the right to assemble.

In the gun-control debate, once again, the opposing sides call each other names, or at least color each other ugly. Pro-gun-control people have been known to portray their opponents as macho types who love violence. Anti-gun-control people have on occasion hinted that their opponents are a bunch of snivelers who will end up sapping the strength of America. And, again, the Constitution is invoked—this time the Second Amendment, part of which says "the right of the people to keep and Bear Arms, shall not be infringed."

Freedom of peaceable assembly at first seems to be uncontroversial. Aside from the fact that it is guaranteed explicitly in the First Amendment, Americans generally respect the right of people to hold public meetings as long as they do it peacefully.

But suppose the Nazis want to parade through your neighborhood. They assure town officials that they will march peacefully, but they do plan to show off their nice new regalia: their swastikas, their brown shirts and shiny boots, their banners of the Third Reich. Do you have to put up with that—especially if you or your friends or relatives are refugees of Nazism? The same can be asked about marches by the Ku Klux Klan, or, from the viewpoint of refugees from Soviet gulags, of marches by the Communist party.

These issues, then, are all highly emotional. They may be connected in other ways as well. The positions people take on them sometimes get tied to political doctrines. Many of those who call themselves "conservatives" are against gun control, for school prayer, and against the right of Nazis to parade. Many self-designated liberals go the opposite way. In his 1984 presidential campaign, President Reagan linked two of the issues by charging that "the same people" who want to "take prayers out of schools" also want to give Nazis the freedom to march. He was referring to "liberal" organizations like the American Civil Liberties Union (ACLU) which have opposed public school prayer and supported the right of Nazis to assemble publicly.

The Video Discussion

It is interesting to see how the panelists in the video debate line up on these issues. Attorney Jeanne Baker, formerly of the Massachusetts branch of the ACLU, opposes public school prayer and supports the right of radicals to march. *Washington Post* reporter Laura Kiernan opposes public school prayer and supports gun control. Those positions seem to fit the "liberal" profile. On the other hand, U.S. Appeals Court Judge William Bauer is opposed to a march by radicals but supports gun control. Those positions are also taken by Assistant Attorney General William Bradford Reynolds. On the first issue these men are "conservative," on the second "liberal." Since they offer coherent arguments for both positions, it seems that the issues are really logically independent of one another. They get linked together in political campaigns—but they don't have to be linked.

The panel moderator is Professor Arthur R. Miller of Harvard Law School.

List of Participants

HON. ARLIN M. ADAMS
Judge
U.S. Court of Appeals
Third Circuit

JEANNE BAKER
Attorney
Baker & Fine
Former General Counsel
Massachusetts Civil Liberties Union

HON. WILLIAM J. BAUER
Judge
U.S. Court of Appeals
Seventh Circuit

HON. GRIFFIN B. BELL
Attorney
King & Spaulding
Former U.S. Attorney General

HON. HARRY T. EDWARDS
Judge
U.S. Court of Appeals
District of Columbia

HON. ORRIN HATCH
U.S. Senator
Utah

HON. SHIRLEY M. HUFSTEDLER
Attorney
Hufstedler, Miller, Carlson & Beardsley
Former U.S. Secretary of Education

LAURA A. KIERNAN
Reporter
Washington Post

ANTHONY LEWIS
Columnist
New York Times

HON. ROBERT R. MERHIGE, JR.
Judge
U.S. District Court
Eastern District of Virginia

JAMES F. NEAL
Attorney
Neal & Harwell

AVI NELSON
Media Commentator and Analyst
WCVB-TV (Boston)

HON. CHARLES B. RANGEL
U.S. Representative
New York

DAN RATHER
Managing Editor
CBS Evening News

WILLIAM BRADFORD REYNOLDS
Assistant Attorney General
Civil Rights Division
Department of Justice

HON. POTTER STEWART
Justice (retired)
U.S. Supreme Court

Program Summary

The program consists of three parts. The first is mainly about public school prayer, though it also touches on the power of the judiciary. The moderator posits a situation in which a number of black youths in the fictional town of Marathon have been murdered by a person or persons unknown.

The local pastor's son was one of the victims. The pastor wants the local public high school to call an assembly at which he will conduct a memorial service for the dead youths and offer a few prayers. The panel is then asked whether his proposal would be all right. Some panelists say that it would violate the First Amendment. To varying extents, others disagree. Some argue that a one-time prayer in school would be all right, but not prayers every day. Others believe that the Supreme Court was wholly mistaken in ever holding that public school prayers violate the Constitution. The conversation then touches upon the power of courts today and whether the Supreme Court can or should be restrained by Congress.

The second part of the program concerns the issue of gun control. The moderator reminds the panelists that all the murder victims are black; the murders, therefore, may have racial overtones. At least that seems to be how some Marathoners feel, and these townspeople have started to buy guns. The City Council decides to ban further sale of guns. May it do so without violating the Constitution? Is it fair for it to do so? The panelists then debate the political, moral, and legal issues connected with gun control.

The third part of the program deals with the right to assemble. The moderator informs the panelists that two opposing groups, a left-wing radical group and the Ku Klux Klan, are planning marches in the town. Hardly anyone in town wants them to march. Should they be allowed to? As the moderator suggests different situations involving various possibilities of violence, the participants take sides on the issue.

I: SCHOOL PRAYER

The issue of school prayer is really part of the larger issue of church-state relations in America. What role should religion play in our political and legal system? How close together, or far apart, should church and state be? To what extent and in what ways should religion in America be allowed to appear in public? Americans today are divided on these critical issues along philosophical and to some extent theological lines. This does not mean, of course, that all religious people favor close church-state involvement and all nonreligious people are opposed. Some religious groups, such as the National Council of Churches, have fought vigorously against prayers in public schools, while there are doubtless many Americans belonging to no religion who see nothing wrong with the practice.

Boundaries of the Dispute

In the introduction to this book, the Constitution was included among the "ground rules." Does the Constitution offer any guidance on these issues? Yes and no. The Constitution mentions religion in two separate clauses in the First Amendment. The first is called the "establishment" clause: "Congress shall make no law respecting an establishment of religion. . . ." The second, called the "free exercise" clause, comes immediately afterwards: ". . . or prohibiting the free exercise thereof. . . ." What does all this mean? We get the sense that boundaries are being laid down. On the one hand, the Framers did not want to set up any particular religion as an official one. But, on the other hand, they meant to protect believers in the practice of their religion. Religion need not be relegated to the purely personal sphere. Its practice, its exercise, was singled out by the Constitution as an area that deserved protection. Thus, even the most outspoken advocates of the separation of church and state would agree that the United States was not meant to have a system of church-state relations such as exists in Communist countries, where the state claims to guarantee the right of religious belief but severely restricts any public display of that belief.

The reader may be puzzled. Are these the only two references to religion in the Constitution—the establishment and the free exercise clauses? What about the principle of separation of church and state? Have we not all heard of a "wall of separation" between church and state? These phrases come up during arguments about church-state relations, and they may well be legitimate interpretations of the spirit of the First Amendment. But they are not in the Constitution. "Separation of church and state" goes back to the Middle Ages, when the doctrine of the two swords (the secular sword and the spiritual sword of Christianity) was widely recognized and appealed to by both spiritual and temporal powers. Indeed, "separation of church and state" can even be traced back to the words of Jesus: "Render unto Caesar the things that are Caesar's, and to God the things that are God's."

Yet the medieval and early modern understanding of that expression did not intend that church and state be completely separate. In the Middle Ages, cooperation between secular and spiritual authorities was the rule; even in the eighteenth and nineteenth centuries, religion played an important role in public and political life. This was particularly true in the United States, as we shall presently see. As for the "wall of separation," the Supreme Court has often used this metaphor, particularly in opinions written by the late Chief Justice Earl Warren and Justice Hugo Black and, more recently, in opinions written by Justice William Brennan. The expression does not come from the Constitution, from statute, or from any official document. It comes from a letter written by Thomas Jefferson to a group of Baptists in Danbury, Connecticut, in 1802. It is not clear why the justices have adopted Jefferson's metaphor. In a way, Jefferson was a Founder, since he wrote the Declaration of Independence and remained a leading thinker during the early years of the nation. Yet he did not sit in either the Constitutional Convention of 1787 or in the first Congress of 1789, which wrote the Bill of Rights.

Jefferson was also something of a freethinker, whereas most of the men who sat in the convention and the First Congress were traditional Christians. The conventional wisdom is that they were Deists—adherents of the view that God wound up the universe like a clock, then retreated and let it run by itself. Actually, as M. E. Bradford has shown (*A Worthy Company*, 1982), most of the Framers adhered to biblical Christianity, which gave God a more active role in the world. The proclamations, speeches, and public statements of presidents and Congresses during the eighteenth and nineteenth centuries were full of references to the Almighty and to the beneficial effects of religion. A case in point is the Northwest Ordinance of 1787, which set aside federal property for schools. It said: "Religion, morality, and knowledge being necessary to good government and the happiness of mankind, schools and the means of learning shall forever be encouraged."

America's Religious Heritage

Lest the advocates of greater church-state involvement take too much comfort from what has been said so far, it is necessary to point out that our early history is a sword that can cut both ways. The argument that America's Founders and early statesmen wanted religion to play a public role is an argument that, in a way, proves too much. Our Founders were not just religious, they were Christian; and they were not just Christian but Protestant. The kind of religion they professed, the kind they kneaded into public life, was Protestant Christianity. It was always the King James Bible that was read at public ceremonies and in public schools. And it was always assumed that America was a Christian nation, in spite of increasing Jewish immigration in the nineteenth century. The question, then, is whether "our religious tradition," so frequently invoked by advocates of school prayer, was in all respects a good tradition. Did it not sometimes foster prejudice and divisiveness?

These questions must be faced by anyone who invokes precedent and history to support disputed claims in the present day. "Fact is," remarks Justice Potter Stewart in the video discussion, "there was an established church in the state of Massachusetts until well into the nineteenth century." Yes, but was that good? Is it what we want today?

Defining a Religious "Establishment"

Let's take a closer look at the establishment clause. What *is* an "establishment of religion"? We know the phrase means at least this: singling out one particular religion for official state patronage and support. In the past, such establishments were the rule.

Even today some nations have them: in England, the Church of England is the established church; in Israel, Orthodox Judaism enjoys establishment status; Sweden has Lutheranism as its established church. These are clear cases of established churches. But what if a particular church is not singled out—what if it is just religion in general that is given official recognition? This brings us to the threshold of the so-called school prayer cases decided by the Supreme Court in 1962 and 1963. Before stepping over the threshold, though, we must mention an earlier case, *Everson v. Board of Education* (1947).

At first glance the decision in this case seems to represent a victory for those favoring closer church-state relations, for the Court upheld the constitutionality of a New Jersey statute providing free bus transportation for children attending parochial schools. The Court's reasoning, in an opinion by Justice Hugo Black, was that this was not aid to religion but to children and parents. In developing his argument, however, Justice Black defined the establishment clause in such a way as to extend it much further than simply aiding one religion. The clause means, said Black, that "neither a state nor the federal government can set up a church. Neither can pass laws that aid one religion, *aid all religions*, or prefer one religion over another" (italics added). Even if government aids *all* religions on a purely evenhanded basis, it is still an "establishment of religion."

The Landmark Case: *Engel v. Vitale*

Now we see the groundwork for *Engel v. Vitale* (1962). The school board in question had composed a purely "nonsectarian" prayer, referring only to "Almighty God." That expression fits all three major faiths in America. Yet the Court struck it down as an establishment of religion. The prayer was in one sense nonsectarian, yet it did not include those children who do not believe in "almighty God." It established religion—perhaps not a particular religion, but religion.

In one respect, Justice Black's opinion was ambiguous. It was not clear whether he objected to the prayer because it was written by public officials (it was composed by the New York State Board of Regents), because it was said in public schools, or both. What if the prayer were not written by any public official but emerged from ancient religious traditions? What if it were not an official prayer but a selection from the Bible, or the Lord's Prayer? Might that make a difference? Anyone looking for such loopholes was bound to be disappointed the following year, when the Court also struck down the reading of the Lord's Prayer and the Bible in public schools: see *School District of Abigton Township v. Schempp* and *Murray v. Curlett* (1963).

Avoiding a Religious "Establishment": Three Tests

Building on all these cases, the Court in 1971 tried to work out a set of principles that would allow the state to benefit citizens who happened to be religious without directly aiding religion. In the case of *Lemon v. Kurtzman* (1971), the Court said:

1. The statute in question must have a clear, secular legislative purpose.

2. The statute must neither advance nor inhibit religion.
3. The statute must not result in "excessive" government "entanglement" with religion.

The *Lemon* tests raise some obvious questions. What is an "entanglement" of government and religion? What is an "excessive" entanglement? Still, the case provides a clearer framework for interpreting the establishment clause than anything the Court had said earlier. The more troubling questions about the ruling are these: Was it a correct framework? If so, has the Court recently begun to abandon it?

Was it a correct framework? The *Lemon* tests are criticized mainly by those who favor the public recognition of religion. They argue that the tests are based on a mistaken understanding of American history. Where does it say that our laws cannot advance religion? As already mentioned, most of the Framers were religious, and many public statements from our early years did champion the advancement of religion. In more recent years a Supreme Court opinion (in the 1952 case *Zorach* v. *Clausen*) gave voice to such sentiments when it stated, "We are a religious people whose institutions presuppose a Supreme Being." In reply, those who favor a "wall of separation" between church and state say that in today's America government should not get into the business of sponsoring religion. They point out that the same justice, William O. Douglas, who wrote the opinion in the *Zorach* case also said, during his dissent in another: "If a religious leaven is to be worked into the affairs of our people, it is to be done by individuals and groups, not by the Government" (*McGowan* v. *Maryland*, 1961, dissenting opinion). Justice Douglas also concurred in the *Engel* decision barring prayers in public schools.

Have recent decisions by the Court been faithful to the framework laid down in the *Lemon* case? Four recent cases have raised this question.

The *Widmar* Case: Religious Exercises in a Public College

In 1981 the Supreme Court decided the case of *Widmar* v. *Vincent*. For four years a group of evangelical students attending the University of Missouri sought and received permission from the university to conduct meetings of their prayer group, called Cornerstone, in campus-owned facilities. (A typical Cornerstone meeting included prayer, hymns, commentaries on the Bible, and the sharing of religious experiences.) Then the university informed the group it could no longer meet there because such meetings violated university regulations barring religious meetings on state campuses. Cornerstone sued, claiming that the prohibition violated, among other rights, their right to free speech and the free exercise of religion. The university countered that to allow such a group to meet on its campus would violate the establishment clause as interpreted by the Court in the school prayer cases. This argument prevailed in the lower federal court, the district court, but that decision was overturned by a federal court of appeals. The Supreme Court, in an opinion written by Justice Lewis Powell, reaffirmed the appeals court decision—in other words, it upheld the constitutional right of the evangelical group to conduct its services on campus.

Isn't that aiding religion? Yes, in a way, the Court admitted. But it only aids religion "incidentally" and therefore does not run afoul of the second criterion laid down in *Lemon* v. *Kurtzman*. The Court seemed to base most of its case not on freedom of religion but on freedom of speech. If a university makes a practice of allowing student groups to meet in its buildings, why should it draw the line at religious student groups? Don't they have a right to speak? The Court's decision was simply meant to ensure that state universities act with strict neutrality toward various groups. Outside of the classroom, its facilities must be open to all student groups; the university must provide an "open forum" to all lawful organizations, religious or secular.

The *Widmar* decision did not create much controversy. Justice Byron White dissented, but on narrow grounds. (He thought a state university should be allowed to let religious student organizations use its facilities but not required to do so.) More recent cases, however, have provoked dissent. The first of these concerns the issue of tax breaks for parents whose children attend religious schools.

The *Mueller* Case: Tuition Tax Deductions

On June 29, 1983, the Court handed down its decision in the case of *Mueller* v. *Allen*. In that case a group of Minnesota taxpayers challenged a provision of state law allowing parents, in computing their state income tax, to deduct all expenses connected with "tuition, textbooks, and transportation" for their children's school attendance. The law was challenged as an "establishment of religion" because it had the effect of aiding church-related schools. Those bringing the suit must have felt on safe grounds, for, only a decade earlier, the Court had decided the case of *Committee for Public Education* v. *Nyquist* (1973). In that case the Court struck down a provision of New York State law which provided tax *credits* for parents of children attending nonpublic schools. (A tax deduction is an amount subtracted from taxable income, while a tax credit is an amount subtracted from the total tax one would have to pay.) But if those objecting to the deduction plan in *Mueller* thought the *Nyquist* decision disposed of it, they did not anticipate the kind of distinctions the Court made in its decision.

In an opinion written by Justice William Rehnquist, the Court made two key distinctions. First, in *Nyquist* the tax credits were narrowly distributed; they applied only to parents whose children attended nonpublic schools. But in this case the tax deductions applied to *everyone* whose children attended *any* school, private or public. Thus, though religion was aided, it was only aided "incidentally," as in the *Widmar* case. Second, a tax deduction is much different from a tax credit, or at least from the kind of credit granted in New York State in 1973. The New York State credit, Rehnquist said, amounted to thinly disguised tuition grants to parochial schools. Under the Minnesota plan, the benefit went to the parents and only indirectly to the schools. In short, the Court believed that the Minnesota tax deduction passed all three tests set down in the *Lemon* case: it had a clear secular purpose, it did not aid religion as such, and it did not result in excessive church-state "entanglement."

Justice Thurgood Marshall, speaking for himself and three other justices, disagreed. Marshall argued in his dissent that the distinction between this case and *Nyquist* was a distinction without a difference. What does it matter whether parents are reimbursed through a tax credit or a tax deduction? Either way they are given financial incentives to send their children to church-related schools. As for the neutrality of the grants—the fact that they apply to the parents of children attending all schools, public and nonpublic—Marshall said this was more apparent than real. Tuition deductions were meaningless for public schools, for public schools do not charge tuition! True, he said, there were also deductions for the cost of gym clothes, pencils, and notebooks, but tuition is by far the largest chunk of parents' expenditures. To allow deductions for it is to help subsidize religious education, and that, he concluded, violates the establishment clause.

Justice Marshall's dissent raises its own questions. How far would he and the other dissenters go in preventing the state from aiding religion? Every time extra policemen are called in to direct traffic in front of churches and synagogues during worship hours, it "aids" religion. If the extra police were not provided, the houses of worship would probably have to hire their own crossing guards or pay more money to the municipal authorities. The Court has already approved the use of taxpayers' funds to pay for busing children to parochial schools (*Everson* v. *School Board*, 1947), and that indirectly "aids" religion, since otherwise the parochial schools would have to work out their own transportation and bill parents for it. How do we distinguish these legitimate "aids" from others that violate the Constitution?

If the answers are not easy, it is because religion *does* have a public dimension in America. We do not force people to worship only in their living rooms. Religion is not purely private. But how public should it be? What is its proper role in our public institutions? These questions were raised by the third recent case involving an alleged establishment of religion.

The *Marsh* Case: Prayers in Legislatures

The legislature of the state of Nebraska, like legislatures throughout the nation, begins each day with a prayer offered by a chaplain. Since 1965 the Nebraska legislature had employed a Presbyterian minister named Robert E. Palmer for this purpose and paid him a monthly salary of $319.75. Chaplain Palmer was not known for the blandness of his prayers. They expressed an identifiable Christian orientation. Here is one example:

> Father in heaven, the suffering and death of your son brought life to the whole world, moving our hearts to praise your glory. The power of the cross reveals your concern for the world and the wonder of Christ crucified.

Ernest Chambers, a member of the Nebraska legislature, objected and brought suit under the establishment clause. He won a partial victory in the lowest federal court (the district court), for the judge said that the chaplain could not be paid without violation of the establishment clause. At the next level, the court of appeals, Chambers won a total victory: the appeals court judge said that the whole practice violated the establishment clause. The case reached the Supreme Court when the state legislature appealed.

Reversing the appeals court decision, the Supreme Court upheld the practice. Writing for the majority in *Marsh* v. *Chambers* (1983), Chief Justice Burger said that opening official deliberations with a prayer "is deeply embedded in the history and tradition of the country." The practice, he said, goes back nearly a hundred years to our First Congress and has continued without interruption ever since. It is also found in our courts. (Burger noted that the very appeals court that overturned the prayer began its session with an invocation: "God save the United States and this Honorable Court." The Supreme Court also begins its session with this invocation.) By itself, the chief justice admitted, the fact that something has gone on for a long time does not mean that it is justified. But if, in addition, the drafters of the provision being invoked against the practice saw nothing wrong in it, then that becomes a weighty argument for its constitutionality. In the case of legislative prayers, the very men who drafted the First Amendment back in 1789 also voted to appoint and pay a chaplain for each house of Congress. The chief justice concluded that to open a legislative body with prayers "is not, in these circumstances, an 'establishment' of religion or a step toward establishment: it is simply a tolerable acknowledgment of beliefs widely held among the people of this country."

There were three dissenters in the case: Justices Stevens, Brennan, and Marshall. Stevens wrote a brief dissent that centered on the sectarian nature of the prayers the Rev. Palmer was offering; the prayers obviously left no space for Jewish beliefs, not to mention those of other non-Christian groups. A more extensive dissent was written by Justice Brennan. Speaking for himself and Justice Marshall, Brennan said that the prayers of legislative chaplains violated all three tests laid down in the *Lemon* case. They did not have a clear secular purpose; they were not neutral in their effect on religion; and they did not avoid an excessive entanglement with religion. Justice Brennan tried to put the best face on the Court's decision. In his view, the Court was simply carving out a narrow category of exceptions to its line of decision since *Engel* v. *Vitale*; his estimate was that it would probably "pose little threat to the overall fate of the Establishment Clause." Yet he was troubled by the Court's decision and especially by its reliance upon our religious history as a way of justifying the prayers. Brennan sensed that this kind of reasoning, if carried very far, could erode the whole line of prayer decisions since *Engel*. If we go back into history—and we do not have to go back very far—we find all sorts of reference to almighty God in official practice, and it is very hard to fit these references into the three-pronged framework in *Lemon* v. *Kurtzman*. Precedent, history, tradition, Framers' intentions—these considerations have been on a collision course with the logic behind the prayer decisions, a logic based on a "wall of separation" between church and state.

Standards for Interpreting the Constitution

If Justice Brennan was struggling with the past in his dissent, he was also struggling with his past self. He forthrightly acknowledged this:

> Moreover, disagreement with the Court requires that I confront the fact that some twenty years ago, in a concurring opinion in one of the cases striking down official prayer and ceremonial Bible reading in the public schools, I came very close to endorsing essentially the result reached by the Court today.

In the earlier case, Brennan had mentioned in passing that prayers in legislatures "might well" be constitutional, since they occurred among consenting adults. Now, however, "after much reflection," he changed his mind. Jefferson's metaphor of the "wall of separation" was controlling, no matter what the practices or thinking of the past implied.

Justice Brennan's dissent amounted to a sensitive exposition of the philosophy embraced by many members of the Supreme Court since the early '50s. In *Brown* v. *Board of Education* (1954), a case studied in Chapter 12 of this book, Chief Justice Warren summed it up: "We cannot turn the clock back." In the present case the philosophy would mean this: Even *if* legislative prayers were a common element of our tradition and history and even *if* the Framers of the establishment clause saw nothing wrong with such prayers, that does not mean they are constitutional. We cannot turn the clock back to 1789 or even 1963. We must interpret the Constitution's meaning *today.* The Constitution, said Brennan, "is not a static document whose meaning on every detail is fixed for all time by the life experience of the Framers." Brennan's is an extremely important—and controversial—philosophy. It lies behind much of the controversy over the Court's decisions not only on prayer but on other sensitive issues such as abortion and affirmative action. It raises the question of what standards the Court is using to interpret the Constitution. If the Constitution is not static, if it is constantly changing, how do the judges know what changes are correct? *How do we know that the judges are not simply reading their own current prejudices and viewpoints into it?*

Here we reach the heart of the present controversy over the Supreme Court's prayer decision. Those who want to insert a prayer amendment into the Constitution or to restrict the Court's authority to hear cases on prayer are not simply saying they disagree with the Court; nor are they saying they want the Constitution changed. They are accusing the Court of tampering with the Constitution, of changing its meaning. In reply, those who defend the Court's decisions accuse the critics of attempting to tamper with it. Both sides of the controversy portray themselves as the defenders of the Constitution.

Lynch v. *Donnelly*: Nativity Scenes

Today's Court is closely divided on church-state issues. This became apparent in a recent case, *Lynch* v. *Donnelly* (1984), concerning the constitutionality of a Christmas Nativity scene sponsored by the town of Pawtucket, Rhode Island. The Nativity scene or crèche—a stable with Mary, Joseph, the infant Jesus, the wise men, and the shepherds—had been owned and displayed by Pawtucket for at least forty years; it was part of a larger Christmas display that included Santa and his reindeer, carolers, and (the Court actually listed these things in its opinion!) "a clown, an elephant, and a teddy bear." Some Pawtucket residents and the ACLU brought suit, charging that city sponsorship of the Nativity scene violated the establishment clause of the First Amendment. By a margin of five to four, the Court disagreed.

The majority opinion, written by Chief Justice Warren Burger, noted that *Lemon* v. *Kurtzman* had two sides. It said that the First Amendment seeks to prevent the "intrusion" of either church or state "into the precinct of the other." But it also said that "total separation is not possible in an absolute sense." Therefore, Burger concluded, Jefferson's famous metaphor of the "wall of separation," while useful, "is not a wholly accurate description" of the real relationship between church and state in America. Burger then went on, as he had done in *Marsh* v. *Chambers*, to provide examples of the legitimate intermingling of religion and state in America; among the examples he cited were presidential proclamations of religious holidays, prayers in Congress, paid chaplains, and officially sponsored art galleries that display religious pictures. Given all this inevitable intermingling, "the Court consistently has declined to take a rigid, absolutist view of the Establishment Clause." Burger mentioned the *Lemon* tests—"secular purpose," probable effect, and the need to avoid "excessive entanglement" of church and state—but he was unwilling to get pinned down on any of them, for, he said, "we have repeatedly emphasized our unwillingness to be confined to any single test or criterion in this sensitive area."

It was precisely the *Lemon* criteria that Justice William Brennan emphasized in his dissent. He was convinced that the crèche had violated them all. A Nativity scene, he said, unlike a Santa Claus or a Christmas tree, re-creates "an event that lies at the heart of the Christian faith." It does not, therefore, have a secular purpose. Also, its effect is to advance a particular religion. Finally, government sponsorship of a crèche creates an "excessive government entanglement with religion." Rejecting Burger's contention that such scenes have become merely traditional expressions of Christmas in America, Brennan said:

> To suggest . . . that such a symbol is merely "traditional" and therefore no different from Santa's house or reindeer is not only offensive to those for whom the crèche has profound significance, but insulting to those who insist . . . that the story of Christ is in no sense a part of "history" nor an unavoidable element of our national "heritage."

How does the reader stand on this issue? What part of the holiday that gets its name from "Christ's mass" is secular? What part is strictly religious? Is it possible to separate the two? What if the crèche were standing alone—minus the reindeer, Santa, clown, elephant, and teddy bear? A case involving just a crèche is now being appealed and may be decided by the Court.

Points to Remember

1. The term "wall of separation" is not found in the Constitution. It was first used by Thomas Jefferson in a letter to a group of Baptists in Danbury, Connecticut.
2. In *Engel* v. *Vitale* (1962), the Supreme Court held that officially composed prayers recited aloud in public school classes violate the establishment clause of the First Amendment. Subsequent Court decisions extended the *Engel* ruling to cover

prayers, like Bible readings and the Lord's Prayer, that are not composed by state officials.

3. In the case of *Zorach* v. *Clausen* (1952), the Court said, "We are a religious people, whose institutions presuppose a Supreme Being."

4. In *Lemon* v. *Kurtzman* (1971), the Court laid down three criteria for testing the constitutionality of statutes touching on religion: (a) the statute must have a secular purpose, (b) it must neither advance nor inhibit religion, and (c) it must not result in excessive government "entanglement" with religion.

5. In *Widmar* v. *Vincent* (1981), the Court said that religious exercises by students on the grounds of a state-run college are protected by the free speech clause of the First Amendment. In *Mueller* v. *Allen* (1983), the Court approved of Minnesota's program of tax deductions for tuition, textbooks, and transportation costs of children attending parochial schools. In *Marsh* v. *Chambers* (1983), the Court upheld the constitutionality of denominational prayers said aloud by a paid chaplain in a state legislature. In *Lynch* v. *Donnelly* (1984), the Court upheld a city-sponsored Christmas display that included a Nativity scene. These four decisions suggest that the current Court majority rejects the notion of an impermeable "wall of separation" between church and state.

The Video Discussion of School Prayer

In the three-pronged test laid down in the *Lemon* case, there is one word that seems particularly pertinent to the video discussion of school prayer. That word is "excessive."

Note that the *Lemon* test does not forbid government entanglement with religion. It forbids "excessive" government entanglement. A good part of the video discussion concerns the meaning of that word as it relates to the town of "Marathon." Over the past year something terrible has been happening in Marathon. Twenty-two black teenagers have been sexually molested and murdered. The perpetrator remains unknown.

Paster Brown wants to hold a religious memorial service in the public school for his son, Jamie, who was one of the murdered children. Is that all right? Some panelists answer the question categorically: No, it is not all right, for it violates the establishment clause of the First Amendment. For a number of others, however, including attorney James Neal, TV commentator Avi Nelson, Justice Potter Stewart, and Judge Arlin Adams, it is all a question of degree. What kind of service will this be? What are its ground rules? How often will it take place? How many people want it? Will it calm tensions? Right at the outset, the question of degree is introduced by James Neal in the form of a metaphor—the camel's nose in the tent.

Apparently, camels are aggressive animals. Once the camel gets his nose in the Arab's tent, there is no keeping out the rest of him. Neal, however, is ready to concede that "I think you can tolerate a little nose in this case." Provided the religious exercise occurs only once, or at any rate rarely, and provided the community is religious, then perhaps there is nothing wrong with this assembly. The moderator, Professor Arthur Miller, decides to push Neal a bit. Suppose the community were composed of a variety of religious and nonreligious individuals: "Twenty-five Baptists, five Hindus, three Jews, two Moonies, six Ethical Culturists, and eight yahoos—and I'll throw in an agnostic and two atheists." Would Pastor Brown's prayer service then be too much "nose"? Not yet, says Neal, though it's "enough." No more nose is allowable.

Laura Kiernan, a *Washington Post* reporter, at first wants nothing to do with the camel's nose, not even the tip of it. "Mr. Neal is making a big mistake." But the moderator is cunning. He gets Kiernan to admit that a nonreligious service for Jamie Brown would be fine. Then he talks about music for it. "Could we play a Bach cantata?" Sensing trouble, she makes a tight-lipped reply: "Could." That is all he needs. "I mean, with words as well as music—all that religious stuff that they say about—" Watching the trap spring shut around her, Kiernan tries to get out by suggesting that they might "screen the music for the service," but then she realizes that this sounds like censorship. So she tries changing the subject to the coercive nature of all prayers in public schools. Even if a child can leave the room during prayers, they put the child into "an untenable position." Still, by the end of her remarks, Kiernan has left perhaps a molecule of the camel's nose in the tent. The moderator has gotten her to agree that not all references to the Deity are unconstitutional in public schools. "I don't think you're injecting religion by singing 'God Bless America'."

So it goes, throughout the dialogue: How much of the camel's nose should be allowed in the tent? How much "entanglement" is "excessive"? Judge Arlin Adams tries a summary formula: if it's "a one-shot affair," if attendance is "voluntary," and if its purpose is "to maintain harmony in a community that's badly divided," then the assembly should pass muster. There are echoes here of the *Lemon* tests. The "secular purpose" in this case is the maintenance of harmony; the neutrality required by *Lemon* might be met by making attendance voluntary; and possibly *Lemon*'s prohibition of excessive entanglement in religion might be met by making this assembly "a one-shot affair." Still, there are strong objections from other panelists to this kind of compromise. Among others, ACLU Attorney Jeanne Baker objects, as does former HEW Secretary Shirley Hufstedler and Judge Harry Edwards. All of them believe that the establishment clause flatly prohibits such an assembly. The moderator teases Hufstedler, saying that she's "hiding behind your First Amendment." Proudly she answers: "Absolutely enwrapped in it."

The reader, of course, will have to make up his or her own mind on this issue. Does the question of a religious establishment admit of degree? Can the camel's nose be in the tent only a little bit? If so, how far? If not, where would this logic take us? Can children sing "God Bless America"? Should "God" be taken off our coins? Where do we draw the lines? There is one question that was not even brought up in the video discussion: What if the exercise were held in the school but after school hours, at the initiative of an evangelical Christian group? Could that be justified under the *Widmar* precedent?

II: GUN CONTROL

"Praise the Lord and Pass the Ammunition" is a World War II song that joins reverence with belligerence. In America the two sometimes go together. It is not unusual for those who call themselves "conservatives"—a term we do not dare to define—to be at once in favor of prayers in public schools and against gun control. With "liberals" (another term of uncertain meaning), positions generally go the opposite way: for gun control and against prayers in public schools. There are plenty of exceptions, however, in both cases. Former Senator George McGovern, often regarded as a superliberal, used to vote against gun-control legislation (probably because he represented South Dakota, a Western state), while almost none of the video participants who support public school prayer oppose gun control.

Are All Amendments Created Equal?

Nevertheless, one finds a seeming inconsistency among the supporters and opponents of gun control. It lies in their attitude toward the Bill of Rights. At one point, the moderator probes this apparent inconsistency. On the one hand, everyone, but particularly the opponents of school prayer, finds the First Amendment loaded with restrictions on government. Government can't conduct school prayers because even nonsectarian ones conflict with the establishment clause. Even a government-approved Bach cantata is suspect! But, on the other hand, everyone seems very casual about the Second Amendment. True, it guarantees "the right to keep and bear arms," but most of the panelists consider that phrase obsolete, or at least severely qualified by the first part of the amendment, which talks about the need for a "well-regulated militia."

Still, shouldn't "the right to keep and bear arms" be taken as seriously as the establishment clause in the First Amendment? The moderator puts it this way to James Neal: "You mean not all amendments were created equal?" Neal answers, "There's a lot of political philosophy grafted onto the words of the Constitution," meaning that the Constitution depends upon the construction we place on it. The moderator counters that it sounds like "this Marathon ordinance [banning handguns] puts the whole camel in the Second Amendment tent." Everyone has been so worried about the least government entanglement with religion. Why are they ready to let the government ban firearms, the Second Amendment notwithstanding?

In part, the answer has already been touched on. The reference to the right to bear arms seems to appear in the context of a state militia; as Judge William Bauer interprets it in the video discussion, it means that "anyone in the militia can keep and bear arms whenever he is in the militia and on duty." But the rejection of Second Amendment claims turns upon larger considerations than simply the context in which "the right of the people to keep and bear arms" appears in the Amendment. Rightly or wrongly, many jurists have concluded that the Second Amendment is a dead amendment, a kind of museum piece of early America. It recalls the days when citizens displayed muskets over their mantelpieces and took them down to join the militia during times of danger. Today, they say, internal defense is more professionalized. The Court's rulings seem to reflect that viewpoint. In 1896, the Court began whittling down the Second Amendment by ruling that it applied only to the federal government, not the states. (And yet, as noted in the Introduction and Chapter 4, the Court has in other cases expanded the scope of the Bill of Rights to apply to the states as well as the federal government.) In 1939, the Court rejected a Second Amendment challenge to a federal law prohibiting the transportation of sawed-off shotguns in interstate commerce. And in 1983, the Court let stand an appeals court ruling that upheld the authority of the village of Morton Grove, Illinois, to ban not merely the sales but the possession of handguns by village residents. Clearly, the Supreme Court does *not* consider all amendments to be created equal.

Leaving aside the question of whether government *may* ban firearms, *should* it ban them? Now the burden of proof is on the government. Since taking away people's guns, or prohibiting the sale of guns, is a limitation on liberty, those who favor such limitations have to give us reasons for taking such actions. What good is gun control?

One obvious good is that it takes away an instrument for inflicting death and injury. Sam Fields, a director of the National Coalition to Ban Handguns, sums up his case for gun control:

> The proposition is simple: for technological reasons a certain type of firearm, the handgun, has become a menace to our society. Measured by any yardstick— law and order, human tragedy, financial—the cost-benefit ratio is overwhelmingly against a system that allows easy access to handguns. A sampling of the tangible and intangible tragedies interwoven in the handgun menace indicates that $500 million is spent annually in hospital care for handgun wounds, that annually, handguns take the lives of over twenty thousand individuals with potential lifetime earnings of $116,000 and that thousands of families are reduced to welfare for want of a breadwinner. . . .

Gun-control advocates like Field point to the experience of England and Japan, both of which have extremely strict gun-control laws. England has a rate of violent crime that is trivial compared to America's, and Japan's rate is almost incredibly low by our standards.

What replies are there to these arguments? B. Bruce-Briggs, a historian and policy analyst, contends that the low crime rates in England and Japan have more to do with the character of the English and Japanese people than with the existence of tough gun-control laws. The Japanese living in America have even lower rates of violence than those in Japan. And the English people, he says, have a "generally deferential and docile character." In contrast, Northern Ireland is exploding with violence—yet it has even tougher gun-control laws than England.

Empirical studies have led some researchers to believe that the possession of firearms may in some cases *deter* violent crime. Political scientists Gary Kleck and David Bordua, in a research article published in *Law and Policy Quarterly* in July 1983, contend that a firearms training program for women sponsored by the Orlando, Florida, police had the effect of dramatically decreasing rapes. The program lasted from October 1966 to March 1967. As a result, Kleck and Bordua claimed, the rape rates plummeted.

For 1966 the rape rate was 35.91 in Orlando, while it was only 4.18 for 1967, a one-year drop of 88%. It cannot be claimed that this was merely part of a general downward trend in rape, since the national rate was increasing at the time. No other U.S. city with a population over 100,000 experienced so large a percentage decrease in the number of rapes from 1966 to 1967, and only Philadelphia could boast of even so large a decrease in actual numbers.

Of course, a carefully supervised program on the use of firearms is different from just letting people buy guns. But the authors cite another example that should be disquieting to gun-control advocates. The city of Kennesaw, Georgia, in 1982 passed an ordinance *requiring* people to buy guns. In the seven months following the passage of that law, only 5 residential burglaries were reported, as opposed to 45 during the same period of the previous year—a decrease of 89 percent!

Yet the evidence for cause and effect in the gun-control controversy is very difficult to pin down. It is hard to say what causes crime to increase or decrease. In the case of Kennesaw, it may simply have been the community's expressed determination to fight crime that deterred potential burglars. Burglars knew that the town "meant business." The town could have shown similar determination in a variety of other ways, such as appropriating more money for the police or organizing citizens' patrols. Burglaries may be down in Kennesaw, but if the law put more guns into people's homes, a different danger may now exist. What worries many gun-control advocates is not the professional criminal but the honest citizen who might get drunk, get cheated at cards, or get into a violent argument and then reach for the weapon that was intended only for "protection."

The questions, then, are both urgent and highly debatable. Is gun control a good and useful policy? Or is it unfair, needlessly intrusive, futile, and counterproductive? In grappling with these questions, the panelists try to avoid absolutes. Is gun control a good policy? Their answer seems to be that it depends upon circumstances.

In Marathon, according to the moderator, community tensions have been growing since the murders came to light and gun sales have sharply risen. The council decides to pass a gun-control ordinance. "You with me, Mr. Reynolds, on the city council?" The man he has turned to is William Bradford Reynolds, the Reagan administration's assistant attorney general. If the moderator expected a negative vote from this "conservative" official, he must have been surprised, for Reynolds immediately agrees. So does everyone else on the panel. The moderator ups the stakes: Suppose the ban extended not only to the sale of guns but to their *possession.* Is the vote still unanimous? No. Now he has lost Griffin Bell, former attorney general (during the Carter administration). But he still hasn't lost Reynolds. "How long are you going to keep the guns? Just take 'em forever, or are you taking them for a temporary period while we're in the middle of a . . . ." When the moderator assures him that it is just until the murderer is convicted, Reynolds again votes yes. So does Charles Rangel, who represents most of Harlem in the House of Representatives. But the moderator loses even Rangel's vote when he ratchets the regulations up another notch, taking away not only handguns but also hunting rifles and shotguns.

Points to Remember

1. Apparently all amendments are not created equal. Discussion participants who favor rigorous enforcement of the First Amendment tend to regard the Second Amendment as an outdated remnant of the eighteenth century. It can be argued that the Second Amendment's guarantee of "the right of the people to keep and bear Arms" was in the context of the need for "A well regulated Militia" and is therefore no guarantee to civilians.
2. In 1896 the Supreme Court ruled that the Second Amendment applied only to the federal government, not the states, and in 1939 it restricted the amendment's application to the federal government. In 1983 the Court let stand an appeals court ruling that upheld the authority of a town to ban the possession of handguns.
3. Whether or not strict gun-control laws will lower the rate of violent crime is the subject of intense controversy. Proponents cite the example of countries, such as England and Japan, that have such laws and very low rates of violent crime. Opponents say that the low crime rates in those countries result not from gun-control laws but from the character of the people. They point to examples that prove, they think, that the ownership of guns may actually decrease crime. Their critics deny that there is any such cause-effect relationship.
4. Most of the participants in the panel discussion think that some form of gun control is justified, at least during tense situations. But when the moderator escalates from the sale of guns to their possession, and finally to the sale and possession even of hunting rifles and shotguns, the panelists begin to fall away. Even the most ardent advocates of gun control seem to be opposed to the confiscation of hunting guns.

Reflections

The question, then, is not whether government has the constitutional authority to regulate firearms. It does have it. The question is how far, as a matter of public policy, it should go in regulating firearms. The reader should think about these questions:

1. Is there a critical difference between banning the *sale* of firearms and banning their *possession*? If so, what is the difference? If not, does that mean that government officials may come into people's homes to make sure they don't have guns?
2. Is there a critical difference between banning firearms only during an emergency and banning them permanently? If so, does that mean that the government must give them back once the emergency is over? What if that itself creates a new emergency?
3. Is it meaningful to distinguish between handguns and hunting guns? If not, does that mean people can have their hunting rifles taken away by the government? If

there is a meaningful difference, what is it? Can't hunting rifles also be used to shoot people?

There are no easy answers to any of these questions. They are meant to provoke thought, not to settle arguments. We are, in a sense, on our own in working out answers, for the Supreme Court has provided us with practically no guidelines beyond its dismissal of the Second Amendment. Perhaps there could come a point where the rigid enforcement of an ordinance prohibiting the possession of guns could raise questions about the violation of privacy rights. If the police came to a person's door demanding the right to search his house for a .22 rifle purchased thirty years earlier, they might end up facing a lawsuit based on the Ninth Amendment, which protects the right of privacy. But this is sheer speculation; there is little precedent to guide us.

In the third area covered in the video discussion, the right to assemble, we have more than reason to guide us. There are some solid precedents. We turn to the topic of freedom of assembly, then, with somewhat more confidence concerning judicial guidelines.

III: THE RIGHT TO ASSEMBLE

Freedom of assembly is strongly protected by the First Amendment, though there are enough exceptions and qualifications to make the moderator's hypothetical case interesting. Professor Miller announces, "There's been a new development in town." It seems that two groups are going to hold demonstrations on the same day and at the same place. One is a radical left-wing group and the other is the Ku Klux Klan. Now suppose the council quickly passes an ordinance stating that permits for assemblies and demonstrations shall be denied when there is a reasonable likelihood of violence? Would that ordinance be constitutional?

This is not an easy call by any means. Let us lay out some of the precedents both ways.

DeJonge v. *Oregon*: Freedom of Assembly Is Fundamental

In the case of *DeJonge* v. *Oregon* (1937), the Supreme Court set aside a conviction under Oregon's "criminal syndicalism" law. Criminal syndicalism was defined in the statute as "the doctrine which advocates crime, physical violence, sabotage, or any other unlawful acts or methods of accomplishing or effecting industrial or political change or revolution." DeJonge was charged with helping to organize and conduct a meeting "which was called under the auspices of the Communist Party, an organization advocating criminal syndicalism." DeJonge countered that the meeting itself was orderly and nonviolent. The highest state court rejected his defense, stating that it was sufficient that DeJonge was involved in the conduct of a meeting sponsored by a violent organization. The Supreme Court reversed the state court, upholding DeJonge.

Two points about *DeJonge* need to be emphasized. First, the decision made freedom of assembly applicable to the states; second, it established once and for all that even nasty, evil organizations have the right to hold peaceful meetings. Let us consider each of these points in turn.

1. *DeJonge* described the First Amendment's clause guaranteeing "the right of the people peaceably to assemble" as "fundamental." On its face the First Amendment seems to apply only to Congress, not to state legislatures. ("Congress shall make no law. . . .") But since the 1920s the Court had begun extending some of the liberties protected in the First Amendment to the states as well. In *Gitlow* v. *New York* (1925), the Court did the same with the First Amendment's guarantee of a free press. Now the Court was saying the same for the First Amendment's protection of the right to assemble peacefully. Central to whether one of the guarantees in the Bill of Rights extends to the states is the question of whether it is a "fundamental" right. True, the word "fundamental" is difficult to define. But the Court at least elaborated on the word if it did not precisely define it. A "fundamental" right is one that cannot be denied without violating those principles of liberty and justice which lie at the base of all civil and political institutions. All amendments are not created equal. It may also be that not all clauses within amendments are created equal. But the *DeJonge* case established that the freedom of assembly guarantee of the First Amendment "is a right cognate to those of free speech and free press and is equally fundamental."

2. *DeJonge* established that even bad, vicious organizations have a right to demonstrate peacefully. Dirk DeJonge participated in a public meeting held under the auspices of the Communist party, an organization that, in the judgment of the state authorities, taught and preached the doctrine of violent revolution. DeJonge himself said nothing about revolution at the meeting, nor did anyone else present. He was being punished solely because he participated in a public meeting that happened to be sponsored by Communists. The Court reversed his conviction because "peaceable assembly for lawful discussion cannot be made a crime." The real question, said the Court, "is not as to the auspices under which the meeting is held but as to its purpose." There was no showing that the purpose was anything other than peaceful.

Application of *DeJonge* to the Marathon Case

How does all this apply to the proposed march in Marathon? First, we know that the right to assemble is a fundamental right: it binds the local Marathon authorities just as it binds the federal government, and it is just as sacred as the right to speak, to publish, and to practice one's religion. Second, *DeJonge* teaches that we should not let moderator Miller stampede us into banning demonstrations by the mere mention of the Ku Klux Klan and "a left-wing radical group." Klansmen and left-wing radicals have as much right to hold public meetings as any other group. To quote *DeJonge* again: "The question . . . is not as to the auspices under which a meeting is held but as to its purpose."

Other Court Rulings

The *DeJonge* precedent upholding peaceful demonstrations is reinforced by others in more recent years. During the '60s and '70s, the Vietnam War and the civil rights struggle generated some interesting precedents, almost all of them favoring the right to demonstrate. In *Garner* v. *Louisiana* (1961), the Supreme Court unanimously reversed the conviction of black student "sit-inners" for "disturbing the peace" by sitting at "white" lunch counters and refusing to leave when asked. The following year, in *Taylor* v. *Louisiana* (1962), the Court reversed the convictions of "freedom riders" who refused to leave the white waiting room at a bus depot. The Court pointed out that, as in the *Garner* case, "there was no evidence of violence. The record shows that the petitioners were quiet, orderly, and polite." In 1963 the Court reversed the convictions of black students who held a demonstration on state house grounds and refused to leave after the time limit set by police officers (*Edwards* v. *South Carolina*, 1963). Following this decision, the Court overturned the convictions of 373 black students on charges of breach of peace after a demonstration in Orangeburg, South Carolina (*Fields* v. *South Carolina*, 1963), and in 1964 it did the same to the convictions of sixty-five black students for demonstrating in front of the city hall in Rock Hill, South Carolina (*Henry* v. *Rock Hill*, 1964). Although the Court rejected the argument of David O'Brien that burning his draft card in public was a form of "symbolic speech" protected by the First Amendment (*United States* v. *O'Brien*, 1968), it upheld the right of a man to wear the American flag on the seat of his blue jeans (*Smith* v. *Goguen*, 1974) and of a high school girl to come to class wearing a black armband to protest American involvement in Vietnam (*Tinker* v. *Des Moines School District, et al.*, 1969).

Applying these findings to the Marathon hypothetical case, we can see that:

1. Klansmen and Communists have a right to demonstrate if their intention is peaceful.
2. They can wear the symbols of their groups—sheets and hammer-and-sickles—even if those symbols make other people angry.
3. Their demonstrations cannot be hampered by arbitrary standards set by public officials.

The *Skokie* Case

A case resembling that hypothesized (from which, indeed, the hypothetical case was borrowed) involved the decision of a neo-Nazi group to hold a march in Skokie, Illinois, in 1977. The decision caused an uproar because Skokie, a community with a large Jewish population (many of them Holocaust survivors), attempted to prevent the march by quickly passing a variety of new laws. No marches could be held in the village if they featured military-style uniforms (a requirement which would have also prevented the Boy Scouts from marching); marchers would have to purchase $350,000 worth of liability insurance; and marchers could not pass out literature that cast aspersions on any group. In practical terms the regulations amounted to a ban on the demonstration. So the Nazis went to court. The American Civil Liberties Union backed them, a move that almost destroyed the organization because it resulted in a massive loss of membership and contributions. Eventually, the Nazis won their right to demonstrate. Though the village appealed the decision to the very threshold of the Supreme Court, the Court rejected its request for a stay.

Other Precedents: *Schenck, Feiner, Beauharnais*

In fairness to those on the Marathon City Council who still feel that the demonstrations by the Klan and other extremist groups should not take place, there are some Supreme Court precedents that point the other way. *Schenck* v. *United States* (1919) was discussed in a previous chapter. That was the case in which Oliver Wendell Holmes, Jr., said that if there is a "clear and present danger" of something government has a right to prevent—violence, in this case—then First Amendment rights can be qualified. In *Feiner* v. *New York* (1951), the Court let stand the conviction of a man who had stirred up a crowd *against* him and was then arrested for disorderly conduct. In a five-to-three opinion, the Court said that it "respects, as it must, the interest of the community in maintaining peace and order on its streets." And in *Beauharnais* v. *Illinois* (1952), the Court upheld the conviction of a man who had distributed racist leaflets in the streets of Chicago and was thereafter convicted of violating a "group libel" statute that punished anyone who distributed literature portraying "depravity, criminality, unchastity, or lack of virtue" in any race or class of citizens. Although many legal authorities now consider the *Beauharnais* decision to be one the Court would rather forget, at least two justices, Blackmun and Rehnquist, considered it "in some tension" with the lower-court rulings protecting the Nazi's right to march in the Skokie case.

The Video Discussion of the Right to Assemble

Armed with this tremendous array of precedents, we can return to the video debate with something approaching confidence. Let us start with this proposition: anyone who wants to ban demonstrations, even demonstrations by vicious people, has a tough row to hoe. Yet the particular facts of this case should give pause even to ardent libertarians. The community is full of tension and suspicion; the murders seem to have racial overtones; gun sales have gone up; violence is in the air. Not content with these facts, the moderator adds more: each group holds press conferences, at which "a total of twelve fights" breaks out. The KKK burns a cross in front of the home of the NAACP's local director. A gun cache is discovered. Somebody on the "Ten Most Wanted" list of the FBI comes to town. Professor Miller adds all this in an effort to get the former ACLU attorney, Jeanne Baker, to agree that maybe the march *can* be banned. She won't agree, though, because "we have a constitutional set of rights that protects a minority group and allows that minority group to make political statements in public." Baker will stick to her principles. The moderator taunts her: "Do I have to bring in the A-bomb?" Yet even that won't do. What is needed, she says, is to show "an imminence of danger at the location of the marches at the time of the marches."

The moderator wonders whether Baker has "allowed doctrine to run riot here," and Judge William Bauer is convinced that she has. He, for one, is "not going to wait around until this thing blows up." Given the facts of this case—two violent groups opposing each other, known criminals involved, dynamite hidden away—he feels he has enough information to justify a ban on demonstrations. Baker is shocked. "In the meantime, the First Amendment has been . . . has been. . . ." "Hasn't blown up," Bauer interjects. "The city is still all right, and God's in his heaven and all's right with the world. The city's still there and nobody's dead and who's been hurt?" But something has been hurt, Baker insists, because "it is a prior restraint of speech. I think the law's very clear that . . . marches and uniforms are symbolic speech."

The law is clear about prior restraint. The reader will recall the discussion of prior restraint in an earlier chapter. *Near* v. *Minnesota* and the Pentagon Papers case make it clear that courts almost never tolerate prior restraint—of speech. But is a demonstration the same as a speech? On that point the law is less clear. David O'Brien's attempt to argue that burning his draft card was a form of symbolic speech was unsuccessful, though the Court has considered armbands and other insignia as forms of speech. But Judge Bauer is not concerned with these niceties of law. He will ban the demonstrations, period, and risk the charge that he has destroyed the First Amendment. "I've done my bit to bring America to its knees, but I've also saved the community from a terrible battle." "You don't understand," Miller says. "The camel's nose is in the tent again."

Reflections

Is it? And if it is, can we allow a bit of nose into the tent, given the circumstances of this case? The reader must work out the answers without any authoritative guide. There are precedents pointing both ways. In one direction is *DeJonge* and all the decisions of the '60s and '70s upholding the right of civil rights and anti-Vietnam demonstrators to assemble peacefully. Pointing the other way are the *Schenck, Feiner,* and *Beauharnais* cases. The last two may no longer be viable precedents, but *Schenck* is still alive. Even Baker respects its famous "clear and present danger" formula. "Now, if there were a set of facts which could be developed in advance and presented to a judge, a set of facts making out a case of clear and present danger, it's possible that a judge could be persuaded." (Note how careful she is to dissociate *herself* from the approval of parade bans. *A judge* could be persuaded.) Finally, the reader should remember that the First Amendment only protects the right of the people "peaceably" to assemble. It does not protect violent demonstrations, and the *DeJonge* case tells us that the *intent* of the demonstrators is critical in judging whether or not it will be violent. All these factors should serve as criteria in weighing the facts of the Marathon case.

Points to Remember

At this point the reader should know:
1. The background facts leading up to the *DeJonge* case (covered in Friendly and Elliott's book) and the major holdings of the case.
2. The issue in the *Skokie* case.
3. The Court's attitude toward "symbolic" speech.
4. The Court's holding in the *Beauharnais, Feiner,* and *Schenck* cases and the meaning of the "clear and present danger" formula.

5. The meaning of the term "prior restraint" and the Court's view of prior restraint. (It may be necessary to review this section in Chapter 8.)

SUMMARY

This chapter has discussed a potpourri of issues: school prayer, gun control, and the right of assembly. All three issues probe the deepest feelings of Americans. These are divisive issues; they tend to polarize people along class, cultural, and religious lines. David Hamlin, who was executive director for the Illinois chapter of the ACLU when it was defending the right of the Nazis to march in Skokie, remembers having tried patiently to explain to a woman why Nazis had the same rights as other people to march. Then, according to Hamlin, this exchange occurred:

> "Young man," the woman asked, "are you Jewish?"
> It did not occur to me to refuse to answer—I am not Jewish.
> "My God," whispered the woman, "I *spit* on you!"

Anecdotes of the same sort could be culled from the various debates over school prayer and gun control since the early '60s. Both sides of the controversies often see each other through the lenses of stereotype and prejudice.

Some school prayer advocates hint at plots by "Godless materialists," while some of their opponents portray them as intolerant bigots with strong ties to the "radical right." Gun-control advocates sometimes resort to stereotyping their opponents as supermacho types, while some on the other side like to brand gun-controllers as "those who would disarm America." The sheer vividness of the imagery frequently obscures the fact that one can be a devout Christian and an opponent of prayers in public schools; an atheist and a critic of *Engel* v. *Vitale*; or a Jew who supports the rights of anyone, even a Nazi, to demonstrate peacefully.

The usefulness of the video debate on these topics is that it brings together advocates of opposing views and reveals them to be human beings, not political cartoons. Though there are cleavages on the panel along the lines of liberal and conservative, they are far from airtight. Here is "archconservative" William Bradford Reynolds, Reagan's assistant attorney general, ready to ban not only the sale but the possession of handguns. There is James Neal, "liberal" Democratic prosecutor of Watergate, who sees nothing wrong, on the issue of prayer in the public schools, in letting some of the camel's nose into the tent. Then there is the moderator—nobody's ally—who prods all the panelists to modify their positions, to get away from speechmaking and move closer to careful analysis and reflection. The effect may be to let some of the air out of the balloons these controversies have inflated, to see both sides—all sides—as human beings grappling with some extremely tough issues. Maybe we ought to applaud the participants for what is after all a joint effort to find solutions.

Still, the controversies will remain, and they will probably wind up in the Supreme

Court. Ever since John Marshall declared it to be "the province and duty of the judicial department" to interpret the Constitution, the Supreme Court has been the storm center of controversies. And given the role of the Court since *Marbury* v. *Madison*, it is hard to see how it can avoid them. If it ducks them, it will be accused of abdicating its responsibilities. If it confronts them and makes a decision, the losing side will accuse it of tampering with the Constitution. The Court seems to be caught in the classic dilemma of "damned if you do and damned if you don't."

The debatable issue is not whether the Supreme Court can extricate itself from controversy; it can't. The issue is whether the Court can discover, or perhaps rediscover, some "objective" standards for decision making. In his conversation with former Supreme Court Justice Potter Stewart at the end of the video debate, Fred Friendly says, "I heard you say once that the Constitution was not a self-executing document." Stewart reaffirms the statement, and both agree that it is the Supreme Court that must do the executing. But to execute a document one must first interpret it, and that brings us to the very nerve of the controversy that lies behind these issues, particularly the issue of school prayer. The question that reaches in and probes the nerve is, very simply, this: Has the Court in recent years been doing more than interpreting the Constitution? Has it been rewriting it?

The question itself is not that new. Different sides on various controversies have raised it since the early nineteenth century. Abolitionists asked it after the *Dred Scott* decision of 1857 declared slaves to be "private property." Supporters of the Roosevelt administration asked it during the 1930s, when the Court struck down New Deal legislation. The difference, however, is that in the past the Court always claimed to be using some kind of legal formula for interpreting statutes. More often than not, these formulas were rigid, abstract, and scholastic, but they were formulas: they had *form*. It is not clear that today's Court majorities use any single formula, or at least one which commands a consensus on the Court. More precisely, there seem to be two competing schools of interpretation, one championed by Chief Justice Burger and Justice William Rehnquist, the other by Justices Thurgood Marshall and William Brennan. (The views of the other justices are less clear; sometimes they seem to go one way and sometimes another.)

The Burger-Rehnquist approach is to seek out the meaning of statutes and constitutional provisions by attempting to reconstruct the views of the Framers. There are a number of ways of doing this: by studying the record of debate at the time the provisions were written, by reading about public attitudes at the time, and by inferring the Framers' intentions. (For example, in *Marsh* v. *Chambers*, the chief justice inferred that the Framers of the establishment clause did not mean to ban prayers in legislatures because they appropriated moneys to pay their own legislative chaplain.) The advantage of the Burger-Rehnquist approach is that, at least in theory, it provides a fairly solid standard for interpretation. The disadvantages appear once it is put into practice. How do we know what the Framers of these old clauses would have thought about many of today's problems? Many of the facts behind today's controversies simply did not exist when the clauses were written. Moreover, to paraphrase Justice Brennan in his *Marsh* dissent, are we to treat the Constitution as a static document, as a piece of crystal that never changes? Or does it not grow and adapt itself to the various circumstances we face today? An approach based on "the Framers' intentions" seems to bind the Constitution to the world of 1787–89.

Then what of the competing philosophy, the one championed by Brennan and Marshall? Quoting himself in an earlier case, Justice Brennan said in his *Marsh* dissent that in light of the "profound changes" in this country over the past two centuries, "practices which may have been objectionable to no one in the time of Jefferson and Madison may today be highly offensive to many persons, the deeply devout and the nonbeliever alike." The conclusion is that it is up to the Court to adapt the Constitution to the "profound changes" that have come over America since the days of the Founders.

The difficulty with this approach to interpreting the Constitution may be the opposite of the difficulty in the Burger-Rehnquist approach: not that it is too inflexible but that it contains no limits on what the Court may do in interpreting the Constitution. All the Court seems to have to do is take its own measure of what is "up to date" for our society, then interpret the Constitution accordingly. It seems to make the Court a legislature—one, moreover, that is not only appointed for life but unfettered by the Constitution. The Court itself becomes the Constitution. As for Brennan's claim that the Court needs to adapt the Constitution to the "profound changes" that have come over our society, the reply can be made that the Constitution possesses a mechanism for keeping itself up to date without the help of the Supreme Court: the amendment process. If two-thirds of both houses of Congress and three-quarters of the states want to change the Constitution in order to adapt it to changing conditions, then it is changed. It is as simple as that.

The last point, about the amendment process, needs to be considered very carefully by all sides to the present controversies, especially the contending sides in the school prayer debate. If, indeed, the Court's decisions on school prayer are as unpopular as some critics claim, then the movement to amend the Constitution to allow school prayer will one day succeed. If, on the other hand, the prayer amendment continues to fall short of the necessary two-thirds vote in Congress, as it did in 1984, then the proprayer side ought to admit that opposition to the Court was not so overwhelming after all. If, however, the prayer movement does finally generate enough steam to push a constitutional amendment through Congress and the states by massive majorities, it will be time for the defenders of *Engel* v. *Vitale* to concede that the Republic has spoken—and that the Supreme Court, notwithstanding its majesty and dignity, has been overruled by the final authority: the people.

Documents

ENGEL V. *VITALE*, 370 U.S. 421 (1962)

Engel was the first of the "prayer cases" of the 1960s. In subsequent years there were later cases, on Bible reading and the Lord's Prayer, but Engel *was the groundbreaking case, making the later decisions predictable. Below are excerpts from Justice Hugo Black's majority opinion in the case.*

Opinion of the Court, Mr. Justice Black.

The respondent Board of Education of Union Free School District No. 9, New Hyde Park, New York, acting in its official capacity under state law, directed the School District's principal to cause the following prayer to be said aloud by each class in the presence of a teacher at the beginning of each school day:

> Almighty God, we acknowledge our dependence upon Thee, and we beg Thy blessings upon us, our parents, our teachers and our country.

This daily procedure was adopted on the recommendation of the State Board of Regents, a governmental agency created by the State Constitution to which the New York Legislature has granted broad supervisory, executive, and legislative powers over the State's public school system. These state officials composed the prayer which they recommended and published as a part of their "Statement on Moral and Spiritual Training in the Schools," saying: "We believe that this Statement will be subscribed to by all men and women of good will, and we call upon all of them to aid in giving life to our program."

Shortly after the practice of reciting the Regents' prayer was adopted by the School District, the parents of ten pupils brought this action in a New York State Court insisting that use of this official prayer in the public schools was contrary to the beliefs, religions, or religious practices of both themselves and their children. Among other things, these parents challenged the constitutionality of both the state law authorizing the School District to direct the use of prayer in public schools and the School District's regulation ordering the recitation of this particular prayer on the ground that these actions of official governmental agencies violate that part of the First Amendment of the Federal Constitution which commands that "Congress shall make no law respecting an establishment of religion"—a command which was "made applicable to the State of New York by the Fourteenth Amendment of the said Constitution." . . .

We think that by using its public school system to encourage recitation of the Regent's prayer, the State of New York has adopted a practice wholly inconsistent with the Establishment Clause. There can, of course, be no doubt that New York's program of daily classroom invocation of God's blessings as prescribed in the Regents' prayer is a religious activity. It is a solemn avowal of divine faith and supplication for the blessings of the Almighty. The nature of such a prayer has always been religious, none of the respondents has denied this and the trial court expressly so found:

> The religious nature of prayer was recognized by Jefferson and has been concurred in by theological writers, the United States Supreme Court and State courts and administrative officials, including New York's Commissioner of Education. A committee of the New York Legislature has agreed.

The Board of Regents as *amicus curiae*, the respondents and intervenors all concede the religious nature of prayer, but seek to distinguish this prayer because it is based on our spiritual heritage. . . .

The petitioners contend among other things that the state laws requiring or permitting use of the Regents' prayer must be struck down as a violation of the Establishment Clause because that prayer was composed by governmental officials as a part of a governmental program to further religious beliefs. For this reason, petitioners argue, the State's use of the Regent's prayer in its public school system breaches the constitutional wall of separation between Church and State. We agree with that contention since we think that the constitutional prohibition against laws respecting an establishment of religion must at least mean that in this country it is no part of the business of government to compose official prayers for any group of the American people to recite as a part of a religious program carried on by government.

It is a matter of history that this very practice of establishing governmentally composed prayers for religious services was one of the reasons which caused many of our early colonists to leave England and seek religious freedom in America. The Book of Common Prayer, which was created under governmental direction and which was approved by Acts of Parliament in 1548 and 1549, set out in minute detail the accepted form and content of prayer and other religious ceremonies to be used in the established, tax-supported Church of England. The controversies over the Book and what should be its content repeatedly threatened to disrupt the peace of that country as the accepted forms of prayer in the established church changed with the views of the particular ruler that happened to be in control at the time. Powerful groups representing some of the varying religious views of the people struggled among themselves to impress their particular views upon the Government and obtain amendments of the Book more suitable to their respective notions of how religious services should be conducted in order that the official religious establishment would advance their particular religious beliefs. Other groups, lacking the necessary political power to influence the Government on the matter, decided to leave England and its established church and seek freedom in America from England's governmentally ordained and supported religion.

It is an unfortunate fact of history that when some of the very groups which had most strenuously opposed the established Church of England found themselves sufficiently in control of colonial governments in this country to write their own prayers into law, they passed laws making their own religion the official religion of their respective colonies. Indeed, as late as the time of the Revolutionary War, there were established churches in at least eight of the thirteen former colonies and established religions in at least four of the other five. But the successful Revolution against English political domination was shortly followed by intense opposition to the practice of establishing religion by law. This opposition crystallized rapidly into an effective political force in Virginia where the minority religious groups such as Presbyterians, Lutherans, Quakers and Baptists had gained such strength that the adherents to the established Episcopal Church were actually a minority themselves. In 1785–1786, those opposed to the established Church, led by James Madison and Thomas Jefferson, who though themselves not members of any of these dissenting religious groups, opposed all religious establishments by law on grounds of principle, obtained the enactment of the famous "Virginia Bill for Religious Liberty" by which all religious groups were placed on an equal footing so far as the State was concerned. Similar though less far-reaching legislation was being considered and passed in other States.

By the time of the adoption of the Constitution, our history shows that there was a widespread awareness among many Americans of the dangers of a union of Church and State. These people knew, some of them from bitter personal experience, that one of the greatest dangers to the freedom of the individual to worship in his own way lay in the Government's placing its official stamp of approval upon one particular kind of prayer or one particular form of religious services. They knew the anguish, hardship and bitter strife that could come when zealous groups struggled with one another to obtain the Government's stamp of approval from each King, Queen, or Protector that came to temporary power. . . .

The Establishment Clause, unlike the Free Exercise Clause, does not depend upon any showing of direct governmental compulsion and is violated by the enactment of laws which establish an official religion whether those laws operate directly to coerce nonobserving individuals or not. This is not to say, of course, that laws officially prescribing a particular form of religious worship do not involve coercion of such individuals. When the power, prestige and financial support of government is placed behind a particular religious belief, the indirect coercive pressure upon religious minorities to conform to the prevailing officially approved religion is plain. But the purposes underlying the Establishment Clause go much further than that. Its first and most immediate purpose rested on the belief that a union of government and religion tends to destroy government and to degrade religion. . . .

It is true that New York's establishment of its Regents' prayer as an officially approved religious doctrine of that State does not amount to a total establishment of one particular religious sect to the exclusion of all others—that, indeed, the governmental endorsement of that prayer seems relatively insignificant when compared to the governmental encroachments upon religion which were commonplace 200 years ago. To those who may subscribe to the view that because the Regents' official prayer is so brief and general there can be no danger to religious freedom in its governmental establishment, however, it may be appropriate to say in the words of James Madison, the author of the First Amendment:

[I]t is proper to take alarm at the first experiment on our liberties. . . . Who does not see that the same authority which can establish Christianity, in exclusion of all other Religions, may establish with the same ease any particular sect of Christians, in exclusion of all other Sects? That the same authority which can force a citizen to contribute three pence only of his property for the support of any one establishment, may force him to conform to any other establishment in all cases whatsoever?

The judgment of the Court of Appeals of New York is reversed and the cause remanded for further proceedings not inconsistent with this opinion.

Reversed and remanded.

Justice Black's majority opinion represented the views of only five members of the Court. Justices Felix Frankfurter and Byron White took no part in the decision of the case, and Justice William O. Douglas wrote a separate, concurring opinion (meaning that he agreed with the majority's holding but not with all the reasoning behind it). The lone dissenter in the case was Justice Potter Stewart, who continues to voice his dissent in the video discussion. Below is his dissent as expressed in the case.

Justice Stewart's dissenting opinion.

A local school board in New York has provided that those pupils who wish to do so may join in a brief prayer at the beginning of each school day, acknowledging their dependence upon God and asking His blessing upon them and upon their parents, their teachers, and their country. The Court today decides that in permitting this brief non-denominational prayer the school board has violated the Constitution of the United States. I think this decision is wrong.

The Court does not hold, nor could it, that New York has interfered with the free exercise of anybody's religion. For the state courts have made clear that those who object to reciting the prayer must be entirely free of any compulsion to do so, including any "embarrassments and pressures." Cf. *West Virginia State Board of Education* v. *Barnette,* 319 U.S. 624. But the Court says that in permitting school children to say this simple prayer, the New York authorities have established "an official religion."

With all respect, I think the Court has misapplied a great constitutional principle. I cannot see how an "official religion" is established by letting those who want to say a prayer say it. On the contrary, I think that to deny the wish of these school children to join in reciting this prayer is to deny them the opportunity of sharing in the spiritual heritage of our Nation.

The Court's historical review of the quarrels over the Book of Common Prayer in England throws no light for me on the issue before us in this case. England had then and has now an established church. Equally unenlightening, I think, is the history of the early establishment and later rejection of an official church in our own States. For we deal here not with the establishment of a state church, which would, of course, be constitutionally impermissible, but with whether school children who want to begin their day by joining in prayer must be prohibited from doing so. Moreover, I think that the Court's task, in this as in all areas of constitutional adjudication, is not responsibly aided by the uncritical invocation of metaphors like the "wall of separation," a phrase nowhere to be found in the Constitution. What is relevant to the issue here is not the history of an established church in sixteenth century England or in eighteenth century America, but the history of the religious traditions of our people, reflected in countless practices of the institutions and officials of our government.

At the opening of each day's Session of this Court we stand, while one of our officials invokes the protection of God. Since the days of John Marshall our Crier has said, "God save the United States and this Honorable Court." Both the Senate and the House of Representatives open their daily Sessions with prayer. Each of our Presidents, from George Washington to John F. Kennedy, has upon assuming his Office asked the protection and help of God.

The Court today says that the state and federal governments are without constitutional power to prescribe any particular form of words to be recited by any group of the American people on any subject touching religion. The third stanza of "The Star-Spangled Banner," made our National Anthem by Act of Congress in 1931, contains these verses:

Blest with victory and peace, may the heav'n rescued land
　　Praise the Pow'r that hath made and preserved us a nation!
Then conquer we must, when our cause it is just,
　　And this be our motto "In God is our Trust."

In 1954 Congress added a phrase to the Pledge of Allegiance to the Flag so that it now contains the words "one Nation *under God,* indivisible, with liberty and justice for all." In 1952 Congress enacted legislation calling upon the President each year to proclaim a National Day of Prayer. Since 1865 the words "IN GOD WE TRUST" have been impressed on our coins.

Countless similar examples could be listed, but there is no need to belabor the obvious. It was all summed up by this Court just ten years ago in a single sentence: "We are a religious people whose institutions presuppose a Supreme Being." *Zorach* v. *Clauson,* 343 U.S. 306, 313.

I do not believe that this Court, or the Congress, or the President has by the actions and practices I have mentioned established an "official religion" in violation of the Constitution. And I do not believe the State of New York has done so in this case. What each has done has been to recognize and to follow the deeply entrenched and highly cherished spiritual traditions of our Nation—traditions which come down to us from those who almost two hundred years ago avowed their "firm reliance on the Protection of Divine Providence" when they proclaimed the freedom and independence of this brave new world.

I dissent.

LYNCH V. DONNELLY, 463 U.S. _____ (1984)

In 1984 the Court decided that a city may include a Nativity scene as part of a city-sponsored Christmas display. The majority opinion in the case was written by Chief Justice Warren Burger. Excerpts follow.

Opinion of the Court, Chief Justice Burger.

We granted certiorari to decide whether the Establishment Clause of the First Amendment prohibits a municipality from including a crèche, or Nativity scene, in its annual Christmas display.

Each year, in cooperation with the downtown retail merchants' association, the City of Pawtucket, R.I., erects a Christmas display. The display is situated in a park owned by a nonprofit organization and located in the heart of the shopping district.

The display is essentially like those to be found in hundreds of towns or cities across the nation, often on public grounds, during the Christmas season. The Pawtucket display comprises many of the figures and decorations traditionally associated with Christmas, including, among other things, a Santa Claus house, reindeer pulling Santa's sleigh, candy-striped poles, a Christmas tree, carolers, cutout figures representing such characters as a clown, an elephant, and a teddy bear, hundreds of colored lights, a large banner that reads "Seasons Greetings," and the crèche at issue here. All components of this display are owned by the city.

The crèche, which has been included in the display for 40 or more years, consists of the traditional figures, including the Infant Jesus, Mary and Joseph, angels, shepherds, kings and animals, all ranging in height from five inches to five feet.

Respondents, Pawtucket residents and individual members of the Rhode Island affiliate of the American Civil Liberties Union, and the affiliate itself, brought this action in the United States District Court for Rhode Island, challenging the city's inclusion of the crèche in the display violates the Establishment Clause, which is binding on the states through the 14th Amendment. The District Court found that, by including the crèche in the Christmas display, the city has "tried to endorse and promulgate religious beliefs," and that "erection of the crèche has the real and substantial effect of affiliating the city with the Christian beliefs that the crèche represents."

This "appearance of official sponsorship," it believed, "confers more than a remote and incidental benefit on Christianity." Last, although the Court acknowledged the absence of administrative entanglement, it found that excessive entanglement has been fostered as a result of the political divisiveness of including the crèche in the celebration. The city was permanently enjoined from including the crèche in the display.

A divided panel of the Court of Appeals for the First Circuit affirmed. We granted certiorari, and we reverse.

This Court has explained that the purpose of the Establishment and Free Exercise Clauses of the First Amendment is "to prevent, as far as possible, the intrusion of either [the church or the state] into the precincts of the other." (Lemon v. Kurtzman, 1971).

At the same time, however, the Court has recognized that "total separation is not possible in an absolute sense. Some relationship between government and religious organizations is inevitable." (ibid.)

In every Establishment Clause case, we must reconcile the inescapable tension between the objective of preventing unnecessary intrusion of either the church or the state upon the other, and the reality that, as the Court has so often noted, total separation of the two is not possible.

The Court has sometimes described the Religion Clauses as erecting a "wall" between church and state. The concept of a "wall" of separation is a useful figure of speech probably deriving from views of Thomas Jefferson. But the metaphor itself is not a wholly accurate description of the practical aspects of the relationship that in fact exists between church and state.

No significant segment of our society and no institution within it can exist in a vacuum or in total or absolute isolation from all the other parts, much less from government. Nor does the Constitution require complete separation of church and state; it affirmatively mandates accommodation, not merely tolerance, of all religions, and forbids hostility toward any.

There is an unbroken history of official acknowledgment by all three branches of government of the role of religion in American life from at least 1789.

Our history is replete with official references to the value and invocation of divine guidance in deliberations and pronouncements of the Founding Fathers and contemporary leaders. Beginning in the early colonial period long before Independence, a day of Thanksgiving was celebrated as a religious holiday to give thanks for the bounties of nature as gifts from God. President Washington and his successors proclaimed Thanksgiving, with all its religious overtones, a day of national celebration and Congress made it a national holiday more than a century ago.

Executive orders and other official announcements of Presidents and of the Congress have proclaimed both Christmas and Thanksgiving national holidays in religious terms. And, by acts of Congress, it has long been the practice that Federal employees are released from duties on these national holidays, while being paid from the same public revenues that provide the compensation of the Chaplains of the Senate and the House and the military services.

Art galleries supported by public revenues display religious paintings of the 15th and 16th centuries, predominantly inspired by one religious faith.

This history may help explain why the Court consistently has declined to take a rigid, absolutist view of the Establishment Clause.

Rather than mechanically invalidating all government conduct or statutes that confer benefits or give special recognition to religion in general or to one faith, as an absolutist approach would dictate, the Court has scrutinized challenged legislation or official conduct to determine whether, in reality, it establishes a religion or religious faith, or tends to do so.

In each case, the inquiry calls for line-drawing; no fixed, per se rule can be framed.

In the line-drawing process we have often found it useful to inquire whether the challenged law or conduct has a secular purpose, whether its principal or primary effect is to advance or inhibit religion, and whether it creates an excessive entanglement of government with religion. (Lemon, supra.) But we have repeatedly emphasized our unwillingness to be confined to any single test or criterion in this sensitive area. . . .

Justice Brennan describes the crèche as a "re-creation of an event that lies at the heart of Christian faith." The crèche, like a painting, is passive; admittedly it is a reminder of the origins of Christmas. Even the traditional, purely secular displays extant at Christmas, with or without a crèche, would inevitably recall the religious nature of the holiday. The display engenders a friendly community spirit of good will in keeping with the season.

Of course the crèche is identified with one religious faith but no more so than the examples we have set out from prior cases in which we found no conflict with the Establishment Clause. It would be ironic, however, if the inclusion of a single symbol of a particular historic religious event, as part of a celebration acknowledged in the Western world for 20 centuries, and in this country by the people, by the executive branch, by the Congress and the courts for two centuries, would so "taint" the city's exhibit as to render it violative of the Establishment Clause.

Justice William Brennan wrote a dissent that was joined by Justices Thurgood Marshall, Harry Blackmun, and John Paul Stevens. Excerpts follow.

Justice Brennan's dissenting opinion.

Despite the narrow contours of the Court's opinion, our precedents in my view compel the holding that Pawtucket's inclusion of a life-sized display depicting the Biblical description of the birth of Christ as part of its annual Christmas celebration is unconstitutional. Nothing in the history of such practices or the setting in which the city's crèche is presented obscures or diminishes the plain fact that Pawtucket's action amounts to an impermissible governmental endorsement of a particular faith.

I am convinced that this case appears hard not because the principles of decision are obscure, but because the Christmas holiday seems so familiar and agreeable. Although the Court's reluctance to disturb a community's chosen method of celebrating such an agreeable holiday is understandable, that cannot justify the Court's departure from controlling precedent. . . .

As we have sought to meet new problems arising under the Establishment Clause, our decisions, with few exceptions, have demanded that a challenged governmental practice satisfy the following criteria:

"First, the [practice] must have a secular legislative purpose; second, its principal or primary effect must be one that neither advances not inhibits religion; finally, [it] must not foster 'an excessive government entanglement with religion.'" (Lemon v. Kurtzman, 1971). . . .

Applying the three-part test to Pawtucket's crèche, I am persuaded that the city's inclusion of the crèche in its Christmas display simply does not reflect a "clearly secular purpose."

Two compelling aspects of this case indicate that our generally prudent "reluctance to attribute unconstitutional motives" to a governmental body should be overcome.

First all of Pawtucket's "valid secular objectives can be readily accomplished by other means." Plainly, the city's interest in celebrating the holiday and in promoting both retail sales and good will are fully served by the elaborate display of Santa Claus, reindeer and wishing wells that are already a part of Pawtucket's annual Christmas display. More importantly, the Nativity scene, unlike every other element of the Hodgson Park display, reflects a sectarian exclusivity that the avowed purposes of celebrating the holiday season and promoting retail commerce simply do not encompass. To be found constitutional, Pawtucket's seasonal celebration must at least be nondenominational and not serve to promote religion. The inclusion of a distinctively religious element like the crèche, however, demonstrates that a narrower sectarian purpose lay behind the decision to include a Nativity scene.

The "primary effect" of including a Nativity scene in the city's display is, as the district court found, to place the government's imprimatur of approval on the particular religious beliefs exemplified by the crèche. Those who believe in the message of the Nativity receive the unique and exclusive benefit of public recognition and approval of their views. The effect on minority religious groups, as well as on those who may reject all religion, is to convey the message that their views are not similarly worthy of public recognition nor entitled to public support. It was precisely this sort of religious chauvinism that the Establishment Clause was intended forever to prohibit.

Finally, and most importantly, even in the context of Pawtucket's seasonal celebration, the crèche retains a specifically Christian religious meaning. I refuse to accept the notion implicit in today's decision that non-Christians would find that the religious content of the crèche is eliminated by the fact that it appears as part of the city's otherwise secular celebration of the Christmas holiday. . . .

Contrary to the Court's suggestion, the crèche is far from a mere representation of a "particular historic religious event." It is, instead, best understood as a mystical re-creation of an event that lies at the heart of Christian faith. To suggest, as the Court does, that such a symbol is merely "traditional" and therefore no different from Santa's house or reindeer is not only offensive to those for whom the crèche has profound significance, but insulting to those who insist for religious or personal reasons that the story of Christ is in no sense a part of "history" nor an unavoidable element of our national "heritage."

SELECTED READINGS

Barker, Lucius J., and Barker, Twilley W. *Freedom, Courts, Politics: Studies in Civil Liberties.* Englewood Cliffs, N.J.: Prentice-Hall, 1972.
Lucius and Twilley Barker have devised a unique method for examining the for-

mulation of civil liberties law. Each section dealing with a civil liberties question concentrates on a single landmark Supreme Court decision. The precedents and circumstances of the case are recalled and the decision itself explained.

Cox, Archibald. *Freedom of Expression.* Cambridge, Mass.: Harvard University Press, 1981.

The Harvard law professor who was the first U.S. special prosecutor during the Watergate prosecutions provides a clear and concise review of case law and principles concerning the First Amendment right of expression. Among the topics Cox considers are political speech; symbolic speech; campaign financing; advocacy; clear and present danger; gag orders; and time, place, and manner regulations.

Dolan, Edward. *Gun Control.* New York: Impact, 1978.

Dolan provides a long-needed, comprehensive overview of the gun-control debate in the United States. Federal and state laws regulating firearms are explained and the history of these statutes is perceptively examined. Dolan also supplies important information on the various organizations and political leaders engaged in this controversy.

Emerson, Thomas I. *The System of Free Expression.* New York: Random House, 1970.

Probably the most ambitious and comprehensive book written to date on the subject of freedom of expression under the U.S. Constitution. The author is professor emeritus at Yale Law School and one of the nation's leading authorities on the First Amendment. His historical, philosophical, and legal analysis covers, among others, the areas of internal security, assemblies, and demonstrations; libel and group libel; and academic freedom. See also his *Toward a General Theory of the First Amendment*, New York: Random House, 1966.

Gun Control. Washington, D.C.: American Enterprise Institute for Public Policy Research, 1976.

This pamphlet provides a brief introduction to federal gun-control legislation and sets out the practical and constitutional issues involved in gun control.

Hamlin, David. *The Nazi-Skokie Conflict.* Boston: Beacon, 1980.

As executive director of the Illinois chapter of the ACLU, David Hamlin moved to support the appeal of an American Nazi group that had been denied a permit to demonstrate in Skokie, Illinois—a town where a significant number of Holocaust survivors live. Despite his revulsion at everything Nazis stand for, Hamlin is convinced that suppression of speech and assembly cannot be tolerated in a free society.

Hentoff, Nat. *The First Freedom.* New York: Delacorte, 1980.

Journalist Hentoff's book begins with symbolic speech and anti-Vietnam protest and ends with the Nazis in Skokie. In between is an engaging history of the principle and practice of free speech in America—whose history Hentoff describes as "tumultuous."

Miller, Glenn T. *Religious Liberty in America.* Philadelphia: Westminster, 1976.

A social, legal, and regional report on religion in America. After recounting the establishment of religious colonies in the seventeenth century, Miller explains the reasons for the movement toward disestablishment in the next century. The effects of scientific and pseudoscientific inquiry (especially Darwinism), slavery, immigration, and industrialization on American religious attitudes are discussed.

Neier, Aryeh. *Defending My Enemy.* New York: Dutton: 1979.

Neier was executive director of the ACLU at the time of the Skokie controversy. He tells the story of the American Nazis in Skokie and of their case in the courts and explains the principles that compelled the ACLU to defend the Nazis' march in order to defend the First Amendment.

Sorauf, Frank J. *The Wall of Separation: The Constitutional Politics of Church and State.* Princeton, N.J.: Princeton University Press, 1976.

Sorauf has studied the litigants, attorneys, strategies, and policy outcomes in sixty-seven church-state separation cases. He is especially interested in litigation initiated by interest groups rather than individuals and in the "test case." His books make it clear that the judicial policy process in general and the politics of church-state relations in particular are very decentralized.

GLOSSARY

Established church. A particular church or sect that is singled out by the government for official patronage and tax support. In England the established church is the Church of England.

Establishment clause. The clause in the First Amendment stating that "Congress shall make no law respecting an establishment of religion. . . ." Justice Stewart and others have argued that this clause was inserted into the First Amendment only to prevent the federal government from setting up an established church. Others, including the majority on the Supreme Court, insist that its purpose was to outlaw any significant state "entanglement" in religion, even if no particular church is singled out for special patronage.

Greensboro and Skokie. On November 3, 1979, in Greensboro, North Carolina, four people were killed by members of the Ku Klux Klan as they demonstrated against the Klan at a rally sponsored by the Workers' Viewpoint Organization, a Communist group. Skokie, Illinois, was the site for a proposed march by neo-Nazis in 1977. Skokie refused them a march permit, and, after prolonged legal battles extending to the Supreme Court, the Nazis won their right to march. They decided, however, to hold their march elsewhere.

Judicial review. The authority of the Supreme Court to hold federal statutes and presidential acts unconstitutional. See further the introduction to this book.

Jurisdiction. The authority of courts to hear and decide certain categories of cases.

Marbury **v.** *Madison* (1803). The historic case in which the Supreme Court first declared that it has the power of judicial review. See **judicial review.**

Norris-LaGuardia Act. A law, passed in 1932, that sharply restricts the power of courts to issue injunctions in labor disputes. Before the act was passed, employers were able to break strikes by getting courts to issue injunctions against them.

Precedent.   Literally, "that which preceded." In Anglo-American law, the fact that a statute or court ruling is not novel but has occurred in the past and has stood the test of time lends weight to it.

Prior restraint. Stopping something before it happens. In American law, prior restraint of speech is almost always struck down by the courts. See Chapter 8 and its glossary entry **TRO.**

Chapter 10
Right to Live, Right to Die

"I will neither give a deadly drug to anybody if asked for it, nor will I make a suggestion to this effect. Similarly, I will not give to a woman an abortive remedy."

HIPPOCRATIC OATH

"Our biggest problem in medicine is not to shorten life; our biggest problem is that we over-treat; we prolong too much."

MILTON D. HEIFETZ, M.D.

THE CONTROVERSY

Every year since 1973, when the Supreme Court legalized abortion, about 1.6 million abortions have been performed in America. The context in which these statistics are viewed depends partly on what we think of the right to abortion. For many, the context is a bright one, suggesting that a new climate of freedom exists in America, one which has finally accorded legal recognition of the right of women to control their bodies. For others, the context is a dark nightmare, permitting a Holocaust of the un-born, the mass killing of defenseless human beings. The conflict between the partisans of these views is bitter and uncompromising. It may be that compromise is impossible, for the quarrel seems to grow out of radically different views of human life and death, human rights and responsibilities, human autonomy and human dignity.

The issues, and the bitterness that goes with them, have spilled into other areas. Again, we can start with the facts. In hospitals and nursing homes all over America, there are terminally ill patients, patients hooked up to respirators, patients near death and in great pain, hopelessly senile and comatose patients. Others, including newborn infants, may live or die depending upon whether operations are performed. Some of these patients are able to make choices, others are not. Most of them have families who love and care for them, who respect their dignity, and are tormented by their pain. In all of these cases, choices have to be made; even choosing to do nothing is a choice. In many cases the choices are forced upon us by technology. In-dividuals who would have died quickly a century ago can now be kept alive for in-definite periods by sophisticated machines. But "alive" in what sense? And what does "alive" mean?

THE ISSUES

In all the cases just mentioned, from abortion to shutting off the respirator of a brain-dead patient, the choices are agonizing. The issues they involve are partly political and legal, but they also have moral, psychological, and even metaphysical dimensions. When does human life begin? When does it end? What are the true signs of such life? Is it possible to be alive, but not in a human sense? Do we ever have the right deliberately to end the life of an innocent person? Is "personhood" defined biologically or in some other sense? Do we have the obligation to keep people alive against their wishes? In considering these questions, what weight should be given to the wishes of the patient, or to those of a pregnant woman? How should the wishes of the family be weighed? What about friends and spiritual counselors? Should the right to end one's life be recognized by statute? Should it continue to be forbidden by statute? Panelists representing a wide range of viewpoints on these issues grapple with them in *Right to Live, Right to Die.*

The Video Discussion

Instead of attempting to summarize the entire discussion at once, it is better to do it part by part. There are really three separate debates, with participants sometimes arguing and sometimes agreeing, depending on the issue. The three issues, nevertheless, are clearly bracketed by the philosophical questions raised above: the questions of life, including "meaningful" life, and death. The three specific parts of the program are, first, the right to die; second, the right to an abortion; third, the issues raised by the "Baby Doe" case involving a retarded infant who died for want of an operation that would have allowed him to swallow.

List of Participants

RABBI J. DAVID BLEICH, PH.D.
Herbert Tenzer Professor of
Jewish Law and Ethics
Yeshiva University

PHIL DONAHUE
Host
Donahue
Multi-Media Broadcasting Co.

HON. JOSEPH A. CALIFANO, JR.
Attorney
Dewey, Ballantine, Bushby, Palmer
& Wood
Former Secretary of Health,
Education and Welfare

REV. ROBERT F. DRINAN, S.J.
Professor of Law
Georgetown University Law Centre
President
Americans for Democratic Action
Former U.S. Representative
Massachusetts

HON. BARNEY FRANK
U.S. Representative
Massachusetts

WILLARD GAYLIN, M.D.
President
The Hastings Center

MEG GREENFIELD
Editorial Page Editor
The Washington Post

MILTON D. HEIFETZ, M.D.
Chairman
Department of Neurological Surgery
Cedars-Sinai Medical Center
Professor of Neurology
University of Southern California

JAMES HOGE
Then Publisher
Sun-Times (Chicago)
Currently Publisher
The Daily News (New York)

HON. HENRY J. HYDE
U.S. Representative
Illinois

MILDRED FAY JEFFERSON, M.D.
Assistant Clinical Professor of Surgery
Boston University Medical School
President
Right to Life Crusade, Inc.

HON. NANCY LANDON KASSEBAUM
U.S. Senator
Kansas

HON. JOAN DEMPSEY KLEIN
Presiding Justice
California Court of Appeal

HON. CAROL LOS MANSMANN
Judge
U.S. District Court
Western District of Pennsylvania

HON. ABNER J. MIKVA
Judge
U.S. Court of Appeals
D.C. Circuit
Former U.S. Representative
Illinois

HON. ALAN K. SIMPSON
U.S. Senator
Wyoming

GLORIA STEINEM
Publisher
Ms. Magazine

HON. POTTER STEWART
Justice (retired)
U.S. Supreme Court

THOMAS P. STODDARD
Legislative Director
New York Civil Liberties Union

I: THE RIGHT TO DIE

Suicide. The word is too brutal, too direct. It sounds harsh. Its meaning is also harsh: "self-killing." The popularity of classical studies in the nineteenth century helped inspire a softer word for it: "euthanasia." The meaning is even softer. It comes from ancient Greek and it means "happy death." By the 1930s, the word had become popular in "progressive" circles. But the word soon was found to have a problem. It is ambiguous. Happy death for whom? "Suicide" was harsh but clear: killing *oneself*. But "happy death" could imply that one might also wish to visit it upon *others*. (Happiness is normally thought of as something that is spread around.) Within a decade these logical possibilities became historical facts. The Nazis began a widespread "euthanasia" program for the "feebleminded" and the "incurably ill." Though the Nazis insisted that the "happy death" was indeed happy, for it was brought about by painless gassing, a public outcry ensued. The euthanasia program was halted, at least until the 1940s, when the gas was used on Jews and other groups.

Because of these historical associations of the term, hardly anyone today advocates euthanasia. Increasing numbers, however, have been joining groups advocating "self-deliverance." These groups, with names like Exit and Hemlock, promote the ending of one's life when the prospect of indefinite pain and hopelessness makes life unbearable. "We are all going to die, and a few of us are going to die badly," said Derek Humphrey, Hemlock's founder, in 1983. In his view, people should be given the right to die painlessly, and by their own hand.

At this time there is no "right to die" recognized by American law. In most states suicide is illegal, though obviously such laws are difficult to enforce. What about giving people advice on how to commit suicide? In 1980, the English group Exit announced plans to publish a how-to book on the subject. The group was promptly served notice by British authorities that its leaders would go to jail if the book appeared. After complaining that this could only mean "tragedy and continued distress and personal suffering" for thousands of sick people, the group abandoned its plans. But a few days after the English group's retreat, Hemlock, its American counterpart, announced that it would publish a similar, if less clinically detailed, manual on suicide. The leaders of the California-based group were undaunted by the section of the California legal code which, like the British law, makes it a crime to aid or abet a suicide. Hemlock's director observed that "the law is there in America, but it hasn't been applied." If it were, it would make an interesting freedom of press case, which the state would probably lose.

What if an individual "aids and abets" a suicide in a more active way, say by shooting or giving an overdose? In most cases American courts, at least in recent years, have mixed condemnation of the crime with lenience toward the criminal. Applying existing state laws, judges and juries have found defendants guilty of homicide but have suspended the sentences, sentenced them to weekend service in hospitals or nursing homes, or otherwise tempered justice with mercy. An editorial in the *New York Times* probably summed up the feelings of many jurors and legal professionals when it commented on the case of an elderly Texan who shot his brother, a man whose brain had been destroyed by Alzheimer's disease and who was being fed through tubes. "One does not wish for the old man's punishment, only for that pause in which society, in the form of a judge and jury, acknowledges the value of a life."

The Slippery Slope

At this point in our history the *Times* editorial probably expresses a widely shared viewpoint: we should have compassion for a tormented mercy killer while still condemning his act as homicide. But the ground is shifting under this consensus. Technology is shaking it. In increasing numbers of cases, the "mercy killer" is not someone who puts a gun to the head of a sick person. It is someone who removes tubes, or withdraws medication, or pulls the plug of a respirator. "Mercy killer" is put in quotation marks because the real issue in these cases is whether it is a case of "killing" or "letting die." The two are different—or are they?

Lest anyone think that this is a debate which neatly divides people according to whether they are "traditionalists" and "modernists," it should be noted that the most traditional institution in the world, the Catholic Church, has taken a stand on death and dying that many modernists, even "secular humanists," might agree with. In 1980, the Vatican issued a set of guidelines ("Declaration on Euthanasia") which, while condemning "mercy killing," stated that under certain circumstances life-support technology may be discontinued. "It is permitted," it said, "with the patient's consent, to interrupt these means where the result falls short of expectation." The "reasonable wishes" of the patient's family as well as those of the patient had to be considered, and doctors may conclude that "the investment in instruments and personnel is disproportionate to the results foreseen."

The Quinlan Case

These guidelines seemed to fit the case of Karen Anne Quinlan, decided by the Superior Court of New Jersey five years earlier (one cleric speculated that they might have been drawn up to quiet the debate among Catholics over her case). After mixing drugs with alcohol, the twenty-one-year-old woman lapsed into what her doctors said was an irreversible coma. Her breathing was assisted by a respirator and she was fed through intravenous tubes. She appeared to be in a vegetative state, curled up in a fetal position, unresponsive to stimuli. The question was whether her parents had a right to order the hospital to shut off the respirator. New Jersey's highest court, holding that the respirator amounted to extraordinary means of keeping a person alive, and taking note of her apparently irreversible loss of significant brain activity, ruled that the machine could be shut off. It was—and Karen Quinlan kept breathing. At this writing she still is breathing and is still being fed through tubes.

Claire Conroy's Feeding Tubes

Very well, suppose we move further along the slippery slope and remove her feeding tubes. That did not happen in the Quinlan case, but eight years later, again in New Jersey, a state judge issued an order that would have allowed the death of Claire Conroy, a senile, terminally ill patient, by the removal of such tubes. It was the first instance of its kind in the United States, but the Quinlan case was cited as a precedent. As in the Quinlan case, the judge said, "Most of us would agree that when a person has been permanently reduced to a very primitive intellectual level or is permanently suffering from unbearable or unrelievable pain there is no valid human purpose to be served by employing active treatment to prolong life." But what is "active" treatment? A respirator differs from feeding tubes in two respects. First, a respirator, a product of more recent technological advances, intimately intervenes in bodily functions: it "breathes" for the patient. Feeding tubes allow nutrients to enter the veins, but the body does the rest of the work. Second, disconnecting a respirator may or may not result in the patient's death (it did not in the Quinlan case), but removing a feeding tube will without fail kill the patient—and it will be a painful death by starvation and dehydration. To disconnect someone's feeding tubes is the same as depriving the person of food and water. On the basis of these distinctions, a court-appointed lawyer for the patient appealed the judge's order to a three-judge panel of the Appellate Division of the New Jersey State Superior Court. On the other side of the issue, a lawyer for the New Jersey Hospital Association called the distinctions between a respirator and feeding tubes "artificial."

While the arguments were being advanced, the higher court stayed the order of the original judge. The feeding tubes remained but the patient died anyway, apparently of natural causes. Both sides, however, appealed in order to get a judgment on the principles in the case. The appeals panel reversed the judge's order, insisting that the removal of feeding tubes would have amounted to deliberate failure to feed the patient. During the oral arguments, one judge in particular was horrified by the Hospital Association's position. She described the removal of feeding tubes as "less humane" than the lethal injection of drugs under the recently enacted New Jersey capital punishment law. Sarcastically, she suggested that "since it was winter at the time, the window in Miss Conroy's room could have been opened so that she could die quicker and less painfully by exposure."

Today's *reductio ad absurdum* becomes tomorrow's "option." The principles of "self-deliverance" may be broad enough to encompass the deliverance of others who no longer have control of their faculties. If pain, not killing, is the ultimate evil, and if Claire Conroy's seemingly vegetative existence causes unbearable pain to her relatives, it follows that the lower court judge's order was provisionally correct. But only provisionally. If the appeals court judge was right that letting someone die from starvation and dehydration is more inhumane than giving the person a lethal injection, then the remarks about leaving the window open in winter need not be taken ironically. Perhaps such an "active" measure should be employed to end the sufferings of Claire Conroy. An even quicker, more certain, and guaranteed-painless method would be a lethal injection. We move further along the slippery slope.

It is hard to say what principle or distinction will halt the slide. All we can do is note the topography. At the bottom is homicide and at the top is the most life-giving attitude toward the sick and the handicapped. It could be drawn like this:

1. Disconnecting respirator of (a) hopelessly comatose
patient who has left a will (orally or in writing) saying
he would not like to live like that.

   2. Disconnecting respirator of (b) hopelessly comatose patient
who has left no such will, but whose family says she should
not live like that.

      3. Removing feeding tubes of (a) above.

         4. Removing feeding tubes of (b) above.

     5. Killing (a).

      6. Killing (b).

       7. Killing terminally ill person who begs for death.

        8. Killing a conscious person against his or her express will.

The list is far from perfect. It could easily be argued that items 6 and 7 should be reversed. A number of intermediate levels might be added. Nevertheless, its point ought to be clear: we are dealing here in stages separated from one another by short distances. In each successive stage downward, the distinctions so important to the stage above seem "artificial," almost metaphysical. Yet at the top practically everyone, even the Pope, finds the practice acceptable, and at the bottom everyone sees a homicide being committed. It is somewhere between levels 2 and 7 that the consensus falls apart. This is the stretch that the moderator, Harvard Law Professor Arthur Miller, explores in the video discussion.

Video Discussion of the "Right to Die"

It seems that eighteen-year-old Bobby Joe Parker, returning from church services on his motorcycle, has met with an accident. He comes into the hospital semiconscious. He needs blood. But his religion, to which he is deeply devoted, forbids blood transfusions, and he has indicated that he subscribes to this article of belief. Apparently, all this is known to the hospital staff. His family cannot be reached for awhile, yet he needs the transfusion immediately or he will die. Since all the doctors on the panel would give him the transfusion, the moderator keeps changing the circumstances to get some disagreement. Suppose he is conscious and refuses the transfusion. Suppose he is not eighteen but forty-five. Suppose his wife is contacted and she agrees with Bobby Joe's position. Suppose the other members of his family also agree that he should not be transfused. The judges are brought into the argument. Is there a "right to privacy" of the patient that overrides the need to preserve his life? Their views differ. The moderator now changes the situation. Bobby Joe's condition has worsened. He has slipped into an irreversible coma and has suffered sustained brain damage. Do you put him on a respirator? Dr. Gaylin wants to talk with the family, so the moderator creates a family by recruiting several members of the panel. They are asked for their votes, as is the "spiritual adviser," a role assigned to talk-show host Phil Donahue. The arguments turn upon the accuracy of the prognosis for the patient, his youth, and the relative weight of family members' preferences.

Again, the moderator changes the facts. This time Bobby Joe is conscious and competent but terminally ill and in great pain. He wants his doctor's help in putting an end to his life. All the doctors resist outright aiding and abetting suicide, though two of them would be prepared to give enough pain-killing medication to drastically shorten his life; these two also suggest that the only factor keeping them from fully acceding to Bobby Joe's wishes is the threat of legal sanctions. The moderator then turns to the lawmakers. Would they sponsor a law that would permit physicians to aid and abet suicide under certain circumstances? Congressmen Barney Frank and Henry Hyde sharply disagree.

"Now, Dr. Gaylin," the moderator says, "I'm bringing Bobby Joe to you one last time. This time, he's a quadriplegic." He is not terminal but life to him has become meaningless. He wants to die. Will you help him? At first Dr. Gaylin resists. Bobby Joe should think it over. Years go by, and he still wants to die. Dr. Gaylin wonders why Bobby Joe can't kill himself without getting him involved. Meantime, the moderator brings in Meg Greenfield of the *Washington Post* and James Hoge, publisher of the Chicago *Sun-Times*. Both would refuse to help Bobby Joe kill himself. Then Dr. Gaylin seems to reconsider his earlier reluctance to help him commit suicide. "I do respect his autonomy, even to the point of taking his life."

Analysis

This first and longest section of the program is the most perplexing. It is in this section that we hear what Fred Friendly calls "agony gasps," expressions revealing that the panelists are struggling more with themselves than with each other. This kind of internal self-struggle is well expressed by Judge Klein in her response to the moderator's question whether she would order Bobby Joe transfused against his wishes. After a long Hamlet-like rumination about Bobby Joe's putative "right to privacy" versus the duty to preserve life, all she can conclude is "it's a toughie."

It is indeed. But perhaps more light can be shed on the tangle of dilemmas if we consider some of the factors Judge Klein and the other participants think are important. Four considerations emerge: Bobby Joe's wishes, his age, his religion, and his family's wishes.

1. *Bobby Joe's Wishes.* This may be the weightiest consideration. Legally, Bobby Joe is an adult (though just barely). In America and throughout the Western world, we assign great importance to the wishes of consenting adults in matters that concern only them. This is particularly true in matters of medical procedure. Before operations can be performed, written consent must be obtained. A blood transfusion is, like an operation, an intrusive procedure. Our bodies are, in a sense, our private property. If we have a right to privacy in our homes, don't we have that right in our ultimate worldly home, our body? Gloria Steinem probably speaks for most Americans, even those who disagree with her on issues like abortion, when she contends that "the power of the state should stop, if at all possible, with our skins." Judge Klein mentioned Bobby Joe's "right to privacy" and talked about the origin of that right in "the First and the Fourth and the Fifth and the Fourteenth and the Ninth [Amendments], and it's around there somewhere like a penumbra." Laughter follows these remarks, but it is doubtful that many know what Judge Klein is talking about. Judge Mansmann does, though, for she also mentions the constitutional justification for "privacy" rights. We'll begin discussing the claim to a constitutional "right to privacy" when we get to the case of *Griswold* v. *Connecticut* (1965) later in this chapter.

2. *Bobby Joe's Age.* Balanced against Bobby Joe's wishes is his age. Legally he is an adult, but he is only eighteen. Drs. Gaylin and Heifetz state that they would not even think twice if Bobby Joe were forty-five or eighty-two; they would honor his

wish not to be transfused and let him die without further thought. The judges agree. The age factor is important to the doctors and judges for three reasons. First, Bobby Joe may not be very mature. He may not really be capable of making a wise decision concerning his future. His commitment to his religion may be shallow, and his willingness to let himself die may be an impetuous impulse instead of a settled conviction. Second, his prognosis may be good. Young people's bodies have great regenerative powers. This fact becomes particularly important when moderator Miller changes the hypothetical in order to put Bobby Joe in an "irreversible" coma, or to make him terminally ill or paralyzed. Doctors cannot always be certain about terms like "terminal" and "irreversible" when it come to the enormous strength in a young person's biological system. The third implication of Bobby Joe's youth is the future that stretches in front of him. Someone sixty-five years old has already lived a long life. Whether he dies now or five years from now—when the acutarial tables say that he will die—is of little consequence compared to the fifty-two years that lie ahead of Bobby Joe.

3. *Bobby Joe's Religion.* This has some importance, but not much, in the minds of the judges and doctors. The First Amendment protects the free exercise of religion, and Dr. Heifetz reminds the moderator that there are precedents in which judges have agreed with patients who were Jehovah's Witnesses that they have the right to forego transfusions. But the doctor is also aware of other Jehovah's Witness precedents involving not an adult but children of believers whom the parents did not want to be treated. In such cases courts have ordered treatment despite the religious objection of the parents. (Indeed, not long after this discussion took place, a court ordered chemotherapy for the child of parents who had refused to provide for it because of religious scruples.) The difference is that in the first type of case the adult is making a decision that concerns his or her own life, while in the second an adult is making a decision affecting someone else. This question of one's own life as opposed to someone else's turns out to be what is controlling. Religion really has little to do with the participants' view of the matter.

4. *Bobby Joe's Family.* "No man is an island," said John Donne, and the wisdom of his observation exposes the critical weakness of the dichotomy between "self-regarding" and "other-regarding" actions. Under the terms of this dichotomy, one can do what one pleases with oneself—get drunk, take drugs, have affairs, commit suicide—as long as it does not adversely affect others. It is a neat distinction, but it loses force once we begin asking what *is* merely "self-regarding." If a married man has an affair, does it concern only himself? If a father gets drunk every night, what happens to his children? And so with Bobby Joe: the question of whether he lives or dies is not purely "self-regarding." Moderator Miller assembles a "family" from members of the panel and asks them whether the plug should be pulled on the respirator. But this particular family seems to be composed of mainly those for whom self-autonomy is the highest value. Only Rabbi Bleich, who plays the father, places supreme importance on the value of life itself, for he would not have Bobby Joe taken off the respirator even if his son had earlier said that he would not want to live in such a state. All the others assume that Bobby Joe would want to be taken off, and vote accordingly. And all the doctors except Dr. Jefferson, a prominent "pro-life" leader, would go along with the

majority vote. (Dr. Heifetz would give a temporary veto to Rabbi Bleich but would eventually turn off the machine if he could not persuade him to go along.) In this case, the family turns into an extension of Bobby Joe. The question is not so much "What is good for Bobby Joe?" as it is "What Bobby Joe would want for himself?"

None of these answers and attempts at answers help us get a firm foothold on the slippery slope, but they provide some hints of where the participants would dig in their heels. Human autonomy and individual choice seem to loom large in the minds of most of the panelists. With the exception of Rabbi Bleich and Dr. Jefferson, all are ready to respect Bobby Joe's desire to be taken off the respirator. (Former HEW Secretary Califano is ambiguous on this question. He would take Rabbi Bleich's legal case, but it is not clear whether he shares his view.) But once we come to more "active" means of ending a patient's life, everyone pulls back. Even Dr. Heifetz, who along with Dr. Gaylin, seems very sympathetic to the philosophy of "self-deliverance," only hints that he would shorten the patient's life by loading him with pain-killing drugs. Nobody is ready to give Bobby Joe a lethal injection or a bullet in the head, though Dr. Gaylin would instruct Bobby Joe's wife on how to kill him "if I'd get away with it." This is not an ethical objection but a prudent concern about staying out of jail. .

Right-to-Die Legislation

The last point raises the question of whether there ought to be a law allowing doctors to aid and abet suicide under certain circumstances, as in the case of a terminally ill individual in great pain. This question is directed to the two congressmen, Barney Frank and Henry Hyde, and the former congressman, Robert Drinan, who is also a Jesuit priest. At first it appears that Father Drinan and Henry Hyde agree ("first time in my life, I think," Hyde says), for both would oppose such legislation. Hyde, a leader of the antiabortion movement, is the author of the "Hyde amendment," which prohibits federal funding of abortions. His attitude toward right-to-die legislation is that it would make doctors immune to prosecution under the homicide law. Drinan's attitude is really quite different. He starts off talking in traditional and religious terms: "From my point of view . . . people are never vegetables," and ending a human life "is God's right alone." But a careful ear to Drinan's words will reveal that he sees nothing wrong, at least from a legal standpoint, in Dr. Gaylin's decision to give Bobby Joe a lethal injection. He just does not want to get Congress involved. "I'm not certain that we should be in this business." However, if the physicians themselves "want to make a code and get that adopted at the local level, I think that might be acceptable."

Congressman Barney Frank has already told the moderator that he would support legislation of the kind described, so he disagrees with Henry Hyde. "Well, Henry, you said a right to life. A right belongs to someone; whose right is it, the right to life?" It is true that no one has a right to kill a handicapped person. "But if I am a desperately ill person in terrible pain, you say there is a right to life; if it isn't my right, who else has got a right to my life?" Hyde starts to answer, "As a practical matter . . . ," but Frank interrupts: "The insurance company?" The laughter that follows this crack drowns Hyde out, but he is able to say that "no one can stop you from committing suicide. As a practical matter, if you want to commit suicide, you know how to do it. . . ." Frank interrupts him: "Would you change the law?" Hyde goes on trying to finish: ". . . but I refuse to assign legal legitimacy to that and say you have. . . ." Another interjection from Frank: "Why?" Hyde finally finishes the sentence: ". . . a right to take any life, even your own." But what have you accomplished, Frank asks, by putting such a law on the books? Hyde replies: "I have not legitimated the act of killing. That's what I've accomplished."

Something has gotten turned around. Originally, it was Frank, not Hyde, who wanted a new law on the books, one that would have allowed doctors to kill terminally ill patients who request death. Hyde was opposed to such a law. But in the heat of the debate, Frank somehow maneuvered Hyde into sponsoring a law against this practice and then was able to question its usefulness. The burden of proof got reversed. Let us restore the original order. Frank wants a law that would allow the practice. Hyde opposes it for two reasons: first, he does not want to legitimize "the act of killing," second, he believes in a "right to life." The first of these reasons is rooted in the heritage of Judeo-Christian morality. The second reason, based upon individual rights, is of more recent vintage. This criterion, as Frank shows, is more vulnerable. For "rights" tend to be associated with individual wants and preferences. What if someone wants to die? How can we speak of his "right" to live if he doesn't want to? Hyde would have been better off developing the first reason, the one based on traditional Western morality. To speak of "rights" gets into the area of the "right of privacy," which is really the cutting edge of Barney Frank's argument. To some extent the argument seems to be accepted by the judges on the panel. If Bobby Joe wants to die at the age of eighteen, it may be necessary to respect his "right of privacy."

Where does this right come from? It is found nowhere in the Constitution, at least not in so many words. But perhaps it is implied. The Fifth Amendment protects our right not to incriminate ourselves. The Fourth Amendment protects us against unreasonable searches and seizures. The First Amendment protects our religious beliefs. What all of these areas have in common is that they border on the intimate. The Constitution does not let the government break into our homes without proper warrants, or inquire into our religious practices, or force confessions from us. Don't all these protections add up to an implied protection of our privacy rights? True, "privacy" is not explicitly mentioned in any of the amendments, but the Ninth Amendment says, "The enumeration in the Constitution, of certain rights shall not be construed to deny or disparage others retained by the people." In other words, just because a right is not mentioned doesn't mean it isn't there. You have a right to play tennis even though it isn't mentioned in the Constitution. If you have that right, how much more obviously do you have the right to personal privacy! Judges Mansmann and Klein both allude to this "right" in connection with Bobby Joe's wish not to be transfused, though they both do it reluctantly, for they want to save him in spite of his wish. In Judge Klein's Hamlet-like debate with herself, one side of her says, "Well, it (the right of privacy) is one of those emanations coming from the First and the Fourth and the Fifth and the Fourteenth and the Ninth, and it's around there like a penumbra." Emanations? Penumbra? What is all this supposed to mean? The only way to answer is to explore the case of *Griswold* v. *Connecticut* (1965).

Griswold v. *Connecticut*: **The Right of Privacy**

In the late nineteenth century a particularly draconian law was added to the books in Connecticut. It banned not the sale or manufacture of contraceptives but their *use*. In theory it might have sanctioned police searches of people's bedrooms for evidence of contraceptives. In practice, of course, this never happened. Griswold was convicted under the statute as an accessory after he gave advice to married couples on contraceptive use. There are few people today who would consider the statute a good one. The question is whether the statute violated the Constitution. The Court was convinced that it did, though it refused to become specific about what clause of the Bill of Rights it violated. The Fourth Amendment protects against "unreasonable searches and seizures," but there was no search and seizure in this case. The Fifth Amendment protects against self-incrimination, but nobody was forced to confess in this case. So the Court relied on "penumbras" and "emanations."

The specific guarantees in the Bill of Rights "have penumbras, formed by emanations from those guarantees that help give them life and substance." The word "penumbra" is derived from Latin and means, literally, "almost shade." In painting, it means the boundary of shade and light, where one blends with the other. An "emanation," according to the dictionary, is "that which issues, flows, or proceeds from any source, substance, or body." What we have, then, are some rather shadowy and indistinct somethings that flow out of the various clauses of the Bill of Rights. They are not the clauses themselves but emanations of the clauses. In the present case we have what the Court called a "zone of privacy" created by various amendments. The Ninth Amendment hints at its existence when it says that the enumeration of specific rights does not preclude the existence of other rights not enumerated. As for the substance of this "zone," it grows out of the right of privacy implicit in the First, Fourth, and Fifth Amendments but it is older than any of them—indeed, "older than our political parties, older than our school system." It is the privacy of the conjugal bond which guards "the sacred precincts of marital bedrooms" against state interference.

This talk of shadows and emanations was too much for Justice Hugo Black. He dissented on the ground that the Court had been unable to cite any single constitutional clause that the Connecticut statute violated. As already noted in Chapter 4, Justice Black was a black-and-white man. He read his Constitution the way a fundamentalist reads the Bible. If the Bible says Jonah was swallowed by a great fish, he was swallowed by a great fish. If the Constitution says "Congress shall make no law" abridging free speech, that means *no* law, not "some laws" or "certain kinds of laws." The Fourth Amendment protects against "unreasonable searches and seizures." For Black the words were simple and clear. They contained no emanations, halos, shadows, or electron flows. They did not add up to a generalized "right of privacy." Without such a specific guarantee, written down in the Constitution, the Court may deplore Connecticut's birth control law but it may not strike it down. "I like my privacy as well as the next one, but I am nevertheless compelled to admit that government has a right to invade it unless prohibited by some specific constitutional provision."

For those who might charge Black with holding a narrow, crabbed view of the Bill of Rights, he had a ready answer: on the contrary, reducing "unreasonable searches and seizures" to "right of privacy" is a narrowing of the Bill of Rights. What if the police searched someone *in public* but conducted the search improperly? If all the Fourth Amendment means is "privacy," then the police could claim that their search, being public and open, was perfectly constitutional.

But if the "privacy" interpretation was "niggardly" in its scope, it was also, Black said, too broad. Black suggested that it had an accordionlike quality. It could be squeezed into a narrow compass and opened out into a very broad one, depending on the mood of five or more Supreme Court justices.

Seven years after the *Griswold* decision, the Supreme Court opened the accordion to lengths that few could have anticipated in 1965. It expanded the "right of privacy" to include the right of women to obtain abortions virtually on demand during the first six months of pregnancy.

Before turning to the issue of abortion, it may be useful to review some of the points made in this section.

Points to Remember

1. The "right to die" is a continuum, a slippery slope. At the one end, even the most socially conservative institution, the Catholic Church, recognizes that we do not have to use all kinds of technological gadgets to keep people alive if they want to die. At the other end, even doctors committed to "self-deliverance" would not put to death a conscious person who wanted to remain alive. The difficulty comes in trying to draw lines along this continuum.
2. The participants in the program draw lines in different ways, but all of them seem ready to consider these factors: Bobby Joe's wishes, his age, his religion, and his family. His wishes seem to be paramount, though the panelists tend to balance them against his age.
3. Out in the real world, courts have approved the unplugging of respirators in certain cases; the most prominent case was that of Karen Quinlan, who still lives. In another case a lower court approved the removal of feeding tubes, though that decision was reversed on appeal.
4. At least two of the judges on the panel lean toward the view that a "right to die" may be included among the rights of "privacy" in the Constitution.
5. The "right of privacy" is nowhere mentioned in the Constitution. However, in the *Griswold* case of 1965, the Court held that it is a "penumbra," formed by "emanations" from the First, Fourth, Fifth, and Ninth Amendments, and applied to the states through the due process clause of the Fourteenth Amendment.

II: ABORTION

As a national controversy, the abortion issue has its origin in *Roe* v. *Wade*, a Supreme Court decision of 1973. Roe (a pseudonym) was blocked by the laws of Texas from obtaining an abortion. Texas law prohibited abortion except to save the life of the mother. Citing the *Griswold* case as a precedent, she appealed to the Supreme Court, charging that the Texas statute was an unconstitutional abridgment of her "right of privacy." By a margin of seven to two, the Court agreed.

The above is a bare-bones statement of this important and controversial decision. What is far more interesting is the flesh of it—a fifty-page opinion by Justice Harry Blackmun.

Roe v. *Wade*: Abortion by Trimesters

Much of Justice Blackmun's opinion was spent in anticipating and replying to the charge that the Court's decision amounted to a fundamental reversal of Western moral tradition. Actually, he said, the laws against abortion in most states are of rather recent origin, dating from the 1820s to the 1890s. The movement to enact these laws was largely composed of doctors and medical associations, and it was based upon the conviction that human life begins with fertilization. But in the long history of the West, the question of when life begins has been a matter of dispute and conjecture. "Ancient religion," Blackmun said, "did not bar abortion," and the Hippocratic oath, which prohibits the prescription of an "abortive remedy," appears to have been subscribed to only by certain sectors of the ancient medical community. Even in the Catholic Middle Ages, theologians could find no agreement on when human life begins. Instead of extending it back to the period of fertilization, they tended to fix its origin somewhere in the period of "quickening," when the fetus begins to move in the uterus, which might be anywhere from forty to eighty days.

It is not immediately obvious why Blackmun delved so extensively into Western history. "So what?" the reader might ask. The medieval thinkers believed many things that were exploded by nineteenth-century science. Because the two eras differed on when human life begins in the womb, does that mean that neither side was correct? But what Blackmun seemed to be saying is that the question of when human life begins is not, properly speaking, a scientific question; it is a philosophical and even theological one. His decision, therefore, was not breaking any new ground in this matter but restoring the sense of uncertainty that prevailed before the nineteenth century. Where uncertainty exists, the state has no right to make laws pretending to certainty. There can be no certainty about when life begins because conception "is a 'process' over time, rather than an event." But Blackmun went on to mark certain critical points in the process. He rejected the view that the state has no interest in a woman's decision whether or not to have an abortion. The state "does have an important and legitimate interest in preserving and protecting the health of the pregnant woman" and it has "still *another* important and legitimate interest in protecting the potentiality of human life" (emphasis Blackmun's). These two interests, the health of the mother and the potential of human life in the fetus, become important during different stages of the pregnancy.

The average period of gestation in human beings is nine months. A pregnancy consists of three "trimesters," or three-month periods. Blackmun asserted that the state's interest increases as the pregnancy progresses. During the first three months (first trimester), the state has no compelling interests. As regards this period, therefore, it may not enact any regulations concerning a woman's right to an abortion. She can get an abortion by any means and in any place she pleases. The state *may* enact abortion regulations affecting the second three months or trimester, but *only* to protect the health of the pregnant woman. The state still has no compelling interest in the life of the fetus. Only with regard to the last trimester may the state enact regulations to protect "potential life." The state, then, may forbid abortions during that last three months. Even then, however, the state may not ban abortions if such a ban would endanger the health of the mother. And "health" is defined broadly enough to encompass not only physical but emotional health.

Blackmun's opinion is puzzling. He said that "we need not resolve the difficult question of when life begins"—and then went on to resolve it. He said that human conception is a "process" rather than an "event," and then went on to speak of a "compelling point" in the process, which sounds like an "event." Whatever we call it, an "event," a "point," a moment when "life begins," Blackmun identified it as the time when "viability" begins. What is "viability"? It means "capability of meaningful life outside the mother's womb." What does that mean? Presumably, it means that if you take the baby out of the womb, it will live on its own. But there is ambiguity in that notion of viability. In a certain sense no newborn baby is viable. It cannot forage for food or protect itself against the cold. Premature babies need even more elaborate support in order to live. They are not viable on their own, yet we all recognize the state's compelling interest in keeping them alive. Some babies, of course, are so premature that they barely cling to life even in incubators, and in that sense they are hardly viable at all. But we are reluctant to say that these already-born babies lose their humanity by their fragility; instead, we try to save them and rejoice when we succeed.

How, then, do we really know the point of "viability" of the fetus when it is still in the uterus? "[I]n the light of present medical knowledge, [it] is at approximately the end of the second trimester." But this is almost an arbitrary figure. In the first place, Mother Nature has only limited respect for human numbering systems. Some normal pregnancies extend beyond nine months; others are shorter. Very seldom are they neatly divisible into three trimesters. That is probably one reason why some second-trimester abortions have resulted in live births. Second, what if medical science is able to push back the date when a prematurely born infant can be saved? Is the Court ready to adjust its "viability" point accordingly? If a five-month fetus can be kept alive just as easily as we now keep alive seven-month fetuses, is the fetus entitled to state protection? Or has the Court tied its concept of "viability" to the medical science of 1973? The Court has not yet had to face this question, but Justice Sandra Day O'Connor raised it in her dissenting opinion in *City of Akron* v. *Akron Center for Reproductive Health* (1983).

The *Akron* Case: Invalidating Abortion Regulations

What will probably be known as the *Akron* case was really five cases, all decided on the same day in 1983. The city of Akron sued the Akron Center for Reproductive

Health, and the center countersued. These two cases were consolidated by the Supreme Court. The Planned Parenthood Association sued the attorney general of Missouri, and he countersued. These two were also consolidated (*Planned Parenthood* v.
Ashcroft). Chris Simopoulos, an abortionist practicing in Virginia, sued the state of
Virginia for prosecuting him under its abortion regulations (*Simopoulos* v. *Virginia*).
Since the *Akron* case was the most important—in the sense that it tested some of the
most comprehensive abortion regulations since the *Roe* decision—we shall focus on it.

In 1978, the city council of Akron, Ohio, enacted an ordinance containing a
series of regulations on abortion. The regulations, it was claimed, were carefully drafted
so as not to conflict with the *Roe* v. *Wade* decision five years earlier. Indeed, some of
the regulations seemed to take their cue from remarks of Justice Blackmun in the *Roe*
case. Blackmun had said that the right to abortion "is not absolute and is subject to
some limitation; and that at some point the state interests as to the protection of
health, medical standards, and prenatal life, become dominant." He had also said that
during the second trimester "a State may regulate the abortion procedure to the extent
that the regulation reasonably relates to the preservation and protection of maternal
health." He cited as an example of such permissible state regulations the specification
"as to the facilities in which the procedure is to be performed, that is, whether it must
be in a hospital or may be in a clinic or some other place of less-than-hospital status."

Akron, then, considered itself within the *Roe* guidelines by its abortion regulations, which required (1) all second-trimester abortions to be performed in hospitals;
(2) either parental consent for abortions performed on girls below the age of fifteen or
else written consent of the girl plus a court order; (3) that no abortion could be performed until a series of statements were read to the patient concerning the abortion
procedure, including the statement that "the unborn child is a human life from the
moment of conception" and that "abortion is a major surgical procedure, which can
result in serious complications"; (4) a twenty-four-hour waiting period between the
time the woman signs the consent form and the time of the abortion; and (5) that the
fetal remains be "disposed of in a humane and sanitary manner." The Court struck
down all of these regulations.

In holding Akron's abortion regulations unconstitutional, the Court was for the
most part affirming a decision made by a lower federal court, a court of appeals. Regulations 2 through 5 were voided by the lower court because they seemed to subvert
the spirit of *Roe* v. *Wade*. But the appeals court upheld regulation 1, requiring all
second-trimester abortions to be performed in hospitals. The Supreme Court reversed.
The reason it gave for its reversal served the three dissenting justices, led by Justice
O'Connor, as a kind of springboard for their critique of *Roe* v. *Wade*.

The Court struck down Akron's hospitalization requirement because of progress
in medical science since 1973. Since *Roe*, abortion techniques have been refined to
the point that early second-trimester abortions can safely be performed on an outpatient basis. Today it may unduly burden a woman to make her go to a hospital for a
second-trimester abortion. *Roe* v. *Wade* was based upon what is called "present medical knowledge." If the *Akron* decision illustrates anything, it is that "present medical
knowledge" keeps changing. But that fact, said Justice O'Connor in her dissent, is
precisely what puts *Roe* "on a collision course with itself."

O'Connor's Dissent: Roe's "Collision Course"

Ironies get piled upon each other when we think of Justice Sandra Day O'Connor. One irony is that her appointment by President Reagan was passionately opposed by the leaders of the pro-life movement, while feminist leaders, virtually all of them pro-choice, supported her appointment. (Pro-lifers had opposed her because of statements she had once made that supported the pro-choice position.) After *Akron* the positions were exactly reversed; pro-lifers discovered in her a wisdom that they had earlier missed, while feminists saw her as just another Reaganite "conservative." The other irony is that the sole woman on the Court vigorously disagreed with a Court decision praised by feminists as a "victory for women."

O'Connor's disagreement reached all the way back to *Roe* v. *Wade*. O'Connor was convinced that Justice Blackmun's "trimester" framework in *Roe* was "on a collision course with itself." The *Roe* decision was based upon two points in a woman's pregnancy: the point at which a woman's health may be endangered by an outpatient abortion and the point at which a fetus is considered viable. The conventional medical wisdom in 1973 was that a woman's health is endangered unless she is hospitalized for a second-trimester abortion. But by 1983 that was no longer the medical consensus, which is why the Court majority struck down Akron's hospitalization requirement. But something else was also happening in the '70s and '80s: medical science was finding ways to keep very premature infants alive. Viability, which was set at about 28 weeks in 1973, was now 25 and even 22 weeks (five and a half months). A second-trimester fetus was now viable, and there was every prospect that the time could be moved to an even earlier point in the pregnancy. "Just as improvements in medical technology inevitably move *forward* the point at which the state may regulate for reasons of maternal health, different technological improvements will move *backward* the point of viability . . ." (emphasis O'Connor's). The collision will come, if it has not done so already, when we have a viable fetus, a fetus which can be kept alive outside the uterus, that can nevertheless be dismembered and disposed of in an abortion clinic. Its viability gives it the right to life, yet it can be routinely destroyed. This is the contradiction which O'Connor saw in *Roe*'s basic philosophy.

Whether the contradiction is real or only apparent, O'Connor's analysis is thought-provoking. Some of the thoughts it provokes are explored in the video discussion of the abortion issue, to which we now turn.

The Video Discussion of Abortion

The moderator, Professor Miller, now turns the discussion to Bobby Joe's sixteen-year-old wife, Mary Jane. She is pregnant, but, finding that her husband is either vegetative or dead at this point, decides to abort. His parents are opposed to the abortion. Can anything be done, legally, to prevent her from having an abortion? The discussion turns to the legal status of abortion, then to whether such questions are better left to courts or legislatures, then to what the moderator refers to as a "Buck Rogers" world in which fetuses can be kept alive outside the womb "almost from conception." If the fetus is removed alive, does it then have the right to live? Some surprising agreements emerge among the panelists, despite sharp exchanges on the issue of abortion.

There are predictable differences of opinion in this area; the lines have been drawn in Congress for a number of years. Congressman Henry Hyde, author of the "Hyde amendment" limiting federal funding of abortion, is the most outspoken in his opposition to it: "If protecting the weak from the strong is what the law is all about . . . that's what antiabortion legislation seeks to do; protect the most defenseless, vulnerable of all creatures, the unborn, the preborn." Equally outspoken on the other side is Hyde's congressional colleague, Barney Frank, who complains that too many pro-lifers in Congress don't think about the welfare of *born* children. "[T]here are people in Congress who will vote against nutrition programs, against housing programs, against programs to protect people against abuse." He and Hyde get into a heated exchange over this charge, which Hyde says is both untrue and irrelevant. Former HEW Secretary Joseph Califano, on the other hand, gets treated rather gently by the pro-choicers on the panel, even though he shares Hyde's pro-life views. Perhaps this is because he balances off ideals against the realities. When asked to be the lawyer for Bobby Joe's parents and make out the best legal case for them, he confesses that "they've got a hard case to make it impossible for Mary Jane to get an abortion."

The most intriguing part comes when the moderator asks Gloria Steinem, publisher of *Ms.* magazine, to imagine a "Buck Rogers" scenario:

> Let us assume the existence of a medical technology that will sustain the fetus almost from conception, outside the womb. Mary Jane is pregnant. . . . Bobby Joe's parents say, "Don't have the abortion. Let us have this procedure performed, let us remove the fetus from Mary Jane's womb, let us sustain it at our cost, and let us bring up the child."

Do Bobby Joe's parents have a right to insist upon this? Steinem first tries answering by formula: the parents have no right to "invade her space." But then she realizes that the formula does not fit the facts, for in this case Mary Jane is bent upon invading her *own* space in order to evict an unwanted fetus; the parents are not interfering with that right, only asking that she let the fetus live. And—surprisingly, no doubt, to some viewers—Steinem agrees with the parents. "All right. If the body space of the individual woman has not been invaded," then yes. Mary Jane "doesn't own that fetus after it is outside of her body."

It seems at first as though Gloria Steinem is a relentless individualist. A woman, she seems to argue, is the landlady of her body. She sets the rules and she allows in whom she pleases. She can evict tenants at will, during any season of the year. But once her former tenants are on the street and still managing to stay alive, she has no business interfering with them—for they, too, are individuals. On closer examination, however, it appears that Steinem's view may be both more subtle and less consistent. What she says is that the woman "loses her exclusive right" once the child is born. In other words, she still retains *some* rights. Rights, then, derive from something other than ownership, for, as Steinem admits, Mary Jane certainly doesn't "own" the born child. But if rights can be derived from facts other than ownership, then what happens to Steinem's doctrine that a woman has *exclusive* rights over her "body space"? Can there be cases in which others have legitimate claims as well?

Points to Remember

1. *Roe* v. *Wade* (1973) held that the "right of privacy" which the Court had derived from the "emanations" of various amendments in the *Griswold* case was broad enough to protect a woman's right to an abortion.
2. *Roe* held that the abortion right was not absolute. It used a trimester framework for deriving the following formula: during the first three months the state may not regulate abortion at all; during the second three months abortions may be regulated, but only for the sake of the woman's health, not to save the fetus. Only during the last trimester may the state forbid abortions, and even then its prohibition may be overridden if the woman can prove that her health, physical or emotional, will be endangered if she carries to term.
3. In *Akron* v. *Akron Center for Reproductive Health* (1983), the Court struck down a series of abortion regulations, including those requiring a twenty-four-hour waiting period, "informed consent" requirements, and compulsory hospitalization for second-trimester abortions. The last provision was struck down because gynecologic medicine now permits outpatient abortions during part of the second trimester.
4. Justice Sandra Day O'Connor and two other justices dissented in the *Akron* case, on the grounds that medical science has put the whole *Roe* framework "on a collision course with itself."
5. In the video discussion, the participants take fairly predictable positions. Some viewers might have been surprised by Gloria Steinem's agreement that a fetus should be protected, if possible, against death while it is being aborted. The position seems consistent with individualism, though Steinem qualifies it by saying the mother still retains some rights over the fetus that survives an abortion.

Reflections

Pregnancy confronts us with another slippery slope. At the one end of the pregnancy is a fertilized ovum, which does not look like a human being. At the other end is a nine-month fetus, which does not look like anything except a human being. Some pro-choice advocates maintain that human life begins at birth, but for many others this position is untenable. They may not agree with the pro-lifers that humanity begins with conception, but their feeling is that it must begin somewhere before the fetus emerges into the world and is called a "baby."

But where is that point? In spite of Justice Blackmun's assurance in *Roe* v. *Wade* that "we need not resolve the difficult question of when life begins," he did appear to hazard an answer: human life begins at the point of viability, the point at which the fetus can live outside the womb. At that point the state may forbid abortions except under special circumstances.

It is just here that the perplexity begins. As Justice O'Connor pointed out in her *Akron* dissent ten years later, *Roe* v. *Wade* may have tied itself to the medical knowledge of 1973, when viability was reached at six months. Today the time required is a bit shorter, and future technologies will probably reduce it still more. Has the Court shown a corresponding willingness to let states forbid earlier abortions? It does not appear so. If anything, the Court has compelled states to allow outpatient abortions at *later* periods.

Adding to the problem is the knowledge derived from contemporary fetology. If, as Gloria Steinem contends, "the brain is the seat of our life," then it should be disconcerting to know that a six-week fetus shows measurable signs of brain activity. Early, legally abortable fetuses also behave in ways that are associated with such activity; they dream, suck their thumbs, avoid needles. All this suggests that the abortion controversy is far from being resolved. For many Americans the problem is as much a "toughie" as the right to die is for Judge Klein.

III: "BABY DOE"

It is not quite accurate to say that Justice Blackmun defined "viability" as the capability to sustain life outside the womb. He inserted a qualifier before the word "life." The qualifying word was "meaningful." But what is a "meaningful" life? The negative of this is more perplexing, perhaps a little frightening: What is a "meaningless" human life? We are talking now about life *outside* the womb. Or are we?

The expression "meaningful life" comes from *Roe* v. *Wade*. Though Justice Blackmun was not addressing the question of an already-born child's right to live, Supreme Court statements in one case often get picked up and applied to a different case. We have already seen this in the contraception and abortion cases. In *Griswold*, the "right of privacy" was derived from "emanations" in the Bill of Rights and applied to the area of contraception. In *Roe*, "privacy" was broadened to cover the area of abortion. This brings us to the new issue: Does the "privacy" protected in *Griswold* and *Roe* also protect the right of a family to let a baby die because, in their opinion, the baby's life would not be "meaningful" if it lived?

In 1982, in Bloomington, Indiana, an infant suffering from Down's syndrome (a form of mental retardation that can be mild or severe—no one knows until the child is at least a year old) was allowed to die of hunger and dehydration when an operation might have allowed him to swallow food. The parents' decision not to have the operation, on the ground that their child was better dead than alive with Down's syndrome, was upheld by a state court. Before the case could be appealed, "Infant Doe," as he was known in the court papers, died.

The case itself, however, acquired a new life, this time in federal court. Shortly after the infant's death, the Reagan administration promulgated a regulation that required the posting of warning signs in hospital nurseries stating: *"Discriminatory failure to feed and care for handicapped infants in this facility is prohibited by federal law."* Violations were to be reported by using an emergency number listed on the signs. The regulation was challenged in federal district court by the American Academy of Pediatrics. The doctors claimed that the regulations would be disruptive and intrusive. Administration officials claimed that the federal law in question, Section 504 of the Rehabilitation Act of 1973, left no doubt about the rights of handicapped infants, for it protected "any person" with substantially limiting mental or physical impairment. Siding with the Reagan administration were a number of organizations representing the handicapped, who submitted a friend-of-the-court brief.

The judge, Gerhard Gesell, sided with the doctors. Conceding that the Rehabilitation Act, "on its face, is open to a broad and all-inclusive interpretation," Gesell stated that the government had gone too far in attempting to apply it indiscriminately to all infants, resulting in regulations that were "arbitrary and capricious."

Many groups, including those representing the pediatric profession, applauded Judge Gesell's ruling. Others were troubled by the implication of his words. Gesell stated (italics added) that "*some* infants born with physical and mental defects *may* well fit within that broad definition" of "person." A "mildly handicapped child whose parents *want him* to benefit from those services" might be a person. That means that a child's "personhood" is dependent in part on its "wantedness." But if Gloria Steinem is correct in saying that Mary Jane "doesn't own that fetus, after it is outside of her body," then the baby's personhood would appear to be independent of whatever plans its parents have for it.

The Video Discussion of "Baby Doe"

Mary Jane's baby is born "severely retarded" and suffering other physical disabilities. He also needs a simple ten-minute operation that will unblock his esophagus, enabling him to swallow. His parents refuse the operation. The moderator turns to the doctors. Will they do it anyway? Dr. Jefferson would, but not Drs. Heifetz and Gaylin. Phil Donahue and Judge Mikva agree with Heifetz and Gaylin. Rabbi Bleich, Joseph Califano, and Thomas Stoddard disagree. Father Drinan says the parents have a legal but not a moral right to refuse the operation.

The surprise, for many, is Thomas Stoddard. The New York Civil Liberties Union, of which he is an officer, is an outspokenly pro-choice organization. But Stoddard, perhaps using Steinem's inside/outside dichotomy, is not ready to extend the right of choice to Baby Doe's parents. "Children do have rights. They have rights from the moment of birth and in *Roe* v. *Wade* they also have rights in the third trimester of pregnancy." He would take the baby's case. Another surprise, though from a different standpoint, is the distinction made by Dr. Gaylin. Given his views on death, it is not surprising that he would not do the operation if the parents objected to it. The surprise comes in the age distinction he makes. If this were a six-year-old or eight-year-old child, he would do the operation. But this is just a baby. "This is brand new."

Does Dr. Gaylin mean that "brand new" human beings have less right to live than older ones? Perhaps the question is misleading. Dr. Gaylin and his colleague Dr. Heifetz do not think of the right to life as something that keeps gradually increasing with age. Instead, in their view, it seems to follow a parabolic path: it goes up along with age to a certain point and then starts descending. A five-month fetus has no claim on life, a "brand new" baby has a qualified claim, and eighteen-year-old Bobby Joe may have more claim than he wants. But after a certain point, the right to life starts diminishing. If Bobby Joe were forty-five, Dr. Gaylin said earlier in the program, "I'd have no argument at all. I'd turn to the next case that needed my time." If Bobby Joe were eighty-five, Dr. Heifetz said, "I wouldn't even think twice."

The doctors' view of a person's right to life seems to correlate with his mental and physical strength. A five-month fetus is hardly viable, a newborn baby is fragile, an eighteen-year-old is near the peak of his power, a forty-five-year-old is starting to lose vigor, and an eighty-five-year-old is fragile once again. Does that mean the doctors would make one's right to live depend on one's strength?

Such questions are no longer academic. They underlie decisions made every day in hospitals throughout the nation. Many of these decisions are made quietly. Others, for one reason or another, generate headlines. One such case became the New York State version of "Baby Doe." This time the patient was "Baby Jane," a female infant suffering from spina bifida (an opening in the spine). Children who suffer from spina bifida frequently suffer from other handicaps as well, including partial paralysis. In Baby Jane's case, it was also suspected that the child's unusually small head signaled possible retardation.

The physicians recommended to the parents that the child be operated upon (the operation involved closing the spine and shunting fluid from the brain), and at first the parents agreed. Then they changed their minds. With the operation, the child would live a number of years, possibly suffering some degree of paralysis and retardation. Without it, the child would probably die within two years. The parents opted for "conservative treatment": the child would be fed and treated for infection, but there would be no operation.

A right-to-life attorney intervened and got a hearing before a state judge. The judge appointed an attorney to represent the child (after which the right-to-life attorney withdrew), and the trial began. During the trial, the court-appointed attorney forced the hospital to produce the baby's medical records. These revealed that the baby's head, while small, was within normal range, and that the prognosis was that, if operated upon, the child would one day walk with braces. The court ruled that the parents had to go ahead with the operation. The ruling, however, was reversed by New York State's highest court, the Court of Appeals.

What seemed to bother the seven members of the Court of Appeals most was the fact that an outsider, not related to the family, had intervened in the case. The court did not directly address the question of surgery; instead, the judges expressed their "distress" that the case was ever brought. In praising the appeals court decision, the *New York Times* distinguished this case from the case of Baby Doe. "He had an incomplete esophagus, which is operable, and Down's syndrome, the consequences of which are impossible to estimate at birth." Baby Jane's prognosis, the *Times* editorial said, was different; the operation would do no more than prolong her existence. To "withhold heroic treatment is to do her no cruelty." Others disagreed, pointing out that operations for spina bifida are not usually considered "heroic treatment." One of the dissenters, *Village Voice* columnist Nat Hentoff, suggested that "conservative treatment" often turns out to be a polite term for infanticide.

In the meantime, the Reagan administration got involved in the case by asking the

hospital for the child's medical records in order to determine whether federal intervention on her behalf was warranted. The hospital refused. The refusal brought the
case into federal courts for the first time. As with the "Baby Doe regulations," the
statute relied upon by the federal government was the Rehabilitation Act of 1973,
which protects "any person" with substantially limiting mental or physical impairment. The administration contended that such a statute ought at least to give the government a chance to examine the child's hospital records. The hospital contended that
the paramount right was the right to privacy of the parents and their physicians.

Points to Remember

1. The treatment of newborn retarded infants is a frontier area of law and ethics.
   The two most prominent cases, involving "Baby Doe" and "Baby Jane," have resulted in court verdicts favoring the family's right to withhold treatment. In the
   latter case, the Reagan administration intervened, bringing such a case to federal
   court for the first time.
2. Earlier, the Reagan administration sought to avoid a repetition of the "Baby Doe"
   outcome by requiring pediatric hospitals to post warnings concerning the violation
   of federal law and a "hot line" number to call. This regulation was struck down
   by a federal district judge.
3. Of the panelists favoring the pro-choice position, only one of them, Thomas Stoddard, volunteered an opinion opposed to the wishes of the family in a case similar
   to that of "Baby Doe." Other pro-choice panelists would draw lines using such
   criteria as age and capacity for self-awareness.

SUMMARY

In the video discussion there has been a logical progression from "inner" to "outer."
The first part of the discussion was largely confined to what people should be allowed
to do to themselves; other people, such as the doctors, were brought in largely as instruments of the individual's will and desire. The second part began to raise the question of what people can do to others, even if the "others" in question may only be
"potential" people for two-thirds of their existence. In the third section the "others"
were without question separate in the biological sense of being removed from the
body. The question, then, really seemed to turn upon whether they were "persons" in
the full sense of the word, whether their life was "meaningfully" human.

   The entire program suggests a slippery slope. At the top is the sovereign self making
decisions about itself. At the bottom is the decision to do something, or let something
happen, to someone else. Whatever remains of traditional strictures against suicide,
American individualism is so strong that we hesitate to invoke the letter of the law
against it. Even Henry Hyde, who staunchly opposes laws permitting doctors to help

people kill themselves, suggests that if people want to do it to themselves, "no one can stop you . . . you know how to do it." At the other end of the slope, though, we get far beyond individualism. We have a retarded baby, an individual unable to make choices, and we have to decide what to do with it. Rugged individualism is simply irrelevant to the facts in the case. We have traveled down a slippery slope and we try, now, to find some place to get a toehold. Is it the baby's intelligence that makes the difference? Its age? Its strength? Its "newness"? In Judge Klein's words: "it's a toughie."

Documents

GRISWOLD V. *CONNECTICUT* 381 U.S. 479 (1965)

In Griswold *v.* Connecticut, *the Court struck down a Connecticut statute prohibiting the use of contraceptives. The Court held that there is a right to marital privacy which extends beyond the legislative reach of the state government. The Court discerned the right to marital privacy in several different amendments to the Constitution.*

Mr. Justice Douglas wrote the Opinion of the Court.

The foregoing cases suggest that specific guarantees in the Bill of Rights have penumbras, formed by emanations from those guarantees that help give them life and substance. Various guarantees create zones of privacy. The right of association contained in the penumbra of the First Amendment is one, as we have seen. The Third Amendment in its prohibition against the quartering of soldiers "in any house" in time of peace without the consent of the owner is another facet of that privacy. The Fourth Amendment explicitly affirms the "right of the people to be secure in their persons, houses, papers, and effects, against unreasonable searches and seizures." The Fifth Amendment in its Self-Incrimination Clause enables the citizen to create a zone of privacy which government may not force him to surrender to his detriment. The Ninth Amendment provides: "The enumeration in the Constitution, of certain rights, shall not be construed to deny or disparage others retained by the people."

The Fourth and Fifth Amendments were described in *Boyd* v. *United States*, 116 U. S. 616, 630, as protection against all governmental invasions "of the sanctity of a man's home and the privacies of life." We recently referred in *Mapp* v. *Ohio*, 367 U. S. 643, 656, to the Fourth Amendment as creating a "right to privacy, no less important than any other right carefully and particularly reserved to the people."

We have had many controversies over these penumbral rights of "privacy and repose." These cases bear witness that the right of privacy which presses for recognition here is a legitimate one.

The present case, then, concerns a relationship lying within the zone of privacy created by several fundamental constitutional guarantees.

. . .

We deal with a right of privacy older than the Bill of Rights—older than our political parties, older than our school system. Marriage is a coming together for better or for worse, hopefully enduring, and intimate to the degree of being sacred. It is an association that promotes a way of life, not causes; a harmony in living, not political faiths; a bilateral loyalty, not commercial or social projects. Yet it is an association for as noble a purpose as any involved in our prior decisions.

Justice Black dissented from the Court's opinion, arguing that there is no general right to privacy that is protected against legislative reach by one or more amendments to the Constitution.

Justice Black, dissenting.

The Court talks about a constitutional "right of privacy" as though there is some constitutional provision or provisions forbidding any law ever to be passed which might abridge the "privacy" of individuals. But there is not. There are, of course, guarantees in certain specific constitutional provisions which are designed in part to protect privacy at certain times and places with respect to certain activities. Such, for example, is the Fourth Amendment's guarantee against "unreasonable searches and seizures." But I think it belittles that Amendment to talk about it as though it protects nothing but "privacy." To treat it that way is to give it a niggardly interpretation, not the kind of liberal reading I think any Bill of Rights provision should be given. The average man would very likely not have his feelings soothed any more by having his property seized openly than by having it seized privately and by stealth. He simply wants his property left alone. And a person can be just as much, if not more, irritated, annoyed and injured by an unceremonious public arrest by a policeman as he is by a seizure in the privacy of his office or home.

One of the most effective ways of diluting or expanding a constitutionally guaranteed right is to substitute for the crucial word or words of a constitutional guarantee another word or words, more or less flexible and more or less restricted in meaning. This fact is well illustrated by the use of the term "right of privacy" as a comprehensive substitute for the Fourth Amendment's guarantee against "unreasonable searches and seizures." "Privacy" is a broad, abstract and ambiguous concept which can easily be shrunken in meaning but which can also, on the other hand, easily be interpreted as a constitutional ban against many things other than searches and seizures. I have expressed the view many times that First Amendment freedoms, for example, have suffered from a failure of the courts to stick to the simple language of the First Amendment in construing it, instead of invoking multitudes of words substituted for those the Framers used. For these reasons I get nowhere in this case by talk about a constitutional "right of privacy" as an emanation from one or more constitutional provisions. I like my privacy as well as the next one, but I am nevertheless compelled to admit that government has a right to invade it unless prohibited by some specific constitutional provision. For these reasons I cannot agree with the Court's judgment and the reasons it gives for holding this Connecticut law unconstitutional.

ROE V. WADE, 410 U.S. 113 (1973)

In Roe *v.* Wade *the Court held that the Fourteenth Amendment's concept of "liberty" includes a "right to privacy" broad enough to encompass the right of a woman to obtain an abortion. The right to abortion, however, is not absolute but diminishes with the increasing maturity of the fetus. During the first three-month period, or "trimester," of pregnancy, the state may enact no regulations on abortion; during the second trimester, it may enact regulations as long as they are reasonably related to the protection of the mother's health (not that of the fetus); only during the final trimester may the state forbid abortions, and even then a woman may obtain one if she makes a valid claim that her life or health (physical or emotional) may be adversely affected by carrying to term.* Roe *was decided by a seven to two majority, whose opinion, written by Justice Harry Blackmun, is excerpted here. The dissenting opinion, by Justice Byron White (joined by Justice William Rehnquist), is omitted.*

Opinion of the Court, Mr. Justice Blackmun.

The principal thrust of appellant's attack on the Texas statutes is that they improperly invade a right, said to be possessed by the pregnant woman, to choose to terminate her pregnancy. Appellant would discover this right in the concept of personal "liberty" embodied in the Fourteenth Amendment's Due Process Clause; or in personal, marital, familial, and sexual privacy said to be protected by the Bill of Rights or its penumbras, see *Griswold* v. *Connecticut*, 381 U. S. 479 (1965); or among those rights reserved to the people by the Ninth Amendment, *Griswold* v. *Connecticut*, 381 U. S., at 486 (Goldberg, J., concurring).

The Constitution does not explicitly mention any right of privacy. In a line of decisions, however, going back perhaps as far as *Union Pacific R. Co.* v. *Botsford*, 141 U. S. 250, 251 (1891), the Court has recognized that a right of personal privacy, or a guarantee of certain areas or zones of privacy, does exist under the Constitution. In varying contexts, the Court or individual Justices have, indeed, found at least the roots of that right in the First Amendment, *Stanley* v. *Georgia*, 394 U. S. 557, 564 (1969); in the Fourth and Fifth Amendments, *Terry* v. *Ohio*, 392 U. S. 1, 8-9 (1968), *Katz* v. *United States*, 389 U. S. 347, 350 (1967), *Boyd* v. *United States*, 116 U. S. 616 (1886), see *Olmstead* v. *United States*, 277 U. S. 438, 478 (1928) (Brandeis, J., dissenting); in the penumbras of the Bill of Rights, *Griswold* v. *Connecticut*, 381 U. S., at 484-485; in the Ninth Amendment, *id.*, at 486 (Goldberg, J., concurring); or in the concept of liberty guaranteed by the first section of the Fourteenth Amendment, see *Meyer* v. *Nebraska*, 262 U. S. 390, 399 (1923). These decisions make it clear that only personal rights that can be deemed "fundamental" or "implicit in the concept of ordered liberty," *Palko* v. *Connecticut*, 302 U. S. 319, 325 (1937), are included in this guarantee of personal privacy. They also make it clear that the right has some extension to activities relating to marriage; *Loving* v. *Virginia*, 388 U. S. 1, 12 (1967); procreation, *Skinner* v. *Oklahoma*, 316 U. S. 535, 541-542 (1942); contraception, *Eisenstadt* v. *Baird*, 405 U. S., at 453-454; *id.*, at 460, 463-465 (White, J., concurring in result); family re-lationships, *Prince* v. *Massachusetts*, 321 U. S. 158, 166 (1944); and child rearing and education, *Pierce* v. *Society of Sisters*, 268 U. S. 510, 535 (1925), *Meyer* v. *Nebraska, supra.*

This right of privacy, whether it be founded in the Fourteenth Amendment's con-cept of personal liberty and restrictions upon state action, as we feel it is, or, as the District Court determined, in the Ninth Amendment's reservation of rights to the people, is broad enough to encompass a woman's decision whether or not to terminate her pregnancy. The detriment that the State would impose upon the pregnant woman by denying this choice altogether is apparent. Specific and direct harm medically diagnosable even in early pregnancy may be involved. Maternity, or additional off-spring, may force upon the woman a distressful life and future. Psychological harm may be imminent. Mental and physical health may be taxed by child care. There is also the distress, for all concerned, associated with the unwanted child, and there is the problem of bringing a child into a family already unable, psychologically and other-wise, to care for it. In other cases, as in this one, the additional difficulties and con-tinuing stigma of unwed motherhood may be involved. All these are factors the wom-an and her responsible physician necessarily will consider in consultation.

On the basis of elements such as these, appellant and some *amici* argue that the woman's right is absolute and that she is entitled to terminate her pregnancy at what-ever time, in whatever way, and for whatever reason she alone chooses. With this we do not agree.

. . .

The Court's decisions recognizing a right of privacy also acknowledge that some state regulation in areas protected by that right is appropriate. As noted above, a State may properly assert important interests in safeguarding health, in maintaining medical standards, and in protecting potential life. At some point in pregnancy, these respec-tive interests become sufficiently compelling to sustain regulation of the factors that govern the abortion decision. The privacy right involved, therefore, cannot be said to be absolute. In fact, it is not clear to us that the claim asserted by some *amici* that one has an unlimited right to do with one's body as one pleases bears a close relationship to the right of privacy previously articulated in the Court's decisions. The Court has refused to recognize an unlimited right of this kind in the past. *Jacobson* v. *Massa-chusetts*, 197 U. S. 11 (1905) (vaccination); *Buck* v. *Bell*, 274 U. S. 200 (1927) (sterilization).

We, therefore, conclude that the right of personal privacy includes the abortion decision, but that this right is not unqualified and must be considered against impor-tant state interests in regulation.

. . .

Although the results are divided, most of these courts have agreed that the right of privacy, however based, is broad enough to cover the abortion decision; that the right, nonetheless, is not absolute and is subject so some limitations; and that at some point the state interests as to protection of health, medical standards, and prenatal life, become dominant. We agree with this approach.

JUSTICE O'CONNOR'S DISSENT IN *AKRON* (1983)

The most comprehensive judicial critique of Roe v. Wade *(1973) came ten years later, in the dissenting opinion of Justice Sandra Day O'Connor in* Akron v. *Akron Center for Reproductive Health, 462 U.S. ____ (1983).*

In the Akron *case a six-member majority, in an opinion by Justice Lewis Powell, invalidated several regulations on abortion passed by the city of Akron, Ohio, on the ground that they overreached the limits on state abortion regulations laid down in* Roe v. Wade.

Among the regulations the Court struck down was one requiring all second-trimester abortions to be performed in hospitals. The Court said that while such a requirement may have been necessary for the patient's health in the past, abortion procedures had now become sophisticated enough to allow second-trimester abortions to be performed in clinics, on an outpatient basis; therefore the hospitalization requirement was an unnecessary impediment to a woman's right to abortion.

Justice O'Connor's dissent went beyond the immediate issues of the case. It questioned the whole "trimester" framework for deciding when and where abortions may be obtained.

The trimester or "three-stage" approach adopted by the Court in *Roe*, and, in a modified form, employed by the Court to analyze the state regulations in these cases, cannot be supported as a legitimate or useful framework for accommodating the woman's right and the State's interests. The decision of the Court today graphically illustrates why the trimester approach is a completely unworkable method of accommodating the conflicting personal rights and compelling state interests that are involved in the abortion context.

As the Court indicates today, the State's compelling interest in maternal health changes as medical technology changes, and any health regulation must not "depart from accepted medical practice." *Ante*, at 2493. In applying this standard, the Court holds that "the safety of second-trimester abortions has increased dramatically" since 1973, when *Roe* was decided. *Ante*, at 2496 (footnote omitted). Although a regulation such as one requiring that all second-trimester abortions be performed in hospitals "had strong support" in 1973 "as a reasonable health regulation," *ibid.*, this regulation can no longer stand because, according to the Court's diligent research into medical and scientific literature, the dilation and evacuation procedure (D & E), used in 1973 only for first-trimester abortions, "is now widely and successfully used for second trimester abortions." *Ibid* (footnote omitted). Further, the medical literature relied on by the Court indicates that the D & E procedure may be performed in an appropriate non-hospital setting for "at least . . . the early weeks of the second trimester. . . ." *Ante*, at 2496. The Court then chooses the period of 16 weeks of gestation as that point at which D & E procedures may be performed safely in a non-hospital setting, and thereby invalidates the Akron hospitalization regulation.

It is not difficult to see that despite the Court's purported adherence to the trimester approach adopted in *Roe*, the lines drawn in that decision have now been "blurred" because of what the Court accepts as technological advancement in the safety of abortion procedure. The State may no longer rely on a "bright line" that separates permissible from impermissible regulation, and it is no longer free to consider the second trimester as a unit and weigh the risks posed by all abortion procedures throughout that trimester. Rather, the State must continuously and conscientiously study contemporary medical and scientific literature in order to determine whether the effect of a particular regulation is to "depart from accepted medical practice" insofar as particular procedures and particular periods within the trimester are concerned. Assuming that legislative bodies are able to engage in this exacting task, it is difficult to believe that our Constitution *requires* that they do it as a prelude to protecting the health of their citizens. It is even more difficult to believe that this Court, without the resources available to those bodies entrusted with making legislative choices, believes itself competent to make these inquiries and to revise these standards every time the American College of Obstetricians and Gynecologists (ACOG) or similar group revises its views about what is and what is not appropriate medical procedure in this area. Indeed, the ACOG standards on which the Court relies were changed in 1982 after trial in the present cases. Before ACOG changed its standards in 1982, it recommended that all mid-trimester abortions be performed in a hospital. See *Akron Center for Reproductive Health, Inc.* v. *City of Akron*, 651 F.2d 1198, 1209 (CA6 1981). As today's decision indicates, medical technology is changing, and this change will necessitate our continued functioning as the nation's "*ex officio* medical board with powers to approve or disapprove medical and operative practices and standards throughout the United States." *Planned Parenthood* v. *Danforth*, 428 U.S. 52, 99, 96 S.Ct. 2831, 2854, 49 L.Ed.2d 788 (1976) (White, J., concurring in part and dissenting in part).

Just as improvements in medical technology inevitably will move *forward* the point at which the State may regulate for reasons of maternal health, different technological improvements will move *backward* the point of viability at which the State may proscribe abortions except when necessary to preserve the life and health of the mother.

In 1973, viability before 28 weeks was considered unusual. The fourteenth edition of L. Hellman & J. Pritchard, Williams Obstetrics, on which the Court relied in *Roe* for its understanding of viability, stated that "[a]ttainment of a [fetal] weight of 1,000 g [or a fetal age of approximately 28 weeks gestation] is . . . widely used as the criterion of viability." *Id.*, at 493. However, recent studies have demonstrated increasingly earlier fetal viability. It is certainly reasonable to believe that fetal viability in the first trimester of pregnancy may be possible in the not too distant future. Indeed, the Court has explicitly acknowledged that *Roe* left the point of viability "flexible for anticipated advancements in medical skill." *Colautti* v. *Franklin*, 439 U.S. 379, 387, 99 S.Ct. 675, 681, 58 L.Ed.2d 596 (1979). "[W]e recognized in *Roe* that viability was a matter of medical judgment, skill, and technical ability, and we preserved the flexibility of the term." *Danforth, supra*, 428 U.S., at 64, 96 S.Ct., at 2838-2839.

The *Roe* framework, then, is clearly on a collision course with itself. As the medical risks of various abortion procedures decrease, the point at which the State may regulate for reasons of maternal health is moved further forward to actual childbirth. As medical science becomes better able to provide for the separate existence of the fetus, the point of viability is moved further back toward conception. Moreover, it is clear that the trimester approach violates the fundamental aspiration of judicial decision making through the application of neutral principles "sufficiently absolute to give them roots throughout the community and continuity over significant periods of time. . . ." A. Cox, The Role of the Supreme Court in American Government 114 (1976). The *Roe* framework is inherently tied to the state of medical technology that exists whenever particular litigation ensues. Although legislatures are better suited to make the necessary factual judgments in this area, the Court's framework forces legislatures, as a matter of constitutional law, to speculate about what constitutes "accepted medical practice" at any given time. Without the necessary expertise or ability, courts must then pretend to act as science review boards and examine those legislative judgments. . . .

The Court in *Roe* correctly realized that the State has important interests "in the areas of health and medical standards" and that "[t]he State has a legitimate interest in seeing to it that abortion, like any other medical procedure, is performed under circumstances that insure maximum safety for the patient." 410 U.S., at 149, 150, 93 S.Ct., at 724, 725. The Court also recognized that the State has "*another* important and legitimate interest in protecting the potentiality of human life." *Id.*, at 162, 93 S.Ct., at 731 (emphasis in original). I agree completely that the State has these interests, but in my view, the point at which these interests become compelling does not depend on the trimester of pregnancy. Rather, these interests are present *throughout* pregnancy.

This Court has never failed to recognize that "a State may properly assert important interests in safeguarding health [and] in maintaining medical standards." 410 U.S., at 154, 93 S.Ct., at 727. It cannot be doubted that as long as a state statute is within "the bounds of reason and [does not] assume[] the character of a merely arbitrary fiat. . . . [then] [t]he State . . . must decide upon measures that are needful for the protection of its people. . . ." *Purity Extract and Tonic Co.* v. *Lynch*, 226 U.S. 192, 204-205 (1912). "There is nothing in the United States Constitution which limits the State's power to require that medical procedures be done safely. . . ." *Sendak* v. *Arnold*, 429 U.S. 968, 969 (WHITE, J., dissenting). "The mode and procedure of medical diagnostic procedures is not the business of judges." *Parham* v. *J.R.*, 442 U.S. 584, 607-608 (1979). Under the *Roe* framework, however, the state interest in maternal health cannot become compelling until the onset of the second trimester of pregnancy because "until the end of the first trimester mortality in abortion may be less than mortality in normal childbirth." 410 U.S., at 163, 93 S.Ct., at 732. Before the second trimester, the decision to perform an abortion "must be left to the medical judgment of the pregnant woman's attending physician." *Id.*, at 164.

The fallacy inherent in the *Roe* framework is apparent: just because the State has a compelling interest in ensuring maternal safety once an abortion may be more dangerous in childbirth, it simply does not follow that the State has *no* interest before that point that justifies state regulation to ensure that first-trimester abortions are performed as safely as possible.

The state interest in potential human life is likewise extant throughout pregnancy. In *Roe*, the Court held that although the State had an important and legitimate interest in protecting potential life, that interest could not become compelling until the point at which the fetus was viable. The difficulty with this analysis is clear: *potential* life is no less potential in the first weeks of pregnancy than it is at viability or afterward. At any stage in pregnancy, there is the *potential* for human life. Although the Court refused to "resolve the difficult question of when life begins," *id.*, 410 U.S., at 159, the Court chose the point of viability—when the fetus is *capable* of life independent of its mother—to permit the complete proscription of abortion. The choice of viability as the point at which the state interest in *potential* life becomes compelling is no less arbitrary than choosing any point before viability or any point afterward. Accordingly, I believe that the State's interest in protecting potential human life exists throughout the pregnancy.

SELECTED READINGS

Beauchamp, Tom L., and Childress, James F. *Principles of Biomedical Ethics*. 2nd ed. New York: Oxford University Press, 1983.

An excellent introduction to the complex web of personal, social, professional, economic, political, and ethical relationships in which health professionals and their clients must make decisions. The volume includes a bibliography, case studies, and the codes of professional ethics of several professional health care associations.

Beauchamp, Tom L., and Perlin, Seymour, eds. *Ethical Issues in Death and Dying*. Englewood Cliffs, N.J.: Prentice-Hall, 1978.

This outstanding collection of essays covers death and dying from the technological, medical, legal, and ethical points of view. Essays address the special problems raised in the cases of infants, children, the elderly, and the comatose; the volume includes several case studies.

Feinberg, Joel. "Voluntary Euthanasia and the Inalienable Right to Life." *Philosophy and Public Affairs* 7 (Winter 1978): 93-123.

Philosopher Feinberg examines voluntary euthanasia in the context of the inalienable right to life as it was understood by Thomas Jefferson and the signers of the Declaration of Independence.

Granberg, Donald, and Denney, Donald. "The Coathanger and the Rose." *Society*, May/June 1982, pp. 39-46.

This article compares the attitudes of members of the National Abortion Rights Action League (NARAL) with those of the National Right to Life Committee (NRLC) on a number of social issues besides abortion. The findings may surprise some readers. For example, "NARAL and NRLC members do not differ significantly on capital punishment" and, except for the issue of the ERA, both take pro-women's liberation positions.

Malone, Robert J. "Is There a Right to a Natural Death?" *New England Law Review* 9 (1974): 293-310.

This brief review of the ethical, religious, and constitutional questions regarding the right to die concludes that "the right to a natural death, with dignity, and without pain . . . falls within the domain of the Ninth Amendment."

Nathanson, Bernard N. *Aborting America.* Garden City, N. Y.: Doubleday, 1979.

The author, a founder and former head of what is now called the National Abortion Rights Action League (NARAL), reversed his views on abortion after he became convinced that the fetus is "a human being in a special time of its development." This book records his activities as an early pro-choice advocate in the '60s and the reasons for his change of heart.

Noonan, John T., Jr. *A Private Choice: Abortion in America in the Seventies.* New York: The Free Press, 1979.

A professor of law at the University of California at Berkeley explores the social and legal consequences of *Roe* v. *Wade* from a pro-life perspective and summarizes the arguments against the legalization of abortion.

Petchesky, Rosalind. *Abortion and Woman's Choice: The State, Sexuality, and the Conditions of Reproductive Freedom.* New York: Longmans, 1984.

Petchesky, a political theorist, argues that the right to secure an abortion is not just a legal right but a social one, based on a woman's fundamental right to control her body. She argues for a more active state role in providing pre- and postnatal counseling and services.

Reagan, Ronald W. "Abortion and the Conscience of the Nation." *The Human Life Review*, Spring 1983, pp. 1-11.

President Reagan sums up the reasons for his administration's opposition to legalized abortion. He concludes that "the transcendent right to life of all human beings" is a right "without which no other rights have any meaning."

Reeves, Robert B. "When Is It Time to Die? Prolegomenon to Voluntary Euthanasia." *New England Law Review* 8, no. 2 (1973): 183-196.

Reeves, a hospital chaplain, sensitively considers the meaning and practice of voluntary euthanasia from the point of view of the individual and society.

Ross, Steven L. "Abortion and the Death of the Fetus." *Philosophy and Public Affairs* 11 (Summer 1982): 232-245.

Ross seeks to separate the ethical and legal questions raised by the killing of a fetus from those raised by performing an abortion. The analysis is particularly important as medical and technological advances make it more likely that aborted fetuses will be "born" alive.

Stinson, Robert, and Stinson, Peggy. *The Long Dying of Baby Andrew.* Boston: Atlantic-Little, Brown, 1984.

The parents of a premature and severely handicapped infant tell how they lost control over decisions regarding their son's care to the "medical bureaucracy." Their story raises significant ethical and public policy questions about the provision of health care to handicapped infants.

Sullivan, Michael T. "The Dying Person: His Plight and His Right." *New England Law Review* 8, no. 2 (1973): 197–216.

A probate judge for Milwaukee County explains the difficult legal and procedural issues of guardianship, conservatorship, and the living will and urges clear legislative guidelines within which dying persons can control their medical care and death.

Westin, Alan. *Privacy and Freedom.* New York: Atheneum, 1967.

One of the country's leading authorities on the constitutional right to privacy explains the origin of the notion of privacy, the importance of privacy in modern democratic society, and the threats that modern technology and some public policies pose to it. Though Westin does not specifically consider the right to live and die, his discussion provides a context within which these rights can be considered.

GLOSSARY

Comatose. In a coma; suffering prolonged unconsciousness.

Down's syndrome. A form of mental retardation accompanied by Oriental-looking eyes; hence sometimes referred to as "mongolism."

Euthanasia. Literally "happy death." A painless killing, usually of oneself, though the Nazis extended the term to refer to others. Self-euthanasia is now often called "self-deliverance."

Hippocratic oath. The ancient medical oath originated by the Greek physician Hippocrates, which includes the promise not to help a woman abort or to prescribe deadly drugs.

Penumbra. Literally "almost shade." Something that lies between two distinct entities and contains elements of both; often referred to as a "gray area."

Right of privacy. The right to be left alone in one's person or dwelling. Such a right is not specifically mentioned in the Bill of Rights, but the Supreme Court has held that it is implied by a combination of the Bill of Rights' provisions.

Spina bifida. A birth abnormality; specifically, an opening in the spine. Children born with the condition frequently suffer other handicaps, including partial paralysis.

Trimester. A three-month period. In *Roe* v. *Wade* (1973), the Supreme Court considered the abortion issue in terms of the three trimesters of a woman's pregnancy.

Viable. In this context, capable of living outside the woman's uterus. In *Roe* v. *Wade*, the Supreme Court defined viability as the capacity for *meaningful* life outside the uterus.

Part Four

Peoples and
States in America

Chapter 11
"...Your Tired, Your Poor."

"Can we doubt that only a divine Providence placed this land—this island of freedom—here as a refuge for all those people in the world who yearn to breathe free?"

RONALD REAGAN, accepting the
Republican nomination, 1980

"Simply put, we've lost control of our own borders."

ATTORNEY GENERAL
WILLIAM FRENCH SMITH, 1983

In 1949 a delegation of American Indians went to Washington to tell American officials about the plight of America's only native peoples. After meeting with Vice-President Alben Barkley the delegation rose to leave. But one old Sioux chief stayed a moment longer to deliver a parting word to the vice-president. "Young fellow," he said, "let me give you a little advice. Be careful with your immigration laws. We were careless with ours."

THE NEW IMMIGRANTS

Today there are many Americans—sons and daughters of earlier immigrants—who would urgently second the old chief's words. They would like to see fewer immigrants coming into our land. Once before, in the 1920s, our country narrowed its gates to people from certain regions of the world by imposing quotas designed to preserve the balance of races in America. But in 1965, during the heyday of the Great Society, that policy was reversed. A series of amendments to the Immigration and Nationality Act put all the world's peoples on an equal footing in terms of immigrating to America. The result, wrote journalist Theodore H. White, was "a stampede, almost an invasion." White considered the change in the law "noble, revolutionary—and probably the most thoughtless of the many acts of the Great Society."

The growth of immigration over the past twenty years has been startling. The restrictive immigration laws of the 1920s, coupled with our Great Depression and World War II, once kept immigration to a low of less than 100,000 annually. But by 1978 annual immigration was more than 600,000, and it has increased every year thereafter. And this is counting only legal immigration. The number of illegal ("undocumented") aliens entering this country is obviously hard to estimate, but the fraction of the total

339

caught every year offers evidence that their numbers have exploded. In all, counting legal and illegal immigrants, many authorities believe that the number of people coming into this country every year is over a million, a level about equal to that of the pre-World War I years, the great period of European emigration.

But most of the new immigrants are not, by and large, European. They come from the Third World. European immigration decreased from 1,300,000 during the 1960s to 842,000 in the 1970s; during the same period, Asian immigration jumped from 362,000 to 1,500,000; African from 33,000 to 87,000; South American from 219,000 to 266,000; and Mexican from 432,000 to 624,000. The largest percentages of immigrants now come from Mexico, the Philippines, Korea, and the Caribbean.

Typically, then, our new immigrants do not sail into New York harbor on steamships. They wash up on Florida beaches in wretched sailboats; fly into Los Angeles ("the new Ellis Island") in crowded 747s; wade the shallow waters dividing Mexico from El Paso, Texas; trek across the burning Arizona desert to Yuma, arriving parched, penniless, and ready to try any kind of work. They come here to flee tyrants and terrorists. They come to join relatives who have already arrived. Above all, they come because America is an island of affluence in a global sea of poverty; here they will earn five to ten times what they made in their home countries. The question is: What will they do to this country—or for it?

THREAT OR BOON?

Many observers see the deluge of immigrants as a threat to our nation's future. Environmentalists focus on the danger of overcrowding. Since immigration now accounts for one-half of all U.S. population growth, they argue that unrestricted immigration is starting to put intolerable pressure on our limited space and natural resources. Labor leaders and blacks worry that new immigrants are taking jobs from poor Americans, making these native workers still poorer by depressing the level of wages. Others are concerned about the impact of the new immigrants on our schools and social services. The Supreme Court has already ruled that children of illegal aliens are entitled to free public education. If the estimated 3½ to 6 million illegal aliens are ever amnestied (declared legal), health and welfare costs will soar.

Still others are worried about the cultural effects of unrestricted immigration. Will America's common language and culture be overwhelmed by peoples who know nothing of our way of life? Will "America" finally become an incoherent collection of nationalities, each cherishing its own ways, none caring about our traditions or future as a nation?

In short, say the critics of immigration, things have gotten out of hand. We have opened our doors wide to the peoples of the planet, and our generosity may overwhelm us. America, says Wyoming Senator Alan Simpson, has become "the patsy of the earth." His view seems to be shared by a majority of Americans. A 1980 Roper poll showed that 9 out of 10 Americans want illegal immigration stopped, and 8 out of 10 want even legal immigration cut back.

But there are other sides to the issue. Some say the problems of immigration have been exaggerated, while its benefits have too often been ignored. America, after all, is a land of immigrants, and these immigrants have brought strength, energy, and productivity to the country. The ancestors of Jefferson, Washington, and Franklin were immigrants. So were the waves of Irish, Italians, Jews, and Slavs who built America's railroads and bridges, mined its ores, poured its steel, grew its crops, manned its sweatshops, and made it one of the most prosperous nations on earth. If these historic immigrants helped make America great, why shouldn't the new immigrants help make it greater? Their skin color and languages may be different, but they have the same energy and grit—the same devotion to thrift and hard work—that turn-of-the-century immigrants possessed.

Cubans in Miami, for instance, have caused the local economy to boom. Indians and Koreans in New York City, running newsstands and fruit markets, have brought new life to declining neighborhoods. In Los Angeles, former Vietnamese "boat people" have already done well enough to start moving to prosperous suburbs. Economist Thomas Sowell has calculated that the average income level of second-generation blacks from the Caribbean now exceeds that of native-born *whites*.

Indeed, the new immigrants may be putting more into the economy than they are taking out. Illegal immigrants pay taxes and Social Security, yet seldom avail themselves of social services for fear of being caught and deported. Jobs taken by immigrants are often the marginal ones in restaurants, hotels, factories, and fields that American workers either avoid altogether or remain in only for short periods. Moreover, despite what environmentalists fear, the new immigrants tend to concentrate in declining city neighborhoods where population is dropping. Without these newcomers, America as a whole would be losing population, for our birth rate has declined to less than the replacement level. And this country still has vast stretches of open space. France—not the most densely populated country in Europe—is four times as densely populated as the United States.

As for the impact of immigration on our culture, in some respects the new immigrants are more traditionally "American" than the Americans. Their commitment to the work ethic would delight Ben Franklin, and their sexual mores are generally pre-Hefner. Their children, either because of or despite bilingual classes, are rapidly learning English and have mastered everything from American cuisine to American slang.

THE UNRESOLVED PROBLEMS

Still, the problems occasioned by mass immigration cannot be ignored. "It is difficult to explain to residents of the community that the Indochinese refugees are drying skinned cats out on the clothesline because they enjoy cats as a delicacy in their country," said the mayor of Santa Ana, California, in his testimony before a congressional committee in 1981. Of course, cultural discontinuities between immigrants and earlier arrivals are nothing new in America. There was much of it during the late nineteenth and early twentieth centuries, when immigrants from eastern and southern Europe began arriving in large numbers. "What kind of American consciousness can grow in the atmosphere of sauerkraut and Limburger cheese? Or what can you expect of the

Americanism of the man whose breath always reeks of garlic?" These sentiments were voiced by an upper-class society woman early in this century. (Walter Lippmann cited them in his book *Public Opinion* as excellent examples of "stereotypes.")

The important difference between then and now is that today's Americans are conscious of something more than cultural tensions with their new neighbors. They also sense a conflict over limited resources. The earlier American belief that there is plenty of land, plenty of work, plenty of everything to go around seems to have declined in recent years, and with it the cushion of indifference between the older arrivals and the new Americans. Sometimes the results can be violent.

In the waters off Galveston, Texas, Vietnamese shrimp boats were set afire after local fishermen complained that the Vietnamese were exhausting the supply of fish. Rocks and bottles were thrown in Denver when Asians were given apartments in a Chicano housing project. When some 6,500 Indochinese moved into the Linda Vista neighborhood of San Diego in the late '70s and early '80s, neighborhood residents suddenly found themselves in competition for welfare, jobs, and housing. The new residents' windows were broken, they found torn-up welfare checks in their mailboxes, and their children were taunted. "We are not callous people," said one American resident. "But when everybody is hungry at the same time, you lose sight of the humanitarian picture."

More recently, thanks in part to the efforts of voluntary resettlement agencies, things have begun to improve in Linda Vista (whose initials now also stand for "Little Vietnam"). But tensions remain in other locations. Some Miami black leaders in 1980 blamed the "Liberty City" black riots on the influx of Cuban refugees, which they claimed sharpened the struggle for jobs. Similar complaints have been voiced by Americans working in the fields, factories, and service industries of the Southwest. Against the claim that new arrivals take jobs Americans turn down can be set the finding of one researcher that illegal immigrants are making $4 to $9.50 an hour, wages many Americans would be glad to receive.

Another distinction needs to be made between today's immigrants and those of the turn of the century. America then was sure of itself—of its destiny, strength, and direction. Because of this, it could absorb and "Americanize" its immigrants. But post-Vietnam America has experienced a crisis of confidence. "Patriotism" has become an embarrassing word in educated circles. Schools are changing the emphasis of their curricula from American to "global" studies. Thus the process of assimilating immigrants through education may have broken down.

THE ISSUES

The issues, then, should be obvious. Is the new wave of immigration a positive development or a threat to the nation's future? Are immigrants taking jobs away from Americans? Or are they stimulating the economy and producing more opportunities for all? Should legal immigration be cut back? Do we need new legislation to stem the tide of illegal immigration?

What proposals have been made for dealing with illegal immigration? Do they have merit? Do any of them violate basic rights? What *are* the rights of aliens in this country? Are they the same as those of citizens? Finally, what will happen if immigration is not curbed?

The Video Discussion

These are among the issues debated by the panelists as they consider immigration and illegal aliens. The moderator of the panel is Columbia Law School Professor Benno Schmidt, Jr. The panelists are:

List of Participants

HON. ARLIN M. ADAMS
Judge
U.S. Court of Appeals
Third Circuit

HON. ARTHUR L. ALARCON
Judge
U.S. Court of Appeals
Ninth Circuit

PETER ALLSTROM
Director of Research
Food and Beverage Trades Department
AFL-CIO

DAVID CARLINER
Attorney
Carliner & Gordon
Immigration Committee
American Bar Association

ROGER CONNER
Executive Director
Federation for American
Immigration Reform

RUDOLPH W. GIULIANI
U.S. Attorney
Southern District of New York
Former Associate Attorney General
Department of Justice

ANTONIA HERNANDEZ
Associate Counsel
Mexican-American Legal Defense
and Educational Fund

REV. THEODORE M. HESBURGH, C.S.C.
President
University of Notre Dame
Select Committee on Immigration
and Refugee Policy

JACQUELYNE JOHNSON JACKSON
Associate Professor of Medical Sociology
Duke University Medical School

GUILLERMO MARTINEZ
Columnist
Miami Herald

HON. DORIS M. MEISSNER
Executive Associate Commissioner
U.S. Immigration and
Naturalization Service
Department of Justice

MICHAEL POSNER
Executive Director
Lawyers' Committee for
International Rights

WILLIAM RASPBERRY
Columnist
Washington Post

JACK ROSENTHAL
Deputy Editorial Page Editor
New York Times

STEVEN R. SHAPIRO
Staff Counsel
New York Civil Liberties Union

HON. MARVIN H. SHOOB
Judge
U.S. District Court
Northern District of Georgia

HON. ALAN K. SIMPSON
U.S. Senator
Wyoming

NINA K. SOLARZ
Executive Director
Citizens' Committee for
Immigration Reform

HON. POTTER STEWART
Justice (retired)
U.S. Supreme Court

MONSIGNOR BRYAN O. WALSH
Director of Catholic Charities
Archdiocese of Miami

Program Summary

The program has three main parts. The first deals with the rights of aliens arriving by sea. Suppose Coast Guardsmen stop a boatful of Haitians headed for the Florida coast. Can they turn it around and send it back to Haiti without first holding formal hearings on the right of its occupants to emigrate to America? Though the panelists differ on this question, everyone seems to agree that alien rights are much clearer once the aliens arrive on American soil.

The moderator then turns to this second question—the rights of aliens who have reached America. What sort of legal protection are they afforded? How long can they be detained? Is detainment really a form of punishment without a trial for acts that are not criminal?

The second part of the program deals with illegal aliens who arrive by land, particularly those who cross the Mexican border. Much of it centers on proposed legislation aimed at curbing illegal immigrants by punishing those who employ them. Are employee sanctions the right way to proceed? Would their implementation violate basic rights?

The third part of the program deals more extensively with the problem of alien rights, particularly as those rights have been interpreted by American courts. How far do they extend? Do the children of illegal aliens have a right to free public education? The Supreme Court has ruled that they do, but some participants are troubled by the

Court's reading of the Constitution and puzzled by its reasoning. These issues are aired, along with the broader issue of whether the Supreme Court has overstepped the boundaries of the judicial branch.

I: IMMIGRANTS ARRIVING BY SEA

The Statue of Liberty stands at the gate of New York harbor. At the base of the statue are the famous lines written by Emma Lazarus:

> Give me your tired, your poor,
> Your huddled masses yearning to breathe free,
> The wretched refuse of your teeming shore,
> Send these, the homeless, tempest-tossed to me,
> I lift my lamp beside the golden door!

Forty or fifty miles off the coast of Florida, some homeless, tempest-tossed Haitians are riding a leaky sailboat bound for America. A Coast Guard cutter intercepts the boat, bringing its passengers aboard in small groups and questioning them about their whereabouts, their visas, their reasons for leaving Haiti. The process takes several hours. None of the Haitians has a visa, and the Coast Guard officials are not persuaded that any of them are entitled to asylum in America. They are told they will not be allowed to land and are sent back to sea—to return to Haiti, to find some other country, or to perish.

This is the scenario that develops at the beginning of the program. It does not come out of a vacuum. A series of true events helped to cause what Senator Alan Simpson calls America's "compassion fatigue."

The Mariel Boatlift, 1980

The events began in April 1980, when 2,000 Cubans seeking asylum crowded into the grounds of the Peruvian embassy in Havana. At first Cuban dictator Fidel Castro sought to stem this flood by posting armed guards around the embassy. Then he announced that the guard would be lifted.

That did it. Within a few days, the crowd had swollen from 2,000 to 10,000. Rallies in various cities of the United States demanded that we grant asylum to those at the embassy. The media weighed in with editorials supporting asylum. President Carter decided to help. Invoking the terms of the Refugee Act he had signed the month before, Carter ordered the admission of 3,500 of the Cubans.

Then events began to take their own course. American friends and relatives of Cubans began sailing empty boats to Cuba and returning laden with refugees. Castro saw this as an opportunity: if Jimmy Carter wanted Cubans, he would have Cubans. Castro invited Americans to sail their boats into the Cuban port of Mariel. He would have Cubans there waiting to be picked up. Soon there were 1,300 boats in Mariel harbor and, true to his word, Castro had Cubans waiting. It soon became clear, however, that only a portion of them were from the 10,000 who had crowded the Peruvian embassy.

Where had the rest come from? Castro had taken at least some—federal officials estimated the figure to be more than 20 percent—from prisons and insane asylums. Cuban government officials called the people "scum." *Granma*, the government-controlled newspaper, said they included "robbers, gamblers, drug pushers and prostitutes" but no really violent criminals. *Granma* turned out to be half right. There were all of the above, but there were also rapists, child molesters, stick-up artists, and murderers among the new refugees.

Almost immediately after the arrival of the Mariel flotilla and before any procedures could be established for screening and processing the new arrivals, crime in the Miami area soared. Soon local officials were reporting that 16 percent of felony arrests in Dade County, Florida, involved recent Cuban emigres. President Carter, who had earlier pledged that the United States would "provide an open heart and open arms" for refugees, began to have second thoughts. Declaring that America would not allow itself to become the "dumping ground" for criminals, Carter ordered all boat captains to turn around and bring their vessels back empty.

But now it was too late. Ferrying Cubans to the United States had become a lucrative business. The Cubans kept arriving. Before the fall of 1980, when Castro shut off the flow, 125,000 had come to our shores. About one in five had police records, though some had been arrested for political rather than criminal offenses. Unlike the first wave of Cuban immigrants in the early '60s, these new arrivals tended not to be wealthy or even middle class. They lacked the education, the business sense, and the connections of the earlier arrivals. How soon, if ever, they will rise to the level of the first wave remains a matter of debate—and concern.

Haitian Immigration, 1980–81

A few months before the start of the Mariel boatlift, Haitians had begun arriving in Florida in significant numbers. By the time the boatlift began, Haitian immigration had started to reach record proportions. The numbers increased throughout 1980 and into 1981. By the time the influx was over, about 15,000 Haitians had entered, though many were detained and eventually sent back.

The controversy really begins here. The charge has been made that the Haitians were victims of a double standard. The Cubans were automatically given refugee status as long as there was no evidence that they had committed serious crimes. The Haitians, on the other hand, had to prove that they deserved to be considered refugees rather than simply illegal aliens. Failing to establish such proof, they would be sent home.

What is a "refugee"? This definition has been the subject of controversy. The term ordinarily refers to anyone fleeing political oppression. In U.S. law, however, this meaning was applied only to those who fled either from Communist or Middle Eastern countries. It did not apply to anyone escaping oppressive regimes in other countries and certainly not to anyone leaving a "friendly" tyranny like the Duvalier regime in Haiti. That definition was changed, however, by a bill President Carter signed into law in March 1980—about the time the Haitian boatlift was getting under way.

The Refugee Act of 1980

The Refugee Act of 1980 defined "refugee" broadly to include anyone from any-where in the world—not just from Communist countries or the Middle East—who has a well-founded fear of persecution from his or her government. It also raised the num-bers allowed to enter this country as refugees from 17,000 to 50,000 and allowed the president, in consultation with Congress, to exceed even that limit in emergency situa-tions. As we have seen, Carter did so to accommodate the Mariel boatlift.

Much of the suffering experienced by Haitian immigrants in 1980–81 resulted from long periods of detention in crowded and unsanitary camps while claims to refugee status were being evaluated by immigration authorities. Had the Refugee Act of 1980 not been passed, most would have been spared the wait. After very brief ques-tioning, they would have been put on the next plane back to Haiti. They did not, after all, come from a Communist or Middle Eastern country. In fact, if the new law had not been passed, there probably would have been no massive boatlift from Haiti. The Hai-tians would have known the futility of risking their lives in a 700-mile journey across open waters to a country that would not accept them. Now, for the first time, they had a chance to be classified as refugees.

For most of the Haitians, these hopes turned to despair during the long wait in de-tention camps. Overcrowding made their situation desperate. Riots caused the author-ities to disperse them to a variety of places—federal prisons in New York, deserted air bases in Florida, army bases in Arkansas and Pennsylvania. When news of the hard-ships of detention drifted back to Haiti, the boatlift slowed. It was finally curbed by President Reagan in 1981, when he ordered the Coast Guard to interdict and turn around ships suspected of carrying illegal immigrants.

The video discussion begins here. We are out at sea with the Coast Guard, and a boatload of Haitians has been interdicted. What are these people's rights? Are they guaranteed the same rights under the "due process" clause of the Fifth Amendment as are people who live in the United States?

As Doris Meissner of the Immigration and Naturalization Service (INS) quickly re-veals, the immigrants interdicted at sea do not have many procedural rights. They are brought aboard the Coast Guard boat, asked for papers, and, when they admit they have none, told to turn around. There are no formal hearings, no judge, no lawyer to defend them. Is that constitutional? No, says U.S. District Court Judge Marvin Shoob.

Judge Shoob does not have a high opinion of Coast Guard officials. "Certainly no yo-yo out on a boat pitching in the Atlantic Ocean is competent to make that decision and say you can't come to the shores of the United States and get the hearing that you are entitled to," he says. Most Coast Guardsmen "have no legal training" and are thus unable to apprise the Haitians of their rights; consequently, the Haitians "might not even know what they should assert to entitle them to come into the United States."

The judge seems to be saying that the Coast Guardsmen should be not just com-petent judges but also defense attorneys for the Haitians. But they are still out at sea! Do constitutional rights apply to aliens even before they have reached American shores? Where will this reasoning take us? Earlier in the program, U.S. Prosecutor Rudolph Giuliani argued that it will take us to a global constitutionalism. "You're outside of the United States and these people are not citizens of the United States. To say that the United States Constitution applied would mean that the United States Constitution applies to the entire world."

Perhaps U.S. Appeals Court Judge Arthur Alarcon has been mulling over that argument. At any rate, he now has a reply to it: "My understanding from . . . high school on is that the Constitution of the United States follows our flag." But if that's the case, replies Giuliani, we should have to fly American judges and defense attorneys around the world, wherever people may claim refugee status. If someone runs into an American embassy in Moscow or Warsaw, we couldn't leave the deliberations to the U.S. authorities there; we would have to airlift judicial teams over. "You have selected a very poor example," Shoob responds, for "anybody that applies to the Russian embassy for refugee status, if he wasn't a refugee when he walked in, he became one now." He means that if the person were not persecuted before, he certainly would be if he ever walked back out.

Who is right in the controversy? U.S. Appeals Court Judge Arlin Adams sympathizes with his colleagues' point of view but concludes that constitutional rights do not extend beyond our shores. He does so reluctantly, because he wants "to see these people have as much of a hearing as . . . [is] deemed necessary to insure their safety and well being." It is a different story, though, when they reach our shores. Here Judge Adams readily agrees that "the language of the Constitution refers to all persons in the United States, whether or not they're citizens."

Well, then, let them reach our shore. "Ms. Meissner," says the moderator, "a couple of these boats get through and a group of Haitians land on a beach in Florida. . . . Now what happens?" They're entitled to a hearing, she says, to determine whether they are bona fide refugees. What happens while they're waiting for the hearing? They go to jail. By this time, Steven Shapiro of the New York Civil Liberties Union has gotten into the discussion. "Are they being punished for illegally coming into the country?" he asks Meissner. Incautiously, Meissner answers: "That is correct." Giuliani corrects her: "It really isn't punishment." It is detention, just as suspects are detained before a trial to make sure they do not disappear.

But, the moderator starts to remind him, when people are charged with crimes, they can put up bail and get out of detention. The difference, says Giuliani, is that in the case of crime the government has the burden of proving people guilty, while in these cases the burden is on the aliens to prove they are refugees. What is more, these people "crashed our borders." We have 150,000 people waiting to come here legally, and you "disserve" them when you encourage illegal entry. You also "create all sorts of dangers for our society, including the danger of communicable diseases." Giuliani may be alluding particularly to the danger of AIDS (acquired immune deficiency syndrome), a leukemia-like disease that some health authorities have found in disproportionate percentages among Haitian emigrants. The moderator then asks where these detained people are kept. In detention centers, Giuliani answers.

MODERATOR: Do they look like jails?
GIULIANI: Yes, they are places where people are held.
MODERATOR: Behind bars?
GIULIANI: They are not held behind bars; they are locked behind bars at night.

These distinctions seem excessively fine to Judge Shoob. We are still keeping people in prison—"and that's what it is, in prison"—while they await a hearing. Judge Shoob thinks that detaining people longer than six months amounts to punishment without a trial. He also claims that some Cuban detainees have been kept as long as three years. But, as the moderator reminds him, the Cubans were part of the Mariel boatlift, which included extremely dangerous felons. Some were and some were not, Shoob answers. "And the government . . . never wanted to make that distinction. They didn't want to face the problem, and still to this day, they don't want to face the problem."

Aside from the length of time the Caribbean "boat people" had to wait behind bars, there is another issue that keeps struggling to surface in this first section. It never really reaches the top, in spite of the moderator's best efforts, though Judge Shoob explicitly mentions it. The issue is the kind of procedural safeguards afforded to aliens. Are they entitled to the same right of counsel, the same protection against improper searches and interrogations, and all the other protections given to citizens of the United States?

Remember that the protections of the Bill of Rights are not limited to citizens. The Fifth Amendment, which guarantees "due process of law," extends to "any person." The Fourteenth Amendment, which prevents states from abridging "due process of law" and "the equal protection of the laws," again uses the word "person" in connection with these guarantees. Since aliens are as much "persons" as the rest of us, they would seem to enjoy the same protections. The trouble—perhaps the glory— is that American citizens enjoy such a wide array of protections, thanks to a series of Court decisions in the '60s, that aliens may have to be given warnings before they can be apprehended, provided with free lawyers, and let out of confinement if it gets too crowded. Furthermore, evidence against them that is seized without warrants may have to be thrown out of court. If aliens get all the same protections as citizens, then to land on American soil is to ensure oneself a safe, free, comfortable home for an indefinite period while the government frets over what to do without getting tripped up by the courts.

Part of this controversy does manage to surface in the third part of the program, when the panelists consider the implications of a 1983 Supreme Court decision forcing states to guarantee a free public education to the children of illegal aliens. Before moving on to the second and third parts of the program, however, the reader should review what has been said so far.

Points to Remember

1. Legal and illegal immigration has risen to record levels in recent years. There is evidence that its rate has reached a million a year or more, the level that existed shortly before World War I.
2. Some observers consider the new wave of immigration a threat to this country's future. Others regard it as a positive development, an infusion of new energy into American society.

3. Two concentrated waves of immigrants in 1980–81 were the boatlifts from Cuba and Haiti, which together brought in more than 150,000 people seeking asylum as refugees. Both groups were detained for long periods, but the Haitians had a heavier burden of proof. The Cubans were detained in order to screen out major felons, but the Haitians were detained until they could prove they were genuine refugees—that is, fleeing political persecution. Those failing to prove this were sent back.
4. The Refugee Act of 1980 changed the legal definition of "refugee." Formerly it had applied almost exclusively to those leaving Communist and Middle Eastern countries. Now it was extended to people leaving any country, even one friendly to the United States, that persecutes them politically.
5. The harsh conditions of the detention camps, along with President Reagan's new policy of interdicting boats bound for the United States, has deterred further Haitian immigration. Some critics deplore what they consider a double standard in our treatment of Haitians and Cubans.

II: LAND CROSSINGS

The second part of the program begins when the moderator moves the discussion to the United States' southern land border. "I want you to assume that I am a twenty-four-year-old . . . Mexican laborer," he says. "I am very poor, I have no work in Mexico, I think I must go to the United States so that I do not starve." These facts, of course, do not qualify our hypothetical immigrant for refugee status. He wants to enter the United States not to flee political persecution but to make money. To enter legally he must apply, wait months or even years, and probably get turned down. So he simply wades across a shallow spot in the Rio Grande and enters El Paso, Texas. There he is approached by border guards.

What happens next? Doris Meissner of the INS tells the moderator that he will be asked his name and where he comes from. The moderator obliges: "My name is Carlos. I have no papers." Meissner politely asks Carlos if he would care to return to Mexico. He replies, "Well, no, obviously not, I just came across." She then gives him a choice: he can be detained for a hearing that may take weeks to convene, or he can go back (with the hope of slipping across next time without getting caught). Carlos chooses the latter.

Carlos is not only a very logical man but he also knows something about the United States-Mexican border. It is 1,900 miles long and extraordinarily porous. Patrolling it on any given day are about 350 agents of the INS. That averages out to one agent for every 6 miles. If Carlos is apprehended, he will be sent back without any penalty. Then he will try again—and again, if necessary—until he makes it. Illegal land crossings are by far the most difficult to stem. They cannot be interdicted, like water crossings, and they require no vehicles that can be easily spotted. The United States cannot build a Chinese Wall on its southern border; even if it could, people would find a way of climbing over it or tunneling under it.

The real question is why Mexicans are so anxious to leave their country for this one. The answer is that they can make five to ten times more than what they make at home. They do so by working in the fields (15 percent), in service industries like hotels and restaurants (50 percent), or in factories (30 percent). Are they taking jobs away from Americans? Or are they filling jobs Americans disdain and helping to make the economic pie larger? The experts continue to disagree on this issue.

One point on which all sides agree, however, is that America is supposed to be a country of laws, and it is bad for those laws to be consistently flouted. American immigration laws *are* consistently flouted on the southern border. The question in the second part of the discussion is what to do about it.

The answers are not simple. One answer, the one debated by the panelists, is the Simpson-Mazzoli bill.

The Simpson-Mazzoli Bill: Employer Sanctions

The Simpson-Mazzoli bill can be traced back to 1978, when President Carter and Congress created the Select Committee on Immigration and Refugee Policy (SCIRP), a sixteen-member group of congressmen, senators, other officials, and prominent citizens appointed to study the problem of illegal immigration. The group included two members also present in the video debate: Republican Senator Alan Simpson of Wyoming and Father Theodore Hesburgh, president of Notre Dame. SCIRP held public hearings in a dozen cities, from Albany, New York, to Phoenix, Arizona, and in March 1981 released its final report and recommendations. The recommendations, in somewhat revised form, soon found their way into a bill jointly proposed by Senator Simpson and Democratic Representative Romano Mazzoli of Kentucky.

The Simpson-Mazzoli bill contained four major provisions:

1. *Amnesty.* The estimated 3½ to 6 million illegal immigrants living in America have become a kind of underclass. Constantly fearful of being apprehended, they put up with the worst treatment by employers while developing no civic attachments or roots in America. Simpson-Mazzoli therefore proposed an amnesty for all illegals who were here as of January 1, 1980. Through this amnesty they could, sooner or later, acquire citizenship.

2. *Beefing Up Enforcement.* The bill proposed funds to hire more agents to patrol the United States–Mexican border. While the present number is obviously inadequate, it argued, intensified patrolling *can* work. The INS's unfortunately named "Operation Wetback" of 1953–54 greatly diminished the flow of illegals from Mexico.

3. *Employer Sanctions.* This was the centerpiece—in the video discussion Simpson calls it the "guts"—of the Simpson-Mazzoli bill. If, as Father Hesburgh notes, jobs are the "magnet" attracting illegal immigrants, then this was an attempt to "demagnetize" the United States. It made it illegal for any employer knowingly to hire an illegal alien.

4. *A Forgery-proof I.D.* If employer sanctions was the centerpiece of Simpson-Mazzoli, here was an essential corollary. We cannot punish employers for hiring illegal aliens unless we give them a dependable and simple way of finding out whether an applicant *is* illegal. Otherwise they may just fall back on their prejudices and refuse to hire anyone with brown skin. Driver's licenses and Social Security cards can easily be

falsified. Therefore, the bill directed the president to come up with "a new, secure system to verify work eligibility." Sensitive to the charge of libertarians that such a national I.D. system might be used by police to stop people on the streets ("Where are your papers?"), the bill added that the I.D. card "would not be required for any purpose except verification of work eligibility."

The Simpson-Mazzoli bill has had a perilous career in Congress. First introduced in 1982, it was passed twice by the Senate but was stymied by the nonaction of the House of Representatives. In 1983 it seemed, for a time, that House action was imminent. In September, House Majority Leader Jim Wright (D-Texas) told Congressman Mazzoli that the bill would come up "before Thanksgiving." Then something happened. After meeting with the eleven members of the House's "Hispanic Caucus," House Speaker Thomas ("Tip") O'Neill said he would kill the bill by not letting it emerge from the House Rules Committee.

O'Neill's reasons seemed to be equal parts speculation and imagination. He feared that President Reagan would veto the bill so as to curry favor with Hispanic voters in time for the opening of the '84 elections. Reagan, who had supported legislation similar to Simpson-Mazzoli, stoutly denied any such planned doublecross, and Attorney General William French Smith announced that "the President would sign the Senate-passed version of the bill today if it was on his desk." (It is doubtful that the president would win much favor among Hispanic voters by vetoing the bill, for its basic content —sanctions against employers who hire illegal aliens—was endorsed by a margin of nearly two to one in a poll of Hispanic citizens.) O'Neill's other reason for opposing the bill was his fear that it would make Hispanics "wear a tag around their necks like the Jews in Germany."

True to his threat, O'Neill killed the bill by tying it up in committee. But after an enormous public outcry—from sources including prominent members of O'Neill's own party and newspapers like the *Washington Post* and the *New York Times*—he started backing down. He promised to let the bill come to the House floor in 1984, though it was clear that House consideration would not be possible until after the 1984 elections.

The Simpson-Mazzoli bill is the main issue of the second part of the program. Debate centers mainly on two of its provisions: employer sanctions and the forgery-proof I.D. system. Father Hesburgh and Senator Simpson spend much of their time describing and justifying the employer sanctions. Again, Father Hesburgh says sanctions will finally "demagnetize" the United States. Senator Simpson adds that we can never enforce our immigration laws "as long as it is legal to hire an illegal." Their views are opposed by Antonia Hernandez of the Mexican-American Legal Defense and Educational Fund, a pressure group defending the rights of Mexican aliens. Hernandez considers employer sanctions both unenforceable and discriminatory. Studies in other countries, she says, show that such attempts don't really stem the tide of immigration. All they do is give employers an excuse to discriminate against brown-skinned people with accents.

The moderator asks Simpson how he responds. Simpson, who has obviously debated Hernandez in the past, says, "I'm going to say to Antonia just what I say to her every time (*laughter*)," which is that employer sanctions are necessary, workable, and, thanks to the forgery-proof I.D. card, utterly nondiscriminatory. Anyone wanting a job, including "people who look like Antonia and bald-headed guys like me," will have to present the card to a prospective employer.

This talk of a national I.D. card opens up another attack on the Simpson-Mazzoli bill. It comes from Appeals Court Judge Alarcon. "I am old enough to have been in Germany during World War II, and traveled across Europe, where people had to show cards to go from city to city." This sounds like a variation on Tip O'Neill's theme that the bill would make Hispanics "wear a tag around their necks like the Jews in Germany." In spite of the bill's explicit assurance that the I.D. card "would not be required for any purpose except work eligibility," the Orwellian image of an internal passport system keeps appearing every time someone mentions it.

Jack Rosenthal, deputy editorial page editor of the *New York Times*, jumps to Senator Simpson's assistance by saying that a national I.D. card is really no more frightening than a credit card. He has "an American Express card, and I think we're in the grip of a kind of romantic view of the past here on the subject of national I.D." He's got his American Express number, and when he calls the theater for tickets he just reads it off. But by these remarks, Rosenthal has unwittingly demonstrated the difference between the world of the *New York Times* and that of Mexican-American immigrants. Hernandez is quick to underscore it. How many poor Mexican-Americans have American Express cards? "In the Southwest right now," she says, "[when] you talk about 'let me see your visa,' the joke is, 'I only carry Mastercharge,' because when they say, 'I want to see your visa,' they're talking about your immigration visa."

From Rosenthal's standpoint, all this may seem beside the point. He was only illustrating the point that I.D. cards need not be threatening. But Hernandez's point is that such items may mean one thing to U.S. senators and *Times* writers and quite another to those who inhabit the back alleys of American society.

Points to Remember

1. The Select Committee on Immigration and Refugee Policy (SCIRP), appointed in 1978 by President Carter, deliberated for three years and issued a report in 1981. Its report became the basis for the Simpson-Mazzoli bill, first introduced in 1982.

2. The Simpson-Mazzoli bill contains four major features: amnesty for illegals who arrived before 1980, beefed-up patrolling of our borders, employer sanctions, and a forgery-proof I.D. system.

3. Its major provisions are controversial. Employer sanctions ("the guts of the bill") are defended as the key to "demagnetizing" America by lowering the incentive of aliens to cross the border. Yet the sanctions have been criticized as an invitation to employers to discriminate in their hiring practices. The I.D. system is supposed to eliminate discrimination by giving employers secure and objective means of determining whether someone is here illegally. However, some worry that the system may threaten civil liberties, especially the liberties of poor aliens.

III: EDUCATION AND WELFARE OF ALIENS

There is one "sleeper" in the Simpson-Mazzoli bill that might present problems if it were ever awakened. That is the amnesty provision. If the 3½ to 6 million illegal aliens now residing in the United States are ever "forgiven" and started down the road to citizenship, it will cost American taxpayers a lot of money.

Presently, according to the calculations of University of Illinois professor Julian Simon, about three-quarters of the illegal aliens in the United States have federal taxes and Social Security deducted from their paychecks. Yet most do not receive welfare or unemployment compensation, either because of ineligibility or fear of being caught if they apply for them. All that would change if they were amnestied. They would then become eligible for every social service, and they would have no reason to fear applying. America now has a variety of welfare programs, from Food Stamps to Aid to Families with Dependent Children, whose costs soared during the decade of the '70s. If these programs were extended to the families of presently illegal aliens, the total annual costs would mean additional billions spent on social services. Estimates place the costs in excess of $10 billion annually.

Indeed, the costs of social services for aliens, both legal and illegal, are already considerable. For the Mariel and Haitian boatlifts alone, the federal government spent about $532 million to handle entry and resettlement costs in 1980. For aliens as a whole, some key court decisions have resulted in costs to the taxpayer that may grow steeply in the coming years.

Lau v. *Nichols*: Bilingual Instruction

In 1974 the Supreme Court decided the case of *Lau* v. *Nichols*, which resulted from a suit by Chinese-speaking students in San Francisco against the San Francisco school system for failure to provide special English-language instruction classes for about 1,800 Chinese-ancestry students who did not speak English. The students said that the school district's failure to provide special English-instruction classes violated Section 601 of the Civil Rights Act of 1964. Section 601 bans discrimination "on the ground of race, color, or national origin" in "any program or activity receiving Federal financial assistance." San Francisco public schools receive large amounts of federal assistance. Therefore, the claimants argued, they have the duty to provide special English-language instruction to Chinese students.

But wait a minute. True, Section 601 bans racial discrimination in teaching programs. But by what kind of acrobatics does that section get turned around to mean that a school district has to provide *special* language instruction for Chinese students? Discrimination means singling out a certain race for inferior treatment. But San Francisco was treating the Chinese just like everybody else—it was *not* singling them out. Now the Court was saying it *had* to.

That may seem a strange interpretation of the 1964 Civil Rights Act. Defending its reading, the Court said it was following the interpretation placed on the law by the Department of Health, Education and Welfare (HEW, now replaced by the Department of Health and Human Services and the Department of Education). HEW issued guidelines interpreting the law to mean that any school district receiving federal money "must take affirmative steps" to rectify students' language deficiencies. By failing to take such steps, San Francisco violated Section 601.

But isn't that a peculiar interpretation of Section 601? Some people might think so, but the Court took note of the fact that another section of the Civil Rights Law, Section 602, gave HEW the power to issue "rules and regulations" for carrying out Section 601. The Court thought it should not second-guess the bureaucrats as long as their rules were reasonably related to the law's intention.

Thus the justices let themselves be guided by the bureaucrats in interpreting the law. But this was just the beginning of bureaucratic leadership on this issue. The Court's decision in *Lau* v. *Nichols* did not require school districts to hold bilingual classes (classes conducted in two languages). All the Court said was that one way to end discrimination would be to teach English "to the students . . . who did not understand the language." But HEW immediately began laying down new rules requiring many school districts to set up "transitional" bilingual programs and to hire bilingual teachers and special "consultants" to supervise them, thus creating whole new bilingual divisions in the schools. About $140 million of federal money is being spent on these programs every year. Millions of additional dollars are spent by the states.

Another Supreme Court decision concerning aliens and their children may also have a high price tag. It was handed down a year before the panelists met to discuss immigration and forms a backdrop to much of the debate in part III. The case was *Plyler* v. *Doe*.

Plyler v. *Doe*: States Must Educate Illegal Aliens

Texas is one of the major transit points for the estimated half-million illegal aliens who slip into the country every year. In 1975, determined that public revenues would not be used to enhance the life of illegal immigrants, the Texas legislature revised its education laws to withhold state money for educating children who were not "legally admitted" into the country. There followed a lawsuit brought by attorneys representing "Doe," an illegal alien.

The suit was successful. The Supreme Court said that withholding state money for the public education of the children of illegal aliens violated the equal protection clause of the Fourteenth Amendment. This clause says that no state shall "deny to any person within its jurisdiction the equal protection of the laws." Texas seized on the phrase "within its jurisdiction" to justify its denial of free public education to the children of illegal aliens. Such individuals, the state said, were not "within its jurisdiction."

The Court rejected that reasoning as specious. The illegals reside "within the State's territorial perimeter" and are subject to the laws of the state. They do not suddenly become nonpersons when the school bell rings. Anyway, the "they" in this case are not the adults who have illegally crossed the border but the children they have brought with them. Because the state of Texas has a grievance against the parents, it is discriminating against their children! Its law is "directed against children, and imposes its discriminatory burden on the basis of a legal characteristic over which children can have little control." Why take it out on the kids?

By depriving these children of an education, the Court added, the state of Texas was doing itself—and the nation—a grave disservice.

It is difficult to understand precisely what the State hopes to achieve by promoting the creation and perpetuation of a subclass of illiterates within our boundaries, surely adding to the problems and costs of unemployment, welfare, and crime.

One of the problems with the *Plyler* opinion is the sweep of its logic. For if the children of illegal aliens have a right to public education, it would seem to follow that they have a right to other public services—welfare, for example. Yet the Court strongly implied that the state does not have to provide them with welfare payments. How can this be? The Court answered the contradiction by saying that education is extraordinarily important. ("What we said 28 years ago in *Brown* v. *Board of Education* still holds true: 'Today, education is perhaps the most important function of state and local governments.'")

But, as Justice Burger asked in his dissenting opinion, is education more important "than food, shelter, or medical care"? The logical conclusion of the Court's reasoning seems to be that the children of illegal aliens have a right to everything other children should have—education, food, shelter, medical care. In fact, they should have a right not to be deported. After all, why penalize the children for the sins of their parents?

If that is indeed what follows, then the children of illegal aliens are—citizens. They have all the rights of minor citizens, and they can't be deported. All you have to do, then, to make your children citizens of the United States is to sneak across the border with them. Of course, the Court would deny that its *Plyler* opinion could be taken to such lengths, but it is hard to see where its lines of distinction could be drawn.

This problem was raised by the dissenters in the case—Chief Justice Warren Burger and Justices Byron White, William Rehnquist, and Sandra Day O'Connor. But the dissent went much further. Written by Chief Justice Burger, it was a wide-ranging, scathing attack on the majority's approach to social problems. It accused the Court of acting like a legislature, trying to make laws instead of confining itself to interpreting them. "Were it our business to set the Nation's social policy," Burger wrote, "I would agree without hesitation that it is senseless" to deprive the children of an education. But it is not the business of courts to make laws; that is the job of legislatures. Maybe the legislature did not do a good job of setting policy in this case. But that does not grant judges the right to redo it. In trying to become an "omnipotent and omniscient problem solver," the dissent continued, this Court "distorts our constitutional function to make amends for the defaults of others." The state of Texas may not have been wise to refuse public education to illegal aliens, but it had as much right to do it as the federal government has not to give them food stamps.

Burger noted that previous cases had already settled these questions: education is not a basic right, and being an illegal alien is not like being, say, a black; it is not a category specially protected by the Constitution against discrimination. "Yet by patching together bits and pieces" of constitutional protections mentioned in previous cases, "the Court spins out a theory custom-tailored to the facts" of this case. Burger called this a "result-oriented" approach, suggesting that the Court was slapping together a theory to get the result it wanted. To put it more plainly, Burger accused five of his brethren of arrogance and hastiness if not outright dishonesty!

Compared with Burger's blistering dissent, the video discussion of the *Plyler* case is rather mild. Yet it is interesting that, despite their differences, the panelists all seem to have trouble grasping the Court's distinction between education and other social services.

As we have seen, the Court in *Plyler* said that states had to supply the children of illegal aliens with education but not necessarily with health services, welfare checks, food stamps, and the like. To the participants, this seems like a distinction without a difference. The moderator asks Nina Solarz of the Citizen's Committee for Immigration Reform whether the Constitution requires that illegal aliens be given access to "welfare, medical benefits. . . ." Maybe he was going to add "and education," but Solarz cuts in. She says they should not get welfare but should get health care on the grounds that they might otherwise spread illness. When Guillermo Martinez, a *Miami Herald* columnist, adds that the children of illegals are entitled to education, Solarz says, "Yes . . . I'm sorry . . . I should have added . . . an education."

Solarz obviously sees no distinction between health care and education. William Raspberry, the *Washington Post* columnist, sees none between welfare and education. In fact, he uses the *Plyler* opinion's why-punish-the-kids argument—which the Court had confined to the sphere of education—to justify giving the children welfare as well. "It seems to me that you're willy-nilly punishing children who can't do anything about it . . . for their parents' illegal status."

Perhaps the reader agrees with Raspberry. Why distinguish between education and welfare? Remember, though, that such an agreement carries a price tag. To extend the full range of welfare services to the illegal aliens of this country will cost American taxpayers about $10 billion annually. Raspberry would take the burden of these costs off state government by making the federal government pick up the tab, but the tab still comes back to the taxpayer. Solarz tries to reassure us by saying that most illegal aliens do not want welfare—but that could change once it was established that they had a constitutional right to it.

It remains for Appeals Court Judge Arlin Adams to give the discussion a little more structure. First, he reminds the participants that the Court made a distinction between education and the other social services mentioned. Only education is mandated by the Constitution. "Having said that," he continues, "I have a difficult time making the distinction between educating the youngster and supplying the youngster with enough food to subsist." After all, what good is it to be guaranteed an education "if you're . . . starving in the meantime, or so sick that you couldn't go to school?"

Yet Adams is not ready to agree that the Constitution mandates that the children of illegal aliens are entitled to a wide range of welfare benefits as well as education. On the contrary, he agrees with the dissenters in *Plyler* that we must distinguish between what we think is right and what is mandated by the Constitution. "Just because the legislature or you or I wish a particular result, [that] doesn't constitutionalize what we wish; we always have to go back to the Constitution and decide whether that matter is covered."

Points to Remember

1. If the illegal aliens now in the United States were ever "amnestied," as provided in the Simpson-Mazzoli bill, it would make them eligible for a number of social services, including Aid to Families with Dependent Children and food stamps. Cost estimates run about $10 billion annually.
2. Court decisions have made aliens, including illegal aliens, eligible for programs in education. *Lau* v. *Nichols* (1974) held that public schools have an affirmative duty to provide special English-language instruction for non-English-speaking students. *Plyler* v. *Doe* (1982) held that states must supply the children of illegal aliens with free public education.
3. Some participants in the video debate would extend the *Plyler* holding to require that the states or the federal government also supply the children of illegal aliens with welfare and health services. Others, notably Judge Arlin Adams, believe the Court majority in *Plyler* went too far in interpreting the mandate of the equal protection clause.

SUMMARY

Over the past fifteen years, we have seen a dramatic increase in the rate of immigration, both legal and illegal. We have also seen a shift in the areas from which immigrants come, from Europe to Asia, Mexico, and the Caribbean. What will all this mean for the future of America? As the video discussion comes to a close, different visions of the future are presented. Senator Simpson, who thinks America has become "the patsy of the world," offers a dark vision. "What's out there in this country right now is stuff, lots of stuff down underneath, it's called . . . for want of a better word, the uglies." You won't hear it here, he says, "it won't be dealt with on top of the table, but let me tell you, after traveling the United States back and forth . . . that stuff is down there."

What stuff? What is "the uglies"? Simpson does not sketch the nightmare in detail, but what he seems to be alluding to is the scramble for limited resources. The scenario is actually borrowed from Thomas Malthus, the nineteenth-century English economist who speculated on what happens when population outruns food supply. Then, Malthus said, there has to be a period of famine and disease, which reduces population again. Of course, Malthus could not anticipate the widespread use of contraception. But that method is only common in northern, industrialized countries. America's new immigrants are escaping from regions where population is still out of

control. How many more can we absorb before we too are in the grips of "the uglies"
the desperate scramble for what is left of America?

There are those who consider the Malthusian nightmare just that: a bad dream, an
illusion. According to Julian Simon, what Malthus leaves out is that human beings are
not just resource eaters but also resource producers. We are more than mouths and
stomachs; we also have hands, and with those hands we *make* things that do not exist
in nature. We *create* wealth. This viewpoint may even lead us to conclude that new
immigration is needed, to compensate for the loss of population in the United States
due to birth control and abortion.

That is the vision of the future offered by Monsignor Bryan Walsh, who directs
Catholic Charities for the Archdiocese of Miami.

> This is relatively still an unpopulated country, compared to the advanced countries
> of the world. . . . And I honestly think that we will be looking for immigrants in
> this country, young immigrants here twenty, twenty-five years from now . . .
> because we won't have our own population to . . . maintain, the way things are
> going.

It is probably safe to say that relatively few Catholic clergymen suffer from Senator Simpson's "compassion fatigue." Their tendency is to welcome immigrants; therefore Monsignor Walsh's position is unsurprising. What may surprise some viewers is
Father Theodore Hesburgh's attitude. Hesburgh shares the views of Senator Simpson.
This may be because he sat on SCIRP with Simpson for four years. (Hesburgh was
made chairman of the committee in 1979.) Was Father Hesburgh "co-opted" into a
hard-nosed attitude on immigration? Or did he simply investigate the facts about unrestricted immigration and find them frightening? Whatever the reason, his vision of
the future is at least as dark as Simpson's.

> We have to face the fact that in the world of tomorrow—and I'm thinking about
> the year 2000—it's not inconceivable that a hundred million people would start to
> march on this or some other country. . . . If you had, for example, a massive fam-
> ine in India, and you had literally tens of millions of people dying of starvation,
> and the population at that point of that country was over a billion, and they knew
> perfectly well there was a lot of food in Venice and Vienna and Paris and Rome
> and other countries in Europe—supposing a hundred million Indians put a sack of
> rice over their shoulders and started to walk on Europe? It could happen, it's not
> a science fiction. Suppose things get so bad in the Caribbean that everybody who
> can make a boat starts heading for the United States? Suppose things get so bad in
> Central America and South America and Mexico that literally millions of people
> start voting with their feet and walking across the border?

This pessimistic vision is reminiscent less of Malthus than of Jean Raspail, the
Frenchman who wrote the 1973 novel *Camp of the Saints*. Raspail's novel pretends to
depict events in the not-so-distant future, when the West is invaded by the starving
multitudes of the Third World. From India alone a whole fleet of dilapidated ships,
caked with rust, makes it way to the southern coast of France. "A hundred ships! . . .

On this Easter Sunday evening, eight hundred thousand living beings, and thousands of dead ones, were making their peaceful assault on the Western World." Raspail's message is that the West will bring on its own destruction by letting the multitudes enter. It will be done in by its own humanitarianism. "You and your pity!" one of his heroes shouts. "Your damned, obnoxious, detestable pity!"

The nightmare vision of a West overrun by the Third World's starving masses puts to the ultimate test the words on the Statue of Liberty: "Give me your tired, your poor. . . ." In the 1980s the nation's lawmakers are being pressured to qualify that invitation, to temper compassion with caution, to do something to slow down the movement of new peoples into this country. Is there something selfish about these demands? Or do they represent an attempt to face hard realities that too many idealists and moralists have ignored? Perhaps they contain elements of both. What is certain is that the opening and closing of America's "golden door" is a process that will be watched very carefully in the coming years.

Documents

PLYLER V. DOE, 457 U.S. 202 (1982)

In this case the Court ruled that a Texas statute denying state funding of education for any children not "legally admitted" into the United States violated the equal protection clause of the Fourteenth Amendment.

Opinion of the Court, Mr. Justice Brennan.

The Fourteenth Amendment provides that "[n]o State shall . . . deprive any person of life, liberty, or property, without due process of law; nor deny to *any person within its jurisdiction* the equal protection of the laws." Appellants argue at the outset that undocumented aliens, because of their immigration status, are not "persons within the jurisdiction" of the State of Texas, and that they therefore have no right to the equal protection of Texas law. We reject this argument. Whatever his status under the immigration laws, an alien is surely a "person" in any ordinary sense of that term. Aliens, even aliens whose presence in this country is unlawful, have long been recognized as "persons" guaranteed due process of law by the Fifth and Fourteenth Amendments. Indeed, we have clearly held that the Fifth Amendment protects aliens whose presence in this country is unlawful from invidious discrimination by the Federal Government.

Appellants seek to distinguish our prior cases, emphasizing that the Equal Protection Clause directs a State to afford its protection to persons *within its jurisdiction* while the Due Process Clauses of the Fifth and Fourteenth Amendments contain no such assertedly limiting phrase. In appellants' view, persons who have entered the United States illegally are not "within the jurisdiction" of a State even if they are present within a State's boundaries and subject to its laws. Neither our cases nor the logic of the Fourteenth Amendment supports that constricting construction of the phrase "within its jurisdiction." We have never suggested that the class of persons who might avail themselves of the equal protection guarantee is less than coextensive with that entitled to due process. To the contrary, we have recognized that both provisions were fashioned to protect an identical class of persons, and to reach every exercise of state authority. . . .

There is simply no support for appellants' suggestion that "due process" is somehow of greater stature than "equal protection" and therefore available to a larger class of persons. To the contrary, each aspect of the Fourteenth Amendment reflects an elementary limitation on state power. To permit a State to employ the phrase "within its jurisdiction" in order to identify subclasses of persons whom it would define as beyond its jurisdiction, thereby relieving itself of the obligation to assure that its laws are designed and applied equally to those persons, would undermine the principal purpose for which the Equal Protection Clause was incorporated in the Fourteenth Amendment. The Equal Protection Clause was intended to work nothing less than the abolition of all caste-based and invidious class-based legislation. That objective is fundamentally at odds with the power the State asserts here to classify persons subject to its laws as nonetheless excepted from its protection. . . .

Use of the phrase "within its jurisdiction" thus does not detract from, but rather confirms, the understanding that the protection of the Fourteenth Amendment extends to anyone, citizen or stranger, who *is* subject to the laws of a State, and reaches into every corner of a State's territory. That a person's initial entry into a State, or into the United States, was unlawful, and that he may for that reason be expelled, cannot negate the simple fact of his presence within the State's territorial perimeter. Given such presence, he is subject to the full range of obligations imposed by the State's civil and criminal laws. And until he leaves the jurisdiction—either voluntarily, or involuntarily in accordance with the Constitution and laws of the United States—he is entitled to the equal protection of the laws that a State may choose to establish.

Our conclusion that the illegal aliens who are plaintiffs in these cases may claim the benefit of the Fourteenth Amendment's guarantee of equal protection only begins the inquiry. The more difficult question is whether the Equal Protection Clause has been violated by the refusal of the State of Texas to reimburse local school boards for the education of children who cannot demonstrate that their presence within the United States is lawful, or by the imposition by those school boards of the burden of tuition on those children. It is to this question that we now turn. . . .

Sheer incapability or lax enforcement of the laws barring entry into this country, coupled with the failure to establish an effective bar to the employment of undocumented aliens, has resulted in the creation of a substantial "shadow population" of illegal migrants—numbering in the millions—within our borders. This situation raises the specter of a permanent caste of undocumented resident aliens, encouraged by some to remain here as a source of cheap labor, but nevertheless denied the benefits that our society makes available to citizens and lawful residents. The existence of such an underclass presents most difficult problems for a Nation that prides itself on adherence to principles of equality under law.

The children who are plaintiffs in these cases are special members of this under-class. Persuasive arguments support the view that a State may withhold its beneficence from those whose very presence within the United States is the product of their own unlawful conduct. These arguments do not apply with the same force to classifications imposing disabilities on the minor *children* of such illegal entrants. At the least, those who elect to enter our territory by stealth and in violation of our law should be pre-pared to bear the consequences, including, but not limited to, deportation. But the children of those illegal entrants are not comparably situated. Their "parents have the ability to conform their conduct to societal norms," and presumably the ability to re-move themselves from the State's jurisdiction; but the children who are plaintiffs in these cases "can affect neither their parents' conduct nor their own status." . . .

Of course, undocumented status is not irrelevant to any proper legislative goal. Nor is undocumented status an absolutely immutable characteristic since it is the product of conscious, indeed unlawful, action. But § 21.031 is directed against chil-dren, and imposes its discriminatory burden on the basis of a legal characteristic over which children can have little control. It is thus difficult to conceive of a rational justi-fication for penalizing these children for their presence within the United States. Yet that appears to be precisely the effect of § 21.031.

Public education is not a "right" granted to individuals by the Constitution. But neither is it merely some governmental "benefit" indistinguishable from other forms of social welfare legislation. Both the importance of education in maintaining our basic institutions, and the lasting impact of its deprivation on the life of the child, mark the distinction. The "American people have always regarded education and [the] acquisi-tion of knowledge as matters of supreme importance." We have recognized "the public schools as a most vital civic institution for the preservation of a democratic system of government," and as the primary vehicle for transmitting "the values on which our society rests." "[A]s . . . pointed out early in our history, . . . some degree of educa-tion is necessary to prepare citizens to participate effectively and intelligently in our open political system if we are to preserve freedom and independence." In addition, education provides the basic tools by which individuals might lead economically pro-ductive lives to the benefit of us all. In sum, education has a fundamental role in main-taining the fabric of our society. We cannot ignore the significant social costs borne by our Nation when select groups are denied the means to absorb the values and skills upon which our social order rests.

In addition to the pivotal role of education in sustaining our political and cultural heritage, denial of education to some isolated group of children poses an affront to one of the goals of the Equal Protection Clause: the abolition of governmental barriers presenting unreasonable obstacles to advancement on the basis of individual merit. Par-adoxically, by depriving the children of any disfavored group of an education, we fore-close the means by which that group might raise the level of esteem in which it is held by the majority. But more directly, "education prepares individuals to be self-reliant and self-sufficient participants in society." Illiteracy is an enduring disability. The inability to read and write will handicap the individual deprived of a basic education each and every day of his life. The inestimable toll of that deprivation on the social, economic, intellectual, and psychological well-being of the individual, and the obstacle it poses to individual achievement, make it most difficult to reconcile the cost or the principle of a status-based denial of basic education with the framework of equality embodied in the Equal Protection Clause.

Chief Justice Warren Burger—joined by Justices White, Rehnquist, and O'Connor—dissented.

Dissenting Opinion, Chief Justice Burger.

Were it our business to set the Nation's social policy, I would agree without hesitation that it is senseless for an enlightened society to deprive any children—including illegal aliens—of an elementary education. I fully agree that it would be folly—and wrong—to tolerate creation of a segment of society made up of illiterate persons, many having a limited or no command of our language. However, the Constitution does not constitute us as "Platonic Guardians" nor does it vest in this Court the authority to strike down laws because they do not meet our standards of desirable social policy, "wisdom," or "common sense." We trespass on the assigned function of the political branches under our structure of limited and separated powers when we assume a policymaking role as the Court does today.

The Court makes no attempt to disguise that it is acting to make up for Congress' lack of "effective leadership" in dealing with the serious national problems caused by the influx of uncountable millions of illegal aliens across our borders. The failure of enforcement of the immigration laws over more than a decade and the inherent difficulty and expense of sealing our vast borders have combined to create a grave socioeconomic dilemma. It is a dilemma that has not yet even been fully assessed, let alone addressed. However, it is not the function of the judiciary to provide "effective leadership" simply because the political branches of government fail to do so.

The Court's holding today manifests the justly criticized judicial tendency to attempt speedy and wholesale formulation of "remedies" for the failures—or simply the laggard pace—of the political processes of our system of government. The Court employs, and in my view abuses, the Fourteenth Amendment in an effort to become an omnipotent and omniscient problem solver. That the motives for doing so are noble and compassionate does not alter the fact that the Court distorts our constitutional function to make amends for the defaults of others. . . .

The dispositive issue in these cases, simply put, is whether, for purposes of allocating its finite resources, a state has a legitimate reason to differentiate between persons who are lawfully within the state and those who are unlawfully there. The distinction the State of Texas has drawn—based not only upon its own legitimate interests but on classifications established by the Federal Government in its immigration laws and policies—is not unconstitutional.

The Court acknowledges that, except in those cases when state classifications disadvantage a "suspect class" or impinge upon a "fundamental right," the Equal Protection Clause permits a state "substantial latitude" in distinguishing between different groups of persons. Moreover, the Court expressly—and correctly—rejects any sugges-tion that illegal aliens are a suspect class, or that education is a fundamental right. Yet by patching together bits and pieces of what might be termed quasi-suspect class and quasi-fundamental-rights analysis, the Court spins out a theory custom-tailored to the facts of these cases.

In the end, we are told little more than that the level of scrutiny employed to strike down the Texas law applies only when illegal alien children are deprived of a public education. If ever a court was guilty of an unabashedly result-oriented approach, this case is a prime example.

The Court first suggests that these illegal alien children, although not a suspect class, are entitled to special solicitude under the Equal Protection Clause because they lack "control" over or "responsibility" for their unlawful entry into this country. Similarly, the Court appears to take the position that § 21.031 is presumptively "ir-rational" because it has the effect of imposing "penalties" on "innocent" children. However, the Equal Protection Clause does not preclude legislators from classifying among persons on the basis of factors and characteristics over which individuals may be said to lack "control." Indeed, in some circumstances persons generally, and chil-dren in particular, may have little control over or responsibility for such things as their ill health, need for public assistance, or place of residence. Yet a state legislature is not barred from considering, for example, relevant differences between the mentally healthy and the mentally ill, or between the residents of different counties, simply because these may be factors unrelated to individual choice or to any "wrongdoing." The Equal Protection Clause protects against arbitrary and irrational classifications, and against invidious discrimination stemming from prejudice and hostility; it is not an all-encompassing "equalizer" designed to eradicate every distinction for which persons are not "responsible."

The Court does not presume to suggest that appellees' purported lack of culpability for their illegal status prevents them from being deported or otherwise "penalized" under federal law. Yet would deportation be any less a "penalty" than denial of priv-ileges provided to legal residents? Illegality of presence in the United States does not—and need not—depend on some amorphous concept of "guilt" or "innocence" con-cerning an alien's entry. Similarly, a state's use of federal immigration status as a basis for legislative classification is not necessarily rendered suspect for its failure to take such factors into account. . . .

[T]he Court's analysis rests on the premise that, although public education is not a constitutionally guaranteed right, "neither is it merely some governmental 'benefit' indistinguishable from other forms of social welfare legislation." Whatever meaning or relevance this opaque observation might have in some other context, it simply has no bearing on the issues at hand. Indeed, it is never made clear what the Court's opinion means on this score.

The importance of education is beyond dispute. Yet we have held repeatedly that the importance of a governmental service does not elevate it to the status of a "funda-mental right" for purposes of equal protection analysis. Moreover, the Court points to no meaningful way to distinguish between education and other governmental benefits in this context. Is the Court suggesting that education is more "fundamental" than food, shelter, or medical care? . . .

Denying a free education to illegal alien children is not a choice I would make were I a legislator. Apart from compassionate considerations, the long-range costs of excluding any children from the public schools may well outweigh the costs of educating them. But that is not the issue; the fact that there are sound *policy* arguments against the Texas Legislature's choice does not render that choice an unconstitutional one.

The Constitution does not provide a cure for every social ill, nor does it vest judges with a mandate to try to remedy every social problem. Moreover, when this Court rushes in to remedy what it perceives to be the failings of the political processes, it deprives those processes of an opportunity to function. When the political institutions are not forced to exercise constitutionally allocated powers and responsibilities, those powers, like muscles not used, tend to atrophy. Today's cases, I regret to say, present yet another example of unwarranted judicial action which in the long run tends to contribute to the weakening of our political processes.

SELECTED READINGS

Blum, Carolyn Patty, ed. *Immigration Law and Defense.* 2nd ed. National Lawyers' Guild. New York: Clark Boardman, 1979-1980.
A lengthy, detailed outline of immigration law, as it has been developed and interpreted by courts, arranged according to chronology and specific issues.
Donohue, John W. "The Uneasy Immigration Debate." *America*, March 20, 1982, pp. 206-209.
A generally proimmigration piece. It points out that while the number of immigrants is at an all-time high, the *percentage* of foreign-born people in the United States is only 4 or 5 percent, compared with 14.7 percent in 1910. It also discusses the Simpson-Mazzoli bill.
Fallows, James. "Immigration: How It's Affecting Us." *The Atlantic Monthly*, November 1983, pp. 45-106.
A comprehensive survey of current immigration laws and immigration in America today, with particular attention to the "new immigrants" from Asia and Latin America: their economic situation, languages, and races. The article is richly researched and superbly written.
Handlin, Oscar. *Immigration as a Factor in American History.* Englewood Cliffs, N.J.: Prentice-Hall, 1959.
One of several books on the subject by a Pulitzer Prize-winning historian, this compilation of personal accounts, newspaper and magazine clippings, and scholarly commentaries makes enjoyable reading for both the general student and the specialist.

Hewett, Sylvia Ann. "Coping with Illegal Immigrants: Reagan Administration Proposals." *Foreign Affairs* 60 (Winter 1981-82): 358-378.

This article offers excellent descriptions and analyses of the problems of illegal immigration and the ways the Reagan administration has tried to cope with them. The writer is executive director of the Economic Policy Council of the United Nations Association.

Keely, Charles B. *U.S. Immigration Policy Analysis.* New York: Population Council, 1979.

In this analysis of the official immigration policy of the United States, Keely traces what he terms the "ambivalent" history of American immigration policy through the 1970s and outlines the theory and practice currently employed by policy makers.

Kessner, Thomas, and Caroli, Betty Boyd. *Today's Immigrants, Their Stories.* New York: Oxford University Press, 1981.

Subtitled *A New Look at the Newest Americans*, this book offers an array of narratives based on the firsthand accounts of both legal and illegal immigrants from the Orient, Latin America, the Caribbean, western Europe, and the Soviet Union. The book includes a comprehensive selection of charts and statistics on immigration.

Law and Contemporary Problems 45 (Spring 1982).

Entirely devoted to U.S. immigration policy, this issue contains a variety of essays, all of them scholarly and rich in data, spanning a range of viewpoints. The introduction is by William French Smith, then attorney general.

North, David S. *Amnesty: Conferring Legal Status on Illegal Immigrants.* 2nd ed. Washington, D.C.: New TransCentury Foundation, 1982.

A collection of three research papers, by the director of the Center for Labor and Migration Studies at the New TransCentury Foundation, focusing on the issue of amnesty for illegal immigrants. Particular emphasis is given to the results of amnesties already conferred in Canada and western Europe. The author then explores the implications such a policy would have for America.

Rips, Geoffrey. "The Simpson-Mazzoli Bill: Supply-Side Immigration Reform." *The Nation*, October 8, 1983, pp. 237-242.

A critique of the Simpson-Mazzoli bill and of current immigration policies. Rips contends that the latest immigration "reform" proposals are hypocritical in light of past American exploitation of immigrant laborers.

GLOSSARY

Asylum. An administrative act by which a government authorizes the entry or settlement of an illegal alien fleeing political persecution.

"Boat people." Those fleeing their native country by boat, often in large numbers, to escape political persecution or economic hardship. Cuba, Haiti, and Vietnam have produced the largest numbers of boat people.

Doe. A court-designated name used to designate persons whose identity the court wishes to protect or whose identity is unknown.

Ellis Island. A tiny island in New York harbor which, from 1892 to 1954, served as the port of entry for more than 30 million immigrants.

Great Society. A series of social welfare programs initiated in the mid-'60s by President Lyndon Johnson in order to wipe out poverty in the United States.

Illegal or undocumented aliens. Immigrants who have entered a country without permission of the country's government.

Orwellian. Of or pertaining to a society completely devoid of both liberty and privacy, such as the society depicted in George Orwell's novel *1984*.

Visa. Official, written permission to enter a country.

Chapter 12
Should Laws Be Color-Blind?

*"Our Constitution is color-blind, and neither
knows nor tolerates classes among citizens."*
JUSTICE JOHN HARLAN, 1896

*"Color-blindness is the goal. There have been
just scores of commentators, courts, and other
thoughtful people that have recognized that the
only way you get to that goal is to indulge color-
consciousness on the way."*
JUDGE HARRY EDWARDS, 1982

The Declaration of Independence asserts that "all men are created equal." Yet America is scarred by a long history of legally imposed inequality. Even after slavery was abolished by the Thirteenth Amendment in 1865, American blacks, other minorities, and women continued to be deprived of some of the most elementary rights of citizenship. In 1896 the Supreme Court gave legal sanction to racial segregation by endorsing the concept of "separate but equal." For nearly sixty years the "separate" part was strictly enforced, particularly in the South, though equality was systematically denied. Even today, despite the Supreme Court's desegregation decision of 1954 and the civil rights statutes of the 1960s, equality of condition remains elusive. In a variety of areas, from the quality of health care to the rate of employment, blacks still remain far behind whites. Their representation in the more prestigious professions is still almost negligible. Comparable imbalances exist for other racial and ethnic minorities as well as for women.

"Affirmative action" is based on the premise that the only way these imbalances can be redressed is by "numerical goals" which ensure that a minimum number of minorities and women are admitted to schools, jobs, or programs of economic advancement. To opponents of affirmative action, such "quotas" amount to discrimination in reverse, which they view as both unjust and unwise—unjust because racial and gender quotas penalize people simply for being white males and unwise because, they contend, quotas increase bitterness and tension without accomplishing their goals.

Is affirmative action a fair and practical means of addressing the problem of inequality? Or is it a form of reverse racism? Should the laws be "color-blind"? Or is it necessary at this point in history to become "color-conscious" in order to undo the effects of past discrimination? These difficult questions have provoked vigorous, often heated debate—a debate that has spilled over into every forum imaginable, from the law court and the political podium to the family dinner table.

368

The Video Discussion

The participants in the video discussion represent a wide spectrum of viewpoints on these issues. Their moderator is attorney Tyrone Brown, a former member of the Federal Communications Commission.

List of Participants

HON. WILLIAM J. BAUER
Judge
U.S. Court of Appeals
Seventh Circuit

HON. ROBERT H. BORK
Judge
U.S. Court of Appeals
District of Columbia

HON. JOSEPH A. CALIFANO, JR.
Attorney
Dewey, Ballantine, Bushby,
Palmer & Wood
Former U.S. Secretary of Health,
Education and Welfare

HON. HARRY T. EDWARDS
Judge
U.S. Court of Appeals
District of Columbia

ELLEN GOODMAN
Syndicated Columnist
Boston Globe

HON. SHIRLEY M. HUFSTEDLER
Attorney
Hufstedler, Miller, Carlson & Beardsley
Former U.S. Secretary of Education

IRVING KRISTOL
Editor
The Public Interest

JIM LEHRER
Associate Editor
Macneil-Lehrer News Hour

ANTHONY LEWIS
Columnist
New York Times

AVI NELSON
Media Commentator and Analyst
WCVB-TV (Boston)

ELEANOR HOLMES NORTON
Professor
Georgetown University Law School
Former Chair
Equal Employment Opportunity
Commission

JUAN U. ORTIZ
City Personnel Director
New York City

ALVIN POUSSAINT, M.D.
Associate Professor of Psychiatry
Harvard Medical School

HON. CHARLES B. RANGEL
U.S. Representative
New York

WILLIAM RASPBERRY
Columnist
Washington Post

WILLIAM BRADFORD REYNOLDS
Assistant Attorney General
Civil Rights Division
Department of Justice

HON. POTTER STEWART
Justice (retired)
U.S. Supreme Court

ALBERT SHANKER
President
United Federation of Teachers

Program Summary

The discussion is divided into three parts. In the first part, the moderator chooses three panelists to portray "candidates for tenure" at a state-run university. One is a white male, one a black male, the third a white female. Their qualifications: all are approximately equal in publications; in terms of teaching ability, the white male is "slightly better" than the white female, and she, in turn, is "slightly better" than the black male. When it comes to nonacademic activities, such as relationships with the community (which contribute to university life), the black male is first, though the other two have also done well. There is only one opening for tenure. The moderator appoints various panelists to a "tenure committee." He asks them which of the three candidates they would vote for and why. He then asks them to explain their votes to those they turned down and asks the disappointed candidates for their reactions.

If the first part of the program is specific and concrete, turning upon a particular case, the second part becomes more general. The panelists debate the pros and cons of affirmative action as a social policy. What are the implications—social, political, and constitutional—of affirmative action? The concept of "color-blindness" is introduced. Various Supreme Court cases on the issue of civil rights are discussed.

The third part of the program is a kind of wrap-up discussion of affirmative action, color-blindness, the difficulty of defining "merit," the persistence of racial prejudice in America, and the role of legal institutions in trying to minimize its effects.

Before getting into the immediate issues raised in the video discussion, we need some historical background. In particular, we need to get a sense of why affirmative action—which is admittedly a controversial and divisive experiment in race relations—has been considered necessary by many civil rights advocates. Whatever positions Americans finally reach on the issue of affirmative action, they must understand the rationale behind it. That rationale is tied to memories and effects of the American past, particularly as they relate to American blacks.

The Career of Jim Crow

"We didn't land on Plymouth Rock, my brothers and sisters—Plymouth Rock landed on *us!*" Malcolm X's observation is well borne out by the facts of American history. Snatched from their native land, transported thousands of miles—in a nightmare of disease and death—and sold into slavery, blacks in America were reduced to the legal status of farm animals. A Supreme Court opinion, *Dred Scott* v. *Sandford* (1857), made this official by classifying slaves as a species of "private property."

This is the heritage, "the stain on our history," as Justice Potter Stewart calls it, whose traces we are still trying to remove. It seemed, for a moment, that they were removed by the Thirteenth Amendment of 1865, which formally reversed *Dred Scott* by making slavery illegal. But the South reacted by passing the "Black Codes," which severely limited the rights of the newly freed slaves, preventing them in most states from testifying in court against whites, limiting their opportunities to find work, and generally relegating them to the status of second- or third-class citizens.

Then came Reconstruction, which seemed like the dawn of a new era to American blacks. Reconstruction was a far-reaching reorganization plan imposed by Congress on the South at the end of the Civil War. Before the defeated Southern states could be readmitted to the Union, they had to guarantee suffrage and equal treatment to blacks. Anyone connected with the former Confederacy was barred from holding office or even participating in political campaigns. The Fourteenth Amendment, passed in 1868, made blacks citizens and promised them "the equal protection of the laws." In 1870 the Fifteenth Amendment was passed, which gave blacks the right to vote. Congress also passed a number of civil rights laws barring discrimination against blacks in hotels, theaters, and other places.

The Reconstruction statutes and amendments were stringently enforced. Federal troops remained in the South, and the army's officers served as administrators for the region. The result was akin to a revolution. The former white power structure was destroyed and replaced by a new one composed of many who had never even voted before, including former slaves. In the South Carolina legislature, blacks outnumbered whites.

But Reconstruction was short-lived. Soon, white vigilante groups like the Ku Klux Klan began to appear; they murdered and terrorized blacks who tried to exercise their new rights. "Legal" ways were also found for circumventing the new laws. "Grandfather" clauses—which limited the right of suffrage to those who had voted before 1867 or were the children or grandchildren of those who had—were attached to state constitutions. Poll taxes, to be paid before voting, were instituted. Whites-only primary elections were established. And there was constant social discrimination against and intimidation of blacks, who were excluded from education and from any jobs except the most menial. By the time the last Union troops left the South in 1877, most of the rights given to blacks during Reconstruction were badly eroded. Over the next twenty years they were wiped out.

The Supreme Court made it all official. In 1883 it declared unconstitutional a key civil rights statute passed during Reconstruction, one that prohibited discrimination in public accommodations. (Not until 1964 would another such federal statute be passed.) And in 1896, in the case of *Plessy* v. *Ferguson*, the Court declared that the state of Louisiana had the right to segregate its railroad cars. The logical—and factual—extension was that all states had the official right to segregate their races in every public facility from washrooms to schools. Thus began the heyday of "Jim Crow" legislation, which in South Africa is called *apartheid* and in America was called "separate but equal." That was the philosophy of *Plessy* v. *Ferguson*, and only one person on the Court, John Marshall Harlan, realized it was a mockery. In his lone bitter dissent he wrote:

> We boast of the freedom enjoyed by our people above all other peoples. But it is difficult to reconcile that boast with a state of the law which, practically, puts a brand of servitude and degradation upon a large class of our fellow citizens, our equals before the law. The thin disguise of "equal" accommodations for passengers in railroad coaches will not mislead anyone, or atone for the wrong this day done.

Another part of Harlan's dissent needs to be quoted. It is frequently cited today by opponents of affirmative action and other race-conscious remedies for the effects of segregation. In reply, proponents of affirmative action say that if Harlan had been listened to in 1896, perhaps affirmative action would not be necessary today. Here is what Harlan said:

> [I]n the view of the Constitution, in the eye of the law, there is in this country no superior, dominant ruling class of citizens. There is no caste here. Our Constitution is color-blind and neither knows nor tolerates classes among citizens.

Not until sixty years later, in *Brown* v. *Board of Education of Topeka, Kansas* (1954), was "the wrong this day done" officially overturned. The *Brown* case actually consisted of four separate cases involving public school segregation, from the states of Delaware, South Carolina, Virginia, and Kansas. The Court consolidated them because they all involved the same issue: whether state-imposed racial segregation violates the equal protection clause of the Fourteenth Amendment "even though the physical facilities and other 'tangible' factors may be equal." This last phrase assumed special importance in the Kansas case. In the city of Topeka, the authorities had built brand-new schools for the black children and recruited the best teachers they could find. They wanted to make sure that the black schools were tangibly "equal" so they could say they were living up to the "equal" part of the "separate but equal" formula.

But it was too late. The theoretical underpinnings of Jim Crow had already been chipped away. Six years earlier President Truman had desegregated the armed forces. Two years earlier the Supreme Court had ordered graduate schools and law schools to desegregate. The NAACP had assembled teams of legal experts who were challenging segregation at every turn. The NAACP's cause was increasingly being applauded by white political leaders. Significantly, the Court's unanimous opinion in the *Brown* case, as announced by Chief Justice Earl Warren, started off by saying: "We cannot turn the clock back to 1868, when the Amendment was adopted, or even to 1896, when *Plessy* v. *Ferguson* was written." In today's world, "separate educational facilities are inherently unequal." Even if state authorities go to great pains to pretty-up the blacks' schools, official segregation violates the equal protection clause of the Fourteenth Amendment.

Race Relations Since the *Brown* Decision

Thus spoke the Supreme Court in 1954. But it is one thing to announce a doctrine, another to see it fulfilled. In fact, separate—and unequal—conditions remained a way of life in the South and elsewhere in the nation, imposed either openly or covertly by state and city officials. In 1957 President Eisenhower had to call federal troops into Little Rock, Arkansas, after the state's governor forcibly barred black children from entering white schools. In the South, social customs, "private" discrimination, and laws were still woven together in a web of humiliation for black Americans. Blacks, for example, were still expected to sit in the back of the bus. Then, one day in 1955, a forty-three-year-old seamstress named Rosa Parks refused to move to the back of a bus in Montgomery, Alabama. She was arrested and fined, but her act sparked a citywide black boycott of the bus company, setting a pattern followed by blacks in other cities. (One of the leaders of the boycott was a young black minister named Martin Luther King, Jr.) Restaurants and lunch counters throughout the South were still segregated. But at the end of the '50s a group of very serious, very earnest divinity students from black colleges began sitting down at "white" lunch counters in Greensboro, North Carolina. Ordered to leave, they refused and were hauled off to jail. Then more black students took their place.

The "sit-ins" were still going on as John F. Kennedy began his campaign for the presidency. Over the next ten years, everything happened quickly. A "new frontier" was promised, and the whole mood of newness and reform may have helped stimulate further demonstrations in the streets. Then came the ugly responses of municipal authorities, viewed, for the first time, in millions of homes throughout the nation. Men and women of conscience were shocked at what they saw: police dogs, cattle prods, and fire hoses used against unarmed and nonviolent demonstrators. A new bipartisan consensus began to form around the need for legislation to put an end to compulsory inequality. Responding to that consensus, Congress passed a variety of new laws. Three are particularly noteworthy: the Civil Rights Act of 1964, the Voting Rights Act of 1965, and the Civil Rights Act of 1968.

The 1964 law outlawed discrimination in public accommodations and employ-ment and established the Equal Opportunity Employment Commission. The Voting Rights Act of 1965 finally broke the back of southern resistance to black suffrage; it authorized the attorney general to appoint federal examiners to register voters in areas from which blacks had been systematically excluded. The Civil Rights Bill of 1968 prohibited discrimination in the sale or rental of housing. Of these three laws, the most interesting for the purpose of this chapter is the Civil Rights Act of 1964, particularly titles VI and VII of it, which *seem* to prohibit any form of racial discrimination, in-cluding discrimination for the sake of affirmative action. The word "seem" is used very deliberately; defenders of affirmative action insist that the language in these provi-sions must not be read literally. Their arguments will be considered later in the chapter.

For now, let us simply conclude that the 1960s produced an enormous, quantum change in the relations between the races in America. By the end of the decade the days of Jim Crow were over. Blacks and whites could mingle freely in public accom-modations. Blacks could vote anywhere, and they flocked to the polls. White politicians everywhere got the message. Segregationist politicians like George Wallace and Strom Thurmond started talking a different language; they were no longer Dixiecrats but "conservatives" or even "populists." Within the space of ten years, a new era was born.

One would like to be able to add "and the stains of Jim Crow finally vanished from the land." Unfortunately, it did not quite turn out that way. Certain effects are still evident: black unemployment remains double that of whites, black life expectancy is a decade less than that of whites, black median income is 55 percent of white income, black infant mortality is twice that among whites, black participation in the higher professions is about 2 percent. If it is crazy to attribute all this to present-day racism, it is no less crazy to imagine that it is completely unrelated to the practices of the past, as if blacks just somehow got themselves into this fix. The ultimate question is what to do about it.

One answer, the answer debated by the video panelists, is affirmative action. The debate has three parts. Let us start with the first.

I: TENURE AT DALTON STATE

Part I introduces the argument by formulating the hypothetical case. Three candidates are competing for *one* tenured position at "Dalton State University." One of the candidates is a black male (the moderator assigns the role to columnist William Raspberry), one is a white female (assigned to columnist Ellen Goodman), the third is a white male (played by media commentator Avi Nelson). Each of these candidates is qualified and competent. All are approximately equal in terms of experience and publications. The white male is a slightly better classroom teacher than the white female, and she, in turn, is slightly better than the black male in classroom performance. However, the black male leads all three in his "contribution to university life"—membership on various college committees, relationship with the community around the college, and so on.

Before proceeding to the question of who gets the job, we ought to take note of what "tenure" means and what Dalton State means in this context.

In the "pilgrim's progress" of a struggling young academic, the question of tenure looms like a great mountain range. On this side of the divide is perennial anxiety about one's future; on the other side is heaven. Loosely understood, tenure means a guaranteed lifetime job in academia. More precisely, it means a teaching position that extends until the mandatory retirement age. From such a position the teacher can be dismissed only under exceptional circumstances, as in the case of highly unprofessional conduct or the abolition of the teacher's whole department or division. Candidates who are turned down for tenure not only fail to receive "lifetime" jobs but have probably lost even their interim jobs at the university. They are told that it's time to move on. Usually an individual "comes up" for tenure after a fixed period of employment, say three or five years, during which time senior colleagues have a chance to look the candidate over and see how he or she performs. Hence the anxiety and the potential for disappointment and anger. To be turned down for tenure is not only a financial blow but a blow to one's self-esteem. Even in the make-believe situation on this panel, the unsuccessful tenure candidates seem genuinely hurt when they hear that they didn't get the job. In real life they might be tempted to start a lawsuit against Dalton State.

Dalton State. The name is revealing, though not much is made of it in the discussion. Because of it, the tenure decision could have legal repercussions. If a candidate for tenure felt he or she was turned down solely because of race, a lawsuit might be a logical move. In that case, it would be significant that this is Dalton *State* University. The equal protection clause of the Fourteenth Amendment says that "no *state*" shall deny any person the equal protection of the laws. On its face, the amendment does not prohibit racial discrimination by private institutions (although Congress and the courts have found bridges into the private sphere, such as an institution's receipt of federal aid and tax exemptions). But at Dalton *State*, a suit might be possible under the Fourteenth Amendment or the Civil Rights Act of 1964.

The *Weber* and *Fullilove* Cases

Here we should introduce the famous *Bakke* case, a major Supreme Court ruling on affirmative action at a state university receiving federal funds. The case ties in directly with the hypothetical case of Dalton State. First, however, we ought to review two cases since *Bakke* that relate to our topic.

The first was *United Steelworkers of America* v. *Weber* (1979). In 1974, under pressure from a federal agency, an aluminum corporation entered into a collective bargaining agreement with a union that reserved for black workers 50 percent of the openings in skills-upgrading programs. Brian Weber, a white worker, was passed over for admission to a training program in favor of a black worker with less seniority. He brought suit under Title VII of the Civil Rights Act of 1964, which prohibits racial classifications that could have adverse effects on people and specifically outlaws discrimination against workers in admitting them to training programs.

The Supreme Court ruled against Weber on two grounds. First, it reminded him that the 1964 Civil Rights Act was aimed at relieving the plight of *blacks*, not whites. Second, said the Court, the 1964 Civil Rights Act "did not intend wholly to prohibit private and voluntary affirmative action efforts." It only prohibited "compulsory" affirmative action programs, ones imposed on employers by the government. In an angry dissenting opinion, Justice William Rehnquist, joined by Chief Justice Warren Burger, accused the majority of grossly misreading both the language and the legislative intent of the Civil Rights Act of 1964. Rehnquist also questioned whether the affirmative action plan was truly "voluntary," since it was instituted as a result of pressure from the federal government.

In *Fullilove* v. *Klutznick* (1980), the Court seemed to go even further in upholding certain forms of racial quotas. There was nothing at all "voluntary" about the facts in that case. Two years earlier, Congress had passed a statute guaranteeing that 10 percent of federally funded local construction work projects go to "minority" contractors ("Negroes, Spanish-speaking, Orientals, Indians, Eskimos, and Aleuts"). Because of this law, a white-owned construction firm was passed over in favor of a minority-owned firm, even though the white firm came in with a lower bid. The white firm sued, claiming that it had sustained economic injury because of reverse discrimination. It argued that the section of the statute setting aside the 10 percent figure violated both the equal protection clause of the Fourteenth Amendment and the due process clause of the Fifth Amendment. (The latter clause says that "no person shall . . . be deprived of life, liberty, or property, without due process of law.") By a five-to-three vote, the Court sustained the statute against these challenges. (Justice Byron White took no part in the case.) While conceding that the program "may press the outer limits of congressional authority," the Court said that it was a legitimate means of redressing the effects of past discrimination.

The *Bakke* Case: "Race-Conscious Remedies"

This brings us to *Regents of the University of California* v. *Bakke* (1978), the case that best fits the hypothetical situation in the video discussion. Although *Bakke* in some respects resembled *Weber* and *Fullilove*, in other ways it was quite different. Unlike *Weber*, it did not involve a private company but a state university, so there was nothing "voluntary" about it. Unlike the situation in *Fullilove*, the program was not mandated by a federal statute—it was strictly a university policy—so it did not come from a co-equal branch of government.

The program at issue was an affirmative action plan at Davis Medical School of the University of California. Davis set aside 16 of the 100 admissions for nonwhite applicants. Those admitted in that category were subject to less rigorous qualifications than the 84 admitted in the regular manner. Alan Bakke, a white male, was turned down for admission, even though his test scores and grades were higher than those of some candidates admitted through the "special" program.

Bakke argued that he was a victim of reverse discrimination: he was discriminated against because he was white. His argument recalled the words of Justice Harlan's dissent in *Plessy* v. *Ferguson*: "Our Constitution is color-blind and neither knows nor tolerates classes among citizens."

Four members of the Supreme Court agreed with the "color-blind" argument. In their view, even well-intended programs that discriminate against people because of skin color violate the Constitution and the Civil Rights Act of 1964. Another four members rejected Bakke's argument. In their view, affirmative action programs of the kind used at Davis are legitimate means of correcting the long-term effects of past discrimination.

If there were eight members on the Court, it would have been a tie. But there are nine, and the ninth member, Justice Lewis Powell, was of two minds. On the one hand, he agreed that there may be a legitimate purpose in increasing the number of minorities in medical school and that this might justify the use of race as a criterion to be weighed in considering an applicant's suitability for admission. However, he opposed the use of "explicit" racial classifications, ones that divide applicants into minority and white groups and then use different standards for each group. (A system of this sort was used at Davis Medical School.) Powell, then, agreed in part with both sides of the controversy. He agreed with the "color-blinders" that Bakke, a white male, had been excluded from the medical school in violation of the equal protection clause of the Fourteenth Amendment. But he also agreed with the supporters of affirmative action that race may sometimes be taken into account in these decisions.

Powell was the Court's "swing" member. His vote tipped the balance in favor of Bakke's claim that he had suffered reverse discrimination. But Powell's vote also put the Court on record as permitting state institutions receiving federal funds to use race as one factor determining a candidate's suitability for medical school. If none of the other members of the Court wholly agreed with Powell, not a single member wholly disagreed with him. His opinion was therefore what lawyers call "the controlling opinion" in the case.

Much of Powell's opinion hinges on the meaning of the equal protection clause of the Fourteenth Amendment. What does this Delphic phrase mean? At least since the *Brown* case, there is a consensus that it means there shall be no discrimination *against* blacks and other racial minorities. But does it permit a bit of discrimination *for* them in certain cases? Putting the matter more precisely, does the equal protection clause permit certain kinds of "color-conscious" remedies for racial imbalance? The five-to-four majority in *Bakke* answered this question very clearly: yes. What Powell's controlling opinion does is to narrow, by carefully defining, the area in which race-consciousness can be used.

What it comes down to is this: race, gender, and ethnic origin can be used provided they are used "flexibly," as factors considered along with a number of other qualities in an applicant. These other qualities could include personal talents, work experience, leadership potential, maturity, and ability to communicate. Even geography could be relevant in some cases. Powell commended the admissions program at Harvard College for its manner of including racial criteria among a whole set of nonacademic criteria. He quoted from Harvard's admissions guidelines: "A farm boy from Idaho can bring something to Harvard College that a Bostonian cannot offer. Similarly, a black student can usually bring something that a white person cannot offer." A program such as Harvard's, Powell reasoned, "where race or ethnic background is simply one element—to be weighed fairly against other elements—in the selection process," does not violate the equal protection clause of the Fourteenth Amendment because it "treats each applicant as an individual in the admissions process and does not insulate the individual from comparison with all other candidates for the available seats." In contrast, the program at Davis Medical School, which assigned "a fixed number of places to a minority group," prevented any competition between individuals of different races and thus unfairly discriminated against whites.

A case can be made that the proponents of affirmative action lost a battle in the *Bakke* decision—and won a war. The decision struck down the particular kind of affirmative action program set up by the University of California at Davis, a program using fixed percentages. But the decision, by five to four, explicitly approved of the use of racial criteria as long as they were used "flexibly," as part of the candidate's overall evaluation. "Color-blindness" was not required by the Fourteenth Amendment.

Undoubtedly, the controlling opinion of Justice Powell in *Bakke* influences the rationales given by some panelists in the video debate. Those who would reject the white male candidate—even though he has the best teaching record of the three—in favor of the black candidate tend to avoid any direct reference to race. Instead, they talk about the black candidate's "particular essences," including his "relationship with the community." (The words are from former HEW Secretary Shirley Hufstedler, but the same idea is expressed by other panelists, including *New York Times* columnist Anthony Lewis and newsman Jim Lehrer.) In this respect, Juan Ortiz, New York City's personnel director, stands out as the lone exception. When asked why he prefers the black candidate, he answers simply and artlessly: "Because he's black." The other proponents of affirmative action find other reasons for stating their preference.

In order to initiate a successful lawsuit on the pattern of *Bakke*, then, Avi Nelson, who plays the white candidate, would have to prove that his merits were greater than the black candidate's. Yet the meaning of the term "merit" seems elusive to many of the panelists. There may be an element of willfulness in this. It seems more than coincidental that the panelists who oppose affirmative action have little trouble with the term, while those who support affirmative action are continually struck by what columnist Ellen Goodman calls "the utter subjectivity of the word 'merit.'" Nevertheless, the fact that the three tenure candidates seem to be no different when it comes to publications (the sine qua non for tenure) and only marginally different in teaching ability and contributions to the academic community makes this case difficult to decide and even more difficult to challenge in court.

Aside from legal challenges, what about the moral case against affirmative action? The most impressive of all the arguments against it in this section is Avi Nelson's. He speaks quietly but with what is obviously deep feeling as he sums up his case against race-conscious remedies. "I'm an individual, and my career and my life I don't think should be sacrificed on the altar of some historical perspective where we say that because, as a society, we made bad judgments and bad decisions in the past, therefore my life has to be sacrificed to make amends." It is a powerful statement. It suggests that innocent individuals are being hurt today because of something others did in the past—a form of retribution repugnant to Western values. But the argument rests on two assumptions that may not be entirely sound. First, it seems to assume that the purpose of affirmative action is retribution against white people. Sensible defenders of affirmative action steer clear of that sort of rationale in favor of more positive, nonjudgmental ones. One recurring rationale—former HEW Secretary Joseph Califano builds his whole case upon it—is the analogy of "disaster relief," or special treatment of people who have been injured. It does not matter whether they have been injured by evil men or by a hurricane. Yet Nelson would argue that other people, innocent people, are going to have to pay for special programs to rehabilitate the victims. Does that mean that the others, those who were not afflicted, can legitimately portray themselves as sacrificial victims?

Second, a guiding premise in Avi Nelson's argument is that candidates for positions at a university must be seen only as individuals, not as members of any race. But can human beings be seen only as individuals? Don't individuals really come in various sizes, shapes, and colors? And aren't some of these characteristics relevant to the life of an academic institution? What about Justice Powell's argument in the *Bakke* case that a person's race might enrich the institution? What about Harvard's admissions guidelines, where they say that if a "farm boy from Idaho can bring something to Harvard College" that a Bostonian cannot, then "a black student can usually bring something that a white person cannot offer"? A university, Juan Ortiz reminds the panelists, "does not exist in a vacuum." It exists "as part of a society." In that context, affirmative action begins to assume a different form than that of "disaster relief." Now it is no longer just a matter of helping people who have been hurt; it is a matter of helping ourselves—enhancing the life of our college. This position is taken by other panelists who support affirmative action. Anthony Lewis favors the practice because it will bring in more black "role models" for the black students. Jim Lehrer favors hiring blacks and females for what he calls "functional" reasons, meaning that they can cover certain stories better than white males can. Both of these statements may contain some weaknesses,* but their strength lies in their concreteness.

The opponents of affirmative action, like author and editor Irving Kristol, keep talking about "merit" and "excellence." "Take the best," says Kristol. But the question is merit in *what* respect, excellence at *what*? In this case, presumably, we mean merit in teaching, writing, and relating to others in the academic community. But are these qualities wholly abstract, or do they tie in with an individual's particular culture? As Anthony Lewis says in the third part of the program: "There is a kind of abstract quality to the discussion of merit as merit. It's a sort of merit in some wonderful land above the sky." That doesn't mean that "merit" is utterly subjective, as Ellen Goodman claims, but it does suggest that it can be colored—the term is chosen carefully—by a variety of considerations, worthy and unworthy. If nothing else, this argument should lead to soul-searching by the members of tenure and promotions committees. Do they need better definitions for some of the terms, like "excellence" and "merit," that they use so readily?

Points to Remember

1. Although the Reconstruction period led to many advances for blacks, most of them were wiped out by the end of the nineteenth century. Terror was used by the Ku Klux Klan and other groups to prevent blacks from exercising their rights, and other, "legal" means, such as poll taxes and "grandfather clauses," were also used to disenfranchise blacks.
2. In 1896, in *Plessy* v. *Ferguson*, the Supreme Court approved of state-imposed racial segregation, justifying it under the principle of "separate but equal." Justice

---

*Viewed from a certain angle, they seem to contain a trace of condescension. In Anthony Lewis's statement, one can almost hear the voice of a college administrator saying, in the privacy of his office: "Well, you know, our black students need their black role models—people they can look up to and aspire to be. Since they can never hope to rise to our standards, we'll find some black professors for them." Moreover, race and gender consciousness is a two-way street. What if Jim Lehrer were to tell one of his female news correspondents: "I'm sorry, but this story is not for you. This is a good football story and we want to have it covered by a male. Functionally speaking, males are better suited for it." Of course Lehrer would say no such thing to any female correspondent, but the logic of his position seems to lead in that direction.

John Harlan dissented, insisting that our laws and our Constitution must be "color-blind."

3. In 1954, in *Brown* v. *Board of Education*, the Supreme Court in effect reversed the *Plessy* decision. Ruling on the issue of public school segregation, the Court held that "in the field of public education the doctrine of 'separate but equal' has no place." It soon made it clear that the doctrine had no place in any other state institution.

4. Great progress was made during the '60s in wiping out official segregation and guaranteeing black voting rights. However, great disparities in conditions remain between blacks and whites. Affirmative action is a strategy aimed at reducing such disparities.

5. In *United Steelworkers of America* v. *Weber* (1979), the Supreme Court upheld an agreement between an aluminum plant and a union to establish a quota for blacks in admissions to a special training program. In *Fullilove* v. *Klutznick* (1980), the Court upheld the constitutionality of a federal public works program requiring that 10 percent of spending be reserved for minority contractors.

6. In *Regents of the University of California* v. *Bakke* (1978), the Court struck down the system of racial categories used by Davis Medical School of the University of California. However, the controlling opinion, by Justice Powell, approved of race-conscious admissions programs provided they are used "flexibly," avoid strict quotas, and use race as only one of a number of factors that may be taken into account.

7. In deciding the question of who gets tenure at "Dalton State," most of the proponents of race-consciousness avoid saying they prefer the black candidate simply because he is black. Instead, they speak of the particular contributions he could make to the academic community. They tend to regard the question of "merit" as one that is difficult to settle by any objective critieria.

II: IS AFFIRMATIVE ACTION FAIR TO ALL?

The highlight of the program's second part is a duel between Irving Kristol and Joseph Califano on the implications of a metaphor. The metaphor is introduced by Califano.

> My analogy would be a race, the New York City Marathon. You take two people. One person's been training for six months for that race. The other one's been in chains, so he can't use his legs. Okay? You put them at the starting line . . . that's what Mr. Kristol's saying, "It's fair, let 'em go, whoever wins the race." Happens that the black man has been in chains, and that the white person's been training.

This brings us back to the "disaster relief" rationale for affirmative action—in this case, the need for some kind of special therapy for the handicapped black runner. Kristol is primed for a reply. His eyes are twinkling. Califano's metaphor, he says, is a "good one," but

> I thought I suggested, and I'd like to make it clear, that I would indeed subscribe to affirmative action, if it meant taking the one chap who had been chained, giving him a good diet, giving him good massage, giving him good training, helping him compete. But I would not put chains around the other guy, and say, "Let's make it more equal. . . ." That is what affirmative action is today, unfortunately.

The moderator detects a possible contradiction, or at least a road to a contradiction. He starts exploring it. Would Kristol support some kind of "massage," some kind of training, for blacks "in the university context"? Kristol: "Absolutely. I mean, if you want remedial activities of all kinds for students who have problems of one kind or another. . . ." Moderator: "What about faculty tenure? That's what we're talking about." But Kristol won't be trapped. "Oh, no, faculty tenure is the finish line, who won." This is an extremely shrewd answer. In the hypothetical example, Dalton State actually *had* an affirmative action program for recruiting black and female faculty members. *There* was the massage-and-exercise program. But now it is three years or five years later. It is time for tenure—the race is at the finish line. What Kristol is saying is that affirmative action programs have to come to an end at some point. We cannot remediate people all through life.

Kristol's answer is shrewd, but is it sound? Is three or five years enough to overcome crippling? Moreover, is there any solid evidence in the discussion that Kristol would have supported Dalton's minority recruitment program? Surely such a system would increase the probability that a white applicant could be turned down in favor of a less qualified black. What then would become of "merit"? There may be at least a hint of contradiction here.

If Kristol were peering over this page he would probably have a quick reply. Irving Kristol does not get flustered in verbal duels. The same cannot be said of one of his allies in the argument, William Bradford Reynolds, President Reagan's assistant attorney general for civil rights. In the next part, Anthony Lewis gets the drop on him.

III: THE WRAP-UP

The great issue in part III is "color-blindness," Justice Harlan's ideal in his famous *Plessy* dissent. Reynolds cites this ideal as the basic reason why the Reagan administration opposes color-conscious affirmative action programs. Anthony Lewis starts off by affirming the ideal. "The Constitution," Lewis says, "is color-blind." Then he adds: "But if I were black, I would find it slightly hypocritical. . . ." He pauses an instant. Then, warming to the subject: "*more* than slightly hypocritical, to have everybody pledging such fealty to that wonderful ideal, after it had been rejected by a vote of eight to one, and ground into the dust in the real world for most of the life of blacks in this country." What is this supposed to mean? That ideals should be discarded because they are not lived up to? That it is now too late for color-blindness? Lewis does not explain. Instead, he suddenly turns to Reynolds and asks, "Do you think it was right for the president of the United States to choose, *probably because of their race and sex*, a black member of the Supreme Court and a female member of the Supreme Court?" (Italics added.)

Reynolds is flabbergasted. He clears his throat. He writhes in his chair. His voice is leaden as he tries to answer:

> I don't think it was wrong to do that. I don't have—again, I think that the selection process should be based on the—president's decisions, determination as to whom he believes is most qualified to sit on that court, weighing all the factors that he's entitled to weigh.

The weakness of this answer encourages Lewis to move in for the kill:

> LEWIS: I think you're avoiding my question, Mr. Reynolds—
> REYNOLDS: I, well, I—

There is more of Reynolds on the program, but he never really recovers from this exchange.

Was it a fair fight? One of the ground rules for these debates is that the panelists must "stick to the hypothetical." The topic is a safely imaginary Dalton State. But Lewis has departed from the hypothetical to ask Reynolds a dreadful question: Was it right for Ronald Reagan (*your boss*) to appoint Sandra Day O'Connor in order to get a woman on the Court, and was it right for Lyndon Johnson to appoint Thurgood Marshall (*before whom your division must argue cases*) in order to get a black on the Court? There is no way Reynolds can answer that question without getting into trouble. If he says, "No, it wasn't right," he has to go back to face Ronald Reagan and Thurgood Marshall. If he says, "Yes, it was right," he would contradict himself on the issue of color-blindness.

One way out of the dilemma would be to challenge the assumption underlying Lewis's question: that Sandra Day O'Connor and Thurgood Marshall were appointed to the Court *because of gender and race*. Reynolds could have turned the tables on Lewis with an answer such as this: "Why, Mr. Lewis, I'm really surprised that you should consider that Justices O'Connor and Marshall were appointed because of gender and race. These two individuals happen to be excellent jurists. They qualify on merit alone. By the way, how long have you harbored these attitudes toward women and blacks?" Such clever, malicious answers occur to us all—after the debate.

The last word on the topic of color-blindness comes from U.S. Circuit Judge Harry Edwards. It is the last word because it comes a few minutes before the end and because nobody replies to it. "Color-blindness," he says, "is the goal," but "the only way you get to that goal is to indulge consciousness on the way." This is a very different kind of color-blindness than the one that Reynolds, Kristol, and Avi Nelson have in mind. Indeed, it is different from the one invoked by Justice Harlan in his *Plessy* dissent. All the others are talking about color-blindness as a process. Harlan was obviously referring to the legal process when he insisted that the "laws" must be color-blind. The rest are talking about the process of awarding tenure. What Edwards means is something different: color-blindness as a result. He does not really mean color-blindness but color-balance: if blacks number 15 percent in the community around Dalton State, there should be 15 percent of them on the faculty. It can be argued that once this balance is attained, people will finally *become* color-blind. But will they? Suppose the percentage of blacks on the faculty begins slipping down again, so that after five years there are only 10 percent on the faculty. Or suppose many more blacks move into the surrounding community, so that a new discrepancy appears between the percentage of blacks on the faculty and the percentage in the community. Won't all this need monitoring? Won't there have to be bureaus to do the monitoring? And don't bureaus have a tendency to perpetuate themselves, in this case by making sure that everyone remains *very* color-conscious?

Points to Remember

1. Former HEW Secretary Joseph Califano compares blacks to people whose past treatment has handicapped them. To expect them to compete on equal terms is like asking someone who has been in chains to compete in a race on equal terms with a trained runner.

2. Author Irving Kristol replies that affirmative action is an attempt to even the odds by putting chains around the white runner.

3. Anthony Lewis suggests that it is hypocritical to endorse "color-blindness" after all the years when it was not practiced in this country. He seems to suggest that the Reagan administration has not been principled in its opposition to color- and gender-consciousness, since it deliberately appointed a female to the Supreme Court.

4. Judge Harry Edwards supports color-blindness as a "goal" but thinks the best way to reach that goal is to "indulge" color-consciousness as a temporary strategy.

SUMMARY

Most Americans feel uneasy about race-conscious remedies for the effects of racism. In both the *Bakke* and the *Weber* decisions, the Supreme Court expressed this uneasiness. Race, the justices said, is a "suspect" category, even when it is used for benign purposes. In *Bakke*, Justice Powell sanctioned its use but insisted that it be used "flexibly," as one of a number of criteria. In *Weber*, the Court consigned its use to the private, "voluntary" sphere, implicitly admitting that the government's use of race-conscious remedies in employment would probably violate the Civil Rights Act. And in the video debate, even the most outspoken advocates of race-conscious remedies, such as Joseph Califano and Judge Harry Edwards, seem to support them only as temporary expedients.

If even the supporters of affirmative action tend to qualify their support, it should not be surprising that opponents like Avi Nelson and Irving Kristol are so passionate in their opposition. To some that passion sounds like extremism and self-righteousness. To others it is evidence of dedication to principle. (These different perceptions probably correspond to the observer's own view of affirmative action.) In terms of recent Supreme Court decisions, the opponents of race-conscious remedies are the "outs," the underdogs, which may be one reason for their intensity. In a free country, the opportunity to be outspoken is one consolation to the losers. The other consolation is the hope of one day becoming winners, or at least of being vindicated by history. Hence the prophetic tone often adopted by dissenters: "Just wait!" There is something of that tone in Justice Harlan's *Plessy* dissent, when he warns that the Court's shallow rationale for segregation will never "atone for the wrong this day done." It also lurks in Justice William Rehnquist's *Weber* dissent. The "racial quota," he warns, is "a creator of castes." It "must demean one in order to prefer another." In legitimizing it, "the Court has sown the wind. Later courts will face the impossible task of reaping the whirlwind."

We know today that in 1896 Justice Harlan was a true prophet. Whether Justice Rehnquist in 1979 was also a true prophet is not for us to determine. If we cannot turn the clock back, we certainly cannot turn it forward. All we can try to do is fashion our own imperfect, fallible views on whether our laws today should be color-blind—or color-conscious in order one day to *become* color-blind.

Documents

PLESSY V. FERGUSON, 163 U.S. 537 (1896)

In Plessy v. Ferguson *the Supreme Court held that the state of Louisiana did not violate the Fourteenth Amendment by establishing and enforcing a policy of racial segregation in its railway system. Justice John Marshall Harlan wrote a memorable dissent to that decision, parts of which are quoted today by both sides of the affirmative action controversy. One statement often quoted by opponents of race-conscious affirmative action programs is Harlan's assertion that the Constitution is "color-blind," which can be found in the excerpts below.*

Justice Harlan's dissent.

In respect of civil rights, common to all citizens, the Constitution of the United States does not, I think, permit any public authority to know the race of those entitled to be protected in the enjoyment of such rights. Every true man has pride of race, and under appropriate circumstances when the rights of others, his equals before the law, are not to be affected, it is his privilege to express such pride and to take such action based upon it as to him seems proper. But I deny that any legislative body or judicial tribunal may have regard to the race of citizens when the civil rights of those citizens are involved. Indeed, such legislation as that here in question is inconsistent not only with that equality of rights which pertains to citizenship, national and state, but with the personal liberty enjoyed by everyone within the United States. . . .

It was said in argument that the statute of Louisiana does not discriminate against either race but prescribes a rule applicable alike to white and colored citizens. But this argument does not meet the difficulty. Everyone knows that the statute in question had its origin in the purpose, not so much to exclude white persons from railroad cars occupied by blacks, as to exclude colored people from coaches occupied by or assigned to white persons. Railroad corporations of Louisiana did not make discrimination among whites in the matter of accommodation for travellers. The thing to accomplish was, under the guise of giving equal accommodations for whites and blacks, to compel the latter to keep to themselves while travelling in railroad passenger coaches. No one would be so wanting in candor as to assert the contrary. The fundamental objection, therefore, to the statute is that it interferes with the personal freedom of citizens. . . . If a white man and a black man choose to occupy the same public conveyance on a public highway, it is their right to do so, and no government, proceeding alone on grounds of race, can prevent it without infringing the personal liberty of each. . . .

The white race deems itself to be the dominant race in this country. And so it is, in prestige, in achievements, in education, in wealth, and in power. So, I doubt not, it will continue to be for all time, if it remains true to its great heritage and holds fast to the principles of constitutional liberty. But in the view of the Constitution, in the eye of the law, there is in this country no superior, dominant, ruling class of citizens. There is no caste here. Our Constitution is color-blind and neither knows nor tolerates classes among citizens. In respect of civil rights, all citizens are equal before the law. The humblest is the peer of the most powerful. The law regards man as man and takes no account of his surroundings or of his color when his civil rights as guaranteed by the supreme law of the land are involved. . . .

The arbitrary separation of citizens, on the basis of race, while they are on a public highway, is a badge of servitude wholly inconsistent with the civil freedom and the equality before the law established by the Constitution. It cannot be justified upon any legal grounds.

If evils will result from the commingling of the two races upon public highways established for the benefit of all, they will be infinitely less than those that will surely come from state legislation regulating the enjoyment of civil rights upon the basis of race. We boast of the freedom enjoyed by our people above all other peoples. But it is difficult to reconcile that boast with a state of the law which, practically, puts the brand of servitude and degradation upon a large class of our fellow citizens, our equals before the law. The thin disguise of "equal" accommodations for passengers in railroad coaches will not mislead anyone, nor atone for the wrong this day done. . . .

I do not deem it necessary to review the decisions of state courts to which reference was made in argument. Some, and the most important, of them are wholly inapplicable, because rendered prior to the adoption of the last amendments of the

Constitution, when colored people had very few rights which the dominant race felt obliged to respect. Others were made at a time when public opinion, in many localities, was dominated by the institution of slavery, when it would not have been safe to do justice to the black man; and when, so far as the rights of blacks were concerned, race prejudice was, practically, the supreme law of the land. Those decisions cannot be guides in the era introduced by the recent amendments of the supreme law, which established universal civil freedom, gave citizenship to all born or naturalized in the United States and residing here, obliterated the race line from our systems of governments, national and state, and placed our free institutions upon the broad and sure foundation of the equality of all men before the law. . . .

For the reasons stated, I am constrained to withhold my assent from the opinion and judgment of the majority.

BROWN V. BOARD OF EDUCATION OF TOPEKA, 347 U.S. 483 (1954)

Speaking for a unanimous Court, Chief Justice Earl Warren in 1954 held that state-imposed segregation of public schools violates the equal protection clause of the Four-teenth Amendment. Warren based his opinion on the findings of social scientists that segregation "generates a feeling of inferiority" among black children and thus has a detrimental effect on their learning ability. Excerpts follow.

Opinion of the Court, Chief Justice Warren.

These cases come to us from the States of Kansas, South Carolina, Virginia, and Delaware. They are premised on different facts and different local conditions, but a common legal question justifies their consideration together in this consolidated opinion.

In each of the cases, minors of the Negro race, through their legal representatives, seek the aid of the courts in obtaining admission to the public schools of their community on a nonsegregated basis. In each instance, they had been denied admission to schools attended by white children under laws requiring or permitting segregation according to race. This segregation was alleged to deprive the plaintiffs of the equal protection of the laws under the Fourteenth Amendment. In each of the cases other than the Delaware case, a three-judge federal district court denied relief to the plaintiffs on the so-called "separate but equal" doctrine announced by this Court in Plessy v. Ferguson, 163 U.S. 537. Under that doctrine, equality of treatment is accorded when the races are provided substantially equal facilities, even though these facilities be separate. In the Delaware case, the Supreme Court of Delaware adhered to that doctrine, but ordered that the plaintiffs be admitted to the white schools because of their superiority to the Negro schools.

The plaintiffs contend that segregated public schools are not "equal" and cannot be made "equal," and that hence they are deprived of the equal protection of the laws. Because of the obvious importance of the question presented, the Court took jurisdiction. Argument was heard in the 1952 Term, and reargument was heard this Term on certain questions propounded by the Court.

Reargument was largely devoted to the circumstances surrounding the adoption of the Fourteenth Amendment in 1868. It covered exhaustively consideration of the Amendment in Congress, ratification by the states, then existing practices in racial segregation, and the views of proponents and opponents of the Amendment. This discussion and our own investigation convince us that, although these sources cast some light, it is not enough to resolve the problem with which we are faced. At best, they are inconclusive. The most avid proponents of the post-War Amendments undoubtedly intended them to remove all legal distinctions among "all persons born or naturalized in the United States." Their opponents, just as certainly, were antagonistic to both the letter and the spirit of the Amendments and wished them to have the most limited effect. What others in Congress and the state legislatures had in mind cannot be determined with any degree of certainty.

An additional reason for the inconclusive nature of the Amendment's history, with respect to segregated schools, is the status of public education at that time. In the South, the movement toward free common schools, supported by general taxation, had not yet taken hold. Education of white children was largely in the hands of private groups. Education of Negroes was almost nonexistent, and practically all of the race were illiterate. In fact, any education of Negroes was forbidden by law in some states. Today, in contrast, many Negroes have achieved outstanding success in the arts and sciences as well as in the business and professional world. It is true that public school education had advanced further in the North, but the effect of the Amendment on Northern States was generally ignored in the congressional debates. Even in the North, the conditions of public education did not approximate those existing today. The curriculum was usually rudimentary; ungraded schools were common in rural areas; the school term was but three months a year in many states; and compulsory school attendance was virtually unknown. As a consequence, it is not surprising that there should be so little in the history of the Fourteenth Amendment relating to its intended effect on public education.

In the first cases in this Court construing the Fourteenth Amendment, decided shortly after its adoption, the Court interpreted it as proscribing all state-imposed discriminations against the Negro race. The doctrine of "separate but equal" did not make its appearance in this Court until 1896 in the case of Plessy v. Ferguson, *supra*, involving not education but transportation. American courts have since labored with the doctrine for over half a century. In this Court, there have been six cases involving the "separate but equal" doctrine in the field of public education. In Cumming v. County Board of Education, 175 U.S. 528, and Gong Lum v. Rice, 275 U.S. 78, the validity of the doctrine itself was not challenged. In more recent cases, all on the graduate school level, inequality was found in that specific benefits enjoyed by white students were denied to Negro students of the same educational qualifications. Missouri ex rel. Gaines v. Canada, 305 U.S. 337; Sipuel v. Oklahoma, 332 U.S. 631; Sweatt v. Painter, 339 U.S. 629; McLaurin v. Oklahoma State Regents, 339 U.S. 637. In none of these cases was it necessary to reexamine the doctrine to grant relief to the Negro plaintiff. And in Sweatt v. Painter, *supra*, the Court expressly reserved decision on the question whether Plessy *v.* Ferguson should be held inapplicable to public education.

In the instant cases, that question is directly presented. Here, unlike Sweatt *v.* Painter, there are findings below that the Negro and white schools involved have been equalized, or are being equalized, with respect to buildings, curricula, qualifications and salaries of teachers, and other "tangible" factors. Our decision, therefore, cannot turn on merely a comparison of these tangible factors in the Negro and white schools involved in each of the cases. We must look instead to the effect of segregation itself on public education.

In approaching this problem, we cannot turn the clock back to 1868 when the Amendment was adopted, or even to 1896 when Plessy *v.* Ferguson was written. We must consider public education in the light of its full development and its present place in American life throughout the Nation. Only in this way can it be determined if segregation in public schools deprives these plaintiffs of the equal protection of the laws.

Today, education is perhaps the most important function of state and local governments. Compulsory school attendance laws and the great expenditures for education both demonstrate our recognition of the importance of education to our democratic society. It is required in the performance of our most basic public responsibilities, even service in the armed forces. It is the very foundation of good citizenship. Today it is a principal instrument in awakening the child to cultural values, in preparing him for later professional training, and in helping him to adjust normally to his environment. In these days, it is doubtful that any child may reasonably be expected to succeed in life if he is denied the opportunity of an education. Such an opportunity, where the state has undertaken to provide it, is a right which must be made available to all on equal terms.

We come then to the question presented: Does segregation of children in public schools solely on the basis of race, even though the physical facilities and other "tangible" factors may be equal, deprive the children of the minority group of equal educational opportunities? We believe that it does.

In Sweatt *v.* Painter, *supra*, in finding that a segregated law school for Negroes could not provide them equal educational opportunities, this Court relied in large part on "those qualities which are incapable of objective measurement but which make for greatness in a law school." In McLaurin *v.* Oklahoma State Regents, *supra*, the Court, in requiring that a Negro admitted to a white graduate school be treated like all other students, again resorted to intangible considerations: ". . . his ability to study, to engage in discussions and exchange views with other students, and, in general, to learn his profession." Such considerations apply with added force to children in grade and high schools. To separate them from others of similar age and qualifications solely because of their race generates a feeling of inferiority as to their status in the community that may affect their hearts and minds in a way unlikely ever to be undone. The effect of this separation on their educational opportunities was well stated by a finding in the Kansas case by a court which nevertheless felt compelled to rule against the Negro plaintiffs:

Segregation of white and colored children in public schools has a detrimental effect upon the colored children. The impact is greater when it has the sanction of the law; for the policy of separating the races is usually interpreted as denoting the inferiority of the Negro group. A sense of inferiority affects the motivation of a child to learn. Segregation with the sanction of law, therefore, has a tendency to retard the educational and mental development of Negro children and to deprive them of some of the benefits they would receive in a racially integrated school system.

Whatever may have been the extent of psychological knowledge at the time of Plessy *v.* Ferguson, this finding is amply supported by modern authority. Any language in Plessy *v.* Ferguson contrary to this finding is rejected.

We conclude that in the field of public education the doctrine of "separate but equal" has no place. Separate educational facilities are inherently unequal. Therefore, we hold that the plaintiffs and others similarly situated for whom the actions have been brought are, by reason of the segregation complained of, deprived of the equal protection of the laws guaranteed by the Fourteenth Amendment.

UNIVERSITY OF CALIFORNIA REGENTS V. BAKKE, 438 U.S. 265 (1978)

In Regents of the University of California *v.* Bakke *(1978), four members of the Supreme Court took the view that admission to a state medical school must be on a completely "color-blind" basis; another four contended that racial criteria may be used by a state for the purpose of overcoming the chronic minority underrepresentation in the medical profession.*

The remaining justice, Lewis Powell, thus had the controlling opinion in the case. As explained previously in this chapter, Powell agreed in part with both sides. He believed that a legitimate justification might exist for using race as a criterion in medical school admissions, yet he opposed "explicit" racial classifications. Below is an excerpt from his opinion.

Justice Powell's opinion.

It may be assumed that the reservation of a specified number of seats in each class for individuals from the preferred ethnic groups would contribute to the attainment of considerable ethnic diversity in the student body. But petitioner's argument that this is the only effective means of serving the interest of diversity is seriously flawed. In a most fundamental sense the argument misconceives the nature of the state interest that would justify consideration of race or ethnic background. It is not an interest in simple ethnic diversity, in which a specified percentage of the student body is in effect guaranteed to be members of selected ethnic groups, with the remaining percentage an undifferentiated aggregation of students. The diversity that furthers a compelling state interest encompasses a far broader array of qualifications and characteristics of which racial or ethnic origin is but a single though important element. Petitioner's special admissions program, focused *solely* on ethnic diversity, would hinder rather than further attainment of genuine diversity.

Nor would the state interest in genuine diversity be served by expanding petitioner's two-track system into a multitrack program with a prescribed number of seats set aside for each identifiable category of applicants. Indeed, it is inconceivable that a university would thus pursue the logic of petitioner's two-track program to the illogical end of insulating each category of applicants with certain desired qualifications from competition with all other applicants.

The experience of other university admissions programs, which take race into account in achieving the educational diversity valued by the First Amendment, demonstrates that the assignment of a fixed number of places to a minority group is not a necessary means toward that end. An illuminating example is found in the Harvard College program:

> "In recent years Harvard College has expanded the concept of diversity to include students from disadvantaged economic, racial and ethnic groups. Harvard College now recruits not only Californians or Louisianans but also blacks and Chicanos and other minority students. . . .
>
> "In practice, this new definition of diversity has meant that race has been a factor in some admission decisions. When the Committee on Admissions reviews the large middle group of applicants who are 'admissible' and deemed capable of doing good work in their courses, the race of an applicant may tip the balance in his favor just as geographic origin or a life spent on a farm may tip the balance in other candidates' cases. A farm boy from Idaho can bring something to Harvard College that a Bostonian cannot offer. Similarly, a black student can usually bring something that a white person cannot offer.
>
> "In Harvard College admissions the Committee has not set target-quotas for the number of blacks, or of musicians, football players, physicists or Californians to be admitted in a given year. . . . But that awareness [of the necessity of including more than a token number of black students] does not mean that the Committee sets a minimum number of blacks or of people from west of the Mississippi who are to be admitted. It means only that in choosing among thousands of applicants who are not only 'admissible' academically but have other strong qualities, the Committee, with a number of criteria in mind, pays some attention to distribution among many types and categories of students." App. to Brief for Columbia University, Harvard University, Stanford University, and the University of Pennsylvania, as *Amici Curiae* 2-3.

In such an admissions program, race or ethnic background may be deemed a "plus" in a particular applicant's file, yet it does not insulate the individual from comparison with all other candidates for the available seats. The file of a particular black applicant may be examined for his potential contribution to diversity without the factor of race being decisive when compared, for example, with that of an applicant identified as an Italian-American if the latter is thought to exhibit qualities more likely to promote beneficial educational pluralism. Such qualities could include exceptional personal talents, unique work or service experience, leadership potential, maturity, demonstrated compassion, a history of overcoming disadvantage, ability to communicate with the poor, or other qualifications deemed important. In short, an admissions program operated in this way is flexible enough to consider all pertinent elements of diversity in light of the particular qualifications of each applicant, and to place them on the same footing for consideration, although not necessarily according them the same weight. Indeed, the weight attributed to a particular quality may vary from year to year depending upon the "mix" both of the student body and the applicants for the incoming class.

This kind of program treats each applicant as an individual in the admissions process. The applicant who loses out on the last available seat to another candidate receiving a "plus" on the basis of ethnic background will not have been foreclosed from all consideration for that seat simply because he was not the right color or had the wrong surname. It would mean only that his combined qualifications, which may have included similar nonobjective factors, did not outweigh those of the other applicant. His qualifications would have been weighed fairly and competitively, and he would have no basis to complain of unequal treatment under the Fourteenth Amendment.

It has been suggested that an admissions program which considers race only as one factor is simply a subtle and more sophisticated—but no less effective—means of according racial preference than the Davis program. A facial intent to discriminate, however, is evident in petitioner's preference program and not denied in this case. No such facial infirmity exists in an admissions program where race or ethnic background is simply one element—to be weighed fairly against other elements—in the selection process. "A boundary line," as Mr. Justice Frankfurter remarked in another connection, "is none the worse for being narrow." *McLeod v. Dilworth*, 322 U.S. 327, 329, 64 S.Ct. 1023, 1025, 88 L.Ed. 1304 (1944). And a court would not assume that a university, professing to employ a facially nondiscriminatory admissions policy, would operate it as a cover for the functional equivalent of a quota system. In short, good faith would be presumed in the absence of a showing to the contrary in the manner permitted by our cases. . . .

In summary, it is evident that the Davis special admissions program involves the use of an explicit racial classification never before countenanced by this Court. It tells applicants who are not Negro, Asian, or Chicano that they are totally excluded from a specific percentage of the seats in an entering class. No matter how strong their qualifications, quantitative and extracurricular, including their own potential for contribution to educational diversity, they are never afforded the chance to compete with applicants from the preferred groups for the special admissions seats. At the same time, the preferred applicants have the opportunity to compete for every seat in the class.

The fatal flaw in petitioner's preferential program is its disregard of individual rights as guaranteed by the Fourteenth Amendment. *Shelley v. Kraemer*, 334 U.S., at 22, 68 S.Ct., at 846. Such rights are not absolute. But when a State's distribution of benefits or imposition of burdens hinges on ancestry or the color of a person's skin, that individual is entitled to a demonstration that the challenged classification is necessary to promote a substantial state interest. Petitioner has failed to carry this burden. For this reason, that portion of the California court's judgment holding petitioner's special admissions program invalid under the Fourteenth Amendment must be affirmed.

In enjoining petitioner from ever considering the race of any applicant, however, the courts below failed to recognize that the State has a substantial interest that legitimately may be served by a properly devised admissions program involving the competitive consideration of race and ethnic origin. For this reason, so much of the California court's judgment as enjoins petitioner from any consideration of the race of any applicant must be reversed.

SELECTED READINGS

Flexner, Eleanor. *Century of Struggle: The Women's Rights Movement in the United States.* Cambridge, Mass.: Harvard University Press, 1975.
This classic history, first published in 1959 and considerably revised by the author sixteen years later, documents the gradually improving civil rights status of women in America. The book first describes the condition of women during the colonial and revolutionary periods and the beginnings of the women's rights movement in the nineteenth century. Advances in education and employment and the passage in 1920 of the suffrage amendment are compared with other social reforms, such as the abolition of slavery and the organization of trade unions. Last, Flexner establishes a context for viewing future social changes relating to the relationship between the sexes.

Glazer, Nathan. *Affirmative Discrimination: Ethnic Inequality and Public Policy.* New York: Basic Books, 1975.
Glazer's thesis is that affirmative action, at least as it developed during the '70s, violates the principle "that the individual and the individual's interest and good and welfare are the test of a good society." He contends that all attempts to divide America into groups deserving or not deserving special consideration in hiring, admissions, and the like are bound to lead to capriciousness, bitterness, and backlash. He also cogently analyzes the shifting criteria used in placing various groups (blacks, Asians, women, Hispanics) into the protected category.

Gross, Barry, ed. *Reverse Discrimination.* New York: Prometheus, 1977.
Since the 1978 Bakke decision, efforts to redress racial imbalances in school admissions and other areas of American life have been widely controversial. The contributors to these thirty-two essays—lawyers, educators, philosophers, and sociologists—use the insights and methodologies of their various disciplines to debate the pros and cons of these attempts.

Jensen, Arthur. *Educability and Group Differences.* New York: Harper & Row, 1973.
Although this book was written by a scientist, its political implications are explosive. Jensen argues for the genetic heritability of intelligence through racial groupings. Not surprisingly, he is pessimistic about the benefits of affirmative action

legislation. Differences in occupation, income, and educability, he feels, are ultimately the result of genetic influences.

Kluger, Richard. *Simple Justice.* New York: Knopf, 1980.
   The importance of the 1954 Supreme Court decision in *Brown* v. *Board of Education* is difficult to exaggerate. In overruling the earlier standard of "separate but equal" of *Plessy* v. *Ferguson*, the Court undermined the legality of racial segregation in every area of public life and helped to spark the civil rights movement of the '50s and '60s. Kluger provides a comprehensive description of the issues, institutions, and personalities behind this epic clash of viewpoints.

Larson, E. Richard, and McDonald, Laughlin. *The Rights of Racial Minorities.* New York: Avon, 1980.
   This easy-reference volume and valuable handbook covers minority rights in several contexts, including affirmative action in admissions and discrimination in education, employment, housing, and public accommodations.

Livingston, John C. *Fair Game?* San Francisco: Freeman, 1979.
   The author seeks to place the public policies regarding affirmative action in philosophical and historical perspective. While chiefly interested in clarifying often misunderstood terms like "affirmative action," "reverse discrimination," "quota," "color-blind," and "meritocracy," Livingston offers a defense of affirmative action and the use of racial quotas.

Rossum, Ralph. *Reverse Discrimination: The Constitutional Debate.* New York: Marcel Dekker, 1980.
   Rossum, a political scientist at Loyola/University of Chicago, carefully guides the reader through the principal legal and constitutional arguments and Supreme Court cases involving affirmative action and/or reverse discrimination.

Sher, George. "Justifying Reverse Discrimination in Employment." *Philosophy and Public Affairs*, 4 (Winter 1975): 159-170.
   Sher looks at the difficult problems raised in diagnosing and remedying the effects of past and present discrimination against blacks and women in employment.

Sindler, Allan P. *Bakke, DeFunis, and Minority Admissions.* New York: Longmans, 1978.
   The dean of the Graduate School of Public Policy at the University of California, Berkeley, tells the full stories of the famous cases brought by Alan Bakke and Marco DeFunis to secure admission by medical and law schools. Sindler also examines the legal and public policy aspects of affirmative action programs in general and racial quotas in particular.

GLOSSARY

Affirmative action. According to Irving Kristol, this term originally meant any program that ordered industries "to go out and search for qualified people." In its present meaning, it stands for any program of recruitment, admission, or award that takes into account the candidates' race, ethnic background, or gender.

"Color-blind."   Unmindful of an individual's race. Opposite of "color-conscious."

Controlling opinion.   The opinion of a Supreme Court justice whose vote tips the balance in favor of a certain result. The opinion of Justice Lewis Powell in the *Bakke* case was controlling because it produced a five-to-four decision in favor of Bakke's claim that he was a victim of reverse discrimination.

Equal protection clause.   The clause in the Fourteenth Amendment that states: "No state shall . . . deny to any person within its jurisdiction the equal protection of the laws." It has figured prominently in many civil rights cases, including the *Brown* and *Bakke* cases.

Minority.   A term of uncertain meaning. In the '50s and early '60s, it generally meant blacks and other non-Caucasians. But as "whites" began to be broken down into constituent groupings, some whites, including those of Hispanic background, began to be included in the "minority" category. Numerically, all distinct ethnic groups in America are minorities, but the term also connotes "victims of past or present discrimination." Using that criterion, other Caucasian groups, such as Italians and Jews, might qualify as minorities, though they are seldom classified as such for purposes of affirmative action.

Role model.   A person in authority toward whom young people can feel an affinity and whom they wish to emulate.

Tenure.   Loosely understood, the guarantee of a lifetime job in academia. More precisely, the status of a teacher whose position extends until the age of retirement and from which a teacher can be dismissed only under exceptional circumstances, such as highly unprofessional conduct or the abolition of the teacher's department or division.

Chapter 13
Out of Many, One

"The powers not delegated to the United States by the Constitution, nor prohibited by it to the States, are reserved to the States respectively, or to the people."

AMENDMENT X, U.S. CONSTITUTION

"The amendment states but a truism that all is retained which has not been surrendered."

JUSTICE HARLAN FISKE STONE,
United States v. Darby (1941)

The name of almost every nation on earth is singular: "England," "France," "*Union* of Soviet Socialist Republics." Ours is plural: "the United *States* of America."

There are good historical reasons for this. Before the American Revolution there were thirteen English colonies in the bottom part of North America. The Revolution turned them into separate and independent states. Soon they were loosely associated under the Articles of Confederation. But the Articles provided only a feeble central government. The new states were surrounded by ambitious foreign powers, troubled by Indian raids and domestic turmoil, saddled with staggering war debts, and engaged in a fierce economic war with one another. Even the most cautious American statesmen agreed that the central government needed something more. But for many, the proposed Constitution went too far. Some old revolutionaries, such as Patrick Henry, fought against its ratification because they feared it would centralize the government too much. Others, like Jefferson, approved of the Constitution but thought it needed a bill of rights to protect the liberties of states and people. Such a bill was added by the First Congress, and it culminated in the Tenth Amendment, which says that all powers not delegated to the federal government are "reserved" to the states or the people.

The federal, or central, government, then, would take care of national defense, foreign policy, the regulation of foreign commerce and commerce among the states, the coining and printing of money, the post office, and the other areas listed in Article I, section 8. Everything else would be up to the states. It seemed like a logical division of power, and within a few years everybody was celebrating the new Constitution. It seemed to breathe new life into the Latin motto that Ben Franklin, Thomas Jefferson, and John Adams wanted written on the Great Seal of the United States (and which is stamped on all our coins today): *E pluribus unum*, "Out of many, one."

But there is a built-in logical tension between "many" and "one." "Many" implies diversity: each state goes its own way and does its own thing. "One" implies conformity: there can only be "one way" of doing certain things if we are to have unity. Soon the logical tension had its counterpart in the real world: there were quarrels between the federal government and some of the states, quarrels about taxes and tariffs, and quarrels about slavery. Seventy-one years after the ratification of the Constitution, they exploded into civil war.

The northern victory in 1865 strengthened the Union. Now secession—leaving the Union—was out of the question, and there were new amendments to the Constitution that limited the power of states. And this was just the beginning of the shift in power from the states to the national government.

Over the next century, other events occurred: the nation became involved in worldwide conflicts that required concerted national action; industries and cities sprang up, and the flow of commerce they fostered paid no attention to state boundaries; American inventors created a technological revolution, and their new inventions —the telephone, radio and TV, mass-produced cars, airplanes—tied the American people together as never before. Finally, the new age produced new national problems, from catastrophic depressions to the poisoning of our environment.

Those American leaders, statesmen, and jurists who fought hardest for a national solution often regarded the states' "reserved" powers as an impediment to progress. The states seemed incapable of exercising their powers properly. Soon, American law and jurisprudence began to qualify the states' "reserved" powers: Yes, the constitutional lawyers said, the states can do certain things, but so can the federal government. Or: Yes, certain powers are reserved to the states, but they can only exercise them in certain ways. Or: Yes, we respect states' rights, but once the states take federal money, they must do what the federal government says. Today, federal standards have overridden state and local practices in a wide variety of areas, from the treatment of prisoners and criminal suspects to the design of school buildings and playgrounds. What bothers many people is the suspicion that there is really not much left of state autonomy. Have the states been so stripped of power that they no longer serve as self-governing units? During the 1960s one senator lamented that the existence of states would soon be of interest only to Rand McNally, the map-making company. Are we closer to that point today?

Ours is supposed to be a federal system, one that apportions some powers to a central government and some to the several states. That was the promise of the Constitution and its Bill of Rights, and it was with that understanding that the Constitution was ratified. But there are also good practical reasons for wanting to preserve our federal structure. First, as James Madison pointed out in No. 10 of *The Federalist*, federalism allows for diversity and choice. If people don't like the practices in one state, they can move to another. To centralize government is to put all the eggs in one basket. If the central government ever becomes oppressive, where can people move? Only out of the country. Second, a federal system offers individual states a chance to experiment. Not long ago the state of Oregon passed a law requiring a deposit on beer and soda bottles; its purpose was to eliminate litter and save energy. The experiment worked, and other states are starting to duplicate it. Other experiments have not worked well, so they were not imitated by other states. The point is that a state can try out a new idea without necessarily inflicting it on the whole nation.

Third, leaving the business of governing up to state and local officials may be the best way of adapting laws to local needs and problems. Local officials are closer to grass-roots America. It is usually easier to see them and talk to them than it is to get through to Washington officials. Washington is much better at handling foreign policy and national defense. Yet in the video discussion, Utah Senator Orrin Hatch complains that Washington officials are now "determining what football fields to play on, where the cars should park," and whether or not your local high school should buy Bunsen burners. Hatch calls this "idiotic." It is hard to quarrel with that.

Where is the quarrel, then? If excessive centralization is idiotic, why not go back to decentralization? One answer is that the good old days of decentralized government were really not so good. Here are some things state officials did in those days: they segregated their schools by race, they discriminated against women, they apportioned their legislatures to give extra weight to rural votes, they allowed businesses to make money by using child labor, and they allowed their police to use third-degree tactics on criminal suspects. Do we really want to bring those days back? Another point to remember is that America has changed considerably since the days of decentralized government. Like it or not, our technology has bound us together, and our modern social problems require coordinated solutions. We need our enlarged federal government. The question, then, is not how to recapture some bygone era but how to reconcile the need for national standards and national action with the need for state and local independence. How can we use the federal government to help us without letting it stifle grass-roots government?

The Video Discussion

There is no simple answer, no neat formula, for answering these questions. All we can do is to keep adjusting the balance by looking at specific cases to see if they weight the scales too much in one direction or the other. That is what the participants in the video discussion try to do with the cases posed by their moderator, Professor Lewis B. Kaden of Columbia Law School.

List of Participants

FLOYD ABRAMS
Attorney
Cahill Gordon & Reindel

HON. ARLIN M. ADAMS
Judge
U.S. Court of Appeals
Third Circuit

HON. LAMAR ALEXANDER
Governor
Tennessee

GREGORY R. ANRIG
President
Educational Testing Service

HON. BRUCE E. BABBITT
Governor
Arizona

JOHN BRADEMAS
President
New York University
Former U.S. Representative
Indiana

ALONZO A. CRIM
Superintendent
Atlanta Public Schools

LLOYD N. CUTLER
Attorney
Wilmer, Cutler & Pickering
Former Counsel to President Carter

FRED GRAHAM
Law Correspondent
CBS News

HON. ORRIN G. HATCH
U.S. Senator
Utah

PAUL G. HEARNE
Executive Director
Just One Break, Inc.

MARGARET MARSHALL
Attorney
Csaplar & Bok

HON. SCOTT M. MATHESON
Governor
Utah

WADE H. MCCREE, JR.
Lewis M. Simes
Professor of Law
University of Michigan
Former U.S. Solicitor General

HON. DANIEL P. MOYNIHAN
U.S. Senator
New York
Former U.S. Permanent Representative
to the United Nations

DIANE RAVITCH
Professor of History and Education
Teachers College
Columbia University

ALBERT SHANKER
President
United Federation of Teachers

HON. POTTER STEWART
Justice (retired)
U.S. Supreme Court

HON. DICK THORNBURGH
Governor
Pennsylvania

HON. PATRICIA M. WALD
Judge
U.S. Court of Appeals
D.C. Circuit
Former Assistant Attorney General
for Legislative Affairs

HON. J. CLIFFORD WALLACE
Judge
U.S. Court of Appeals
Ninth Circuit

Program Summary

The program is divided into three parts. In the first part the moderator raises a hypothetical case in which a handicapped child who wants to attend a local school cannot

do so because the school lacks ramps and other facilities for wheelchairs. The federal government helps the state pay for education to the handicapped but requires that the children be "mainstreamed," sent to school with the nonhandicapped, whenever that is appropriate. The moderator questions various panelists—a school superintendent, a state governor, an advocate for the handicapped, present and former members of Congress—to test their reactions and probe their views.

In the second part of the program the moderator pretends to be the president. Concerned about the decline of educational standards, he plans to sponsor a bill to provide salary supplements for teachers. But the bill will also stipulate that any state accepting the salary supplements must require four years of science, math, computer science, and a foreign language of all its high school students. The moderator asks various state governors whether they would be willing to take the aid package with such strings attached to it. He sounds out other panelists on the issue of grants-in-aid and federal standardization in the field of education.

In the third part of the program the discussion becomes more general; it also raises the question of the role of courts as referees in federal-state disputes. Among the issues considered: What is the purpose of federalism? Have courts been fair to the states? What fields are properly left to states, and when is federal intervention necessary? Has federal involvement helped or hurt education?

I: MAINSTREAMING THE HANDICAPPED

In the early 1970s a study by the federal Office of Education showed that only about half the nation's 8 million handicapped children were receiving an adequate education; 2.5 million were receiving an inadequate education; and 1.75 million were getting no education at all.

Such findings moved federal and state judges to rule that states had to provide education for the handicapped, even if that meant paying for special buildings, facilities, and transportation. These rulings threatened to break the budgets of financially pressed school districts. The National Educational Finance Project has estimated that the average cost of educating a handicapped child is 1.9 times that of educating a normal child. Where would all this extra money come from?

In 1975, Senator Harrison Williams of New Jersey and Representative John Brademas of Indiana suggested that the federal government pick up the tab. Their suggestion took the form of a bill which they jointly sponsored and which, when it became law in November of that year, was called the Education for All Handicapped Children Act. Its stated purpose was to ensure that all disabled children receive "a free appropriate public education which emphasizes special education and related services designed to meet their unique needs." The act provided increasing amounts of federal aid to the states to help pay for education of handicapped children. In 1976 the amount was supposed to be $100 million, in 1977 it would increase to $200 million, in 1978 to $378 million, and so on; for 1982 and beyond it would reach the level of $3,160,000,000 annually. A generous gift—one that the states, already forced by courts to educate their handicapped children, could hardly refuse. But there were strings attached. Once a state accepted the money, it would have to meet a number of stipulations in the act.

One stipulation was that the state must follow federal criteria for determining what should be considered a specific learning disability and what procedures should be used for diagnosing the problem. Another was that state school districts must set up individualized learning programs for each handicapped child; each program must set forth annual goals, short-term objectives, and the specific services to be provided for each student. There must also be an individual conference between the parents, the child, and the child's teachers as soon as the child enters the school, anther conference later in the year, and yearly conferences thereafter. Still another stipulation was that the child must be "mainstreamed"—taught with nonhandicapped children instead of being consigned to a special school—wherever that is possible or "appropriate." If that seems like a lot of federal intrusion into a traditionally local concern, there is even more in the act. That is the "price," as it were, of grants-in-aid.

Grants-in-Aid: Federal Money, Federal Control

Most Americans regard education as a local concern. It was not among the functions delegated to the federal Congress in Article I, section 8. Therefore, it seems to belong to those powers "reserved" to the states by the Tenth Amendment. Yet the Education for All Handicapped Children Act gets the federal government involved in the minutiae of school administration. Of course, the states are under no obligation to accept the money. They can always turn it down and educate their handicapped children as they see fit. Or can they? Federal and state judges have been telling the states that they must educate the handicapped on substantially equal terms as they do the nonhandicapped. And the only way they can do that is to increase their education budgets sharply. The states don't have that kind of money. So their "choice" is really not much of a choice. They have to take the money, and with it the federal interference in state affairs. In that respect the act is a typical grant-in-aid.

Although federal grants to states go back to 1802, it is only in the last generation that they have played a major role in state affairs. In the 1950s such grants amounted to about $5 billion annually, less than 12 percent of what states and localities raised from their own resources. Today federal grants are close to $100 billion annually and constitute more than 30 percent of the amount state and local governments raise themselves. The increased money has brought increased regulations. In 1960, few regulations were imposed on states and localities. By 1980, however, there were 223 sets of direct federal orders regulating states and localities, and another 1,036 sets of orders that were conditions for receiving aid, such as the stipulations listed in the Education for All Handicapped Children Act.

The prospect of increased federal interference in an area once reserved to states and localities was one reason for President Ford's opposition to the act when it was before Congress. He signed it only because it passed by such huge margins (in the House by 404 to 7, in the Senate by 87 to 7) that a veto would easily have been over-ridden. But in signing it he complained about the bill's "vast array of detailed, complex and costly administrative requirements which would unnecessarily assert federal control over traditional state and local functions." Whether or not Ford's complaint was justified, he was right about the growth of new administrative requirements: no sooner was the law enacted than the bureaucrats went to work "implementing" it.

The law required that the handicapped be educated with the nonhandicapped where appropriate. The bureaucrats interpreted that to mean that states and localities must start remodeling old schools to provide elevators, ramps, and other "barrier-free" accommodations for wheelchairs, and that the schools must begin hiring special teachers to help handicapped children keep up with the nonhandicapped in the schools. These regulations entailed new expenditures, for which the states were supposed to be compensated by the new federal grants; but construction and other costs often overran the amount that the states got back from the federal government. Some state and local officials began wondering whether the whole package was worth it. Now they had more expenses, more regulations, and—in case they failed to comply—the threat of political and legal pressures from organizations representing the handicapped.

This brings us to our hypothetical case. The moderator asks CBS law correspondent Fred Graham to imagine that he has an eleven-year-old son, Andrew, who is paralyzed from the waist down. Andrew is in a wheelchair, yet he wants to go to school with the other kids on his block. The school district tells Graham that it can't accommodate Andrew at the neighborhood school, which was built in the 1930s and has no access ramps or elevators. Andrew will have to go to a special school for the handicapped, which is on the other side of town. "You and Andrew are very upset about this, think it would be bad for him, and you're determined to fight it. What's your first step?"

Graham is convinced that he has a strong cause for legal action against the school district, but he will first try persuasion. The moderator introduces him to Alonzo Crim, Atlanta's school superintendent, who will play the superintendent of this school district. Graham asks Crim why he won't help Andrew get into school with the other, nonhandicapped kids in his neighborhood. All he has to do is build some access ramps, install an elevator, maybe hire a few new teachers. "You can do a wonderful thing . . . and . . . all it is going to require is, perhaps, a little bit of cost." Crim is sympathetic but says his district is strapped for money. As for federal aid, Crim implies that the federal government has welched on its commitments. "The federal government pledged, over a period of years, that it would encumber [pay for] up to 40 percent of the costs of special education and it never exceeded 12 percent."*

John Brademas, the congressman who sponsored this legislation in the House (he is now president of New York University), tries scolding Crim. "I think you should be aware, Mr. Crim, that in your school system, you're way behind the times." All Andrew requires is a "*de minimus* expenditure." Now Graham, too, is going to get tough. He says, "I'm going to take this to the media." It is, indeed, a perfect media

*This was another prediction of President Ford in 1975. In signing the bill, Ford said, "Unfortunately, this bill promises more than the federal government can deliver. . . . Even the strongest supporters of this measure know as well as I that they are falsely raising the expectations of the groups affected by claiming authorization levels which are excessive and unrealistic" if federal spending is to be brought under control. See *Congressional Quarterly*, 1975, p. 656.

story: Graham will talk about the district's "high salaries to administrators" coupled with its callous treatment of "this little child" who just wants "to go to school with his . . . neighbors and friends." Television can dramatize this story as no other medium can. There could be shot of a TV reporter asking the school superintendent why he can't accommodate a handicapped child, with the superintendent saying something about money, followed by a close-up shot of Andrew saying, "I just want to be educated with the other kids. I know I can make it." No public official wants to play the heavy in that scene. The power of the media could be one reason that this very expensive piece of legislation passed Congress by such overwhelming margins. Nobody who runs for office cares to be seen as Ebenezer Scrooge.

Since Crim is appointed rather than elected, he may be able to weather the evening news programs. Still, it looks as though his troubles are just beginning. Now he has to deal with Paul G. Hearne, executive director of Just One Break, Inc., a pressure group for the handicapped. Hearne knows all the ins and outs of "handicap" politics. He will go to the local committee on the handicapped, which all communities must now have, to pressure the school board into modifying the school. In response, the local committee demands a hearing before the state school board. The moderator appoints Diane Ravitch, a well-known writer on educational issues and a professor at Columbia's Teachers College, as head of the school board. Ravitch announces the results of the hearing: "We determine that . . . inasmuch as he doesn't need special education and should be mainstreamed, we've ordered the local school board to, forthwith, admit him to the regular school and deal with the problems." So, even without going to court, Graham has gotten Andrew into the local school.

Now all the school district has to do is come up with the money for the ramps, elevators, and other facilities and services for Andrew. Albert Shanker, head of the United Federation of Teachers, suggests two alternatives. The decision "will result either in somebody finding additional money, which is pretty rare these days, or . . . in great internal shifts in money." Crim mentions one "internal shift" that may be necessary. Right now the schools are spending great amounts of money to remove cancer-causing asbestos that was put into the schools years ago. He may have to divert money from that project in order to build access ramps. This prompts Hearne to jest that perhaps "you should take all that asbestos and make a ramp out of it."

After further discussion of the controversy, which has somehow gotten into court after all, the moderator confronts the cosponsor of the act: "Mr. Brademas, what happened to the idea that schools are the responsibility of the local government?" Brademas answers that, first, local and state governments were not meeting their responsibilities, and, second, that nobody forced them to take the federal money. "That's my idea of Hobson's choice," replies Arizona's Governor Bruce Babbitt. Thomas Hobson (1544?-1631) ran a rent-a-horse service in England and required each customer to "choose" the horse nearest the door. A Hobson's choice, therefore, is one in which a person must take what is offered or nothing. "That's no choice at all," says the governor.

Then he hits on an idea. He calls up Crim and tells him that he, Crim, has to accommodate Andrew. *But* there will be a little present for his district if he does. "Now there's a lot of state money . . . that comes to you in the form of discretionary grants.

You take this kid, make it work, and I'll see if I can load a little extra onto some of these special grants for textbooks." Amid laughter, Crim says, "Thank you, Governor." Governor Scott Matheson of Utah likes Babbitt's way of sweetening the compliance process. "I've learned a lot from Governor Babbitt already. (*laughter*)" So maybe the bureaucratic process is not so stifling when it comes to the creative use of grants-in-aid. Babbitt seems to be able to shift moneys from one area to another to encourage local school officials to make changes. This is not exactly a Hobson's choice!

Points to Remember

1. *E pluribus unum*, "Out of one, many," reminds us that our nation developed out of individual states. Our nation retains its plural name.
2. The Tenth Amendment says that all powers not delegated to the federal government or denied to the states are reserved to the states or the people.
3. The Civil War ended slavery and made it impossible for a state to secede from the Union. Since the Civil War, a number of other developments, including our involvement in world wars and the revolution in technology, have helped unify the nation. As a result, some people fear that the states may become obsolete.
4. States serve at least three functions: they help preserve diversity, they serve as laboratories for political experiment, and they adapt government to local needs.
5. Grants-in-aid provide money to help states finance programs in areas traditionally reserved to the states. But such aid usually comes with strings attached, which give the federal government control. Some people feel that this control has become excessive. Others feel that federal intervention is necessary, since the states have often failed to meet their responsibilities.
6. The Education for All Handicapped Children Act of 1975 provides states with funds to help educate the handicapped. It gets the federal government involved in the details of curriculum planning, student-teacher relationships, and the construction of school buildings. In the hypothetical case explored by the panel, a local school district is compelled to modify a school so that a handicapped child can be "mainstreamed."

II: FEDERAL CURRICULUM STANDARDS?

"It's a time in the not-too-distant future," says the moderator, "and I've just been elected president of the United States." The new president is deeply worried about the crisis in American education. Convinced that we're far behind the Russians and the Japanese, he is determined to catch up. He wants to push through Congress a program that will provide high school teachers with annual salary supplements. It is not clear yet whether teachers will have to work a longer school year in order to get the extra money. But one stipulation will definitely be contained in the aid package: every high school benefiting from the teachers' supplements must require four years of English, math, science, and a foreign language from every student.

The moderator turns to Lloyd Cutler, former counsel to President Carter. "Mr. Cutler, what do we have to do to get it passed?" Before Cutler can answer, New York Senator Daniel Patrick Moynihan breaks in. "Mr. Cutler, would you yield?" Mr. Cutler yields. Moynihan points out that public school teachers aren't the only teachers in this country. What about those in parochial schools? Will they get money, too? Cutler tells the moderator he'd better "make your peace with the senior senator from New York." Okay, says the moderator, who else do I have to talk to to get this bill passed? Cutler: "Oh, you've got to talk to Brother Shanker over here." He means teachers' union chief Albert Shanker.

Shanker has been reading a sheet of paper handed to the panelists before the discussion. The paper outlines the hypothetical cases, though it leaves the moderator free to change them any way he likes. On the paper it says that teachers would get an extra $5,000 in salary supplements but that they would have to work twelve months a year for it. Shanker doesn't like the last part. "Have you ever been locked in a room with thirty-five kids for ten months a year and you are going to take away my two months during the summer?" All right, replies the moderator, you've convinced me. The teachers' contract stays at ten months but the teachers will still get their extra $5,000. "I'll take it," says Shanker.

Now that he has delighted Shanker and at least quieted Moynihan, the moderator starts looking around for more support. He goes to the state governors with his package—and meets what is at best a mixed reception. Governor Babbitt of Arizona tells him that there is already a "revolution" in the states. The states are upping teachers' salaries on their own, and the moderator's new offer will "lay the deadening hand of the United States Congress on this issue, and you are going to be maligned in history for having stopped a revolution that's already under way." It is not clear whether Governor Babbitt objects to the federal money or the federal standards. Possibly both. Governor Lamar Alexander of Tennessee also opposes the moderator's bill. He explains his opposition in terms of the particular roles of federal and state governments.

> Congressmen and presidents ought to worry about what you usually worry about in Washington, which is welfare and taxes and debt and minor scandals and things like that, and leave to us in the local governments better schools and what's going on in the third grade.

The moderator presses him. "Why?" Well, replies Alexander, a long time ago we divided up the jobs. "The states can't figure out what to do about national defense, and neither can you have much to do with the quality of public education. . . . You've done what you can. Now leave it to us."

Governor Dick Thornburgh of Pennsylvania is more amenable. Having watched the moderator and Shanker cut a deal, he figures that he and the moderator can also do some bargaining. "I'm looking at a package that would bring about a half a billion dollars into Pennsylvania," he says. What he wants is a "block grant," a grant for general educational purposes that does not get specific about standards and has few strings attached to it. "In other words," the moderator says, "you'll take the money. I can keep my standards." That does seem to be what Thornburgh has in mind. He complains that the bill's attempt to dictate "a very tight four-year curriculum . . . leaves very little movement at the school district level to decide what priority needs of a particular community have to be met."

Professor Ravitch agrees. She thinks this proposal has too much stick and not enough carrot. You need a "large carrot," she says, maybe more than $5,000 per teacher. And the stick must be minimal, "one year of math and science," just enough to encourage states to stiffen their own standards. She worries that the moderator may be aiming at "a national curriculum and national tests," which states would vigorously resist.

Senator Hatch now delivers a far-reaching criticism of federal aid to education. Earlier in the program Hatch complained about the "idiotic" application of federal standards to local football fields, parking lots, and high school Bunsen burners. Now he talks not just about the standards but the money itself. "I think that as federal government expenditures have gone up through the years . . . scores and other telltale signs of education quality have gone down." Albert Shanker has heard this criticism before, and he is anxious to reply. He says:

> Mr. President, you should know that federal money was not wasted and that your program has a good deal of merit, because those federal funds were targeted toward poor kids, blacks and Hispanics, and they're the only ones whose scores have gone up in the last fifteen years, and they are the only ones who are going to college in much greater numbers, so this story about federal money going in and the scores going down just isn't right.

The moderator now changes the focus of the discussion from the wisdom of the proposed law to its constitutionality. He asks Professor Wade McCree, who was solicitor general in the Carter administration, if the president has the authority to formulate standards for local schools. McCree sees no constitutional problem, for "the appropriations power of Congress permits it to attach certain restrictions and limitations on the use of its money." But he worries that if the restrictions get too detailed, "they might be found to offend concepts of federalism." The moderator asks him to explain, whereupon McCree says something very interesting. "Well," he says, "the federal government, of course, is the creature of the several states, and it . . . holds powers that the states surrendered to it."

Is the federal government simply "the creature of the several states"? The issue was addressed in a historic Supreme Court case, *McCulloch* v. *Maryland* (1819).

McCulloch v. *Maryland*: A Union of People

We quoted from this case in the Introduction. In his opinion in the case, Chief Justice John Marshall said, "We must never forget, that it is a *constitution* we are expounding." Marshall meant that our great charter is not like a set of statutes. It does not try to spell out everything in detail. It leaves room for the federal government to grow and adapt itself to changing circumstances.

It was the growth of the federal government that was at issue in the case. In 1816 Congress passed a law setting up a "Bank of the United States." The bank was meant to serve as a convenient means of encouraging investment in federal projects and enlarging national revenues. It was bitterly resented by many of the states, which saw it as an institution that intruded into state domains. To retaliate against it, the state of Maryland required the bank's Baltimore branch to pay an annual state tax of $15,000 or else pay a stamp tax on each bank note it issued. The bank's Baltimore cashier, McCulloch, refused to do either, and he was sued by the state.

When the case of *McCulloch* v. *Maryland* reached the Supreme Court, Chief Justice Marshall noted that it raised two issues. First, does the federal government possess the authority to charter a bank? Second, if it does, does Maryland have a right to tax the bank? Leaving aside the second issue, let us concentrate on the first. Where does the federal government get the authority to charter a bank?

Nowhere in the Constitution does it explicitly say that Congress has any such authority. However, in Article I, section 8, a number of other powers are given to Congress, including the power "to borrow money on the credit of the United States," "to regulate Commerce with foreign Nations, and among the several States," and to lay and collect taxes for the defense and "general welfare" of the nation. Then, at the end of Article I, section 8, we find this grant of power: Congress may "make all Laws which shall be necessary and proper for carrying into execution the foregoing powers."

The "necessary and proper" clause is sometimes also called "the elastic clause" because it can be used to stretch the power of the federal government. All the government has to show is that a certain action it has taken is "necessary and proper" for carrying out one or more of the powers assigned to it in Article I, section 8. For this reason the necessary and proper clause is also called the "implied powers clause," since it gives the federal government powers not explicitly written down in the Constitution. In this case, what the federal government had to do was to demonstrate that a federally chartered bank was "necessary" for carrying out the powers delegated to it in Article I, section 8.

Very well, then, said the lawyer for the state of Maryland, what is so necessary about the bank? Does the federal government really need a bank? It had gotten along without one for more than thirty years. Why all of a sudden was a federal bank necessary and proper?

Marshall answered that question by launching into a discussion on the meaning of the word "necessary." The word, he said, admits of degrees. "A thing may be necessary, very necessary, absolutely or indispensably necessary." The bank may not be "indispensably necessary," but it is necessary in the less urgent sense of "convenient" or "appropriate." Once Marshall gave the word that construction, the rest was easy. For Maryland would be hard-pressed to show that the bank was not a convenient or appropriate means by which the federal government could carry out its powers to tax and spend, borrow money, and do many of the other things it was given the power to do in Article I, section 8. If these powers are legitimate, Marshall said, then any means appropriate for carrying them out is also legitimate—from which it follows that the federal government has the power to charter a bank, even though that power is not written down in the Constitution.

Marshall's decision was severely criticized. It was charged that he was riding rough-shod over the rights of the states. Back in 1787 representatives of the states had gener-ously surrendered some of their states' powers to a central government; now the cen-tral government was grabbing more power, including powers reserved to the states by the Tenth Amendment. And Marshall was aiding and abetting it! The federal govern-ment should remember its origin: it is nothing more than a creature of the several states, for it is the result of a compact between them.

Marshall anticipated this criticism in his opinion. (Its premises were in the argu-ment of the attorney for Maryland.) He answered it by flatly denying that the federal government *is* a creature of the states. Look at the history of our Constitution, he said. It was *drawn up* by representatives of the states in 1787. But when it came from their hands it was "a mere proposal." It had to be ratified to become official, and the ratification was not by state legislatures but by conventions of the American *people.* The federal government, then, "proceeds directly from the people." It is ordained and established in their name (the Constitution begins, "We the people of the United States"), and has been ratified by them. "The government of the Union, then," said Marshall, "is emphatically and truly a government of the people," not of the states.

This brings us back to the video discussion, and to the remark of Professor McCree. He has said that the federal government, "of course, is the creature of the several states." Oddly, no one challenges this statement except Senator Moynihan, and Moy-nihan seems to have mixed up John Marshall with James Madison. He says, "Madison was of the view that the Constitution was not created by the states but by the people of the states."

Of course, Marshall's reading of constitutional history may be wrong. The lawyer for the state of Maryland in the *McCulloch* case was a man named Luther Martin. Mar-tin was one of Maryland's delegates to the Constitutional Convention!

Marshall's interpretation was bold, perhaps presumptuous—but it has prevailed. Today, our country is considered to be a union of people rather than a compact of states. States have independent powers, but they can neither secede from the Union nor interfere with the rightful authority of the federal government.

The emphasis, of course, is on "rightful" authority. All the panelists agree that it is neither legitimate nor wise for the federal government to barge into areas best left to state and local governments. The education of children, or at least its particulars, seems to be one such area rightly set aside for state and local governments. No one on the panel is more eloquent in defense of such local decision making than Tennessee Governor Lamar Alexander:

> People want to have some control over the decisions that affect their lives the
> most every day. Is the third grade good? Is the road in front of their house paved?
> Is the water they drink clean? And most of that should be decided at a local level.

Later in the program, Governor Alexander says that if the Constitution were being rewritten and the question came up as to "who should be in charge of educating our children in Hendersonville, Tennessee," the people in his state would say: the local community first, the state second, and "keep the federal government entirely out of it." Although some panelists, such as Senator Moynihan, favor an expansive role for the federal government in the field of education, Alexander's statement commands a wide consensus.

Even Floyd Abrams, the attorney who has sometimes had to defend the *New York Times* from challenges by state and local officials, sounds like a staunch advocate of local autonomy as he sums up the consensus:

> All we're saying is that there has to be . . . some line over which Congress and the president can't go and that when you get into an area so historically local as education and educational qualifications and the content of education, that's well over the line.

In the end, it seems that the moderator's bill has little chance of passage; even if it does pass, the governors on this panel won't take the money with such strings attached to it. Even Governor Thornburgh finally backs out of the deal he was considering earlier in the program.

Points to Remember

1. Most members of the panel are opposed to detailed federal curriculum standards.
2. Constitutionally, the federal government could set such standards if they were tied to grants-in-aid. Once states take federal money, they can be required to meet federal standards.
3. In the case of *McCulloch* v. *Maryland* (1819), the Supreme Court held that the federal government could charter a bank, even though the Constitution says nothing about national banks.
4. The Court's reasoning in *McCulloch* was based on the premise that Congress can do anything "necessary and proper" for carrying out its legitimate powers. The Court defined "necessary" as "convenient" or "appropriate."
5. In *McCulloch* the Court held that the federal government is not a mere creature of the states. It results from a union of the people.

III: FEDERAL-STATE RELATIONS, THE ROLE OF COURTS

In *McCulloch* v. *Maryland*, Chief Justice Marshall used a formula to sum up the permissible reach of federal power: "Let the end be legitimate, let it be within the scope of the constitution, and all means which are appropriate, which are plainly adapted to that end, which are not prohibited, but consist[ent] with the letter and spirit of the Constitution, are constitutional." In other words, the federal government can pass any law it pleases just as long as the law helps to implement the government's constitutional powers and is not prohibited by the Constitution. That is a recipe for expansion, and the federal government took advantage of it in subsequent years to build roads and railways, buy and sell public lands, regulate commerce and navigation, fund public works projects, punish crimes against the federal government, create new agencies, admit new territories, and prohibit business practices that it deemed harmful.

It was in just this last area, business regulation, that the federal government began to run into resistance from the courts. Let us back up a bit and explain how the cases got into the courts to begin with.

After the Civil War, American industry began to expand dramatically. New technologies helped to spawn new industrial techniques and even whole new industries. As businesses expanded, they opened up branches in many states. Soon a variety of industries, like steel making, coal, petroleum, and mining, were all interconnected by railroads. Labor unions also began to grow, though they were fiercely resisted by the heads of industries. Strikes, riots, and even shooting wars between labor and management frequently erupted. Many other social problems also appeared, from unhealthy and dangerous working conditions to price-rigging and the sale of contaminated food products. Rather timidly at first, the federal government began to take some steps toward dealing with these problems. But by the early years of the twentieth century, it was already encountering opposition in federal courts. The courts challenged the federal government's right to regulate business. They said that business should be regulated—if at all—by state governments.

The Constitution says: "Congress shall have Power . . . To regulate Commerce with foreign Nations and among the several States, and with the Indian tribes." But early in this century American courts started reading the commerce clause narrowly. Instead of talking about commerce "among the several states," a general expression that allows for expansion, they started using the term "interstate commerce," which is found nowhere in the Constitution. They then distinguished between *inter*state and *intra*state commerce, meaning by the latter the kind that goes on within state boundaries and can't be regulated by the federal government.

What did that leave for the federal government to regulate? Not much. It could regulate railroads, even *intra*state lines if their rates affected interstate commerce. But it could not regulate businesses that remained stationary, like factories and mines, unless the government could show that a business's practices "affected" interstate commerce. And in demonstrating that effect, the federal government had to show that it was "direct" rather than "indirect." It all got very complicated, and led lawyers into subtle arguments about the "flow" of commerce in and out of the states. The end result was this: the federal government was largely stymied in its efforts to regulate business. One of the best-known cases involving a restrictive interpretation of the commerce clause was decided by the Court in the midst of the Great Depression. It was *Schechter Poultry Corporation v. United States* (1935).

"The Sick Chicken Case"—Again

The *Schechter* case was discussed in Chapter 1. It was popularly known (for reasons not entirely clear) as "the sick chicken case." It involved a poultry slaughterhouse in Brooklyn, whose owner was convicted of violating federal regulations concerning wages, working hours, and trade practices. Schechter challenged the constitutionality of the regulations on two grounds. First, he said, they resulted from an unconstitutional delegation of legislative power. Second, Schechter argued, his business was not involved directly in interstate commerce—it was purely intrastate—so it was beyond the reach of the federal government. The Court agreed with Schechter on both counts.

The first issue, the delegation of legislative power, was discussed in Chapter 1. It is the second issue that interests us here. Can the federal government regulate the business and labor practices of a Brooklyn poultry slaughterhouse? The Court said no.

If Schechter were running some big beef slaughterhouse in Chicago, the Court reasoned, then his business would be involved in a "flow" of commerce that could be considered interstate. The Chicago slaughterhouses bought cattle from the West, killed them, and sold their meat to dealers in other states. The cattle flowed into Illinois, then flowed out, in a continuous "stream" of commerce. But Schechter's chickens took a one-way ride. They were trucked into Brooklyn, but their meat never left New York. It was all sold locally. Nor could it be said that the prices Schechter charged or the wages he paid affected interstate commerce in any direct way. This, then, was a case of intrastate commerce, which Congress has no authority to regulate.

It is hard to say what John Marshall would have thought of the *Schechter* decision. Quite possibly, he would not have liked it. It was based on the dichotomy of "interstate" and "intrastate" commerce, terms that Marshall never used. He interpreted the commerce clause broadly, leaving much discretion in the hands of the federal government. This, of course, is sheer speculation, for the times had changed greatly and the facts in the case were much different than those in the cases Marshall had decided. What we know for sure is that many people at the time were furious at the Court for its *Schechter* decision. Here was our nation, gripped by the worst depression in its history, with a quarter of its workers unemployed, and the Court was limiting the power of the federal government to regulate business. It was fiddling while Rome burned! The Roosevelt administration was secretly relieved that the Court had struck down the law that had been used to regulate Schechter—it wasn't working well anyway —but it was worried about the Court's apparent willingness to strike down other pieces of legislation that might be necessary to fight the depression. So President Roosevelt sought to change the direction of the Court's decisions. His plan was to "pack" the Court.

The Court Since 1937: A Change of Direction

There is nothing in the Constitution that says the Court has to have only nine members on it. The numbers are set by Congress. All right, said Roosevelt in 1937, let us increase the size of the Court to fifteen. He, of course, would appoint the other six, and that would tilt the balance on the Court in his direction. This transparent attempt to tamper with the Supreme Court alienated even Roosevelt's congressional supporters, and the plan was killed in committee without reaching the floor of Congress. But in the meantime the Court started changing its line of decisions. What happened was that Justice Owen Roberts, who often voted to strike down federal legislation in closely divided cases, began switching to the other side. That tilted the balance in favor of upholding the laws. Roberts's move has been called, probably unfairly, "the switch in time that saved nine."

The Tenth Amendment: A "Truism"?

By the end of the 1930s, the Court's new direction was made more emphatic by the death or retirement of the Court's older members and their replacement by Roosevelt appointees. Now, almost invariably, the Court upheld statutes regulating commerce and stopped making so many fine distinctions between in*ter*state and in*tra*state. In 1941, for example, in the case of *United States v. Darby*, the Court upheld the Fair Labor Standards Act of 1938. The act prohibited the shipment in interstate commerce of products made by employees who were paid below a minimum standard and had worked longer hours than a maximum limit.

Twenty-five years earlier, the Court had struck down a piece of legislation similar in spirit. It was a law banning the interstate shipment of products made by child labor. The Court invalidated the law because, it said, Congress was attempting to reach inside the state and regulate intrastate practices. Now the Court was being asked by Darby, a Georgia lumber manufacturer, to make a similar ruling. Darby argued that the obvious purpose of the Fair Labor Standards Act was not to regulate interstate commerce, which Congress had a right to do, but to regulate a business located within Georgia, which it had no right to do. That right was "reserved" to the state by the Tenth Amendment.

The Supreme Court disagreed with Darby. Its opinion, by Justice Harlan Fiske Stone, stated that Congress's motive in regulating commerce was not for the Court to question. Congress had a right to limit the shipment of goods in interstate commerce even if its real motive was to eliminate substandard labor practices. Anyway, if workers are being underpaid in one state, the practice will spread to businesses in other states. Otherwise, how can they compete with Georgia's products? But that kind of reasoning practically eliminates the distinction between interstate and intrastate commerce, since every business in one state could have effects outside that state.

What happened to the Tenth Amendment? What about the "reserved" powers of the states? Stone's answer was that the Tenth Amendment "states but a truism that all is retained which has not been surrendered." In other words, there never was much substance in the Tenth Amendment. All it says is that if the federal government doesn't have the power, then the power is retained by the states or people. The purpose of the amendment, Stone implied, was more psychological than anything else; it simply was meant to "allay fears" that the states could not exercise the powers left to them. No doubt Jefferson and Madison would be surprised by Justice Stone's rather casual dismissal of the Tenth Amendment. The Court itself in recent years seems to be taking the amendment more seriously, as we shall see presently.

For now, it is enough to see how this historical background affects the video discussion. Governor Babbitt of Arizona wishes we could bring back some of the spirit of the pre-1937 Court, when the judiciary closely scrutinized federal legislation that seemed to intrude into the states. Babbitt likes "the idea of the Supreme Court as a referee in a striped shirt at the fifty-yard line between the contending forces of federal and state government." Now, alas, "the Supreme Court has pretty much walked off the field," which means that "the federal government can win this ball game, carry the ball, dictate the rules, and do whatever it wants." Governor Matheson of Utah disagrees. "That's the last way I would like to see public policy settled." He does not want to see the Supreme Court any more involved than it already is in settling federal-state disputes. Instead of using the Court as a referee, Matheson favors "getting the players together and all recognizing we want to solve that problem."

Senator Hatch agrees with his colleague from Utah and has harsh words for the Court. "The Supreme Court has done more to take away the rights of the states than any entity of the government in existence today." In a way, Governor Babbitt and the two panelists from Utah, Matheson and Hatch, are talking about different Supreme Courts. Babbitt is praising the *Schechter* Court, which kept a watchful eye on states' rights. Matheson and Hatch are criticizing the modern Court, which, Hatch contends, has "expanded the commerce clause and the general welfare clauses of the Constitution to embrace almost everything."

But what if the Court again started invalidating federal laws for intruding into the state domain? In one case the modern Court did just that. The case was *National League of Cities* v. *Usery* (1976).

The *Usery* Case: Protecting State Power

At issue in the *Usery* case was the constitutionality of some 1974 amendments to the Fair Labor Standards Act. The original act, which was upheld by the Court in the *Darby* case, in effect compelled employers to comply with certain minimum-wage and maximum-hours requirements set by Congress. Yet the act had specifically exempted state governments from any of its requirements. They could pay their employees whatever they saw fit to pay and establish any kind of working hours they wanted. But, beginning in 1966, Congress started amending the act to make it apply to state agencies. In 1974 Congress made the application even more explicit. The amendments passed said that the term "employer" used in the act "includes a public agency," and such an "agency" included "the government of a State or a political subdivision thereof." The National League of Cities challenged the amendments, charging that they represented a federal intrusion into the affairs of the states. They won their case by a six-to-three margin in the Supreme Court.

The majority opinion, by Justice William Rehnquist, conceded that Congress had the power to regulate private business. But, he argued, these amendments were directed "not to private citizens, but to States as States." Congress was really telling state governments how to run their shops: what hours they could work their employees, what wages they had to pay them. That was really striking at the heart of state independence.

Rehnquist talked about the hardships that the new amendments would cause state governments. California, he said, would have to increase its annual budget by $8 million to $16 million to meet the new requirements. He also said the amendments would take away needed discretion in the hiring of state workers. A state might wish to employ persons with minimal training for certain routine jobs and pay them less than the minimum wage; it might want to hire teenagers in the summer and pay them less than federal standards. The 1974 amendments "would forbid such choices by the states." Their only choice would be to raise more revenue from angry taxpayers or to fire state employees.

Granted, Rehnquist said, any private employer regulated by the Fair Labor Standards Act could face a somewhat similar dilemma. But a state government is no mere private entity. It is "itself a coordinate element in the system established by the framers for governing our federal union." State autonomy is guaranteed by the Tenth Amendment.

Brennan's Dissent: For Judicial Self-Restraint

The dissent in *Usery*, by Justice William Brennan (joined by Justices Marshall and White), is full of irony, all of it completely unintended. The dissent is really a very earnest denunciation of judicial lawmaking. This Court, Brennan said, is substituting its own idea of what is desirable for that of Congress. The Court has "manufactured an abstraction without substance, founded neither in the words of the Constitution nor on precedent," and used it to invalidate a law it didn't like. The decision reflects nothing more than the Court's "displeasure with a congressional judgment."

What makes all this ironic is that precisely such criticisms have been made of many opinions Justice Brennan has delivered or joined. For example, when Brennan talks about the Court's reliance on an "abstraction," critics of the Court's decisions on school prayer (Chapter 9) and abortion (Chapter 10) could ask: What are "separation of church and state" and "right of privacy" if not abstractions? Neither is found anywhere in the Constitution, and there were scarcely any precedents for either before the 1960s. In both areas the Court has been accused of substituting its own idea of what is "desirable" for the judgment of elected lawmakers. And in both these areas Justice Brennan was allied with those who struck down legislative enactments.

This is not to single out Justice Brennan as being the only member of the Court with an apparent double standard. The same could be said of other members, including the author of the *Usery* opinion, Justice Rehnquist. Rehnquist's approach seems to be the mirror image of Brennan's. In cases like school prayer and abortion, he opposes judicial intrusion into areas he thinks should be settled by legislators. But in other cases, like this one for example, he thinks the judiciary has the duty to strike down laws. Sometimes, then, Rehnquist believes in "judicial self-restraint," meaning the reluctance to overrule legislative decisions; at other times he believes in "judicial activism," meaning very close scrutiny of laws to see whether they violate the Constitution.

The same can be said of Brennan, though he applies his standards differently. He is suspicious of any law that interferes with what he would call "personal liberty," while Rehnquist squints very hard at laws that interfere with "economic freedom." Though it is often hard to distinguish between these two categories (Is prayer simply "personal"? Is economic freedom "impersonal"?), they seem to explain the justices' shift back and forth between activism and self-restraint. Such reversals have been going on in the Court for some time. Years ago, the late Justice Felix Frankfurter observed that "it all depends on whose ox is being gored."

Points to Remember

1. In *McCulloch* v. *Maryland* and other cases, Chief Justice Marshall gave the federal government great latitude in lawmaking. But in the early twentieth century the Court narrowed the permissible scope of federal legislation by excluding the federal government from in*tra*state commerce. In the *Schechter* case of 1935, the Court invalidated a federal law that sought to regulate "intrastate" industries whose effect on interstate commerce was indirect.
2. In reaction to *Schechter* and other such rulings, President Roosevelt sought to "pack" the Court, increasing its membership from nine to fifteen. Congress rejected Roosevelt's plan, but in the meantime the Court started approving federal laws that regulated businesses.
3. In *United States* v. *Darby* (1941), the Court allowed the federal government to impose wage-and-hour standards on industries. In *Darby* the Court seemed to dismiss the Tenth Amendment as a mere "truism" that added no new meaning to the Constitution.
4. In the video discussion, Governor Babbitt of Arizona says he wishes the Court would go back to playing referee in contests between the federal government and the states. He thinks it has left the field to the federal government. However, Utah's Governor Matheson and Senator Hatch are worried about judicial intervention. They fear that an active judiciary can only broaden federal power.
5. In fact, in the *Usery* case of 1976, the Court did rule against the federal government, striking down some 1974 amendments to the Fair Labor Standards Act. The amendments would have imposed federal wage-and-hour standards on state governments. The Court said that the amendments constituted an improper interference with the independence of states. Justice Brennan and two other justices dissented, charging that the Court was not interpreting the Constitution but imposing on Congress its own views of what is "desirable."

SUMMARY

What is unusual in this video discussion is the absence of sharp exchanges. There are, of course, differences of opinion. Senator Moynihan and Albert Shanker tend to welcome grants-in-aid and do not worry much about federal standards, while others, like Senator Hatch, are wary of them. But these are differences more of emphasis than of fixed principle. Senator Hatch, in fact, voted for the Education of All Handicapped Children Act, and he readily concedes that states have in the past been derelict in fulfilling their responsibilities. Moynihan and Shanker, for their part, seem more thoughtful than combative about their positions. This session is not what Barbara Mikulski would call a "street fight." The tone is philosophical, not pugilistic.

More punches might have been thrown if this discussion were taking place not in 1983 but 1963, especially if it included some of the Southern governors of that period. At that time there were violent clashes between police and civil rights demonstrators in the Southern states, and showdowns had already occurred between Southern governors and federal authorities. Even in the North there were tensions between the states and Washington. Many legislatures were heavily weighted in favor of rural interests, and federal judges were just starting to challenge the apportionment schemes that caused the "tilt." In general, state governments still savored of an America that had disappeared years ago. Their procedures were often antiquated, their pace leisurely, their recordkeeping haphazard. Challenges to their traditional ways were often met with indignation; the challengers were called "outside agitators" and even "Communists." But since then a civil rights revolution has occurred; state legislatures have become more representative; and state governments have been modernized, so that they now attract some of the most talented people in the nation.

In the video discussion, Fred Graham sums up this history by recalling the changes that have occurred since he began his career as a journalist:

> When I got into journalism, my first stories were the civil rights revolution in the deep South and the massive resistance that was occurring across there and the violence. And what was wrong with federalism then was that a lot of our governors were not the quality of people they should have been. Certainly, our state supreme court justices were not—they'd abdicated their responsibility. A lot of our legislatures were malapportioned and they were not what they should have been. And what's happened is that, as we've seen with the governors here today, and others we know, the quality of state leadership is so much better now than it was in those days, that the situation is righting itself.

These conciliatory remarks from a journalist who has usually taken the federal government's side may be taken as signs of a new era. Among spokesmen for the federal and state governments, the mood is no longer confrontational. Both sides have lowered their guards. Twenty years ago it would not have been likely that a civil rights-conscious attorney like Floyd Abrams would have talked about the limits of rightful federal presence in the states, or about the need for local control of education.

Abrams can take such positions today because local control does not have, or at any rate does not have to have, the kind of meaning it had in the early '60s in some regions of the country. The term is no longer a smoke screen for racial segregation, unrepresentative legislatures, and do-nothing government. Instead, "local control" now has a chance of recovering some of the meaning it had for Thomas Jefferson and other patriots at the time the Constitution was adopted. For them it meant that citizens could get involved in making the political decisions that most intimately affected their lives. That is why they insisted on the "reserved" powers guarantee in the Tenth Amendment, which Jefferson called the "bedrock" of the Constitution.

Documents

MCCULLOCH V. MARYLAND, 4 Wheaton 316 (1819)

In 1816 Congress incorporated the Bank of the United States. Two years later the state of Maryland required all banks not chartered by the state to pay taxes to the state. McCulloch, cashier of the Baltimore branch of the bank, refused to pay the taxes, and Maryland sued him. He appealed to the Supreme Court, charging, among other things, that Maryland's tax on the bank was unconstitutional. Maryland countered that the bank itself was unconstitutional. In the excerpts reprinted below, Chief Justice Marshall gives the Court's reasons for sustaining the constitutionality of the bank. (Omitted is the second issue Marshall discussed in the case—whether Maryland could tax the bank.)

Opinion of the Court, Chief Justice Marshall.

The first question made in the cause is, has congress power to incorporate a bank? . . . The power now contested was exercised by the first congress elected under the present constitution. The bill for incorporating the Bank of the United States did not steal upon an unsuspecting legislature, and pass unobserved. Its principle was completely understood, and was opposed with equal zeal and ability. After being resisted, first in the fair and open field of debate, and afterwards in the executive cabinet, with as much persevering talent as any measure has ever experienced, and being supported by arguments which convinced minds as pure and as intelligent as this country can boast, it became a law. . . .

In discussing this question, the counsel for the state of Maryland have deemed it of some importance, in the construction of the constitution, to consider that instrument not as emanating from the people, but as the act of sovereign and independent states. The powers of the general government, it has been said, are delegated by the states, who alone are truly sovereign; and must be exercised in subordination to the states, who alone possess supreme dominion. It would be difficult to sustain this proposition.

The convention which framed the constitution was, indeed, elected by the state legislatures. But the instrument, when it came from their hands, was a mere proposal, without obligation, or pretensions to it. It was reported to the then existing congress of the United States, with a request that it might "be submitted to a convention of delegates, chosen in each state by the people thereof, under the recommendation of its legislature, for their assent and ratification." This mode of proceeding was adopted; and by the convention, by congress, and by the state legislatures, the instrument was submitted to the *people.* They acted upon it, in the only manner in which they can act safely, effectively, and wisely, on such a subject, by assembling in convention. . . . From these conventions, the constitution derives its whole authority. The government proceeds directly from the people; is "ordained and established" in the name of the people; and is declared to be ordained, "in order to form a more perfect union, establish justice, insure domestic tranquility, and secure the blessings of liberty to themselves and to their posterity." . . . The government of the Union, then, is emphatically and truly, a government of the people. In form, and in substance, it emanates from them. Its powers are granted by them, and are to be exercised directly on them, and for their benefit. . . .

Among the enumerated powers, we do not find that of establishing a bank or creating a corporation. But there is no phrase in the instrument which, like the articles of confederation, excludes incidental or implied powers; and which requires that everything granted shall be expressly and minutely described. Even the 10th amendment, which was framed for the purpose of quieting the excessive jealousies which had been excited, omits the word "expressly," and declares only that the powers "not delegated to the United States, nor prohibited to the states, are reserved to the states or to the people"; thus leaving the question, whether the particular power which may become the subject of contest, has been delegated to the one government, or prohibited to the other, to depend on a fair construction of the whole instrument.

The men who drew and adopted this amendment had experienced the embarrassments resulting from the insertion of this word in the articles of confederation, and probably omitted it, to avoid those embarrassments. A constitution, to contain an accurate detail of all the subdivisions of which its great powers will admit, and of all the means by which they may be carried into execution, would partake of the prolixity of a legal code, and could scarcely be embraced by the human mind. It would, probably, never be understood by the public. Its nature, therefore, requires, that only its great outlines should be marked, its important objects designated, and the minor ingredients which compose those objects, be deduced from the nature of the objects themselves. That this idea was entertained by the framers of the American constitution, is not only to be inferred from the nature of the instrument, but from the language. Why else were some of the limitations, found in the 9th section of the 1st article, introduced? It is also, in some degree, warranted, by their having omitted to use any restrictive term which might prevent its receiving a fair and just interpretation. In considering this question, then, we must never forget, that it is a *constitution* we are expounding.

Although, among the enumerated powers of government, we do not find the word "bank," or "incorporation," we find the great powers, to lay and collect taxes; to borrow money; to regulate commerce; to declare and conduct war; and to raise and support armies and navies. . . . A government, intrusted with such ample powers, on the due execution of which the happiness and prosperity of the nation so vitally depends, must also be intrusted with ample means for their execution. The power being given, it is the interest of the nation to facilitate its execution. It can never be their interest, and cannot be presumed to have been their intention, to clog and embarrass its execution, by withholding the most appropriate means. . . .

The argument on which most reliance is placed, is drawn from the peculiar language of this clause. Congress is not empowered by it to make all laws, which may have relation to the powers conferred on the government, but only such as may be "necessary and proper" for carrying them into execution. The word "necessary" is considered as controlling the whole sentence, and as limiting the right to pass laws for the execution of the granted powers, to such as are indispensable, and without which the power would be nugatory. That it excludes the choice of means, and leaves to congress, in each case, that only which is most direct and simple.

Is it true, that this is the sense in which the word "necessary" is always used? Does it always import an absolute physical necessity, so strong, that one thing, to which another may be termed necessary, cannot exist without that other? We think it does not. If reference be had to its use, in the common affairs of the world, or in approved authors, we find that it frequently imports no more than that one thing is convenient, or useful, or essential to another. . . . A thing may be necessary, very necessary, absolutely or indispensably necessary. To no mind would the same idea be conveyed by these several phrases. This comment on the word is well illustrated by the passage cited at the bar, from the 10th section of the 1st article of the constitution. It is, we think, impossible to compare the sentence which prohibits a State from laying "imposts, or duties on imports or exports, except what may be absolutely necessary for executing its inspection laws," with that which authorizes congress "to make all laws which shall be necessary and proper for carrying into execution" the powers of the general government, without feeling a conviction, that the convention understood itself to change materially the meaning of the word "necessary" by prefixing the word "absolutely." This word, then, like others, is used in various senses; and, in its construction, the subject, the context, the intention of the person using them, are all to be taken into view. . . .

We admit, as all must admit, that the powers of the government are limited, and that its limits are not to be transcended. But we think the sound construction of the constitution must allow to the national legislature that discretion, with respect to the means by which the powers it confers are to be carried into execution, which will enable that body to perform the high duties assigned to it, in the manner most beneficial to the people. Let the end be legitimate, let it be within the scope of the constitution, and all means which are appropriate, which are plainly adapted to that end, which are not prohibited, but consist[ent] with the letter and spirit of the constitution, are constitutional.

That a corporation must be considered as a means not less usual, not of higher dignity, not more requiring a particular specification than other means, has been sufficiently proved. . . . If a corporation may be employed, indiscriminately with other means, to carry into execution the powers of the government, no particular reason can be assigned for excluding the use of a bank, if required for its fiscal operations. To use one, must be within the discretion of congress, if it be an appropriate mode of executing the powers of government. That it is a convenient, a useful, and essential instrument in the prosecution of its fiscal operations, is not now a subject of controversy. . . .

After the most deliberate consideration, it is the unanimous and decided opinion of this court, that the act to incorporate the Bank of the United States is a law made in pursuance of the constitution, and is a part of the supreme law of the land.

NATIONAL LEAGUE OF CITIES V. *USERY,* 426 U.S. 833 (1976)

In National League of Cities *v.* Usery, *the Supreme Court held that the Congress's power under the commerce clause does not extend to the power to prescribe minimum wage and maximum hours standards on states and their employees. The decision was by a margin of five to four.*

Excerpts from the majority opinion, written by Justice William Rehnquist, are reprinted below.

Opinion of the Court, Mr. Justice Rehnquist.

The original Fair Labor Standards Act passed in 1938 specifically excluded the States and their political subdivisions from its coverage. In 1974, however, Congress enacted the most recent of a series of broadening amendments to the Act. By these amendments Congress has extended the minimum wage and maximum hour provisions to almost all public employees employed by the States and by their various political subdivisions. . . .

Appellants in no way challenge these decisions establishing the breadth of authority granted Congress under the commerce power. Their contention, on the contrary, is that when Congress seeks to regulate directly the activities of States as public employers, it transgresses an affirmative limitation on the exercise of its power akin to other commerce power affirmative limitations contained in the Constitution. . . .

Appellants' essential contention is that the 1974 amendments to the Act, while undoubtedly within the scope of the Commerce Clause, encounter a similar constitutional barrier because they are to be applied directly to the States and subdivisions of States as employers. . . .

This Court has never doubted that there are limits upon the power of Congress to override state sovereignty, even when exercising its otherwise plenary powers to tax or to regulate commerce which are conferred by Art. I of the Constitution.

It is one thing to recognize the authority of Congress to enact laws regulating individual businesses necessarily subject to the dual sovereignty of the government of the Nation and of the State in which they reside. It is quite another to uphold a similar exercise of congressional authority directed, not to private citizens, but to the States as States. We have repeatedly recognized that there are attributes of sovereignty attaching to every state government which may not be impaired by Congress, not because Congress may lack an affirmative grant of legislative authority to reach the matter, but because the Constitution prohibits it from exercising the authority in that manner.

One undoubted attribute of state sovereignty is the States' power to determine the wages which shall be paid to those whom they employ in order to carry our their governmental functions, what hours those persons will work, and what compensation will be provided where these employees may be called upon to work overtime. . . .

In their complaint appellants advanced estimates of substantial costs which will be imposed upon them by the 1974 amendments. Since the District Court dismissed their complaint, we take its well-pleaded allegations as true, although it appears from appellee's submissions [that] resolution of the factual disputes as to the effect of the amendments is not critical to our disposition of the case. Judged solely in terms of increased costs in dollars, these allegations show a significant impact on the functioning of the governmental bodies involved. [California, for example,] which must devote significant portions of its budget to fire suppression endeavors, estimated that application of the Act to its employment practices will necessitate an increase in its budget of between $8 million and $16 million.

Increased costs are not, of course, the only adverse effects which compliance with the Act will visit upon state and local governments, and in turn upon the citizens who depend upon those governments. [F]or example, California asserted that it could not comply with the overtime costs (approximately $750,000 per year) which the Act required to be paid to California Highway Patrol cadets during their academy training program. California reported that it had thus been forced to reduce its academy training program from 2,080 hours to only 960 hours, a compromise undoubtedly of substantial importance to those whose safety and welfare may depend upon the preparedness of the California Highway Patrol. . . .

Quite apart from the substantial costs imposed upon the States and their political subdivisions, the Act displaces state policies regarding the manner in which they will structure delivery of those governmental services which their citizens require. The Act, speaking directly to the States *qua* States, requires that they shall pay all but an extremely limited minority of their employees the minimum wage rates currently chosen by Congress. It may well be that as a matter of economic policy it would be desirable that States, just as private employers, comply with these minimum wage requirements. But it cannot be gainsaid that the federal requirement directly supplants the considered policy choices of the States' elected officials and administrators as to how they wish to structure pay scales in state employment. The State might wish to employ persons with little or no training, or those who wish to work on a casual basis, or those who for some other reason do not possess minimum employment requirements, and pay them less than the federally prescribed minimum wage. It may wish to offer part time or summer employment to teenagers at a figure less than the minimum wage, and if unable to do so may decline to offer such employment at all. But the Act would forbid such choices by the States. The only "discretion" left to them under the Act is either to attempt to increase their revenue to meet the additional financial burden imposed upon them by paying congressionally prescribed wages to their existing complement of employees, or to reduce that complement to a number which can be paid the federal minimum wage without increasing revenue.

This dilemma presented by the minimum wage restrictions may seem not immediately different from that faced by private employers, who have long been covered by the Act and who must find ways to increase their gross income if they are to pay higher wages while maintaining current earnings. The difference, however, is that a State is not merely a factor in the "shifting economic arrangements" of the private sector of the economy, but is itself a coordinate element in the system established by the framers for governing our federal union. . . .

. . . Congress has attempted to exercise its Commerce Clause authority to prescribe minimum wages and maximum hours to be paid by the States in their capacities as sovereign governments. In so doing, Congress has sought to wield its power in a fashion that would impair the States' "ability to function effectively in a federal system," *Fry*, 421 U. S., at 547 n. 7.* This exercise of congressional authority does not comport with the federal system of government embodied in the Constitution. We hold that insofar as the challenged amendments operate to directly displace the States' freedom to structure integral operations in areas of traditional governmental functions, they are not within the authority granted Congress by Art. I, § 8, cl. 3.

Justice Harry Blackmun wrote a separate, concurring opinion in the Usery *case. Justice William Brennan wrote a dissenting opinion, which was joined by Justices White and Marshall. Justice John Paul Stevens wrote a separate dissent.*

Below are excerpts from Justice Brennan's dissent.

Dissenting opinion, Mr. Justice Brennan.

The Court concedes, as of course it must, that Congress enacted the 1974 amendments pursuant to its exclusive power under Art. I, § 8, cl. 3, of the Constitution "[t]o regulate Commerce . . . among the several States." It must therefore be surprising that my Brethren should choose this bicentennial year of our independence to repudiate principles governing judicial interpretation of our Constitution settled since the time of Mr. Chief Justice John Marshall, discarding his postulate that the Constitution contemplates that restraints upon exercise by Congress of its plenary commerce power lie in the political process and not in the judicial process. For 152 years ago Mr. Chief Justice Marshall enunciated that principle to which, until today, his successors on this Court have been faithful.

"[T]his power over commerce . . . is vested in Congress as absolutely as it would be in a single government, having in its constitution the same restrictions on the exercise of the power as are found in the constitution of the United States. *The wisdom and the discretion of Congress, their identity with the people, and the influence which their constituents possess at elections, are . . . the sole restraints on which they have relied, to secure them from its abuse. They are the restraints on which the people must often rely solely, in all representative governments.*" *Gibbons* v. *Ogden*, 9 Wheat 1, 197, 6 L.Ed. 23 (1824) (emphasis added).

---

*The reference is to *Fry* v. *United States*, 421 U.S. 542 (1975), where the Court sustained *temporary* federal wage controls as applied to state employees. The ruling was narrow—it hinged in part on the emergency nature of the controls—and the majority opinion recognized the significance of the Tenth Amendment in protecting the states' "ability to function effectively in a federal system." (G. McK.)

Only 34 years ago, *Wickard v. Filburn*, 317 U.S. 111, 120 (1942), reaffirmed that "[a]t the beginning Chief Justice Marshall . . . made emphatic the embracing and penetrating nature of [Congress' commerce] power by warning that effective restraints on its exercise must proceed from political rather than from judicial processes."

My Brethren do not successfully obscure today's patent usurpation of the role reserved for the political process by their purported discovery in the Constitution of a restraint derived from sovereignty of the States on Congress' exercise of the commerce power. Chief Justice Marshall recognized that limitations "prescribed in the constitution," Gibbons v. Ogden, restrain Congress' exercise of the power. Thus laws within the commerce power may not infringe individual liberties protected by the [First, Fifth, or Sixth Amendments]. But there is no restraint based on state sovereignty requiring or permitting judicial enforcement anywhere expressed in the Constitution; our decisions over the last century and a half have explicitly rejected the existence of any such restraint on the commerce power. . . .

My Brethren thus have today manufactured an abstraction without substance, founded neither in the words of the Constitution nor on precedent. An abstraction having such profoundly pernicious consequences is not made less so by characterizing the 1974 amendments as legislation directed against the "States *qua* States." [M]y Brethren make no claim that the 1974 amendments are not regulations of "commerce" [My] Brethren are . . . repudiating the long line of our precedents holding that a judicial finding that Congress has not unreasonably regulated a subject matter of "commerce" brings to an end the judicial role. . . .

The reliance of my Brethren upon the Tenth Amendment as "an express declaration of [a state sovereignty] limitation" not only suggests that they overrule governing decisions of this Court that address this question but must astound scholars of the Constitution. For not only early decisions, Gibbons v. Ogden, McCulloch v. Maryland, and Martin v. Hunter's Lessee, hold that nothing in the Tenth Amendment constitutes a limitation on congressional exercise of powers delegated by the Constitution to Congress. Rather, as the Tenth Amendment's significance was more recently summarized: "The amendment states but a truism that all is retained which has not been surrendered. . . ." United States v. Darby. . . .

My Brethren do more than turn aside longstanding constitutional jurisprudence that emphatically rejects today's conclusion. More alarming is the startling restructuring of our federal system, and the role they create therein for the federal judiciary. This Court is simply not at liberty to erect a mirror of its own conception of a desirable governmental structure. If the 1974 amendments have any "vice," my Brother Stevens is surely right that it represents "merely [a] policy issue which has been firmly resolved by the branches of government having power to decide such questions." . . .

It is unacceptable that the judicial process should be thought superior to the political process in this area. Under the Constitution the judiciary has no role to play beyond finding that Congress has not made an unreasonable legislative judgment respecting what is "commerce." My Brother Blackmun suggests that controlling judicial supervision of the relationship between the States and our National Government by use of a balancing approach diminishes the ominous implications of today's decision. Such an approach, however, is a thinly veiled rationalization for judicial supervision of a policy judgment that our system of government reserves to Congress.

Judicial restraint in this area merely recognizes that the political branches of our Government are structured to protect the interests of the States, as well as the Nation as a whole, and that the States are fully able to protect their own interests in the premises. Congress is constituted of representatives in both Senate and House *elected from the States*. Decisions upon the extent of federal intervention under the Commerce Clause into the affairs of the States are in that sense decisions of the States themselves. Judicial redistribution of powers granted the National Government by the terms of the Constitution violates the fundamental tenet of our federalism that the extent of federal intervention into the State's affairs in the exercise of delegated powers shall be determined by the States' exercise of political power through their representatives in Congress. See Wechsler, The Political Safeguards of Federalism . . . , 54 Col.L.Rev. 543 (1954). [Any] realistic assessment of our federal political system, dominated as it is by representatives of the people *elected from the States*, yields the conclusion that it is highly unlikely that those representatives will ever be motivated to disregard totally the concerns of these States. . . .

SELECTED READINGS

Elazer, Daniel J. *American Federalism: A View from the States*. 2nd ed. New York: Crowell, 1972.
  Political scientist Elazer values federalism as an equal partnership between central and state governments. He argues that the partnership reflects important regional and sectional differences in the United States and is essential for managing the nation's growing economic complexity.
Horowitz, Irving Louis. "From the New Deal to the New Federalism: Presidential Ideology in the U.S. from 1932 to 1982." *The American Journal of Economics and Sociology* 42 (April 1983): 129-148.
  Professor Horowitz of Rutgers University takes the New Federalism of the Reagan administration as a point of departure for examining the ideological, economic, and political aspects of federalism from the Roosevelt administration to the present. He argues that the New Federalism of the '80s is essentially a demand for reduced federal controls and increased local and state controls, and that it represents a movement of middle and elite working-class groups rather than of big business.
McConnell, Grant. *Private Power and American Democracy*. New York: Random House, 1970.
  In this excellent volume, McConnell explores the theory and promise of federalism as understood by the Constitution's Framers and the founders of American polity; he then shows how the practice of federalism falls short of that theory and promise. In particular, McConnell explores the anti- or nondemocratic ironies that characterize American political thinking and ideology.

MacMahon, Arthur W., ed. *Federalism: Mature and Emergent.* Garden City, N.Y.:
Doubleday, 1955.

This lengthy volume, a classic in the field, includes twenty-six articles on the
theory and practice of federalism inside and outside the United States. Of particular importance are MacMahon's essay "The Problems of Federalism: A Survey"
and Franz Neumann's "Federalism and Freedom: A Critique."

Publius.

The most important resource for studying American federalism, from both historical and public policy perspectives, is *Publius: The Journal of Federalism.* The
following numbers, each devoted to a particular topic, are especially valuable: *The
Federal Polity*, 3 (Fall 1973); *The Suburban Reshaping of American Politics*, 5
(Winter 1975); *Republicanism, Representation, and Consent: Views of the Founding*, 9 (Spring 1979); *The Study of American Political Culture and Its Subcultures*,
10 (Spring 1980); *Covenant, Polity, and Constitutionalism*, 10 (Fall 1980).

Riker, William H. *Federalism.* Boston: Little, Brown, 1964.

An excellent short introduction to the principles and practice of federalism. Placing American federalism in both historical and comparative perspective, Riker
explains the values a federal form of government is supposed to establish and promote. He also discusses why the federal form has become so popular in this century in all regions of the world.

Storing, Herbert. *What the Anti-Federalists Were For: The Political Thought of the
Opponents of the Constitution.* Chicago: University of Chicago Press, 1981.

This slim volume introduces Herbert Storing's and Murray Dry's seven-volume collection of Anti-Federalist papers: *The Complete Anti-Federalist* (Chicago: University of Chicago Press, 1981). It is an excellent summation of the values and goals
of those who sought to retain the structure of government provided for under
the Articles of Confederation.

GLOSSARY

Block grant. A type of federal grant-in-aid for a specified field, such as education,
which allows state and local governments to use their own discretion in deciding
how to spend the money.

Commerce clause. The clause in Article I, section 8, of the Constitution which says
that Congress shall have the power "To regulate commerce with foreign nations,
and among the several States, and with the Indian tribes."

Hobson's choice. A "choice" that does not really present much of a choice. Named
after an Englishman who ran a livery service and made each customer "choose"
the horse that was nearest the door.

Judicial self-restraint. The sparing use of the judicial power to strike down statutes
passed by legislatures; the assumption that the statutes are constitutional unless it
clearly appears that they violate the letter and spirit of the Constitution. Opposite
of *judicial activism.*

Local control. The tradition in America of giving the power to pass laws regulating local affairs to units of government based in the localities.

Malapportionment. A condition in which the electoral districts that make up a legislature are grossly unequal in voting populations. This has the effect of giving voters in the sparsely populated districts more representation than those in densely populated districts. For example, districts with 5,000 voters and with 50,000 voters may both get only one representative. In the 1960s the Supreme Court held that such malapportionment violates the principle of "one person, one vote."

Necessary and proper clause. The clause at the end of Article I, section 8, that gives Congress the power "To make all laws which shall be necessary and proper for carrying into the execution the foregoing powers. . . ." Also called the *elastic clause* because it stretches the power of the federal government, and the *implied powers clause* because it gives the federal government powers that are not explicitly granted by the Constitution.

Reserved powers. The powers set aside for the states or the people in the Tenth Amendment. The amendment says that all powers not delegated to the federal government nor denied to the states are "reserved" to the states or the people.

Appendix:
The Constitution
of the United States

The Constitution of the United States of America

WE THE PEOPLE of the United States, in Order to form a more perfect Union, establish Justice, insure domestic Tranquility, provide for the common defense, promote the general Welfare, and secure the Blessings of Liberty to ourselves and our Posterity, do ordain and establish this CONSTITUTION for the United States of America.

Article I.

SECTION 1. All legislative Powers herein granted shall be vested in a Congress of the United States, which shall consist of a Senate and House of Representatives.

SECTION 2. The House of Representatives shall be composed of Members chosen every second Year by the People of the several States, and the Electors in each State shall have the Qualifications requisite for Electors of the most numerous Branch of the State Legislature.

No Person shall be a Representative who shall not have attained to the Age of twenty-five Years, and been seven Years a Citizen of the United States, and who shall not, when elected, be an Inhabitant of that State in which he shall be chosen.

[Representatives and direct Taxes shall be apportioned among the several States which may be included within this Union, according to their respective Numbers, which shall be determined by adding to the whole Number of free Persons, including those bound to Service for a Term of Years, and excluding Indians not taxed, three fifths of all other Persons.] The actual Enumeration shall be made within three Years after the first Meeting of the Congress of the United States, and within every subsequent Term of ten Years, in such Manner as they shall by Law direct. The Number of Representatives shall not exceed one for every thirty Thousand, but each State shall have at Least one Representative; and until such enumeration shall be made, the State of New Hampshire shall be entitled to chuse three, Massachusetts eight, Rhode-Island and Providence Plantations one, Connecticut five, New-York six, New Jersey four, Pennsylvania eight, Delaware one, Maryland six, Virginia ten, North Carolina five, South Carolina five, and Georgia three.

When vacancies happen in the Representation from any State, the Executive Authority thereof shall issue Writs of Election to fill such Vacancies.

The House of Representatives shall chuse their Speaker and other Officers; and shall have the sole Power of Impeachment.

SECTION 3. The Senate of the United States shall be composed of two Senators from each State, chosen by the Legislature thereof, for six Years; and each Senator shall have one Vote.

Immediately after they shall be assembled in Consequence of the first Election, they shall be divided as equally as may be into three Classes. The Seats of the Senators of the first Class shall be vacated at the Expiration of the second Year, of the second Class at the Expiration of the fourth Year, and of the third Class at the Expiration of the sixth Year, so that one-third may be chosen every second Year; and if Vacancies happen by Resignation, or otherwise, during the Recess of the Legislature of any State, the Executive thereof may make temporary Appointments until the next Meeting of the Legislature, which shall then fill such Vacancies.

No Person shall be a Senator who shall not have attained to the Age of thirty Years, and been nine Years a Citizen of the United States, and who shall not, when elected, be an Inhabitant of that State for which he shall be chosen.

The Vice President of the United States shall be President of the Senate, but shall have no Vote, unless they be equally divided.

The Senate shall chuse their other Officers, and also a President pro tempore, in the absense of the Vice President, or when he shall exercise the Office of President of the United States.

The Senate shall have the sole Power to try all Impeachments. When sitting for that Purpose, they shall be on Oath or Affirmation. When the President of the United States is tried, the Chief Justice shall preside: And no Person shall be convicted without the Concurrence of two thirds of the Members present.

Judgment in Cases of Impeachment shall not extend further than to removal from Office, and disqualification to hold and enjoy any Office of honor, Trust or Profit under the United States: but the Party convicted shall nevertheless be liable and subject to Indictment, Trial, Judgment and Punishment, according to Law.

SECTION 4. The Times, Places and Manner of holding Elections for Senators and Representatives, shall be prescribed in each State by the Legislature thereof; but the Congress may at any time by Law make or alter such Regulations, except as to the Place of Chusing Senators.

The Congress shall assemble at least once in every Year, and such Meeting shall be on the first Monday in December, unless they shall by Law appoint a different Day.

SECTION 5. Each House shall be the Judge of the Elections, Returns and Qualifications of its own Members, and a Majority of each shall constitute a Quorum to do Business; but a smaller number may adjourn from day to day, and may be authorized to compel the Attendance of absent Members, in such Manner, and under such Penalties as each House may provide.

Each House may determine the Rules of its Proceedings, punish its Members for disorderly Behavior, and, with the Concurrence of two thirds, expel a Member.

Each House shall keep a Journal of its Proceedings, and from time to time publish the same, excepting such Parts as may in their Judgment require Secrecy; and the Yeas and Nays of the Members of either House on any question shall, at the Desire of one fifth of those Present, be entered on the Journal.

Neither House, during the Session of Congress, shall, without the Consent of the other, adjourn for more than three days, nor to any other Place than that in which the two Houses shall be sitting.

SECTION 6. The Senators and Representatives shall receive a Compensation for their Services, to be ascertained by Law, and paid out of the Treasury of the United States. They shall in all Cases, except Treason, Felony and Breach of the Peace, be privileged from Arrest during their Attendance at the Session of their respective Houses, and in going to and returning from the same; and for any Speech or Debate in either House, they shall not be questioned in any other Place.

No Senator or Representative shall, during the Time for which he was elected, be appointed to any civil Office under the Authority of the United States, which shall have been created, or the Emoluments whereof shall have been encreased during such time; and no Person holding any Office under the United States, shall be a Member of either House during his Continuance in Office.

SECTION 7. All Bills for raising Revenue shall originate in the House of Representatives; but the Senate may propose or concur with Amendments as on other Bills.

Every Bill which shall have passed the House of Representatives and the Senate, shall, before it become a Law, be presented to the President of the United States; If he approve he shall sign it, but if not he shall return it, with his Objections to that House in which it shall have originated, who shall enter the Objections at large on their Journal, and proceed to reconsider it. If after such Reconsideration two thirds of that House shall agree to pass the Bill, it shall be sent, together with the Objections, to the other House, by which it shall likewise be reconsidered, and if approved by two thirds of that House, it shall become a Law. But in all such Cases the Votes of both Houses shall be determined by Yeas and Nays, and the Names of the Persons voting for and against the Bill shall be entered on the Journal of each House respectively. If any Bill shall not be returned by the President within ten Days (Sundays excepted) after it shall have been presented to him, the Same shall be a Law, in like Manner as if he had signed it, unless the Congress by their Adjournment prevent its Return, in which Case it shall not be a Law.

Every Order, Resolution, or Vote to which the Concurrence of the Senate and House of Representatives may be necessary (except on a question of Adjournment) shall be presented to the President of the United States; and before the Same shall take Effect, shall be approved by him, or being disapproved by him, shall be repassed by two thirds of the Senate and House of Representatives, according to the Rules and Limitations prescribed in the Case of a Bill.

SECTION 8. The Congress shall have Power To lay and collect Taxes, Duties, Imposts and Excises, to pay the Debt and provide for the common Defense and general Welfare of the United States; but all Duties, Imposts and Excises shall be uniform throughout the United States;

To borrow money on the credit of the United States;

To regulate Commerce with foreign Nations, and among the several States, and with the Indian Tribes;

To establish an uniform Rule of Naturalization, and uniform Laws on the subject of Bankruptcies throughout the United States;

To coin Money, regulate the Value thereof, and of foreign Coin, and fix the Standard of Weights and Measures;

To provide for the Punishment of counterfeiting the Securities and current Coin of the United States;

To establish Post Offices and post Roads;

To promote the Progress of Science and useful Arts, by securing for limited Times to Authors and Inventors the exclusive Right to their respective Writings and Discoveries;

To constitute Tribunals inferior to the supreme Court;

To define and punish Piracies and Felonies committed on the high Seas, and Offenses against the Law of Nations;

To declare War, grant Letters of Marque and Reprisal, and make Rules concerning Captures on Land and Water;

To raise and support Armies, but no Appropriation of Money to that Use shall be for a longer Term than two Years;

To provide and maintain a Navy;

To make Rules for the Government and Regulation of the land and naval Forces;

To provide for calling forth the Militia to execute the Laws of the Union, suppress Insurrections and repel Invasions;

To provide for organizing, arming, and disciplining the Militia, and for governing such Part of them as may be employed in the Service of the United States, reserving to the States respectively, the Appointment of the Officers, and the Authority of training the Militia according to the discipline prescribed by Congress;

To exercise exclusive Legislation in all Cases whatsoever, over such District (not exceeding ten Miles square) as may, by Cession of particular States, and the acceptance of Congress, become the Seat of the Government of the United States, and to exercise like Authority over all Places purchased by the Consent of the Legislature of the State in which the Same shall be, for the Erection of Forts, Magazines, Arsenals, dock-Yards, and other needful Building;—And

To make all Laws which shall be necessary and proper for carrying into Execution the foregoing Powers, and all other Powers vested by this Constitution in the Government of the United States, or in any Department or Officer thereof.

SECTION 9. The Migration or Importation of such Persons as any of the States now existing shall think proper to admit, shall not be prohibited by the Congress prior to the Year one thousand eight hundred and eight, but a tax or duty may be imposed on such Importation, not exceeding ten dollars for each Person.

The privilege of the Writ of Habeas Corpus shall not be suspended, unless when in Cases of Rebellion or Invasion the public Safety may require it.

No Bill of Attainder or ex post facto Law shall be passed.

No capitation, or other direct, Tax shall be laid, unless in Proportion to the Census or Enumeration herein before directed to be taken.

No Tax or Duty shall be laid on Articles exported from any State.

No Preference shall be given by any Regulation of Commerce or Revenue to the Ports of one State over those of another: nor shall Vessels bound to, or from, one State, be obliged to enter, clear, or pay Duties in another.

No Money shall be drawn from the Treasury, but in Consequence of Appropriations made by Law; and a regular Statement and Account of the Receipts and Expenditures of all public Money shall be published from time to time.

No Title of Nobility shall be granted by the United States: And no Person holding any Office of Profit or Trust under them, shall, without the Consent of the Congress, accept of any present, Emolument, Office, or Title, of any kind whatever, from any King, Prince, or foreign State.

Section 10. No State shall enter into any Treaty, Alliance, or Confederation; grant Letters of Marque and Reprisal; coin Money; emit Bills of Credit; make any Thing but gold and silver Coin a Tender in Payment of Debts; pass any Bill of Attainder, ex post facto Law, or Law impairing the Obligation of Contracts, or grant any Title of Nobility.

No State shall, without the Consent of the Congress, lay any Imposts or Duties on Imports or Exports, except what may be absolutely necessary for executing it's inspection Laws: and the net Produce of all Duties and Imposts, laid by any State on Imports or Exports, shall be for the Use of the Treasury of the United States; and all such Laws shall be subject to the Revision and Controul of the Congress.

No State shall, without the Consent of Congress, lay any duty of Tonnage, keep Troops, or Ships of War in time of Peace, enter into any Agreement or Compact with another State, or with a foreign Power, or engage in War, unless actually invaded, or in such imminent Danger as will not admit of delay.

Article II.

Section 1. The executive Power shall be vested in a President of the United States of America. He shall hold his Office during the Term of four Years, and, together with the Vice-President, chosen for the same Term, be elected, as follows.

Each State shall appoint, in such Manner as the Legislature thereof may direct, a Number of Electors, equal to the whole Number of Senators and Representatives to which the State may be entitled in the Congress: but no Senator or Representative, or Person holding an Office of Trust or Profit under the United States, shall be appointed an Elector.

[The Electors shall meet in their respective States, and vote by Ballot for two persons, of whom one at least shall not be an Inhabitant of the same State with themselves. And they shall make a List of all the Persons voted for, and of the Number of Votes for each; which List they shall sign and certify, and transmit sealed to the Seat of the Government of the United States, directed to the President of the Senate. The President of the Senate shall, in the Presence of the Senate and House of Representatives, open all the Certificates, and the Votes shall then be counted. The Person having the greatest Number of Votes shall be the President, if such Number be a Majority of the whole Number of Electors appointed; and if there be more than one who have such Majority, and have an equal Number of Votes, then the House of Representatives shall immediately chuse by Ballot one of them for President; and if no Person have a Majority, then from the five highest on the List the said House shall in like Manner chuse the President. But in chusing the President, the Votes shall be taken by States, the Representation from each State having one Vote; A quorum for this Purpose shall consist of a Member or Members from two-thirds of the States, and a Majority of all the States shall be necessary to a Choice. In every Case, after the Choice of the President, the Person having the greatest Number of Votes of the Electors shall be the Vice President. But if there should remain two or more who have equal Votes, the Senate shall chuse from them by Ballot the Vice-President.]

The Congress may determine the Time of chusing the Electors, and the Day on which they shall give their Votes; which Day shall be the same throughout the United States.

No person except a natural born Citizen, or a Citizen of the United States, at the time of the Adoption of this Constitution, shall be eligible to the Office of President; neither shall any Person be eligible to that Office who shall not have attained to the Age of thirty-five Years, and been fourteen Years a Resident within the United States.

In Case of the Removal of the President from Office, or of his Death, Resignation, or Inability to discharge the Powers and Duties of the said Office, the same shall devolve on the Vice President, and the Congress may by Law provide for the Case of Removal, Death, Resignation or Inability, both of the President and Vice President, declaring what Officer shall then act as President, and such Officer shall act accordingly, until the Disability be removed, or a President shall be elected.

The President shall, at stated Times, receive for his Services, a Compensation, which shall neither be encreased nor diminished during the Period for which he shall have been elected, and he shall not receive within that Period any other Emolument from the United States, or any of them.

Before he enter on the Execution of his Office, he shall take the following Oath or Affirmation:—"I do solemnly swear (or affirm) that I will faithfully execute the Office of President of the United States, and will to the best of my Ability, preserve, protect and defend the Constitution of the United States."

SECTION 2. The President shall be Commander in Chief of the Army and Navy of the United States, and of the Militia of the several States, when called into the actual Service of the United States; he may require the Opinion in writing, of the principal Officer in each of the executive Departments, upon any subject relating to the Duties of their respective Offices, and he shall have Power to Grant Reprives and Pardons for Offenses against the United States, except in Cases of Impeachment.

He shall have Power, by and with the Advice and Consent of the Senate, to make Treaties, provided two-thirds of the Senators present concur; and he shall nominate, and by and with the Advice and Consent of the Senate, shall appoint Ambassadors, other public Ministers and Consuls, Judges of the supreme Court, and all other Officers of the United States, whose Appointments are not herein otherwise provided for, and which shall be established by Law: but the Congress may by Law vest the Appointment of such inferior Officers, as they think proper, in the President alone, in the Courts of Law, or in the Heads of Departments.

The President shall have Power to fill up all Vacancies that may happen during the Recess of the Senate, by granting Commissions which shall expire at the End of their next Session.

SECTION 3. He shall from time to time give to the Congress Information of the State of the Union, and recommend to their Consideration such Measures as he shall judge necessary and expedient; he may, on extraordinary Occasions, convene both Houses, or either of them, and in Case of Disagreement between them, with Respect to the Time of Adjournment, he may adjourn them to such Time as he shall think proper; he shall receive Ambassadors and other public

Ministers he shall take Care that the Laws be faithfully executed, and shall Commission all the Officers of the United States.

SECTION 4. The President, Vice President and all civil Officers of the United States, shall be removed from Office on Impeachment for, and Conviction of, Treason, Bribery, or other high Crimes and Misdemeanors.

Article III.

SECTION 1. The judicial Power of the United States, shall be vested in one supreme Court, and in such inferior Courts as the Congress may from time to time ordain and establish. The Judges, both of the supreme and inferior Courts, shall hold their Offices during good Behaviour, and shall, at stated Times, receive for their Services a Compensation which shall not be diminished during their Continuance in Office.

SECTION 2. The judicial Power shall extend to all Cases, in Law and Equity, arising under this Constitution, the Laws of the United States, and Treaties made, or which shall be made, under their Authority;—to all Cases affecting Ambassadors, other public Ministers and Consuls;—to all Cases of admiralty and maritime Jurisdiction;—to Controversies to which the United States shall be a Party;—to Controversies between two or more States;—between a State and Citizens of another State;—between Citizens of different States;—between Citizens of the same State claiming Lands under Grants of different States, and between a State, or the Citizens thereof, and foreign States, Citizens or Subjects.

In all Cases affecting Ambassadors, other public Ministers and Consuls, and those in which a State shall be Party, the supreme Court shall have original Jurisdiction. In all the other Cases before mentioned, the supreme Court shall have appellate Jurisdiction, both as to Law and Fact, with such Exceptions, and under such Regulations as the Congress shall make.

The trial of all Crimes, except in Cases of Impeachment, shall be by Jury; and such Trial shall be held in the State where the said Crimes shall have been committed; but when not committed within any State, the Trial shall be at such Place and Places as the Congress may by Law have directed.

SECTION 3. Treason against the United States, shall consist only in levying War against them, or in adhering to their Enemies, giving them Aid and Comfort. No Person shall be convicted of Treason unless on the Testimony of two Witnesses to the same overt Act, or on Confession in open Court.

The Congress shall have power to declare the Punishment of Treason, but no Attainder of Treason shall work Corruption of Blood, or Forfeiture except during the Life of the Person attained.

Article IV.

SECTION 1. Full Faith and Credit shall be given in each State to the public Acts, Records, and judicial Proceedings of every other State. And the Congress may by general Laws prescribe the Manner in which such Acts, Records and Proceedings shall be proved, and the Effect thereof.

SECTION 2. The Citizens of each State shall be entitled to all Privileges and Immunities of Citizens in the several States.

A Person charged in any State with Treason, Felony, or other Crime, who shall flee from Justice, and be found in another State, shall on demand of the executive Authority of the State from which he fled, be delivered up, to be removed to the State having Jurisdiction of the Crime.

No Person held to Service or Labour in one State, under the Laws thereof, escaping into another, shall, in Consequence of any Law or Regulation therein, be discharged from such Service or Labour, but shall be delivered up on Claim of the Party to whom such Service or Labour may be due.

SECTION 3. New States may be admitted by the Congress into this Union; but no new State shall be formed or erected within the Jurisdiction of any other State; nor any State be formed by the Junction of two or more States, or parts of States, without the Consent of the Legislatures of the States concerned as well as of the Congress.

The Congress shall have Power to dispose of and make all needful Rules and Regulations respecting the Territory or other Property belonging to the United States; and nothing in this Constitution shall be so construed as to Prejudice any Claims of the United States, or of any particular State.

SECTION 4. The United States shall guarantee to every State in this Union a Republican Form of Government, and shall protect each of them against Invasion; and on Application of the Legislature, or of the Executive (when the Legislature cannot be convened) against domestic Violence.

Article V.

The Congress, whenever two-thirds of both Houses shall deem it necessary, shall propose Amendments to this Constitution, or, on the Application of the Legislatures of two-thirds of the several States, shall call a Convention for proposing Amendments, which, in either Case, shall be valid to all Intents and Purposes, as part of this Constitution, when ratified by the Legislatures of three-fourths of the several States, or by Conventions in three-fourths thereof, as the one or the other Mode of Ratification may be proposed by the Congress; Provided that no Amendment which may be made prior to the Year One thousand eight hundred and eight shall in any Manner affect the first and fourth Clauses in the Ninth Section of the first Article; and that no State, without its Consent, shall be deprived of its equal Suffrage in the Senate.

Article VI.

All Debts contracted and Engagements entered into, before the Adoption of this Constitution, shall be as valid against the United States under this Constitution, as under the Confederation.

This Constitution, and the Laws of the United States which shall be made in Persuance thereof; and all Treaties made, or which shall be made, under the Authority of the United States, shall be the supreme Law of the Land; and the Judges in every State shall be bound thereby, any Thing in the Constitution or Laws of any State to the Contrary notwithstanding.

The Senators and Representatives before mentioned, and the Members of the several State Legislatures, and all executive and judicial Officers, both of the United States and of the several States, shall be bound by Oath or Affirmation, to support this Constitution; but no religious Test shall ever be required as a Qualification to any Office or public Trust under the United States.

Article VII.

The Ratification of the Conventions of nine States shall be sufficient for the Establishment of this Constitution between the States so ratifying the Same.

DONE in Convention by the Unanimous Consent of the States present the Seventeenth Day of September in the Year of our Lord one thousand seven hundred and Eighty seven and of the Independence of the United States of America the Twelth. In Witness whereof We have hereunto subscribed our Names.

G° WASHINGTON
Presidt and deputy from Virginia

New Hampshire.

JOHN LANGDAN
NICHOLAS GILMAN

Massachusetts.

NATHANIEL GORHAM
RUFUS KING

Connecticut.

WM SAML JOHNSON
ROGER SHERMAN

New York.

ALEXANDER HAMILTON

New Jersey.

WIL: LIVINGSTON
DAVID BREARLEY.
WM PATTERSON
JONA: DAYTON

Pennsylvania.

B. FRANKLIN
ROBT. MORRIS
THOS. FITZSIMONS
JAMES WILSON
THOMAS MIFFLIN
GEO. CLYMER
JARED INGERSOLL
GOUV MORRIS

Delaware.

GEO: READ
JOHN DICKINSON
JACO: BROOM
GUNNING BEDFORD jun
RICHARD BASSETT

Maryland.

JAMES McHENRY
DANL CARROLL
DAN: of ST THOS JENIFER

Virginia.

JOHN BLAIR—
JAMES MADISON Jr.

North Carolina.

WM BLOUNT
HU WILLIAMSON
RICHD DOBBS SPAIGHT,

South Carolina.

J. RUTLEDGE
CHARLES PINCKNEY
CHARLES COTESWORTH PINCKNEY
PIERCE BUTLER

Georgia.

WILLIAM FEW
ABR BALDWIN
Attest:

WILLIAM JACKSON, *Secretary.*

Articles in Addition To, and Amendment Of, the Constitution of the United States of America, Proposed by Congress, and Ratified by the Legislatures of the Several States, Pursuant to the Fifth Article of the Original Constitution.

Article I.

Congress shall make no law respecting an establishment of religion, or prohibiting the free exercise thereof; or abridging the freedom of speech, or of the press; or the right of the people peaceably to assemble, and to petition the Government for a redress of grievances.

Article II.

A well regulated Militia, being necessary to the security of a free State, the right of the people to keep and bear Arms, shall not be infringed.

Article III.

No Soldier shall, in time of peace be quartered in any house, without the consent of the Owner, nor in time of war, but in a manner to be prescribed by law.

Article IV.

The right of the people to be secure in their persons, houses, papers, and effects, against unreasonable searches and seizures, shall not be violated, and no Warrants shall issue, but upon probable cause, supported by Oath or affirmation, and particularly describing the place to be searched, and the persons or things to be seized.

Article V.

No person shall be held to answer for a capital, or otherwise infamous crime, unless on a presentment or indictment of a Grand Jury, except in cases arising in the land or naval forces, or in the Militia, when in actual service in time of War or public danger; nor shall any person be subject for the same offence to be twice put in jeopardy of life or limb; nor shall be compelled in any criminal case to be a witness against himself, nor be deprived of life, liberty, or property, without due process of law; nor shall private property be taken for public use, without just compensation.

Article VI.

In all criminal prosecutions, the accused shall enjoy the right to a speedy and public trial, by an impartial jury of the State and district wherein the crime shall have been committed, which district shall have been previously ascertained by law, and to be informed of the nature and cause of the accusation; to be confronted with the witnesses against him; to have compulsory process for obtaining witnesses in his favor, and to have the Assistance of Counsel for his defence.

Article VII.

In suits at common law, where the value in controversy shall exceed twenty dollars, the right of trial by jury shall be preserved, and no fact tried by a jury, shall be otherwise reexamined in any Court of the United States, than according to the rules of the common law.

Article VIII.

Excessive bail shall not be required, nor excessive fines imposed, nor cruel and unusual punishments inflicted.

Article IX.

The enumeration in the Constitution, of certain rights, shall not be construed to deny or disparage others retained by the people.

Article X.

The powers not delegated to the United States by the Constitution, nor prohibited by it to the States, are reserved to the States respectively, or to the people.

Article XI.

The Judicial power of the United States shall not be construed to extend to any suit in law or equity, commenced or prosecuted against one of the United States by Citizens of another State, or by Citizens or Subjects of any Foreign State.

Article XII.

The Electors shall meet in their respective states and vote by ballot for President and Vice-President, one of whom, at least, shall not be an inhabitant of the same state with themselves; they shall name in their ballots the person voted for as President, and in distinct ballots the person voted for as Vice-President, and they shall make distinct lists of all persons voted for as President, and of all persons voted for as Vice-President, and of the number of votes for each, which lists they shall sign and certify, and transmit sealed to the seat of the government of the United States, directed to the President of the Senate;—The President of the Senate shall, in presence of the Senate and House of Representatives, open all the certificates and the votes shall then be counted;—The person having the greatest number of votes for President, shall be the President, if such number be a majority of the whole number of Electors appointed; and if no person have such majority, then from the persons having the highest numbers not exceeding three on the list of those voted for as President, the House of Representatives shall choose immediately, by ballot, the President. But in choosing the President, the votes shall be taken by states, the representation from each state having one vote; a quorum for this purpose shall consist of a member or members from two-thirds of the states, and a majority of all the states shall be necessary to a choice. And if the House of Representatives shall not choose a President whenever the right of choice shall devolve upon them, before the fourth day of March next following, then the Vice-President shall act as President, as in the case of the death or other constitutional disability of the President.—The person having the greatest number of votes as Vice-President, shall be the Vice-President, if such number be a majority of the whole number of Electors appointed, and if no person have a majority, then from the two highest numbers on the list, the Senate shall choose the Vice-President; a quorum for the purpose shall consist of two-thirds of the whole number of Senators, and a majority of the whole number shall be necessary to a choice. But no person constitutionally ineligible to the office of President shall be eligible to that of Vice-President of the United States.

Article XIII.

Section 1. Neither slavery nor involuntary servitude, except as a punishment for crime whereof the party shall have been duly convicted, shall exist within the United States, or any place subject to their jurisdiction.

Section 2. Congress shall have power to enforce this article by appropriate legislation.

Article XIV.

Section 1. All persons born or naturalized in the United States, and subject to the jurisdiction thereof, are citizens of the United States and of the State wherein they reside. No State shall make or enforce any law which shall abridge the privileges or immunities of citizens of the United States; nor shall any State deprive any person of life, liberty, or property, without due process of law; nor deny to any person within its jurisdiction the equal protection of the laws.

Section 2. Representatives shall be apportioned among the several States according to their respective numbers, counting the whole number of persons in each State, excluding Indians not taxed. But when the right to vote at any election for the choice of electors for President and Vice-President of the United States, Representatives in Congress, the Executive and Judicial officers of a State, or the members of the Legislature thereof, is denied to any of the male inhabitants of such State, being twenty-one years of age, and citizens of the United States, or in any way abridged, except for participation in rebellion, or other crime, the basis of representation therein shall be reduced in the proportion which the number of such male citizens shall bear to the whole number of male citizens twenty-one years of age in such State.

Section 3. No person shall be a Senator or Representative in Congress, or elector of President and Vice-President, or hold any office, civil or military, under the United States, or under any State, who, having previously taken an oath, as a member of Congress, or as an officer of the United States, or as a member of any State legislature, or as an executive or judicial officer of any State, to support the Constitution of the United States, shall have engaged in insurrection or rebellion against the same, or given aid or comfort to the enemies thereof. But Congress may by a vote of two-thirds of each House, remove such disability.

Section 4. The validity of the public debt of the United States, authorized by law, including debts incurred for payment of pensions and bounties for services in suppressing insurrection or rebellion, shall not be questioned. But neither the United States nor any State shall assume or pay any debt or obligation incurred in aid of insurrection or rebellion against the United States, or any claim for the loss or emancipation of any slave; but all such debts, obligations and claims shall be held illegal and void.

SECTION 5. The Congress shall have power to enforce, by appropriate legislation, the provisions of this article.

Article XV.

SECTION 1. The right of citizens of the United States to vote shall not be denied or abridged by the United States or by any State on account of race, color, or previous condition of servitude—

SECTION 2. The Congress shall have power to enforce this article by appropriate legislation.

Article XVI.

The Congress shall have power to lay and collect taxes on incomes, from whatever source derived, without apportionment among the several States, and without regard to any census or enumeration.

Article XVII.

The Senate of the United States shall be composed of two Senators from each State, elected by the people thereof, for six years; and each Senator shall have one vote. The electors in each State shall have the qualifications requisite for electors of the most numerous branch of the State legislatures.

When vacancies happen in the representation of any State in the Senate, the executive authority of such State shall issue writs of election to fill such vacancies: *Provided,* That the legislature of any State may empower the executive thereof to make temporary appointments until the people fill the vacancies by election as the legislature may direct.

This amendment shall not be so construed as to affect the election or term of any Senator chosen before it becomes valid as part of the Constitution.

Article XVIII.

SECTION 1. After one year from the ratification of this article the manufacture, sale, or transportation of intoxicating liquors within, the importation thereof into, or the exportation thereof from the United States and all territory subject to the jurisdiction thereof for beverage purposes is hereby prohibited.

SECTION 2. The Congress and the several States shall have concurrent power to enforce this article by appropriate legislation.

SECTION 3. This article shall be inoperative unless it shall have been ratified as an amendment to the Constitution by the legislature of the several States, as provided in the Constitution, within seven years from the date of the submission hereof to the States by the Congress.

Article XIX.

The right of citizens of the United States to vote shall not be denied or abridged by the United States or by any State on account of sex.

Congress shall have power to enforce this article by appropriate legislation.

Article XX.

SECTION 1. The terms of the President and Vice President shall end at noon on the 20th day of January, and the terms of Senators and Representatives at noon on the 3d day of January, of the years in which such terms would have ended if this article had not been ratified; and the terms of their successors shall then begin.

SECTION 2. The Congress shall assemble at least once in every year, and such meeting shall begin at noon on the 3d day of January, unless they shall by law appoint a different day.

SECTION 3. If, at the time fixed for the beginning of the term of the President, the President elect shall have died, the Vice President elect shall become President. If a President shall not have been chosen before the time fixed for the beginning of his term, or if the President elect shall have failed to qualify, then the Vice President elect shall act as President until a President shall have qualified; and the Congress may by law provide for the case wherein neither a President elect nor a Vice President elect shall have qualified, declaring who shall then act as President, or the manner in which one who is to act shall be selected, and such person shall act accordingly until a President or Vice President shall have qualified.

SECTION 4. The Congress may by law provide for the case of the death of any of the persons from whom the House of Representatives may choose a President whenever the right of choice shall have devolved upon them, and for the case of the death of any of the persons from whom the Senate may choose a Vice President whenever the right of choice shall have devolved upon them.

SECTION 5. Sections 1 and 2 shall take effect on the 15th day of October following the ratification of this article.

SECTION 6. This article shall be inoperative unless it shall have been ratified as an amendment to the Constitution by the legislatures of three-fourths of the several States within seven years from the date of its submission.

Article XXI.

SECTION 1. The eighteenth article of amendment to the Constitution of the United States is hereby repealed.

SECTION 2. The transportation or importation into any State, Territory, or possession of the United States for delivery or use therein of intoxicating liquors, in violation of the laws thereof, is hereby prohibited.

SECTION 3. This article shall be inoperative unless it shall have been ratified as an amendment to the Constitution by conventions in the several States, as provided in the Constitution, within seven years from the date of the submission hereof to the States by the Congress.

Article XXII.

SECTION 1. No person shall be elected to the office of the President more than twice, and no person who has held the office of President, or acted as President, for more than two years of a term to which some other person was elected President shall be elected to the office of the President more than once. But this Article shall not apply to any person holding the office of President when this Article was proposed by the Congress, and shall not prevent any person who may be holding the office of President, or acting as President, during the term within which this Article becomes operative from holding the office of President or acting as President during the remainder of such term.

SECTION 2. This article shall be inoperative unless it shall have been ratified as an amendment to the Constitution by the legislatures of three-fourths of the several States within seven years from the date of its submission to the States by the Congress.

Article XXIII.

SECTION 1. The District constituting the seat of Government of the United States shall appoint in such manner as the Congress may direct:

A number of electors of President and Vice President equal to the whole number of Senators and Representatives in Congress to which the District would be entitled if it were a State, but in no event more than the least populous State; they shall be in addition to those appointed by the States, but they shall be considered, for the purposes of the election of President and Vice President, to be electors appointed by a State; and they shall meet in the District and perform such duties as provided by the twelfth article of amendment.

SECTION 2. The Congress shall have power to enforce this article by appropriate legislation.

Article XXIV.

SECTION 1. The right of citizens of the United States to vote in any primary or other election for President or Vice President, for electors for President or Vice President, or for Senator or Representative in Congress, shall not be denied or abridged by the United States or any State by reason of failure to pay any poll tax or other tax.

SECTION 2. The Congress shall have power to enforce this article by appropriate legislation.

Article XXV.

SECTION 1. In case of the removal of the President from office or of his death or resignation, the Vice President shall become President.

SECTION 2. Whenever there is a vacancy in the office of the Vice President, the President shall nominate a Vice President who shall take office upon confirmation by a majority vote of both Houses of Congress.

SECTION 3. Whenever the President transmits to the President pro tempore of the Senate and the Speaker of the House of Representatives his written declaration that he is unable to discharge the powers and duties of his office, and until he transmits to them a written declaration to the contrary, such powers and duties shall be discharged by the Vice President as Acting President.

SECTION 4. Whenever the Vice President and a majority of either the principal officers of the executive departments or of such other body as Congress may by law provide, transmit to the President pro tempore of the Senate and the Speaker of the House of Representatives their written declaration that the President is unable to discharge the power and duties of his office, the Vice President shall immediately assume the powers and duties of the office as Acting President.

Thereafter, when the President transmits to the President pro tempore of the Senate and the Speaker of the House of Representatives his written declaration that no inability exists, he shall resume the powers and duties of his office unless the Vice President and a majority of either the principal officers of the executive department or of such other body as Congress may by law provide, transmit within four days to the President pro tempore of the Senate and the Speaker of the House of Representatives their written declaration that the President is unable to discharge the powers and duties of his office. Thereupon Congress shall decide the issue, assembling within forty-eight hours for that purpose if not in session. If the Congress, within twenty-one days after receipt of the latter written declaration, or, if Congress is not in session, within twenty-one days after Congress is required to assemble, determines by two-thirds vote of both Houses that the President is unable to discharge the powers and duties of his office, the Vice President shall continue to discharge the same as Acting President; otherwise, the President shall resume the powers and duties of his office.

Article XXVI.

SECTION 1. The right of citizens of the United States, who are eighteen years of age or older, to vote shall not be denied or abridged by the United States or by any State on account of age.

SECTION 2. The Congress shall have power to enforce this article by appropriate legislation.